Acclaim for Nicholas Shakespeare's

BRUCE CHATWIN

"A sensual and erudite writer, [Shakespeare] has a deep understanding of Chatwin's feverish wanderlust and emotional turmoil. . . . [His] book does the very best thing any biography can do: it sends you racing back to the author's work." —*Chicago Sun-Times*

"Shakespeare's ultimate accomplishment . . . is in making Bruce Chatwin—that icy vapor who darted, often maddeningly, just behind his sentences—finally corporeal. Here is Chatwin in the flesh, the too-pretty blue-eyed Wunderkind stripped of pretense, stripped of myth but at last warmly and tremendously human." —*Salon*

"Boswell's *Life of Johnson* and Shakespeare's *Bruce Chatwin* are the two inspirational benchmarks for biography writing. . . . A beautiful and completely absorbing book." —Peter Oliva, *The Vancouver Sun*

"Meticulously crafted. . . . In the crucial task of assessing Chatwin's achievement Shakespeare does a first-class job."　　　　　　　　　　　　*—The Seattle Times*

"The biographer who is an accomplished novelist brings two invaluable assets to his task—the ability to tell a gripping story and a genuine understanding of the creative process. Both these assets are amply demonstrated in this monumental life of Bruce Chatwin."
　　　　　　　　　　　　　　　　　　—The Toronto Star

"Shakespeare's deliciously gossipy and scrupulously fair-minded book navigates the labyrinthine complexities and contradictions that made his subject so irresistibly seductive."　　　　　　　　　　—Francine Prose, *Elle*

"*Bruce Chatwin* ranks among the best recent literary biographies, and any reader with an interest in how a writer's life shapes his or her art will find much to ponder in Shakespeare's revelations."　　*—The Plain Dealer*

"If you're a diehard Chatwin fan—and his books inspire cultishness—you'll want to read every one of these 600 pages."　　　　　*—The Washington Post Book World*

"Shakespeare's biography is a curious kind of cabinet in its own right, a place full of wonders and strangenesses, where Chatwin's charms sit side by side with his contradictions."　　　　*—The Globe and Mail* (Toronto)

"In Nicholas Shakespeare, Chatwin has found the right biographer. This is a magnificent work of empathy and detection."　　　　　　*—The Sunday Times* (London)

"Quite simply, one of the most beautifully written, painstakingly researched, and cleverly constructed biographies written this decade. Shakespeare has a quite extraordinary empathy for his subject, whom he portrays with humor, warmth, and an eye for telling detail, creating a book almost as original, intelligent, and observant as those by Chatwin himself."
　　　　　　　　　—William Dalrymple, *Literary Review*

Nicholas Shakespeare

BRUCE CHATWIN

Nicholas Shakespeare is the author of *The Vision of Elena Silves,* winner of the Somerset Maugham Award; *The High Flyer,* for which he was nominated one of *Granta*'s Best of Young British Novelists in 1993, and *The Dancer Upstairs,* chosen by the American Library Association as the Best Novel of 1997. He grew up in the Far East and lives in London.

ALSO BY NICHOLAS SHAKESPEARE

The Vision of Elena Silves
The High Flyer
The Dancer Upstairs

BRUCE CHATWIN

BRUCE CHATWIN

Nicholas Shakespeare

ANCHOR BOOKS
A Division of Random House, Inc.
New York

FIRST ANCHOR BOOKS EDITION, JULY 2001

Copyright © 1999 by Nicholas Shakespeare

All rights reserved under International and Pan-American Copyright Conventions. Published in the United States by Anchor Books, a division of Random House, Inc., New York. Originally published in the United Kingdom by Harvill in association with Jonathan Cape, London, and subsequently published in hardcover in the United States by Nan A. Talese, an imprint of Doubleday, a division of Random House, Inc., New York, in 2000.

Anchor Books and colophon are registered trademarks of Random House, Inc.

The Library of Congress has cataloged the Nan A. Talese/Doubleday edition as follows:
Shakespeare, Nicholas, 1957–
Bruce Chatwin / Nicholas Shakespeare. —1st ed. in the United States of America
p.   cm.
ISBN 0-385-49829-2
Includes bibliographical references (p. 601) and index.
1. Chatwin, Bruce, 1940–1989—Criticism and interpretation.   2. Travelers' writings, English—History and criticism.   3. Travelers in literature.   4. Travel in literature.   I. Title.
PR6053.H395 Z88 2000
823'.914—dc21
99-036474

Anchor ISBN: 0-385-49830-6

Author photograph © Renate von Mangoldt
Book design by Terry Karydes

www.anchorbooks.com

Printed in the United States of America

10   9   8   7   6   5   4   3   2   1

for Gillian
and to the memory of
Tommy and Eduardo Davies of Gaiman

THE
CHATWIN
FAMILY TREE

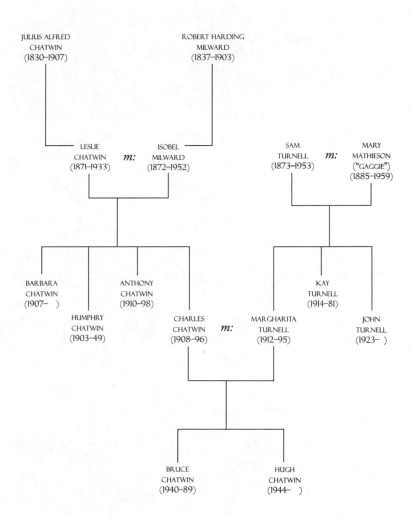

JULIUS ALFRED
CHATWIN
(1830–1907)

ROBERT HARDING
MILWARD
(1837–1903)

LESLIE
CHATWIN
(1871–1933)

m:

ISOBEL
MILWARD
(1872–1952)

SAM
TURNELL
(1873–1953)

m:

MARY
MATHIESON
("GAGGIE")
(1885–1959)

BARBARA
CHATWIN
(1907–)

ANTHONY
CHATWIN
(1910–98)

KAY
TURNELL
(1914–81)

HUMPHRY
CHATWIN
(1903–49)

CHARLES
CHATWIN
(1908–96)

m:

MARGHARITA
TURNELL
(1912–95)

JOHN
TURNELL
(1923–)

BRUCE
CHATWIN
(1940–89)

HUGH
CHATWIN
(1944–)

Contents

◦━━◦

Acknowledgments

This biography could not have been written without the encouragement of Elizabeth Chatwin, who gave me unrestricted access to her family papers as well as to Bruce Chatwin's notebooks, letters and medical records. It is impossible to acknowledge adequately her help. I am also indebted to Hugh Chatwin for sharing with me detailed memories of his family's past and for his patience in correcting drafts of early chapters.

Bruce Chatwin burned many of his papers in the summer of 1986 ("I turned arsonist and destroyed heaps of old notebooks, card indexes, correspondence"). What remains of his archive is deposited in the Modern Western Manuscripts room of the Bodleian Library. The 41 boxes are not to be opened to the public until 2010. Boxes 31 to 35 contain the 85 notebooks, dating from 1962 to 1988.

For access to collections of Bruce Chatwin's papers and related material, I would like to thank Colin Harris and Judith Priestman at the Bodleian; Mike Bott and the Jonathan Cape archive at Reading University; the Churchill Hospital in Oxford; the department of Archaeology at Edinburgh University; Marlborough College; Deborah Rogers Ltd; the Burns Library in Boston; and the Patagonian Institute in Punta Arenas.

I would like to express my immense gratitude to the following for letters, diaries and unpublished manuscripts: Murray Bail, John Barnett, Sybille Bedford, Shirley Conran, Ben Gannon, Shirley Hazzard, James Ivory, Judith Jesser, John Kasmin, Kate Foster, Lala Leach, the late James Lees-Milne, Tom Maschler, Desmond Morris, David Nash, Keith Nicholson Price, David Plante, George Steiner, Jean Raspail, Kenneth Rose, Miranda Rothschild, Stewart Sanderson, Petronella Vaarzon-Morel, Gillian Walker, Cary Welch, and Francis Wyndham.

For permission to use unedited tapes of their interviews, I would like to thank Colin Thubron, Suzanne Hayes of the Adelaide College of Technical and Further Education, Uki Goni of the *Buenos Aires Herald* and Robyn Ravlich of the ABC.

I am also grateful to the following for their comments on work in progress: Peter Adam, Clare Alexander, Jan Dalley, Robert Erskine, Dan Franklin, John Hatt, Adam Low, Ted Lucie-Smith, Guy Norton, Ian Pindar, Peter Ryde, Peter Washington, Hermione Waterhouse, Paul Yule.

In the writing of this book I owe an enormous debt of gratitude to a large number of people around the world who gave me their recollections. In Britain, I would like to thank the following for accounts of Chatwin's early life: the late Charles and Margharita Chatwin, the late Anthony Chatwin, Barbara Chatwin, Bobbie Chatwin, John and Joyce Turnell, Gavin Anderson, Corbyn Barrow, John Crowder, Juliet Hubbard, John James, Susan Kinnersley, Patrick Lawrence, David Lea, and Irene Neal. *Chatwin's schooldays:* Andrew Bache, Pat Barber, Michael Cannon, Michael Fea, Ivry Freyberg, Robin Garran, Trevor Gartside, Peter Hadfield, Tony Haines, Ewan Harper, John Hartland, Caroline Hayman, Philip Howard, Tim Jackson, Dick Longfield, Alan MacKichan, Christopher Massey, Tim O'Hanlon, David Parry, John Peregrine, Thomas Pye, Nigel Roberts, David Rogers, David Smith, Robert Smith, Nick Spicer, Richard Sturt, John Thorneycroft, Ronald Ward, and David West. *Chatwin in London:* Jane Abdy, Nigel Acheson, Peter Adler, Gloria Birkett, Ann Cadogan, Susannah Clapp, James Crathorne, Richard Day, Kenelm Digby-Jones, Adrian Eales, David Ellis-Jones, Peter Eyre, Richard Falkiner, Jocelyn Fielding, Magouche Fielding, Rowena Fielding, Sven Gahlin, the late Martha Gellhorn, Christopher Gibbs, Sue Goodhew, Janet Green, Nigel Greenwood, Carmen Gronau, Guy Hannon, David Heathcoat-Amory, Mary Henderson, Frank Herrmann, the late John Hewett, Derek Hill, Howard Hodgkin, Julia Hodgkin, Jonathan Hope, Rebecca Hossack, Sarah Hunt, Sara Inglis-Jones, John Kerr, Samira Kirollos, Marcus Linell, Dorothy Lygon, John Mallet, Sandy Martin, Katherine Maclean, Anne Miller, the late Teddy Millington-Drake, Felicity Nicholson, John Pawson, Anthony Pitt-Rivers, Julian Pitt-Rivers, Michael Pitt-Rivers, Peregrine Pollen, Howard Ricketts, Salman Rushdie, Simon Sainsbury, Brian Sewell, William Sieghart, Judith Small, Anthony Spink, John Stefanidis, Michel Strauss, Emma Tennant, James Thackera, Patrick Trevor-Roper, Guler Tunca, Tilo von Watzdorf, Michael Webb, Jason Wilson, and Patrick Woodcock. *Chatwin in Edinburgh*: Chris Houlder, Richard Langhorne, Fiona Marsden, Roger Mercer, the late Stuart Piggott, Marjorie Robertson, Rosanna Ross, Anthony Snodgrass, the late Tamara Talbot Rice, Charles Thomas, Ruth Tringham, Alex Tuckwell, Trevor Watkins, and Rowan Watson. *The writing of* The Nomadic Alternative: Gillon Aitken, Emmy Bunker, the late Quentin Crewe, Bess Cuthbert, Ann Farkas, Oliver Hoare, Peter Levi, Harry Marshall, John Michell, John Nankivell, Bob Parsons, Deborah Rogers, Chris Rundle, Natasha Spender, the late Stephen Spender, Peter Straker, Jeremy Swift, Wilfred Thesiger, Charles and Brenda Tomlinson. *Chatwin at the* Sunday Times: Eve Arnold, Celestine Dars, Hunter Davies, James Fox, Colin Jones, David King, Roger Law, Magnus Linklater, Meriel McCooey, Philip Norman, Michael Rand, David Sylvester, Valerie Wade, and Barny Wan. *Chatwin in Wales*: the late Penelope Betjeman, Lucy Chenevix-Trench, George Clive, Mary Clive, Jasper Conran, Ali and John Cotterell, Michael Cottrill, Olive and Clive Greenway, Vivian and Jacqueline Howells, Jean the Barn, Paul Kasmin, Matthew and Sybella Kirkbride, Paul and Penny Levy, Diana and George Melly, Mary Morgan, Tom Oliver, Alan Silver, Martin Wilkinson, Stella Wilkinson. *Chatwin's illness*: David Curtin, Michael Elmore-Meegan, Bent Juel-Jensen, Richard Staughton, Kevin Volans, Kallistos Ware, and David Warrell.

I would like to thank the following for their time, and invariably their hospitality.

Ireland: Alison and Brendan Rosse, and Desmond Fitzgerald. *Stockholm*: Peter, Lennart and Elsa Bratt. *Paris*: James Douglas, André le Fesvre, Jean-François Fogel, Loulou and Thadee Klossowski, James Lord, David Sulzberger, Ian Watson, and Edmund White. *Geneva*: George Ortiz. *Germany*: Hans Magnus Enzensberger, Niko Hansen, Werner Herzog, Michael Kruger, Michael Oppitz, and Manfred Pfister. *Prague*: Martin Hilsky, Clovis and Lizzie Meath-Baker, and Diana Phipps. *Budapest*: Rudi Fischer. *Spain*: Lynda Pranger. *Italy*: Roberto Calasso, John Fleming, Hugh Honour, Beatrice Monti, the late Gregor Rezzori, Matthew and Maro Spender, and Maurizio Tosi. *Greece*: Paddy and Joan Leigh Fermor, and Nikos Theanu. *India*: Sunil Sethi, and Paddy Singh. *Nepal*: Lisa and Tensing Choeygal. *Tangier*: Richard Timewell. *Benin*: Colin and Clothilde Barnes, Gilberto Gil, François Paraiso, Milton Monteiro Ribeiro, Henriette de Roux, Dana Rush, Karim da Silva, Martine de Silva, Doig Simmonds, Honoré Feliciano de Souza, Simone de Souza, and Norberto Prosper de Souza. *South Africa*: Bob Brain, Barbara and Jim Bailey, Sean and Fiona Baumann, Christine Hodges, Clive and Irene Menell. *Argentina*: Jesse Aldridge, Guillermo Alvarez, Robert Begg, Ignacio and Teresita Braun-Menendez, David and Ann Bridges, Jacqueline Caminos de la Carreras, Raul Cea, Tommy Davies, David and Peggy Fenton, Harold Fish, Ingebord Frazer, Paula Goldstein, Adrian and Stephanie Goodall, Jimmy Gough, Daphne Hobbs, Owen Ap Iwan, Yolanda Jamieson, Judith Jesser, Ruth Lamm, Kenneth and Diana Mcallum, Archie Norman, Rogelio Pfirter, Alma Arbusova de Riasniansky, Fabio Roberts de Gonzalez, Luned Roberts de Gonzalez, Tegai Roberts, Pascual Rosendo, Carlos Saenz, Alejandro Tirschini, Nicholas Tozer, Ofelia Veltri, Albina Zampini, and Jorge Torre Zavaleta. *Chile*: John Rees, John Barnett, Rose Eberhardt, and Mateo Martinic. *Brazil*: Noah Richler, Amanda Shakespeare, Rasbutta da Silva, and Pierre Verger. *The United States*: Bruce and Loretta Anawalt, Lynn Block, Clarence Brown, Nell Campbell, Carole Chanler, Gertrude Chanler, John and Sheila Chanler, Ollie Chanler, Freddy Eberstadt, Barbara Epstein, Grey Foy, Sarah Giles, Robert Hughes, Harmer Johnson, Bill Katz, Ward and Judith Landrigan, Michele Laporte, Lisa Lyon, Kynaston McShine, Gita Mehta, Keith Milow, Werner Muensterberger, John Richardson, John Russell, Elisabeth Sifton, Helene Sieferheld, Jim Silberman, Judith Small, Susan Sontag, Pattie Sullivan, Donna Tartt, Paul Walter, Cary and Edith Welch, Jessie Wood, and Gillian Walker. *Toronto*: Greg Gatenby. *Australia*: Carl Andrew, Geoff Bagshaw, Margaret Bail, the late Pam Bell, Richard Buckman, Paul Cox, Robyn Davison, Jenny Day, Nin Dutton, Ben Gannon, Jenny Green, Thomas Keneally, Dick Kimber, Lydia Livingstone, Les Murray, Anne-Marie Mykyta, Pam Nathan, Rob Novak, Christopher Pearson, Toly and Alexis Sawenko, Leo Schofield, Gary Stoll, Kath Strehlow, Phillip Toyne, Penelope Tree, Clinton Tweedie, Val Vallis, and Daphne Williams. *New Zealand*: Philippa Davies.

I have made every effort to trace copyright holders. I greatly regret any omissions, but these will be rectified in future editions.

Lastly, my deepest thanks go to Gillian Johnson and to Christopher MacLehose.

Nickolas Shakespeare, Old Wardour, 1999

The author would like to thank Hugh Chatwin, Elizabeth Chatwin, Bob Brain, Diana di Carcaci, Lady Ivry Freyberg, Werner Herzog, James Ivory, Harmer Johnson, John Kasmin, Diana Melly, Chris Rundle, Kath Strehlow and Paul Yule for the loan of photographs from their private archives. Thanks are also due to Linda Amory, Jerry Bauer, Corbis Images, the *Daily Mail*, Stewart Meese, Thames & Hudson Ltd, Times Newspapers, The Powerhouse Sydney and Topham Picturepoint for permission to use photographs from their collections.

Individual credits are listed in the illustrated sections to be found between pages 110 and 111 (1942–1963), 302 and 303 (1965–1976) and 494 and 495 (1977–1985).

As you are not unaware, I am much travelled. This fact allows me to corroborate the assertion that a voyage is always more or less illusory, that there is nothing new under the sun, that everything is one and the same, etcetera, but also, paradoxically enough, to assert that there is no foundation for despairing of finding surprises and something new: in truth, the world is inexhaustible.

—JORGE LUIS BORGES,
Extraordinary Tales

BRUCE CHATWIN

1.

~~~

Fire

"Was he a cold fish?" I asked

"A fish?"

"A cold person."

"He was hot and cold. He was all things."

—BC, FROM "AMONG THE RUINS"

ON FEBRUARY 1984, an Englishman with a rucksack and walking-boots strides into a bungalow in the Irene district of Pretoria. He is six feet tall, with fair hair swept over a huge forehead and staring blue eyes. He is only a step ahead of the illness that will kill him. He is 43, but he has the animation of a schoolboy.

Bruce Chatwin had come to South Africa to see the palaeontologist Bob Brain after reading his book *The Hunters or the Hunted?*. It was, Bruce wrote, the book he had "needed" since his schooldays, and it had re-awoken themes that had been with him a long time.

"This is a detective story, but rather an odd one," begins Brain's classic text on early human behaviour, based on 15 years' excavation at the Swartkrans cave near Johannesburg. Brain's analysis of fossilised bones raised the possibility that Early Man was not a savage cannibal, as had been generally held, but the preferred prey of one of the large cats with whom he shared the open grasslands of Africa. Around 1,200,000 BC the roles were reversed when *homo erectus* began to outwit his predator, the *dinofelis* or false sabre-tooth tiger.

What had given man the upper hand? "Everything," says Brain, "is linked to the management of fire." But 30 years of exploring and digging in caves over southern and Saharan Africa had failed to produce evidence of fire prior to 70,000 BC, by which time *dinofelis* had been extinct a million years.

Bruce called Brain's book "the most compelling detective story I have ever read". As a schoolboy he had held that "everyone needs a quest as an excuse for living". Brain's findings promised a key.

For two days Bruce engaged Brain in conversations which he described as "the most stimulating discussions in my life". They spoke of Birmingham, where Bruce had grown up and from where Brain's father, finding England restrictive, had departed for the Cape. They spoke about Brain's son Ted, who died at 14 months when he choked on a piece of apple, teaching Brain—painfully—to live his life as though each day might be his last. And they spoke of the origin of evil.

Bruce seized on Brain's discoveries to support his conviction that human beings were "not that bad" and that the predator instinct was not essential to our nature. If the leopard-like cat had preyed on our ancestors, then man in his origins was not necessarily aggressive. He lived his life in fear, *dinofelis* watching him from the shadows.

Bruce—who called the cat "the Prince of Darkness"—amused the older man. Brain says, "He understood 'the Prince of Darkness' as a psychological necessity. He thought we had lived so long with prowling nocturnal predators they had become part of our make-up. When we no longer had these animals in bodily form, we invented dragons and heroes who went off to fight them." Discussing, for instance, Uccello's painting of St George in the act of lancing the dragon, Bruce seemed to think this was an illustration of what had actually happened. Brain had misgivings about this nostalgia for "the Beast we have lost". Nevertheless, it excited him to watch Bruce take his work and run with it. "Chatwin was like a nineteenth-century synthesiser," says Brain. "There is a place again for that kind of generalist, someone who can wander among specialised fields and pull things together. Otherwise it's very compartmentalised and syntheses don't really occur." The two men talked late into the night and on the following day they drove to the cave at Swartkrans.

FROM THE CAVE entrance on a hill of pink dolomite it is possible to see, 40 kilometres to the south-west, the skyline of Johannesburg, and to the east, the dumps of chalky rock from the goldmines of Krugersdorp. Close as it is to one of the most dangerous cities in the world, Swartkrans is always tranquil. Black eagles looking for rock rabbit glide above slopes dotted with white stinkwood, and here and there are bright red flowers.

Brain completed his book in a hut nearby. Bruce, too, sensed a place of special significance. He wrote in his notebook: "Good feeling at Swartkrans."

He was familiar with the excavation procedure. With Brain and the site foreman, George Moenda, he took up a position close to the west wall. The three started to dig into a patch of calcified earth with plastic-handled screwdrivers. At 10 a.m. one of them found a bone tool. A second grey bone looked like a scraper. "Turned out to be gnawed by a porcupine," recorded Bruce. Over the course of 19 years, Brain told him, the cave had yielded more than 100,000 specimens like these. They had been digging in the west wall for half an hour after lunch when Moenda prised from the earth, alongside an arrangement of three stones, a cracked fragment of antelope bone. Beige white on the outside, blackened on the inside, the bone was speckled with dark patches, as if burned.

George handed it round. It had a soapy feel.

Brain was not a demonstrative man. He had so often set out to find confirmation of his thesis, suffered so many false alarms. But this time he was visibly moved. "This bone is remarkably suggestive!"

What they were looking at would eventually be validated, in 1988, as man's first known experimentation with fire. It would predate by 700,000 years the previously oldest find, at Choukoutien in China. "That was the first convincing evidence for the earliest use of fire in any human context anywhere," says Brain. "It was a very astonishing moment."

BRAIN WAS QUICK to speculate. This bone provided a partial explanation of how our ancestors escaped the continual threat of predation. He reconstructed the scene: a thunderstorm at the beginning of summer, the yellow grass, dried to a parchment in the winter sun, a lightning-struck bush, and *homo erectus* dragging back to his cave this elusive substance, which coming with flashes and thunder must have had a magical significance.

Man's use of the fire-struck bush represented for Brain the "crucial step in the progressive manipulation of nature . . . so characteristic of the subsequent course of human affairs". It would not, of course, guarantee permanent protection: another half million years would pass before man could make fire to order. But it offered intermittent respite.

Bruce gave his own account of that day in a letter to Colin Thubron: "When visiting the excavation at Swartkrans with Bob Brain, one of the questions uppermost in my mind was man's use of fire: the myth of Prometheus is absolutely crucial, to my mind, in understanding the condition of the First Man—since it is with fire that Man could adequately protect himself at night from the predators.

"Bob and I discussed the pros and cons of the first hearth over lunch. Then, in the first few cubic centimetres which we—or rather the foreman George—excavated that afternoon, there were some fragments of bone which looked most definitely charred! Since the level in question would date somewhere close to 2 million [1.2 million is now the accepted figure], I got very excited—though he, sanguine as ever, was inclined to pooh-pooh the discovery. This morning, however, I had a letter in which he says the bones were definitely burned. In other words, I may, conceivably, have turned up at Swartkrans on the day the world's earliest hearth was found."

The Swartkrans discovery has not been challenged and Brain remains convinced that here, more than a million years ago, there occurred the first step which released our ancestor from his subservience to big cats.

BRAIN TOOK FOUR more years to excavate the next eight metres. Close to the end of his life, impatient to have the finding registered, Bruce wrote from Vienna in 1987. "Do I take it that the bits of blackened bone were burnt? And does this mean that the use of fire *has* been found with fossils associated with *H. Habilis* [*sic*]. Or is that going too far?" Not until the following year was Brain able to demonstrate with confidence, microscopically and chemically, that the 260 charred pieces of antelope bone constituted good evidence of "the earliest use of fire". In December 1988, the results were announced on the cover of *Nature* magazine. Bruce was dead before the news reached him.

Bruce never, except in letters, wrote about the events on 2 February, 1984. His discretion owes much to his respect for Brain: Swartkrans was his life's work. But somehow it is typical that Bruce should have been party to this crucial archaeological discovery. So many of the threads of his life come together on that dolomite hillside: the uncanny good luck, the speedy in-and-out, the all-suggestive fragment, the speculative theory, the fascination with provenance and the origin of things. At last, he had scientific evidence to support his belief that man was not a bloodthirsty and cannibalistic aggressor, as authorities like Dart and Lorenz would have him.

Bruce hammered out his theory on the telephone to Colin Thubron.

"I got this wonderful call out of the blue," says Thubron. "He was terrifically geared up about it. After all, what could be more important than trying to diagnose the origins of evil in the world? I remember his charge of intellectual delight. He wanted to share it with someone. *He had held the bone in his hands.* 'Colin, I've just been down in South Africa and I've been at the moment that they uncovered the earliest discovery of the domestic hearth, which puts back the discovery of fire to . . .' and so on, then bang, down the telephone went and Bruce had disappeared for a year or two years."

Thubron wrote down what Bruce had said: "If the sources of aggression are directed not against other human beings, but against the wild beast etc, then our condition is OK." The glitter-eyed cat disappeared, according to Bruce, at the same time as humans developed speech. He told Thubron, "It was through language that the earliest hominids saved themselves." Language was the medium of uniting against "the Beast".

The discovery at Swartkrans was a glorious affirmation of the work on which Bruce had been engaged for 16 years. On his return to England he signed a contract with Tom Maschler at Cape for the book he now decided to entitle *The Prince of Darkness Is a Gentleman.*

THE EVIDENCE OF fire had suggested to Brain the "perfectly valid speculation" that language, and so storytelling, might have evolved from a need to issue warnings about our predator. "Language came into being," Brain says, "out of a need for far more precise communication and identification of objects and circumstances, and for more elaborate audible signals."

Our earliest stories were vessels for preserving vital information about how to survive: water supply, plant location and, possibly, the whereabouts of *dinofelis.* Brain makes no extravagant claims, but he does say that when fire was available, it lengthened the daylight hours and encouraged people sitting around the flames to discuss what they had done during the day. He calls fire a "social facilitator" and says that it promoted language because people had to be within the arc of firelight. "If they strayed outside, they were in mortal danger."

The significance of fire was not lost on Bruce. From childhood he was fascinated by the priest-like figures who tended its flames. "Shamanism," he declared at the beginning of his writing career, "has always been connected with mastery over fire." His identification with shamans endured right to the end. In a hospital bed in Oxford, he wrote in what would be his last notebook: "Aren't all true healers—from the prehistoric shaman on—all 'thundermen'?" In his failing hand he added, "the feminised man, healer, songmaster etc. always set apart in every tribe . . . Appeased. Honoured. Essential. The superior man." They were almost the last words he wrote.

For Bruce, as for "the early guardians of fire", stories were not just entertainment: they concerned his own survival too. "Man is a talking animal, a storytelling animal," he wrote in one of his black notebooks. "I would like to think that he talked his way out of extinction and that is what talk is for."

BRUCE CHATWIN'S GIFT for instant intimacy meant that a lot of people felt they knew him. As often as not, it was the perishable intimacy of a first encounter. What impressed the Australian poet Les Murray was not the dazzle but the loneliness it concealed. "He was lonely and he wanted to be. He had those blue implacable eyes that said, 'I will forget you, I will reject you because neither you nor any other human being can give me what I want'." He reminded Murray, forcibly, of T. E. Lawrence.

Stephen Spender was also reminded of Lawrence. "Two hundred years ago, Bruce might have conquered a large slice of Empire and he probably would have died early and been buried in Afghanistan. He didn't like England, but that is very English too. The British Empire, after all, was based on people trying to get away from Britain."

Bruce professed a distaste for Lawrence, as he did for anyone with whom he might be compared. "I hate T. E. Lawrence. Well, I think I do. Incredibly unpleasant." Yet he was powerfully attracted to the myth and, like Lawrence, travelled as much to leave one self behind as to find another. "He is in the tradition of Drake, Cavendish, Darwin, Bridges," says Professor Zampini, who entertained Bruce in Patagonia. "For a long time the only way to be universal was to be English. You are an island open to the sea which takes you everywhere." Bruce's father was a sailor. "At heart we are an island of buccaneers and pirates," Bruce told André Malraux.

"If he'd lived in the nineteenth century," says Sandy Martin, an antiquities dealer who knew Bruce at Sotheby's, "he would have got a backer, a peer who fancied him, and been a good archaeologist and discovered something." This may account for his attraction to nineteenth-century figures: shipwrecked sailors who have lost everything and start again on the tip of the world; Europeans who create kingdoms in Patagonia; Portuguese who have the run of the Slave Coast. Ordinary folk, in other words, who leave the suburbs to reinvent themselves royally in the sticks.

In the late twentieth century, Bruce had to be "a Stanley of literature", according to Gregor von Rezzori, exploring places which everyone else had passed over. "He was attracted to small countries like Dahomey, where he might have felt quite powerful," says the American novelist David Plante. "His attitude seemed to be: 'Except for the fact it's too late, I might have run the Empire. But I certainly have a right to it in a retrospective way because I know more about it than anyone else.' With Bruce, knowledge and fantasy became power."

He was English in the way of Lawrence and Burton, distancing himself from where he came from. "Being an Englishman makes me uneasy," he said. "I find I can be English and behave like an Englishman only if I'm not here." His Englishness trailed him everywhere. It was part of him, from the way he talked, dressed, walked into any room confident of a delighted welcome. He had the self-confidence bred of the public school system, the English knack of being able to talk on all manner of subjects while being only half as knowledgeable as he was able to convey; and of disappearing—just like that. Neal Ascherson describes this trait, the smile of the Cheshire cat: "To be unfindable and untraceable—that is an English dream! It is an idea of liberty which allows the individual to be 'present' only when he or she chooses, but to retain the right and capacity to melt away."

He called England "*le tombeau vert*", the green tomb, and to a friend in Sydney began a letter: "a quick note *in extremis*, i.e. from London". The wife of Carlos Fuentes assured him, "You're not English at all." He looked pleased. He liked to misquote the actress Arletty, telling how his nationality was one thing—"but *mon cul* is *international.*"

He was everything the English distrust. Stylish. Passionate. A lover of theory and of the French; and obsessive, which we dislike in particular.

NOT LONG AFTER the momentous meeting with Brain, Chatwin stepped off a plane to Melbourne and for 48 hours non-stop, it seemed, he talked to the German film director Werner Herzog. "It was a delirium, a torrent of storytelling," says Herzog. "It went on and on, interrupted by only a few hours of sleep. When I think of Bruce Chatwin now, I think of the ultimate storyteller. It's the resonance of the voice and the depth of his vision that makes him one of the truly great writers of our time."

In Italy, he liked to descend without warning on the art historian, Hugh Honour. "The moment he got out of his car he began talking," wrote Honour. "He never made any conventional opening remark. There was never any 'how ghastly the traffic is nowadays on the *autostrada*'. He would launch straightaway into an account of some new friend he had just made, of some new place he had just seen or some wonderful and extraordinary object he had found—and bought for a song. A brilliant mimic with a sharp ear for absurdities of phrase and voice, he could impersonate people I knew so brilliantly that I never doubted the accuracy of those I hadn't met, Jacqueline Kennedy or Mrs Gandhi for instance, who were two of his stand-by party turns. And his gossip was without malice. He cherished his sacred monsters as part of his mental collection of the unusual. For he collected people just as he collected objects—and ideas and words. He was fascinated by the idea of the *Schatzkammer*, those sixteenth- and seventeenth-century collections of natural and artificial curiosities and his own 'collection', which mostly remained in his head, rather resembled them. His mind was filled with an extraordinary jumble of the abstruse, the exotic, the savage and the sophisticated."

"I'm at my happiest," Chatwin used to say, "having a good old yakking conversation."

Telling stories was how he gave of himself. "For all his hypocrisies, snobberies and curmudgeonliness, he was a giver," says the Indian journalist, Sunil Sethi. For the writer Sybille Bedford, "Having him around was having extra oxygen in the air." He reflected his listeners back on themselves in heightened colours. "He made you participate in what, in that moment, did not seem to be a fantasy," says Francis Wyndham, who in 1972 recruited him to the *Sunday Times*. "One was included in it, even though he did *all* the talking. But he made me feel he was talking because of me, which explained the sense of exhilaration. That was part of his charm: he made me feel pleased with myself." Nin Dutton drove with Chatwin over four days from Adelaide to Brisbane. "The whole time we were driving, Bruce never stopped talking, and he was never boring ever, ever. His over-exuberance was one of his gifts, that's why a lot of women adored him. He made them feel three times their size."

Chatwin's storytelling engaged all his faculties: his youthful looks, his savage mimicry, his peacock voice—both invigorating and crushing at the same time, and "always on the edge of mirth". To the novelist Shirley

Conran, the combination was impossible to ignore. "He looked like a knight of medieval legend and if you found yourself sitting next to him on a bus you'd find it disconcerting and you'd drop your shopping bag. And you'd be likely to find him on a bus, discussing the merits of Sainsbury's cream crackers and how much cheaper they were in Fortnum's; and two weeks after you'd given him your address, you'd receive a box of Fortnum crackers and a note: '*This* is what I mean'."

As a young man he was stocky and resembled a big baby. He had fair hair brushed flat over a square head, which was slightly too big for his body, and huge blue eyes that never seemed to blink. "I fixed her with my well-known arctic stare," he wrote of the anthropologist Margaret Mead. "It made her profoundly nervous." People have compared the adult Chatwin to a German admiral, a curate, a fallen angel, an unfledged baby sparrow, a farmer, a St Bernard, but the image fixed in most minds is that of a pink-cheeked schoolboy, slightly bumptious, with Robert Louis Stevenson's ability to render those he met "slaves to a rare, authentic and irresistible charm". He had, like Stevenson, a child-like rather than a childish approach to life. "His style was to be the beautiful soft child-boy who's not quite real, like a boy in an English school whom others have a crush on," says the film director James Ivory. "He was like that and he stayed like that. He was a Rupert Brooke." His looks matched the way he dressed. "He had a perfect outfit that nanny could have put out for him: khaki shorts, white polo shirt, wonderful white floppy hat, sandals, socks," says Jessie Wood, with whom he stayed in Greece in the 1960s. "He had a theory you didn't get corns if you wore socks." There was always the sense he was conscious of his effect. "You're like Baron Münchhausen," Howard Hodgkin told him once. "How?" Bruce asked. "Was he pretty?" Vain he was, but not completely confident about his looks. "Well, I suppose I'm fairly good-looking, but not *that* handsome. And rather moley," he told the art critic, Ted Lucie-Smith. He felt his British voice sat on his personality "like a layer of slime". For all that, a great many thought him irresistible. "He was amazing to look at," says Susan Sontag. "There are few people in this world who have the kind of looks which enchant and enthral. Your stomach just drops to your knees, your heart skips a beat, you're not prepared for it. I saw it in Jack Kennedy. And Bruce had it. It isn't just beauty, it's a glow, something in the eyes. And it works on both sexes."

Part of his appeal was his humour, a combination of innocence, vulnerability, mimicry, rescued from slapstick by an English taste for the absurd. "He was one of the two funniest people I've known," says Salman

Rushdie. "He was so colossally funny you'd be on the floor with pain. When his stories hit their stroke, they could simply destroy you."

He was a superb mimic. In his imitations there was the hilarity of the jousting knight who was sometimes less St George than he was Don Quixote. "He had a laugh like a wild hyena, whoops and away it went," says Nin Dutton. "In the outback, he'd have had a chorus of kookaburras to keep him company. They sit in a tree and laugh like mad. They'd have imitated every word he said."

Chatwin had Evelyn Waugh's "delicious gift for seeing people as funny". His most common word in conversation, noticed the Australian novelist Murray Bail, was "mad". "It was a description of honour. He didn't like ordinary people. He wanted them extraordinary. 'Everyone's *quite* mad,' he would say, speaking in italics and bulging his eyes." He could give others the same impression. "There was something inhuman about him when he got excited," says Sybille Bedford, "a mad horse, large eyes with lots of white."

The performance was physical. As he watched his audience come forward on their chairs, affirming him, he grew and so did his stories. "He went straight into a performance," says his friend, Jonathan Hope. "He'd sit bolt upright, ramrod back, his eyes popping, and roar off in fourth gear on his *idée fixe* of that week or hour." His voice had the speed of the eighteenth-century Sotheby's auctioneer George Leigh, pitched, it was said, "somewhere between the *affettuouso* and the *cadenza*." He reminded Hope of Danny Kaye, a Chatwin favourite, who was able to convince an audience entirely by phonetics that he was speaking in Hungarian. Hope could seldom follow Chatwin's stories to their conclusion. "But he would conjure up incredible images. Evening in the Atlas mountains, the sky an exquisite cerulean blue, the stars coming out one by one and the wonderful *sang de boeuf* of the North African desert. Sometimes it would get so exhausting that I'd say: 'Could you just show me a photograph?' "

He rehearsed his stories "like Churchill, muttering in the bath," says Chatwin's wife, Elizabeth. "He was always playing a kind of role: you could see him cooking up how he was going to do it. He was so excited when he got to someone's house: he'd drive up, slam on the brakes, jump out and rush into the house—and I'd have to turn the engine off and shut the car door." Elizabeth Chatwin did not believe he intended anyone necessarily to believe his stories. "But if they did, he went further."

———

CHATWIN WAS A storyteller first, but not until the last third of his life did he write the stories down. "I've always loved telling stories," he told Thubron. "It's *telling* stories for what it's worth. Everyone says: 'Are you writing a novel?' No, I'm writing a story and I do rather insist that things must be called stories. That seems to me to be what they are. I don't quite know the meaning of the word novel."

Stories were Chatwin's central obsession: digging for them, bringing them to the surface, sharing them. "He was looking for stories the world could give him and that he could embellish," says Salman Rushdie, who travelled with him through Central Australia. "He didn't give a damn whether they were true or not; only whether they were good."

Chatwin was very theatrical, but he was also deeply serious. His stories concealed as much as they revealed and he hid inside them. He talked as he wrote, to keep something at bay, with an intensity to convince whoever was listening, or reading, that his dragons were not peculiar to him. He told his stories right to the last, going up to bed, stopping on each step of the stair for five minutes, going out to the car, as he drove off leaning out of the window, till the moment he died.

In this he shared the malleability of all-knowing Proteus, eluding questions by changing into a lion, a serpent, or fire. "His whole life was spent transforming," says the actor and theatre director, Peter Eyre. As long as he was talking he could not be questioned.

As with a child, he could invoke in his audience a tenderness towards something easily shattered. "He was very scared," says Rushdie. "He was telling stories to keep the Jungle Beast away, the false sabre-tooth, whatever it is." Rushdie had no doubt what this Beast was: "The Beast is the truth about himself. The great truth he's keeping away is who he is."

SAY ALMOST ANYTHING of Bruce Chatwin and the opposite is also true. There seem to be as many Bruce Chatwins as people he met. "I sometimes think he wasn't a person: he was a scrum," says the art critic, Robert Hughes. "I think I hardly knew him, there were so many of him," says Sheila Chanler. The American artist Michèle Laporte likened him to a mirror. "Often people talk about him and end up talking about themselves."

"Something in him spoke to an impulse, a fear that is universal," says his American editor, Elisabeth Sifton. "The Beast is the truth about ourselves, for *each* of us." Perhaps this accounts for why so many feel proprietorial about him. According to Wyndham, it is a rare person who remains neutral. "People feel some attitude has to be taken about Bruce, as if you define yourself by how you react to him." Rushdie says: "You have to agree or disagree. Everything he did, he did very noisily and that creates a response." Anthony Powell recorded in his diary after watching *On the Black Hill* on television: "I always feel there was something a bit phoney about Chatwin." Andrew Harvey, reviewing *The Songlines* in the *New York Times*, spoke for a younger audience. "Nearly every writer of my generation in England has wanted, at some point, to be Bruce Chatwin; wanted, like him, to talk of Fez and Firdausi, Nigeria and Nuristan, with equal authority; wanted to be talked about, as he is, with raucous envy; wanted above all to have written his books . . ." He was, wrote Harvey, "a writer no one who cares for literature can afford not to read."

Bruce's endeavour might seem to be old-fashioned, uniting him to the earliest fireside storytellers, but there is something prescient in his insistence that everything is linked. In his best stories, he gives us licence to travel freely. He introduces us to people and to texts we would not otherwise have encountered. He makes the world tidier, simpler, more exciting: a place to sample, at ease with anybody. His vision is both aristocratic and populist. And it is adventurous. In some ways he was a tremendous snob, but he was not a climber. "He wanted to *be* there, to *know* everything," wrote Hugh Honour. "He had a great appetite for life."

What is compelling about Bruce Chatwin is easily lost in a din of bright lights and colours, incessant chatter and a crowded address book where Jackie Onassis is listed next to an Oryx herder. He is so noisy that you cannot hear him; so good-looking that you cannot see him; his work so restrained and cool that you cannot feel him. "His fastidiousness is a disguise," says Rushdie, "and, oddly, that disguise is what most readers would think of Bruce. They refer to the characteristics of the prose."

Where the work is transparent, unencumbered and deceivingly clear, his life is deliberately opaque. "We know nothing about him at the book's end," Alasdair Reid grumbled in the *New Yorker* when reviewing *In Patagonia*. In fact, Bruce is himself more mysterious and subtle than anything he wrote. It is this elusive quality which had led him to the cave in South Africa.

Returning to Swartkrans a decade on, Bob Brain reflects on the day there with Bruce. "Such moments come to you in remote places. It's as if the curtain that separates us from a broader vision is briefly lifted. We're tied to a sequential time sequence, it's the only way evolution can work—otherwise everything happens at once. But every now and then the process falters and we look through a chink at, I suppose, the eternity religions speak of. When this happens, it's such a startling experience that you hanker after it when you're back in the world of sequence. I think that's what Chatwin did: when he returned to the sequential world, he found it tiresome and set off on another expedition."

II

"Let's Have a Child," I Said

> *Do you know, my dear, that "Chatwin" is Old*
> *English for "spiralling ascent"?*
> —BC TO HIS WIFE

BRUCE CHATWIN CAME from a middle-class family without pretensions, but in his imagination—and sometimes in his behaviour—he was exalted, a young prince. In July 1968, he accompanied Stuart Piggott, his professor of archaeology at Edinburgh, to Moscow. "He really is splendid & resourceful & gloriously autocratic," Piggott noted in his journal. "When on the train an inspector speaking German asked if we were *Erste Klasse* Bruce said haughtily, 'Of course we are! Look at us!' He was under the impression that the man had asked if we were *aristocrats!*"

The impulse to re-create himself was present from an early age. "On the Yorkshire Moors aged three or four, I remember my grandmother shouting to my mother over the field: 'Be careful! Be careful! The gypsies will take him.' And seeing a whole line, just over the hedge, of gypsy caravans moving up a lane and then a gypsy boy, very brown, on a piebald pony stripped to the waist riding by and being envious in some way or another."

To be stolen by gypsies was a better fate than to be Bruce Chatwin from Birmingham. In one of the five schools he attended before he was eight, he told pupils he was an orphan.

In Australia, the man on whom he had based the hero of *The Songlines*—that is to say the closest he came to using the device of an alter ego—tried to find out about Chatwin. "Bruce was not the sort of person who liked talking about himself. If you wanted to ask him what he thought about something or what he knew, you could never shut him up. But if you wanted to find out about where he came from and about his family, somehow the subject drifted on to something else and before you knew it he was drawing out information from you. He didn't say anything to give you a handle on his inner personal life." He talked sparingly, if at all, of his ancestry or his family. "For most of his life he wanted us to think him so unique that he didn't actually have parents," says Jonathan Hope. Some people supposed that he was hiding his family away. A German aristocrat, one of Bruce's lovers in the 1970s, said: "A middle-class conventional morality haunted him. He had a chip on his shoulder about his background, a critical way of dismissing the years before."

From what he has written and said to friends, he was not ashamed so much as protective of his parents. Hard-working, honest and straightforward, they laboured after the Second World War to put behind them the mistakes and humiliations of their forbears and to build a new life. But as secrets gnaw so Bruce would have absorbed the unspoken. "We were taught at Marlborough," says his brother Hugh, "that the sins of the fathers are wrought upon the sons even unto the third and fourth generations. He was, in a sense, a grandchild of shame."

IN ONE OF many attempts to make sense of a book on nomads, which dogged him for 20 years and which he never published, Bruce wrote: "This book is written in answer to a need to explain my own restlessness—coupled with a morbid preoccupation with roots." From his mother, he derived his restlessness; from his father, an appetite for genealogy.

The Chatwins had a firm sense of their place. They were honourable sitters and servers: lawyers, architects, button-makers, builders who stayed put. If they strayed it was to bring back and to make Birmingham better.

The name Chatwin is a variant spelling of Chetwynde and derives from a hill in Shropshire once owned by Lady Godiva. Bruce Chatwin's passion for provenance led him to believe that his name came from the Anglo-Saxon Chettewynde and that it meant "a winding path" or "a spiralling ascent". But he referred only to the suffix, *windan*. Chette is harder to fix. It might stem from *Catta*, a nickname for cat; or from *Caté*, "a chatterer". Chatwin most probably meant "Chatterer's Corner".

There is a portrait of the first recorded Chetwynde in the Bayeux Tapestry, a tall, beaming spear-holder. He was so tall that the designer had to squeeze his name Turald beside his sword-belt, instead of over his head. Turald was a Norman from Rouen who served with William the Conqueror. His spoil would be part of Lady Godiva's manor.

The Domesday Book has Chetwynde as a demesne of 300 acres with a priest, a mill and two eel fisheries and values the manor at 50 shillings. Turald, who owned 13 properties in Shropshire, treated it as waste ground. It is from this giant Norman, who took the name de Chetwynde, that the Chatwins most likely descend.

The Chetwyndes were knights, mill-owners and sharp-eyed business-men. About one of them, George I, lately arrived from Hanover, com-plained: "This is a strange country. The first morning after my arrival in St James', I looked out of my window and saw a park with walks and a canal, which they told me was mine. The next day Lord Chetwynde, the Ranger of the Park, sent me a brace of fine carp out of my canal and I was told I must give five guineas to Lord Chetwynde's servant for bringing me my own carp out of my own canal in my own park."

Bruce inherited the Chetwynde acumen. He was ruthlessly protective of his interests. "My trouble is that, under a somewhat bland mask, I am from my Sotheby's days a rather hard-nosed business pro," he wrote to his literary agent in 1987. "Not for nothing did I once draw up a new form of draft contract, revolutionary in its day, which ultimately gave the art auc-tion business a new flexibility."

Little is known about the Chatwin branch until the nineteenth cen-tury, despite efforts to elevate them higher by Bruce's great-uncle Philip, a leading force behind the Birmingham Archaeological Society. They were probably groomsmen to the Chetwyndes who came into the Black Coun-try looking for work. The first known Chatwin, who died in 1810, was a builder from Halesowen, five miles west of Birmingham. The second was a button-manufacturer who patented a method of making cloth buttons which, for the first time, would have no metal visible. A century on, Bruce's father Charles—John Chatwin's great-great-grandson—remained a connoisseur of hand-stitched garments. After dancing with a friend's wife at the Pytchley Hunt Ball, Charles Chatwin ran his fingers down the back buttons of her dress. "Mmm, I don't suppose you made *those* yourself."

BRUCE WAS CONSCIOUS of his Birmingham background and minded being put down by public school boys. One night near Faizabad he was stung into argument by the poet and Jesuit priest Peter Levi. "Peter was scorning Birmingham and aroused me to a certain sense of fury." He took pride in the captains of industry in his ancestry. References to Birming-ham run through his books and in certain company he would talk in a

Birmingham accent. But he was aware, like his forbears, of the difference between middle class and gentry. Because of their regional accent, Victorian industrialists once they had money would often rather go to Vienna, even to southern Chile, than risk being disdained as provincial in London.

What was true of Bruce's distant cousin Charles Milward, who settled in Patagonia, was true of him. "The extraordinary thing about Milward is that he could never shake off Birmingham," Bruce wrote to his parents from Punta Arenas, where Milward had built himself a house in the image of his father's rectory.

Nor would Bruce in all his travels shake off the influence of his father, a wise old sailor and a sound lawyer for whom everything had to be right.

Charles Chatwin's earliest memory was of George V's coronation in 1911. Aged three, he stood on the corner of Maas Road and waved a Union Jack. He remembered a man wearing a leopard-skin beating a drum.

He was a robust child who suffered from a form of epilepsy, *petit mal*, and was educated at home until he could be trusted not to have seizures in public. His Edwardian history came straight from his mother's leather-bound copies of *Punch*. As an adult, he would describe his favourite cartoon, which depicted the problem of taking life head on. A man asks George, the gardener: *Why do you always pull the barrow instead of pushing it?*

George: *Because I hate the very sight of it.*

"That made me laugh."

He grew up to be a big, socially awkward, decent man and bossy as some shy people are. He had apple red cheeks and sharp, bridge-deck eyes which remained blue all his life. "They are the eyes of a man who has never known the meaning of dishonesty," wrote Bruce, who inherited their colour. "They have never tempted him to anything mean or shoddy."

Bruce's father was a doer, not a dreamer. He had a photographic memory and could assimilate information quickly. "I never read novels," he said. "I prefer law reports." His two enthusiasms were amateur dramatics and mucking about in boats at Barnt Green reservoir and on the south coast. He fell into the Law, his father's profession, because there was little money to train him as a doctor, which he would have preferred. In 1933 his father died young and Charles became sole practitioner of Messrs. Gem & Co. at 2 Bennetts' Hill, Birmingham.

He channelled his healing compassion into his legal practice, winning respect as a fair-minded solicitor who specialised in family law from cradle to grave: land, inheritance, wills and settlements. "As a lawyer, I did not want to know what happened to bring about a divorce, but I felt sorry for both." He sorted out people's businesses and did his best to keep his clients away from litigation. "If you don't want to go to court, go to Charles Chatwin," clients said to each other. Not having an academic background, he laboriously wrote his contracts in longhand. "A lot of his work was holding hands with old ladies after they'd been burgled," says Guy Norton, son of the senior partner. "Charles was very good at that." He was a President of the West Midlands Rent Assessment Panel and sat on boards of the Children's Hospital and the Commercial Union. "I am," he said, "a very pink conservative."

Favourite among Charles's clients were the Quakers and Unitarians who had helped make Birmingham the Second City, "the City of a Thousand Trades". He was influenced by their uprightness, their nonconformity, their ethos of interdependence—for instance, the sharing of capital assets. His good friend was the Quaker lawyer, George Barrow, who worked next door at Wragge & Co. They talked boats incessantly. In 1934, together they bought for £130 a six-ton gaff cutter, *Noctiluca*, named after the marine life which cause the sea's phosphorescence. In the same year, they took down the wall between their offices to allow them to communicate more easily. Charles amalgamated his practice with Wragge & Co., as one of five partners, on a salary of £600.

Barrow remembers his partner as a tolerant man, patient, always on to the latest gadget. "He didn't lose his wool. He was expansive, but never about personal affairs." To Patrick Lawrence—also of Wragge & Co. and another co-owner of Charles's boats—Charles Chatwin gave the impression of an inward, Pickwickian figure. "Charles was one of the most sensible men I've ever met. If there was some scandal, he'd quietly not let the file go outside his office. In the nicest possible way, he swept that sort of thing under the carpet. He wasn't surprised by human frailty, but he was going to make sure he didn't have it himself."

One day Barrow telegraphed from London: COMING HOME. BRINGING LUNATIC. The Master of Lunacy had agreed that Barrow's client, "a lunatic so found by inquisition", might be committed to Charles's custody while Barrow was on holiday. The young man, who had run off with a nurse and married her, stayed with the Chatwins at West Heath Road, where he turned out to be adept at cards. "Mrs Chatwin," says Barrow, "was delighted to have him as a bridge player."

Unmarried in his late twenties, Charles lived at home with his widowed mother, Isobel. He rolled his own cigarettes and wore a dark blue suit, dressing as his partner recalls "one down from a city solicitor, one up from a country solicitor". He was strong, prudent, common-sensical—and impeccable. "From the rest of us, he would come in for some 'heavy-duty' teasing for being stolid, forbearing and virtuous," says Hugh, his youngest son. "Two more different and complementary people than Charles and my mother Margharita are hard to imagine."

Charles was on a train to London to attend a party when he first set eyes on Margharita, a young woman with long legs and brown eyes. "Brown eyes are naughty eyes," she would tell the infant Bruce on her knee.

Charles was too shy to introduce himself, but on returning to Birmingham he told his mother about "the jolly nice girl" he had seen. Two weeks later he walked into the drawing room and was astonished to find her talking to his mother. Margharita Turnell had been offered a job with the local MP, Ronald Cartland, and was in need of lodgings. Isobel Chatwin, who led the Woman's Branch of the King's Norton Conservatives, insisted she stay with the Chatwins. "Hands off, this one's mine," Charles said to his brother Anthony, who had a way with the girls.

One evening three months later, Charles drove her in his Austin 10 to Far Forest and proposed. He was 30. She was 26.

"MOTHER NEVER LIKED to talk about the past," says Hugh. "A lot of pain there. Not a rejoicing thing."

Margharita Turnell came from Sheffield. "You can tell people from Sheffield by the way they look at knives," she said. One of her father's jobs had been in cutlery. The Turnells were sheet-metal workers, railway guards, corn merchants. Bad luck and disappointment clung to them, their history one of spiralling descent. At school Margharita was nicknamed Toenail or Turnip.

Turnell means "hill overgrown with thorn bushes". The English Turnells were Huguenot emigrants. Margharita's family traced themselves to an argumentative mercer from Tickhill, on the outskirts of Sheffield.

Margharita's grandfather, Sam Turnell, had been a commercial traveller in the wine trade who sailed to Australia for his health and died on the journey. Sam's wife was born in scandalous circumstances to a young heiress who became pregnant by the music master and ran away with him to Ecclesfield, where he scraped a living as the church organist. Sam's brother, William, was a railway guard who was crushed to death between the buffers at Penistone.

Bruce's grandfather, Margharita's father, was also named Sam. On his marriage certificate he called himself an architect, but most likely he was helping out his architect brother, Ernest. As a young man, Sam liked to tap-dance and ride a tram to the moors to shoot grouse. He looked good on a hard polished floor, or in bowler hat and breeches galloping a horse across the sands. His favourite phrase was "Watcha cocky"; his keenest hobby, to draw meticulous plans of houses that were never built.

By the time Bruce knew him, Sam Turnell was a thin, melancholy man with a nose he would say had been broken by a cricket ball and a face that went on forever. He had brushy brows and long narrow hands that he kept thrust into the pockets of his tweed suit, to hide the nails he bit. He wore this suit, buttoned with a single button and a narrow black tie, even to the beach. "Sam had the face of a sad clown," wrote Chatwin in *On the Black Hill.* "Nets of red string covered his eyeballs and his eyelids seemed to rustle as he blinked. The presence of an attractive woman drove him to acts of reckless flirtation."

"I adored him," wrote Bruce. "He was a great walker and I preferred to walk with him over the Yorkshire Moors rather than play with children my own age."

MORE OFTEN THAN not, Sam Turnell walked to escape his wife, a headstrong, superstitious woman who had been raised in Aberdeen, in a middle-class Scottish household with a butler. Mary Mathieson's father had married and lost two fortunes and she was supposed to have had relatives in the Indian army. This partly explained, to Bruce, her dark tan. Somewhere in her Highland past there was also a story of gypsies.

Bruce's grandmother had plenty of Romany temperament. "I like to think she *was* a gypsy," wrote Bruce, "a changeling perhaps or a castaway left at the Manse." She wore gold earrings, collected brass and took pride in her wonderful legs that she would show off at the least provocation. An effigy of a black cat was important to her and the correct hanging of a horseshoe. "An addict of the Ouija board and horoscopes, she was also given to any kind of gambling. Her husband lost his last penny in the slump, so she 'made do' betting on the horses". Once she invested a pound on "Grackle" in the Grand National and the horse came in at 33-1. A later bet of six shillings each way financed her son's engagement ring.

Bruce knew his grandmother as "Gaggie". Forty years later, in the backlands of Brazil, he would find her gypsy double under a jackfruit tree.

GAGGIE HAD ARRIVED in Sheffield, after her father's death, to keep house for her brother, a doctor practising in Broomhill. When her brother married, she rowed with his wife and never spoke to either again. Desperate for somewhere to live she moved in with Sam Turnell, the tap-dancing "architect", who lived next door.

They married in October 1911. Sam was 38, Mary 27. Her inheritance enabled them to settle in an elegant house in Broomhill. Bruce's mother, the eldest of their three children, was born in February, 1912. Known to her family as "Margie", Margharita was named after Sam's favourite flower.

Sam was now working for Jonas & Colver, the knife manufacturers. He rose to become a manager. "Then, evidently, he did something wrong," says his son, John Turnell. The firm despatched him on a mysterious mission to South America.

In 1927 he lost his job altogether. Margharita was at home when he came in and told her: "The steel works have gone bust." He remained unemployed until the mid-1930s, living off his wife's capital, but Gaggie's money ran out and the Turnells moved from their pillar-fronted house into smaller and smaller lodgings, finally settling in 136 Sandygate Road, a semi-detached with a green-painted dining room, three ducks flying up the wall and a fine view over the Rivelin valley across the hen-house roof.

"They had friends when they had money, and then they didn't have so many," says John Turnell. Possessions were sold. It became difficult to keep up appearances. Gaggie felt Sandygate Road demeaned her and hated it. Then, in about 1935, Sam found a job as a quantity surveyor for a firm making metal windows. (Bruce, casting him in rosier lights, claimed he sold stained glass). Sam worked for Mellowes until he retired, but the pay was meagre. He was living a cut above the breadline with a wife and three children. The only supplementary source of income was that brought in by Gaggie from the horses. She regretted having married him. They fought continually. Slowly, the marriage unravelled. "Sam, you're useless, Sam!" Gaggie would snap in a thickening Scots accent.

To escape Sandygate Road, Sam walked the moors. He took John with him and later Bruce. They walked past the Three Merry Lads pub, past Red Mires dam, past Ashopton—now under water—and back along

Manchester Road. All day, sometimes 20 miles a day, said John, who complained it put him off walking. "We all wanted to escape home."

The experience of walking the moors with his grandfather would germinate Bruce's conviction that the human frame is designed for a day's march. "When people start talking of man's inhumanity to man it means they haven't actually walked far enough."

BRUCE'S MOTHER WAS 14 when Sam lost his job at Jonas & Colver. Gaggie, to remove Margharita from the house, sent her to Dieppe to stay for six months with the parents of her French governess. She returned home speaking French, with a taste for French magazines and clothes. Unable to afford new dresses, Gaggie, from cut-outs and curtains, taught Margharita how to design her own. Margharita said: "We were brought up poor as church mice, but Gaggie *always* made sure we were properly turned out."

Margharita sought refuge from the grime of Sheffield in parties and matinées. Hugh ascribes his brother's appetite for the exotic to their mother's passion for European fashion and American films. She loved going with her sister Kay to the cinema, identifying with the heroines. Her favourite film was *Gone With the Wind*. She confided to Hugh, whom she took to see it, that Scarlett's predicament, sitting in a house with no money and taking down the green velvet curtains to cut into a dress, was similar to her own situation in Sandygate Road. Both of her siblings would later work in films; Kay as a continuity girl, John as an actor, and afterwards as a cost controller at Denham Studios. "If you've got good eyesight, and are quick, and know where to look, you'll see me in the farewell speech of *Goodbye Mr Chips.*"

For Margharita, the most accessible theatre was Sheffield's political stage. She worked as an assistant for the local Conservatives, looking after old ladies and organising whist drives in Sheffield, Blackpool and Wales. In 1934, aged 21, she moved to London, sharing with Kay a one-bedroom flat in Great Portland Street. She canvassed the Paddington ward for Conservative Central Office, until the chief agent sacked her "for giggling at the policy".

In the winter of 1937, Margharita caught the train to Birmingham with a recommendation to join the team of Ronald Cartland, MP, brother of a young romantic novelist, Barbara. She was coming back from her interview when Charles Chatwin boarded the train.

BRUCE LIKED TO think of his mother as glamorous. In *On the Black Hill* he cast her as Jo Lambert: "a strange, long-legged woman, with scarlet lips and nails, and sunglasses set in wedges of white Bakelite . . . She had always been famous for her taste and her ability to 'make do' on a shoe-string." He detected in her lively brown eyes "suggestions of Southern ancestry" and told friends that Margharita had been a cabaret performer. If ever she danced, it was probably to perform demure turns as part of her fund-raising activities for the Conservative Party.

To Hugh, their mother was "morally very correct, with a bit of Scarlett O'Hara trying to burst out". Sensitive to her lack of formal education, she played at not being bright, but she could think fast, "flirt with the best" and was always looking at the funny side of people.

She was a giggler, but her vivacity camouflaged a nervous side. She used to talk to herself. "The first sign of madness," she would say dismissively when caught by her children. Robert Erskine once found Bruce on top of a double-decker bus having so fierce a discussion with himself that he did not dare to interrupt.

Charles and Margharita married on 28 September 1938, at Ranmoor Church in Sheffield. At the wedding, there was a sense that the shy and socially awkward groom had been rescued by this vivacious woman. A Chatwin cousin told Margharita: "You caught him in the nick of time."

THE CHATWINS HONEYMOONED west of Cannes and moved, on their return to Birmingham, into "Namura", a rented semi-detached in Barnt Green, backing onto the railway station. They could not afford a home of their own: Margharita, when she transferred her account from London to Birmingham, had ten pence in credit, the whole of her wealth.

The picture of family life anticipated by Charles may be seen in his present to Margharita that Christmas: Mrs Beeton's *Household Management*. Charles, sharing Mr Beeton's every expectation, was anxious soon to start a family. "War was imminent. We'd been married a year. 'Let's have a child,' I said."

In the summer of 1939, they departed on a short touring holiday of Wales. Bruce was conceived in a hotel south of Aberystwyth. "Then the war came and our lives were broken up," said Charles.

On the outbreak of war, Margharita announced to Barbara, Charles's sister: "I shan't be able to do any war work. I'm going to have a baby." She was eight months pregnant when Charles, who had joined the R.N.V.R., received his papers ordering him to Chatham where he would spend a year square-bashing, digging trenches and learning elementary pilotage.

Without Charles, a nerviness set in which could only be remedied by moving. Margharita's greatest fear was to have soldiers billeted on her, so without consulting anyone she gave up the lease on "Namura" and went to stay with her parents near Sheffield and there she gave birth to Bruce on the evening of 13 May 1940, in the Shearwood Road Nursing Home.

BRUCE WAS BORN at 8.30 p.m., at the end of a hot day. "I don't remember it ever raining on Bruce's birthday," said Margharita, whose superstitious nature matched her mother's.

She remembered "not a particularly easy birth, but an incredibly beautiful child". Her son had the Chatwin blue eyes, the high forehead and long nose of the Turnells, and a big head. One of the myths he elaborated for himself was Bruce the Baby: he would tell friends that he was so golden, blue and pink he was selected in a competition in 1942 to be the baby on the Glaxo food tin. He retained an exemplary sense of his own uniqueness. Aged 40, while watching a children's nativity play in Wales, he so identified with the angel who appeared to Mary that he was moved to write on the programme: "I am that Star."

Margharita never divulged to him the comment made by the maternity nurse: "He's so beautiful. He's almost too beautiful to live."

He was christened on 16 June at St John the Baptist, Dronfield. The Reverend Richards had fallen asleep and had to be fetched by John Turnell. The two of them ran, shoulder to shoulder, through the church's swing doors and in a hasty service he was baptised Charles Bruce. His mother had chosen Charles, after her husband. Her husband, then tramping about a square in Brighton, had chosen Bruce, after some remote Scottish ancestors.

A SWAYING NIPPLE and a shower of gold. These, Bruce claimed, were the first images of a nomad child on coming into the world. What were his? Probably, a mildewed wall in Quoit Green House, Dronfield, the latest of his grandparents' lodgings.

Margharita and her baby left Quoit Green House after a few weeks. In Birmingham, Charles's mother Isobel Chatwin, worried by the danger of enemy bombardment, put pressure on her daughter-in-law to look for a safer place. Margharita found furnished rooms on the seafront at Filey, a resort on the Yorkshire coast where she had spent her holidays. There, Gaggie insisted on joining her. Sam was reluctant to lose his hard-won position as a quantity surveyor and stayed in Dronfield. In any case, "he was told there wasn't room," said Margharita.

31, The Crescent, the setting of Bruce's first conscious memories, was a ground floor flat facing the beach. "I watched the convoys of grey ships as they passed to and fro along the horizon. Beyond the sea, I was told, lay Germany. My father was away at sea, fighting the Germans."

In their ground floor flat, Gaggie conferred on Bruce the affection she had withheld from Sam. She fed her grandson halibut oil laced with orange. She toasted bread for him on a gas fire in the bedroom and played with him on the sand.

In that confined space Gaggie's temperament led to friction. "My mother was one of those awful pram-rockers," said Margharita, who liked to carry her baby. She was annoyed by Gaggie's insistence on rocking the pram every time Bruce shouted. They had their first row. Bruce heard a cry, soon familiar: "the carriage door closing—we're off!"

For the next five years—a period of "fantastic homelessness"—Bruce was "passed around like a tea-urn". "All my early recollections are of travelling—from great aunts to friends to rented flats . . . the most dismal boarding-house kind of lodging. The whole idea of going somewhere else was always exciting."

Bruce's experience was not unique: everybody was on the move at that time, letting their houses, having guests in, avoiding the bombs. But once his mother started moving she could not stop. Anxious not to settle, and on the run from her domineering mother, Margharita shuttled with her son back and forth, on the railways of wartime England, between Filey and a dozen addresses in Birmingham, Stratford, Baslow, Buxton, Leamington Spa. Hugh says: "She was the one who instigated the moves. *She* was the gypsy."

"All this frenzied agitation of the times communicated itself to me," Bruce wrote in *The Songlines*. "The hiss of steam on a fogbound station; the double clu-clunk of carriage doors closing; the drone of aircraft, the searchlights, the sirens; the sound of a mouth-organ along a platform of sleeping soldiers."

Home was a suitcase: a roll-up canvas holdall, with bags at both ends, and a solid black Revelation trunk known as the Rev-Robe. The trunk opened up like a wardrobe and Bruce had use of two of the drawers—for his clothes and his Mickey Mouse gas mask. "I knew that once the bombs began to fall, I could curl up inside the Rev-Robe and be safe." But those to whom he spoke of the Rev-Robe noticed real pain. "Quite definitely a scar," he wrote in his notebook about the effect of those homeless years.

THE CHIEF INFLUENCES in his early life were women and elderly cousins. Most of his wartime addresses belonged to great-uncles, great-aunts and grandparents. The time spent in their company encouraged his sympathy for old people.

In Stratford, he stayed with Charles's spinster aunts, Grace and Jane. Like Clovis in Saki, Bruce caricatured them a little too colourfully. Grace, the more extrovert, takes credit for first smelling out his tall stories. She kept chickens and owned a fat spaniel that farted and so did she. "Don't poof, Amber. Amber, *do* stop that!" She was deaf and carried a black box, covered in leather, an aid she held in front of her so Bruce was puzzled where to address his remarks. Bruce said she had lost her lover in the Great War, in which she had been a nurse, and never looked at a man again. No one else had heard of Aunt Grace's soldier lover. Grace said, "I'm afraid Bruce doesn't know whether he's telling the truth or not."

He liked walking around Stratford with Grace. In a little tweed coat and velvet collar he appointed himself guardian of Shakespeare's tomb. "Long before I could read, Aunt Gracey had taught me to recite the words engraved on the tomb-slab:

Bleste be ye man yt spares these stones
And curst be he yt moves my bones.

Only once did he see his great-aunt angry, one summer evening in 1944 when he peed in the bath. "If you ever do that again, Boney will get you." To make the threat more vivid she drew a bicorn hat on legs: Bonaparte, the Beast with which she had been disciplined as a child.

Aunt Jane, the elder and wittier sister, was a thin-faced artist. As a young woman she had lived on Capri. Her room was littered with not very good watercolours: turbaned Indians, churches, sailing boats and almost naked men with exiguous turquoise slips. Bruce called her Miss Catharine Tuke in *On the Black Hill*. "The canvas that fascinated Benjamin showed a beautiful young man, naked against a blue sky, pierced through and through with arrows, and smiling."

She was still painting at 84 and knew the names of all the English rugby players. Once Bruce learned to read, Jane became his favourite. "She was a tireless reader of modern fiction. Later, she would tell me that American writers wrote better, cleaner English than the English themselves. One day she looked up from her book and said 'What a wonderful word *arse* is!'—and for the first time I heard the name Ernest Hemingway."

The first writer Bruce met was his great-uncle. Philip Chatwin lived in modest gentility in Leamington Spa, a moustached teetotaller with spectacles on the end of a long, narrow nose. Once at Cowes, a doctor's wife mistook him for Nansen, the Norwegian explorer, and it was only with difficulty that he could convince her otherwise. Philip was an architect, with a passion to repair old buildings. Scarcely a church in Warwickshire had not benefited from his restoring hand. Bruce wrote, "My old great-uncle was the architect in charge of the Beauchamp chapel which is where I got my feeling for history." In the school holidays Philip would show Bruce his excavations, for example at Weoley Castle. Among the items he had dug up were the mouthpiece of a trumpet and a wooden *pissoir*.

Philip was renowned for his academic leanings, for his patronage of archaeological societies, for his fussy collection of material important to public archives. He was also an obsessive genealogist. He kept careful notes on the Chatwin ancestors and Bruce always wanted to see him at the end of term. He became a surrogate grandfather from whom Bruce would learn his family history. "I must go and see Great Uncle Philip because I like talking to him."

III.

∽♦∼

The Cabinet

*According to Aboriginal theory, the ancestor first
called out his own name and this
gave rise to the most sacred and secret couplet or
couplets of his song. Then he named
the place where he had originated, the trees or rocks
growing near his home, the
animals sporting about nearby, any strangers who
came to visit him and so forth . . .*

—THEODOR STREHLOW,

Songs of Central Australia

DURING THE SECOND world war, the young Bruce was often with his paternal grandmother in a south-western suburb of Birmingham. The house, 198 West Heath Road, had bow windows with stained-glass motifs, and a long lawn down to fields and the stacks of the Austin Motors factory.

Isobel Chatwin was a stoical character with undeniable presence. "She was a big lady," said Irene Neal, who cleaned house. "When I hung her bloomers on the line they used to come down to the ground." She filled a chair especially made for her and in later years had to be lifted out of bed.

Isobel had been a film censor, a prominent Conservative activist and, since 1932, a Justice of the Peace. When war broke out, she was vested with the power of execution in the event of a German invasion.

By the time her grandson came to stay, Isobel had been a widow ten years. She smelt of Mornay Carnation soap and, though enormous, she dressed well. In winter, she wore woolly two-pieces; in summer, pure silk dresses with large cuffs.

"Like a duchess she was," Irene Neal remembers.

One day Isobel brought a stubby lad into the kitchen. "This is my grandson, Bruce."

Irene Neal replied: "He looks a proper little Bruce, Mrs Chatwin. A little toughie." The four-year-old boy wore short trousers and a tweed jacket. "If I'd known he was going to die as a young man, I'd have given him a big kiss."

WHILE IRENE WAS cleaning the house, Bruce would chase Isobel's huge cat, Monty, round the elm tree in the garden or under the kitchen stove. But his greater pleasure, to be enjoyed when his grandmother occupied the magistrate's bench, was to steal into the dining room and gaze into her cabinet.

The cabinet was a wedding present, a solid piece of Victorian mahogany. The top half lifted off and consisted of three shelves behind glass doors that locked. Brass-handled drawers made up the base, also locking. Isobel had made her wedding present into "the family museum". Behind the panes, she arranged little odds and ends handed down over generations from her late husband's family, the Chatwins, and from her family, the Milwards. To each a narrative was attached.

In Isobel's absence, Bruce admired these objects through his reflection. Once he was old enough, he was permitted to play with them on the carpet. He wrote in his unpublished nomad book: "The mother gives her child 'things' to play with, handle and name; these things are the contents of his environment and the very stuff of his or her intelligence."

His grandmother's cabinet was a sort of Narnia. He reached through it into a fantastical world of lions, unicorns and ice queens where he would make his home.

TWO SNIPPETS OF RED AND GREEN PLAID;

THE FIRST WORN BY THOMAS ARBUTHNOT AT

THE BATTLE OF SHERIFFMUIR, 1715;

THE SECOND WORN BY BONNIE PRINCE CHARLIE IN EDINBURGH, 1745.

Bruce's grandfather Leslie Chatwin was a "tubby fusspot" who was "mad keen" on his Scottish relations. From ancestors in the '15 and '45 rebellions Bruce inherited his love of king-makers and collaborators, and his Christian name.

A distant cousin was the Thomas Arbuthnot who proclaimed Bonnie Prince Charlie the rightful King of Scotland and England on the steps of the Mercat Cross. Bruce warmed to Thomas's resourceful daughter, Isabella. She had distracted one of the English redcoats looking for her brother, and once her brother had escaped (dressed as a servant girl), married the pursuer.

All his life Bruce made a show of pricking against his Christian name, complaining it was something you would only call a dog or an Australian. In fact, he owed it to the surname of Isabella's son-in-law, Alexander Bruce, a tax collector.

Determined Jacobites, the Bruces inherited Bonnie Prince Charlie's plaid in the distressing shape of two pairs of bedroom slippers. "Disliking the desecration," they had taken the shoes to pieces, preserving each fragment as if a relic of the true cross.

They were also fond of porcelain. On the cabinet's three shelves were remnants of a fine collection, these known as "Bruce china".

RICHTER'S ANCHOR BLOCKS.

Following the instructions on the box, Bruce assembled the brightly-coloured bricks, the Victorian equivalent of Lego, into "a miniature crib", "an entrance to an Armenian cemetery" and "a lighthouse with candle".

Bruce at Marlborough flirted with the idea of joining the family architectural business, but his mathematics was not good enough. These toys belonged to his great-grandfather Julius Alfred Chatwin, a restless, energetic entrepreneur who had founded the firm with his name.

The Chatwins blossomed under Julius Alfred, known as "Timmy". Well-mentioned in Pevsner, he grew up to be a prolific architect of churches, fire stations and banks. In 1851, after erecting an arena for the Birmingham Cattle Show in steel, brick and glass, he travelled to London to serve an apprenticeship with Sir Charles Barry. He designed details for Barry's House of Lords and was able to observe Queen Victoria open the new building from a hole in a roofbeam.

Julius Alfred was outward-looking, one of the few Chatwins who did not restrict himself to Birmingham, and he was blessed with a draughtsman's memory. Once in a pea-soup fog he guided a crowd to safety by placing his hands against the closest wall and feeling his way along the street until he recognised, on the facade of a gentleman's club, some of Barry's mouldings. Bruce would enact a similar rescue operation on his honeymoon. "There's an awful lot of Bruce in Julius Alfred," says Hugh.

After four years with Barry, Julius Alfred returned home to start his own practice. Working within convention, he built ably in a variety of styles: Gothic for churches, Renaissance for almshouses, Italianate for banks. His 80 Lloyds banks, constructed mainly in the shape of small palazzos, included the head office in London, the first commercial building in the capital to have electric light.

His best-known work was the baroque chancel of Birmingham Cathedral, with a window by Burne-Jones. The donor, Miss Wilkes, rebelled against the presence of oxen at her stained-glass crèche. "I wish 'The Nativity of Our Lord'," she said, "not a Cattle Show."

He never completed his most interesting commission. In 1880, a maharajah asked him to design a Glass Palace. Everything was to be made out of richly-cut glass—glass walls, glass stairs, glass columns, surrounded by glass terraces and fountains, and open to view. Erected on a nickel-plated frame the palace was to cost more than £100,000. Then, on the day his council met to approve the project, the Maharajah went riding and his horse took an ominous fall. He interpreted this as a sign to cancel the commission.

Julius Alfred Chatwin was also Vice-President of the Birmingham Society of Artists. He was interested in art, provided it did not cost much, and crammed his large mansion in Edgbaston with a collection of pictures. Although he had become wealthy, after his marriage he had resolved never to spend more than £5 on a painting. The single exception was a dish of flesh-tinted peaches by Etty. He owned a painted Antwerp cabinet, earmarked for Bruce, a Guarneri violin, and a collection of 30 David Coxes which he had partly inherited from his father and of which "not half a dozen" were genuine. At the Society's annual dinner, "almost always one of Chatwin's Coxes came up for criticism."

WHITE PORCELAIN CHRISTENING MUG WITH THE GOLD INSCRIPTION: LESLIE BOUGHTON CHATWIN, 13 AUGUST 1871.

Julius Alfred's eldest son was Bruce's grandfather. Leslie Chatwin was an overworked lawyer whose heart was in the theatre and the sea. A pipe-smoking Edwardian, he had an untidy handlebar moustache and a sense of humour which was not everyone's cup of tea. People liked to hear him reading in Northfield Church, of which he was churchwarden. He had a good voice and his father's memory. On stage, he could recite the whole of Kipling's *Just So* story about a dog.

Recognised in amateur dramatic circles, Leslie believed you could produce Shakespeare by employing village actors with no previous the-atrical experience. He tested his theory, annually, in Northfield village hall.

In the evenings, once supper was cleared, he set about writing his own plays. In 1913 the Birmingham Rep produced Leslie's *Re Pilgrage,* about the inventor of an anti-fouling paint, designed to make ships cleave faster through the water. "It wasn't very successful," said Bruce's father. Stephen-son's kettle inspired another one act play. As the pressure rose, Charles Chatwin had to make the kettle rattle with a stick and wire.

Sailing was Leslie's other passion. At Merton in 1890, he had founded the Oxford University Yacht Club. He designed his boats on the dining table in West Heath Road and built them in the garage, his children hold-ing down the wood so that he could hammer in the rivets. He named his boats after herons and grebes and raced them every weekend on the reser-voir at Barnt Green, four miles away.

Through his marriage Leslie Chatwin would be tainted by a scandal which affected his legal practice. In the First World War, he found a job forwarding post to soldiers. "We were very much the reverse of well-to-do," said Charles.

ISOBEL MILWARD'S PHOTOGRAPH ALBUM.

The family albatross was the Law, thrust around the Chatwin neck by the Milwards. In 1902, the 31-year-old Leslie married Isobel Milward. She was 32, and belonged, as the newspapers put it, "to one of the oldest and best-known families in Worcestershire". Their union fulfilled the ambi-tion of her father, Robert Harding Milward, to draw in "the builder Chatwins" to his powerful legal clan. The cabinet was probably his wed-ding present. Almost immediately Leslie discovered he had married into a family with things to hide.

The Chatwin virtues were memory, craftsmanship, business nous— open, sedentary qualities. Through his Milward grandmother, Bruce had acquired the genes of adventurers, corner-cutters and embezzlers.

Isobel's album was locked in a drawer. A photograph, dated 1898, shows a slender woman posing on a camel in Egypt. Her father, at the time a prosperous solicitor, stands stiffly in front of her. A few months separate him from a scandal that had repercussions well into Bruce's lifetime.

The Milwards came from Redditch where they had made needles and fish hooks since the eighteenth century. In 1703 John Henry Milward started his firm at Washford Mills. A forward-looking proprietor, he was credited with the creation of the August bank holiday and with initiating the payment of wages on Friday afternoon, to ensure that his men went home to tea. Soon everyone was making needles in Redditch.

Isobel's father, "one of Birmingham's most prominent figures", had not gone into the needle business, but like her husband had studied law. The senior partner of Milward & Co., employing 50 clerks, Robert Harding Milward was held in high esteem in the Midlands. "It is questionable whether a more remunerative practice existed outside London and the whole of the country."

Milward acted for the firm that laid the first Atlantic cable and was trustee of several large estates, the money of which passed through his books. "In those days, your solicitor acted as banker," said Charles. "If he went bust, your money went too."

An ambrotype of Milward at 25 shows strong, sensuous features: black mutton chops, hands contentedly on chest—and eyes which steer away from the camera. Suave, imperturbable, courteous, a man of beaming affability, he was promoted at his trial as "the *beau idéal* of the family lawyer."

By far his most prestigious client was the Duke of Marlborough, whose marriage to the heiress Consuelo Vanderbilt he brokered. Milward suggested she would need money to spend, say, a million pounds. And a personal wedding present to the Duke of £10,000, to clean his dirty lake. The advantageous terms he established were to plant in generations of East Coast American breasts a suspicion of Englishmen—as Bruce discovered when he married into the Chanler family, friends of the Vanderbilts.

At some point Milward appears to have overreached himself. In 1897 the Duke wrote him a letter dispensing with his services "for grose incompitanse [*sic*]".

Thanks to his ducal connections, Milward had built up "an ample standard" of comfort. He kept substantial house near Bromsgrove, with 13 servants, and was treasurer of the Birmingham Triennial Festival, putting on a special train for the convenience of principal singers. His clients' money often backed his largesse and he used it to entertain well. Bruce wrote, "He was a friend of Richter, the Wagnerian conductor; of Madame Patti, and of Charles Gounod . . ." His dismissal knocked the stuffing out of him.

Milward's extravagance matched his recklessness. After losing his most important client, he was caught by the slump at the end of the Boer

War. Drawn into a number of wildcat schemes, he became desperate in his speculations. When the Indian rubber tyre came out, he made the fatal miscalculation of sponsoring, instead, the leather tyre. At the Cox Tyre Company, losses accumulated rapidly. He began to dig into the money entrusted to him by his remaining clients.

On Saturday, 27 September 1902, Milward was arrested at Ashton Under Mill on his way to meet the 11.39 train from Evesham. Dressed in a grey lounge suit and white gaiters, he was driven by horse and trap to a court where, as usual, he cut a splendid figure. The charges to be considered "were of a most grave character". He was not given bail.

At his trial, he was accused of defrauding 200 creditors, owing one £38,000. His gross liabilities amounted to more than £100,000. All he had in the world, he said, was £2 11s 11d.

Pronounced guilty, he was asked to say a few words. His mutton chops had greyed and he appealed for leniency in "a somewhat weak and nervous manner": "I am in my 65th year. My mother died at 65, my brother at 65. I have only just recovered from a terrible attack of brain fever and apoplexy caused by these terrible events."

The Lord Chief Justice, ignoring his appeal, committed Milward for his "haphazard business methods" to six years in Parkhurst Prison. He left the dock with the warder's help.

At Parkhurst, Milward became prison librarian, but the authorities released him after he suffered two further paralytic seizures. He died on 18 September 1903, speechless with aphasia. But his death was not the end of the matter.

THE EFFECT OF the "Milward affair" on the Birmingham Quaker circles which comprised Leslie Chatwin's clients was explosive. Milward's wife moved to Malvern to escape the pointed fingers, while the question occupying Edgbaston was whether his glamorously dressed daughters would continue to worship at Edgbaston Old Church. Bruce's grandfather, who had just married into the family, felt a special kind of horror.

"Now this has happened," Leslie asked a relative of the convicted man, with whom he used to commute to Five Ways station, "would you mind if we didn't travel in the same carriage?"

But he could not avoid the scandal undermining his business. Through the Law and through his marriage, the Chatwins were associated with the Milward mess. At West Heath Road, Leslie kept his shame hidden. In 50 years, it was a subject concealed from his children and grand-children, never to be mentioned. Leslie's son Anthony learned of it first as a teenager, from a girlfriend. The story reached as far as Sheffield, where, 36 years later, it mortified Charles to discover the scandal was known to his in-laws. He refused ever to discuss his grandfather with his children. "That's all from long ago," he would say if Milward's name came up. "His name was taboo," wrote Bruce.

The image of his great-grandfather loomed over Bruce Chatwin's life. After Isobel died in 1953, he found Milward's court suit and sword in a tin trunk, last used when the Duke of Marlborough became Lord-Lieutenant of Ireland. "Dressed as a courtier, sword in hand, I dashed into the draw-ing room shouting 'look what I've found!'—and was told to 'take those things off at once!'" It was the one time Bruce saw his father angry.

Milward's disgrace became a Chatwin party piece. In 1962, at a din-ner in Istanbul, Bruce used it to delight a daughter of the last Turkish Sul-tan, after which he noted with satisfaction in his journal: "All were very intrigued to hear of my great-grandfather . . ." Six years later, at a lunch with Kenneth Rose and two South American girls, he was at it again. Rose wrote in his diary: "Bruce tells us that his great-grandfather was a cele-brated swindler, who cheated the then Duke of Marlborough out of many millions as his family solicitor. 'He cheated old women out of their few pounds, too . . .' Bruce has tried to get his father to talk about the case, but cannot get a word out of him. He asks me to see what I can discover."

Rose at the time was working on the Churchill archives. Bruce re-sponded enthusiastically to what he was able to uncover. "A real opera-tor—£108,595.15.11 is no mean sum. If only he hadn't been found out!"

Friends noticed that what appealed to Bruce was the idea of a conman ripping off a lot of toffs. "Every writer is a cut-purse," he was fond of say-ing. "The art is to make one's thefts as invisible as possible." Theft, pla-giarism, pick-pocketing, these were writers' skills. The art critic Ted Lucie-Smith knew him from 1959. "Bruce was a great intellectual thief. He had no respect for intellectual property."

Another friend, Stella Wilkinson says: "He did have a dodgy side, a tremendous lot of the street urchin in him. A quality that education can't give you."

ISOBEL CHATWIN TOOK consolation in a large family. She was one of ten children. Her sisters were models of rectitude, and married pillars of the church; her brothers rather the reverse. After "the surprise", as it was referred to by the Milwards, they scattered.

With the help of Philip Chatwin and an elderly aunt, Bruce unravelled their fates. Henry fled to South Africa where he became town clerk of Durban, dying of fever soon after. Geoffrey worked as a barrister in Cairo where his wife went "off it" and died by swallowing a small bit of chain. Bickerton, an engineer in the Broken Hill gold rush, "did a 100 things and nothing". At 44, he enlisted in the Great War and was badly gassed, after which he lived "rather rakishly" in Gloucestershire. Robert— "a wild one!"—was a wanderer with a gift for languages and a large stomach. He could hold his liquor better than anyone else and held a great deal. He was in charge of the railway between Alexandria and Damascus and went mining turquoise in Egypt, south of Wadi Halfa. Emir Faisal gave him a dress of honour, the robe eventually taking pride of place in Bruce's dressing-up box.

But Isobel's favourite relation was an insubordinate, snub-nosed cousin who travelled further than the lot of them.

A SCRAP OF GIANT SLOTH FROM PUERTO NATALES, PATAGONIA.

Isobel's cousin, Charles Milward, the son of a Birmingham vicar, rebuilt his life on the uttermost part of the earth. Birched as a child for telling lies, he escaped his father's vicarage and went to sea aged twelve. He sailed the Horn 40 times, until he was shipwrecked there in 1898, on his first voyage as captain. Sacked by the shipping company, he settled in Punta Arenas where with a German partner he bought a forge to repair ships. For twelve years he was British Consul.

In the year of Robert Harding Milward's trial, Charles Milward befriended a German gold-panner who was blowing up a cave near Puerto Natales to obtain specimens of a prehistoric animal. The discovery, in perfect condition, of a Giant Sloth, or mylodon, excited European scientists into believing the animal must recently have been alive. Scraps of mylodon were sought by natural history museums and Charles Milward was in a position to supply them.

Sometime in 1902 or 1903, he sent a piece of this mylodon to his cousin Isobel as a wedding present. The skin, a good-sized tuft, was a fragment of reddening, coarse hair attached to a card with a pin. It was wrapped in paper and kept in a pillbox.

"We knew it came from abroad 'cause it was in the cabinet, see," says Irene Neal, one of whose duties was to dust and polish the contents.

"Everything in the cabinet had come from abroad. It was Mrs Chatwin's pride and joy, even to the piece of fur."

Neal was not sure what the fur was. "Whatever it was, we knew it was precious, same as all the little knick-knacks that were in there. The house-keepers, especially the one Edna, she couldn't look at it. Oh no! *I* had to pick it up and move it when they were cleaning the cabinet out. It used to put the creeps up me, an old bit of blacky, browny, bristly stuff as didn't look very nice at all, the sort of thing you didn't want to pick up. It was not until I had me grandsons as I learnt about dinosaurs. I thought it was only monkey fur."

Charles Chatwin believed the slothskin to be a dinosaur's. "The one thing I could think of was the ditty: '*When the brontosaurus saw us in the prehistoric days. . .*.'" His father's misattribution landed Bruce in hot water. "You know how all children dream about monsters," he told an Argentine interviewer. "I had this very, very highly developed fantasy about what this animal looked like—and then, of course, my bitter disappointment to discover brontosauri were reptiles and I was told by my science master not to tell terrible lies."

The hairy remnant became Bruce's favourite object. "Never in my life have I wanted anything as I wanted that piece of skin."

FOR BRUCE, THE lockable cabinet in West Heath Road was a sustaining metaphor and it informed both the content of his work (faraway places, one-offs, marvels, fakes, the Beast) and its style (patchwork, vitreous, self-contained). The shelves and drawers were a repository for collecting, movement and story. Bruce's life would enact all three. "For those who are awake, the cosmos is one," he wrote in his notebook, quoting Heraclitus. He hated to see a collection broken up.

The art critic, Robert Hughes, says, "a very important component of Bruce's imagination is his admiration for *Wunderkammer*". Hughes remembers Bruce's enthusiasm for a little-known, meticulous drawing by Dürer, of the mutant pig of Landser: a portentous creature with eight legs. "He liked the off-beat. He liked the monstrous. He liked things that suggested an inadvertent crack in the seamless world of cause and effect."

The phenomenon of the *Wunderkammer* began in Vienna as a response to the wonder of America. It domesticated our terror of a dangerous new world, the monsters seething on the peripheries of the medieval map. To create a *Wunderkammer* was to cast the world in your own light.

It contained, according to historian Steven Mullaney, "things on holiday, randomly juxtaposed and displaced from any proper context . . . Taken together, they compose a heteroclite order without hierarchy or degree, an order in which kings mingle with clowns." A defiance of category was crucial.

These cabinets of curiosities were also mirrors. They reflected the collector's extraordinariness, his journeys to marvellous places, his encounters with marvellous people, and—important when considering Bruce—they offered up a neat metaphor of a world picture that they replicated in miniature. "If nature speaks through such metaphors," wrote the seventeenth-century musicographer Emmanuel Tesauro, "then the encyclopædic collection, which is the sum of all possible metaphors, logically becomes the great metaphor of the world."

The collections Bruce most admired were the Pitt-Rivers museums in Oxford and Farnham; the Cabinet des Médailles in Paris, where he proposed to his wife; the Volkerkunde in Vienna. In 1967, like the narrator of his novel *Utz*, Bruce stopped off in Vienna on his way to Prague: "The Imperial mantle of *1125*!! with gold lions attacking camels on a scarlet ground is the most wonderful thing I ever saw," Bruce wrote to his wife. "The sword of Charles the Bold has a narwhal tusk sheath and handle, and I must say I am more than resigned to the extravagance of a tusk since seeing the unicorn presented to the Emperor Rudolf, one of the inalienable treasures of the Habsburgs together with a sumptuous Byzantine agate bowl, once considered to be the Holy Grail."

Isobel Chatwin's mahogany wedding gift from Chamberlain, King and Jones was in the solid tradition of these *Wunderkammer*. With the development of British maritime power and the scientific voyages of Cook, Darwin and Huxley, most middle-class drawing rooms had a flat, glass-topped table which lifted to reveal "conversation pieces" to prove where the traveller had been. Some of the marvels turned out to be fake—the mermaid tail inevitably a piece of dried hake with a monkey sewn on. But many were genuine curios.

Isobel's family museum was as formative in its influence on Bruce as the collections of the Habsburg Emperors in Vienna and Prague were on the Meissen collector, Utz. In his last novel Bruce reaches back to his four-year-old self, to the young Utz visiting his grandmother's castle outside Prague and standing on tip-toe before her vitrine of antique porcelain and saying: "I want him." The slothskin has been recast as a Meissen harlequin with a leering orange mask. "He had found his vocation: he would devote his life to collecting . . ."

Werner Muensterberger, a friend of Bruce and the author of a study of the psychology of collecting, suggests that the collector is only too aware of the futility of his compulsion: "a chronic restiveness that can be cured only by more finds or yet another acquisition". Muensterberger, himself a collector and intimate with the "tyrannising" dedication of his calling, believes the collecting passion is an instrument "to allay a basic need brought on by early traumata". The infant looks to alternative solutions for dealing "with anticipations of vulnerability". For the young Bruce, always on the move, the objects in the cabinet became a fixed compass. In desiring to hold on to them, he alleviated, temporarily, his dread of being alone. "Things," he wrote in his notebook, "are substitutes for affection."

In his grandmother's dining room in West Heath Road, Bruce became one of the Prague *curieux*, seeking an explanation for all things. The building bricks, Isobel's photograph album, the tartan scraps were all part of the same plaid. No less than for Utz, his porcelain collector, "this world of little figures was the real world"—and the bombardments of the Second World War were "so many noises off".

Most travel writers colonise a territory. Bruce kept moving. Each of his books explores a different part of the world. They cooked in his head a long time, but the cabinet was his departure point. It was a centre of order, a larder for his daydreams, and the objects in it his toys, his routes to knowledge. Charlie Milward's hairy remnant belongs to *In Patagonia*; Uncle Humphrey's seed necklace to *The Viceroy of Ouidah*; Leslie's christening mug and the "Bruce china" to *Utz*; the Victorian walker's compass and pocket sun-dial to *The Songlines*.

"I'd polish the cabinet so it came up really lovely," says Irene, the cleaning lady. "It must have held raptures for him."

IV

War Baby

*To Freud we owe the insight that the character of the
human adult is already formed for better or worse
between the ages of 3 and 5.*
—BC, NOTEBOOKS

"BRUCE WAS A RAY of sunshine from the day he was born," said Margharita. Reluctant to put down roots while Charles was away at sea, she threw her energies into her son. He was a typical war baby, coddled by an anxious mother, fussed over by a team of elderly, mostly female relatives for whom he was the hope of the tribe. For four years, until his father's return and the birth of his brother Hugh, Bruce was the uncontested man of the house.

Margharita was by nature highly strung. Her nerves frayed with a husband at sea. Frightened by images of Charles being Stuka-bombed in the North Atlantic, she would shout out "Charles! Charles!" and talk as if he were in earshot. Bruce would come running to ask what was the matter.

"Nothing, darling."

She retreated into herself. "I hated news. I became a hermit, a complete and utter escapist." She avoided war work, anything that might risk exposing her to bad news. "I was always doing something else when the news was read." When John Amery was hanged, she did not want to know the details. When Aunt Grace suggested she take a job at a Royal Label factory down the road, she dug in her heels: her job was to look after Bruce until Charles came back.

Mother and son were extremely close. She read to him every night. His favourite book was *The Flower Fairies*. By the age of three he knew the names by heart. She said, "Once I threw out some flowers and Bruce found one which wasn't quite dead. 'Mummy, you mustn't do that. It's beautiful and still alive.' I felt very humble." They paid homage to that early bond throughout his life, signing letters to each other: "Love you pieces".

Then in the spring of 1943, the tenuous idyll they had created was ruptured when Bruce's father came back for a month's leave. This was the first of half a dozen visits he would make while serving in the Navy. Writing in his thirties, Bruce described the effect of this turmoil: "desperate attempts on my part to escape, if not mythically, by the invention of mythical paradise."

MARGHARITA HAD NOT seen her husband for two years. Charles had sailed in April 1941 on the new light cruiser *Euryalus*. Margharita took Bruce to Chatham to wave him off, but they were not allowed to be on the quay.

After a stint in Scapa Flow in the Orkneys, the *Euryalus* was despatched to protect the Malta convoys and joined the Eastern Mediterranean Fleet in Alexandria. Charles's attitude was: "I'm in this blooming war and until it's over I'm going to regard it as a job to be done." The "chaps" went ashore for nightlife, but not Charles. On alternate nights he kept watch beside the ASDIC, scanning the horizon for torpedo bombers. It was his sharp eyes that first spotted the trail of enemy smoke off the Libyan coast, prior to the battle of Sirte that put the Italian fleet out of the war.

People who served with him remarked on his bravery. He rose through the ranks quickly, one of the youngest in the R.N.V.R. to get captaincy. Switched to a minesweeper, he operated out of Malta as a watch-keeping officer until, just outside Valletta harbour, a mine ripped a 20-foot hole in the hull. In the spring of 1943, his ship limped into Sheerness, from where he telegraphed Margharita in Filey urging her to come to London.

Margharita left Bruce behind with Gaggie and joined Charles in the Carlton Hotel. They reached Filey a few days later. Charles, preparing for their first proper meeting, gave his son an olive-wood camel from Port Said. He joked to Bruce: "I bought this ship of the desert in case we had to escape from Rommel."

Bruce was wary of this man who had previously existed in a photograph beside his mother's bed, "gazing squarely at the camera from under the patent leather peak of his naval officer's cap". Bruce kissed this face before going to bed. Even so, he felt Charles's features "didn't quite belong".

In *What Am I Doing Here*, Bruce wrote about his first memory of his father, aged three: "He took us bicycling near Flamborough Head, the grey Yorkshire headland that Rimbaud may have seen from a brig and put into his prose-poem "Promontaire".

"He rigged up an improvised saddle for me on his crossbar, with stirrups of purple electric wire. I pointed to a squashed brown thing on the road.

" 'What's that, daddy?'

" 'I don't know.'

"He did not want me to see something dead.

" 'Well, it looks to me like a piece of hedgehog'."

Charles detected a guardedness in his son. "He was quite polite, but he didn't recognise me. It was slightly: 'Who's that man who's come to live with us?' " Bruce felt more fury than he let his father see. In Filey, he contended, his father "found a family rather united against him. My grandmother, mother and I formed a little nucleus: I tried to pretend he was *that* man, he *wasn't* my father."

Charles walked him to Filey Brigg, played with him on the sand, and after a month he was gone.

This stay was unusually long. In five years, father and son saw each other on snatched visits during Charles's standard 48-hour leaves. At the height of the U-boat war he arrived in Cardiff harbour in command of his own ship. In January 1944, Bruce and Margharita travelled by railway to Port Talbot and had lunch aboard H.M.S. *Cynthia*. Charles had brought the minesweeper all the way from Seattle.

Once on board, Bruce stood on the bridge and yelled down the intercom. He later wrote: "The place I liked most was my father's cabin—a calm, functional space painted a calm pale grey; the bunk was covered in black oilcloth and, on a shelf, there was a photograph of me." Ever since then "the rooms which have really appealed to my imagination have been ship's cabins, log cabins, monk's cells . . ."

Charles had promised to bring Bruce a banana, but somewhere in the Gulf of Mexico the bunch rotted. Instead, he gave his son a huge conch from the Mona Straits. Bruce wrote, "He said you could hear the wind and the waves of the Caribbean Sea if you put your ear up close. I decided that my shell was a woman and we called her Mona . . ."

Just at the point when the stranger was changing shape into his father, he would set off again. For Bruce to watch Charles depart during the war was a source of confusion and pain. Alone once more with a downcast and apprehensive Margharita, he steeled himself. Thirty-six years later he would sit in a train beside the Tagus, after separating from a lover, and write in his notebook: "Now moved to tears for one of the only times in my life." Then he added: "My father always to be departing."

IN THE SUMMER of 1943 until the following spring, Bruce attended a kindergarten in Filey. The Bluebird School cost three and a half guineas a term and faced the sea. "The house and garden are delightfully situated and there is an excellent air-raid shelter." Bruce found it hard to conceal his boredom. Once he was sent in disgrace to a spare room and when Margharita asked what he had been doing that day, he replied: "Spitting out of the window." Miss Taylor, the headmistress, told Margharita: "This child is different from the others."

In Birmingham, Bruce's Aunt Barbara discovered his habit of setting off down a track to see where it led. On Lickey Hill, she waited while he wandered out of sight. "There's a pig up there and it goes honk, honk, honk," he informed her, and he performed a snuffle with his nose. "He noticed everything," said Margharita, who was struck by her son's turn of phrase. Seeing snow for the first time in Birmingham, he pointed: "Look, Mummy. God spitting." Another time, he asked, "If I poke a hole in the sky, will God drop it?"

He preferred the company of older people. They interested him and he got on well with them. "Are you a *very* old lady?" he asked Mrs Nunwick in Filey. He had few friends of his own age. Billeted in Barnt Green with the James family, Margharita witnessed the distress of five-year-old John James. "I was in the kitchen and suddenly this little boy ran in and said: *'That bloody Bruce!'* I don't know what he had done."

Nor, today, can John recall. John's sister, Susan, remembers "an isolated little boy with a large head in comparison to the rest of his body, self-contained in the world—and very close to Margharita."

THE BIRTH OF his brother on 1 July 1944, destroyed the "tight nucleus" Bruce had known with his mother

The new baby placed more demands on Margharita. Bruce wrote in his nomad book of how "the arrival of a new-born brother or sister in his mother's arms provokes his jealousy and works towards later tensions . . . nomad history is wracked with the quarrels of brothers." Like most elder brothers, he felt "a slight trauma of rejection". When he had a runny nose and a lot of phlegm, he would say matter-of-factly to Hugh: "You got the better milk." It was during this period that some aspect of him locked, remained a child. A number of his friends, people who went on happily being his eternal hosts, saw in him someone who wanted others to take care of him. "He always sought father and mother figures," says Diana Melly, who would look after the adult Bruce in Wales. His pathological need to embroider dates from Hugh's birth. After the classic shock of the new arrival he had to pout more, be more charming, to keep his position.

Bruce wasted no time in establishing who was king of the castle. He claimed that the first word he heard Hugh pronounce was "Bruce". In October, he hijacked Hugh's christening ceremony. Hugh says, "I remember Bruce as a child saying he was christened on Shakespeare's grave. That was nonsense. It was borrowed from the fact that *I* was christened at the font of Holy Trinity, Stratford. By extension, he was being re-christened in order to assume the Bard's muse."

Soon after Hugh was born and before Charles came back, Margharita moved the boys to the pokiest lodging of all, "a small and hideous cottage" which had once been a café. Here, on the moors behind the Derbyshire village of Baslow, Bruce found—after his grandmother's cabinet—his second compass point. Ignoring his brother, he explored the surrounding countryside with his grandfather, Sam.

Forty years later, he revisited Baslow, intending to introduce his nomad book with an account of their walks. He found the bungalow transformed back into "The Cottage Café", with fake pine panelling, squeeze-me ketchup containers. The fireplace had been bricked in and the room glowed in the light of red lampshades.

Bruce, retracing his steps, was led as by a gunpowder trail to his childhood. "This is the room where I bent over my brother in his cot and he pulled at my nose and said my name months before he uttered another word. The small triangle of grass once seemed interminable to me. The hill behind the house where I raced the James children. My grandmother in the kitchen. Sound of laughter." He wanted to know how they had all fitted in.

His favourite walk led up onto the moors, through some woods, to a bald outcrop of weathered rock known as the Eagle Stone. This stone he understood to be "a pivotal point" in his life. Encouraged by Sam, he used to clamber on its sheer sides, run his hands over the graffiti covering its base. "Sam said there was an old 'un buried there. Or else it was a horse's grave, or a place where the Pharisees danced. His father had once seen the

fairies—'Them as 'ad wings like dragonflies'—but he could never remember where . . ."

Once in the Sudanese desert, Bruce would stumble on an almost
identical rock. "I became convinced I had discovered an archaeological
curiosity of the greatest importance. The experts obdurately expressed
their lack of interest. And it was a long time before I realised that my will
to believe its significance was coloured by emotional involvement over
which I had little control."

The walk to the Eagle Stone shaped the pattern of Bruce's future ex-
plorations. If collecting was one impulse, walking was the other. "My subsequent travels, imaginary or real, are of course relatively unimportant.
But I would say at the outset that I value my ambivalence highly. I avoid
head-on collisions, and attack surreptitiously or just walk out. I accumu-
late things rapidly and with financial success, then suddenly dispose of
them in an ill-tempered and impulsive way. I have never felt any real attachment to a home and fail to produce the normal emotive response
when the word is mentioned—except when travelling . . ."

v.

From Brothel to Piggery

These restricted horizons merely inflamed
Lewis's passion for geography. He would pester
visitors on "them savages in Afriky."
— On the Black Hill

A PROPER FAMILY required a proper house. On leave in 1945, Charles Chatwin learned through Wragge & Co. of an eviction order on a plain terraced house "on the wrong side of the Hagley Road" in Birmingham. A police spy had confirmed to the landlord that the house in Stirling Road was being used to entertain the army. The house was a brothel.

Charles acted swiftly, taking a two-year lease and agreeing to buy the upstairs wardrobes from the Madame, "a straighforward elderly lady, not particularly pleased at being turned out". For several months, American soldiers would ring up Margharita and ask for "Effie".

Charles returned to *Cynthia*, leaving his wife and sons to settle in on their own. Bruce said: "My bedroom window looked out on a Satanic mills landscape, with factories belching smoke and a black sky. The curtains had a fearful pattern of orange flames and like many children I had terrible dreams of the Bomb, of wandering through that blackened landscape with my hair on fire."

The Bomb, like Boney, grew into a vivid spectre.

Enrolled at Garry House nursery school in Fountain Road, Bruce was terrorised by the headmistress, a punctual and religious spinster who gave lectures on "nuclear attacks and fireballs". In between lessons, he beat drums and cymbals, made toys out of cardboard and played in the garden in good weather.

Charles still had Channel minesweeping duties, though the war in Europe was over. He towed a noisy "toad box" to set off acoustic mines. "I had a feeling it was suitable to lawyer, a regular performance." His last naval operation, which earned him the D.S.C., was to sweep the Oslo

Fjord and carry the Crown Prince of Norway back to his kingdom. He spent V.J. Day in an Antwerp hospital with jaundice, and on recovery eagerly accepted his "free pass to civilian life": a de-mob suit, hat, raincoat and a pair of walking shoes.

Bruce accepted the prospect of his father's return without fanfare. "One day my mother came upstairs with a newspaper in her hands saying, 'Wonderful news! Your father's coming home,' but I could only feel sick, looking at the mushroom cloud we'd all learnt about—Hiroshima had been bombed, it had finally happened."

Stirling Road—and Birmingham by implication—was forever associated in Bruce's mind with Hiroshima and freezing winters. The rooms were dreary and lacked central heating. "The house absorbed the damp like a sponge," Bruce wrote in *On the Black Hill*. "Mouldy rings disfigured the whitewash and the wallpaper bulged." He caught bronchitis and for two winters coughed up green phlegm. In later life, he returned to Birmingham only once. In 1980, he caught the train to Moor Street and from the window took in the Industrial Revolution housing; the slates, as though covered in coal dust; the puddles on top of the flat roofs. "The absolute hideousness," he wrote in his notebook. For Bruce, Birmingham was always a place to leave.

LIKE MANY YOUNG couples after the war, the Chatwins had to learn how to be a family for the first time. Mrs Beeton had no advice on coping with the war's aftermath: the shortages, the rationing and the receiving home of a husband you barely knew.

For himself, Charles picked up with his clients easily at Wragge & Co., but the situation in Stirling Road worried him. Bruce was in "bronchial misery" and a depressed Margharita was unable to shake off glandular fever. Common sense urged him to move house, but how and where? "My father," says Hugh, "was 95 per cent predictable and serious. Then all of a sudden he could do something wild."

As if in answer to a prayer, Charles's senior partner alerted him to a smallholding in the countryside twelve miles south of Birmingham. Brown's Green Farm had been carved out of the 5,000 acre Umberslade Estate to house old Mrs Muntz, who had died. The five-bedroomed turn-of-the-century dower house stood empty at the end of a long shale drive with two ponds, a kitchen garden, a staff cottage, paddocks and a ten acre field. The land on either side had been laid out as a shooting estate within tenanted farmland that had hardly been touched since the Great War. Visible through dark Scots pines was the spire of Tanworth Church, recently restored by Uncle Philip.

The house itself was "fairly derelict". The pebbledash had been painted 30 years before with tallow fat and whitewash, and the walls were patchy and grey. The property was for rent at £98 per annum on a repairing lease and the tenant would have to put in electricity.

Charles had no capital for a farming venture: all that he had was tied up in the goodwill of his law firm. "Ordinarily, a country life doesn't come to Birmingham people until *after* you've made your money," he argued to himself. "But can I turn the whole thing round?" He discussed with Margharita the sacrifices they would have to make. Husband and wife had been brought up in different steel towns. Country life was unlike anything they had experienced. The problem with Brown's Green was its isolation. As Margharita pointed out, there were no immediate neighbours, no shops, no buses to get around. Once they left their drive, all journeys had to be by car—and Charles's first car after the war was a "temperamental old Lanchester". There were no convenient state schools, so the boys would have to be sent to boarding school. And the tuberculosis scare? People were warning that the change of milk—straight from the cow instead of bottled and pasteurised—could take the children off. But Charles spelled out the logic: fresh air, fresh food on the table and a fresh start for each member of the Chatwin family. Why not go for it?

Charles's sister Barbara liked to boast that the Chatwins "did things— as opposed to the Milwards who sat behind high hedges and pondered their wealth". Charles had an adventurous elder brother who had emigrated to West Africa where he worked for the Gold Coast Railway. Humphrey Chatwin was Bruce's godfather and the favourite of the family. He was four years older than Charles, the same gap that separated Bruce from Hugh, and a romantic figure whose bold action Charles now sought to emulate by getting his family out of Birmingham. Though only twelve miles away, the relocation proved as life-altering as Humphrey's to Takoradi.

The family moved to Brown's Green in April 1947 during a famously long frost. There were 27 burst pipes and the snow was hedge-high. "Bruce was thrilled to bits," said his mother. His bedroom window looked out over the pigsties and his immediate delight was to sit perched on the window-sill, taking in the scene and waggling his legs. Several times Margharita, heart in mouth, feared to attract his attention lest he fall.

BROWN'S GREEN BECAME a safe haven after the horrors of war. Charles turned his eleven-acre holding into a small working farm much like "The Vision" in *On the Black Hill.* A Birmingham lawyer during the week, at weekends he invented himself as a food-producer with encouragement from the Ministry of Agriculture. He was allowed to set off farming losses against tax on his legal fees. He could afford a handyman, Mr Hayward, a home-help, Mrs Eden, and one reliable vehicle.

In 1949, short-circuiting the waiting list for a new car, Charles exchanged the Lanchester for a grey Ford delivery van, fitting it with removable wooden Spitfire seats for back passengers. With this all-purpose workhorse, he was able to visit clients, take the children on excursions and collect feed stuff for his livestock. The evil-smelling swill, known as "Tottenham Pudding", came in huge aluminium tubs to feed an eventual tally of 37 pigs. He also kept geese, ducks and 200 chickens. Covered in fluff, with her hair done up in a washerwoman's scarf, Margharita butchered and plucked the fowl. Engaged in a daily and productive occupation, she slowly rid herself of panic-attacks.

"We were brought up as country children, tied to the rhythm of the seasons," says Hugh. "The neighbouring tenants and labourers, who were rooted in 'proper' farming, became our main friends; mutually supportive at harvest time, during outbreaks of foot-and-mouth and fowl pest."

As Charles had hoped, the clean air and wholesome food improved the health of his wife and son. Thirty-five years later, Bruce conjured a bucolic picture of life at Brown's Green in *On the Black Hill.* Many of the characters, names and incidents appear as they were in his childhood and are taken directly from his family and neighbours. Bickerton, a wayward Milward cousin, becomes Reggie Bickerton, who perishes of alcoholism in Kenya; Bruce's grandfather Sam becomes Sam the Wheeler, with his sad clown's face and his porcelain statuette of a chubby-cheeked gentleman; the twins Lewis and Benjamin, in their physical resemblance and behaviour, become Bruce and Hugh.

"A special flavour of our childhood," says Hugh, "is that while we enjoyed romping in Lewis and Benjamin's rural playground—damning the infant River Alne with pebbles, pausing to wave at the passengers in passing puffer-trains so that they would be bound to wave back—we were also rejoicing in a much better time than we had known, had heard about, had witnessed at Birmingham's bomb sites. We knew that everything was getting better."

On sunny days, the boys helped Mr Hayward with his farming chores: they collected and scrubbed the eggs before they went off to the packing station, mixed the chicken mash, constructed wire pens for the ducks, fetched the milk from Kemp's Farm half a mile away, drove the large black sows, Charlotte and Louise, to be served at Hemming's Farm up the road and when Charles was away rode the pigs around the farm yard, holding them by the handle-bar ears and trying to stay on. "We mourned the ones that had to go off to be baconed," says Hugh. "They came home in canvas bags to hang in the box room."

As soon as they were old enough the boys joined in local field sports. They went ferreting in the hedge rows and learned to handle guns. Bruce was not squeamish. He shot wood pigeon from his window and chased the chickens with a bow and arrow. David Lea, who had known him at Garry House School, visited Brown's Green during the harvest rabbit shoot. "I remember the powerful smell of inside-of-rabbit."

And on the wet days? "We sat at the kitchen window and raced raindrops," says Hugh. "Or collected and played with Dinky toys on the kitchen table, getting under Mother's feet on her endless round of cooking and baking." Margharita took pleasure in spoiling her husband and boys. "My chaps," she called them.

Space to accommodate her parents had been Margharita's consideration in moving to the country. Sam and Gaggie had run out of money and both were heading for a Poorhouse end. They came to stay, in rote, as a last stepping stone before nursing homes in Leamington Spa. In 1950, Bruce's grandfather, no longer able to endure life with Gaggie, fled from their rented semi in Ickenham and turned up on the Chatwins' doorstep. "Old Sam had come to live at the Vision and slipped into a second childhood. He wore a moleskin waistcoat, a floppy black cap and went around everywhere with a blackthorn stick." Bruce and Hugh loved to go on walks with him down the Mile Drive from Umberslade Hall to Tanworth, some of which are vividly recalled in the novel. "It's our path!" they'd shout, if they happened to meet a party of hikers. The sight of a bootprint in the mud was enough to put them in a towering rage—and they'd try to rub it out with a stick.

They met few people. Five or six cars passed a day and Bruce would hide with Hugh in the grass and throw gravel at them. Hugh was known as "The Squeaker", or "Queekie", always wanting to catch up. "It was more like growing up with an uncle than a brother."

The farm was Bruce's world until he was 14. "Brown's Green taught us how to think independently," says Hugh. "As soon as we had bicycles we had freedom." With Hugh, Bruce delivered the parish magazine on the ten mile round circuit to Henley-in-Arden. There they indulged in ice-cream before Bruce dragged Hugh up the Roman settlement at Beaudesert. Aged ten, he had no fear about making expeditions to the flea-market in Birmingham's Bull Ring to buy caged birds or goldfish. "If we came home with a Java sparrow," Hugh says, "it was because we'd in-spected the atlas first to find out where Java was. From there we'd move to Woolworth's, to buy little nuts, bolts and screws for the sleek balsa wood catamarans which Bruce created to his own design. Then on to the stamp shop in Needless Alley; then onto the H.M.V. record shop where we would listen to 78s of Noel Coward and Fats Waller. At some stage we would go to the cartoon theatre and take in our view of the world via Movietone News."

The Ford van gave Charles and his family freedom to travel beyond Birmingham. On summer weekends, the family's social life revolved around the reservoir at Barnt Green Sailing Club. Bruce handled a square-nosed pram dinghy with skill, but was not at all happy at sea. In 1948, for their first holiday, he went coastal cruising on the five-ton *Ripple* out of Torquay. He promptly felt sick. "He longed for death and for the waves to wash over him," says Hugh. "I went below and taunted him. 'Up and down, up and down.' I had a cast iron stomach and I could get my own back at him for being four years older, at last."

There was no avoiding the sailing. By 1952, the Chatwins shared *Sun-quest*, a beamy 40-footer with a flush teak deck, built for sailing round the world. She was kept at Bursledon on the Hamble where they spent every third weekend. In an essay he wrote at Marlborough, Bruce caricatured the family outing: "Once a year there comes a morning when my father, instead of sauntering down to breakfast with a customary frown, bounces downstairs, eats five times more breakfast than usual, and capers about as if he were 20. The reason for this outburst is a visit to the most important member of the family, the yacht. Through his veins surges the blood of Drake and Hawkins; bowler hat gives way to yachting cap, and his thoughts run far above his bevy of secretaries and Mrs A.'s will.

"My mother also transforms herself from the wife of a respectable lawyer, and chairman of all sorts of philanthropic committees, into a pi-rate's spouse. She dresses to the part with tight black trousers, canvas shoes and a massive blue sweater, a savage scarf tied round her head in true pi-ratical fashion, and a pair of earrings that would have delighted Captain

Kidd. This uniform has become *de rigueur* for all yachtswomen from Bembridge to Salcombe and has even appeared in *Vogue*.

"My brother adopts the urchin look, jeans and a terrible piece of headgear with a bobble on it. Only myself and the dog are upset. I loathe going to sea . . ."

Sunquest WAS A rare luxury. There was no money spare. The war, his determination to be good and not to be observed doing anything but good, had reinforced Charles's correctness. Because of the Milward scandal, he went out his way never to be thought grasping. This extended to not paying himself properly. To neighbours like the James children it appeared that he struggled a bit. "The idea got through to us that they weren't nearly as well off as some of our friends."

At home he found himself without his ship's company and the object of ribbing by his wife, sons and father-in-law. Sam, enjoying his second childhood, set no sort of example, cheating at cards and encouraging the boys to lapse into a full Yorkshire dialect. "Let's say 'fower' till daddy comes." The house was full of laughter, often aimed at Charles's virtue. Once, he came home to discover Margharita and Bruce giggling uncontrollably after Bruce had said of a woman in Tanworth Church: "A woman with a bottom like that can do *anything*."

Bruce himself never tolerated being teased. According to Elizabeth, "If you teased him he took it personally, as if you didn't like him. He always took everything you said seriously." Combined with occasional laspes into gullibility, this made him a natural target for teasers such as Jonathan Hope. "I told him, quoting a line from *In Patagonia*: 'When you laugh like that your mouth unfurls like a red flag.' Bruce threw his napkin at me. 'Stop it!'"

Friends and relations were always commenting on how the genes were apportioned between the children. The father's fair hair and blue eyes went to Bruce, along with the mother's temperament. Her brown eyes and dark hair passed to Hugh, and the father's dogged pragmatism.

Where Margharita was instinctive, going straight to the point without knowing how she arrived there, Charles was rational to the point of pedantry. He had the Milward bossiness, an answer to how everyone should behave, and he had the knack of annoying Margharita by asking: "What's the other side of the story?" She once rebelled, flinging an enamel jug against the kitchen wall. "Why do you always address me like a public meeting?"

In spite of their different temperaments, the marriage worked. For the most part, Margharita was compliant. She busied herself in farm work or mending her husband's shirts, his suits. If she felt cut off, she never said so. She liked a gossip with her friends in the Women's Institute, afterwards entreating: "Don't tell Charles I told you." They were liked and trusted as a couple. There was only one serious argument played out before the children. "Mother," says Hugh, "was adamant that what was in one's blood formed character that would not change. Father was the opposite. He believed that if people's environment could be improved then they could be persuaded to behave better." Bruce constantly resurrected their argument in his work. All his questing, Hugh believes, can be distilled into a single question: Do we have a capacity to behave better towards our neighbours than we do? Hugh sees this question lurking behind the puzzled look in Bruce's early photographs. "Don't frown," Margharita would tell him.

Physically, Bruce was almost identical to Charles. He was called Charles at school, and frequently this was how he signed himself. But the relationship was more respectful than close. Even if Charles was not a controlling figure, Bruce never wanted to disappoint his father. "His whole childhood was governed by not letting Charles down," says Elizabeth. "He would say: 'I don't want my father to think badly of me'." As a result, they kept a Victorian distance. "That Bruce did not unbottle his emotions was a Father-influence," says Hugh. "It was a matter of personal *responsibility* to keep them in check."

Bruce, after he left home, moved between extolling his father's virtues from a distance and recoiling from his way of life. He lived always conscious of his character: his above-board honesty, his "absolute fairness and tireless, unostentatious work for others". But he did not share the same aspiration: "Imagine the horror of being stuck in your father's creation," he wrote in his notebook in Patagonia. And yet he admired Charles his ability to be happy. Years later in Africa, Bruce had this dream of his parents: "Margharita in her blue dress with the orange and green cummerbund and Charles in tails, dancing in the moonlight. I felt that, in their way, they are the most romantic couple on earth."

———

CHARLES TREATED BRUCE from the start as a small adult with no baby talk. He passed on to him a habit of precision and self-expression honed from the legal trade: at the end of each day he would expect Bruce to describe his. "If Bruce had been to a tea-party," Charles said, "I would ask him to tell me properly where he'd been, who he'd met, what their names were, because I thought it was important he should become articulate."

He directed Bruce to answer the telephone, taught him to throw his words out and not to mumble. "I was keen for him to talk. Once he started, he never stopped."

Bruce grew not only articulate, but adept at covering his tracks. "He would always give an answer," says Elizabeth. "I taxed him on it: 'Why do you do that?' 'Oh well, better to give you an answer.' He wanted to shut me up."

Apparent to the whole family was Bruce's phenomenal memory. By the time he was seven, said Margharita, he would chant the whole of "The Walrus and the Carpenter" in his bath.

In the 1970s, Meriel McCooey, fashion editor of the *Sunday Times* magazine, asked Bruce: "Where do you think it all began?"

"I'll tell you exactly," said Bruce. "I was two years old. My parents were running for a train and dropped me on my head. After that I was a genius."

Genius was a word he got hold of early. Aged seven, he told Hugh: "Erasmus says it is possible to be a great genius *and* a complete fool." Hugh replied: "Then *you*, Bruce, must be a *great* genius." Charles was doubtful. "A genius to me is someone who has a rather one-track mind and that was exactly what he hadn't got. Unusual is the right word."

Charles linked Bruce in his mind to another remarkably precocious young boy. In the 1920s Charles had met the *Daily Telegraph*'s theatre critic W. A. Darlington. On Leslie Chatwin's invitation to judge a night of one-act plays, Darlington had stayed in West Heath Road and impressed Charles with the story of his father, the son of a poor yeoman farmer from Cheshire with a startling gift for languages. At the age of eight he would lean over the bridge on the Montgomery Canal and talk in Welsh to the bargemen. He picked up Romany from tramping miles after gypsy caravans and spoke Xhosa. In Russia, he visited Tolstoy whose wife chatted to him for ten minutes without having the least notion that he was not Russian. Bruce, said Charles, possessed something of the older Darlington's photographic recall.

Hugh was also conscious of his brother's talent. "I used to watch him amaze the adults. He'd mug it up. He could absorb any piece of information and then try and make a connection with it—and when it couldn't all fit together, he'd make up the rest of it. For me, he'd wear a sign on his forehead: 'Don't disturb. I am thinking. When I am ready to talk to you, I'll do so.' Then he'd come out with his stories, fully prepared."

Hugh reckoned that "60 per cent" of the content of his brother's stories was true, the rest embellishment. "It was the story that counted and Bruce was a witness to the story. 'Come on, Bruce, surely it didn't happen like that,' we'd say. And it hadn't. But something *had* happened. We would all look at each other and coax him to continue: 'Yes, and then . . . ?' "

"When Bruce told you a fact," said Charles, "you could rely on it. When he told you an opinion, that was different. He had a pretty vivid imagination. As a child, he had an imaginary friend, Tommy, who talked to him a lot and to whom he would tell stories."

In the summer of 1947, Bruce was already testing his more hair-raising stories on pupils at Innisfree House, a private kindergarten catering for children from the R.A.F. station in Wythall. His teacher was Mrs Clifton, her name unchanged in *On the Black Hill*, where she is described as "a buxom woman with milky skin and hair the colour of lemon peel". Mrs Clifton, who taught him elocution, is responsible for the first written estimation of Bruce. "Fluent—too much emphasis on some words," she wrote in her first report, placing him eighth out of 16. Her comment the following term was, "Good memory—rather monotonous tone." He was generally "careless" and in arithmetic "below standard", while achieving "very good preliminary work" in literature.

Never more than an average pupil at Innisfree, he was by his own account only interested in journeys and maps. "I was a tremendous fabulist." In one story he had "absolutely nothing" to do with England. "I startled the class by pointing dramatically at the White Sea on the classroom atlas, and held their attention with a confident revelation. My parents were not my parents at all. I was a Russian orphan. I described in graphic detail my escape across the frontier to safety. Dead of winter, sledges, panting huskies and black pine trees. Guns of the soldiers blazed on the frozen river. Blood in the snow. I was the only survivor. So brave. One little girl sobbed and burst into tears. The headmistress suggested to my mother I might see a psychiatrist."

His love of embellishment was noticed by David Lea, his Birmingham friend, who, one summer, stayed overnight at Brown's Green. "Bruce's parents had gone out. We were sleeping upstairs when we heard the sound of the door opening downstairs, and very quietly someone coming in. Bruce said: 'I don't think there's been a murder here for *years*.' He crept to the banister in his pyjamas and looked over. Mrs Eden, the home-help, had forgotten something. It was a moment of real fright." Lea presumed a murder had taken place. It had, but somewhere else.

ON 8 DECEMBER 1949, when Bruce was nine, his uncle Humphrey was murdered by his cook-boy in West Africa. Humphrey Chatwin was 46. One of the first students at Pangbourne Naval College, he had worked—like Charles Milward—for the New Zealand Shipping Company. In 1946, he was appointed pilot in the Marine Branch of the Gold Coast Railway. He lived with his wife and young daughter in Takoradi harbour where, in Chatwin tradition, they sailed a twelve-foot dinghy with a sliding gunter rig. The staff included Loggart Wadedai, a Nigerian known locally as "the boy who never smiled".

Humphrey had already experienced a premonition about Loggart. While on leave in the summer of 1949, he showed Charles and Margharita a photograph of his staff. He pointed at his cook-boy, one of whose duties was to prepare meals on a stove Humphrey had constructed from old aircraft parts. "I don't trust that one."

On his return to the Gold Coast, Humphrey dismissed Loggart for refusing to clean the brassware. Leaving the house, Loggart was caught lifting Humphrey's silver. Told to open his bag, he stabbed Humphrey.

"Bruce's version," says Hugh, "is that the man was so angry at being dismissed that he came back at the dead of night to monogram Uncle Humphrey between the shoulder blades."

News of the tragedy was slow to reach Birmingham. Isobel Chatwin read about it in the paper over breakfast. "She was in such an upset state," says Irene Neal. At the death of her favourite son, Isobel's health declined.

For a while it looked as if Bruce and Hugh might gain a sister, Humphrey's daughter Philippa. Charles offered to adopt her. "I wrote saying there's a gap in our family and we very much would like to have had a daughter." Eventually, it was decided that Philippa would live with relations in New Zealand.

Charles and Margharita never talked of the tragedy, yet it affected their sons. "If I had nightmares," says Hugh, "it was about getting a knife stuck in me. Black Africa was something to conquer. When I left school, I went to Africa to purge that fright." Nor could Bruce forget his uncle's "sad end in Africa". He knew about Humphrey from the things kept in Isobel's cabinet. He had played on the carpet with his cowrie shells, used on the Gold Coast as coins, and tried on his witch doctor's silver bracelet and the seed necklace from Takoradi. But the strongest link with his murdered uncle was the large black trunk that arrived at Brown's Green containing Humphrey's possessions.

The trunk became the boys' acting box and was stored in the "box room" with the bacon. Into it went Robert Milward's robe from Emir Faisal; Leslie Chatwin's Shakespeare costumes; Isobel Chatwin's enormous crinolines from the 1890s; and several evening dresses, embroidered in silk and satin, which had belonged to Aunts Gracey and Jane. Also, some cast-off bonnets courtesy of Margharita.

If sailing was Charles's one indulgence, dressing up was Margharita's. "Whatever else was needed, mother could still have her dresses," says Hugh. She cut some herself, as Gaggie had taught her, from patterns in English and French magazines. For others, she went to a dress-maker in Leamington Spa whose most elaborate creation was a ball-gown in primrose satin with flounced sleeves and a whalebone corset. Copied from a black and white photograph in a biography of Gertie Lawrence, this was so voluminous that when she wore it for the first time to a hunt ball, Bruce and Hugh had to turn their mother upside down to fit the whole confection in the back of the car.

Bruce involved himself in Margharita's pleasure. "You can say she was Gertie to Bruce's Noel," says Hugh. Bruce knelt beside his mother while she turned the pages of her *Queen,* her *Tatler,* her *L'Officiel,* admiring the colour, line and cut of dresses. (His first articles for the *Sunday Times* would be interviews with French fashion designers of this period.) "I love it when Bruce comes back," Margharita told Pat Barber, his housemaster at Marlborough. "Whenever I go shopping for clothes he's very good at advising me about what I should get."

Not having daughters, Margharita enthused him with her idea of female glamour. She enrolled him in Miss Jepson's dance classes in a room off the Hagley Road, where he learned to dance waltzes and quicksteps— and "to hold a woman properly". Twenty years later, Bruce spoke of all these things while walking with James Lees-Milne. "He was," wrote Lees-Milne in his diary, "his mother's darling. He saw his father only during his rare leaves from the [Navy], and when he appeared in the home Bruce resented his intrusion. His mother, an unwise woman, doted, even dressed him up in her clothes for fun when he was a child of six."

Margharita denied that she had ever decked Bruce in her clothes, except for school plays, but Bruce enjoyed creating this fiction in *On the Black Hill*: "One drizzly morning, the house was unusually quiet and when Mary heard the creak of a floorboard overhead, she went upstairs. Opening the door of her bedroom, she saw her favourite son, up to his armpits in her green velvet skirt, her wedding hat half-covering his face. 'Psst! For heaven's sake, she whispered. Don't let your father see you!' "

Whether or not Charles approved of his son dressing up in female clothes, he did encourage a full use of the acting box for charades. He believed, like Leslie, that amateur dramatics were good for children. The brothers took turns to appear downstairs before family and guests. Unable to wear Harding Milward's court suit, Bruce squeezed into Aunt Gracey's evening dress, in a curly ginger wig and long-drop marcasite earrings. Disguised as a length of brick in the Wall Suit from his grandfather's production of *A Midsummer Night's Dream*, he would recite: "Oh wall, oh wall, oh sweet beloved wall, wherefore thy chink?" His attraction to explorers like Burkhardt and Burton, who passed themselves off as Arabs, began in his parents' drawing room where he elevated Robert Milward's robe into the "golden headdress" of T. E. Lawrence, and was very cross when it got lost. In these improbable attires, he and Hugh sung the words of Jack Buchanan and Noel Coward, taken from records they had bought in Birmingham. "He impersonated Coward perfectly," says David Lea. "It was him doing his thing."

AFTER THE FALSE start at Stirling Road (the house was later demolished in a slum clearance programme), Charles had succeeded in giving his children a country childhood, an environment where they could find and develop their calling. Hugh followed his father into a profession, living a settled existence, but Bruce fixed his eyes elsewhere. He abandoned the pastoral and chased the excitement that he imagined had driven his globe-trotting uncle to Africa. Bruce was ten when Humphrey's trunk appeared at Brown's Green. In the same year, 1950, he put his hand down a rabbit hole and extracted a piece of iridescent glass which he was convinced was Roman. It gave him the idea of starting his own collection along the lines of Isobel's family museum. For his tenth birthday he made it plain that nothing would be more acceptable than a miniaturised version of his grandmother's cabinet. After a tour of junk shops, the family settled on a glass-fronted specimen-cabinet with a tiny padlock, bought in Moseley for 10s.

"When we'd finished playing with our Dinky toys, sometimes we'd look at Bruce's collection," says Hugh. "He'd open it up when he'd found something new to say about the objects." The collection consisted of odds and ends: glass ornaments of a dachshund and a kangaroo acquired in the Bull Ring; a miniature set of blacksmith's tools; a wooden saucer from Norway dated 1945, a fragment of meteorite. But the prize exhibit was the piece of "brontosaurus" given to him by Isobel. (Bruce claimed that this was thrown away when she died in 1953, but according to Hugh and Charles, it was lost in 1961 when the Chatwins moved to Stratford.)

Too large to fit in the cabinet was "Mr Johnson", a four-inch figurine in the shape of a Toby jug fat man. Mr Johnson did not come from the Bull Ring, but was a gift from Sam and lived on Bruce's bedroom shelf. Bruce, before his death, requested the porcelain statuette be lodged in the Bodleian Library, along with 41 boxes of papers and notebooks.

Mr Johnson is a portly gentleman in a Homburg and long green coat, and in his right hand he holds a lavender-coloured Gladstone bag. Curling in brown script around his base are the words: *I am starting for a long journey.*

VI.

〰

I Know Where I'm Going

The sad thing was, we never saw him very much
after school. He disappeared out of our lives.
—MARGHARITA CHATWIN

AT THE END of April 1948, Bruce was sent away to Old Hall School in Shropshire. After completing one week, he sat down to write to his parents. His first surviving letter shows him alert to the miraculous and the forbidden.

"Old Hall, Wellington, 2 May

"Dear Mummy and Daddy, It is a lovely school. We had a lovely film called The Ghost Train. It was all about a train the come into the station every year at mid-night and if any one looked at it they wold die. I am in the second form.

With love from Bruce"

He would spend the next ten years at boarding school: a fifth of his life. A public school education gave him his accent, his manners and his Englishness. In Bruce's case, the experience of being cooped up between the age of seven and 18 meant that he would never sit still for long.

Old Hall, a former coaching inn set in 25 acres, had been transformed in the mid-nineteenth century into a preparatory school for the sons of the professional classes of the Midlands. It was the personal fiefdom of Paul Denman Fee-Smith, a stocky and energetic bachelor with a swarthy complexion who dressed in bold checks. Once a shipping clerk, he had bought the school with a bank loan in 1926. He advertised it as "The Best Preparatory School in England" and there was rumoured to be a waiting list—although when Charles Chatwin enquired what standard was expected of Bruce, the reply came: "If he could read, that would be marvellous."

Fee-Smith was the son of an impecunious clergyman and one of four brothers known as Fee, Fi, Fo and Fum. He was a man of rigorous Christian beliefs. He took a cold bath every morning and used the cane freely for bad work or talking after lights out. To the boys he was known as "Boss".

Boss was everywhere. "Totally all pervasive," says John Thorneycroft, a contemporary of Bruce. Boss produced the school plays, coached games, operated the film projector, read the lesson in chapel and every Guy Fawkes Night was a spectral figure letting off fireworks.

Britain having won the war, Boss saw himself training a new generation for Empire. "Still in my time, four years after Bruce," says Hugh, "we were the chosen, the leaders who would rebuild the empire in the wake of Scott of the Antarctic, Winston Churchill, Sir Edmund Hillary." Bruce's stamp collection was drawn exclusively from the British colonies.

THE FORD VAN which carried the pigswill from Birmingham also took Bruce to Old Hall. For five years, he shuttled with his school trunk from Shropshire to Brown's Green through the outskirts of Wolverhampton. Most children felt homesick in their first term. Brown's Green had fostered Bruce's self-sufficiency. He was content, even cheerful.

"Dear Mummy, This is only a short letter to ask you if you could get me some rubber bands 'Love you pieces'." The regime was spartan, but homely. With five others Bruce shared a wooden-floored dormitory overlooking the Arcle woods, some flowering cherry trees and a pond where on summer evenings he floated his model boat "Lobster", a white and green sailing boat, 18 inches long, which had belonged to his late uncle Humphrey.

He wore a maroon and grey uniform, with a cap and blazer. At the end of each fortnight Boss summarized his class's achievements before the school. Each boy was awarded plus or minus marks, according to whether he rose or fell below his personal ability standard. And a "Black" for discipline.

One of the few friends Bruce kept from Old Hall was Andrew Bache, whose father made weighing-machines in West Bromwich. Bache met him on their first day. "He had very fair hair, cut short, and a head too big for its body—almost a perfect square in all directions, like an Oxo cube." Everyone remarked on this huge head.

In the adult Bruce, many people thought they saw a schoolboy. Charles Bruce Chatwin the schoolboy left virtually no impression at all. To most of his school friends and masters, he was an unexceptional student who, though articulate, did not distinguish himself. He was not sporty. He was not academic. He was not naughty. Making a certain amount of noise, he earned the nickname "Chatty". He did not much care if his marks were good, or if he scored a try on the rugby pitch. He was pleasing himself and in pleasing himself he was quietly banging in the rungs of his independence.

"He could do pretty well if interested," said Charles. "If he wasn't interested, he'd do damn badly." In Lent 1951, he won the form prize. But he was often "inclined to be inattentive". He would be a haphazard speller all his life. Inconsistency was a regular complaint; also irresponsibility. "I came second in the term order. I didn't want to be first as it is to much of a fag." Boss noted Bruce's restlessness in his first report: "He is rather a careless worker & his attention soon wanders. He is still very young & hardly out of the egocentric stage; his behaviour is childish & very noisy at times!"

After assembly, and twice on Sundays, the boys trooped into a small chapel where they sang hymns to a hand-pumped organ. In Bruce's first term, Boss arranged for a gramophone company to record the choir singing "I waited for the Lord", but the recording was marred by sparrows. Bruce was not in the choir: "He has very little vocal ability," reported Miss Davies, his Welsh singing teacher. Nevertheless, he was exercised by the scale with which she used to stretch his ranges, sung to the words "Why do the nations so furiously rage together?" To Hugh, this was just chord practice. "But Bruce would go on thinking. Why *do* the nations so furiously rage together? And he wouldn't let it go. He'd give it 25 per cent extra and he always did that."

Organised High Anglican religion was an essential underpinning in Boss's preparation for Empire. "Mr Fee Smith gave a very good sermon this morning," Bruce wrote on Sunday, 6 March 1949. In spite of his motto, "Christianity cannot be taught: it can only be caught," Boss enjoyed preaching. Miracles were his favourite topic. Wearing white ecclesiastical regalia with cope and coloured shawl, he advised the boys about their prospects for Heaven, if they were good, and about the sure fires of Hell, if they were not. Boss introduced Bruce to Bunyan's pilgrim and to Jeremy Taylor's sermons, whom Bruce would say was "the only seventeenth-century English writer worth reading". Just before Bruce's confirmation, on 24 November 1952, Boss transfixed a group of boys with his true story of someone who on the point of death saw the face of God, survived, and came back to describe his vision.

Fee-Smith invited Bruce to enter a world of absolute values, black and white, without moral ambiguity. With his "melodious singing voice" and child-like views of the Bible, Bruce's headmaster is recalled in the character of the preacher Gomer Davies in *On the Black Hill*: "In a low liturgical voice, he began, 'I see your sins as cat's eyes in the night. . .'." It was Davies who would give to the twins' father, Amos, the colour print of "The Broad and the Narrow Path": depicting, on the left side, "The Way to Perdition"—smart people "drinking, dancing, gambling, going to theatres"; and on the right, "The Way to Salvation"—people going to Church.

THE 108 PUPILS were taught by a dozen or so masters, a lot of them shell-shocked. After the war, the shortage of well-trained teachers explained the presence of some characters who would have found a comfortable billet in Evelyn Waugh's Llanabba. Divinity was taught by an especially nervous ex-officer who stammered, French by a master who had lost his ear. He always looked the other way in photographs and during Assembly would sit at the back with his lost ear to the wall. Then there was the Captain Grimes figure who would mark your book "and his hand would be fiddling with your bottom". Boss was also known to enjoy a tickle. "There were a number of activities going on which were pretty odd," says Thorneycroft. "He'd make us swim in an open air pool, for instance, and we were not allowed to wear our trunks until we'd passed the test. I never could get the rationale behind that."

Lunch was eaten at 1.05, off a trolley wheeled by small, fierce Annie from the Black Country. A little farm in the grounds provided vegetables, milk from eight cows, and eggs. Food rationing continued until 1954 and it was drummed into the boys how lucky they were. But the diet was austere: a pat of margarine; boiled potatoes; fried fish that came off the bone in chunks. "The top was all right," says Bache, "but if you turned it over and looked at the bottom, it was quite awful." And for pudding, chocolate pudding with a thick skin.

On Monday, Tuesday and Friday afternoon Bruce played games. "He was at a disadvantage because sport was not his thing," says Bache. "Playing soccer he'd be likely to kick you and not the ball." Boss observed: "He does not show very much aptitude for football . . . but his swimming has improved." In his last year Bruce played for the rugby fifteen, where he operated "as a clumsy but hard-working forward, full of determination".

It was in the improbable arena of boxing that he shone. On 18 March 1951, Bruce wrote home: "I boxed in the ring on Monday against a tough. I won 5–3. I am in the final for the Junior Cup. I have got a very good chance."

The "tough" was Philip Howard, who before stepping through the ropes had agreed a pact with Bruce that they would try to avoid hitting each other while appearing to do their best. "One of us hit the other on the nose very early on, and after that it was fireworks," says Howard.

The ordeal took place in Hall, before the whole school, and Boss made the boys strip to their waists while matron stood by to mop their bloody noses between rounds. Savoring the physicality of the contest, Boss wrote that Bruce proved "a hard, relentless hitter and gives the impression of immense solidity".

In the boxing ring, Bruce's "do or die spirit" was good for Boss to see, never more so than in the "magnificent" final against Butler-Madden, written up by Boss in the school magazine. "It looked as if the power and weight of Chatwin would prove superior. The first round bore this out. Butler-Madden was in great trouble. Then came the transformation in the second round—Butler-Madden decided to go all out and go all out he did. He proved to have the superior stamina and Chatwin had had enough by the end. This was one of the finest performances seen in Junior Cup battles."

"DEAR MUMMY PLEASE could you get me a box of marbles because I have not got any. 'Love you pieces' Bruce."

Bruce's letters from Old Hall give a narrow but valuable glimpse of his school life. The week's highlight was the Saturday film in Hall. An early cinematic experience was *The God of Creation,* showing the handiwork of the Lord at high speed: a rose hurtling into bloom, a magnified survey of the Milky Way and the life history of a caterpillar in a very few seconds. Most of the films were adventure stories. "We had a film called I know where I'm going, it was about a girl that went to mary a man in Scotland, and she was going to catch a boat it was a very rough sea, they nerly got washed up on to the beach when the got caught in a werlpool."

Travellers were invited to give lantern lectures. In Bruce's first term the nephew of the explorer Cherry Kearton gave a talk on the African veld illustrated with photographs of man-eating lions taken at "suicidal proximity", and Captain Jopp, in a lecture entitled "High Adventure", showed slides of his "thrilling flight" around the Matterhorn.

On Sunday nights in winter, Boss invited boys to sit before a log fire in his drawing room while he read aloud from *Jamaica Inn, Beau Geste* and *The Prisoner of Zenda*.

Bruce was less interested in fiction than in true adventure stories.

"Dear Mummy and Daddy Please could you get me a Romany Book, called *Out with Romany by Medow and Stream*. Because I want it for a friend of mines birthday. Yesterday we had a lantern lecture on a man's uncle who went to Africa to exploring and he took a lot of photographs on big game and natives. In my book *Wild Life* there are two photographs. One of some Rock rabbits, and another of a jackel. It was very nice. I hope you are well. Please will you send a book called *The Open Road*. Tell Hugh it wont be long rill I come home. Please will you save these stamps till I come home. When you see Aunt Gracie next tell her I send my love. 'Love you pieces' Bruce."

A storyteller is most influenced by the kind of stories he first thrills to. Bruce's first books, bought at Hudson's bookshop in Birmingham with 10s 6d tokens, were about sailing round the world: *Sopranino, Blue Waters and Shoals, The Venturesome Voyages of Captain Voss*. Because of Old Hall's connection with the explorer Shackleton—his father had been a pupil—the library was stocked with Joshua Slocum, Richard Henry Dana, Jack London, Lucas Bridges.

—"I have just got a book out of the senior library called *We didn't mean to go to sea* which tells you how to sail a 5-ton cutter. I hope I will learn something from it."

—"I took a very interesting book out of the library called *Heroes of the South Pole*.

—"Please don't send me any comics when I am ill. They bore me. A boy's magazine such as *Boy's Own* would be much more appreciated. Your affectionate son, Bruce."

His mental world was dominated by South Sea islands and deserts. His favourite writers were "the odd ones, the Victorian ones". The Rev. Skertchley, who had travelled among the Amazons of Dahomey ("one of the surrealist books of all time"); Henri de Monfried's *Hashish*; Blaise Cendrars. He also scanned the *Times* atlas. "Some children obviously play with toys, some children play with computer games and I played at a very,

very early age with an atlas. It was the only thing that interested me, to go to X and Y and Z, to see it all." He considered the schoolroom atlas as "sort of one's back door" and in the Old Hall library he pored over the wind chart to decide that Patagonia was the safest place to hide in event of a cobalt bomb.

Lastly, there was the hobbies room. "Conjouring has taken itself in the school and I am very interested in it. I am making some tricks myself."

BRUCE HAD BEEN brought up by Margharita, Gaggie and his great-aunts to be someone special. At the end of his first term he was welcomed back to Brown's Green according to his specific instructions. The greeting he demanded was similar to that of a sailor returning from the war: chocolate mousse and a banner of towels above the shale drive, painted with the words "Welcome home, Bruce!"

At school this Little Prince behaviour did not command sympathy. John Thorneycroft thought him boastful and self-important. On at least four occasions Boss had to caution his parents against a manner which tended to prejudice others against him. "I am sure he is straight and dependable. But he is not popular at the moment with his fellows & appears to be regarded as conceited."

He annoyed masters, too. "On Monday I had the wacking, for refusing to give a chit in, which was not true. I was beating the master (Mr Poole) in an argument. He knew he was loosing so he said 'Well, it's too late now I have reported you to Mr Fee Smith, and he told me to write you out a chit'."

Despite his prowess in the ring, Bruce was not one of Boss' favorites, but Fee-Smith did try to help him locate and cultivate his strengths. Not being shy, Bruce was summoned to talk with parents. "I was awfully embarassed yesterday, some weomen and one man sat on our bench while we were watching the match. I had to entertain them." Boss also encouraged him on to the stage.

Acting was the activity Bruce enjoyed most at Old Hall. "He was a damned good actor," says Thorneycroft, still able to remember Bruce's Orsino. Bruce's first stage role, in December 1949, was a highwayman in A. P. Herbert's *Fat King Melon and Princess Caraway*. The reviewer called him "a good-looking chap". The following year, Boss asked him to play the part of Bottom in *A Midsummer Night's Dream*. "The play is going on quite well now. Boss has put a lot of imagination in it. I think that if acted propaly it will be very nice." The play was performed on 14 December 1950. "Perhaps pride of place should go to Bottom the Weaver," wrote the reviewer. "A very young member of the cast this one, who had a lot to do and did it with great gusto. Ass's head or no ass's head you did well, 'sweet bully Bottom' . . ." In December 1951, he played the love-lorn Orsino in *Twelfth Night* ("to excellent results"); in December 1952, a wicked uncle in *Babes in the Wood* ("and what a nasty uncle to have!") and in March 1953 he was Baptista in *Taming of the Shrew*. "For a boy to play the part of a doddering old man is always difficult, but Chatwin played Baptista's part so convincingly as to make it appear easy."

THE HIGHLIGHT IN the Old Hall calendar was Guy Fawkes Night.

Bruce always wrote about this in his letters ("Yesterday the fireworks were absolutly wizzard. There were 130 rockets, 14 cathrine weels, 4 christal fountains and a lot more"). However, on 5 November 1951, weeks after the defeat of Clement Attlee's Labour government, there occurred what Hugh Chatwin describes as "a big shock" in his brother's life. Boss celebrated the Labour defeat by changing Guy Fawkes into Attlee—and, together with an effigy of Mrs Attlee, he tossed him onto the bonfire.

The spectacle of Mrs Attlee's blazing pumpkin hat deeply distressed the eleven-year-old Bruce. Crying at the memory of it, he told Margharita: "Mummy, how could he do-o-o this?" Hugh believes that Fee-Smith's subversion of Guy Fawkes Night marked Bruce's moral awakening. "He realised that he thought differently from people around him."

Neither Bache nor Thorneycroft remember Attlee being burned. Nor did Bruce make any mention of it in his Sunday letter. "I enjoyed the fireworks last night. They made a very good display indeed."

IN THE SUMMER of 1953 Bruce passed his Common Entrance into Marlborough. In his final address, Boss exhorted Bruce to "hold on to the lovely things in life", and issued this warning: "It is most important to make a good start: if you start the wrong way it becomes difficult to get back on the right road again. A man who was travelling one spring time in the North of Canada when the frost was breaking up and the roads were well nigh impassable saw this notice at a cross-road: 'Take care which rut you choose: you will be in it for the next 25 miles'."

Apart from his performances in the school play, Bruce's five years at Old Hall passed largely unnoticed in the school annals. "If you were to say, 'This is the boy who is going to be Bruce Chatwin'," says Bache, "I would have said: 'No, I don't think so'."

VII.

ᏫᎥᎳᎳᎧ

The English Schoolboy

. . . he finds difficulty in remembering facts and only
the bizarre or trifling really appeals to him.
—ROMAN HISTORY REPORT FOR
MICHAELMAS, 1956

IN SEPTEMBER 1953, after a sailing holiday on the Hamble river, Bruce's parents drove him in their old black Rover to begin his first term at Marlborough College.

Charles had considered Winchester, but it was "out of pocket reach". For an annual fee of £291, he could, however, afford Marlborough College: it is unlikely that "he had to sell a Stradivarius to pay the school fees", as Bruce was overheard claiming 20 years later. Further in Marlborough's favour, there was a family connection. Charles's uncle, Parson Tom Royds, had been there. He claimed the cooking had ruined his health.

Founded in 1843 for the education of the sons of poor clergy, Marlborough retained a strain of militant Anglicanism that filtered into the boys and expressed itself on the playing fields. Bruce participated in the 1956 Army Cadet Corps camp with boys of the Catholic school Stonyhurst, after which one parent complained to the Master: "Although the boys from Stoneyhurst do not mind if rolls of lavatory paper are thrown at them and they are called 'Papist bastards', it makes a very bad name for Marlborough."

Five more years of institutionalised life, with Chapel every day, compulsory games and a regime of tireless jocularity would leave a mark on Bruce as difficult to forget as the smells: the cheap disinfectant, the burned toast, the monkey-cage reek of the changing rooms. If the experience did not damage Bruce, it made him impregnable.

BRUCE SAID HE was "mostly ignored" in his five years at Marlborough and that the obsession with Ciceronian prose and its composition almost put him off the written word for life. "They made the classics incredibly uninteresting and English literature was left out completely," he claimed. "We never read Jane Austen or Dickens, and I haven't read them even now." But he did write an essay in the Classical Lower Sixth on *Pride and Prejudice*. "Jane Austen was a comedian; her outlook was always humorous. And even when she penetrates into one of her characters with knife-edged clearness, she always does so with a smile on her lips."

Whatever he decided in retrospect, at the time Bruce did not regard his time at public school as disagreeable. As with his prep school, he joined in everything, from beagling to the cadet force camp. Elizabeth Chatwin says, "he seemed to enjoy it, but not really to want to admit it."

He was fortunate to spend his first year in Priory. The pleasant out-of-College junior house with two acres of grounds sloping down to the Kennet was situated in the middle of town. Miss Bachelor was Priory's "Dame" or matron, smallish with a pronounced bosom that was discovered to be inflatable. In due course it was pricked. No one ever identified the culprit. "But one day during breakfast half of it slowly went down," says Bruce's friend Nick Spicer. "Froggy" Cornwall was Priory's house-master, "the lineal descendant of the landlady", as another master put it. It was said Froggy had once been brilliant at something, but whatever that was no one could recollect. He taught divinity with not much brio and when a friend of Bruce's wrote that without evil the idea of good would be meaningless Froggy added in the margin: "Oh dear! I suppose you are right. But I don't like to think of its being so." But he was a compassionate man and sensitive enough to realise how much secret unhappiness a place like Marlborough could breed. His report for Bruce at the end of his first term read: "He is somewhat dreamy and vague about the place & he might try to be less so—for our benefit."

Conditions were no less spartan than at Old Hall. The boys in Priory slept in beds separated from each other by a tiny locker just large enough for brush, comb, handkerchief, a couple of books and a little box for collar studs. Boys had to bring their own blanket. At night the windows had to be open and on very cold nights Bruce would pile onto his bed his dressing gown, overcoat, and lovat tweed jacket. "We looked like a row of paupers," said one boy.

Twice a week he took a bath, jumping into someone else's water.

The routine of Bruce's life can be seen in his first letter home, one of two to survive: "I am thoroughly enjoying myself here and I am settling down well . . . I have made several friends already. I get on very well with Edwards. I have made friends also with a boy called Ghalib, whose father is a Turk. The food in Priory is excellent . . . Don't bother to send on the cycle-clips as we have to cycle in shorts. I dont know what the master's name is yet and he is always called the master . . . My bicycle has proved invaluable as we have to clear out of the house for one hour every day and we have 3 half holidays a week. Please will you send me some books because for an hour in the evening we have to read. I have seen all the other ex Old Hall boys except Hanlam . . . Most boys here play the trombone. But I don't think I will have enough time."

In his second year, Bruce moved into B2, a senior in-College house designed by the architect who had built Strangeways Prison. B2, after Priory, came as a bit of a shock: a stone building with a darkly painted central well and railings to stop boys throwing themselves over. Perhaps the most dismaying discovery for the 13 new boys was The Woods, a vast tiled block of 30 doorless toilets.

BRUCE'S PREFERRED IMAGE of himself at Marlborough is recorded by Redmond O'Hanlon, a student at the college several years later. O'Hanlon remembers as a ten-year-old hearing his elder brother Tim talk in riveting terms about a boy at school. "There were Roman emperors—who did mysterious things to women and horses and dogs—and there was Chatwin, who knew all there was to know except Latin and Greek. So handsome that the classics master never bothered him, he sat quietly at the back of the classroom and read French novelists whose characters had habits that were almost as exciting as those of the Roman emperors: if you did Chatwin's prose translations for him, he'd tell you all about it, whole stories. In fact, Chatwin was a bit like an emperor himself, Tim said, except that he was tall and blond and really more like a Visigoth—he was the only man in the sixth form who wasn't worried about exams, who never gave university entrance a thought. He wouldn't do a syllabus; you never caught him swotting Cicero in the Memorial Library. Oh no—he read books *that no one else had ever heard of,* that's what he did."

Bruce might have enjoyed this version of himself, but Tim O'Hanlon, who sat next to him for a year in the Classical Lower Sixth, can recall no such character. The Chatwin he does remember was someone unremarkable. "We never expected to hear from him again." Richard Sturt, who spent an Easter holiday travelling with Bruce to Rome, says: "I don't remember him ever achieving any distinction at all."

"I was *hopeless* at school, a real *idiot*, bottom of every class. I was also innumerate," Bruce told Australian radio. "It was a classic education to produce a dumb-bell."

At Marlborough, his academic work can be summed up by the Master, Tommy Garnett, whose succinct report for Lent 1954 read: "Curiously patchy." There are complaints of his disorderly mental processes, his vagueness and bewilderment, his resignation, his insouciance to everything. "His answers often contain considerable material, but the important point is missed." Nor did he impress his mathematics master. Nor his biology master—"I have failed to capture his interest". In the opinion of his classics master "Bolly" Lamb, "he must learn not to need to be the driver."

Caught reading Flaubert under his desk by the master who taught him Latin composition, A. F. Elliott, Bruce said: "Once you've been with Caesar into one of his battles, the rest are all much the same."

Bruce's talents remained submerged for his first two years. Nick Spicer says, "It's difficult to know how Bruce's specialness could have manifested itself at Marlborough because he had a subterranean habit of thinking and that would not have been recognised. If there is such a thing as a clubbable loner, that was him."

The extent to which he merged into the background was observed by an older boy, Peter Ryde. Not until Ryde read his obituary did he identify Bruce with the Chatwin he had known as "Charles". "We didn't use Christian names much, but in those days when we did he was always Charles. What he couldn't stand was being called Charlie, because Charlie Chatwin was uncomfortably close to Charlie Chaplin. I could not even have told you what the B stood for." (The only "Bruce" Ryde knew at Marlborough was the Labrador belonging to "Bolly" Lamb). He says: "I do remember that I thought of him as someone who was biding his time."

Bruce and Ryde were members of a group that called itself The Estate Agents, formed for the benefit of committed games-haters who were allowed to spend their afternoons doing practical things like building walls, felling trees and making ash paths to the gym. "He seemed entirely self-possessed, very much his own person and with his own agenda, which he did not necessarily choose to reveal. He was competent, efficient and tireless—a good person to have as a partner. I have a vivid memory of the two of us, billhooks in hand, hacking a pathway through a vast tangle of blackthorn for four or five afternoons and subsequently burning the cleared brushwood in a huge bonfire. It was Charles's determination rather than mine that carried us through. But quite the most memorable feature was his voice, pitched low for his age, and with a most unusual timbre—a bit like one of those brassy middle-aged women with an impossibly deep suntan and too many bangles."

About his accent, Bruce was both self-conscious and unrepentant. "We are what others have made us," he wrote in his nomad book. "Psychologically I may be a bum, but with a voice like mine, what's the use? If I had a Cockney or an American accent, it would be a fake. As it is, I am landed with an accent that sounds the biggest fake of all."

It was a natural stage voice. "The memory of his performance at the age of 16 as the Mayor in Gogol's *Government Inspector* even now produces a glow of pleasure," was the opinion of a younger boy, Anthony Ellis. A junior English master Alan MacKichan had cast him as the Mayor "because he had natural authority and could cope perfectly happily without my intervention".

His most successful role was his first, Mrs Candour in *School for Scandal* which was performed over three days in November 1954. For Ryde, who played Sir Benjamin Backbite, Bruce's performance "remains as definitive an interpretation as, say Edith Evans's Lady Bracknell". Under the headline, "Chatwin's Mrs Candour a personal triumph", the *Wiltshire Advertiser* concurred. "She swayed and sailed magnificently across the stage, indeed, on occasions it was difficult to realise that a boy was taking the part . . ."

TED SPRECKLEY, WHO taught Bruce English, was one of perhaps two masters who discerned his interior cast of mind. "That boy's got something," he told Charles. "When I give boys free reading they read Neville Shute. Bruce will read Edith Sitwell and ask me what an ornamental hermit is." The Edith Sitwell was *Planet and Glow-Worm*, an anthology arranged as a common-place book and recommended to Bruce by an old lady in Marlborough's White Horse Bookshop. He would base *The Songlines* on its structure.

The other master was Hugh de Weltden Weldon, who taught Bruce Latin from 1956. "He was the only person who caught my imagination," Bruce told Elizabeth. "I couldn't have survived Marlborough without him."

Weldon arrived a year before Bruce. School lore holds that when he

met the long-jawed Master for his interview, he mistook him for the butler and handed him his hat and gloves. Tall, effete, amusing, with a Hit-
lerite lock of black hair across one eye, Weldon was an enigma.
Nicknamed "The Cat" for his secretive manner, he had the menacing air
of a Gatsby. There was rumour of a broken marriage and many recall the
frisson that enveloped the class when he explained that he never travelled
without a Beretta ("Always aim for the fleshy parts"). "He would tell
everyone with great relish that he'd lost a ball during the war," says David
Nash, who would work with Bruce at Sotheby's and was best man at his
wedding.

Feline, with a smart precise voice, Weldon gave the impression of a
raffish *bon viveur*. He drove a pre-war Rolls Royce and bought his shoes
at Lobb and alone of the staff taught in his gown because it kept the chalk
dust off his tailor-made suits. After Cambridge, where he had been known
as "The Queen of Christ's", he had worked as a wine merchant and was
sometimes to be seen crossing the court to his rooms carrying two or three
bottles of the finest vintage. A superb cook, he hosted elaborate dinner
parties behind his damask-covered door, this only to be entered after hearing the cry of "*'trez*!" He collected first editions of Robert Graves, was
scholarly on country houses, for which he had compiled an extensive card
index, and had written an unpublished biography of Apollo.

"He was absolutely Bruce's cup of tea," says Nash.

Weldon was not pedagogic, attacked all stuffiness, and was rooted re-
freshingly in the outside world. "I trust he is corrupt. I like my priests corrupt," he said of a new chaplain. He once got two boys drunk on a glass
of water, suggesting it was gin. Latin seldom occupied more than half the
lesson. The topics then discussed covered everything from university life
to the latest films and the possible effect of nuclear explosions on the
weather. "He encouraged us to question accepted attitudes and opened intellectual doors where the existence of doors had never been suspected,"
says Ryde.

Weldon had no time for the mere poseur, but was quick to perceive
and nurture genuine originality. "He treated Bruce as an equal and that
had a great effect on Bruce," says Hugh. Marking Bruce 6 = out of 13 in
Roman History, Weldon wrote: "He has a smooth and elegant style but is
still too fond of the byways of historical accident. He would much sooner
write an intimate memoir of Julius Caesar than a factual account of his
Gallic wars. But then who would not? Unfortunately the examiners demand fact."

From Weldon, Bruce learnt about cooking, fine wine and texts not on the curriculum—among them Robert Byron's *The Road to Oxiana*.

Charles Chatwin had been stationed at Scapa Flow when the banana boat carrying Robert Byron to Egypt was torpedoed off the north coast of Scotland. In a short life—he was 35—Byron had travelled to Russia, China and Tibet. *The Road to Oxiana* was a candid account of a journey made in 1933 through Persia and Afghanistan in search of Seljuk tombs— tall, cylindrical mausolea whose existence was known to Byron only through some "inadequate photographs". Bruce put his descriptions of Islamic architecture "at least in the front rank as Ruskin" and raised the book "to the status of 'sacred text', and thus beyond criticism".

The effect on Chatwin of *The Road to Oxiana* was comparable to the effect of Charles Doughty's *Arabia Deserta* on T. E. Lawrence. Each wrote an introduction to his favourite text. "It was my bible," said Bruce.

Bruce set about imitating his hero, who had written the book in a house on the Downs just outside Marlborough. He aped Byron's dislike of Rembrandt, of Shakespeare ("*Hamlet*—That emotional hoax," wrote Byron). He "slavishly" copied Byron's prose style and itinerary. "Because I felt the death of Robert Byron so keenly, I sought out his friends and pestered them for their reminiscences." In the opinion of James Lees- Milne, the two would have got on. "Robert would have delighted in Chatwin, whom by the laws of nature he should have survived to know. He would have been amused by his self-sufficiency, his panache and charm, and have admired his splendid presence." Different from Bruce in that he was not physically attractive—"his oval face with long disdainful nose recalled a Queen Victoria in her middle-aged widowhood"—Byron shared elements of Bruce's personality, among them an "absolute and positive conviction" that he was right, a revulsion for the common-place, and a low threshold of boredom.

BRUCE'S MODEST PERFORMANCE in the classroom was no handicap. "The only thing that mattered was how good you were at games," says Nash. Bruce's record undermines his claim that he loathed organised games. He captained his house rugby team, hunted with the school beagles, took pride in swimming the fastest breaststroke and was a member of the school sailing team, the Longshoremen.

Only in "sweats"—cross-country runs on the Downs—was his discomfort blatant. "When he went running," says one contemporary, Ewan Harper, "his legs went sideways instead of straight and one never imagined he would get anywhere. The idea that he would walk the world as he did, nothing suggested that."

But the "sweats" did bring him this consolation: they opened up his mind to the barren surrounding countryside. They led him along chalk ridges pierced by solitary thorn trees, to the burial barrows of Silbury, sights which had fired another Marlburian, Louis MacNeice:

> . . . here in the first
> Inhabited heights of chalk I could feel my mind
> Crumble and dry like a fossil sponge, I could feel
> My body curl like a foetus and the rind
> Of a barrow harden round me to reveal
> Millennia hence some inkling of the ways
> Of man before he invented plough or wheel.

Like MacNeice before him, Bruce took advantage of his freedom to explore the area's neolithic sites. Devil's Den and Merlin's Mound lay within easy reach of his bicycle or "grid", as did the Horse's Eye at Uffington; and further afield, the circles of Avebury and Stonehenge, where on Midsummer Mornings a small but determined group cycled to watch the sun rise over the helestone.

A regular destination in his first year was Silbury Hill, five miles away. One summer's day he and Nick Spicer cycled to this "place of unexplained mystery" and the largest man-made earthwork in Europe. Spicer says, "As we climbed the hill, Bruce talked excitedly about a Golden King buried there." With a glass jar they trapped some lizards. "We caught three or four, brought them back, and kept them in the common room by the radiator. It was something we had in common: the understanding of mysteries, the collecting of things to be examined in glass jars."

The neolithic Long Barrow at West Kennet was another mysterious site. In 1954, the archaeologist Stuart Piggott came to excavate it, uncovering two vaults leading off the burial chamber. Piggott, who would eventually encourage Bruce to read archaeology at Edinburgh, had a connection with Marlborough through the school's head of biology. In Bruce's second year, Piggott sought the assistance of 30 Marlburians to shift the flint rubble at the Long Barrow. Bruce was probably among this group and present at the lecture Piggott delivered that summer to the Archaeological Society.

Officially, Bruce needed permission to ride beyond a ten-mile radius, but it was never refused. At the end of his second term, he and Philip Howard, his boxing partner at Old Hall, cycled 95 miles home.

BRUCE'S WANDERLUST WAS not shared by many of his schoolmates. Nash remembered how boys in his house took pride in the fact they had never left England. "One housemaster's son was proud that he had never left Wiltshire."

Nevertheless, there was a tradition of mountaineers at Marlborough College: Geoffrey Winthrop Young in the 1890s, Edward Garnett Kempson in the 1920s. In Bruce's first year, the Master announced an un-equalled achievement for the school: the successful scaling of Mount Everest by an expedition led by Col Hunt and containing two other Old Marlburians. Bruce was at a lecture with slides showing their frozen faces and the wind-shredded remains of a Swiss tent, "forming a very vivid im-pression of rivers rushing with snowmelt, bamboo bridges, forests of rhododendrons, Sherpa villages and yaks."

Bruce told the BBC: "I always had an idea that abroad was where I belonged." A book he bought at this time was Robert Louis Stevenson's *An Inland Voyage* in which a coachman speaks of his desire to travel. "How he longed to be somewhere else, and see the round world before he went into the grave. Poor cage bird! Do I not remember the time when I my-self haunted the station, to watch train after train carry its complement of free men into the night, and read the names of distant places on the time-bills with indescribable longings?"

Until he was 14, Bruce's experience of abroad consisted in family sail-ing holidays to France. Then at the end of his first year at Marlborough, he was offered the chance to spend the summer in Sweden with a Swedish boy of his own age.

THE BRATT FAMILY contacted Charles through a friend. Would Bruce like to stay the summer at their lake-house south of Stockholm and teach English to their son, Thomas?

In June, Margharita saw him off at Tilbury on the S.S. *Patricia* with a box of liqueur chocolates for Mrs Bratt. He shared a cabin with a young man who was hoping to become a monk and who said his prayers through the night in Latin. "And another who I think was a Polish Jew who snored all night," he wrote. "What with snoring and Latin I did not get much sleep." On landing he was searched for contraband cigarettes by a Swedish customs officer who mistook him for a Frenchman.

Lennart Bratt's family was well known in Sweden. His father Ivan, a physician, had initiated a programme to control Swedish drinking habits. The Bratt "system", in place for 40 years, rationed alcohol consumption to four litres a month. Bruce's destination had been used by Ivan Bratt as his summer resort.

Bruce spent nearly two months at the farm of Lundby Gard on the edge of Lake Yngaren. The farm was remote. He wrote to Margharita: "There is not a shop for miles and everything has to be ordered, so my £10 may come back unmolested." The estate comprised several houses around a white flagpole and seemed more like a village than a farm. Built in the early nineteenth century, the pine houses were painted blood red with iron oxide from the copper mine mixed with water. One day Bruce would paint his own house near Nettlebed with the same Swedish oxide. "It's a pity I didn't bring my camera because it is so beautiful a country." He responded to the northern architecture: the clean lines of the roofs, like up-turned hulls, the clear, simple colours decorating the woodwork and the scrubbed pine floors of the interiors. "I understood his sense of colour when I visited Sweden," says Elizabeth. "Pale grey and pale green and ochre, not primary colours. You can see it in all his flats."

Bruce and Thomas shared a room which had not long before been used as a gaol. Bruce wrote, "I had expected Thomas to be fair-haired etc, but he has jet black hair and dark skin which makes him look like an Italian." Bruce's task seemed simple enough: to talk to him in English. They ate meals of pike, perch and Ryvita; they visited Viking graves under the ash trees; they sailed in the square-rigged dinghy, "Terna". But to Mrs Bratt's dismay, they did not get on. She says, "I tried in every way to make them do things together. I even hired a canoe. Such a mistake!" The two boys paddled the canoe 15 miles without exchanging a word.

According to Bruce, Thomas was interested only in gramophone records and detective novels. According to Thomas's younger brother Peter, the fault lay with Bruce. "I remember an extremely dull boy running around with a net," says Peter Bratt. "It's a strange thing, a boy of 14 mostly interested in collecting butterflies and putting needles through them. We thought it was disgusting. It occurred to us to put a snake in his bed, a black and yellow snake, but they can bite and my mother would have been angry. Just to tease him, we put nettles in his bed, but he never complained. He never said anything. We were a bit disappointed."

Having nothing in common with the boys, Bruce sought the company of their great-uncle, Percivald.

IN MANY RESPECTS, Percivald Bratt filled the space left by Bruce's grandfather Sam, who had died a year before in a London hospital. Percivald had trained to be a dentist, but his nerves failed him and he had spent the greater part of his salaried life as an actuary. "Work is the hell of your life," he said—a refrain taken up by Bruce, who described employers as "professional time-wasters".

Percivald never dressed before three. He wore a monocle, a brown Manchester-tweed suit like Sam, and carried a watch on a gold chain. Most of the time, he read. He had no academic qualification, but he was a man of wide erudition and his tastes ranged from the poetry of Karl Feldt to the *Spectator*, which arrived each week. He kept his books upstairs, in a glass cabinet on legs. He made Bruce read Duff Cooper's biography of Talleyrand and Chekhov in Constance Garnett's translation.

Cut off from time and space, Percivald was old-fashioned, quiet-voiced and fanatically tidy. He was always combing the gravel outside his gate in the Bratt "village" and once after Thomas marked his walls with greasy hands, he changed the wallpaper. He loved porcelain and he owned twelve plates from the time Charles XII, the Warrior King. When his daughter dropped one of them, he talked about it every day for three weeks until Great Aunt Eva just smashed them all. After that no one mentioned plates.

Partial to acting, Percivald's idea of charades was to perform The Panama Canal.

Soon Bruce was spending all his afternoons with Percivald, drinking tea out of gold cups (which Percivald claimed had been rescued from a sunken boat in the Atlantic) and learning the secrets of Swedish chandeliers (the Swedes were the only people who understand about chandeliers, said Percivald, because they understood about ice). One afternoon, Bruce was permitted to handle Percivald's wooden casket with mother-of-pearl inlay. Percivald had bought this in North Africa as a young man. Once, in a fit of intense depression, he had abandoned his wife and his comfortable life and travelled into the Sahara, filling the casket with fine sand. No one was allowed to touch it, but on occasions he would open the box to sift its contents. Ten years later, under similar stress, Bruce would take a similar journey into the desert.

For Thomas Bratt, the summer exchange had been a wash-out—the following year, instead of staying with Bruce at Brown's Green he opted for another family in the Isle of Wight—but for Bruce it was a turning point. "He came back years older," said his mother, whom he had bought a simple white porcelain dish. "That summer opened his eyes to abroad." Hugh remembered his brother arriving home with "the MAD, MAD eyes of a nineteenth-century explorer".

BRUCE RETURNED TO Marlborough more confident of his tastes. Peter Medawar's *Memoir of a Thinking Radish* presents a clue to his evolving personality and anxiety.

Medawar, at Marlborough in the 1920s, diagnosed the English disease "snobismus . . . the irresistibly exigent impulsion to appear before the world as somewhat grander and more important in point of family, schooling, wealth, friends and worldly distinction than one really is . . ."

Every public schoolboy has to cope with other people's perception of his privilege, which can easily be understood as snobbery. Bruce was a pin-pricker of cant; at the same time, he was susceptible to snobismus. In his fourth year, he was elected Secretary of the Shakespeare Society. "It is fearfully select and membership is only by invitation," he wrote in the school magazine. "To ask openly is taboo." Bruce's ambitions revealed themselves in the Society's correspondence, including "our most treasured possession—a letter, on pink note-paper, from Mrs Arthur Miller, regretting that she was unable to address us."

Mrs Miller was then the most famous actress in the world. The photographer Eve Arnold, who knew them both, says the one person who jostles into her mind whenever she thinks of Bruce Chatwin is Marilyn Monroe. "They have the same blondness. The same giggling delight in themselves. And the same ability to manufacture a persona."

Bruce gave himself airs. In his first term at Marlborough, Hugh overheard another boy ask of him: "Is that Lord Chatwin's brother?" He told another boy the good news that his father had been left a multi-storey car park in someone's will, and this would mean a source of bottomless income for the family. Charles Chatwin explained the reality: "I was acting for a client, Ralph Pearce, who had built such a car park and I kept my car in it."

Bruce's muse continued to be Noel Coward. In B2's small common room, he sat at a piano or beside the gramophone in a silk dressing gown. At meetings of the Literary Society he wore a yellow cravat and a carnation in his buttonhole and adopted the theatrical gesture of "characteristically sweeping his long blond hair away from his eyes with an extended palm".

Sleeked back with brilliantine, the hair reminded the chaplain's daughter of Elvis Presley, but Bruce's superiors in the corps did not approve. He reported back to Hugh how the sergeant at corps camp had admonished him on parade:

"Come 'ere, *you*, yer long-haired in-divid-u-*el*, oo ja fink you are, Oliver Cromwell?"

"Neoh. Charles the First."

In imitation of Coward, he cheered up a C.C.F. session in eight inches of snow with the words: "Gentlemen, I think we shall dress from the left today."

Apart from running, corps was the activity he enjoyed least. The Literary Society was more up his street. This met three times a term in "Monkey" Murray's study. Members read out their own compositions or listened to talks over mulled wine served by Miss Venables, the dining-hall superintendent. Bruce read out poems he had written, including this fateful drama of the boulevard, "The Teddy Boy":

When gin was cheap, and sin was rife,
In bed-clothes grimed and torn
His mother, aged fourteen, expired
The moment he was born

With sunken eyes and boot-lace ties
With leer and lecherous grin,
In coffee bars and cinemas
He bathed himself in sin.

The crooked prodigal of the earth,
Depraved and loose in will,
He cannot help but swear and drink
And some day come to ill.

Poor fool! He met his reckoning hour,
The hour that such must meet.

He felt a knife cut through his back
And crumpled to his feet.

ON 25 MARCH 1958, the master R. J. F. Cook, one of whose end-of-term specialities, hugely in demand, was to read out, complete with appropriate voices, the Llanabba chapters of Evelyn Waugh's *Decline and Fall*, gave a paper to the Literary Society on "The Art of Collecting". He urged members "to collect something throughout their lives".

Bruce's collecting began in earnest after an accident. At the beginning of Michaelmas 1955, he was hit on the head while playing rugby and lost the focus in one eye. Charles immediately brought him home to recuperate. It turned out not to be serious, but problems with Bruce's eyesight would recur, exacerbated by an incorrectly prescribed pair of bifocals.

In the Birmingham eye-hospital, he began to enjoy listening to recorded readings of the very classics he had ignored in the classroom. Austen and Dickens were fresher to him on the gramophone than in print. He spent the rest of that term recuperating at Brown's Green. Margharita was glad to have her elder son to herself again. She helped him with his French ("Mother, you know absolutely *nothing*!") and in his flower-arrangement for the Royal Leamington Spa Horticultural Society. His entry, a bowl of flowers and foliage "arranged for effect", won second prize.

He used his convalescence to redecorate his bedroom. He painted it dove grey after the farm on Lake Yngaren, filled it with blue furniture, and hung the walls with red and gold fleck material from a Hungarian in Stratford who had assisted in furnishing the *Queen Mary*.

His mind wandered naturally from decorating to collecting. His first antique, bought in Burford on one of his journeys back to Marlborough, was a red Venetian vase for a single flower. He gave it to Margharita.

His early acquisitions were pictures, small bits of furniture, chairs, anything he could carry on his bicycle. A popular source was Pullen's of Ramsbury, an eight-mile "grid" ride. Old man Pullen did house clearances and piled his barns with attic junk. Bruce bought from him a twelve-foot Piranesi etching of the Antonine Column and a portrait in oils. He told his friend Richard Sturt: "I paid 10s and I believe it to be school of Rembrandt and worth an absolute fortune." All Sturt could see was a filthy black and "very dingy" canvas.

In 1957, during the Easter holiday, Sturt accompanied Bruce to Italy. One night in Florence, Bruce came staggering back to their *pensione* under the weight of a marble table top. "Isn't it wonderful? I paid 100 lire, but I think it's Napoleon III and worth £500."

"It was the most hideous thing I'd seen," says Sturt, "the colour of puke. He lugged it bent double across Europe on the train—*and* he was right."

After Florence, Rome disappointed. "Ripped off by taxi-driver," Bruce wrote in a postcard home. "Went on tour of Rome today with Father O'Flaherty, Richard's friend, and tomorrow morning, together with several thousand other people, we are going to an audience with the Pope himself. Frankly, except for the Coliseum, the arch of Constantine, and Trajan's column, the Roman remains are rather dull to compare with the fantastic Medici palaces and the like."

That same summer, eschewing the family sailing holiday, he borrowed Charles's van and drove to the south of France, returning with a cane-seated high chair. It made a pair with his first major furniture acquisition, a grey Louis XVI chair costing £2 10s. Both pieces requiring restoration, he bought a set of wood chisels and stripped them down in the box room.

In recognition of this passion, Bruce's parents gave him a book on French furniture. He wrote to thank them, the book reassuring him on several points. "Firstly that it is justifiable to refurbish French furniture completely, and secondly that the two chairs are definitely genuine (though I'm not entirely happy about the table, but anyway good reproductions of a century ago are now nearly as valuable). The second chair really is a rarity, it appears; square-backed Louis XVI *bergère* chairs with that standard of carving and those *spiral* legs are very very highly sought after . . ."

Bruce gave the poet Peter Levi the impression of a *wunderkind* with a fabulous eye who became the bane of antique dealers in the Marlborough area. Levi says, "A deputation of antique traders got together and discovered it was always the same boy who bought something and promptly sold it on for a hugely increased price, and so they went to the headmaster. Bruce told me this. He knew what something was. 'Ah ha, but that is an Outer Mongolian coat or a sheep's eye-warmer from Victorian Patagonia'."

Bruce, in his genius for self-promotion, reminded Nash of T. E. Lawrence. "He had this ability to make you believe he was a born aesthete and passionately pursuing the aesthetic life since he was 16. I'm not sure."

Nor is there evidence for a deputation to the Master. So far as is known Bruce's "collecting" amounted to less than a dozen pieces and was limited by what he could afford, which was not much.

Hugh Weldon stored Bruce's "collection" until he had his own study. In Lent 1957, he moved into a ground floor room in New Court and set about transforming it. "He has gone to earth in his newly acquired and newly-decorated study this term and so I have not seen that much of him," reported his housemaster, Jack Halliday. Furnished with Bruce's acquisitions and a brownish chaise longue, the room had mauve curtains and white, lime-striped wallpaper. His study-companion, Michael Cannon, says: "We'd get the porter knocking on the door: 'Excuse me, sir. I just want to show these parents a typical study'."

CANNON, ALSO FROM Birmingham, was a good games-player. Through him, Bruce got to know Raulin Guild. "We were a triumvirate," says Cannon. Guild became one of Bruce's best friends. Guild's sister Ivry says her brother was someone Bruce "would like to have been". Senior Prefect, captain of games, a friend of Prince William of Gloucester, he was a rare and gifted young man. "He was one of the very few really remarkable people I have known," Bruce wrote to Ivry after Guild died in 1966. Following a memorial service, at which a plaque was erected at his local church showing a figure resembling Guild, Bruce wrote again to Ivry: "It was as though we were all celebrating the gift of life. I don't think anyone missed Raulin because he was quite emphatically *there* in everything we said and did. The sculpture is very beautiful. I think you did very well to commission it."

He risked more in a letter written on the same day to another friend: "I had to assist Prince William of Gloucester unveil a memorial plaque to a mutual friend who died, and imagine the shock when we saw the memorial underneath the veil—a sculpture of a boy, naked and beckoning in a Michaelangelesque way with the caption under '. . . of all sorts enchantingly beloved.' Not far from the truth and that was the trouble."

IN THE SUMMER of 1957, "Bolly" Lamb borrowed his best friend's shotgun and two cartridges and walked to the top of a field where he shot dead the Labrador "Bruce", and then himself. He was engaged to be married to the Literary Society's caterer, Miss Venables. A rumour went round that he had gone drunk one night into the dormitory, pulled back the blankets and fondled a boy, whose father had reported him.

At Marlborough in the early 1950s there was homosexual activity of various kinds and degrees. Unlike the college today, it was an exclusively male society: dances were arranged "against" St Mary's Calne, not "with". The only girls to be seen in the place were the darners and menders who came in from the town and were known as the Winks. The term gave rise to jokes about "having 40 Winks", though in practice, as Ryde says: "Most of us took one look and shuddered."

In the majority of cases, what occurred was not innate homosexuality—or its nineteenth-century term, "dissipation"—but rather burgeoning sexuality taking the only outlet available.

"It would be wrong to suppose we spent our entire time with our hands in each other's pockets," says Ryde. "But if homosexuality wasn't a way of life, it was certainly a way of thought, an integral part of one's general frame of reference. A scarcely-veiled undercurrent of homoerotism was part of the very air you breathed." Garnett, who arrived as Master in 1952, was concerned enough about the problem, which he referred to simply as "it", to call all boys in Senior Houses to a meeting in the Memorial Hall. "He had a lisp so when he said 'Sit down' everyone had a good laugh," says Ewan Harper. " 'I'm here to talk about "it",' he began. He understood 'it' went on and 'it' was not to go on and anyone caught doing 'it' was *out*." Even today, Guy Norton remembers his shock at hearing Garnett say, " 'I have no objection to mutual masturbation, but I will not tolerate small boys being led astray by big boys'."

In Lent 1954, during Bruce's second term, Garnett conducted an inquisition. Over a period of many weeks, he personally grilled dozens of boys who were obliged under considerable pressure to tick off on a school list the names of any boys they had had sex with. The boys would be sent for in turn, and so on it went. "It was a dreadful time which left a good many emotional scars," says Ryde.

It is now impossible to know the extent to which Bruce was involved. The only accounts we have emanate from Bruce himself. In 1977, he described to a friend in Brazil a homosexual experience with another boy after a rugby match. To Cary Welch, he spoke of going off with a gypsy boy. Welch says, "He didn't specify what went on, but there was definitely a sexual attraction."

No one at Marlborough remembers Bruce's gypsy boy. The affectation that had started to appear towards the end of his school career was understood to be foppishness rather than a sign of budding homosexuality. Robin Garran, his head of house in B2, says there was "no chit-chat—and I would have known." Cannon is adamant that nothing went on between Bruce and Raulin Guild, or anyone else. "One or two people used to sleep together out on the Downs; but I swear black and blue that Bruce wasn't one of them. He wasn't particularly that way; he wasn't particularly anything really." It is much more likely that Bruce was excited by Raulin's elder sister.

BRUCE MET IVRY GUILD in his last term. Thirty years later, only weeks before he died, he made a special journey to Munstead to tell Ivry what a crystallising experience had been her arrival in his life. "I never forget that moment. You epitomised everything I thought mattered. You knocked me for six."

On Sunday, 20 July 1958, Ivry motored down from London with Emeric Pressburger, the film producer who had written *The Red Shoes*. Arriving in a huge Bentley, coloured in two shades of greeny-yellow, they caused a sensation. Ivry says, "We turned into the college court and sat looking like a couple of millionaires." Within seconds the car was surrounded by boys, among them Raulin and Bruce. Ivry, dressed like a 1920s Flapper in a green suede hat, slid out of her leather seat. From the boot of the Bentley she unpacked her gifts. "Emeric had brought a chocolate cake from Madame Prunier, especially ordered for Raulin, and some smoked sturgeon from Czarda in Dean Street, along with fresh horseradish cream."

Bruce responded in the manner of Paul Pennyfeather seeing Margot Beste-Chetwynde (pronounced Beast Chained) alight from her Rolls Royce at Llanabba school sports day. "I suddenly represented something he wanted to be a part of," says Ivry. "I was Bruce's first taste of London glamour and sophistication."

Ivry and Emeric took the two boys out to lunch. In the afternoon Raulin brought his sister to Bruce's study where they consumed the cake. ("Awfully nice to give us such a wonderful lunch—and the cake!! Oooh!! You really must think I am starved. It's an absolute beauty," Raulin wrote the following day.) About Bruce, he had warned Ivry: "This is the most fascinating man with whom I think you'll have a great deal in common." As her brother had predicted, she found Bruce "vital and intensely bright".

Ivry Guild's visit may have inspired Bruce's essay on "Cars & Character". "You can tell a man's character from the vehicles he owns and the way in which he drives them," he wrote. A white Allard showed moral depravity and an addiction to drugs; a Rover exemplified the solid world of solicitors and accountants, and whereas the owner of a black Rolls Royce—"or, just permissibly a midnight blue or olive green one"—gave clear indication of his or her social respectability, the owner of a red or white one most certainly did not: "Indeed he is probably a property speculator in Birmingham." And Birmingham, his father's city, was definitely not what Bruce wanted for himself.

In his third year at Marlborough, Bruce had planned to try for a place at Oxford. His housemaster hoped that his desire to read Classics at Merton—the college of his grandfather and of Robert Byron—would give him "the stabilising influence and the ambition to be achieved, which I think he has lacked up till now." But then National Service ended. The university had abruptly to find room for a whole extra generation of students. It meant that Bruce might have to delay coming up for two years. Worried about the financial implications—he had had to borrow from the bank to pay for the fees at Marlborough—Charles failed to encourage Bruce to push for a place at Oxford. "I told him: I'm not keen on paying when you don't know what to do." In the absence of a firm purpose, Bruce was unwilling to contradict his father. Charles did nothing to conceal his satisfaction. "When it was decided that I should not go to the University," joked Bruce in his essay on sailing, "it was the sign for instant celebration and the purchase of a new yacht."

If later in his life Bruce regretted that he had not gone to Oxford and blamed his father, at the time he turned the decision to his advantage. It singled him out. "You're all so boring," he told Michael Cannon. "You're all going to Cambridge. I'm going to do something else."

"I remember thinking, it was rather brave," says Cannon.

Bruce proposed a stage career. In March 1958, he had directed a successful production of *Tons of Money*, for which Margharita had supplied the dresses. "I congratulate him on his direction," wrote his by now desperate housemaster. "The undoubted success he had on the stage in Memorial Hall shows that he is extremely capable at organising other people, while the unsatisfactory reports in this folder show that he is not very capable at organising himself. In the holidays Bruce simply *must* get to grips with himself, and with his father's aid, *must* evolve a plan for his future."

Charles Chatwin shrank at the prospect of his son as an actor. He wondered if Bruce might not be interested in a career in the family's other business: architecture. "He could draw and I felt he had the ability to create buildings." Here two problems arose. Bruce was no good at maths ("He has been feeling his way very slowly in the realms of Calculus"); and if he was going to study architecture, he insisted on doing so at the Architectural Association in London. Charles would not agree. He had inherited his forbears' aversion to the capital. "He felt London was dangerous," says Hugh, denied four years later on the same grounds. "London experience may be a good thing—but not straight from boarding school, living away from home for the first time."

Bruce's second idea was a job in Africa. Marlborough had strong connections with the colonial service. On leaving school, several boys went to work in Northern Rhodesia, including Guild. However, when Bruce proposed his African plan, it was Margharita who objected. In Africa Uncle Humphrey had met his "sad end" and the Mau Mau rebellion in Kenya was still fresh. It was "obviously quite unsafe", she told him.

Then, in *Vogue*, Margharita read an article about a firm of fine art auctioneers. She canvassed Charles. "What about Sotheby's for Bruce?" Mastering his reluctance to send Bruce to London, Charles contacted one of his clients, a chartered surveyor who had sold at Sotheby's a Monet "of a train going over a bridge". On 15 April 1958, enclosing Guy Bartleet's letter of introduction, Bruce wrote to Peter Wilson at Sotheby's. "I am very anxious to learn the best way of making a career in Fine Art. If you would find time to see me before I go back to school on May 1st, I should be most grateful." A meeting was fixed.

The interview went well. "I very much enjoyed meeting your son and shall look forward to seeing him again during the summer," Wilson informed Charles on 7 May. He had asked Bruce to get in touch in June, when it would be known whether there was a vacancy. "If there does happen to be a job available," Bruce wrote to Wilson, "I am very keen to take it."

And there matters rested. A meeting proposed by Wilson for 3 July fell in the middle of Bruce's A Levels. (He would get passes in Latin, Greek and Ancient History). Two further appointments were cancelled at the last minute, one coinciding with the family's sailing holiday to St Malo. At last, on Friday, 26 September, an interview took place with Richard Timewell, Head of Furniture in the Works of Art department.

"I was told he had just left Marlborough," says Timewell. "It's very difficult, when you're trying to engage someone, to ask the right questions. I said to him: 'Do you know Avebury Manor?' I'd had a lot to do with the sale of that house. 'Oh, yes,' he said. 'I used to go as a paid guide on Saturday afternoons.'* He was then able to go through the house room by room and describe everything and say what it was. I was enormously impressed. I took him on."

Bruce liked to remind Margharita that he had accepted the job with her in mind, to honour her wishes. "I was sent to Sotheby's very much against my will by my mother who decided it would be much better for her precious little child to be working in the safe firm of fine art auctioneers than to travel to Kenya." Years later, sick and dying, he told her. "Mummy, you ought *never* to have let your little boy go to London at 18."

---

* Research has not been able to verify this, but Bruce was always going to tea with Avebury Manor's owner, Sir Francis "Sissy" Knowles, the school's head of biology and an expert on prawn's eyes.

VIII.

ᗕᗦᔕᗩ

The Smootherboy

An emporium where nobody expects you to buy, a
museum where all the objects are changed once a
week like the water in a swimming pool . . .
—CYRIL CONNOLLY, SOTHEBY'S
Yearbook, 1960–1

A LITTLE AFTER 9.30 P.M. on 15 October 1958, Sotheby's new chairman Peter Wilson raised his gavel to auction seven Impressionist masterpieces. He had staked his career on this moment, the culmination of two years of intense negotiation with the estate of the German-Jewish collector Jakob Goldschmidt. Goldschmidt's executors had first approached Christie's, traditionally auctioneers to the nobility, requesting a big social splash. Sir Alec Martin had pulled a long face at the suggestion of an evening sale with bidders in black tie and evening dresses, and was not impressed by the expectation of a lower than usual commission. The executors next sounded out Sotheby's, auctioneers to the carriage trade. Peter Wilson revelled in special terms. He would arrange the sale on the far side of the moon if that was what the estate wanted.

Maximum publicity, as stipulated, attended the event. The first evening sale since the eighteenth century; television news cameras for the first time; and 1,400 ticket holders in evening dress, including Margot Fonteyn, Kirk Douglas and Somerset Maugham.

Wilson was a charismatic auctioneer. "He could make each person in turn think only you and he had this special understanding of this work of art," says Peregrine Pollen, his former assistant. Within five minutes Wilson had sold three paintings. The sixth lot was Cézanne's *Garçon au Gilet Rouge.* When the bidding stopped at £220,000, double the price ever paid for a modern picture, Wilson cast his gaze around the room. In a calm voice, he said: "What, will no one offer any more?"

"That," says Pollen, "snapped the elastic." Gasps broke into applause.

This was not only a world record, but by such a large margin that for a number of years Impressionist paintings did not go for auction anywhere else. In the span of 21 minutes the fortunes of Sotheby's, the art world and of London's place in it, had shifted. It was, for Bruce, a piece of good fortune to be joining the firm that autumn.

UNTIL WILSON'S APPOINTMENT as chairman, Sotheby's had operated like a quiet and rather scholarly family firm in a more innocent time. It comprised four departments, a staff of about 60 and a representative in New York whose secretary forwarded letters. Publicity consisted of a modest advertisement placed in *The Times*. After the Goldschmidt sale, Wilson took Sotheby's by the scruff of its neck and expanded the number of departments from four to 15. Marcus Linell, the porter whom Bruce was hired to assist, says: "It can only be described as the Wild West. We were a tremendously ignorant bunch of people with extraordinary confidence, being sent off to Paris, Switzerland, New York. It was the exceptional moment, rather than the exceptional person." Linell likened the experience to riding in a troika. "You were panting behind, thinking, 'My God! What a marvellous life this is'."

Bruce rode the crest of this expansion. "There is no doubt in my mind," says David Nash, who worked alongside Bruce in the Impressionist department, "that Sotheby's was the main stimulus of Bruce's life, whether he likes to admit it or not." He learned how to look at an object and to describe it compactly. Sponsored by Sotheby's, he travelled to countries where these objects originated and in Robert Byron's footsteps to Afghanistan. Sotheby's enabled him to meet a network of aesthetically-minded, rich, enquiring young people. It also introduced him to his wife.

Yet after three years the loathing set in. "I suddenly had a horror of the so called ART WORLD," he wrote to a friend, "and though I went on to be a Director of Sotheby's everything about the firm filled me with claustrophobia and disgust."

BRUCE ENTERED SOTHEBY'S as a numbering porter in the Works of Art department at a salary of £8 a week. For his first season, he took the tube from Ealing Broadway to Victoria. In the evening he returned to his uncle John's house at 111 Cleveland Road, Ealing, a semi-detached Wimpey house built in the 1930s. He did not discuss his work. "He was finding his way," says John Turnell. "He went into that job relatively cold."

The dealer Jane Abdy met him during these early days. "He was stocky, thickly built and looked like a country boy." Speaking in a piping voice, Bruce struck Abdy as unsophisticated, with an enthusiasm and a bounciness which her Oxford contemporaries would have considered "most odd". Brian Sewell, the art critic, that year started work at the rival house, Christie's. "It is easy to forget how pure Bruce was at that stage," he says. "There was a frankness and honesty about him. He would have made a very good priest." To the dealer Robert Erskine, Bruce looked like a young curate "rather wet behind the ears". The transformation from chubby-cheeked Marlborough *ingénu* to "Smootherboy" would take place, in the words of one who had known Bruce since childhood, "in a phenomenally short time".

BRUCE'S FIRST DUTIES in the Works of Art department were to shift and dust European and Oriental ceramics, glass, majolica, and tribal antiquities. His job was to locate each object on the storage shelves where it might have stayed for months, dust it, place the owner's name against a lot description, and safely stack it on the trolleys to take up to the sale room. "Whenever there was a sale," he said, "I would put on my grey porter's uniform and stand behind the glass vitrines, making sure that prospective buyers didn't sticky the objects with their fingers." Soon he was bored by the menial tasks required of him.

For three weeks he shared a room with John Mallet, a junior cataloguer in ceramics. Mallet says, "We were supposed to be cataloguing ceramics, including Chinese; sculpture from the fall of the Roman Empire to Rodin, objects of *vertu* and miniatures. Bruce would go for the objects that appealed to him and leave me with the boring things." Mallet found him bumptious, "a slightly phoney figure" interested in silly ideas. "He said he had written a thesis on 'Sausages as phallic symbols'. This didn't interest me a great deal. I had my doubts as to what he was up to. It seemed confidences of a most horrific kind were waiting to be prised out of him."

Marcus Linell, the department's other numbering porter, was technically his boss. "Bruce would wander around where he wanted. When sales went on view, there would be 35 lots missing and things were misnumbered and dirty. After four months I went to Jim Kiddell and said: 'This is hopeless, he simply won't concentrate on doing the job.' The next thing I'm told, he's going to work in furniture."

The Head of the Furniture department was Richard Timewell, who had interviewed him, but hardly had Bruce landed there before Timewell was visited by Peter Wilson, who wanted to discuss his young charge.

Wilson had great faith in the ideas of the young. He said to Timewell: "I really think that boy would do well in the Modern Picture department. Would you give him up?"

"The fact Bruce was nice looking didn't do him any harm," says Timewell. "For quite a while he was Peter's very blue-eyed boy."

JUST HOW BRUCE attracted the Chairman's attention is not certain. Bruce told Michael Cannon that he had caused a stir by translating the Greek inscription on an amphora. Since most public schoolboys of the period knew Greek—and Bruce's Greek was not very good—this hardly sets him apart. He told Susannah Clapp that he remained unnoticed until, "loitering near a Picasso gouache of a harlequin, he was approached by a man 'looking like a birdman in a blue fedora and suede shoes' who asked him what he thought of the picture. 'I don't think it's genuine,' pronounced the porter." The birdman was Sir Robert Abdy, art buyer for Gulbenkian. Abdy, impressed, passed on the comment to Wilson.

In the spring of 1959, Wilson set about injecting energy in his two favourite departments, Modern Pictures, which included Impressionist sales, and Antiquities, where, in 1937, he had been given his own head as a cataloguer. "Wilson's text told stories and made connections that went beyond the bare recital of facts," wrote Robert Lacey. "One ring had been found in the tomb of a dramatically murdered duke, another in the bed of the river Oise . . ."

Under Wilson's wing, Bruce began to move between both departments as a junior cataloguer. Antiquities answered directly to Wilson and was "a convenient term which may denote anything from a Sumerian clay tablet to a carved head from darkest Africa". It took up a tiny room in the basement and consisted of Bruce; a secretary, Felicity Nicholson; and an outside adviser whose job was to come in once or twice a week to give his expertise. This was Wilson's friend, John Hewett. The two had been business partners since the 1950s; they lived next to each other in Kent and Wilson had been Hewett's best man. Second only to Wilson, Hewett was a crucial figure in Bruce's apprenticeship.

Hewett was a Bond Street dealer, but he virtually ran Antiquities. A dapper figure with a spade beard, he liked to glide silently into a room and make a theatrical display of pulling from an expensive tweed pocket a waistcoat button or a fifth-century gold marvel or a shell. He did not ask Bruce, "What is it?" Rather, he dropped it into his palm and with his ox-eyes on him waited for Bruce to comment.

Ted Lucie-Smith who used to hang around Hewett's shop and run errands for him, says, "He made objects available and he endowed them with magic. He was interested in natural curiosities almost as much as works of art. Bruce acquired from him the feeling that an object which was a wonder of nature was as satisfying as a work of art." Hewett's taste, not confined to any period or culture, was for simplicity of form.

One clique thought Hewett a genius. He did not disabuse them. He relied on his taste and on his *gravitas*, supported by long silences, to a greater extent than on his expertise, which though real was not as encompassing as his supporters might believe. He could be generous, often allowing Bruce to buy an expensive object and pay over a long period, or to exchange a lesser thing for a finer one. But, says Lucie-Smith, "there always came a day when he was determined to screw you for a better deal."

Hewett was an odd ally for PCW, as Wilson was known. "He was a rampant heterosexual," says Lucie-Smith, "and came from a different layer of the English class system." A self-taught man who still spoke in "a faint Cockney whine", Hewett had remade himself as a shaman-dealer. Raised in Ealing, where his grandfather had a horse and cart removals business, his first love was botany—a passion he also encouraged in Bruce. Before the war he had worked as apprentice gardener in a great house in Middlesex. Wounded while serving as a batman in the Scots Guards in Algeria, he convalesced in Naples, and there discovered his aesthetic appetite. He was an expert in fifteenth-century carpets, the history of travel in the South Seas and Africa. His special love was for tribal and ethnographic specimens collected by botanists and sailors.

Bruce's photographic memory acquired a new depth of focus under Hewett's tuition. He learned to look with close attention to detail and to remember what he had seen. "Hewett taught Bruce how to hold something in your hand and feel it and *really* look at it," says Elizabeth. "Not just look, but look intensely. Bruce used to look at something in changing lights until you got pretty fed up, but it did mean that he never forgot a thing." The designer John Stefanidis once discussed with Bruce some chairs in the Villa Malcontenta that he was keen to copy. "You don't have to copy them," said Bruce. "I've got the precise measurements."

In 1828, Joseph Haslewood drew up for his friend Samuel Sotheby *Hints for a Young Auctioneer of Books.* His first rule: "Consider your catalogue as the foundation of your eminence and make its perfection of character an important study." One hundred and thirty years on, John Hewett made the Sotheby's catalogue just that. In the Antiquities cubby-hole, he taught Bruce to condense an object to its purest form and to use few words vividly so that there could be no mistaking one item for another. Bruce had to produce a succinct description of the object's history, weight and size so as to maximise its value. By the process of cataloguing thousands of objects and dipping into arcane reference books, he learned how to transfer graphic ideas into words. It was the exact skill of a botanist or a sniper.

The entries were distilled and spare, at first glance dull.

A Syrian limestone relief of an antelope being attacked by a spotted beast of prey, 15 in by 11 1/2 in 1st millennium BC
—found at Amouda, North of Aleppo, in September/October 1959

But the Chatwin style begins here.

A Bajokwe wooden figure of a squatting ape, baring its teeth and holding a fruit in its hand, the eyes inlaid with bone. 13 in.

Many of the skills Borges acquired through cataloguing books for the Miguel Cané municipal library, Bruce picked up in Antiquities.* As his first editor, Susannah Clapp, observed: "The cataloguer's habits—of close attention, the chronicling of a mass of physical detail, the search for a provenance and the unravelling of a history—can be seen in the structure of his paragraphs and plots, and in his project of objectivity."

Hewett also gave Bruce licence to go out and ham it up. He encouraged him to attach a story to each object: where it came from, why it was interesting, who owned it. Bruce soon grew nimble at exploiting the connection between story and salesmanship. Brian Sewell envied his gift of the gab. "He had extraordinary social grace and not the smallest embarrassment in dealing with anybody. He picked a thing up—a wretched bit of terracotta—and handled it in such way that the intending buyer felt it must be by Michelangelo."

* Utz, the Prague collector, also "had a poorly paid job as a cataloguer in the National Library".

Bruce took as much interest in the owner as the object. Until Peter Wilson's arrival as chairman, few members of the general public attended auctions. This now changed. Spear-headed by Brigadier Stanley Clark, a deft advertising campaign coaxed into the saleroom anyone who had £100 to spend. Works of art were promoted as affordable and, better still, as investments. About the whole performance—for a spectacle is what it became—was woven a spell of fun and the hint of rags turning into riches. Sotheby's continued to welcome Armand Hammer, but he had to rub shoulders with "the little old lady with the Ming vase which had always been used as an umbrella stand".

The little old lady was Bruce's speciality. He explained to Colin Thubron how important Sotheby's had been to fashioning his narratives. Antiquities began to supply a daily stream of characters with amazing stories. "When I was there the whole of life became in its better moments a sort of treasure hunt and that technique of treasure-hunting and being rewarded or not rewarded is, I suppose, the way in which I do research on a story.

"For example a letter comes from an old woman in an old folks' home in Tunbridge Wells saying she's seen in the papers Sotheby's have sold a Benin head. She has a Benin head because her father was a doctor on the Benin expedition and so you go down and see this marvellous old lady.

"She says: 'Do you smell something here?'

"I say, 'Not particularly.'

" 'Yes, you can. Sniff. Smell it.'

"So I went like that. 'What is it?'

" 'I'll tell you what it is. Caca. Everybody in this place is incontinent'."

The woman pointed to the Benin head on the floor and asked how much it would fetch. "It's perfectly genuine. We were in Cape Town and I remember my father telling the servants to wash it down because it was covered in blood, *human blood*. And they put the hose pipe on it and the yard was red with blood for days."

The head *was* genuine, Bruce sold it and the woman used the money to sail back to South Africa. "She had a marvellous time in Cape Town and she died on the way back and was buried at sea. Many people in the world are *yearning* for that kind of destiny."

In the tearoom at Sotheby's, there was a phrase, "doing a Bruce". It meant wrapping up something in a bit of myth and making a story out of it.

FOR BRUCE IN his first two years here, Sotheby's functioned as a cabinet of curiosities that was constantly replenished. To observe Hewett and Bruce together was, says one dealer, "like watching a young puppy with a silent block of marble". Hewett said, "He was at a very impressionable age then. Coming into Antiquities, he was confronted by the whole gamut of civilisation. We catalogued, we sorted out what was rubbish, what was a fake and we decided what to illustrate."

A photograph shows Bruce holding an African mask against shelves stacked with a Greek pot, a Thai head, a New Guinea head, a Roman torso, an Assyrian relief, a fake Benin bronze. Having to make snap judgements on objects so diverse, Bruce's connoisseurship developed at a great rate.

Hewett said, "He was a good pupil, was willing to learn. He'd pick something up and say, 'This is jolly good,' and I'd say, 'It *is* jolly good, but what is it?' It might have been 50,000 BC to the present day. And I'd say, 'It's Rumarian, 3rd millennium BC. Read Leonard Woolley's book about Ur.' I pushed him to read about everything. I'd send him to research on a piece we weren't sure about—say to the British Museum or the Ashmolean, wherever there were other examples. I've had very little experience of anyone cramming knowledge into such a short space of time. He was the quickest I've known."

One day, in a consignment of Japanese Netsuke carvings, Bruce picked out a little ivory figure carved like a crescent moon, of a man with his arms up. It was the same size and shape as the others, but Bruce identified it as Polynesian, something of great rarity. It sold for £600. On another occasion he went into a shop in Ludlow and ignoring everything else fixed on what seemed to be a walking stick: it was one of the flag-poles from a doge's barge. The owner had no idea.

Hewett said, "If you put ten things on a table, Bruce would pick out the best one. Basically, he had a strange thing, rather unfashionable now, which is called a good eye."

BRIAN SEWELL SAYS of it, "The eye is indefinable, but those who have it know so, and know it to be the instrument through which informed in-

tuition works; it is connected with a knotting of the stomach and a
clenching of the bowels; it may break a sweat on a man's brow, or make
him breathless as angina." Sewell once witnessed an "eye" responding to a
picture of scant quality. " 'If that's a Romney, my cock's a lettuce.' "

He says, "Bruce would come into my room at Christie's. 'Gosh, isn't
that so, so beautiful,' and it might be something I hadn't noticed. He
didn't know what it was, when it was done, who did it; but he knew it had
quality. He could bring it out of the mire."

He responded to the object, not its label. "He didn't care whether it
would be by Fra Angelico," says Robert Erskine, then running the St
George's Gallery. "I would be interested in something which had a historical point to make. Bruce was not so much interested in the meaning. He
knew things like a docket, but to put something, say, in an eighteenth-
century context didn't interest him. He'd see it frozen. His reaction was
totally aesthetic."

In this Bruce modelled himself on Hewett. He believed that beauty
was inherent in objects of great seriousness or of human endeavour and
that things were genuine because *he* felt, intuitively, that they *were* so.

Those lucky enough to have the eye could trade on it. Bruce wrote,
"The Directors at Sotheby's assumed that people like myself had private
incomes to supplement our wretched salaries. What was I to do? Exist on
air? I earned myself a little extra by trafficking in antiquities . . . Almost
everyone in the art business was at it."

He bid at Sotheby's under the name "Winchat". (On 16 July 1962, for
instance, Winchat paid £30 for an Attic marble funerary stele.) He told
Jane Abdy that Wilson had arranged for him to have a credit account in
order to buy, an arrangement she found "rather odd". He bought more expensive items in partnership.

Hewett was Bruce's entrée to a circle of collectors on whom he would
depend for his financial survival. The introductions were made in
Hewett's Park Street office or in the saleroom at Sotheby's, around a horseshoe table covered in green baize. This circle remained a constant factor
in Bruce's life. They dealt. They swapped objects, sometimes lovers, and
they prided themselves on having "the eye".

Some had great wealth. The millionaire George Ortiz, whom Bruce
called "Mighty Mouse", was the wide-eyed and energetic grandson of the
Bolivian tin magnate Simon Patino. Since 1949, Ortiz had been using his
fortune to build a collection of art from the ancient world. Rich enough
to rely on his maverick intuition alone, he bought objects he loved. He
was responsive to a Benin bronze, a Corinthian helmet or an Easter Island

canoe paddle—provided each object "took my breath away". Ortiz's Harvard room-mate was Cary Welch, the son of an architect of recital halls, who lived and taught in Boston. Welch shared many of Ortiz's tastes, competed with him, and collected Indian miniatures and nomadic art. Thirdly, there was the Hon. Robert Erskine, a coin and antiquities dealer, who was "half-rich". Bruce entered into an arrangement with Erskine, an Old Etonian whose father was Governor of Madras in the 1930s. Erskine put up the money, Bruce provided the Sotheby's list of clients, and they shared the profit. The partnership proved so successful that when Bruce was made a director, he was told quite specifically to deal with Erskine no longer.

At the head of the green baize horseshoe, controlling the market, sat John Hewett.

TED LUCIE-SMITH used to accompany Bruce to the Portobello Road on Saturdays. "When you look at the origins of Bruce's taste, the much touted 'eye', you realise he wasn't an intellectual. He was basically parroting and popularising borrowed ideas. He didn't have a really solid education. He didn't have the application, and he wasn't sufficiently systematic to acquire a solid foundation even later. He was a maker of bower-birds' nests, with ideas as well as with the objects he gathered around himself. He flourished best where aspects of Brancusi, say, intersected with aspects of ancient and ethnographic art."

Bruce's ideas about objects, says Lucie-Smith, derived not only from André Malraux's *Musée Imaginaire* but from Ludwig Goldscheider's *Art without Epoch*—"in particular Goldscheider's refusal to 'hierarchise' art and his tendency to suggest that things drawn from popular culture and 'high art' objects could be equivalents."

Bruce's aesthetic obsession compressed itself into the activity of *seeing*. He caught immediately uniqueness of form, whether of an ivory nose bone from the Solomons or a stainless steel chair. He later transferred his focus on to people and to books. "He would look at this bottle," said the writer Gregor von Rezzori, "in the same way as he looked at a person, a phrase."

In painting, he liked Piero della Francesca (above all his *Resurrection*), Altdorfer, Hercules Seghers and Turner's watercolours. He did not like Rembrandt or modern art. "He was utterly blind to contemporary art," says John Kasmin, the modern art dealer. Among favourite twentieth-century artists were Braque, Matisse and Cézanne. His favourite Cézanne was an oil sketch of Mont St Victoire "with literally about ten brush-strokes on a plain white primed ground . . . reduced to almost Malevich-like abstraction." It was, Bruce wrote, "one of the most breathtakingly beautiful paintings I have ever set eyes on." He told Malraux that English art was at its best "when it is really English and its great artists, like Palmer and Blake, are lonely eccentrics".

His visual taste responded most intensely to tribal art and antiquities. Following Hewett's lead, Bruce took to walking around with simple objects from the Antiquities shelves which fitted in his pockets: a Sumerian head, $3/4$ inches high, made of white shell from the third millennium BC, an Hawaiian bone figure of a woman, a late Parthian coin . . .

On Friday lunchtimes in the Blue Boar near Piccadilly, Bruce showed these off to a small group of Marlburians who worked in the City, among them Nick Spicer. "It was a little ritual. We'd wear our old school tie. He'd bring the coin or his catalogue notes and talk to us as if we would be interested." But their paths had diverged since the days when they bicycled to Silbury Hill. "I felt he was inhabiting a different world, giving us a gift we didn't appreciate."

Bruce, in defiance of Sotheby's rules, took many of these antiquities home. "He wanted to look at them longer," says Welch.

IX.

༄

The Imps

INTERVIEWER: *How long did it take you to become an expert on the Impressionists?*
BC: *I should think about two days.*
—ADELAIDE, 1984

AFTER LODGING FOR two months with his uncle and aunt in Ealing, Bruce moved to digs in St John's Wood. Six months later, in the summer of 1959, he took a lease on a mews flat behind Hyde Park Corner. His chairman approved. Bruce, he told everyone, was the only person who lived within a mile of the office. The flat was three rooms over a garage where a mechanic tuned sports cars and across the street from the Horse Guards' stables. Bruce painted the interior stark white and invited a lodger to pay half the rent. Anthony Spink, the future chairman, worked at the family firm of coin and medal dealers. He had been introduced to Bruce through an elderly cousin of Charles. He says of the flat, "There was a white-painted floor; a nasty blue carpet in the bedroom, which we shared to begin with; and a skylight. My mother thought we ought to have chintzes; but Bruce built a jousting tent in the sitting room and put his bed inside."

They rubbed along for a year, but had little in common. "He gave the impression of being strongly squirearchical," says Spink. "It would be 'Warwickshire,' not Birmingham." Once Spink brought a Canadian archaeologist back to the flat to find Bruce "flouncing around" in a dressing gown, standing over a blow-heater. "He wasn't ever a person I felt totally at ease with."

The only friend Spink recalls Bruce inviting home was Ivry Guild. "She was here a lot."

———

RAULIN'S SISTER WAS one of few people Bruce knew in London when he first arrived. After researching at the Victoria & Albert, he often turned up at Ivry's house at 34 Boscobel Place. She says, "I never knew when he was coming. The doorbell rang and there he'd be, bright piercing eyes looking at me, completely sure of a welcome." One day Ivry decided to do up her bedroom. Bruce took over. He chose a crazy French wallpaper, pale blue with enormous daisies. Then Ivry decided she could not afford it and they painted the room pink. "Whenever you talked to him, you were the most important person and whenever he was around, you felt awfully happy."

One weekend during the summer of 1959, Bruce and Jane Abdy stayed a weekend at the Cornish home of "the birdman in a blue fedora". Robert Abdy was then courting Jane. Bruce, acting as chaperone, managed to spirit her off for a rare heart to heart. She says, "We walked in the large garden among French-sculptured nymphs and topiary. Bruce had a photograph of Ivry in his jacket pocket. He'd take out the photograph and say: 'Isn't she pretty? I want to marry her, but she's four years older. What do I do, what do I do?' I was Bruce's agony aunt. Ivry was his first real love. He was madly in love and kept on saying: 'Can I propose?' But he was worried about this gap."

Abdy tried to reassure Bruce. Of course, it could work. The four years difference wouldn't matter in time. But at Christabel Aberconway's June party, Ivry met Col. Paul Freyberg, a Guards officer with a Lutyens house. Sad, worried, disappointed, Bruce turned to Abdy once more. "Paul has come along. Have I got a chance?" Again, Abdy urged him on.

Oblivious to this drama, Ivry married in July 1960. As she drove to church, she saw Bruce by himself in the middle of road at the end of the drive. He held up two paintings: "Ivry, these are your wedding presents."

Curiously, neither Ivry nor their mutual friend Robert Erskine suspected the nature of Bruce's feelings. Erskine says, "I was not ever aware that Bruce was part of Ivry's life." Already, Bruce was compartmentalising his world. Not yet 20, he must have felt some need to connect, even if that initial step meant performing the rituals of courtship he observed around him. Lucie-Smith says, "Several women among those he made a play for or fancied were apparently totally unaware of him as a sexual being of any sort."

Another girl who was the object of Bruce's admiration was Sarah Hunt, a student at the Courtauld. Starved of friends who knew about painting, Hunt, the daughter of a Harley Street doctor, fell in with Bruce not long after he started at Sotheby's. They saw each other for lunch.

Bruce took her to dances, to the Fitzwilliam Museum in Cambridge. Both were shy and gauche, and they shared an interest in Byzantine art. Hunt found him "not at all witty to talk to". He did not seem to her suited to being a young man. "He had quite solemn, adult clothes for his age and looked extremely owlish, with a big head. He definitely got better looking." There was an embarrassing episode when he tried to kiss her after a dance in the Chilterns, in front of a house on a hill.

Hunt's affections were spoken for by an engineering undergraduate at Cambridge. In May 1960, the month in which Ivry announced her engagement, Nigel Craig wrote to Hunt from King's College: "Why were you so unkind to Bruce Chatwin? He wanted to go back with you, but you thought him too boring, too little worth bothering with. But you don't have to bother with him really. All you have to do is talk about nothing."

By summer, their friendship had faded. Hunt says, "It never occurred to me he could be of interest to anybody. I never thought about him since." Looking back, she believes the one place where he felt secure was in his work. "He was growing in confidence by the week."

BRUCE'S CONFIDENCE WAS linked to a new responsibility for Impressionist sales.

John Rickett was the administrative head of Modern Pictures. He had been a close friend of Wilson, but was not running the department with the emphasis Wilson had in mind. A large, moody man with unruly, gingerish hair and delicate hands, who played the harpsichord, Rickett was interested most in English pictures and obsessed in particular by the work of Richard Dadd. Ignoring him, Wilson used Bruce as a lever to split up Modern Pictures. He gave Bruce responsibility for cataloguing a group of 49 Matisse bronzes belonging to Mr and Mrs Theodor Ahrenberg of Stockholm. Bruce said, "There came a moment when the rather ancient cataloguer of the department was away and so I chipped in and I said, 'Well, I'd better catalogue them.' And I did. And then I was an instant expert. So it really took me the time it took to write the catalogue—which I think was one evening of my time—and then suddenly, absolutely overnight from knowing nothing at all, I was somehow acclaimed as an instant expert and had views. And then I had to start learning very fast, of course."

Peregrine Pollen recalled a certain amount of resentment that someone so junior had been given such an important collection to catalogue. But Bruce did an elegant job. From this time on, Wilson made Bruce responsible for cataloguing Impressionists. Rickett remained nominally in charge, but by October 1960. "Imps" was in effect a separate department answering to the chairman.

"IMPS" WAS GLAMOROUS and identified itself with the world of fashion. Where dealers in Antiquities tended to be "a lot of Birmingham colonels who'd fought the Japanese", Impressionists attracted Greek shipping money; also the presence of royalty and stars of stage and screen.

Bruce's secretary was Sue Goodhew, a pretty debutante who also worked for John Rickett. She says, "Our office was opposite the Capuccino Café in St George's Street. We used to watch the men go in and out of the tarts' rooms above, and the tarts used to watch us typing."

A keen horsewoman, she was known as "Fidget" or "Corporal of Horse Goodhew" and reputed to have a string of boyfriends in the Life Guards known as "Goodhew's Own". Wilson liked to scurry around looking for the daughters of families with great possessions to work on the front desk: "Fidget" had landed her job through connections with the Earl of Lanesborough, whose pictures Sotheby's sold.

Goodhew says of Bruce, "He was a volatile person to work for. One moment he was in good form. The next he was not." One way to defer his dictation was to plead for an imitation of Noel Coward. "I would sit back while he sang 'In a bar on the piccolo Marina . . .' Sometimes we'd do a duet from *A Room with a View*, and he'd sing, 'I've been cherishing through the perishing winter.' In winter I'd have to wear gloves until my fingers were warm enough for typing."

Bruce would come in at 9 a.m. "We'd do the post together," she says. "Obituaries would go round and if he knew them he'd write a letter of condolence." The stock letter, drafted by Peter Wilson, asked the bereaved not to overlook Sotheby's. "The catalogue will be a monument to your deceased wife/husband's taste and judgement."

If Bruce had no lunch date they might eat a sandwich at the Capuccino. "He'd tease me about my boyfriends. 'Going out with the Cavalry tonight?'" It did not cross her mind to include Bruce in her invitations home to Sutton Bonnington. "Never entered my head. I didn't know he'd been to public school, but I realised he didn't come from the same background. I couldn't see him going back at the weekend to hunt."

Her attitude explained to Lucie-Smith why Bruce became so highly competitive in his new position. "He wanted to show the boys from Eton that he was better than they were and he was irritated that the Fionas on the front desk did not like him or take him seriously."

Goodhew remembers the sort of smart visitor with whom Bruce dealt on a daily basis. She would grab a file and walk back to gawk at Gregory Peck, Alain Delon, Omar Sharif, David Niven . . . "One lunch, I was in the Imps, totally alone eating cheese and pickle, and the doorbell rang at the St George's Street entrance and I opened it and there was Elizabeth Taylor dressed from head to foot in leopard skin."

When there was an Evening Sale, Goodhew would wear a cocktail dress and show clients to their seats. "It was a very social time." Sometimes she accompanied Bruce on a valuation. One hot day they drove to Essex to see a prospective client, Bruce singing Noel Coward all the way. "When we arrived, the man came to the door and looked in amazement at both of us." Bruce, dressed in a flat French beret, denim shirt and jeans, seemed too young to know anything and sometimes it backfired. One French client told him: *"Vous êtes trop jeune pour être expert."*

"BRUCE LOVED TO be the centre of gossip, conversation, everything," said John Hewett. The press cuttings confirm his talent for self-promotion.

—The *Daily Mail*, 25 June 1959. The sale of the "Westminster Rubens" for £275,000, a new world record for a painting. Although he had been there but half a year, he occupied the centre of the picture.

—The *Sphere*, 28 January 1961. Photographed on his own this time, the caption reads: "Mr Bruce Chatwin, already regarded as an expert on antiques".

—The *Daily Mail*, 24 November 1964. Another world record. Lot 32—*A Tahitian Woman and Boy*, by Gauguin. He is shown lifting the painting. "It was Chatwin who arranged the Gauguin sale," declares the paper. "Sotheby's had a call from Mrs Austen Mardon, American-born widow of a tobacco company director. She has nine children, lives in Ardross Castle, Ross-shire. She said she had a painting to sell. Chatwin went to Scotland, was staggered to see the Gauguin hanging in a bedroom. Its whereabouts had been unknown for 40 years."

The newspaper suggests that it was Bruce who discovered the Gauguin, star lot in one of the biggest sales of Impressionist paintings and drawings ever held. In fact, Mrs Mardon—who had bought it in 1923 for £1,200—knew perfectly well what the painting was. It boiled down to good luck that Bruce had gone on the valuation. He was accompanied by John Kerr, the expert in old books. They stayed a night in the castle with Mrs Mardon and her daughters. Kerr says, "They were faintly out of this world. Over dinner, we were told how they had toured all over Canada with the Gauguin in the boot of their car. One day they had stopped for a picnic in the snow and had driven off leaving the Gauguin behind."

The next morning, Bruce had to go on another visit. Kerr elected to take the Gauguin back to London by train. Bruce, strongly feeling it should not go in the guard's van, booked the painting its own sleeper compartment. Kerr says, "We booked it in a child's name, parcelled it carefully and at Inverness gave it to the Inspector, who said: 'This has to go in the van.'

" 'No, here's the ticket for it,' said Bruce.

"The guard gazed at us rather quizzically: 'But there's nae bairn in there'."

Such stories did the rounds in Mrs Ford's tearoom on the top floor of Sotheby's. Bruce's unstinting confidence more than compensated for his lack of training, experience and expertise. David Nash accompanied Bruce to the Parsee dealer Heeramanek in New York, then contemplating a sale of Buddhist and Hindu sculptures. "Bruce was enormously impressive at discussing in learned terms thirteenth-century Vijayanagara culture. I'd never heard of it. I thought: 'My God, this man knows everything.' Only later, I realised he'd read it up the night before."

"He had the right manner," says John Kasmin, "a mixture of bluff, a good eye and an ability to deal with the rich. You have to assume everyone's more uncertain than you. Being a tiny bit confident reassures everyone—like a doctor's bedside manner when he doesn't know what you've got." When Kasmin sought his opinion on a ninth-century Indian bronze, Bruce took the pin out of his lapel and scratched the patina. Kasmin says, "It's a manner you acquire at Sotheby's. It was mildly reassuring."

TRAINED BY HEWETT, Bruce had developed a sure eye. The historian Kenneth Rose never forgot the manner in which Bruce swept into an Irish country house, declaring: "Henry Moore is a fake and Barbara Hepworth is a fake Henry Moore—a fake fake."

Most of the time, his assurance proved justified. He told Peter Levi how he went into a famous gallery in New York, saw a bronze horse and suddenly observed that it had a casting line right through it like a toy soldier. "He thought: 'That is a technique the Greeks never used.' It had to be withdrawn. Not unnaturally when he was seen coming in, it was like the arrival of the Goths. What appalling thing was going to happen next?"

Fakes, on the other hand, were a product of Sotheby's success. Encouraged by spiralling prices, a former Egyptian ballet dancer, Fernand Legros and his friend Elmyr de Hory, made a living on the island of Majorca painting Modiglianis, Derains and Dufys. Their fakes were "terribly obvious" to Bruce who spotted Legros early on. "I remember him making the most incredible scene at Sotheby's and I said to the porter: 'Please help me to get this gentleman out onto the pavement'." The pair stayed at the Dorchester or Claridge's. "If a dealer said that he wanted a Miró sketch or a Dufy watercolour, they'd actually go and paint it in the morning and put it on the radiator to dry." Bruce only had to smell the paint.

His growing confidence expressed itself flamboyantly. In June 1963, David Ellis-Jones, who had joined the Impressionist department, was labouring doggedly on the William Cargill sale. "Bruce had been away on a trip at the wrong time of the year. On the first day of the sale this hurricane comes in and very grandly points at a Renoir drawing of a nude: 'Oh, that's ghastly, I even think it's a fake.' He looked around and said, 'That's a fake. That's a fake. That's a fake,' and walked on. You had to take stock. We then investigated all of these and withdrew them from the sale. And he was right."

Ten years later, Bruce's friend Tilo von Watzdorf held the first serious sale of modern American art at Sotheby's. "A couple of months before, Bruce sails in and sees a Jackson Pollock on the floor, a 1951 black and white head of a man. 'That's a fake.' I was annoyed because I'd worked so hard, I'd already checked that picture with colleagues in New York and Bruce had never had anything to do with contemporary art or Pollocks. He'd just shot from the hip. 'Bruce, listen, give me a break for once.' Then the moment the catalogue came out, Sotheby's was served an injunction by Marlborough Fine Art. It was a fake, made in north Italy. He was triumphant."

Bruce's readiness to pronounce this or that a fake could be tiresome to those around him. To Peregrine Pollen, the theatricality seemed modelled on Joseph Joel Duveen who when asked by J. P. Morgan to admire five of his Chinese porcelain beakers, looked at them, took a walking stick and smashed two. Nor was the Chatwin eye infallible. The daughter of Lord Carnarvon's head digger once offered Bruce and Erskine a purple faience Ushabti figure with Tutankhamen's inscription. She said, probably truthfully, that it had been given to her father by Carnarvon himself. Erskine was about to buy it, until Bruce shook his confidence. "Bruce took me aside and said: 'It's a fake.' That unhitched me. 'It's not,' I said. 'It is,' he said. 'It's an absolute bloody fake.' I didn't buy it. It wasn't a fake, but he was in 'it's a fake' mood. Everything was a fake when he was in that mood."

Mrs Clarke, whose husband Tim was Head of the Porcelain department, spoke for not a few people within Sotheby's when she said, "We thought *he* was a bit of a fake."

IMPRESSIONISTS, UNLIKE ANTIQUITIES, was not a field in which there could be unlimited discoveries. Wilson found the paintings: Bruce catalogued them. The information came mostly from the back of the picture. Since this was illustrated in the catalogue, it did not require description. Bruce had to detail the artist, the title, the medium, the size, the owner, where the painting had been exhibited, which books it had appeared in.

The part of the process Bruce enjoyed best was travelling, at the firm's expense, to verify a painting. Each Impressionist artist had spawned an "expert" who gave out certificates of authenticity: Paul Brame in Paris for a Degas; John Rewald in New York for a Gauguin. Some artists were yet alive to deliver their own assessment. In Paris, Bruce met Braque, dressed in a lilac track suit. "I had a marvellous morning sitting in Braque's studio while he painted one of those great birds, which actually was his soul going out through the studio roof." Braque looked at Bruce's photograph. "I've got very feeble eyes, can you tell me whether it's a fake or not?" Bruce told him it was. "He said, '*Bon.*' He signed the photograph. 'That this is not by me'."

Bruce admitted to Colin Thubron: "It was obviously great fun for a little kid from Birmingham to suddenly find himself in the company of Braque, Giacometti and Picasso." As for the experience of dashing round the world and pontificating "with the maximum arrogance" on the value or authenticity of works of art, "I just took to it."

He loved the rushing about, the whole business of being in a bustle. Postcards to Brown's Green snapshot a hectic itinerary. "Had amusing time in Paris and Rome." "Went to Matisse chapel, Vence." And from New York: "An average of 4 parties a day, 4 times the work, 4 hours sleep, 4 times as expensive—and I'm fine. B."

Although Bruce did not see his parents often, he conveyed to his mother fragments of his life that he knew would enthral. On 4 May 1960, he invited her to see the Pierre Balmain Summer Collection and a Preview of French Impressionist Pictures, including *La Solitude* by Corot. Tickets cost three guineas. The dress was black tie.

Hugh says, "He put Margharita back in touch with her London before the war." Seeing mother and son together John Hewett thought they were brother and sister.

"Guess where I've been, Mummy."

"Buckingham Palace?"

"No, Clarence House."

He had been to deliver a picture to the Queen Mother.

The Corot sale, which took place in the same month as Sarah Hunt dismissed him as "too boring", marked a break with the schoolboy commuter from Ealing. From the spring of 1960, Bruce mixed with the cream of the *beau monde*.

Whatever pain he suffered over Ivry's marriage was soon forgotten. "Have just got Avril's [Curzon] mother's invitation for the 24th with a note from A. saying that you're having a dinner party," he wrote to Ivry on 10 October 1960. "Should love to come." Within a year of her visit to London, Bruce was able to tell Margharita of how, while holidaying at Este near Venice, he had taken tea with the Duke and Duchess of Windsor. The Duke, who was dressed in yellow from tie to toe, spoke in a faint American accent. "What was Wallis like?" Margharita wanted to know. The Duchess had told Bruce, who was suffering from jaundice, to put on some dark glasses and to catch the next plane home.

Bruce's host at Este was a young English artist, Teddy Millington-Drake, a grumpy and mischievous Old Etonian who spoke in a slow drawl. "He came for the weekend and stayed six months," he complained of Bruce who, after he started writing, liked to stay with him in Patmos and Tuscany. Millington-Drake was the son of the diplomat Sir Eugen, ambassador to Montevideo at the time of the *Graf Spee*'s sinking; his mother, Lady Effie, was the daughter of the first Earl of Inchcape. He was 27 when he met Bruce, at dinner with the frame-maker, Alfred Hecht. "Teddy was an unrepentant queer long before such things existed," says Lucie-Smith, who had known him at Oxford as a camp dandy in jeans with chintz turn-ups. "Bruce envied him his ease with his sexuality. He had only minimal artistic talent, but he did have money. He held up a distorting mirror of what Bruce wanted and all he didn't want to become.

Exploiting Teddy, just a little, was a way of getting on terms with his own mixed feelings." Their friendship endured until Bruce's death.

In 1961, Millington-Drake had rented the 35-room Villa Albrizzi at Este. He hung Indian Rajput textiles on the wall and down one wall painted the words of a favourite poem of Bruce's, Baudelaire's *"Invitation au Voyage"*:

> *Là, tout n'est qu'ordre et beauté*
> *Luxe, calme et volupté.*

That summer, Millington-Drake invited Bruce in a party with Colette Clark and Emma Tennant. For much of the visit Bruce lay in bed, yellow-faced with the jaundice he had contracted "from a needle giving me an anti-histamine shot for a mosquito bite in Sicily". Hugh Honour was another visitor. He wrote: "The talk that summer of this brilliant adolescent was all about recent sales of Impressionist and other modern paintings and was very different from his later conversation. It was smart and acid." With his head propped against the pillow in a French Empire bateau-lit, Bruce resembled to Emma Tennant "a Germanic folk-tale hero, a grown-up Hansel who has leapt from the cage where the wicked witch imprisoned him." On her return to England she would spend a surprisingly chaste weekend with him in Great Bedwyn. "Bruce," she wrote, "is a man with no woman in him, no wish for women either."

One day at Este, Bruce felt well enough to visit Bertie Lansberg, an 80-year-old Brazilian of German-Jewish extraction who had bought and restored Palladio's Villa Malcontenta. As he walked through Lansberg's hall Bruce pointed to a lump of marble half hidden under a console and exclaimed: "Look! A Greek kouros!" It turned out to be ten inches from the buttocks and pelvis of a greyish marble kouros. "Lansberg was delighted," wrote John McEwen in his tribute to Millington-Drake, "and immediately said he would give it to Chatwin who, to Millington-Drake's embarrassment, kept him to his word, returning with a sack to claim it the following week." Tennant was with him when he collected it. "What does Bruce do, to secure his prize? I remember only an interminable wait, with Teddy's small figure, very dapper as ever in a dark linen jacket, wandering around the artefacts and pictures, sighing as if once again disappointed . . ."

Bruce smuggled his gift out of Italy in the lower bunk of a sleeper. The fragment became known as "The Bottom".

1   2   3   4

1. The baby Bruce in 1942. "He's so beautiful, he's almost too beautiful to live," the midwife said. [Courtesy of Hugh Chatwin]

2. Bruce, an undistinguished schoolboy, in 1952. "If you were to say, 'This is the boy who is going to be Bruce Chatwin'," says a contemporary, "I would have said: 'No, I don't think so'." [HC]

3. Bruce in 1958, shortly before he started at Sotheby's. "It's easy to forget how pure he was at that stage," says Brian Sewell. [HC]

4. Bruce in 1986, after collapsing in Zurich. These photographs were taken for a visa to West Africa, where he hoped to die. [HC]

This cabinet, passed down through the Chatwin family, first belonged to Bruce's paternal grandmother, Isobel Chatwin. It was his childhood "cabinet of curiosities", a doorway to fantastical lands and the inspiration for many of his books.
[Stewart Meese]

The Chatwins claim descent from Turald (*d*.1121), a messenger from Rouen who fought at the battle of Hastings. He was so tall that in the Bayeux tapestry his name is squeezed in beside him. [HC]   (*Above right*) Bruce's paternal great-grandfather. Julius Alfred Chatwin (1830–90) was a prosperous Birmingham architect. The portrait is drawn from memory by one of his assistants. [HC]

The Chatwins were tainted by the scandal surrounding Bruce's maternal great-grandfather Robert Harding Milward (1837–1903). Milward (*left, standing*) in Egypt with his daughter Isobel (Bruce's grandmother) in 1898, the year the Duke of Marlborough sacked him "for grose incompitanse". [HC]

Charles Chatwin in 1940 just before he joined HMS *Euryalus*. In civilian life, he was a lawyer. When Bruce was three, he would kiss this photograph before going to bed. [HC]

Bruce's mother, Margharita Turnell in 1938. Hugh Chatwin describes their mother as "morally very correct, with a bit of Scarlett O'Hara trying to burst out". [HC]

The war baby: Margharita and Bruce on the coast at Filey in Yorkshire in 1942. "Bruce was a ray of sunshine from the day he was born." [HC]

Hugh and Bruce on the steps of 2 Stirling Road, Birmingham in 1947. When the family moved to the country, the life of the two brothers mirrored that of Lewis and Benjamin in *On the Black Hill*. "Bruce was more like an uncle to me," says Hugh. [HC]

In 1947, the Chatwins moved from Birmingham to Brown's Green Farm. This food-producing smallholding was the family home until 1961. Bruce shot pigeons from the window and rode on pigs across the yard. [HC]

Bruce at Marlborough College in 1955: "I was *hopeless* at school, a real *idiot*, bottom of every class." [HC]

Bruce in the Antiquities cubby-hole at Sotheby's c. 1960. His compact prose style owes much to his having catalogued hundreds of diverse objects. The experience, he claimed, made him blind. [UPI/Corbis-Betmann]

Antiquities auction, 28 June 1965. Bruce (*circled*) caught between his mentors: John Hewett (*bearded, right*) and Sotheby's chairman Peter Wilson (*on podium*), whom he called "the Beast". [Harmer Johnson]

The Impressionist department was more glamorous than Antiquities. Bruce in 1964 with the Gauguin that he was "staggered" to see hanging in a Scottish castle, its whereabouts unknown for 40 years. [Daily Mail/Solo]

Bruce's first love, Ivry Guild, with
her brothers, Raulin and John. "You
epitomised London glamour," he told
her. Raulin, who was one of Bruce's
best friends at Marlborough, died in 1966.
[Terence Donovan/The Lady Freyberg]

Bruce in 1963. "Think of the word
charming," says Miranda Rothschild.
"Think of the word seduction . . .
He's out to seduce everybody,
it doesn't matter if you are male,
female, an ocelot or a tea-cosy." [HC]

WILSON, SEEKING TO prise from Christie's their traditional clients, trained his young men to cultivate connections and to nourish their contacts. The saying went that both auction houses dealt in the three Ds: Divorce, Debt and Death. The difference between them was that at the death Christie's would send a wreath to the funeral while Sotheby's sent a representative. Increasingly, Bruce became Wilson's representative. "He was a bird-dog," says Lucie-Smith. "When someone had got something, Bruce was sent to get it out of them. There are a lot of nutty people in the art world and they come no nuttier than those who have inherited. He was good at managing nuts."

Such a collector was George Spencer-Churchill who lived near Oxford. One day Bruce drove down to Northwick Park with Robert Erskine, George Ortiz and Peter Levi. Bruce, says Levi, was extremely witty and distinctly smartish. "It wasn't name-dropping, although names were dropped." They drove in Erskine's 1936 Aston Martin, and Bruce told a story about a car drive with Picasso. "Someone in the car said to Picasso, 'I don't know what's to happen about Princess Margaret's marriage. She looks very glum.' Picasso talked over his shoulder: 'It's perfectly simple, she bathes him too much. Everyone knows you shouldn't wash a commoner's back'." Levi was impressed. "I'd heard people make jokes about Snowdon, but no one who'd been in a car with Picasso."

They arrived at Northwick Park where Spencer-Churchill had laid out his collection of Greek and Etruscan bronzes on a square table in a ranked pyramid with the largest in the centre. Among the bronzes was one modern toy soldier, brightly coloured, and he would ask the question, "All are BC: except one. Which is the AD one?"

"He'd been shot through both temples, which left him a bit strained," says Levi. "His habits were so odd that he had the dining room wired and if someone upset him he'd turn up the music, Wagner, very loud. He was known always to put water in the claret and when he invited us to supper, he said: 'I only have a boiled egg, you know'."

Taking up a gold weight made of haematite, Spencer-Churchill rubbed the back of Bruce's neck with it.

Declining supper, the four escaped to the Lygon Arms and ordered a magnum. Levi asked Bruce: "How do you know these marvellously funny people?" It was his job, Bruce said. He *had* to know them. "If they have stuff which they one day might sell, better it comes to us than to Christie's." In the event, Spencer-Churchill sent his collection to Christie's.

UNTIL HE TURNED against it, Bruce revelled in the names, the gossip and his contacts in this country house world. He exhibited a genius for taking on the plumage of his prey. "If seriousness was required, he was good at that," said Hewett. "If he went for a walk, or sailed, he immediately fell into the role. He *was* a chameleon, but a nice one."

Then there was his talent for mimicking the people he met. A vigorous social life offered him plenty of scope to "do the police in different voices", as T. S. Eliot wrote of Dickens. Bruce was a mimic after the manner of Gustave Flaubert and Konrad Lorenz who, he wrote, "became the wretched jackdaws". He remembered books and objects and people with his grandfather Leslie Chatwin's total recall. "Bruce on form could be the song the sirens sang," says the artist Howard Hodgkin, who met him at this time. "You could be sitting with him and suddenly he'd be the Countess of Sutherland or Mrs Gandhi or Diana Cooper or almost anyone you could think of. In a crowded restaurant you wished you weren't with him." There was an additional quality to his mimicry. He did not transform his voice into the other person: they co-existed. There was Bruce's voice and, within that, the echoing tones of the person he was imitating. "This gave the hallucinatory feeling of being confronted by two people," says Lucie-Smith. Bruce—and Bianca Jagger's mother, as it were, selling *refrescos* on a beach in Nicaragua. "Talking to Bruce," says the collector Werner Muensterberger, "you could see how he got carried away with his own fantasy and even in his imitation of people how he elaborated on them: it was close, but not exactly what he had seen or heard. Someone who embellishes like that is seeing themselves as the exception: 'It could only happen to me'."

At various moments he would lose himself so completely in the role that he lost the scent and became the person he was mimicking. By 1961, the subject of Bruce's favourite imitations was his boss at Sotheby's.

WILSON WAS SHAPED like a penguin, tall and slightly portly. His face was smooth and unlined and he had narrow, darting blue eyes which looked amiably down his nose. The only time he went out of doors was to admire his garden or to shoot (which he did badly).

Bruce called Wilson "The Beast" (a nickname given to him by the New York art journalist, Leo Lerman). He can be glimpsed in *On the Black Hill:* "The antique dealer was entirely at his ease. He eyed the room up and down; turned a saucer over, and said, 'Doulton'; peered at the 'Red Indian' to make sure it was only a print; and wondered whether, by any chance, they had any Apostle spoons."

With a sleepy, slightly hesitant voice that proved effective particularly in America, Wilson was a prime example of "the export Englishman". He was the son of a rakish Yorkshire baronet known as "Scatters" Wilson—so-called after his habit of carelessly leaving money about the room. It was not a trait Wilson inherited, for he never kept money on him and always took the back roads to his French chateau to avoid the motorway tolls. A late developer, he believed that people who suffered unhappy childhoods came out best in life. Described by his mother as looking like a periwinkle that might have strayed into a meadow, Wilson made no impact at Eton except to win a prize for a wild flower arrangement, an honour he shared with Bruce. Unable to pass his first year history exams at Oxford, he left to work for Spink's, then Reuter's where he was sacked for not learning shorthand. From there, he sold advertising space in the *Connoisseur* before joining Sotheby's in 1936 as a porter in the Furniture department.

Thereafter Sotheby's consumed his life, apart from a spell during the war as an intelligence officer in Gibraltar and Bermuda. His code number was 007, but his acquaintance with the traitors Blunt, Maclean and Burgess stoked stories that he was the Fifth Man. "Nothing would surprise me, that he was the Fifth, Sixth or Seventh man," says the art historian, John Richardson. "He was incredibly sly, devious, clever, dishonest, manipulative." His Byzantine cast of mind, useful in counter-intelligence, was equally so in the art world, which tended to thrive on tight, cell-like cliques. Several Sotheby's directors were former spies.

Wilson was icily cutting when he wanted to be, but he was a man of exquisite charm. "He did control people to a degree you wouldn't believe possible," says Elizabeth Chanler, who worked in his office from 1962. "You'd see clients coming in bristling with rage and stamping and the steam coming out of their ears. And they'd go out like lambs, smiling. He knew exactly how to touch people. Bruce had this in a different, less sinister way."

Wilson lived in London in Garden Lodge, a huge house with a ballroom rented off Tomas Harris, the dealer friend of Burgess and Maclean. The house was a monument to his taste and judgement. Wilson's interests ranged from medieval bronzes to narwhal horns. He kept a chateau near Grasse and a country house in Kent, Stone Green Hall (sometimes known as "Stone Groin Hall") which he shared with his former manservant, Harry Wright, an ardent gardener and gambler for whom he acquired a grocery.

Whatever his fancies, Sotheby's was Wilson's first passion. He built up the firm by a combination of imaginative flair, enthusiasm and ruthlessness. He would stop at nothing to bring a work of art to Sotheby's—even if he had to chip it off the wall himself. John Mallet says, "I remember cataloguing the limestone Romanesque head of a bearded prophet. PCW [Wilson] was the seller. It was attributed to a rather specific area of France. 'How do we know?' I asked. 'Well,' explained Wilson's office, 'the chairman knocked it off a ruined abbey there'."

He would go anywhere for a sale and once he had got there talk about anything except the object he had come to see, until the very last second. "Then," says Peregrine Pollen, "he made you feel that you were unbelievably perspicacious to have bought it and he was the only person who could possibly sell it for you because he understood your cleverness." He deployed the same flattery on his staff.

"He was a great leader," says Howard Ricketts, who had replaced Bruce in the Furniture department. "But he had his favourites whom he later destroyed. If you got into his orbit, woe betide you: he burned you up."

Bruce admired his chairman's *savoir faire* and dedication. He liked to imitate Wilson holding an auction and quietly knocking "this pretty little thing" down to himself via the sales clerk. "Sold to Mr Patch . . ." He adopted the same languid mannerisms, the same intonations, the same elaborate reaction to works of art. "I've always heard about your wonderful collection of pictures . . ." Wilson tells a client in *What Am I Doing Here*. Bruce adds: " 'Always' was 30 seconds beforehand."

Sometimes it was hard to work out where conscious imitation stopped. "Bruce modelled himself entirely on PCW," says James Crathorne, who joined the Impressionist department in 1963. "Literally, he talked like him. They would go round speaking to each other in the same voice, with the words lengthened out." Once Crathorne listened in bewilderment while they discussed Brancusi's ovoid sculpture, *Le commencement du monde*. "Too mmmmarvellous. What a woonderful Brancusi. So beautiful." A more normal response, says Crathorne, would have been to say: "That is a lovely thing." "But this was an emotional reaction. They were vehemently angry to think people did *not* understand."

Something else struck Crathorne. "When they looked at the Brancusi they didn't hold hands, but they were touching each other. It was an enormously close physical tie."

With Wilson's arm on his shoulder, the schoolboy was tipped into what Lucie-Smith called "a world of baroque monsters".

The Art Smuggler

The trouble is, Bruce wanted to be Genghis Khan,
but he would have preferred living in Byzantium.
—ALISON OXMANTOWN

LIKE A STENDHAL character who arrives from the provinces to the city, Bruce suddenly bloomed. Andrew Bache had known him as a lethargic pupil at Old Hall. He was surprised at the change he found on a visit from Cambridge in the early 1960s. "He seemed to be enjoying life, belting round London in a little car. There was an inquisitiveness, a curiosity, a great flowering of mind. He'd become worldly-wise."

Guy Norton grew up with Bruce near Brown's Green and was a contemporary at Marlborough. He remembers how intimidated Bruce had been in his early days in London. "He used to ring up a lot and ask me round and cook dinner." Norton saw him again two years later. "He wasn't the same person at all. It was a fantastic change, very fast and dramatic. You either sink or swim in London—and Bruce very much swam."

In Grosvenor Crescent Mews, Anthony Spink observed his flat-mate's transformation with a degree of wariness. He was struck by how intrigued Bruce was by the marriage of the interior decorator David Hicks to Pamela Mountbatten. Spink recalled an odd incident. "One weekend when I'd been away, he gave me the impression he'd been visited by Lord Mountbatten. 'I met Mountbatten at the weekend. He came round here and you'd be *amazed* what happened'."

In July 1960, Spink moved out of Grosvenor Crescent Mews. Bruce did not seek another lodger. Instead, he shed all the furniture and arranged for Hugh to repaint it during his school holiday. "I want you to come and see London," Bruce told him, "before you decide to bury yourself in Birmingham."

Bruce had chosen a particular shade of white, impressed by the archi-

tecture he had seen on holiday in Greece. In 1986, he would write to his
architect John Pawson, then converting his flat in Eaton Place: "I suppose
it's because I've lived at various times in the incomparably beautiful white-
washed houses of Greece and Andalucia that dead white walls, in England, always used to be just that: dead . . . what I'd like is something the
colour of milk (if there is such a thing)."

Howard Ricketts says, "Everything was white, including the bed covers." Knowing he collected art nouveau, Bruce offered Ricketts an Emile
Gallé glass vase. "It was the last piece in the flat. He was like a child,
chucking everything out from pique."

In his 1973 essay, "The Morality of Things", Bruce described the acquisition of an object as a Grail Quest—"the chase, the recognition of the
quarry, the decision to purchase, the sacrifice and fear of financial ruin,
the Dark Cloud of Unknowing ('Is it a fake?'), the wrapping, the journey
home, the ecstasy of undressing the package, the object of the quest un-
veiled, the night one didn't go to bed with anyone, but kept vigil, gazing,
stroking, adoring the new fetish—the companion, the lover, but very
shortly *the bore*, to be kicked out or sold off while another more desirable
thing supplants itself in our affections." He asked himself: "Do we not
gaze coldly at our clutter and say, 'If these objects express my personality,
then I hate my personality'?"

He was frustrated at not being able to use his "eye" to collect for himself. Every day he exercised his taste, was asked his opinion on what museums and collectors would then buy, which he had catalogued but could
not himself afford to bid for. For a while the only decorations he tolerated,
pinned up in the kitchen, were cut-outs in the style of Matisse. Lucie-
Smith says that he had fallen in love with a particular Matisse, a simple
image of a white china fruit dish drawn in chalky outlines and piled with
oranges. The painting was coming up at auction with a £15,000 estimate.
"It dated from Matisse's austerest period, before he went to Nice. Bruce
was threatening to sell everything he had to buy it. He was in lust for it."

His austerity was short-lived. Not long after stripping bare his flat, he
began to refurbish it once more into a "dandified" interior. This purge-
and-binge cycle punctuated his life. The textile dealer Jonathan Hope had
never seen anyone with two natures at such odds. "Half of Bruce despised
being European and longed to be a Mauritanian nomad, renouncing
everything; the other half was a worldly, acquisitive collector with an eagle's eye for the unusual who longed to go riding with Jackie Onassis. It
was a permanent battle of values." The peremptory *non-sequitur* which is

the hallmark of his prose is no less true of his character. Hugh Honour wrote, "He was a split personality, at any rate in this respect, and his extraordinary vitality and sharpness of perception owed much to the inner conflict of his two obsessive urges, the one sparking off the other."

Bruce had learned from his father the sailor's economical use of space. Even in his collector phase, the flat was never cluttered. His ideal house was a three-windowed Hausa mud hut in which he stayed in 1972. The outside was "the texture of a good-natured bath-towel". Inside, a pillar supported a vault of thornbush logs. The door was made from a crate of canned pineapples from the Côte d'Ivoire and the bed was an old French military camp-bed covered with camel leather. "It is home. I am happy with it," he wrote in his notebook.

Bruce's white-scraped floor and his careful arrangement of objects sought to emulate a hut, a tent or an Ingres interior, but the effect betrayed to Lucie-Smith his decorative taste. "He was full of decorator *pronunciamenti*, giving me specific injunctions and saws. 'With flowers, it is mandatory to see the stem'."

Howard Hodgkin has the Grosvenor Crescent flat in his 1962 painting *Japanese Screen*. It shows Bruce as "an acid green smear", turning away from his guests, Cary and Edith Welch. The dealer Christopher Gibbs remembers Bruce "entertaining sparely, deliciously, beneath a blackened silver screen painted with aquatic plants by some observant Japanese botaniser. Did we eat our scrambled eggs and white truffles off *blanc de Chine* or the blue-sprigged porcelain of the Duc d'Angoulême? At any rate there were dhurries of dirty cream and washed indigo, there was a Tilly Kettle of a young Indian girl smoking a hookah, scrolls, drawings, and objects revealed with becoming ceremony. And there were books and spears and fish hooks from Polynesia, even books about fish hooks and about tomahawks and round towers and taboos and totems."

One night, Hodgkin dined at the flat with the collector Villiers David. "It was incredibly elegant and tidy, as if a photographer was about to arrive." The bedroom had a futon and a duvet, the first Hodgkin had seen. The desk was a sheet of thick plate glass on two trestles, with lots of blue writing paper in piles. The paintings, hung at eye level if you were sitting in a chair, included an eighteenth-century oval relief portrait, French, of a man in a wig, and landscape drawings by Cros and Le Roiseau. His Louis XVI chair was now upholstered in shiny black leather. He had bought from Lucie-Smith a Japanese Ngoro lacquer tray; and swapped his Piranesi of the Antonine Column for the skin of a small tiger shot by the Maharajah of Bikaner in the 1930s and given to Robert Erskine's mother. Plus "The Bottom".

Hodgkin, looking at the skylight, said to Villiers David: "What Bruce needs is a huge chandelier."

"Dear boy, where would he get money from?"

In despair, Bruce replied, "I can cook. I could always make a living by cooking."

"He really minded about not having money," says Hodgkin, "and nobody was quicker to say in his inimitable way: 'Could be valuable, you know.' He was always thinking he'd found something valuable, that the philosopher's stone was lurking in the next antique shop. He was forever a dealer."

Bruce's friendship with rich collectors like Villiers David, Welch and Ortiz encouraged him to spend more than he could afford. Kenelm Digby-Jones, who succeeded Peregrine Pollen as Wilson's assistant, made him a member of the St James's Club, where he dined on Sundays. "Bruce didn't mind putting on a dinner jacket at all." He bought a *Messerschmitt* bubble car and at work he began to stand out by virtue of his clothes. Discarding his stiff collars, his knotted ties and brogues, he began to dress in light grey suits, tailor-made from Henry Poole in Savile Row, and silk ties and slip-on shoes.

Ortiz says, "He liked to live well, but he told me he didn't have enough money. How can you submit a young man to a first-class flight to Chicago to see the Campbell's soup man, be met by his chauffeur, drive to his huge estate full of Impressionist paintings—and not be affected?"

BRUCE MADE MONEY dealing during his holidays. One attraction of working for Sotheby's was the long summer break. He would set off abroad without telling anyone where he was going. "His idea of a holiday," says Nash, who went with him to Afghanistan, "was to go where no one could reach him on the telephone." Lucie-Smith says, "Bruce understood the value of absence and not just in his art."

In his first summer, July 1959, he had gone, alone, on a walking tour of eastern Sardinia. He wrote, "It was terrifying to walk at dusk up the main street of Orgolos, the legendary 'home' of the Sardinian bandit, looking for a bed and having every door slammed in one's face." Finding Sardinia impossible in the heat, he headed for Tarquinia on the mainland, to explore the Etruscan painted tombs. The journey showed him to be a delicate traveller. He wrote to his parents: "My nose bled solidly for no apparent reason the day before yesterday for $1^{1}/_{2}$ hrs."

In December 1961, Bruce made the first of two journeys to the Middle East with Robert Erskine, who knew dealers in Cairo. Erskine says, "We were wheeling and dealing in antiquities and we thought, 'Why not go to the source?'"

It surprised Erskine to discover how raw a traveller was his companion. "I don't think Bruce liked travelling by himself. He was always worried about his stomach." Arriving in Cairo on 17 December, they stayed in a little hotel, The Golden Tulip. Bruce opened his suitcase. It was stuffed with pills. When he discovered in Erskine's valise a pill he did not have, he purloined the pillbox and added it to his own. "It was another example of the collector," says Erskine.

Inevitably, Bruce's stomach suffered. The principal dealers insisted on inviting them home to "pretty revolting" meals. Women peeped through the keyhole, while the host stood behind, not eating but offering more food and watching like a hawk, dish after dish. "Bruce was aghast. He thought he would catch every single disease—and did."

Bruce's Teutonic looks were appreciated by the Arabs. Erskine says, "I was in some shop in Luxor looking at coins when I heard: 'Robert, Robert, rescue me!' There was the sound of many running feet and Bruce burst in, followed by a mass of people who went away with a hang-dog look. Then we were sitting in Luxor station, waiting for the train, and a man suddenly jumped between us and said to Bruce: 'You are my brother. I will never leave you.' We had to push him off."

They spent Christmas Day on the Nile, taking a Sudanese railway steamer from Aswan to Wadi Halfa. Lunch posed a new threat. The waiter served a blancmange topped with a green leaf to resemble a Christmas pudding. Then, beaming like anything, he poured petrol over it from a can and set the creation alight.

Erskine found Bruce an imaginative traveller and fun to be with. As they wandered through the Temple of Hathor at Denderah, Bruce was seized by the idea, which he intoned in French, of buying the place and turning it into a grand hotel in which immensely rich American women could live out their last years. They would call the hotel The Hathor, after the goddess of love, and there would be another hotel for men, The Horus in the Temple of Horus at Edfu, 80 miles up the Nile. Erskine says, "He had this daydream, imagining the dining room over there, the bar obviously here, aspidistras, magenta lighting, Marlene Dietrich singing in the cabaret and plots of desert behind where they would be buried in grand, quasi-Egyptian tombs."

On 6 January, the extent of Bruce's naïveté declared itself as they prepared to leave Cairo with their spoils. In three weeks, they had bought much good material. In Luxor, while poking around a heap, Bruce had picked out a few bits of wood that turned out to be the parts of a 3,000-year-old stool. Erskine had also acquired some heavy Pre-Dynastic stone pots. Now the difficulty was to get them out of the country. It was not strictly legal then to take antiques out of Egypt.

One of Erskine's dealers in Cairo claimed to have arranged for the customs officers to be bribed so that their cases were not looked at. "Bruce was in an absolute funk about this kind of thing. Quivering all over. 'Oh my God, I feel very ill. You'd better go.' Finally, we went through customs. When no one stopped us, he became a different person. He was like a fish which changed colour," says Erskine. "A terrible old funker."

It had been a profitable trip. A piece of Mycenaean silver bought for £90 fetched £250. Bruce paid £5 for the stool, and sold it to an American dealer for $300.

XI.

⟡

A *goût de monstres*

The ugliest men loved the most beautiful things.

—U TZ

"I T'S EXPENSIVE, SPENDING time with rich people," says Robert Erskine. "They never think of paying for anything." Bruce's superiors watched his extravagance with alarm. In New York, where he had arrived in March 1960 to open the American office, Peregrine Pollen received a letter from Wilson. "PCW was worried about what to do with Bruce. He couldn't live within his income and was always sending in expenses for far more than anyone had anticipated." Pollen wrote back. "I said that Bruce would be a brilliant business-getter, but that he was never going to live within his income because he had rich friends and there was no point in sending him where he couldn't pay his way." Pollen suggested that Bruce be given a proper expense account. "Not hearing back from PCW, I assumed that is what happened."

When the 1961 auction season opened in October, Bruce had been at Sotheby's three years. He held the reins in both Antiquities and "Imps". But as the appetite for these paintings grew Wilson decided Impressionist sales were too important to be left in the hands of his protégé alone.

In November 1961, Bruce turned up at work and was taken aback to discover two new faces: Michel Strauss, who was to run the department with him; and David Nash, who was to be a porter.

Nash—or "Nashpiece"—Bruce knew from Marlborough. After leaving school, he had worked as a gravedigger in a Wimbledon cemetery and as an electrical engineer at the Horton lunatic asylum. He knew nothing about art and his interview reflected the amateurishness which still reigned. "PCW asked me what I was interested in. I wasn't interested in anything, so I said Impressionist painting. I'd been on a day trip to the Monet exhibition at the Tate because it meant a day in town."

Michel Strauss posed more of a threat. Four years older than Bruce, he had been at Oxford, Harvard and the Courtauld. His grandfather was an important collector of Impressionists. His stepfather was the philosopher Isaiah Berlin. "I was 25," says Strauss, "with a degree in history of art, and came from an intellectual, cultured background. Bruce was unpleasant and difficult. He wouldn't help at all."

Their rivalry came to a head in barely a month over the sale of 35 Impressionist paintings belonging to William Somerset Maugham. Frightened by a spate of burglaries in his neighbourhood in France, the author had decided to consign the paintings to Sotheby's. For many years they had given him pleasure. "Now," he wrote, "they were an anxiety."

In January 1962, the collection arrived. Bruce and Strauss agreed to catalogue the pictures together at 9.30 the following morning. Strauss arrived to find that Chatwin had been in the office since 5.30 a.m. He had catalogued the lot on his own. "He was very competitive."

After the Maugham sale, Bruce and Strauss—whom Bruce nicknamed "Shellers"—settled into a respectful professional relationship. Socially, they never mixed, but Strauss became the sane core and it was felt that Wilson had successfully played one against the other. The department would have collapsed with Bruce alone in charge; with Strauss alone, it would have lacked the desired zest.

Bruce was still the blue-eyed boy, but he exasperated those who worked with him. "He was not a team player," says Judith Landrigan. "He'd come in late, leave early, was never around when the crunch was on. It was Michel who organised, answered letters, wrote the catalogue, met the printer's deadline."

David Ellis-Jones says that while Bruce moved at "a young prima donna's speed", others had to clean up the mess after him. "If anything got too hot, he was off to Antiquities." Ellis-Jones called him "Chatswein".

When Sue Goodhew had to leave she gave her successor, Sarah Inglis-Jones, some advice:

"1. When Bruce dictates too fast tell him to go slower

2. When he gets in a temper shout back

3. If he throws anything at you, throw it back."

This last tip referred to an incident with a snake.

AT MARLBOROUGH, BRUCE had collected lizards in glass jars. At Sotheby's, he kept for a short while a six-foot white and black royal python.

One day, about to set off for Paris, he had asked Goodhew a favour.

If she was in London over the weekend, would she feed his python, which was housed in a suitcase beside his radiator?

"No, I won't," said Goodhew, who was terrified of snakes.

"It's terribly easy, you must just go in and I'll give you some white mice."

"I absolutely refuse."

"You spoilt little deb!"

Then he picked up a blue volume of Benizéit's *Dictionnaire des Artistes*. The book hit Goodhew on the corner of her forehead, blackening her eye. "I was so shocked I burst into tears and ran from the room. I had to go to the doctor and wear a velvet eye patch."

Bruce was guilty enough to bring her a Hermès scarf back from Paris. He told her he had smuggled the snake past customs under his shirt with a coat over him.

"I hope it hugs you to death," Goodhew said.

The Congolese python belonged not to Bruce but to a wealthy young American living in Paris, Jimmy Douglas. Douglas had bought the snake from Harrods' pet department when staying with Bruce. In Paris, where he kept his pet in a fishtank in the bathroom, the python gained a speedy notoriety. "Rather like Bruce, it got talked about," says Douglas. "You'd find it wandering around on the bed. Sometimes I'd force-feed it hot-dogs. Otherwise I'd give it white mice." The novelist Françoise Sagan, invited to dinner, reacted to the feeding ritual with the same horror as Goodhew. She stuffed the mice into her handbag, later releasing them to maximum effect on the floor of La Coupole. Salvador Dali wore the snake as a turban on a television show, while Bruce scarfed it around his neck to the opening of the "New Jimmy's" night-club where, placed on a table, someone mistook it for a modern ashtray and stubbed out their cigarette. "The python," says Douglas, "started to uncoil."

AT SOME MOMENT, the bird-dog became the prey. It was one reason Bruce gave Lucie-Smith for leaving Sotheby's: "I can't face being chased around one more beach umbrella by one more lady in palazzo pyjamas."

Lady Peel, the former actress Beatrice Lillie, was always ringing in a fluster from the South of France: *"Içi Lady parle qui Peel."* From New York, there was the wealthy Mrs Brummer, whom Bruce impressed to such an extent in the course of cataloguing her late husband's collection, that she told him: "Ah Bruce, the eye of my husband Ernest is alive in you."

Not only women chased him. Collectors in the main were homosexual. "Many were queer beyond description," says Peregrine Pollen. "There was the creature supposed to have been the catamite of the Cardinal Archbishop of Prague. He used to breeze in to sales wearing grey flannel trousers and a double-breasted jacket. When accosted by Carmen Gronau, in charge of Old Masters, he would flap this open—to reveal a naked torso." James Crathorne once had to make a valuation for an American collector, "a frightfully camp creature in Milwaukee who did awful things with his quite big dog."

Wilson favoured the personal touch. He knew his protégé's value in this market. Pollen says, "He knew how the most hard bitten, iron-jawed businessmen could be completely naïve when it comes to works of art. The same person who might have crushed Bruce to dust on the futures market would, if the subject was a Matisse, listen to him mouth open, ears flapping." Here again Wilson deployed his genius for promotion and for encouraging different attitudes to works of art. To invest in a Matisse was not only a demonstration of wealth, but of artistic sensibility: it showed you had taste. The Florida rich were especially susceptible to this line of thinking, says Lucie-Smith, but they tended not to get on with Old Etonians like Pollen.

"Bruce, on the other hand, bowled them over."

"I'M QUITE SURE that physical things happened and he must have had to contend with that," says Brian Sewell, who spoke from his own experience at Christie's.

In the majority of cases, Bruce was an innocent fêted by rich men: the Bey of Albania, Paul Adamidi Frahseri Bey, who looked like a retired brigand and stayed at the Ritz; the Bey's friend, Douglas Cooper, heir to an Australian sheep-dip fortune at whose villa in the south of France Bruce probably met Picasso. ("Douglas took a tremendous shine to Bruce who was fairly adept at wriggling out of range while batting an eyelid at everything in sight," says John Richardson, who lived twelve years with Cooper.) Then there was the mildly talented painter Villiers David, who told Bruce: "You're not sensual enough."

It was perfectly obvious to Lucie-Smith, if not to Villiers David, that

Bruce would not succumb. Watching Bruce's pursuit by a series of rich and elderly collectors, Lucie-Smith was put in mind of a pull-along croc-odile, popular at the time, with a mechanism which made its jaws snap at a butterfly balanced on its head. "Bruce's relationship to a certain kind of sacred monster resembles that between butterfly and crocodile: a great deal of flapping and agitation and colour, with the crocodile thinking at any moment he's going to swallow this satisfying morsel. Of course, it's set up so the crocodile never succeeds."

In fact, one crocodile did get to eat the butterfly. In July 1963, Bruce went on a visit to Glenveagh castle in Donegal. The owner, Henry McIl-henny, was a collector from Philadelphia whose grandfather had migrated from Ireland and invented the gas meter. McIlhenny, then in his fifties and not a timid person, had approached Sotheby's to have Glenveagh's contents appraised for insurance. Wilson selected Bruce for the task.

The castle was five miles from the gates and the guests dressed for din-ner. Another guest was Giacometti's biographer, James Lord, who kept a diary. He says, "I know they went to bed together. Henry did the seduc-ing. He was very boastful about it to me. He called him, 'Bruceykins'."

Brian Sewell identified with Bruce's predicament. "He told me of a hugely embarrassing night in a castle in Ireland. What do you do? There is a certain outrage in one's reaction. If there is one thing a young homo-sexual really resents, it's that homosexuality being taken for granted as be-ing in the gift of someone else. Bruce hadn't anyway come to terms with his homosexual drive. The last thing in the world he'd want, or need, is to have to contend with an exploitation of that homosexuality for the ad-vantage of Sotheby's."

This is exactly what Wilson called upon him to do in the spring of 1962.

Having catalogued the Somerset Maugham sale, Bruce was satisfied that he had completed his duties. Shortly before the sale, however, the old man changed his mind. Had it not been for Bruce, says Kenelm Digby-Jones, the sale might have been cancelled. "Maugham had been to the dentist. He had toothache, he was old, he said he wouldn't sell. The sale was two days away. PCW nearly had a fit. He took a huge sigh. 'I need a drink.' He was a diabetic. It was the first time I'd seen him drink. It was late, about 9 p.m. Then he had this brilliant idea of wheeling in Bruce."

His hair freshly washed (on Wilson's instructions), Bruce went to meet Maugham at the Dorchester. "Somerset Maugham recognised Bruce as a bit of live bait: exactly what he was. It was very cynically done. Bruce didn't have to do anything but talk about Maugham's toothache and the sea and calm him down. But it was one of the things Bruce got miffed about."

Bruce supplied more details to Maugham's grandson, Jonathan Hope. As he entered the room Maugham's companion, Alan Searle, said: "He wants you to go and sit next to him." Bruce complied—whereupon Maugham reached out a hand.

"His awful old fingers going through my hair!" he told Hope. He added that Maugham, in his opinion, was the most over-rated writer of the twentieth century. Bruce wanted Hope to believe that, because he had allowed Maugham to ruffle his hair, he had secured the whole collection for Sotheby's. But that was only part of it. "He wanted to emphasise how grotesque was the atmosphere of corruption and oiliness. He implied he had to do this on other instances, tart up clients, soften them up, charm people to get money out of them, and he became quite hysterical at the recollection, bouncing up in his chair, saying 'I hated it, I hated it!' "

CHATWIN'S FIRST STORY "Rotting Fruit" is based in part on a Maugham figure and seems to contain everything Bruce knows and feels, and it was written at about this time. The unpublished story had its origin in one of Bruce's most elaborate comic routines. Lucie-Smith says, "I heard it several times over and laughed until I was nearly sick." He suggested that Bruce put it down on paper.

Not one of Bruce's colleagues imagined for him a career as a writer. Hewett said, "If you had told me he would have been a famous writer, I never would have believed it. I would have thought his ambition was wealth, to buy things for his own personal collection." Another who worked with him says: "He didn't appear to be able to string two words together on paper."

Lucie-Smith was the only committed writer Bruce knew. He ran a poetry circle called The Group, celebrated in its time, whose members—including Peter Porter, Peter Redgrove and George MacBeth—met at Lucie-Smith's house every Friday. "I didn't ask Bruce to The Group because he expressed no interest. Anyway, it never occurred to me. He and the membership would have been oil and water. When Bruce finally became interested in my status as a writer, it was for two reasons. I told him

he should write things down because some of his 'narratives' were so
funny, and it was very much part of The Group philosophy that *anyone*
could write if they really wanted to. Secondly, I was almost certainly the
only member of his fairly close circle who had a literary agent." His agent,
Deborah Rogers later became Bruce's agent.

The story which Lucie-Smith told him to write down reveals a narrator wrestling his confusion into a drama that celebrates—as it subverts—
the excesses of the art world. The story is transparently autobiographical,
a display case of rare clues to Bruce's emotional life. It is overlong, unfo-
cussed, undigested, and it is unlikely that he showed it to anyone.

"Rotting Fruit" was Bruce's only attempt to deal in fiction with this
homosexual world. He resuscitated it for the director James Ivory, thinking it would make a marvellous film. "I have a *goût de monstres*," Bruce
wrote to Ivory in 1971, "but this was the best ever and I ended up feeling
the deepest compassion for him." The monster was a combination of
Somerset Maugham, Peter Wilson and "an elderly slum property developer from Miami" who came each year to London. Bruce named him
Norman Scott Lauderdale and cast him as the seedy protagonist.

Not much happens in the story except for a series of charged encounters between the dying Norman and the young narrator, who at one
point is despatched to Portugal, where he is required to dress in powder
blue hip-hugging pants and a pink shirt and to perform Nazi salutes for
the delectation of Norman's large photographer friend, Seymour Ross.
Norman and Seymour are archetypes for all the rich homosexual collectors whom Wilson had sent Bruce to charm. The young narrator is called
Peter.

Events are triggered by Peter's reception at Sotheby's of a pink and
faintly scented letter from Miami decorated with bees and bearing the initials NSL, an unmistakable jibe at the type of letter which often landed
on Bruce's desk:

> *I am in possession of a painting by Henri Matisse—Les Lilas—signed
> and dated 1916. I desire to sell this work as soon as possible and I
> understand from an acquaintance that you can assist me. I shall stay at
> the Dorchester Hotel from June 8 through June 15 and would be pleased
> to hear from you.*

Probably Bruce had in mind the same Matisse that he had wanted to
buy. The narrator visits Norman in his hotel room ostensibly to discuss its
sale, but the encounter is quickly complicated by Norman's attraction to

the young art dealer. Norman's face "resembled a Venetian blind. The mouth was thin and the lips colourless. He had a tendency to salivate at the corners." He flatters Peter ("They tell me you are very brilliant") and invites himself to dinner at Peter's modest flat.

"Was his interest in me sexual or financial? I dreaded either. Where was the famous Matisse?"

Norman's car, "a vast grey Rolls Royce" with a grey chauffeur to match, recalls Ivry's dramatic arrival at Marlborough. Even the contents of Norman's dinner parcel faithfully reflect Ivry's picnic: Prunier's bouilla-baisse, Charbonnel and Walker chocolates, Chateau Montrachet 1956. Norman's father, a Pittsburgh steel millionaire "whose furnaces lit up the Allegheny river", points directly forward to the family Bruce would marry into, while Norman's hypochondria carries a self-mocking reference to Bruce's own: he arrives with a pigskin bag containing "a battalion of pills", arranging these in neat formations around his plate.

Norman admires Peter's apartment, the Japanese screen illuminated by a single spotlight. "Its austere chastity appeals to me." He becomes expansive, the wine unlocking the saga of his Miami childhood, the huge house on a coral beach with a swimming pool painted by a fashionable New York artist with images of copulating crocodiles, the sadness he had to endure when his parents ran to ruin ("he didn't stop beating her till she threatened to throw herself over the parapet") and finally his own inexpressible beauty as a boy. "I was the most beautiful thing you ever saw . . . when Mother and I walked into Maxim's, the band stopped playing, the people stopped talking, they rose to their feet and they cheered." As an adult, however, he had to hide behind "a thick curtain" which he could pull down at will.

At this point the story becomes most obviously autobiographical: the mask slips and Chatwin the writer begins to call his narrator by his own name.

"I assure you, Bruce," says Norman, speaking of the protective curtain, "it has saved me a lot of heart aches and misty eyes."

Next morning they go to Aspreys, where Norman makes Bruce spend all his money on a glittering chromium unicorn.

"Why a unicorn, Norman?"

"Why a unicorn?" he repeated with feeling. "Because it reminds me of you . . . *fantastic beast.*"

IN "ROTTING FRUIT" Bruce's obsessions, ambivalence and inexperience come tumbling out: his taste for Matisse and Noel Coward; the austerity that comes from not being able to afford the art he wants; above all, his panic over challenges to what Norman deprecatingly calls "your iron-clad chastity". Although Bruce keeps detached, there are moments when Norman is anxious to close the distance.

The pursuit of the elusive Matisse ends in a hotel in Estoril where Norman sends him for the weekend to meet a "very dear friend" whom he warns is "sick like me, very sick. You'd like him. He's very artistic."

Bruce arrives at the hotel where the story and the writing degenerate into a stock camp fantasy. The cowboy photographer, Seymour Ross, offers Bruce $200 if he will pose for him. "Salute me. Salute me," orders Ross. "Nazi salute. Nazi salute . . . Click your heels."

Finally, Ross collapses on the bed, the camera between his legs. He lies panting for a full minute, then snarls at Bruce to get out.

As he escapes to the seafront, the narrator reflects: "I was unable to decide whether I had been sexually outraged or not. NO. NO. I danced. I jumped in the air, vaulted over the railings and on to the beach kicking the sand. I howled with laughter. It was far too funny. That wasn't outrage." But it is not clear whether Bruce is happy to have preserved his "iron-clad chastity", or if he is experiencing the first exhilaration of the voyeur.

WILSON FILLED SUCH a presence in Bruce's life that he is distributed over all three characters in "Rotting Fruit": the narrator Peter, the art collector and the deviant photographer. He had opened the door to Bruce's sensuous delight in objects, but how much further their own relationship went is harder to know. Bruce's mannerisms undoubtedly grew more camp as he aped Wilson and it was no secret within Sotheby's that the chairman was attracted to Bruce, and felt possessive of his young blood. In Mrs Ford's tearoom there was a joke:

Q: Where do you look for PCW when you can't find him in his office?
A: Behind the tallboy.

"The tallboy," says Brian Sewell, "was Bruce."

Opinions divide as to whether the joke had substance. Hodgkin believes "they definitely had an affair." Lucie-Smith disagrees. "Bruce was clever at keeping old men on heat without ever delivering the goods. His sense of the ridiculous would have prevented him. The whole relationship bears the mark of unrequited love, but Bruce manipulated him for what he could get out of it."

Sewell probably gets closest to the truth. "I'm convinced he was not PCW's lover. Wilson wanted Bruce body and soul and it made it easier for him if Bruce pretended, so it didn't look a footling, idiotic pursuit. It was a very kindly act on Bruce's part."

Even if not physical, their relationship carried the emotional charge of an affair. To at least one person Bruce intimated that the flirtation may have gone too far. He told Ivry that Wilson wanted him to come and live with him in a mews house. "He's very, very possessive and it's very, very awkward. I don't know how long I can take it."

The Somerset Maugham sale had marked a watershed in Bruce's relationship with Wilson. He began to rebel against "the Beast's" exploitation.

BRUCE, LIKE HIS own description of the Russian Bohemian poet Sergei Esenin, married to Isadora Duncan, was "a blonde innocent who awoke the tenderest emotions in both sexes". It was impossible to be indifferent to him, even if he was indifferent to so many others. Peter Adam, an arts documentary-maker for the BBC, described him as "that dangerously charismatic man who had seduced us all". He says: "Many people genuinely loved Bruce or fell in love with him. It was not difficult to do so." Bruce, who shied away from intimacy, was less able to reciprocate. Gregor von Rezzori said, "He was not loving at all, he couldn't care less. But who loves a loving person?"

After Ivry Guild became engaged and Spink left the flat, Bruce embarked on a string of short-lived relationships with both sexes. Most were furtive, schoolboy affairs, as with Teddy Millington-Drake. "It didn't last very long and then we became great friends," said Millington-Drake. "We were all very juvenile in those days. We didn't take our love affairs seriously." Bruce realised the affair was over when he arrived at Este and found Millington-Drake and the designer John Stefanidis in identical bathrobes.

His involvement with Michael Ricketts, the 23-year-old brother of Howard, Bruce's colleague at Sotheby's, was more serious. An unpublished poet, Michael worked for Oxford University Press and was a friend of

Harold Nicolson and Edith Sitwell. Howard Ricketts sometimes joined them for dinner at the Fiddler's Tower in Beauchamp Place. He says, "It was a closet period, pre-Wolfenden. There was a lot of blackmail going on. Bruce knew that I knew, but he kept it as quiet as possible." Observing them together, Howard Ricketts thought: "My brother hasn't totally cracked this relationship." He felt that Bruce's sex life was something perceived by him as being quite separate. "He viewed himself as apart from himself."

This detachment is a recurring trait. Few came close. At the point where his lovers might want to talk personally, Bruce would be incapable.

After Michael Ricketts, Bruce was involved for 18 months with a rich young art dealer whom he had met through Hewett. Bruce, he says, was "a cold fish" with a limited emotional attention span. "You had only a part of him." With the detachment came confusion about his sexuality. "He wasn't 100 per cent gay. I'd put him 70/30. I don't think he was ever happy about being gay. He was not a fulfilled gay man."

Jane Abdy says, "When he gave in to his homosexuality he was disgusted with himself, which explained the rest of his life, which was a flight from reality—going to Edinburgh, going to Patagonia, always to be fleeing. He became like Orestes after the murder of Aegisthus, I thought, pursued by furies. This disgust was never there when I first knew him."

TWENTY-FIVE YEARS later, Bruce reported to his doctor at the Radcliffe Hospital in Oxford that he had been "bisexual since youth". It was a measure of his privacy that, six months before his death, not even his parents or his brother knew.

He was a sexual kaleidoscope, even to himself: at each arbitrary formation a plausible identity. To some he was homosexual, to some heterosexual, to some he was bisexual, to others he was asexual. ("I couldn't imagine anything worse than going to bed with him," says one woman. "Nothing.") To all, he was secretive. "There was something about him which made sure you wouldn't ask," says Robert Erskine. One might have expected him to share confidences to friends like Lucie-Smith or Sewell, both undergoing the same anxieties, but he did not. "There was never a crack," says Sewell. "Not a word." Lucie-Smith says: "We all construct our personalities and sometimes we construct them at different rates. I was going through the difficulties and the demons, but because

Bruce made the jump so quickly he was never at ease with himself as he might have been. Like the *Just So* rhino, he had crumbs inside his skin; he never settled."

James Lees-Milne, himself bisexual, wrote in his diary: "I think of Bruce with fascination and a certain repulsion. He was one of the most physically attractive mortals. I used to tell him he looked like a fallen angel . . . I recall one evening when B and I were alone for dinner at Alderley. He and I sat before the fire, drinking and talking far into the night. I wondered, should I ask him to stay the night, and decided not. Just as well perhaps. He was very beguiling stretched along the rug in a cock-teasing attitude. He was, with all his intense vanity, discreet. Yet on this occasion admitted that he could never decline to sleep with male or female, if pressed, but once only. Nonce with me."

Something old-fashioned in his behaviour recalls the example of an older generation, like E. M. Forster's, who always thought his homosexuality was something distasteful for the world to know. "Bruce is demonised as an arch closet queen," says Francis Wyndham. "He wasn't, but he was reserved and he didn't glory in his homosexuality. I think he looked upon it not as a handicap, rather as something he wished otherwise. He wanted to be heterosexual, which is unfashionable now when one should be happy to be gay."

Homosexuality was illegal until 1967, despite the publication of Sir John Wolfenden's report ten years before arguing that homosexual activity in private should no longer be a criminal offence. "Nobody took any notice of the law," says William Davis, who met Bruce at this time. "You just didn't stand in the middle of the park." If Bruce stood in the park, he did not talk about it—unless the experience took place at a safe remove from Mother England. But he frequented bars like The Rockingham in Soho, The Calabash in the King's Road, The Establishment Club—"always with groups of rather rich young queens, Americans in Paris," says the actor Peter Eyre. "I was almost embarrassed by him. He was inadvertently *tapette*. He used to wear these smart suits and had a sweet, piping upper-class voice which he dropped later. He had the complete identity of the young queen."

Eyre says: "There was no question of Bruce pretending not to be homosexual with his friends who were," but he noticed Bruce's very English resistance to talking about himself. Once, speaking of someone they both knew, Eyre said: "He can't come to terms with his sexuality."

"Oh, my dear," said Bruce. "Sexuality."

IF BRUCE SPOKE openly to anyone, it was to Werner Muensterberger, a psychoanalyst whose patients had included James Dean. Muensterberger knew Bruce from the early 1960s. He says, "I have never seen anyone in all my life who kept his sexuality so private." It surprised Muensterberger when, one evening in the 1970s, Bruce sat with him till 3 a.m. "What excited him personally was to observe two people in action." Bruce told Muensterberger how when staying with a couple in South America, he had burst in on them while they were making love. Instead of leaving the room, Bruce urged them: "Please go on." He described the scene to Muensterberger "in technicolor".

"He was a looker, an observer, much more than a participant," says Muensterberger, who analysed Bruce's homosexuality as a way of avoiding involvement or commitment. "For him, homosexuality was mainly a curiosity. It had the element of being adventurous. His travelling was another form of voyeurism."

To Colin Thubron, Bruce's sexuality went a long way to explaining his fascination with crazed people out of their context, for the ambiguous, the odd, the peculiar. "Homosexuals have an instinct for dealing with the world as abnormal. The assumption that we're all a bit abnormal is less likely to occur to people who feel integrated in the norm of things. Bruce assumed, and was drawn to the assumption, that the extraordinary was everywhere. A lot of his celebration of the world was for its sheer peculiarities: 'Life is peculiar. Everything is really mad. Not just me'."

JUST AS HE was too garrulous to be a great dealer—"You have to leave a silent space in which they take the hook," says Lucie-Smith—so his loud voice got in the way of romance. There must be moments of silence in a relationship. "Bruce was like a well-shaken bottle of champagne," says a friend. "He wasn't one of my best lovers," says Christina Camerara, who had an affair with him in the early 1970s. "He talked too much."

After "Rotting Fruit", Bruce rarely spoke and never wrote directly on the subject of his sexuality. What prevail are the theories and observations of those men and women who were either his lovers or close enough to witness his liaisons. Lucie-Smith says that Bruce was "active with partners at or near his own level of class and education, passive with what might

be described as rough trade". Bruce once described to Lucie-Smith a partner's picture of himself in the sexual act—"brows knitted and eyes bulging
like a Japanese god". Lucie-Smith was impressed by an aspect of Bruce's
description. "He's floating above himself, seeing himself from the outside—or else seeing himself through his partner's eyes. Which of us is
so self-conscious that we would take a snapshot of ourselves in that
moment?"

The Japanese god was how Bruce wanted to appear, a self-image he
approved of. "Aesthetically, all his references are not to the human world
but to the art world. He told me he once went to bed with a famous ice-
skater: it was as if he had succeeded in animating a Greek statue and taken
it to bed."

There was often denial over what had taken place. "When Bruce was
crazy about someone, he was crazy about them," says Lucie-Smith. "Once
it was all over, he sometimes blotted the whole thing from his mind." One
of his lovers was, for a brief period in the late 1970s, Peter Adam. "He
liked the idea of sex better than sex itself," says Adam. "He liked many
ideas better than their reality." Adam was of German extraction, cultured,
confident of his attraction. One night in 1978 he invited Bruce to a dinner party. "Bruce came in wearing a white T-shirt, a pair of jeans. I was
properly dressed in a suit. He didn't pay the slightest attention to me and
I got flirtatious. I thought: 'What can I do so he takes notice?' I've rarely
been so determined and so furious. So I go and do the cheapest thing I
can think of. I went into the kitchen, where I was making pasta, and
poured the hot spaghetti water over me. I went into my bedroom and
changed into jeans and a T-shirt, exactly what he was wearing—and suddenly he paid attention." Bruce stayed the night, but afterwards asked
Adam not to tell anyone. Adam says, "I've hardly known anyone say that.
It's schoolboy behaviour. He had a very bad relationship with himself."

Intensely private people can still be intimate, but Bruce's privacy was
generally not about protecting the intimacy he shared. Many of those who
had loved Bruce speak of his frigidity, his emotional unwillingness, his
lack of connection. He told Howard Hodgkin how he had got into bed at
last with someone he craved. "But," he said, "it was just like making love
to a beautiful machine."

"Just *think*," said Hodgkin, "how many people have felt the same way
about you."

Susan Sontag met Bruce in New York in 1979 and observed the
strange sexual avidity in which he engaged at that time. "He slept with
everyone, once: it goes with being a great beauty. His sexuality was like his

possessions, a means of engaging and also of not engaging with the world. He was profoundly solitary and therefore conducted his sexual activity as a way of connecting with people. At such an industrial rate it meant not an exclusive or intensifying connection: it meant he *had* a connection. 'I know this person because I've slept with him/her.' It gave him the right to call someone next time he was in town. There were no rules about it."

HE FELT A stronger urge towards his own sex, but was also powerfully attracted to women. Francis Wyndham noticed how "he convincingly expressed a desire for young rather sexy girls. I know that wasn't a fake." He would have infatuations with them—especially if they had a touch of the exotic, like Samira Kirollos, a Copt whom he took to a ball in Cowes. Another young woman to whom he responded was Ursula Digby-Jones.

No one could have embodied more satisfyingly Bruce's childhood history for himself. In 1956, Kenelm's tall, blonde wife had escaped her native Hungary and been shot as she crossed the border into Austria. A German officer brought her to the British Embassy in Vienna where a First Secretary looked at this dishevelled woman in a fur coat and asked if she had a passport.

"No, I have this." She gave him a slim volume of *The Waste Land* and, said Kenelm, "never looked back."

Bruce tried to seduce Ursula after the opening of the nightclub at which he had worn Jimmy Douglas's python. He followed her back to her hotel room, squeezed a foot in the door. "She threw me out."

Someone who did not reject his advances was Gloria Taylor, a former Chanel model with a fringe and high cheekbones who ran the Dior boutique in Conduit Street. Gloria was the sister of the actor Malcolm Mac-Dowell. Known as "the naughtiest girl at school", she was right out of the world of Margharita's magazines. She had met George Ortiz in Paris and Ortiz had introduced her to Hewett and Hewett, in the winter of 1962, introduced her to Bruce. She says, "One night after dinner at Robert Erskine's we went out and had an affair. I thought I was a bit of a baby snatcher. John Hewett looked at me askance."

Bruce called her "Glor" and liked the fact she worked for Dior. She found him painfully shy, despite his bluster. "He always had to make statements and justify himself. He couldn't relax and be calm. Something was goading him. Somehow, he was always on the go."

One weekend, Bruce took her sailing and he changed completely.

"I've never seen a change like that. His real courage came to the fore. From being butterfly twittery, he became calm, bold, even-tempered, the master of himself and of the boat. You felt safe." Their affair continued through 1963. "It was like being with someone who wasn't always there. There wasn't a cosy niceness afterwards. He never said he was in love with me." Then Bruce told Gloria he had met an American woman who owned a car and would take them to Wales.

XII.

෴

Elizabeth

I think he was fascinated by my voice.

—ELIZABETH CHATWIN

ELIZABETH CHANLER WORKED as Wilson's secretary. She was two years older than Bruce, small, alert and bubbly, with a deep stripe of shyness. "The one truly delightful thing about you," a friend wrote to her at this time, "beside your occasional spontaneous overflow of healthy animal spirits is your lack of that talent known as ego-inflating."

She lived in a cold flat in Chelsea with two friends from Radcliffe, where she had been at college, and Wilson's grey parrot. She was engaged to be married to an American living in Boston.

Bruce told a friend that he first met Elizabeth on a dig in Persia. By the end of the day they had fallen into the sack "like two warm rabbits". They met, in fact, at Sotheby's. From her desk Elizabeth watched him talking with a client. "I could see him from behind, in a double-breasted charcoal grey suit with a high, stiff detachable collar, standing there, looking at something, his blond hair sticking up." She had read *The Lord of the Rings* at Radcliffe: Bruce was like Strider.

Bruce took no special notice of her to begin with. After he had an operation on his varicose veins, Elizabeth visited Bruce in Fitzroy Square Nursing Home. He lay eating from a pot of caviar, a gift of Simon Sainsbury. "He never offered me any. Then he asked me to buy him a Hermès diary. When I found out how much it cost, I said, 'No'." He invited her to dinner at Grosvenor Crescent Mews, but cancelled at the last moment because there would be too many women. "He had awful manners in lots of ways."

He paid Elizabeth more attention following his first visit to America in the winter of 1961, from which he returned wearing a bright red and yellow lumberjacket and a red hat with a baseball brim and ear flaps. He was, Elizabeth observed, thrilled with it. "You can't wear that!" she shrieked. "It's a farmer's outfit."

His fascination with America woke him up to Elizabeth, the only American at Sotheby's. On subsequent visits to New York, he learned how her Catholic East Coast pedigree, from a small, aware, élite coterie of old money, was so exclusive as to be almost impenetrable. "As recherché as your rare bit of porcelain," says Kasmin. "When it's related to an amusing, well-read, clever, alert girl who's working for your boss, it can seem rather attractive."

On hearing Elizabeth tell a story about a housefly in a New York apartment, Bruce felt: "This was a woman I could marry."

ELIZABETH WAS BORN into two of America's most prominent clans.

Daisy Terry, her father's mother, had been a friend of Henry James, who praised her as "the only truly cultured woman in America". Daisy was an immensely strong character who kept a diary in German, rode to hounds and played piano to concert standard. Aged 85 and living in a Boston hotel, Daisy was described by *Harper's Bazaar* as "a challenging presence in a world where such quality is rare". Elizabeth knew her as "a very old lady, blind in the one eye with a black patch—and tunnel vision in the other".

Elizabeth was shaped by Daisy's world—eccentric women interested in art and travel—rather than by her immediate family, who were "desperately conventional". Her mother, Gertrude Laughlin, was descended from worthy and solid Protestants who pretended to be Scottish, but came from the Irish west coast and got rich quickly. They owned the country's largest steel mill, in Pittsburgh, where they founded banks and built ships. They stood at the opposite end of the trade to the Turnells of Sheffield.

Her father was Rear-Admiral Hubert Chanler, a slight, trim Catholic who collected Tiffany clocks, large cars and terrifying French poodles that he named after favorite wines and deployed like battleships. Known as "Bobby" because she could not say Poppy, her father was, says Elizabeth, "a Victorian figure without any leavening sense of the ridiculous". In Paris, he had once met, completely unwillingly, Léger, and could not understand why his friends the Murphys "had this gear box from a Ford car on their mantelpiece". Bobby would become one of Bruce's stock characters. No one imitated him better: "My career in the Navy's been rather strange. People start talking about me as a tea-time admiral!"

Years later, Bruce wrote to Cary Welch about Elizabeth's father. He had observed "the Admiral" glowering at the guests to a party he and Elizabeth were throwing for Millington-Drake in the Chanlers' New York apartment. " 'I am Admiral Chanler; I don't know who you are; but then I don't know anyone here and this is my house.' By this time he had had far too much to drink having started at 4 p.m., and started to make such observations as, 'There are many people here who, under normal circumstances, I would regard as of questionable honesty,' singling out in particular a friend of mine called Tristram Powell, ex-Eton, son of the novelist Anthony Powell, as a 'very suspicious man with a beaky nose'." The Admiral encouraged his wife to grill Bruce at dinner about the marital status of everyone present. Bruce wrote, "I would love to have invented so bizarre a sex life for each of the characters in turn that they would have a whole-dark-Geneseo-winter-full of conversation and speculation. THEY NEED IT."

AT THE END of his life, Bruce started to write a novel based, in part, on the Chanlers. Late on, he saw an attractive subject in Elizabeth's family—their eccentricities (sometimes teetering on insanity), their reckless Bohemianism and the Jamesian wealth which they had used to furnish houses in Washington and New York. "My dear, the loot!" Bruce told his American editor, Elisabeth Sifton.

The family historian, Lately Thomas, wrote that the Chanler mix of genes was "a volatile mixture about as unstable as nitroglycerine". The first-known Chanlers, like the Chatwins, were Normans who had settled in England. They were self-assured, cosmopolitan, excitable, with a weakness for adventure. The American branch began with the Rev. Isaac Chanler, who left Bristol in 1710 for Charleston, Carolina. Isaac's son was the author of *Hysteria: its causes and aspects*, a study of some relevance to subsequent generations. These included: William Backhouse Astor, a furious hoarder, and Sam Ward, an unrestrainable spender of three fortunes. Elizabeth's father could trace himself to Peter Stuyvesant, the last Dutch governor of New York, and a rebel who liked to plough his land in a court suit to show his contempt for King George III. The two chief distinguishing Chanler traits were an exceptional self-sufficiency and a distinctive, attention-compelling "Chanler voice", both of which Elizabeth inherited.

Bobby brought her up to believe the Chanlers were "an unofficial royalty". But a series of scandals dented recent Chanler history and Bobby, like Charles Chatwin, went a long way to conceal these. It fell to Elizabeth's first cousin, a lawyer for Alger Hiss, to fill in the gaps at family re-unions and weddings—before Bobby came steaming over. She says, "He hated us finding out about family skeletons. We found everything out sideways, under the table." She passed the details on to Bruce.

Bobby's immediate Chanler relations were both eccentric and profli-gate. His father, Winthrop or "Wintie" Chanler, had been a grandchild of John Jacob Astor. Orphaned young, he inherited an income of $80,000 per annum. He did little but travel and hunt. One of his daughters, when asked his profession replied: "He practised fox-hunting." He hunted everything else too. Moufflon in Sardinia, lions in Morocco, chamois in the Alps.

"Grandpa had a fantastically good time," says Elizabeth. "He once agreed to meet Grandma in London. She got there, having come on a boat with her family, to find a note: 'I've gone big-game hunting in the Rockies'."

Wintie's three brothers also did what they wanted. The middle one, Willie, a friend of Theodore Roosevelt, pursued life as an adventurer un-til losing a leg. He smuggled arms to Cuban rebels; fraternised with Butch Cassidy in New York; and instigated, with 200 cowpunchers, an unsuc-cessful revolt against a Venezuelan dictator. In the course of an expedition to British East Africa, he gave his name to a species of antelope, *Cervi-capra chanlerii*, and to a waterfall. Chanler Falls has since dried up. "Like all Chanler enterprises it has come to nothing," says Elizabeth.

The older brother Armstrong, a lawyer married to a highly strung novelist, suffered from progressive paranoia until he was committed to Bloomingdale asylum after re-enacting Napoleon's death scene. On the eve of Thanksgiving, 1900, he escaped the asylum, leaving behind this note to his doctor: "My dear Doctor, You have always said that I am in-sane. You have always said that I believe I am the reincarnation of Napoleon Bonaparte. As a learned and sincere man, you, therefore, will not be surprised that I take French leave. Yours, with regret that we must part. J. A. Chanler"

Bob Chanler, his youngest brother, was an artist who married the Ital-ian prima donna Lina Cavalieri. She deserted him for a Russian nobleman after persuading her infatuated husband to transfer to her all he possessed in exchange for $20 a week pocket money.

This prompted Armstrong to wire Bob: WHO'S LOONEY NOW?

BRUCE WAS NOT alone in mistaking blue money for big money. Because of the Astor connection it was assumed that the Chanlers enjoyed access to considerable wealth. Bruce's friend, the journalist James Fox, says, "At the beginning, Bruce used to infer that Elizabeth owned three quarters of New York—which, as it turned out, she didn't." In fact, the money came from Gertrude's family. All Bobby inherited from the Astors was Sweet Briar, a 200-acre estate in fox-hunting country near Geneseo in New York State. "When I die," he told his eight children, "all you'll get from me is cigarette money."

Required to earn his living, Bobby tried his damnedest not to be eccentric in the manner of his father and uncles. He could mend anything beautifully and wanted to be a sculptor, but Daisy forced him into the Navy. He served in China, on a Yangtsee gunboat, and in Constantinople. Aged 23, he met the nine-year-old Gertrude Laughlin at a diplomatic party thrown by her father in Athens. Fourteen years later, while working as an aide-de-camp at the White House, he married her in a ceremony hailed by the *Evening Star* as "one of the most important of the season". Shortly afterwards Bobby was transferred and the couple moved to San Diego, California, where on 16 November 1938, Elizabeth was born.

LIKE BRUCE, ELIZABETH knew what it was to be the eldest child of a father at sea. Until she was seven, she thought of him as a photograph. "Where's Bobby?" Gertrude once asked. Elizabeth replied: "He's on the bureau." In Hawaii, scene of her earliest memories, her father became known, because of the blackout, as "The Man Who Comes and Goes in the Dark".

In 1941, Bobby was posted to Hawaii on the heavy cruiser *Minneapolis*. On 4 December, Gertrude arrived on the island with Elizabeth and her new-born brother, John. Three days later Elizabeth was playing on the beach when the boy from next door said: "They've bombed Pearl Harbor." Elizabeth ran to tell Gertrude. Then aeroplanes roared overhead. She looked up and saw red circles under the wings. Taking both children, Gertrude left Hawaii and went to stay with her parents in Washington. Bruce would later cite the Japanese attack on Pearl Harbor "to illustrate our murderous propensity".

Gertrude's father, Irwin Laughlin, was a compulsive collector who had retired from the diplomatic service to Meridian House, an airy French-style home which he built and decorated with drawings by

Boucher and Fragonard, eighteenth-century French furniture, and Oriental screens from his bachelor years in Japan—where, unbeknown to his family, he had left behind an illegitimate daughter. It was the lure of Irwin Laughlin's collection for Peter Wilson which led Elizabeth, eventually, to a job at Sotheby's.

Laughlin was important in Elizabeth's early life. From her grandfather she gained an attachment to antique mirrors, chandeliers and embroidery. Meridian House, with its large staff and walls painted to resemble grey silk, was one of several substantial homes in which she grew up.

Bobby remained at sea. The *Minneapolis* had been absent from Pearl Harbor at the time of the Japanese attack. But a year later, news reached Washington that she had been engaged in action in the Solomon Islands. On 1 December 1942, a torpedo sliced off her bow and the cruiser, 15 feet down in water, was engulfed in flaming gasoline. Bobby, as Damage Control Officer, was subsequently awarded the Silver Star for his part in directing the repairs.

Elizabeth's childhood was more peripatetic than Bruce's. She had crossed the Pacific twice by the age of three. After the war she came to live in a palace in Rome where, in 1946, Bobby had been appointed Naval Attaché. At the Assumption convent school, Elizabeth learned Italian and calligraphy. She had terrible handwriting. Bobby, replying to a letter, wanted to know: "Why didn't you write it a little more carefully . . . I have very little time to spend on trying to decipher bad handwriting. Your Bobby."

He had more time than he cared to admit. His naval career did not end splendidly. After three years in Rome, he requested sea duty and was turned down. There were too many captains and technology had changed. Bobby's last command was the repair ship *Hector* on the American west coast, anchored within the breakwater. From *Hector* he transferred to working two days a week on the veterans' disability board. In April 1952, he was given the rank of rear admiral on retirement and he clung to it tenaciously.

BOBBY RETIRED TO Sweet Briar. The farm had been left him by his mother. Daisy walked out of the house with what she was wearing, leaving everything behind, including the painting which she had at different times promised to each member of the family.

He came home intending to set the world on fire as a farmer and horsebreeder. But shortly after taking up residence, his horse "Mainstay" stepped in a woodchuck hole and Bobby broke his collarbone. A year later he still came down to dinner with a wide elastic bandage wrapped under his dress shirt.

In retirement, he became an irascible disciplinarian. His eldest son John says, "He had preconceived notions, some of which were based on his naval training, on how children should be brought up."

He raised them as Catholics. Every week in summer a priest visited the private chapel to say mass and afterwards came to breakfast. When a new priest addressed Bobby as "Mr Chanler", he said gruffly: "I'd really rather be called Admiral." His main source of information was the *Tablet* which he read cover to cover.

He was constantly laying down laws. There was a correct procedure for cutting cheese. No parking on the lawn. No trousers for women. At home, the eight children changed for lunch and supper.

After dinner, for which he wore a maroon smoking jacket, he staggered into the library and closed the door. He forbade books to leave the house. If there was a gap in his shelves it enraged him. "Did you take a book out of Bobby's room," wrote an anguished Gertrude to Elizabeth, *"La Princess des Ursins?"* He had read the complete works of Henry James twice and *Seven Pillars of Wisdom* three times, once aloud to his mother. But apart from the *Tablet* he was not a serious reader. One of the few contemporary books on his shelves was *The Bridge Over the River Kwai*. Suspicious of most writers, he blamed Scott Fitzgerald for his Uncle Teddy's drinking problems.

ELIZABETH WAS NOT allowed out with young men before her eighteenth birthday. Until then, an 11 p.m. curfew was enforced. Bobby did not like her watching television and only grudgingly permitted visits to the Riviera cinema in Geneseo.

Drink increased his rigidity. He was not supposed to drink because he had pancreatitis. But he laced his consommé with sherry and drank two and a half bottles of smoky red wine a night. And before going to bed, he took a bottle upstairs on a silver tray.

With Gertrude he enjoyed a powerful attraction, but she had a difficult time of it. He conducted their serious arguments in French, which he spoke fluently, shifting to Italian once his children learned French. A lot of their arguments had to do with Elizabeth.

ELIZABETH GREW UP the most independent of eight children. She learned to cope with the heckling of a large family. Bobby doted on her, but she bore the brunt of his discipline. "She was difficult, precocious, with a good mind," says Gertrude. "And very determined if she wanted something."

As a baby she screamed incessantly. "I hate being told what to do. I remember going on a steam train and when we got into the compartment I was furious. I wanted to get into the engine with all the excitement and noise."

Only one person could control her, Fuddy, the children's governess. Miss Kathleen Fogarty was an emaciated, common-sensical Irish Catholic from New Brunswick. Over her white uniform she wore a full-length raccoon coat so that, from the rear, herding everyone down the aisle in church, she looked like a raccoon. Elizabeth may have been the first granddaughter of millionaire grandparents, but Fuddy made her finish everything on her plate. "Anybody caught looking at themselves in the nude, she'd go after them. 'Never look at yourself in the mirror!' she'd say. So I hardly ever do."

Elizabeth, like Bruce, was a sickly child. She suffered from asthma. If she ate raw wheat during harvesting, half an hour later she would not be able to breathe. She also had a condition that came to be known as "Lib's Tongue", aubergines, tomatoes and walnuts in particular making her blow up. Most debilitating, she had rickets, probably from Vitamin D deficiency. She grew up with the stoicism of a child who has a physical handicap. "Lib is someone who lives in the present very much," said her best friend Gillian Walker. " 'That's who I am and I'm going to make the best of it.' There is no self-pity."

HER CONDITION DID not prevent her from riding. Her grandfather had been Master of the Genesee Hunt, in the saddle at the time of his stroke. From the age of twelve Elizabeth was riding three times a week to hounds.

Animals were her passion. At Fox Hollow School in Massachusetts she decided she wanted to be a vet. "I was always rescuing game-cocks and chickens and when we did biology I liked to cut up animals. We started out with earthworms and progressed to pregnant cats."

At 17, she applied to Scripps College in California to study biology and was accepted. Months afterwards she received a letter at school. Rear-Admiral Chanler had withdrawn the application. He regarded vets as second class doctors. And he did not want her in California for the same reason Charles Chatwin had not wanted Bruce to be in London. Bobby thought California was "a bad place".

She was 17 when she reached breaking point with Bobby. It was a small incident, one that occurs in households everywhere. She had invited a friend to stay, Didi Drysdale, who persuaded her to put on lipstick. "I forgot I even had the lipstick on." Elizabeth came downstairs to where the family was sitting. "She looked so pretty and alive," remembered her brother Ollie. Then Bobby saw her face and screamed: "GO UPSTAIRS AND WASH THAT OFF IMMEDIATELY."

"That did it," says Elizabeth. "For years and years and years I didn't carry on a conversation with him. He never apologised. I don't think he knew what he'd done. Once I went to Radcliffe, I was gone."

Bruce wrote the incident into his second novel *On the Black Hill*: "She would steal off to Rhulen and come back with cigarette smoke on her breath and rouge rubbed off around her lips . . . He called her a 'harlot'."

ELIZABETH MAJORED IN history at Radcliffe, but after her tutor absconded she studied what she wanted: Russian and Byzantine history, Indian art, and a course in Dante from an Italian who hated correcting papers. Thwarted from her true vocation—to study biology in California—she did not work hard.

Radcliffe was the female branch of Harvard, but segregated for sleeping purposes. Her floor mates were Pattie Sullivan and Gillian Walker, whose father was the Director of the National Gallery in Washington. When Elizabeth came to live in London, Pattie and Gillian joined her as lodgers.

Gillian says, "She was interested in odd things, not in what others thought. She wasn't solitary, but she made up her own world."

Bobby found it difficult to relinquish her. He forbade her to work as a waitress in the summer and she was not to go away for the weekend, unless with a family relation. He wrote often with news of the farm, the

horses. "You might drop us a line . . . In the absence of official information to the contrary, we believe you are still alive, but we have nothing else
to go by—so sit down and tell us what you have been doing and what you
would like to do about all those invitations we have been forwarding,
which Mummy says are for the 'short season' in Washington in June."

On 24 November 1956, the month of her eighteenth birthday, Bobby
introduced Elizabeth to society at a ball in Meridian House. Dressed in
the same whites he would wear at Bruce and Elizabeth's wedding, he led
her in a dance before the orchestra that had played at his own wedding.
From this night on, she was permitted to meet young men.

Her first boyfriend at Radcliffe was Upton Brady, one of a sunny-
faced group of American-Irish brothers whose father was a teacher and
assistant headmaster at Portsmouth Priory. Then, when she moved to
New York, she fell in love with Upton's elder brother Francis. Nicknamed
Buff, he was a gentle, poetic, depressive soul who had failed to complete
his philosophy major at the University of Pennsylvania and worked as a
flight controller and then as a systems analyst who sent a device to the
moon. She says, "He was much less complicated than Upton: athletic and
very good-looking, with Irish blue eyes put in by smutty fingers." Soon
Buff wanted to marry her.

Elizabeth procrastinated. She worked for a private charity in the Bronx
and laid out pages for scientific magazines. By now she knew her vocation:
if not a vet, she would work for Sotheby's. In 1958 she had spent all summer as a volunteer at the Freer Gallery in Washington. In the following
summer she visited London and found it, as she wrote to Gertrude, "really
neat". Her visit coincided with the sale at Sotheby's of half the collection
at Meridian House, including 141 black chalk drawings by Fragonard from
his first Italian journey and Jean-Michel Moreau le Jeune's *N'ayez pas peur,
ma bonne amie*. Her grandfather's collection was sold so cheaply that Elizabeth, when she understood more, believed a ring had been involved.

On 16 June 1959, she turned up at Sotheby's "having found that I
could just walk in". Quite by chance, some of her grandfather's lesser objects were being auctioned that day in a sale of Antiquities. She wrote to
Gertrude: "I got there early, fortunately, as it was a tiny room and there
was a big rush after a while. Fascinating sorts of people."

The chances are, Bruce was in that room. It may even have been the
first sale he catalogued.

IT WAS NO secret that Wilson hired Elizabeth to get at the rest of the Laughlin collection. She says, "I got in because I had collecting in my background. That was the carrot. I used it like anything." At the New York office in the Corning Building, Peregrine Pollen employed Elizabeth as a secretary. But her ambition was to spend a year in Sotheby's in Bond Street. As a child she had read *An English Year*, by Nan Fairbrother, which might have described the life led by Margarita and Bruce in his childhood. "It's the book of my life. Her husband's at war. She's living in the country. It made me want to live in England."

In September 1961, Sotheby's offered her a secretarial position in London and arranged a visa. Was two years all right?

She left New York on the *Queen Elizabeth*. Her mother saw her off with an enormous trunk that would double once she got to London as a dinner table. Gertrude had always been slightly psychic. "I remember thinking: 'Well, she's gone. She will stay in Europe'." On the quayside, she burst into tears.

"She was crying and I didn't know why she was crying," says Elizabeth. "I thought, 'Honestly, it's too silly, too dramatic, why shouldn't I go?' It never occurred to me I wasn't coming back."

ELIZABETH ARRIVED IN time for the Sotheby's season at the end of September. She was told she was replacing a girl who'd put her foot through a painting. "It's the most appallingly inefficient place under the sun, but that has lots of advantages, and besides everyone is so nice." From now on she wrote to Gertrude every week.

Wilson was particularly solicitous. He gave Elizabeth tickets to the theatre. He sent her out to buy Bittermints, ruining her teeth. One weekend he invited her home to Kent. "The house is heated and was absolutely boiling and it's full of odds and ends he has collected including a narwhal's horn which I covet." He proved a good boss, undemanding and jokey. He was always bringing objects into the office, a grey stone yoke, an Aztec carving. "I'd say: What's that? What's that? What's that? I asked questions all day long." Her duties were not onerous, although, she told Gertrude, "he is apt to call up at the weirdest times and rang at 11.30 last night to tell me to forge his signature to some documents he had forgotten to sign."

Once, when recovering from jaundice and knowing her fondness for animals, he asked Elizabeth to look after his parrot. "Birdbrain" was the size of a pigeon and could sing "Three Blind Mice" and miaow. Having lived on the edge of the Cromwell Road, the bird could also make traffic noises. It followed Elizabeth everywhere. "I like having him except that I have to keep the electricity heater on all day which is going to be pretty expensive, but maybe I can charge it to PCW with any luck."

In January 1962, she moved into 38 Tedworth Square, a second floor flat in Chelsea. Sharing the weekly rent of fifteen guineas were her floormates from Radcliffe. Gillian Walker had come to study at the Courtauld; Pattie Sullivan to work at Morgan Guaranty.

The three of them took off at weekends in Elizabeth's grey left-hand drive Volkswagen Beetle. "I would lean out of the right-hand window and tell her if it was safe to pass," says Pattie. "She had strange economies. She refused to buy new glasses, and either borrowed mine or held her hand over the missing lens, which was discouraging when she was driving."

She found London expensive. Three dollars bought her a pound. Her correspondence to Gertrude includes a steady stream of requests, for peanut butter, nylon toothbrushes—"The English ones are simply hopeless and go all squashy immediately"—and Bonnie Doon knee socks. "I wish I could come home just for a few days: all the clothes in *Vogue* are so nice, much nicer than any here."

For all Wilson's pleasantness, her job at Sotheby's lacked excitement. He was often away in New York, "so I spend most of the day reading and doing the crossword . . . However, it does tend to get boring after a while and I sometimes think there isn't much point in coming to work at all."

A few weeks later, she wrote again: "Boy, are we bored." On 28 November 1962, after a year in London, she decided to come home for good. Part of her decision had to do with a series of telephone calls from Bufton Brady, her boyfriend in America. "No one except Gill knows this yet, so don't say anything. Buff and I are thinking of getting married in June if everything works out."

AFTER MONTHS OF feeling lonely and wretched, Buff had written to her from Boston. "Dearest Liz, I've hemmed and hawed my last; something definite must be done now before we both go mad. So. I now make my final stand with the following conditions . . . namely I must either be married to you or 'washed up' . . . There you have it in a nutshell, Elizabeth Chanler, all you have to do is say the word and we're off . . . You can take me or leave me now quite easily. I await you and your answer by the first of the coming year. It will be too late otherwise. Love always, Buff."

Elizabeth, treating her engagement rather in the manner of an awful secret not to be revealed under any circumstances, promised Gertrude to come home once she had sorted out her car. Since she was not a British resident, the American-registered Volkswagen needed to be out of the country by the following year or else she faced a fine.

On 9 September, 1963, Elizabeth wrote to Gertrude. The car had safely left by boat for Baltimore. "Now about me, the thing is that I will not be coming for a little while."

IN THE MIDDLE of April, as Buff had prepared to receive her in America, Elizabeth had driven Bruce to the West Country. They climbed Maiden Castle above Dorchester and walked along a deserted pebble beach.

Bruce soon took to ringing Tedworth Square. "He would talk for hours," says Elizabeth. "I could never find out what he wanted. He wasn't saying, 'Do you want to go to the movies?' I think he was fascinated by my voice. But he was obviously lonely. When we got married, he would say: 'It's so marvellous. When I come home, I'm not alone. There's someone here'."

Bruce was still involved with Gloria. His bubble car had blown up after a collision with a lorry, and he did not hesitate to press Elizabeth into the role of chauffeur. Elizabeth drove them to Wales. They stayed with Wilson's ex-wife, Helen Ballard, near Ledbury, and in the morning they went pony-trekking on the hills above Llantony.

Their affair began in a bed and breakfast in Gloucestershire on another excursion to Llantony. Bruce sang most of the way. Cole Porter's "You're the tops", Jack Buchanan, from *Me and My Girl*, "The sun has got his hat on and he's coming out today," and yards of Noel Coward dialogue.

"He was more fun to be with than almost anyone I knew," says Elizabeth. "When he started writing he became slightly less fun. But at Sotheby's, he was happy-go-lucky and he was singing because he was free of Sotheby's. It was like being let out of a strait-jacket."

Their destination was Llantony Abbey Hotel on the eastern slope of the Ewyas valley, the most beautiful of the Welsh border valleys. The hotel was built out of part of a ruined Augustine priory. The grit-stone arches dated from the twelfth century, framing mountains that had cast their spell on visitors since the time of the Norman Marcher Lords.

Hemmed in on three sides, the valley measured "no more than three arrow shots in width". Today, its beauty is unchanged, savage, remote.

The little hotel had no telephone. Bruce was required to send a reply-paid telegram. He was excited to find that his grandparents had written their names in the hotel guest book. Isobel and Leslie Chatwin had bicycled here over the Gospel Pass from Birmingham. Bruce and Elizabeth rode little Welsh ponies up onto Hay Bluff and the heathery ridge he would call "the Black Hill". "This is where my heart lifts," he told her. He had been conceived in Wales. He knew the valley below from his schooldays at Marlborough, when he had bicycled to Capel-y-ffin. Neither Welsh, nor English, the strange, uninhabited moorland resembled the Derbyshire moors of his early childhood. Elizabeth says, "It was a part of the world he liked best." Together they walked Hay Bluff, like Amos and Mary in *On the Black Hill.* "He walked ahead, brushing aside the gorse and the bracken, and she planted her footsteps in his."

Llantony became Elizabeth's favourite destination with Bruce, but the grey Volkswagen taxied him to other places. Their motoring expeditions resembled those of Lotte and the twins in Bruce's novel: "They visited megalithic tombs, crumbling abbeys, and a church with a Holy Thorn. They walked along a stretch of Offa's Dyke and climbed Caer Cradoc where Caractacus made his stand against the Romans . . . Their interest in antiquities revived."

Bruce showed Elizabeth things she would never have done without him. She says, "He was the best person to travel with. He'd done his research. There was always a point to it. What really turns me on is people's brains, I'm afraid. He just did have a marvellous mind. I knew then I would be more homesick for England than I would ever be for America."

Meanwhile, Gertrude fretted in Geneseo. Since November she had been anxious to announce her daughter's engagement in the newspapers. What was happening? Elizabeth stalled. "I like getting mail at Sotheby's, but could you put PRIVATE in large letters on the outside of the envelope as sometimes they don't look and open them." Gertrude at last entrusted her cousin Ernest with the mission of finding out. Over a lunch at the Connaught, Ernest Iselin, once a diplomat, told Elizabeth a decision had to be made concerning Buff. "Are you really going to marry this man?"

She wrote to Buff, regretting she had led him on. She says, "He was a much weaker character than me and I'd have beaten him to pieces. It's no good marrying a character whom you're going to destroy. I'd have bullied him. I couldn't bully Bruce. That was the great attraction."

———

SOTHEBY'S ROMANCES WERE common. Six office marriages occurred in Bruce's time. But nobody suspected a relationship between the chairman's secretary and the chairman's blue-eyed boy. Digby-Jones once spotted the pair having lunch at the St James's Club and told Wilson. "How extraooorrrdinary," said Wilson, and forgot about it. Nobody knew, not even Elizabeth's flat-mates.

Bruce and Elizabeth did not talk about their affair between themselves. "I was terrified he'd feel trapped and disappear," says Elizabeth. "He'd have run a mile if I was being possessive."

She had known about Gloria and about other girlfriends. "I remember him discussing one French girl, small and blonde, the daughter of a dealer. At one point he said he was going to marry her. I thought she was very inappropriate." Elizabeth was aware also of homosexual relationships. "I'd known he'd had boyfriends. It didn't matter. I knew this was how Bruce was."

In July 1964, after another visit to Llantony, Elizabeth wrote to her Radcliffe friend Eleanor Macmillan: "Is it love or not? I don't think so, but for me it will be the most marvellous bright thing to remember . . . This guy looks like everyone's idea of a golden-haired child. As a matter of fact I'd simply *love* to have a little boy by him. He'd be indescribably beautiful & fantastically clever. I don't suppose I could get away with it without being married."

ONE MORNING, WHEN Bruce was out of the office, Bruce's secretary composed "a husband horoscope". This is how Sue Goodhew defined the attributes of the ideal Sotheby's spouse: "He will live in the country, in a medium-sized Georgian or Queen Anne House, probably in Hampshire, Wiltshire or Berkshire. He will either farm vaguely, or commute each day. He will be about 30, with a red face, but very nice and kind and amusing." The couple would have a spaniel, a labrador, and four children. "She will occasionally be asked to open the village fete and will attend all the hunt balls faithfully . . . Altogether she will lead a normal happy country life. She will occasionally come up to London to do some shopping (Harrods) and have her hair done (André Bernard's). She will drive a Morris Traveller car and husband will have a Jaguar (perhaps). Son will go to

Eton and daughters to a Horsey Establishment. Staff will consist of one gardener and his son, and one daily lady to help in the house when necessary."

Elizabeth did not wish this picture of married life, but she conceived a personal fantasy. She would buy a smallholding with chickens. Bruce would spend the weekends. "I never figured he would want to get married. I figured: 'We can go on like this'."

In this manner, Bruce and Elizabeth kept their relationship secret for two years.

XIII

Afghanistan

*I come from a very middle-class family of
lawyers and architects. Travel was an immense
relief—it got rid of the pressure from above and from
below. If you're out on the road, people have to
take you at face value.*

—BC, TO MICHAEL IGNATIEFF

IN THE SUMMER of 1962, the 17-year-old Hugh Chatwin, on the last leg
after a 10,000-mile hitch-hike from Cape Town via Cairo, bumped into
his older brother in Rome.

"Bruce!"

"Hugh!"

Like Stanley and Livingstone, they shook hands in the middle of the
Via Veneto. Bruce was on his way home from Greece; Hugh from a five-
month odyssey through Africa.

Bruce had urged Hugh to see Africa before he started his training as
a surveyor. Where Bruce at Marlborough had been inspired by Robert Byron, Hugh had read *Cape Cold to Cape Hot* by Richard Pape, an out-of-
work bomber pilot who had driven an Austin A55 from Nord Cap in
Norway to South Africa. Bruce, aged 22, had furnished Hugh with a list
of addresses and his portrait camera.

Not for another year did Bruce attempt a comparable journey. In the
summer of 1963, he made the first of three visits to Afghanistan with his
friend Robert Erskine. Their object was to buy antiquities and to follow
Byron's footsteps in *The Road to Oxiana.*

Bruce rented the Grosvenor Crescent Mews flat to the American
dealer, Hélène Sieferheld. He said, giving her a copy of *The Road to Oxiana*: "This is what I'd like to be." In September 1960, he had retraced Byron's journey through the Greek islands to Crete. That holiday had made
him eager to go further, to cross the Persian border into the Hindu Kush

and to fulfil an adolescent fantasy. His journal would show a conscious imitation of Byron: the appreciation of recondite stonework; the nicknames for rulers (Bruce's pseudonym for Nasser, "the Smiler", is like Byron's "Marjorie Banks" for the Shah of Iran); the same romanticising of the masses. "He's always talking about young gazelles," says Erskine, who performed the role of travelling companion occupied in that book by Christopher Sykes.

The journey lasted only three weeks, plotted in the vaguest of terms and with scant understanding of the culture. Yet it planted the seed of Bruce's yen for Central Asia—"with its pale green rivers and Buddhist monasteries where eagles wheel over the deodar forests and tribesmen carry copper battle-axes and wreathe vine leaves round their heads as they did in the time of Alexander."

BRUCE PLANNED TO meet Erskine in Cairo after first spending a week in Turkey. On 19 August 1963, he flew to Istanbul. "Sotheby's sounded healthy on the telephone and mercifully far off," he scribbled in his notebook. "I loathe jet aeroplanes." Ten years later he would write in his Patagonia notebook, after a flight to Rio Gallegos: "Yesterday afternoon confirmed my opinion that air travel is often the longest method of travelling from A to B."

In Istanbul, his hostess was a Sotheby's contact: Guler Tunca, a beautiful and well-connected glass collector. Guler lived with her husband and son in a white timber house on the Bosphorus. "Bruce appeared very young and unable to fend for himself," she says. "But don't you believe it. He was as cunning as you could hold together."

Guler introduced Bruce to her neighbours, a family of young Ottoman princes and princesses. "The mother is one of the most beautiful women I've ever seen, and radiated a sort of animal attraction," Bruce wrote in his journal. As he lay stretched out in the sun beside the Bosphorus, a large erratic speedboat appeared, containing another prince, more girls. Bruce dived into the water. Untypically, he confided his insecurities. "In their company I felt sickly, weak, hideous and incompetent. They converse in five different languages at once and look healthy."

He explored Istanbul's museums and markets with Guler's son Ahmed and her friend Ziah Sofu. "To the bazaar with its sweaty crowds to see Mustafa Kent, an antiques dealer in a courtyard . . . After an affable talk a hand twists a newspaper package through the window. Unwrapped, it contains a Roman bronze, some 18 in. high, genuine, rather hideous, the Farnese Hercules. Ziah remarks 'Good musculature, isn't it, Bruce, eh,' and strokes its hard patina fondly."

He visited a caravanserai with Ziah—"which is just as a palace ought to be, a series of places to picnic"—and Haghia Sophia. As it had Byron, the building overwhelmed Bruce. "The infinity of this creation transcends everything. It makes the cross beams and cornice of a Greek temple pedestrian and earthly, the dome of St Peter's like a glorified soap bubble."

The rest of his time was taken up by Guler's friends. One evening he was invited to a diplomatic dinner where he sat next to an attractive girl.

" 'Do you live here all the year round?' I asked.

" 'No, I study in Grenoble and then we have houses in Lago de Maggiore, Beverly Hills and Japan'."

Out of his depth, Bruce invoked the scandal in his family. "All were very intrigued to hear of my great-grandfather who died of a tumour on the brain in Ventnor jail in 1902."

Reunited with Erskine in Cairo, his joy at meeting a kindred spirit was palpable. "What a relief to laugh again with Robert! whose arm is pale pink from his injections." Avoiding dinner invitations with local dealers, Erskine and Bruce made two or three local trips, one in an ancient Chevrolet to the Maidan pyramid. Bruce's contemplation of the monument was interrupted by a boy who extracted an English vocabulary from inside his underwear. "The most useless document I have ever seen. The first subject was the Army. The second Love. Under the section Love the 8-year-old would learn in English the following: 'I love, you love, he loves, a bachelor, a prostitute, my mother, my father, my sister, my brother, a sailor, a virgin, Darling, A nice boy, etc., etc.'."

Their departure from Cairo's Shepherd's Hotel two days later was a comic nightmare. While Erskine settled the bill, Bruce went to collect their luggage. "In half a minute the landing was filled with characters expecting to be tipped . . . they began to announce their titles like characters in a Medieval play. 'I am the Washerwoman.' 'I am the Room Steward.' 'I am the Breakfast Steward.' 'I am the Chamber Maid.' And so on. In a fury I screamed that no one would get one cent unless I was given some help with the luggage. Nobody moved. I picked up too many suitcases and fell over a slippery rug on my left rib. Smug smiles from the onlookers. Conspiracy to prevent me to take the luggage in the lift. Ten piastres to the lift boy succeeded. Hobbled out of the lift to find Robert fuming about the bill."

"On to Beirut, that sluttish city, where the Middle East becomes too sharp by half without the charm," Erskine wrote to his mother. "We were only there a day, to see a horrid old merchant who tried his best to peddle fakes at us." In an apartment full of modern French furniture mauled by woodworm, the dealer Fouad Alouf produced a marble head of Alexander the Great, telling Bruce: " 'I have refused $20,000. All the archaeologists are agreed that mine is the only head of Alexander. It has his neck and ears.' Perhaps, but the face was almost entirely missing."

On 3 September, they landed in Teheran. The tight-hipped uniforms of the policemen and the gesticulating copper statues of Reza Shah reminded Bruce of a Berlin suburb from the 1920s. "Considering the very great beauty of Islamic architecture in antiquity," wrote Robert, "the Persians seem to have lost absolutely everything they had in the way of taste and refinement. They are rude to the point of nausea." Mr Naj, a Pakistani from Manchester, bemoaned his fate to Bruce. "He cannot find English Baby Food and wonders that all Persians are corrupt and dishonest. 'I tell you quite frankly, sir, I wish I had never left England'." Next day they travelled to Meshed, close to the Afghan border, a pale, mud-coloured city with jade-painted doors and bricks arranged in tweed-like patterns. The superb mosque architecture included the Shrine of Meshed, covered in sheet gold. "It looks fantastic in the evening sunlight," wrote Erskine, "glowing like the moon, with its two gold-covered minarets standing over it, side by side." He described for his mother the figures they cut: "At the moment I'm dressed exactly like a Rider Haggard character—khaki drill shorts, Australian bush hat, water bottle at belt. Very outpost of Empire and a source of immense amusement to Persian population!" And so they prepared to enter Afghanistan.

It took several days to organise the journey from Meshed. They left in one of the oil tankers departing for Kabul. The driver arrived eleven hours late. "We drove with him for a 100 miles in acute discomfort and apprehension," Bruce wrote to Margharita from Herat. After five hours of "cataclysmic jolting" the driver discovered he had lost his papers. At midnight in the middle of nowhere he let out a piercing scream: the receipt for his petrol load had blown away. He would have to return to Meshed. They passed an uncomfortable night in the lorry. At dawn, Bruce caught the driver escaping in a gale. "He meant to leave us in charge of the tanker until his return two days hence."

They abandoned the tanker and got an immediate lift on an Afghan trading lorry of great character heading for Turbat-i-Sheikh Jam. The lorry delighted Bruce. It was constructed like a little cottage with drawers, and cupboards and covered with painted decorations: windmills, stags at bay,

robins in snow-landscape and other motifs "culled no doubt from Mem-
sahib's Christmas cards 30 years ago!" The cargo, wrote Erskine, appeared
to be "crates of Japanese contraceptives. Symbol of progress!"

The first Afghans Bruce met responded warmly to him: "an Afghan
truck driver greatly admired my ears."

Deposited in a wayside café, they waited in the heat until, finally, a
convoy of four brand-new Land Rovers "driven by dashing Afghans"
agreed to take them across the border. Under the stare of wild-looking
border guards with fixed bayonets—including one wearing a Southdown
Bus Company overcoat—they were through. "Our arrival in Afghanistan
was a moment of rare excitement," Bruce wrote in his journal. "A moon-
less night and a howling gale blowing great clouds of sand across our
path."

BRUCE STRAINED IN his journal for Byron's sophistication, later dropping certain episodes into *The Songlines*. According to Erskine, the material Bruce left out is just as interesting. Erskine, for instance, remembered
the "dashing Afghans" who carried them over the border as "a group of incredibly laid back, dark-glassed young men who were working every conceivable racket, including smuggling vodka. When we got to the Park
Hotel in Herat at 2 a.m. we began to thank them profusely and they said:
'Where's the money?' Things got nasty, Bruce emptied his pockets and I
have a strong memory of it being very humiliating. We had got it wrong.
The dashing Afghans had sold us a lift, but we didn't realise it."

Bruce saw what he expected to see from his Marlborough reading of
Byron. "No sumptuary laws here," he wrote of Herat, responding to the
sight of silk cloaks worn jauntily off the shoulder and turbans of impossible proportions in yellow and blue. "Pompeii must have looked like this."
At first, his glances were rewarded. Herat was an entirely Eastern city, with
no traffic lights or factories. "The bazaar is really Arabian nights! It's marvellous here!" Erskine told his mother.

Bruce explored the city. An aged weaver wore a white sharkskin smok-
ing-jacket decorated with Swastikas. In the fruit stall, a wrapping of pink
silk gauze protected the peaches from flies. Under the peach trees, Bruce
watched professional scribes write letters. "On the desk were the entire letters of Herat for one day (about 30). Stamps are kept in a rose-printed
chintz bag." Most incredible was the bazaar, which he visited in a curricle

jingling with bells and hung with red pom-poms. "All women are in yash-maks. The men storm about with artificial ferocity, flashing dark and disdainful glances. In fact, their eyes are made up, but then the outward appearance is all important."

Descending through an arch, Bruce found himself in a vast cara-vanserai, with two layers of arches, built in the time when Herat was one of the great trading posts in Asia. "Alas, the trans-Asiatic camel trains don't come there any more, but this arcaded enclosure has another use. It has become a clothes market largely for women." From every arch, multi-coloured gowns flapped in the wind. They were not ordinary clothes. "A genius has bought up a gigantic horde of American ladies dresses." Sitting under a peach tree and a blue sky of wheeling kites, he itemised the cuts to Margharita:

"From Maine to Texas, from Chicago to Hollywood the wardrobes of thousands of American ladies over 40 years are hanging into the breeze. Gowns that could have been worn by Mary Pickford, shiny black velvet with no back, or by Clara Bow, red lace and bead fringes, Jean Harlow, flamingo-pink crêpe off the shoulder with sequin butterflies on the hips, Shirley Temple, bows and pink lace, the folk-weave skirts they square-danced in, the crinolines they waltzed in, fiery sheaths they tangoed in, utility frocks they won the War in, the New Look, the A line, the H line, the X line, all are there, just waiting for some Afghan lady to descend from her mud-built mountain village and choose the dress of her dreams all to be closely concealed under her yashmak. I am sure she will get far more pleasure from it than its original owner."

The Afghanistan Bruce encountered had changed since Byron's visit in 1933. A zealous restoration programme had ruined many of the minarets and domes in *The Road to Oxiana*. In Herat, Bruce visited the Mausoleum of Gohar Shad. Set up for it by Byron's description, his heart sank as they drove up to the newly constructed walls. "Furiously impatient to see the buildings for which I had travelled so far, I ran the length of the wall, found an open gate and bounded up an orderly garden planted with rows of pines and mulberry trees, artificially contrived beds of geraniums and petunias . . . My hopes are raised at the sight of the dome of the Mausoleum rising above the pines, to be dashed as I approached. Since Robert Byron wrote, the whole thing has been ham-fistedly restored and restored to look like a pump station in buff brick."

They were also on a buying trip. After they let it be known that they were fully prepared to buy ancient things someone came up and whispered "I have golden helmet". Imagining some splendid Achaemenid object, they agreed with much shushing to be led down a tiny street. Under a bed was a bundle—and out it came: a Prince of Wales Dragoon Guard's helmet, left over from one of the Afghan wars.

A little apprehensive at having to take an Afghanistan internal flight, they pressed on to the capital. Kabul had a welcome freshness after the heat of Herat, but architecturally it resembled a Balkan town, with ugly modern bungalows sprawling into the suburbs. Outside Kabul, they traced Byron's steps to Babur's tomb, one of the architectural marvels of the Mughal Empire, where they experienced another letdown. Shah Jahan's white marble pavilion, built in the 1640s and resembling a blown-up ivory casket, was in ruins. At dinner with the British Council representative, they met the Afghan official in charge of cultural affairs. Bruce laid into him. " 'Why,' we asked, 'should a beautiful little building that is irreplaceable be allowed to disappear at the expense of the hideous concrete fountain that plays outside the Khyber Restaurant?' " The effect was instantaneous. His interest aroused, Mr Manash asked: "How much would it cost to mend the pavilion?" Erskine guessed: "Oh, $10,000." Manash thought for a moment, nodded and said, "Yes, good!" Erskine realised that Manash thought he was offering to buy the pavilion. "I whispered to Bruce, 'Oh my God, he's going to sell it to us!' We fled."

At the pool of the International Club they swam with the Duke Ellington band, but Kabul held few other attractions. "Robert is sick and tired of the place. 'It isn't a city, it's a concrete camp where nothing works.' He has become very morose." Whenever Bruce asked what he wanted, Erskine replied, "Cambridge College Ale."

On 24 September, after exploring the Ghorbend valley and making a dash over the Khyber into Peshawar, they returned to the Afghan capital. They had spent £1,050 on antiquities in Afghanistan, bringing the total cost of the expedition to £4,451. "We pray that the aeroplane will leave," wrote Bruce.

BRUCE'S SECOND TRIP to Afghanistan, the following summer, was more focussed. He had met Elizabeth, he was fed up with Sotheby's and he was seeking a deeper purpose. Having exhausted Robert Byron, he moved from buildings to botany.

A botanist friend, Admiral Furse, had been forced to abandon a mission from Kew Gardens to bring back a sample of cow parsley growing only on the northern slopes of the Hindu Kush. Bruce, hoping Kew might offset his expenses, decided to complete the Admiral's quest. Bruce's mission would be compromised by his susceptibility to illness.

He was, as Erskine had discovered, a terrible hypochondriac. "If Bruce had a cold, it was an extraordinary thing," says his doctor in London, Patrick Woodcock. "If he described to you a minor epileptic fit and a discharge from his nose, it took time to realise he was in fact only describing a sneeze."

Sunil Sethi, an Indian journalist who accompanied him through Utar Pradesh in 1978, says that "travelling with Bruce was like travelling with your 88-year-old maiden aunt. No piece of luggage was ever good enough. The weather was never right. It was too hot, too cold, too damp. He was the mother of all Mrs Gummidges."

Bruce was more of a risk-taker in his work than in his travels, but he did get ill. "He was never very strong," says Elizabeth. "He would cut himself, and go septic over and over again. Then he would put it out of his mind and be furious if I mentioned it: 'I'm never ill!' "

Bruce had originally planned to take Elizabeth with him. At the last minute, it was decided they would meet up in Lebanon on his route back from Afghanistan. Instead, he chose for companion his Sotheby's colleague, David Nash. "It was the most exciting thing I'd done," says Nash. "Bruce was hot-headed and opinionated, but wonderful company."

The atmosphere of an expedition surrounded the preparations. The equipment included a large flower press and a Stilton for the ambassador, which stank by the time they reached Kabul. On the way to the airport, Margharita stopped off at a garden supply shop to buy the trowel with which Bruce was to dig up the cow parsley.

Nash decided to keep a journal.

In Kabul they sought permission to visit the Karma valley in Nuristan, the source of the parsley. Just before catching the bus for Jalalabad, Bruce felt his stomach heave. "I wake up in the morning at 5 and know that something is wrong. Clamminess, violent rumblings of the stomach. Get out of bed, a dash to the rather primitive bathroom and appalling diarrhoea." The attacks continued on the bus, from which he disappeared, Nash recorded, "clutching a handful of notepaper". At last they arrived in Jalalabad. "B is sick and immediately makes full recovery. Afghan servant solemnly comes to empty bucket containing 3 half-chewed pills."

By 5 o'clock the worst was over and they went in search of the local general, who after much ceremony settled down to write a long letter on their behalf to his friend the Governor of Chigar Serai, in whose province the plant was rumoured to be found.

In the morning, they boarded a pea-green bus smelling of decaying curds. Every time the engine needed water an alarm bell went off and a character in a Chitrali cap filled an old billycan from the stream. "The driver," Bruce wrote, "was in a furiously excited frame of mind. Whether it was general high spirits or hashish was difficult to decide. In any event he revved his accelerator to a song of his own composition with an English refrain for our benefit. 'Jesus Christ goddamn son of a bitch,' these were the only words of English he knew."

The grinding journey took them through a basin of emerald maize fields and rice paddies. At midday, they arrived at Chigar Serai, Bruce still feeling delicate. "My stomach gave a few rumblings and so I munched a few sulphur tablets. This had an instant effect and before long the place was seething with people demanding pills."

At 9.30 p.m. the Governor appeared. They gave him the General's letter, explaining their purpose with the aid of two old maps and his 12 words of English. The Governor, "who has hazy visions of the whole of Nuristan as a tourist's paradise", expressed enthusiasm for what he can only dimly have understood since both their maps turned out to be quite useless. "We have the Survey of India of 1947, which is largely compiled from hearsay and guesswork." In the second map, which misplaced villages, reduced their names to gibberish and gave misleading altitudes, the Governor's area of jurisdiction was left largely blank.

Not much wiser about their enterprise, the Governor agreed to provide an escort of a soldier and four men, one to act as guide and three to carry the kit bags and the flower press. "This works out at approximately 1s which couldn't under any circumstances be called unreasonable."

While the expedition was assembled, Bruce made exploratory rambles. Returning from one walk, he discovered Nash had been offered three small boys and a bunch of grapes. The youths looked like "boys from Marlborough", identically attired in pastel green pants, brown shawls and Chitrali caps. For the rest of their journey, they would be mobbed by boys, many with blond hair and blue eyes, which disconcerted Bruce. "One of them aged about 6 had his eyes very heavily painted with antimony and would shoot alluring sidelong glances. This had a very disturbing effect as he had in every other respect exactly the appearance of an English prep school boy." Bruce tried to photograph one boy, but was made to feel acutely embarrassed. "There was an expression of deep resentment in his eyes. He obviously felt that we looked the same and knew not why the difference between us was so wide."

At last, on 22 August, Bruce's expedition to locate Admiral Furse's parsley stood ready. Accompanied by three porters and a Turkik soldier called Ahmed they set off along a narrow gorge beside a fast flowing stream full of large trout. They walked for four hours, the flower press humped on a porter's shoulders in a winding sheet. Suddenly, outside a shuttered teahouse, there appeared a boy carrying his little sister. The girl was about two years old and dressed in a red frock decorated with little silver coins. "The whole of her stomach and thighs were a terrible, septic, pustulant mess," wrote Bruce. "Her brother told me that she had been stung by hornets and there were no less than 20 bites below her waist, nearly all septic."

Through his medicines Bruce seemed to gain his most direct access. "I did my best with the limited medicines I had and bandaged all the septic wounds with an antiseptic cream while the child screamed piercingly and I gave her brother an anti-histamine pill for her in case they swelled up again." His treatment proved effective. When, five years later, Bruce returned to this valley with Peter Levi and Elizabeth, he was remembered with touching gratitude for saving the girl's life. "The reservations of thousands of years break down if you carry medicine," he realised. "The doctor is the unveiler."

For lunch, the porters gathered wild cherries, pomegranates and tiny figs. "Having been reduced to the ultimate stage of diarrhoea four days ago, I now find I am almost totally congested." Soon they reached the most propitious spot for the parsley, near the village of Wama. Leaving Nash with the men, Bruce climbed 100 feet up a mountain stream. "I collected a thistle-like plant which I hadn't seen before, three exiguous rock plants, one of which was aromatic when crushed and two small sedges from the stream." Then, while hunting for his specimen among small bushes of holly oak, Bruce fell and scraped the skin off his arm.

His injury signalled an abrupt end to the expedition, recorded in feeble pencil. "Awoke at 5 a.m. feeling terrible, arm swollen, bandages a smelly mess with temperature of 100, bites from black flies, oozing yellow fluid. Nothing to do but return." In panic, worried that he might develop gangrene, Bruce set off by himself, leaving Nash to follow with the porters. He had failed to notice that Nash was himself feverish with dysentery. Miserable, on an empty stomach, Nash walked the 30 kilometres back to Kandeh, where the bus had dropped them. There, to his fury, he found Bruce seated in a chair of state under a tree, at the centre of a colourful crowd, "looking as fine as could be".

Neither could wait to leave Afghanistan. On 27 August, they arrived at Kabul airport for a flight to Peshawar. Their departure was recorded by Nash.

"Insoluble problem with the customs official.

"CO: You cannot leave, sir, you have no exit visas.

"B: What is this, then, if it is not an exit visa? B. flourishes a piece of paper printed in Persian hieroglyphics.

"CO: Oh no sir, that is not an exit visa, that is a request from the tourist office to the police dept asking them to provide you with an exit visa.

D: J.C! What are you going to do about it then? That plane leaves in an hour. If it leaves without us, there will be hell.

"CO: You will have to get proper exit visa from the police, but to-day is Friday and the police office is shut. The next plane leaves on Wednesday!

"Explosion!

"B. disappears to rout the Police Dept out of bed, gets our visas stamped by an official in his pyjamas whose friendship was immediately won by B.'s vociferous complaints about the inefficiency of the Tourist Dept; and by saying that he is reporter from *Time* magazine and so would the officer please get the King on the telephone as he wished to lodge an official complaint and get the entire Tourist Dept sacked."

Bruce's bluff had worked, but the trip which had begun with such serious intent had ended shambolically. "We are leaving Afghanistan, not without a sensation of the utmost relief," he wrote. They had not managed to get the cow parsley specimen and there was another worry. He had been hoping to join Elizabeth in Lebanon, had requested the Embassy in Kabul to relay any cables, but he had not heard from her.

XIV.

ॐ

The Chattys

When I got married, Bruce said: "That's marvellous,
that's marvellous. Now it means you can travel."

—JAMES FOX

ONE EVENING IN 1963, John Rickett, the director in charge of Pictures, invited Marcus Linell, who had worked alongside Bruce as porter, to dinner in Kensington Square.

"Who do you think is going to be next Chairman of Sotheby's?" Rickett asked.

Linell replied without hesitation: "Bruce Chatwin."

Bruce was then 23. The fact he was considered Chairman material at this age by his colleagues was noteworthy, but in the context of Wilson's treatment of up-and-coming stars it was not the compliment it seemed. Wilson burned most of his favourites, including Rickett who, until the splitting of his department, had considered himself the front runner for the succession.

Bruce revealed his misgivings to Cary Welch. "Am given over to much private melancholy . . . as to my own future," he wrote after Wilson's audacious purchase of New York's premier auction house, Parke-Bernet, in the summer of 1964. "It's like a game of snakes and ladders and as far as Sotheby's are concerned, I have slid down the snake to square one. This means that to go up the ladders again it will be a question of threats, imbecilic charm, insinuous manoeuvring and a better spy-ring. One day I shall kick the whole thing in the pants and retire to Crete. Sorry to be so devious—the details I'll fill in when I see you . . . This is my ambition—BOTANIST written in my passport. The sale of works of art is the most unlovable profession in the world."

Bruce's disillusionment sharpened as he watched the man in charge of his department go, literally, mad.

The fact of John Rickett's schizophrenia was not generally known outside Modern Pictures. It had first manifested itself with an intense pre-occupation with the work of Richard Dadd, the Victorian artist who axed his father to death in a railway carriage, believing him to be the devil. Rickett owned one Dadd and had written a paper on him. One day he surprised one of the secretaries with the declaration: "You know, Anne, I'm going to have a baby by Richard Dadd."

Rickett lunched regularly at the Westbury Hotel, and the effect of alcohol with his medication multiplied his delusions. One lunchtime, he invited along Anne Thomson's husband Paul, who worked for him in the Picture department. After lunch, Rickett picked up a sharp carving knife and said: "I'm going to kill the first person I see in Sotheby's and I hope it's Katherine Maclean [then Wilson's personal assistant]."

He was not joking. A secretary who went into Rickett's office one afternoon was alarmed to find him stabbing his desk and called a porter to remove the knife. This happened several times. Rickett once accosted Elizabeth Chanler with a knife, "but did not say what he wanted". On another occasion, an injection had to be administered through his suit while Kenelm Digby-Jones held him down. Katherine Maclean wrote to Elizabeth: "Poor thing, I feel very sorry for him basically, but the awful thing is I find it hard not to get the shivers whenever I am left alone with him . . ."

Susceptible to dramas in his vicinity, Bruce began to somatize the stresses and the pressure he was feeling, the accumulation of five years at Sotheby's.

BRUCE'S MISFORTUNES HAD multiplied from the moment he left Kabul. A postal strike prevented him from meeting Elizabeth in Lebanon. "He never got my cables at all," she complained to Gertrude. On his return to London, where he had leased Grosvenor Crescent Mews on condition he might store his belongings while in Afghanistan, he found the locks changed. Denied entry by the French photographer who had taken the lease, he was threatening to hire "two goons from Soho" to batter down the door when his father, the guarantor of the lease, stepped in. Bruce lost his christening mug, several drawings, all his books and his kitchen equipment. He moved into a small flat in Mount Street, a short walk from Sotheby's.

At work, Wilson's acquisition of Parke-Bernet demanded of Bruce a succession of transatlantic flights that exhausted him. "I felt sort of trapped by New York and having to turn up at 3 a.m. to get my post done." He wrote: "However enthusiastic my response might be to works of art, however strong my desire to possess them, and however beguiling the atmosphere of the world's largest auction house, I became convinced it [Sotheby's] would drive me insane."

Two important sales consumed his energies that autumn. On 16 and 17 November 1964, Sotheby's held the sale of the Ernest Brummer collection of Egyptian and Near Eastern Antiquities. Bruce had catalogued this collection with Elizabeth. An Impressionist sale, four days later, included Cézanne's *Les Grandes Baigneuses*. Interviewed by the *New York Times*, Bruce promoted himself above Michel Strauss. "Bruce Chatwin, head of the Impressionist and Modern Painting Department of Sotheby's, said Cézanne's 'Bathers' had a 'profound' influence on Picasso and Braque. He says the last comparable work to come on the market was 'Boy in a Red Waistcoat' in 1958 which sold for £222,000."

The National Gallery in London acquired the painting for £500,000, once more a record. In a letter to Murray Bail, Bruce explained that the painting was then owned by Madame de Chaisemartin, "a deafening barrister, who specialised in the cases of poor Algerian immigrants on murder charges. I thought she was terrific. It was I . . . *Je garde mes souvenirs* . . . who set in motion the deal whereby the *Grandes Baigneuses*, then hanging in the maids' corridor, was bought by the National Gallery." How he managed this is unclear.

By his own account, Bruce went blind after these sales. "I manufactured a nervous eye complaint, which I came to believe in and then suffered from. This was interpreted in many ways." Integral to his myth, his blindness was said to precipitate his need to view "distant horizons".

The initial symptoms were real enough, a flare-up of his 1955 complaint from the rugby pitch. He described the problem to Welch: "Am rather depressed because the focussing in my right eye has packed up. Apparently the result of over-doing it in America . . . Am not intending to return until I can *SEE*." He had flown back from New York to Dublin, hired a car, driven to Donegal, and while sleeping in a four-poster bed, had put on the light and seen nothing—just a weak glow from the lamp. In the morning, one eye had recovered while the other remained foggy.

On 31 December 1964, Bruce visited the eye specialist Patrick Trevor-Roper. By now, the problem was not confined to his eyesight. "He described a multiplicity of symptoms," says Trevor-Roper. "He had feelings of fatigue, discomfort and vague subjective unease. He not quite hallucinated: he fantasised. 'When I look upward I feel brown clouds'."

Trevor-Roper discovered a latent squint. The effort of trying to pull it straight had caused the stress. He ascribed Bruce's condition to pressure from Wilson and the result of "a bright, sensitive rather neurotic young man trying to cut a dash". He recommended Bruce give up concentrated work and get away from the office. Bruce told him, "I'd like to go away and write"—the first time he had vouchsafed such an ambition.

Trevor-Roper said, "If you can afford to take six months off, that's what you must do. Go away and write." He had designed an eye hospital in Addis Ababa, "staffed by hopeless Bulgarians", and travelled every year to anglophone Africa, so perhaps the desert had emerged in their conversation as a choice of location.

In February 1965, Bruce set off for a long spell of recuperation in the Sudan.

BRUCE MADE MUCH of the damage to his sight, blaming it on the awfulness of Sotheby's. After he left, he expressed a disgust for collectors whose only passion was to possess, for the dull weekends he had had to spend in their Long Island houses. "It was all to do with *having* and *holding* and *hoarding* and I became less and less impressed." If they already owned a couple of Matisses, they were *de facto* interesting in the Wilson scheme. "In fact, they're not that interesting at all." Welch wrote to agree: "Collectors, after all, are the world's least mature and yet hardest-driving types. They are also in 99 per cent of the cases horrible, corrupt human beings—wildly egotistical, selfish as all hell, ruthless, scheming, dishonest, and utterly miserable. Ugh. What hellish trash (except for the ones we know and like)."

"Things," reflects the narrator in *Utz*, "are tougher than people. Things are the changeless mirror in which we watch ourselves disintegrate. Nothing is more ageing than a collection of works of art." The atmosphere of the art world conjured up for Bruce the image of the morgue. "In the end you felt you were working for a rather superior kind of funeral parlour," he told Thubron. "To give you an idea as to how it was, each morning there came round the *Times* obituary column and it had to be ticked off by any of the partners to see who had died . . ." People would say: " 'All those lovely things passing through your hands,'—and I'd look at my hands and think of Lady Macbeth." Then, as he told Thubron, warming to his theme, he developed sores, rather like stigmata, on his palms. "These works of art, however wonderful they may have been, were literally going to kill me. There and then."

Bruce's breakdown, which he laid at Sotheby's door, was as much personal as professional and it involved more than one layer of distress. He conveyed something of this to Wilson's assistant Kenelm Digby-Jones after collapsing on his way to Dorset during the same autumn.

Digby-Jones was taking Bruce "to do a job" at a private museum in Farnham, owned by George Pitt-Rivers, which housed the best collection of Benin bronzes in the country. The Pitt-Rivers "job" had already become a symbol of everything Bruce disliked about Peter Wilson's Sotheby's. On this day, however, Digby-Jones had no doubt as to what lay behind Bruce's collapse and it had nothing to do with Benin bronzes.

On the way to the museum, Digby-Jones stopped at Heathrow to drop off his wife, who was flying to Paris. "I went to have a pee, came back—and there was Bruce buried in Ursula's bosom, in floods of tears and shaking like a leaf." Digby-Jones at once drove Bruce back to London to see a doctor. "He was in a bad way. It was genuine, no messing. He kept saying: 'I'm in such a muddle, I don't know what to do.' He thought he was going blind. He said it was because he hated Sotheby's. I knew it was a bit of that, but really it was a struggle with himself and the stress of his sexuality."

BRUCE'S RELATIONSHIP WITH Elizabeth, which had begun surreptitiously more than a year before, had reached a watershed. When he came back from Afghanistan, Bruce discovered that Elizabeth was making moves to leave Sotheby's.

Elizabeth had never in this time considered herself faithfully attached to Bruce. "I went on seeing other people, although if that had got back to Bruce he would have been put off." Nevertheless, her reluctance to leave him can be traced in the variety of jobs she considered and rejected from 1963 onwards. In September 1963, she was to take up a position at the Freer Gallery in Washington where she had worked as a volunteer. At the last minute she baulked at the prospect of having only two weeks' holiday. Throughout 1964, her letters to Gertrude describe flirtations with the Freer, the Frick, a teaching project in south India. "What I really want to do is bum around with no time limit and no fixed address." This attitude exasperated her punctilious father. "You only seem to make plans of the most fluid kind and can change them more or less on the spur of the moment." On 29 December 1964, two days before Bruce went to see Trevor-Roper for the first time, Elizabeth wrote to her mother with news of her latest project: to spend six months in Spain, filming black-winged kites.

Not holding out hopes for marriage—"You couldn't bank on Bruce"—Elizabeth packed her trunk and gave away "Birdbrain", who flew out of a window in Norfolk and froze to death. Clearly, unless Bruce acted he would lose her.

LIKE HIS SWEDISH friend, Percivald Bratt, in a time of personal crisis Bruce sought his solution in the desert. Wilson raised an eyebrow. "I'm sure there's something wrong with Bruce's eyes, but I don't know why he has to go to the Sudan."

One answer lay with Gloria Taylor, Bruce's old girlfriend, on whom Khartoum had exercised a cathartic spell. A three-week holiday in Africa had changed her life.

In October 1963, "Glor" had been with Robert Erskine to Egypt and the Sudan. One night they sat in the Muglani gardens where the Blue and White Niles met. There they awaited the arrival of a contact: Tahir, a diffident member of the Mahdi clan whose grandfather Siddig El Mahdi had won the Sudan's independence from Britain. "Tahir arrived at midnight," says Gloria, "an amazing vision wearing a white jellaba and shoes of white camel leather. He was 35, slim, blue-black, and he spoke the most beautiful English." By the third day they were inseparable. Erskine came home on his own.

"I wondered why there was no resistance," says Gloria. "Everyone just said, 'Oh hello', when they saw me. On his deathbed, the Imam had predicted: 'Tahir will marry a foreigner and you're all to accept her.' When we went to meet his mother, she treated me like a long lost friend."

Gloria and Tahir married in December after a visit to England. In Kent they stayed with John Hewett. Gloria's anxious father sent her brother, the actor Malcolm MacDowell, to check. "Malcolm rings him: 'Are you sitting down, Dad? You know that phone you're holding? Well, that's the colour. As black as your phone'."

Bruce arrived in Khartoum on February 5, 1965. He had written to Gloria to say he needed bright, glaring light. He had brought Tahir a purple shirt recommended by David Niven after striking up a conversation with the actor in a shirt-maker's in Jermyn Street. Bruce found Gloria heavily pregnant in a tiny flat with a huge, balustraded terrace beside the Mahdi palace. He stayed with them a week, sleeping on the terrace.

Bruce longed, as Gloria had done, to hatch into something else. "We'd have long conversations about where he was going with his life," she says. "He was trashing everything. 'It's burning me up. I can't stand this much longer. I have to get an education'." Tahir, who had studied at Cambridge, urged Bruce to go to university: it would discipline his thoughts.

Bruce was restless after a week in Khartoum. "Couldn't sit still for five minutes, our Bruce. Unless he was on a quest," says Gloria. Then, at a wedding party, he met Abdul Monhim, a geologist who was leaving on an expedition to the Red Sea Hills to look for kaolin deposits the very next day. "I asked if I could go along and he said I could."

The journey was a "great turning point". He had arrived in Khartoum glutted on the art world, on "women who sent their Renoirs to be relined as often as their faces". Now he found himself in close quarters with someone who took pride in getting rid of everything he owned. The less Abdul Monhim had, the richer he became. "He was the utter swing of the pendulum, but I found him the most fascinating person that I'd ever met."

They headed on camels towards the Rift Valley, riding at a gallop through flat-topped acacia. Bruce discovered "the joy of going on and on". The country was harsh, glinting rocks and shining gorges with white thorns. The biblical landscape recalled the engravings of his favourite Dutch artist, Hercules Seghers. When he found the rock that resembled the Eagle Stone in Derbyshire, he experienced a homecoming. "The word 'homecoming' in that sense is the idea of returning to some kind of original landscape." Close to Ethiopia, he was riding through the Valley of Shadows. "It was, like so many things in life, completely accidental that we should have ended up there."

Here, in the Eastern Sudan, Bruce experienced his first taste of nomadic life. The tribe was the Beja, "the Fuzzy-Wuzzies of Kipling"—people who had been mentioned in the Egyptian annals 3,000 years ago. "They are sensationally idle, and truculent as well. Most of the morning for men is taken up by a fantastic mutual coiffure session." The Beja had long curly hair that they anointed with goat's grease. "The hair would contract at three in the afternoon and pour down their shoulders and by evening was a round fuzzy ball in which they could sleep." They carried buff hides and wandered around without tents. "I was overwhelmed by the simplicity of the lives of those people and struck by the idea that you were much happier if you carried nothing with you." Bruce told Michael Ignatieff: "They started my quest to know the secret of their irreverent and timeless vitality: why was it that nomad peoples have this amazing capacity to continue under the most adverse circumstances, while the empires come crashing down."

Bruce afterwards sought parallels for his desert epiphany in the example of two previous travellers to the Sudan. In 1930, Wilfred Thesiger had crossed the country of the Danakils. "The Danakil journey," Bruce wrote in a review of *Desert, Marsh and Mountain* "set the pattern for a life that turned into a perpetual tramp through the wilderness." On that dangerous journey, Thesiger had crossed the tracks of the other and earlier traveller: Arthur Rimbaud. Bruce came to identify with the French poet. In his mind their situations were similar. "As Rimbaud was passing through his '*saison en enfer*', he realised that the Beast was winning. He made a last ditch stand to avoid suicide or mental collapse, and took to the perpetual pilgrimage of the road." In Bruce's opinion, Rimbaud's abrupt departure was not a failure: it was a cure. "Among the testicle-hunting Danakil in the leopard-coloured lands of Ethiopia, tracking his way '*par des routes horribles reppellant l'horreur présumé des pays lunaires*,' a country of tearing thorns, black acacia trees, glinting schists, and shimmering white salt pans, he found himself again. He reaffirmed his identity, just as Proust found his in re-walking the 'ways' of childhood . . . In his search for mental calm, Rimbaud found that he was a small-time honest provincial bourgeois from Charleville. This is what he was. This he could not change."

After six weeks away, Bruce returned to London by way of Crete and Athens from where, on 10 April, he wrote to his parents: "I shall return by sea and land as the aeroplane for CERTAIN does me no good. Eye took ten days to recover after KHARTOUM-ATHENS. Much better now, in fact am very fit."

Bruce's camel ride in the Sudan not only opened his eyes to the world of the nomad. In the desert he reached a decision over his future with Elizabeth.

ELIZABETH HAD NOT heard a word from Bruce while he was gone. On February 24, she wrote to Gertrude: "I am going on this bird photographing business fairly soon—maybe within the next three weeks." But still she dragged her heels, reluctant to set out. Then at the end of April, her telephone rang at work. Bruce spoke in a whisper. "They don't know I'm back, so don't say anything. Can you have lunch?"

She met him at his new flat in Mount Street. Looking sunburned and well, Bruce told her about the Sudan. Then he asked: "Do you want to come to Paris for Easter?"

Bruce went ahead by train. Elizabeth drove him to the station, planning to follow by air. On the platform, he gave her a little grey leatherette box, not to be opened until the train had left. She opened it in her car. Inside, pale gold in colour, was a Greek electrum ring of the fifth century BC. The intaglio was a wounded lioness with her head thrown back, pulling a spear from her side. "Not entirely suitable as an engagement present," he would much later write of it. "But I think it the loveliest Greek ring I ever saw."

Elizabeth was overjoyed. "It came from out of the blue. Usually people drop hints, but Bruce never did. I was very surprised that he was willing to be married. Only when he went into the desert did he change his outlook." She had no doubt of the answer she would give him.

Bruce waited at Le Bourget to meet her. The following day he took her to the Cabinet des Médailles in the Louvre. Here in this gigantic hall of curiosities, assembled by the Kings of France, Bruce proposed. Elizabeth was looking at some coins when Bruce said: "Do you want to keep the ring?" It was as cryptic as Amos's proposal in *On the Black Hill*, when Amos, having shown Mary the farm he hopes to buy, slips an arm around her waist and says: "Could you live in this?"

HE HAD DITHERED to the last. In Khartoum, he had told Gloria that Elizabeth meant a lot to him, but he wasn't going to get married. As late as 21 April a postcard to his parents spoke of a plan to spend Easter in Rhodes, then climb Mount Ida.

It fell to Cary Welch to play a decisive role. Welch was older and could offer the advice which Bruce found it impossible to solicit from his father. Also Welch was married to Elizabeth's cousin, Edith. "I knew Elizabeth to be very special, an admirable, good, flexible person, someone who could be depended on."

Over breakfast at the Cappuccino, Welch strongly encouraged him.

He described Bruce as "a psychological nomad" and felt the stability of marriage would benefit him. "If ever I did anything that was crucial, it was when I gave him the real nudge which I think was necessary."

SHY BY NATURE, private and keen not to be teased by the older Sotheby's porters, Elizabeth kept news of their engagement to herself. One person Bruce told was Ivry. "The deed is done, and in about three months I'll no longer be a free man. Secrecy is rather necessary for a bit, partly because we both find the word fiancé(e) difficult to pronounce with the right expression."

Gertrude and Bobby were kept in the dark until the last moment. Elizabeth informed them over the telephone during a discussion about her grandmother Daisy's 103rd birthday celebrations.

In Geneseo, the Chanlers were perplexed. They could not distinctly remember Bruce, whom they had met for an unremarkable weekend in Dublin in the middle of May when Elizabeth was already engaged. Gertrude was initially cautious, but Elizabeth allayed her mother's fears. "Everything is perfectly lovely and we are very happy, so don't worry about a thing. Bruce takes care of (al)most everything anyway." By 22 June, Gertrude had adjusted to the news: "We are certainly glad we saw Bruce as it would be very queer to have to wait till he got over here! It is really so exciting & we are thrilled even though it is hard to seem enthusiastic over the transatlantic phone!"

The Chanlers' initial failure to recollect Bruce was rooted in Bobby's dislike of the English. Gertrude, writing earlier in the year to Elizabeth, confessed that she had lost her taste for England "partly because Bobby doesn't really seem to like it". Well-established in Bobby's psyche was the cautionary tale of his mother's friend, Consuelo Vanderbilt, and Consuelo's marriage to an English fortune-hunter—arranged as it happened by Robert Harding Milward. Elizabeth had an inkling of how her father might take the news. "Bobby didn't like me to marry out of the US. He didn't say so at the time, thank goodness. He said rather grumpily, 'I suppose you'll give up your citizenship?' I said, 'No'. But when my sister Felicity came to be an *au pair* here, they said to her: 'Don't marry an Englishman'."

Whatever was their true reaction, Elizabeth's parents concealed it. Gertrude wrote to Margharita Chatwin: "We are so pleased that you like Elizabeth. We too are very pleased to have Bruce for a son-in-law as we liked him so much when we saw him in Ireland. At the time we did not realise that all this was so serious as we had been hearing Bruce's name mentioned casually for some time. It is all very exciting etc."

Over one matter the Chanlers dug in their heels. Elizabeth was a practising Catholic. "One thing you must do," Gertrude wrote to Elizabeth, "is see what can be done about Bruce getting the required religious instructions . . . This is all very important." Bruce, she said, needed to know what he was letting himself in for, or else there might be grounds for annulment.

"I do hope you will not worry about my not being a Catholic," he replied to Gertrude. "I have always been brought up according to the Church of England, as were both my parents. A few relations of my grandfather's generation were Catholic converts. I am absolutely willing, not to say anxious, that any of my children shall be brought up as Catholics, and I intend to talk to a great friend of mine Peter Levi who is a Jesuit. I know you'll agree that it would be a great mistake to take steps in this direction just at this moment. All I can say is that at the time I left school I was influenced strongly by Catholicism and have an entirely open mind about the future."

Through Peter Levi he found a Jesuit priest to give Pre-Câna instruction, the sessions to take place alternately in Father Murray's rooms off Mount Street and in Bruce's apartment, conveniently nearby. "I've got a small flat in Mount Street just opposite the Connaught Hotel. We have decided we would prefer to live there for the time being rather than face a major upheaval just now. It's a bit like a couple of state-rooms on a liner, but its advantages are its economy, cupboard space, living-in housekeeper in the basement, and the fact that it is 2 minutes flat from Sotheby's."

Meanwhile, Bruce wondered how to address his prospective in-laws. "I haven't an idea what to call you. I've discussed it for an hour, but [Elizabeth] has offered no constructive suggestion. I'm amazed by the elaborate detail of her letter. Not a word to tell you how happy we both are, and how much we look forward to the end of August and seeing you again."

WHEN NEWS OF their engagement leaked out, their circle of friends were thunderstruck. "The idea of Bruce getting married seemed absolutely bananas," says Howard Hodgkin. James Crathorne spoke for many within Sotheby's. "Hearing Bruce was to marry Elizabeth was one of the most startling bits of information. Rather like Kennedy being assassinated, I remember where I was." The astonishment extended even to close friends. "I thought Bruce wasn't the marrying kind," says Elizabeth's flat-mate, Pattie Sullivan, who had supposed they were, at best, "buddies". Robert Erskine learned about it as he walked through a square in Chelsea. Suddenly, he saw people looking up and heard someone yelling out of a top floor window. "It was Bruce. He was practically falling out in his urgency to tell me. 'Robert, I'm getting married!' "

This surprised Erskine: it seemed so sudden. "I thought I knew him pretty well, but I had no idea that he had even a lady to think of getting married to. Elizabeth is splendid, though she is not apparently so. If Bruce was going to get married, I assumed it would be to a gorgeous blonde."

In Mrs Ford's tearoom, there were, Hewett said, "one or two *looks*". An extreme reaction was that which occurred halfway through a dinner party thrown by Paul and Anne Thomson. Bruce and Elizabeth announced their engagement. "I'll never forget," says Anne. "Paul positively spat his spaghetti out."

No one was more astonished than Peter Wilson, under whose nose the courtship had taken place. Elizabeth wrote to Gertrude: "We told Katherine and PCW last Friday & then ran. They were really flabbergasted."

On 12 July, the engagement was announced in the papers. Elizabeth flew to Boston to prepare for her wedding. Bruce wrote to Ivry: "We're getting married in their family chapel on their estate which is at the back of beyond in New York State near the Canadian border." He would follow six weeks later by boat.

ELIZABETH'S GRAND AMERICAN connections were not abhorrent to Bruce. He talked "endlessly" to friends like Hugh Honour about her family. "One could tell he was happy she was very well born." He told Hodgkin soon after their engagement that she had "more than a million" in the bank. Hodgkin says, "He didn't marry her for money, but money did matter a lot to him." This figure of a million had certainly not derived from Elizabeth, brought up by Bobby never to mention such matters. She says, "Bruce did say to me once: 'Do you have a little money?' I said, 'It's a little, that's all it is.' But we never discussed a sum. I'm sure he would have liked it to be more." The legendary Chanler wealth, like the legendary Chanler Falls, had long since dried up.

A part of him was taking refuge. Bruce worked in a world where homosexuality was not stigmatised, yet he came from a background which did not approve of homosexuality. This dilemma had driven him to Khartoum. He may have hoped, like Brian Sewell, that "homosexual behaviour is something you grow out of", and that he could follow the model of his parents' successful marriage. "He respected them more than anybody," says Anne Thomson. "He didn't want to let them down." What he aspired to was something not too distant from Sue Goodhew's horoscope ideal: a family life and a relationship that was public, comfortable and supportive. He believed the happiness that marriage and a family would bring might outweigh any sexual urges. It was his greatest luck to find Elizabeth Chanler.

Bruce's parents approved of his choice. "The thing about Elizabeth is she knows everything," said Charles. Elizabeth was likewise enchanted by Charles and Margharita. "I knew Bruce was OK when I met his parents."

Bruce had told his parents that he was marrying Elizabeth because "she's got a very good head for heights". Only when pressed by his brother did he go further. Hugh put the question to Bruce while walking down Bond Street. "I asked why he was marrying Elizabeth after all the beautiful women he had known: Ivry, Samira, Gloria . . ." Bruce stopped in the street and replied: "To stop myself going mad."

Hugh understood Bruce to be saying, stormed by his nervous collapse: "This is my anchor."

ELEANOR MACMILLAN WAS in the bathtub when she opened Elizabeth's letter with the news. "I thought I'd drown from the joy of it all . . . Married—do you realise what you're saying???"

Elizabeth had not lightly entertained the idea of marriage to Bruce. "I had no expectations. Bruce said well before I married: 'I will always want to go off by myself.' So it was understood at the time and I was perfectly happy to accept that." Since a young girl, she had made a promise to herself: never to be dependent on her spouse. When still at Fox Hollow School, she was shocked to hear how a close neighbour, Reverdy Wadsworth, had choked to death while eating in a steakhouse with his wife. "They'd never been separated . . . She went to pieces and I thought: 'I must not be like that.' You have to have something to fall back on. If we'd had children, that would have been a tie to fall back on and probably Bruce would have been different. Mind you, he'd have taken them off before you could say 'knife'."

Elizabeth, too, may have hoped that marriage and a family would change things. "I knew Bruce was ambidextrous. He was never obvious about it and it embarrassed him that he had this tendency, but he wasn't going to give in to it completely. Looking back, I think he was very uncomfortable at having got himself into this situation, but given his background he didn't see any alternative, and he thought men living together completely unnatural. Once I said: 'What about famous couples like Benjamin Britten and Peter Pears?' Bruce said, 'No, it's still not right'."

BRUCE'S "EYE" WAS never better demonstrated than in his choice of a wife. They had a community of interest. Both had grown up on farms; loved art, travel, independence. Both had the Navy and steel in their blood and shared a way of looking at the world. Bruce was continually startled by Elizabeth's originality and lack of self-consciousness: she was never moved by what people thought she ought to be doing or thinking. He admired her, needed her honesty and she made him laugh. "Do you normally keep your stockings in the 'frig'?" he wrote once she had flown to America.

"When he met her, he'd met his match," says John Stefanidis. "She knew as much, if not more than he did. It was checkmate." The marriage was not universally understood, yet it made good and lasting sense. It would be unorthodox—but that worried neither. Elizabeth came from a line of eccentric women accustomed to letting their husbands roam.

To "Glor" at a dinner in Cambridge Place in 1979, Bruce remarked: "I was attracted to Elizabeth because she had a touch of the tar brush." He pursued this line with the photographer, Eve Arnold. Elizabeth, he said, was an octoroon from New Orleans. The story was not entirely a Chatwin invention and had its origins in the eighteenth century and a black girl impregnated by a Chanler on their Carolina estate. The Chanlers, generally, were sandy-coloured, but thanks to this infusion a swarthy complexion popped up in each generation. Bobby's cousin Chanler Chapman had been dark, and so was Elizabeth.

She was not a threateningly feminine woman, yet Bruce described her to Gregor von Rezzori wearing a Balenciaga coat in such a way that the writer imagined a blonde, long-legged beauty. "I remember that piercing and original vision he had of her. He transformed her."

His transforming vision was not always active. There would be painful passages and periods of separation. Bruce had "smart" friends who were slower to see Elizabeth for what she was; sometimes, to his discredit, he appeared to go along with them. Frequently, he went off with other people. He behaved like a little boy with Elizabeth, says Julia Hodgkin. "Always running away from home, setting off with his belongings tied in a kerchief to a stick, knowing that, come nightfall, mummy would come down the road looking for him."

Throughout their marriage Elizabeth remained steadfast. Mindful of Reverdy Wadsworth, she had the ability not to be emotionally clinging. There was a matter-of-factness in her acceptance of whatever he did. She had made her decision about him and her love was constant. Bruce was the person who could most share the way she saw and lived in the world, and it was plain to Gillian Walker that Bruce felt the same way about her. "His life as it was constructed resembled a circus tent. Everything else can go on, but it has to have a pole to keep it in place. That centering is vital for someone who has a passion for the variety of experiences that the world can offer. Elizabeth was pivotal. Without her whatever chaos there was in his life would have pulled Bruce away from himself."

He needed someone both to run away from and to come back to and he found in Elizabeth that person. "He was dreadful to her," says Gloria, "but he stayed." Ivry Freyberg had no doubt about his motives. "There was no question but that he was in love with Elizabeth. She was a completely new animal, so unlike an English girl. He told me: 'I've found this most fantastic American and I'm mad about her'."

BRUCE SOON MISSED his fiancée. Communication was not easy. Telephone calls were expensive and complicated to book. He wrote tenderly, often. "Letters are all very well, but by the time they reach they are old hat. Can you imagine what it must have been like in the 18th century, with the husband disappearing for *years* to India, and with a postal service of three *months*? I now have all the right papers signed by Church, notaries and State. I assume that it is all right to bring them over with me? My Uncle Anthony just came in with an unbelievably hideous and special metronomic clock which was exhibited in the Great Exhibition. There is also a postcard signed Alfred . . . it shows a long Italian tunnel with apparently no ending. How right is he? I can't lay my hands on it just now, but will send it on. The sight of you at the docks will be worth all this trial. Love, love, love, Bruce."

Bruce was pleased with his priest: "Father Murray is a real treasure."

He occupied his spare moments with house-hunting and sorting through wedding presents. "Why don't you say for wedding presents credit at John Hewett, 173 New Bond St W1?" He looked forward to every conversation. "Am much cheered this morning by your telephone call, the Host and the weather. No houses on the market. Chairs, blinds, etc., all arriving soon, must shampoo carpet. A million hugs!" He signed one letter "All is love."

Elizabeth's list of wedding presents to Gertrude included a do-it-yourself-sauna, a holder to store maps in a car "as one day we will go to Afghanistan etc. by land", subscriptions to American *Vogue* and the *New Yorker*, and a blini iron. "Bruce is frightfully fussy about cooking things, as he likes to make elaborate dishes from time to time." One choice of present prompted a panicked letter from Bruce. "My Dear Liz, After our telephone conversation I had a sleepless night. The real reason for my insomnia was . . . the recollection of a conversation we had before you left, a conversation of which I only just [realise] the horrendous implications. You said that you were going to learn how to work a *deep freeze*!!

"Now all week I have been instructed about the evils of paganism and heresy. I have learned the implications of life everlasting, the light of Heaven, the darkness of Hell, and the mist of Purgatory. But I now find myself faced with the greatest HERESY known to man, the DEEP FREEZE.

"Imagine if you were put in a deep freeze. Your outward form might remain, but where would your soul be? Flitting about the Fields of Asphodels or knocking at the Golden Gate. But vegetables have no souls; they die. It is a major article of my faith never to eat dead vegetables. A doctor friend of mine nearly dropped down dead in Harley Street as a result of eating dead vegetables. It is a complaint known as scarlatina. So give up all this nonsense of a deep freeze, do not deprive me of the pleasure of eating fresh food in its due season and learn to make a proper apple pie and the best chowder."

BRUCE ARRIVED IN America in the middle of August. Worried about his son's eyes, Charles insisted that Bruce sail with them on the Dutch ship *Statenden*. "I reckoned it a good idea for Bruce not to fly over, to relax." As they sailed into Manhattan harbour Charles won the ship's sweepstake. The box of Havana cigars augured well.

Bruce had not seen Elizabeth for seven weeks. They stayed in David Nash's New York apartment and visited the Dumbarton Oaks collection in Washington, meeting old Mrs Bliss. When conversation turned to the smuggling of artefacts from Turkey, Bruce began: "Ignorance is—" "Happiness," interjected Mrs Bliss.

At Dumbarton Oaks, they were enraptured by a Peruvian wall hanging of parrot feathers from a species of papagayo now extinct. The Incas had prized these feathers over gold. "I want one of those," Bruce told Elizabeth. "Fat chance," she said.

The chance came a day or two later in New York. Immediately before leaving for Geneseo to get married, they visited John Wise, a pre-Columbian dealer, who in his room at the Westbury Hotel unravelled to their astonishment a pristine checkerboard of blue and yellow parrot feathers. Wise's rectangular hanging, possibly intended for an Inca temple, formed part of a cache discovered in a big earthenware drum near the River Ocoña. Max Ernst owned one. And Nelson Rockefeller. This was the last.

John Wise was a friend, wrote Bruce, "a man of enormous presence and a finely developed sense of the ridiculous". He asked how much money they had on them. Bruce had nothing. Elizabeth looked into her purse. "I happened to have our wedding money on me." The total was $150, given to both Bruce and Elizabeth to buy presents.

"Well, it's a wedding present," said Wise.

"It was the nicest thing he could have done," says Elizabeth.

The ancient feathers celebrate many Chatwin elements: rarity, patchwork, simplicity, flight. Bruce, who was prepared to sell anything, twice teetered on the brink of letting them go. He pulled back on both occasions. The Peruvian hanging became one of the very few objects he could never bear to part with. "To Bruce, it was the sun and the sky—a sacred object," says Elizabeth.

ON 21 AUGUST 1965, Bruce and Elizabeth were married by Abbot Boltwood in the chapel at Sweet Briar Farm. The guests had lunch on the lawn and the Admiral, spruce in his full naval whites, served Californian champagne.

The Chatwin contingent was Charles and Margharita; Hugh; the photographer Derry Moore and David Nash. Bruce had asked Nash to be his best man on condition he did *not* give a speech.

This prohibition did not prevent Elizabeth's younger brother Ollie from rising to his feet after lunch. The sight of Elizabeth kneeling at the altar and wiggling her feet playfully had moved him to deliver an oration. When they heard that their sister was to marry an Englishman, he said, the family had naturally been curious to know what he was like. On a single day, they had put him through his paces, making him participate in tennis, horse-riding and a water-skiing session on Lake Conesus. The conclusion was: "He's a lot like us."

Bruce had succeeded in charming even those Chanler women who found him on first impression "alarmingly handsome". Determined not to have him as an enemy, Bruce had paid conspicuous attention to Elizabeth's father, so much so that Ollie was amazed to observe them disappear into the library and Bobby close the door. So far as he knew, this favour had only ever been bestowed two or three times.

A single cloud cast a shadow on the ceremony. Two days before the wedding, the parish priest in Geneseo, Father Carron, had handed Elizabeth a pamphlet spelling out 32 reasons why she should not marry a non-Catholic.

Otherwise, it was a midsummer day with cicadas singing everywhere. Pattie Sullivan considered it one of the nicest weddings she had known. A friend of Elizabeth, Jane Lyons, wrote to the bride: "I hate to be trite, but I have never seen two people so well matched—that makes it sound like figures or vases. He is just as impressive as you are."

No one was more pleased than Bruce's mother: "I think of Bruce's and Elizabeth's as THE WEDDING," Margharita wrote to Gertrude.

THE CHATWINS HONEYMOONED off the Maine coast. Elizabeth's father had heard Bruce liked sailing. Without consulting either of them, Bobby had chartered a 42-foot yawl.

Nor, as it turned out, were they sailing away on the beautiful pea-green boat by themselves. Cary and Edith Welch would join them on another yawl owned by Billy and Mea Wood.

They drove together to Cold Harbor, Maine. On the way they stopped at a roadside café where there were name-badges for sale. Cary became "Earl", Edith "Darlene", Elizabeth "Maxine" and Bruce was "Max". From then on, "Max" and "Maxine" were their pet names for each other.

The Chatwins' yawl had been badly rigged, but Bruce knew how to handle her. They sailed east for a week. The shoreline was a rocky, flat-forested wilderness with tiny villages. Beyond P'tit Manan, the wind dropped. Bruce, in the faster vessel, steered for the lobster harbour of

Cape Split. As he passed through the breakwater, their boat struck a rock not marked in the charts. "We put it in subsequently," says Elizabeth. Luckily, the hull was not broached.

There, in the dead calm, Cary and Edith Welch joined them with Billy and Mea Wood. That night a thick fog descended and in the morning they could not see their hands before their faces. For three days they lay marooned in the small harbour. In the Wood kitchen, the three couples gorged on lobsters caught by a brawny preacher-woman. Bruce reread his childhood copy of Slocum. Elizabeth wrote thank-you letters. They could not do much but eat and walk. They took long walks in a forest infested with old cars "like wounded sculptures", which the locals used for target practice. "It felt as if we were trespassing on the set of *Bonnie & Clyde*," says Welch.

On the last day a storm blew away the fog. It was dark by the time the wind dropped. The Woods having left by road, the Welches joined the Chatwins on their boat. They decided to risk sailing by night. Elizabeth lay on the bow, looking for rocks. Edith read the charts. Bruce set his course by the flashes of the lighthouse.

"It was a curious honeymoon," says Elizabeth, who had never before spent so much time with Bruce. "But then I hadn't been on any other." As for Bruce, he was proud of his safe helmsmanship in the fog. He felt he had proved himself, demonstrated nerve and sinew. Everything was going to be all right.

XV.

༄

Out of His Depth

*My career was the reverse of most people's in that I
started as a rather-unpleasant little capitalist in a
big business in which I was extremely successful and
smarmy, and suddenly I realised at the age of 25
or so that I was hating every moment of it. I had
to change.*

—BC to MICHAEL IGNATIEFF

AT THE END of September, after a hot and dusty month in New York, the Chatwins sailed to London for the new auction season. "In as much as I foresaw the future, it was Sotheby's," says Elizabeth. "I just assumed it would go on."

The flat at 119a Mount Street proved unsuitable in every way. Bruce had removed the books from the shelves to give his wife room, but the kindness was too little. The flat was tiny and decorated with oriental austerity rather like Charles's galley on the *Sunquest*: the kitchen was in the cupboard and the sink came from a chandler's shop. Everything precious not on display was wrapped in tissue paper and concealed in wooden boxes inside a cupboard.

Bruce was chiefly pleased with the yellow bathroom. On the wall he had hung a gouache of blue and red toothbrushes taken from a French provincial salesman's album, a painting which confirmed to Hodgkin the deep-seated conventionality of his taste. It was the mischievous Hodgkin who was responsible for the bright yellow. He had caught Bruce snooping in his studio—"I'm looking for a colour for my bathroom," Bruce explained with a grin. Annoyed, Hodgkin brought along on his next visit a tube of artist's quality cadmium yellow. "This is the *only* colour for your bathroom wall," he said. "It must be shiny and it must be dense."

"Really?" said Bruce. "That sounds *very* expensive."

"Think of the colour of skin against this yellow," said Hodgkin.

It cost £125 to cover all four walls. Bruce explained to a visitor: "I've always wanted to live inside an egg." To Lucie-Smith, the Mount Street flat—which had no view—was more "like a very posh crackle-glazed prison cell".

Into this confined space Bruce and Elizabeth arrived from America with 15 pieces of luggage. When Elizabeth on the spur of the moment accepted the gift of a female ginger kitten havoc ensued. The cat immediately fouled Bruce's perfect yellow bathroom, initiating a lifelong exasperation with her pets. "I didn't know Bruce hated cats," says Elizabeth. "It drove him up the wall. At least it wasn't a dog."

Elizabeth had accepted the cat in anticipation of a country house overrun with mice. The finding of this house was now a matter of urgency. As Margharita confided to Gertrude, it was even more important for Elizabeth than for Bruce "as she will be much more tied as soon as she has family responsibilities."

Bruce had hoped to keep two establishments: the London flat and a country house in North Oxfordshire, where they had seen an eighteenth-century vicarage. But during October he became aware for the first time just how limited his wife's finances were. If they pooled their incomes, they could just afford one home.

Elizabeth's share of the Astor estate was "31 cents annually", while her mother's fortune was strictly entailed. In 1958, Gertrude had endowed each of her children a capital sum of $250,000, kept in trust at the Mellon bank in Pittsburgh. The capital provided $8,000 dollars in a good year and could not be touched.

"Our situation is not at all good," Elizabeth wrote to Gertrude. "Bruce is now getting £3,000 a year & I get about £1,600. The total of £4,500 will after US & English taxes be reduced to something like £3,500 or less . . . And as Bruce earns more, the tax on *my* income goes up so that it pays him to work less, if you see what I mean."

Sympathetic, Gertrude wrote on 18 October with welcome news. "I have arranged that there will be plenty of money available for the house when you find one." While Bruce worked, Elizabeth house-hunted: one week in London, one week in the country. By November the hunt had widened to Dorset with Hugh and Charles joining in. A promising old priory came to nothing when Hugh—who had completed his training as a surveyor—prodded the plaster and found dry rot. Bruce kept Gertrude up to date. "No luck with houses so far. The market is apparently depressed at the moment and we may have to wait till spring because that's the time people put them on the market."

IT SHOULD HAVE been a glorious homecoming: the young and talented honeymooner returning to assume his new directorship.

He had been appointed a director in the summer and at the age of 25 his name was now on the masthead. The directorship was the fulfilment of a promise by Wilson. "Wilson told him that if he stayed, he would be one of a small group of new directors—about three—who would eventually control the whole firm," wrote Kenneth Rose in his diary, after a conversation with Bruce in 1968. But the Beast groomed many of his favourites for positions they would never fill. The promotion was not the advancement it appeared to be. Bruce kept from Elizabeth the extent of his disappointment until after their wedding.

In March 1965, the board of Sotheby's comprised nine directors. Bruce imagined he would be the tenth, with a vote and a share. He was not alone in his expectations. When the announcement was made, soon after Elizabeth flew to America to prepare for their marriage, Bruce discovered that eight others had been given identical encouragement, two of them—Marcus Linell and Howard Ricketts—younger than himself.

Among the new appointments was Richard Day, in charge of prints and drawings. Summoned to the office of the financial director, Day found Bruce already sitting down. "Bruce was the first in, the catalyst for all of us. I was the second. He was amazed to see me. He realised if I was a director, there would be others. Slowly, the others turned up. Howard, Marcus, Michel . . . He wasn't best pleased."

Those who filed into the room were not invited to join the ruling élite. They were to be subsidiary directors without voting rights. "They were called directors," says Pollen, "but they weren't the executive committee."

Because of a new tax law, there was a waiting period of several months before the partnership came into effect. Meanwhile, Bruce was expected to attend board meetings. On 23 October, he wrote to his mother-in-law, who had agreed to loan him the £6,500 he needed to buy his shares: "I've been going to board meetings for the first time and more often than not they're long and tedious, but sometimes they are very funny especially when all my own contemporaries stand on their dignity and get pompous and silly."

Bruce felt able to contribute little. Too many directors crowded the boardroom and there was a joke: "standing room only". Also, the feeling that a meeting had already taken place. "He felt utterly betrayed," says Elizabeth. "I remember a lot of rage." The powerlessness of Bruce's new position was driven home when one of the élite, Graham Llewellyn, queried Bruce's expenses.

Had Bruce been appointed a full director, Elizabeth believed he might have remained at Sotheby's. "It was typical of PCW. He thought he was going to get away with it. But he had come up against someone as strong willed as he."

ELIZABETH'S OBSERVATION TO her mother after two months described the tempo that prevailed all her married life. "I've discovered there's no point in planning on anything as Bruce's schedule is always changing. You have to leave everything open always." In November, they stayed in Birr Castle with Elizabeth's friends Brendan and Alison Oxmantown. The United Nations had posted Brendan to West Africa and his mother was throwing a farewell party. "Lady Rosse is amazing and calls everything dear, darling beloved, including butlers and the Queen . . . The Press rang up one night while we were there and she did a marvellous imitation of an old Irishwoman till they hung up." Conversation that weekend concentrated on the Oxmantowns' destination, Dahomey. Once the capital of the slave trade, the country would be the setting for Bruce's novel *The Viceroy of Ouidah*.

A plan to spend Christmas in the Sudan was cancelled, but in early December the Chatwins travelled with Hewett and Felicity Nicholson to Leningrad. Bruce explained to Gertrude: "John Hewett and I have always wanted to see the archaeological stuff in the Hermitage and so we've cooked up an expedition."

Immediately after Christmas, Gertrude received another letter from Bruce, this time from Paris. "We are sitting in an Italian restaurant and the woman next to me is a blonde with a *khaki* face. E. and I are speculating how it got that way because she is not a negress. E. has eaten an enormous pizza, half a chicken, and is now proposing to embark on an elaborate sweet. Nobody would say she doesn't eat! But what really irks me is that she doesn't appear to get any fatter while I blow out like a balloon."

Bruce had definite ideas about how his wife should dress. From Sotheby's he had bought her a big-sleeved Victorian dress in brown and grey taffeta. He also insisted that she wear a pair of real tortoise-shell glasses.

He was in Paris with Elizabeth to catalogue Helena Rubinstein's collection of African and Oceanic sculptures. "Helena Rubinstein wore a lot of people out during her long life, and she retains that capacity in the grave. We work from 9 till 8 in the evening and we still get nowhere . . . I'm going to insist that E. gets paid a fortune."

The Rubinstein sale took place on 21 April 1966, fetching £516,320. Bruce at the gavel maintained an open phone link with New York. More than 40 dealers squeezed into the boardroom and a Brancusi bronze called *Bird in Space* sold for £50,000 in 75 seconds. It was Bruce's last major sale.

AFTER SEVERAL FALSE starts the Chatwins found a house.

Bruce had been advised by Hewett, who lived in Kent "practically underneath a mound", that you never wanted a home with a view. "He was so much in thrall to Hewett, that this is what we were after," says Elizabeth, who would have preferred the open spaces of Wiltshire. One day she drove down the Ozleworth valley, in Gloucestershire. "I thought: this is *great*, it doesn't have a view."

Holwell Farm was a pink, seventeenth-century house set in 47 acres near the town of Wotton-under-Edge. It was perched on a steep slope and almost derelict. There was no central heating, limited electricity, and the kitchen was permeated with the stink of untrained tomcats. It required a new roof, new beams, complete redecoration.

The house was beautiful. "All the bluebells and primroses and cowslips are out so it is very pretty, rain or not," Elizabeth wrote to Gertrude. "We like it better every time we see it." She was able to foresee a country house in the image of her favourite book.

In April, Gertrude advanced £17,000 to buy Holwell Farm. They planned to move in on 9 May. The builders would have finished their work by the autumn. "The main thing is for you to own the house and not the house own you," warned Elizabeth's cousin, O'Donnell Iselin. They little suspected that the house was like a Hobbit hole, sunless for three months of the year.

IN APRIL 1966, after a protracted and complex procedure, Bruce officially became one of eight second-tier partners. He may have felt insulted about his directorship a year before, but at the time he had not judged it an issue on which to leave. He was viewed as Wilson's heir. "None of us had any doubt but that he would be at the head of Sotheby's in due course," says Brian Sewell. Then, in the early summer of 1966, he resigned.

The fuse had been lit in the Sudan. Bruce, walking down Bond Street with Wilson, had surprised his chairman by spitting onto the pavement like a Bedouin. "He realised then that I'd changed." The desert had restored his eyesight. "I was never at all able to focus on Sotheby's again."

He maintained that the decision to resign came to him after a revelatory "flash" in the boardroom. "I decided I didn't want to spend not only the rest of my life with these people, but another week and I resigned . . . Just like that."

He presented several reasons. He was piqued at his status; he was bored by his work in the Impressionist department, where there was no longer much movement of first-rate paintings to explore or exploit; he had grown sick of the auctioneering process. "Two days in the auction room brought back a flood of gruesome memories," he wrote to James Ivory in 1972. "The nervous anxiety of the bidder's face as he or she waits to see if she can afford to take some desirable thing home to play with. Like old men in nightclubs deciding whether they can really afford to pay that much for a whore. But things are so much better. You can sell them, touch 'em up at any time of the day, and they don't answer back."

But there may be an additional explanation for his resignation. Near the end of his life Bruce became fixated on one particular drama, little known at the time, which was being played out in the back-room between his two mentors, Wilson and Hewett.

Bruce always told friends he could have written a devastating biography of Wilson. "If he had lived into his eighties, he might have turned the saga of PCW into a *Viceroy of Ouidah*," says the Islamic art dealer David Sulzberger, in whose London and Paris homes he would write that book. "He said he had the goods on PCW. He didn't say it threateningly, but the goods existed and he had the low-down and thereby lay a tale." Sewell suspected that Wilson was directly behind Bruce's decision to leave. "I believe that relationship came to an end over a piece of outright dishonesty by Wilson in which the collaboration of Bruce was necessary."

In the late 1970s, Bruce went for a walk with James Fox to Downton

Castle in Shropshire and revealed how he had more or less hijacked its contents for Sotheby's. "I was a very fierce salesman in those days." To Jane Abdy, he boasted how he once saw a François II cabinet coming up for sale. "Bruce removed the pillars, bought it at the sale, and put the pillars back on afterwards." His capacity for subterfuge is hinted at in a letter written in 1960 to his former master at Old Hall, Edward Peregrine. The subject was a Fra Angelico panel, one of two owned by Peregrine. Bruce had sold the first successfully through Sotheby's, but he conducted the sale of the second panel privately, finding the dealer and charging commission. He wrote, "Sotheby's name must on no account be used in connection with St Anthony Abbot and it must appear that the decision to sell only one stems entirely from you." He made a further request. "Please would you not do anything without my being in the picture as it would not make things easy for me here. Enclosed is a photograph for you to have, but it is essential not to show it to *anyone* yet."

The letter is rare because, amazingly, no archives for Sotheby's exist prior to 1972. This is surprising in an institution whose activities play so central a role in late twentieth-century cultural history. It makes the task of establishing what went on difficult. A number of people have tried, among them Frank Herrmann in the official history of the firm. Four other attempts to write the story of Sotheby's were abandoned, one, by a friend of Wilson, the American art journalist Leo Lerman, in unsatisfactory circumstances. In 1964, Lerman arrived in London at Wilson's request and had use of a temporary office. "Once he began to stir the surface," says his partner, Grey Foy, "there were so many dicey aspects. He didn't want to know where the horse was buried. He withdrew." Lerman told Elizabeth that what he had learned was too litigious. "He could not write the true story because Wilson would not accept it." That may be why, when Lerman heard of Bruce's resignation, he wrote a letter of congratulation. "You must tell Bruce that I admire him enormously—his brave departure from the firm & his marvellous determination. Do, please, tell me in minute detail all about Bruce's departure, the Beast's reaction—everything . . . Tell me, tell me."

SIX MONTHS BEFORE he died, on 27 August 1988, Bruce focussed his rage against Wilson and Hewett. He claimed to have resigned from Sotheby's because he was being forced by them to sell the Pitt-Rivers collection "fraudulently" to America.

This was the tale he might have written, in Cary Welch's words "a nasty novel to undo the wretched crook of the 'ahtworld' ".

The deal involving the Pitt-Rivers museum in Farnham is labyrinthine and mired in secrecy. The truth of its dispersal stays out of reach, spread around the world with the contents of a miraculous collection. The story involves the museum, the tight circle of gentlemanly rogues of which Bruce had become a part, and the descendants of a Victorian nutter, Lieutenant-General Augustus Henry Lane Fox Pitt-Rivers.

Pitt-Rivers is respected as the father of modern archaeology. He established a methodology, insisted on accurate records and brought to his find-spots the same scientific analysis as when examining the 477 men and officers of the 2nd Royal Surrey Militia: "all the men were measured naked, except the officers". A cold man, prone to violence, he once slashed his daughter's face with a riding crop. Unmoved when she was killed by lightning on her honeymoon, he reserved his emotions for Egyptian boomerangs, Benin bronzes and the scale models of his digs. He spent his fortune on two ethnographic collections. The most famous he endowed to the University of Oxford as a teaching museum. From 1881, he housed some of his most treasured pieces in a private museum near his Dorset home. Bruce had been on his way to this museum with Digby-Jones when he suffered his nervous collapse.

The Farnham collection, housed in a converted farmhouse school for gypsies, was varied and remarkable. Intended for pottery, locks and keys, it grew to embrace ethnographic works from West Africa and the Pacific. Outstanding were the contents of Room Nine: 240 works of art from Benin retrieved as bounty by British troops during an expedition in February 1897.

The bronze plaques, heads and figures ranged from the sixteenth to the nineteenth century. The rituals behind them would find an outlet in *The Viceroy of Ouidah*. For the present, these Benin bronzes, the largest collection in private hands, were the nub of Bruce's quarrel with Sotheby's.

By the time he came to know the museum, ownership of the collection had passed to the General's grandson, an ethnologist of Fascist sensibilities who had worked in the South Seas. Captain George Pitt-Rivers possessed the best command of invective of anyone Bruce had met and was, of all the collectors he dealt with, the oddest. Interned in Brixton in 1940 for his political beliefs, Captain George was a convinced Mosleyite who disciplined his son Julian—"because I'd fought on the wrong side in the war, i.e. against Hitler." He is said to have cut out arrows in his cornfields to guide Goering's Luftwaffe and everything in his house at Hinton St Mary was German, including his car and his dog. His sexual habits were mysterious, but a nurse with whom he ran off to Genoa reported them as "rather terrifying". He was, on the other hand, passionately anti-homosexual. When his eldest son Michael was imprisoned for the offence in 1952, he disowned him, explaining to everyone it was the doing of that Jew Churchill. Of Maidstone prison, Michael says: "I had an extraordinary prison life because I was used to lunatic associations. It was just like going home."

In 1959, seeking an expert to reorganise the Farnham museum, Captain George had approached Hewett, Bruce's overlord in Antiquities. "I knew a lot about Benin," said Hewett. "I went down, took stuff out of cases and correctly labelled it." Hewett and his partner Sandy Martin sometimes visited once a week. Often they took Bruce. What began in innocence, removing valuable Benin masks and heads from damp cases and making an inventory, by degrees became something else.

In 1927, Captain George had reached an important agreement with the Inland Revenue: death duties would be exempted so long as the Farnham museum remained intact. By the 1960s, the museum was in a terrible mess and no longer open to the public (although accessible by appointment until 1966). The total takings, claimed Captain George, barely covered the cost of the heating. Defeated, he offered the museum to the nation. "They wanted a capital endowment of £600,000, and for him to have nothing to do with it," says his third son, Anthony. "The one time he tried to do something good, he was rebuffed."

"Then George got a little more cranky," said Hewett. "His income was £70,000 a year and he spent £75,000. He started to get keen to sell and he turned to me, a dealer in Bond Street."

The acts committed were not illegal since the museum was private—but under the terms of the 1927 agreement the collection had to be kept intact. Clear beyond doubt is that a lot of people made money from the break-up of the Pitt-Rivers collection.

What was sold, and to whom, is impossible to trace. One reason was the mysterious disappearance of the catalogue, a meticulous and encyclopaedic copy with watercolour drawings that listed all accessions made between 1881 and 1900. Captain George, travelling across Paris or Vienna, inadvertently left it in a taxi. Thereafter it was impossible for the Inland Revenue to point a finger.

Captain George's second son was Julian Pitt-Rivers, an anthropologist who worked in Iraq with Seton Lloyd. He was in no doubt that something fishy was going on. "When I was still on speaking terms with my father, I went to see what was in the museum, in particular a small white ivory Benin head which I had liked. At last, I discovered the head hung unnecessarily high up over a doorway so it could not be seen from close to. *I understood at once it was a copy.* I then realised Stella, my father's common-law wife, was selling off bits of the museum."

Stella Howson-Clive was the daughter of a Midlands industrialist. She was a large, striking figure with a wicked sense of humour and a streak of white through her dyed black hair. "She met my father in the Ritz, having tea," says Anthony, "and they discovered both had been in prison during the war." They never married. Stella changed her name by deed-poll to Pitt-Rivers. George being famously mean and Stella being on the contrary seriously extravagant, she frequently needed to replenish her funds. Directed by friends in the art world, she set her sights on the Farnham museum.

Captain George, through Hewett, discreetly sold several items. When he fell ill, Stella picked up the flame with a steadier passion. Needing money to subsidize "Stelladoux", her house in France, and her French lover, a conman from Marseille called Raoul Maumen, she made of the museum at Farnham her milch-cow. By the mid-1960s rumour was rich. Locals talked of lorries arriving at the museum late at night. Duplicates of the objects sold were arranged through Hewett so that she could pretend the originals were still there. Hewett's partner, Sandy Martin, confirms that Putzel Hunt (Hewett's third partner, based in Ireland) had a Benin mask copied at this time.

Captain George died in June 1966. He had secretly agreed before his death to sell Stella the museum. No one in the family, not one of his three sons, knew about this arrangement. "I asked Lord Goodman to bring a law suit, to find out what had happened," says Michael. "But it had been so cunningly done, it was practically impossible to find out. Goodman said to me, 'I don't know how much you've got to spend on this case, but if you want to take it to its logical conclusion, it will cost you a million pounds, and you may not win'." Michael decided not to pursue the case. By then, it was too late. Immediately after Captain George's death, Stella left for France to join her lover, while at Farnham it was discovered that in effect a clearance sale had taken place. Apart from some potsherds and British antiquities, the major treasures had been scattered to dealers and private collectors in New York, Switzerland, France and Germany. "Naïve as my father was, he did not think Stella was a great white hope," says Anthony, "but he cannot have imagined how quickly the snouts would be in the trough."

UNDER THE TERMS by which she was able to buy the museum, Stella had been required to find between £50,000–80,000. (The most modest estimate calculates the museum to have been worth five times this figure.) Kenelm Digby-Jones had known George from the 1950s, when he was at the Courtauld. He was also a friend of Stella. He became her adviser. Aware of Peter Wilson's predilection for special terms from the days when he worked as his assistant, Digby-Jones contacted his former boss. Wilson was prepared to advance Stella a loan on the understanding that she would sell the collection at Sotheby's when George died. The Sotheby's chairman perceived the Pitt-Rivers collection as a honey pot that he could syphon into Sotheby's to boost sales. He advised George to set up a trust with Stella as sole beneficiary.

One does not know what stories Bruce was told, or how far he was in cahoots with Wilson. But he must have known Wilson and Hewett were up to *something*. One weekend he drove down with Elizabeth. The museum was locked. They were let in by a Peruvian butler. Inside, Elizabeth remembers glass cases containing astonishing "lur" bronze horns and ivory leopards. Wilson and Hewett were there too. "They all said: 'You haven't seen this, you don't know anything about it, you're not to tell anyone.' It would have cost Bruce his job if he'd said anything."

Bruce was presumably brought in as Head of Antiquities on the understanding that he would take charge of what would have been a stunning catalogue and public sale. "The party line to him was: 'Stella's going to inherit: what do you think these things are worth?'" says Elizabeth. His function in the affair was to identify the plums and put a valuation on the individual pieces.

But the sale did not come to pass. Stella suddenly turned everything on its head. To Digby-Jones, she announced a change of mind. There was to be no public auction; she would, of course, repay to Sotheby's the loan that had enabled her to buy the museum. "Nobody loved me then," says Digby-Jones.

Stella had decided to sell privately, piecemeal and secretly, to buyers outside Britain. Why had she changed her mind? Julian Pitt-Rivers has no doubt. The breaking up of such a unique if little known collection, not to mention the covenant, would have caused a public outcry and the Government might have refused an export licence.

Furthermore, Stella wanted her money abroad. She needed to keep "Stelladoux" going. After George's death, she lived there with Maumen, whom she married. "She married him to become a French citizen," says Julian, "and therefore acquire the rights to export the loot into France and Switzerland."

THE BEST PIECES from the Pitt-Rivers museum did not go to Sotheby's, but the people who helped Stella to sell the major plaques, heads and early period musketeers were Peter Wilson and John Hewett.*

In 1966, Elizabeth wrote about Hewett to Gertrude: "Bruce used to trust him till he started finding out a few things recently." As adviser to the Antiquities department, Hewett had access to confidential information. He could get hold of a photograph before the catalogue came out and line up a private client. The Antiquities auction records for this period reveal that Hewett, the Sotheby's expert, bought, on average, 10 per cent of each Sotheby's sale. On 3 July 1961, for instance, he bid successfully under three different names: Hewett, Hewitt, Hewitt K. J. His presence was warmly felt at important auctions. On the opening day of the Ernest Brummer sale, catalogued by Bruce and Elizabeth, Hewett bought 29 out of the 101 lots. There was nothing illegal about this: as adviser to collectors and museums, he had every right to buy the whole sale if he had instructions. But he used his privileged position.

Hewett and Wilson were very close. "That gang," says Richard Falkiner, Bruce's opposite number at Christie's, "would open Machiavelli's eyes." Wilson was Hewett's best man; they lived cheek by jowl in Kent; and they played both sides of the street. One of their tricks involved fake telephone bids. For the Goldschmidt sale in 1958, Wilson arranged a telephone line to connect Hewett's office with the auction room. "They were indirectly forcing up prices," says Sandy Martin. "They were bidding on behalf of Sotheby's to push clients up."

Jack Hunt and his wife Putzel were two other members of the circle. Because of their political affiliations—conservative in the tradition of

---

* A quantity was sold at Sotheby's. Between 1965 and 1977, items continued to trickle through the Antiquities department. Marcus Linell remembers paying Stella in cash—which she carried out in a suitcase. The pieces were on the whole average.

Captain George—the couple had to live in Ireland, where they dealt in medieval works of art. Wilson, Hewett and the Hunts formed an association with Wilson, not able to buy for himself, conducting, through Hewett, lucrative deals outside Sotheby's.

The Pitt-Rivers collection became such a deal.

To begin with, Wilson was furious to have lost the sale for Sotheby's. When he understood the reason, he said admiringly: "My God, what a piece of footwork!" But there would be no question of Wilson ever leaving the scene. "Peter Wilson did not like to lose," wrote Robert Lacey. He was there at the trough. "I *know* Peter Wilson was involved in liquidating the Benin collection," says Julian Pitt-Rivers.

The best pieces were diverted out of England through an offshore company based in Ireland, and reshipped to the continent to avoid exchange control. Hewett knew the dealers and collectors who would buy. "I sold pieces to the US, to France, everywhere save in England," he admitted shortly before his death. One of his clients was George Ortiz. One evening Hewett invited Ortiz to dine at his flat in Seymour Walk. Before dinner they drank two glasses of claret. Then Hewett said: "Oh, by the way, I know you don't buy this stuff. I want to show you something." Hewett went upstairs, brought back an object which he plonked on the radiator shelf. Stella, he explained, was selling one or two things from the Pitt-Rivers collection. Ortiz found himself staring at the great Yoruba cult head, known as "Bulgy Eyes". Ortiz, as Hewett expected, said: "I must have it." Ortiz was required to pay in Swiss francs, into a Swiss bank account.

"It was all private deals," says Elizabeth. "And it went on for years."

FOR AS LONG as Bruce supposed the Pitt-Rivers collection was promised to Sotheby's, he might have found a means to square his conscience. "Bruce wasn't particularly devious himself about commercial activity," says David Nash, "but he did admire it in other people. He probably felt this was some cunning ruse."

Or if only minor pieces were being sold privately. But this was not the case. The best pieces were leaving the country, going to people he knew anyway. "Bruce was very angry at John Hewett because he had the plums," says Martin.

George Ortiz, who bought two Benin bronzes from the collection, was aware of Bruce's distress. "He did talk to me. He thought they'd misbehaved horribly." Bruce's anger struck Ortiz as an emotional thing, as if he was implicated but not getting anything out of it himself. Ortiz, after considering the evidence, gives this explanation: "Either Bruce *was* involved and didn't feel he had got a fair share; or he felt he shouldn't have been involved and regretted it—'I will leap out of the picture.' Or he felt he had been abused."

The first possibility was discounted by Hewett himself. If Bruce could have profited from the Pitt-Rivers museum, said Hewett, he would have done so. But he did not. The one item Stella gave Bruce, a Roman bronze doorknocker, turned out to be a fake.

Lucie-Smith opts for the second explanation. Flanked by Wilson, Hewett and the Hunts, Bruce cut the figure of a child trailing after adults. "Bruce fantasised about being a dealer, but he was out of his depth and increasingly panicky. It probably dawned on him very gradually what was happening, and it probably disillusioned him more to find Hewett up to his neck than to discover the same thing about Wilson. Moral revulsion might have played a part, but he also suspected that he might finish up as the fall guy. And, of course, he was riveted by the whole thing as 'story': the errant Stella and her conman; the notion of being on the inside; knowing what other people didn't; hinting and not telling."

A creeping self-disgust is also likely. The Pitt-Rivers collection was, in its way, a larger version of his grandmother's cabinet. Had Bruce, because of his "eye", been brought in sneakily to disperse what he responded to most?

This might explain why, in one of the last fragments he wrote, Bruce launched into Wilson. In 1988, while assembling stories and pieces of journalism for *What Am I Doing Here*, he composed "The Duke of M" knowing that his death was imminent. The portrait is a rare sample of Bruce being ungenerous in print and it reads as if all his sorrows could be laid at Wilson's door. In the piece, the chairman of Sotheby's is asked by a disgusted Spanish grandee to leave the house in the middle of lunch after Wilson starts to tell his host how much his Guardis would fetch at auction. "A most disagreeable experience," the grandee tells Bruce—"after *our* agreeable experience."

GEORGE PITT-RIVERS died on 16 June 1966. In the same month, a dinner was held in Paddington. It was a beautiful, warm evening. Ward Landrigan, head of jewellery at Parke-Bernet, had found a place to sit in the garden when Wilson joined him. All of a sudden Bruce hove into view. His face was flushed. He looked upset. Bruce accosted Wilson and angry words were exchanged. "I don't want to be part of this," Bruce said. "I don't care about *it* or *you*." It wasn't just a business discussion, says Landrigan, who listened appalled. Wilson, spluttering and embarrassed, backed off. Bruce left the party.

This was the backdrop against which Bruce resigned. But by then the die was already cast. To the surprise, even irritation, of the Sotheby's board, he announced his intention, at the age of 26, to study archaeology at Edinburgh.

XVI.

༄

The Archaeologist

> *I met him in a television studio in England. We*
> *looked at the chit-chatting intellectuals around us*
> *and he whispered in my ear: "Did you ever get a*
> *degree at university? No? Thank God, neither did I."*
> —BREYTEN BREYTENBACH

"PLEASE DON'T HAVE a fit," Bruce wrote to Gertrude on 24 June 1966, informing her of his departure from the firm. "We'll survive, and before you know it Lib will be turned into a SCHOLAR! I'll write soon: I'm sorry it's all so precipitate, but it's no use chewing it over and over once one's decided to take the plunge."

His mother-in-law needed delicate handling. She had bought their house in Gloucestershire. Furthermore, she had lent Bruce the money to buy his director's share. "I am afraid that the art world, at least the world of art dealing, is coming to a grinding halt," he wrote a fortnight later. "It is no longer the reasonably civilised occupation it was five years ago."

Bruce had been contemplating the idea of university for at least four years. Like many autodidacts he did not think he knew enough: "the worst of all tragedies is the plight of the semi-educated," is a phrase which recurs in his notebooks. He regretted not having taken up his place at Oxford and envied the academic foundations to the careers of Cary Welch and Robert Erskine. The idea had presented itself again during his visit to Leningrad in December 1965.

At the Hermitage, Bruce stood fascinated before the embalmed body of a Pazyryk chief buried in a soaring headdress. His skin was covered in ancestral tattoos of "fantastic beasts". There were horned and winged monsters and on his right shin a creature like a catfish. The finest tattoos had patterned his chest, the curator told Bruce, but his stomach had decomposed not long after the archaeologist Rudenko brought back the body to Leningrad in 1933: the state morgue had refused to store the body without a birth certificate.

He was a nomad recovered from a tomb of ice on the Mongolian border. "He was deep-frozen in perfect condition in that first winter more than 2,000 years ago. His body lay in a carved coffin, stuffed with hemp . . . his concubine was laid beside him."

The image of this Altai herdsman, his protective tattoos and his tent of thick white felt "with springy cut-out appliqués like a Matisse collage" branded itself on Bruce's imagination. On his return to London, he borrowed Rudenko's report from Robert Erskine, once an archaeologist at Cambridge. Without telling Erskine, he began to look into archaeology degrees. He let Cary Welch in on his plan, who was discouraging. "I know, from experience, that you are too alive for the academic world. People like us in fact make the best scholars because we have ideas and earthiness. But the universities are dominated entirely by the cerebral types . . . In short, DON'T sign yourself up for dreary years of academia. Leave that stuff to the eunuchs." But he did agree to write on Bruce's behalf to Stuart Piggott, Professor of Prehistoric Archaeology at Edinburgh. Bruce's meeting with Piggott at the end of May decided him, as he wrote to Gertrude. "He has hardly any students to start with and will be able to take the whole thing tutorially, and he is also one of the finest archaeologists in the world." Since the subject was so vast and complex there was no time to be lost. "I took a very rapid decision, and it is arranged that I start in October."

On 14 July, Welch wrote in a different vein to Bruce: "Edith promises to send a loverly letter to her cousin Gertrude all about how sound archaeology is, what a fine man St P is, what a grand party Preuss is, and zo on."

BRUCE NEEDED GURUS. Piggott, one of the world's experts in neolithic and bronze age studies, would now replace Wilson as his mentor.

Bruce had known of Piggott already at Marlborough, of course, when he excavated West Kennet Long Barrow. His idiosyncratic career appealed to Bruce, who had not impressed anyone the last time he had written an essay. A published poet, the 56-year-old Piggott described his academic background as "very unedifying", twice having failed his school certificate in mathematics. He went up to Oxford when he was 36 and became a professor without ever having taken a degree. In 1946, his breakfast was interrupted by a telegram from his wife: "You have been offered the Abercromby Chair in Archaeology at the University of Edinburgh, God help us."

Piggott's mind was open and enquiring. He was as interested in the history of ideas as in British neolithic pottery. He wrote his thesis on the seventeenth-century antiquary William Stukeley and was as happy in bronze age Wessex, or among the Scythians, as in the pre-history of India, where he had spent three wartime years in aerial intelligence. His excavation reports were clean and precise. He refused to reduce archaeology to graphs. The job of the archaeologist was to tell a story. "What we like to call our thinking may be as much conditioned by the fears and prejudices of the early mammoth-hunters as by the speculative thought of the Greeks." Eventually, he would tire of archaeology, because it could not follow his flights of fancy. At the time of his meeting with Bruce, he had just published *Ancient Europe* (which included an illustration of his friend Cary Welch's Siberian plaque), a survey of the archaeological evidence "from the beginnings of agriculture to classical Antiquity".

Blue-eyed, with a long nose and slightly overweight, Piggott was popular with his students. But he was a difficult person to know and his humour concealed a depressive nature. This melancholy streak, exacerbated by arthritis, came out in his poetry and, most graphically, in a photograph of himself lying at the bottom of a prehistoric burial site he had excavated, curled up in imitation of a dead body and clutching a gin bottle.

He contributed a column to the *Scotsman* under the by-line "Gastronome" and treated visitors to his top-floor flat in the New Town to the same dishes as he served his readers. (A Piggott staple was Kaspin, consisting of jelly consommé, curried mayonnaise and Danish lumpfish.) His friends included Penelope Betjeman, John Piper and Agatha Christie whom he described as "great fun and very shy". The same might have been said of Piggott. His wife Peggy had left him during the 1950s, ending up with T. E. Lawrence's brother. Something lay unresolved from their marriage. Emotionally restrained, he was flirtatious with ideas and relished strong intellectual relationships.

On 15 July, he met Bruce for lunch at 46 King Street. Piggott recorded the meal in his diary: "*oeufs mollets en gelée*, cold salmon trout with mayonnaise, tomato and cucumber salad, strawberries *arrosées* in brandy & with cream; cheese; bottle of chilled Sancerre. Bruce C. very good value and should be a pleasure to teach."

"SOTHEBY'S IS HAVING fits, of course," Elizabeth wrote to Gertrude. She had left Wilson's employ soon after her engagement was announced, but Bruce's parting was not so amicable. Lerman was eager for details. "Is it verity that Richard Came called your Bruce a *cad*?" Bruce had also received from Graham Llewellyn a patronising letter insisting Sotheby's keep his pension. "With each day that passes, the fatter their arses," Bruce wrote to Elizabeth.

Wilson kept Bruce to the bitter end, not releasing him until 5 p.m. on the day before Edinburgh required him to register. He had to take the sleeper to Edinburgh. He travelled in high spirits to the land of his Bruce ancestors. Soon after his arrival, he sent a postcard to his Marlborough study-companion, Michael Cannon: "Change is the only thing worth living for. Never sit your life out at a desk. Ulcers and heart condition follow."

BRUCE HAD AN Indiana Jones notion of archaeology. "I saw myself as an archaeological explorer." He was fired by the examples of André Malraux; of Alexandre Dumas, whom Garibaldi had appointed director of excavations; of Prosper Mérimée who had worked as an enthusiastic Inspector of Monuments. But his attention wandered when confronted by the detailed work. "Bruce had no patience at all, he wanted to find everything immediately," says Erskine, who had studied under Piggott. "He went into archaeology thinking he'd be the next Howard Carter, walking into a room of Egyptian antiquities—and not spending his time with his bottom in the air, in the mud, groping around some sodden Mesolithic site. When he had to face academic discipline and piles of old pots, which actually tell you about a culture, he found it incredibly boring." Bruce once told Erskine: "I've always been interested in the marvellous."

BRUCE USUALLY SAT in the front row of the lecture room at 19 George Square. The notes from his first week hint that all is not well. Megalithic burial sites in the vicinity of Edinburgh, he finds "*Totally bewildering!* Piles of stones everywhere." He recorded the lecturer's definition of archaeology: a series of methods to gather information about the past which depended on the analysis of results obtained by those methods. And next to it, underlining the word three times, Bruce wrote: *"Terrifying."*

Sitting behind him would be 40 undergraduates, seven or eight years younger. Rosanna Ross came directly from a convent school in Edinburgh. "We were sitting in our anoraks and there was this beautiful man in the front row who turned round and amiably scrutinised us." Rosanna had never travelled further than Dorset: Bruce had twice been to Afghanistan. He had worked or moved in circles his fellow students could not fathom. He dressed in bright red corduroys and delivered his essays typewritten.

There was a feeling among the students that Bruce was engaged in exclusive activity with the professor and this provoked jealousy. He was very much the apple of Piggott's eye. Some of the students assumed he was a faculty member because he came in through the door reserved for lecturers.

He provoked people inside the class and out. All students were required to spend four weeks of the year on an approved excavation. In March 1967, Bruce joined an army of diggers at the late neolithic ceremonial complex of Llandegai near Bangor, searching for changes in soil colours. It was a wet, messy site and the weather bitterly cold and snowy. Something Bruce said or did annoyed one of the workmen, a large, red-faced Liverpudlian. "He held Bruce down, his hands on his lapel, beating his head against an upturned wheelbarrow," says Alex Tuckwell. "For a second we froze. But Bruce was unruffled: 'Oh, I say, don't be so childish'." The site supervisor calmed the man down and Bruce shrugged off the incident, but the matter did not end there. Richard Langhorne observed through his field glasses a number of workmen turning a portable field toilet upside down, with Bruce inside.

FOUR WEEKS INTO his first term, Bruce found a letter at the Archaeology Department addressed to him in pink and blue inks. It was from a strange cousin of Emma Tennant: the aesthete, Stephen. "I'm dedicating a poem to you in my new volume. It's called 'The Supreme Vision'." Bruce wrote to Elizabeth: "One can only pray to God it will never be published."

To Bruce's embarrassment, Tennant's decorative envelopes continued to arrive throughout his first term at George Square. "Edinburgh must be

very handsome in sombre autumn . . . you do sound studious. What period are you studying? Boadicea? Camelot? Constantine? Bion?" The letters stopped abruptly when Bruce thought to advise Tennant that he was
married.

He attended fifteen lectures a week: on the archaeology of the British
Isles, European history, Sanskrit. In addition, he was expected to write
four essays a term. The libraries stayed open until 7 p.m. and he worked
until they closed. He was not going to be beaten by younger students. In
July 1967, he received the Wardrop Prize "for the best first year's work".

Bruce was fortunate to have as lecturer in his first year the Dark Age
specialist Charles Thomas. It was Thomas who first excited Bruce's interest in the Welsh settlement in Patagonia. He set essays on the pre-history
of bicycles, scissors and trousers and encouraged Bruce to understand how
far wrong we can go by making inferences out of material objects. In his
first essay for Thomas, Bruce was asked to imagine himself an archaeologist of the year 6000 AD who had been dropped on a deserted St Giles.
What was the nature and function of the building? From the banners and
plaques dedicated to Highland regiments, Bruce deduced the grey stone
High Kirk of Scotland to be rampantly military. The essay does not survive, but among his notes for it is a pencil sketch of a bronze plaque.
Bruce's drawing shows a sick-looking man lying on a couch with a feather
in his hand: Saint-Gaudens's relief of Robert Louis Stevenson.

Eight years later Chatwin wrote a review of James Pope-Hennessy's biography of Stevenson. It is evident to anyone who knows the life that the
two share many characteristics: the "dusty knapsack", the penetrating eyes
"brimful of banter", the "captivating egotism", the frequent glancing at
their own reflections. Like Stevenson, Bruce had developed an infection
which seemed to send him blind. They had, it seems, a similar manic
laugh: Stevenson's uncontrollable laughter could only be stopped by
someone bending his fingers back. And they had the same effect on an audience. Exposed to the radiation of Stevenson's character, wrote Pope-
Hennessy, people remained captive forever after.

Stevenson's life in Edinburgh especially intrigued Bruce. This "gaunt
northern capital," he wrote, was the key to understanding the Scot. "Edinburgh is a place of absolute contrast and paradox . . . In no other city in
the British Isles do you feel to the same extent the oppressive weight of the
past. Mary Queen of Scots and John Knox are a presence. The dead seem
more alive than the living. There is a claustrophobic, coffin-like atmosphere that makes Glasgow, in comparison, seem a paradise of life and
laughter. Moderate health is virtually unknown. Either people enjoy ro-

bust appetites, or they are ailing and require protection. Heady passions simmer below the surface. In winter the city slumbers all week in blue-faced rectitude, only to explode on Saturday evenings in an orgy of drink and violence and sex. In some quarters the pious must pick their way to church along pavements spattered with vomit and broken bottles."

IN NOVEMBER 1966, Bruce bought a three-year lease for £7 a week on a flat on the Royal Mile. 234 Canongate was a nasty building with a good address, developed by the Edinburgh Corporation into apartments. Flat 6, up three flights of concrete steps, had views through small square windows over the gorse-grown Salisbury Crags of Arthur's Seat. This was to be the Chatwins' Edinburgh base for two years.

Bruce ordered wall-to-wall coconut matting and filled the flat with furniture from Salvation Army shops. He and Elizabeth shared one of the two bedrooms. He invited another first year student, Rowan Watson, as a lodger to share the costs.

Watson was one of few students Bruce befriended. He had travelled and had spent nine months excavating Uthong, a seventh-century site in Thailand. Bruce had known his father—head of Chinese antiquities at the British Museum—and was aware that Watson was not enjoying himself at his digs.

Watson lasted only a year at Edinburgh, finding the academic diet not concentrated enough, but he admired his landlord. "Bruce was like an older brother to me in a bloody awful year of my life." Bruce lent Watson his dinner jacket for the Freshers' Ball and cooked Mediterranean dishes with couscous and olive oil. Bruce's dress impressed Watson as much as his cooking. He strode into lectures in jeans and ankle-high desert boots, and at the flat wore a nineteenth-century Dayak hat to study in. But his Sudanese jellaba provoked comment. "I remember coming back with some rather shaky students. They were amazed to see someone in a nightdress."

Bruce, who could cope with exotic places, could not cope with Edinburgh. At first he worked too hard to notice, but he came to agree with Stevenson that it possessed "one of the vilest climates under heaven". In winter, the city fell dark at 3.30 p.m. and a gloom settled on the flat-fronted tenement buildings. For Stevenson, as for Chatwin, "there could scarcely be found a more unhomely and harassing place of residence".

Bruce's confirmation of a place at university had arrived on the same day as the contract for Holwell Farm was signed. Had he received his acceptance a few days earlier, Elizabeth believes, they would have redirected their efforts and bought a house in Edinburgh. "Now we have to cope with the house & a flat in Edinburgh and a million things," she wrote to Gertrude.

They had taken possession of Holwell Farm in the first week of May, renting a small lodge across the fields at Ozleworth Park while the house was redecorated. They spent three days scything nettles. Bruce hired a gardener and an architect. "I'm going to make that barn into a playroom," Elizabeth told her neighbour, Brenda Tomlinson. She wrote to Gertrude: "Allowing for the worst, the architect said not to get upset if the house was only ready in the middle of November!!" It would be more than a year before they moved in.

Elizabeth bore the brunt of this divided life. She stayed behind to prod the workmen during most of Bruce's first term. "Everything takes FOREVER in that part of the world." Five weeks to install a stove; the same time to connect the telephone in the lodge.

The valley's bitter climate was another concern. From November until February a hoar frost settled on the house. "It looked as if it had a spell on it." As winter set in, she felt beleaguered. She wrote to Gertrude on 2 November, "I'm sitting here feeling more or less like an icicle." Jackdaws rattled in the chimney and armies of flies came in from the cold. "They get into everywhere including the oven and I find them buzzing in my handbag all the time." Sending Bruce's love, she warned Gertrude that he would never be a reliable correspondent: "He hardly even writes to me . . . and then only scribbles notes giving orders."

"I still think that the 9 in. tiles would be nice in the dining room . . . They might look very well laid diagonally, but I'm not sure about that. I think you can get Dutch Delft copies with the little figures in the middle." Three days later he worried about the pink exterior. "I also want to see about getting some crushed terracotta for painting the house. I think the Rokeby colour needs toning down a bit for Glos. Would the Victorian curtains be nice in the back bedroom?"

ELIZABETH SUPPORTED BRUCE in his decision, but she had expected a different life. During his first year, she shuttled back and forth from Ozleworth to Edinburgh in a grey Citroën grocer's van which, like her, protested at the journey. "I've never hated a place like Edinburgh."

The Canongate flat was "as bad as could be" . . . Pink panels decorated the outside of the building, which was entirely inhabited by English tenants. Inside, the rooms were ill proportioned and cheaply built, with undercoat only on the woodwork and doors that would not shut. A coke-fire back boiler took four hours to warm water for a bath. There were no hooks, shelves or rails. The toilet leaked.

The city was in bleak contrast to swinging London. She found the people mean-spirited and primitive, with temperance in full blast. When she asked for salad in the North British Hotel, the waitress asked: "How do you do it?" The Italian in the local vegetable shop would break a £5 note for a penny. Edinburgh society was strait-laced, its boundaries tightly drawn and invitations limited to high tea. "Social life was women in tweed suits and terrible hats, with no style or life or movement," says Elizabeth. "In winter no one entertained, simply hibernated."

The days were short, the weather cold with strong gales. "At one point there were gusts of up to 90 or 95 [m.p.h.] and sometimes you could hardly walk," she wrote in March. "It's quite exciting for a while, but not for weeks and weeks."

To occupy herself she started learning Russian. But as Piggott noted in his diary: "Elizabeth is angry and sulky here and . . . hates the whole business of his coming up as an undergraduate."

BRUCE OFTEN VISITED Piggott in King Street when Elizabeth returned to Ozleworth. 20 December: "Bruce to dinner, smoked salmon and venison, *ananas au cognac* . . . I became bored as he stayed until 1.30 a.m. oh my God. I suppose he was enjoying himself, but oh when will the young realise that three hours is the ideal time to come and stay for a meal?" In February, Bruce invited himself to dinner again, "revealing all in the same breath and too obviously that Elizabeth had gone back to their Gloucestershire house and sounding rather gay and relieved about it." Piggott wondered why he had never been asked to the Canongate. "All very odd." He wondered how long the marriage would last. He also wondered whether Bruce "has homo. tendencies". Penelope Betjeman, a mutual friend who talked to him during a ride in her pony trap, had divulged "much entertaining gossip on, *inter alia*, Bruce: certainly a 'flaming homo' says P."

THE SEXUAL CLIMATE in Edinburgh was no more tolerable than the weather. Bruce cut out from the *Times* and kept in his notebook an article reciting the response of the Church of Scotland to the 1967 Act implementing the Wolfenden Report. Homosexuality was a "grave and growing evil which had incurred God's wrath in the past and would do so again".

It was at this time, in May 1967, that Bruce renewed his acquaintance with Andrew Batey, a young architectural student from California. They had met aboard the *Statenden*, on Bruce's way to be married, when a dextrous bartender mixed them pousse-cafés and cocktails of coloured layers. Bruce's experience moved him to propose in 1972 "the Batey story" to the director James Ivory. "My feelings are now totally numb and dispassionate. Quite good to start off on the *France* or some such liner with the seduction—for the hell of it—by a young, ravishing American of an older less ravishing Englishman (young don?) on his way to get married and the subsequent chaos."

Ivory agreed that it was "potentially wonderful material for a film".

Bruce was "very, very keen" on the willowy Batey, says Elizabeth. Their encounter on the ocean may explain why, in 1979, he told Bill Katz that while still on board the *Statenden* he had had second thoughts about going through with the marriage. He had sought out his father, who is supposed to have said: "If you think your mother and I have come all this way for nothing, you are sadly mistaken."

Bruce's father did not recollect any change of heart. Nor could he recall Batey. But on the ship's arrival in New York, Elizabeth's former flatmate Gillian Walker threw a cocktail party for Bruce in the Dakota building, and she remembered him. "Bruce had in tow some man he'd found on the boat. Even at the time it seemed a funny thing to do. He spent the night on some cushions."

When Gillian visited Elizabeth in Edinburgh two years later she was surprised to find Batey. "I remember going with Elizabeth for a walk and asking if she was happy and she said: 'Yes'. She clearly didn't want to talk about it, and I remember being quite startled and then thinking: 'That's Elizabeth.' She makes a commitment to something and it's private and is not judgmental. At some level she had accepted Bruce loved her and he had this relationship with her that was very important to both of them, and he had these gay affairs."

Batey visited Bruce in Edinburgh and Ozleworth, and pestered him to go travelling. "My friend Mr Batey wants to come and look at the architecture of Alvar Aalto," Bruce wrote to Welch, "but I'm not sure if it's a good idea as he's wildly unreliable and unpunctual, and as I have work to do, it would be a distraction."

On 15 July, having barely settled in with Elizabeth at Holwell Farm, Bruce set off for Central Europe with Batey. He kept Elizabeth apprised. In Brussels, they failed to get into the Stocklett Collection. "Then we went to Aix and looked at Charlemagne and the *Schatzkammer* where there are some objects that nearly made me die, especially the engraving on the back of the cross of Lothan and Richard of Cornwall's sceptre. We separated at Cologne after looking over that monstrous cathedral." He planned to meet Batey again in Bulgaria once he had completed an excavation near Prague.

On 17 August, Elizabeth wrote to Gertrude: "Andrew left on Tuesday to join him in Sofia and they were then going to Turkey together." This leg of their trip was not a success. To Bruce's irritation, Batey was so beguiled by Chatwin's contacts in Istanbul that he stayed put. "My Turkish friends almost ate him up entirely," Bruce wrote to Gertrude, "and although he was supposed to come to the wilds of Anatolia with me he never left the city for five weeks. I warned him in advance that it would happen if he weren't firm-minded and it did."

Batey hovered about the Chatwins until his marriage to a childhood sweetheart in October 1968. By then relations had soured. Batey was suspected of going off with too many things. (From Bruce he absconded with a blue faience Egyptian gaming piece; from Erskine, with a silver coin of Augustus that Batey gave to the doorman of the Ritz as a tip.) Batey's impulses were "all too clear" to Welch who described it to Bruce as "a case of his being extremely, deeply upset by his 'queer' tendencies, which make him love you. His preoccupation with your possessions results in his wanting souvenirs. Things to him are equatable with love (as usual). As he dare not in fact love you, he loves your stuff which he must have. This is a kind of fetishism."

PIGGOTT CHANGED HIS mind about Elizabeth after staying overnight at Ozleworth. "She was very welcoming and kind and good fun and it may all have been shyness." Bruce "ran around like a pleased dog". But all was not well.

February 5, 1968: "Bruce rang up and said he'd just bought some venison on impulse and would I come and eat it with him and Ruth if he could get hold of her." Ruth Tringham, a red-haired Marxist, was a research fellow back after a year in Russia, where she had been the first westerner to excavate in Moldavia. She had bought the Chatwins' Citroën van and remembered the negotiations principally for "this huge tension going on between them".

At the appointed hour Tringham and Piggott turned up, but, wrote Piggott, "Elizabeth had suddenly and unexpectedly returned and gone to bed (I suspect in anger rather than the alleged migraine) and so an unholy chill was in the air and though Bruce's cooking was marvellous I didn't stay late and I really felt embarrassed. Bruce of course in a state of nervous volubility. He was like a small boy who in his parents' absence has asked in some disreputable children he wasn't supposed to play with, and had raided the larder for them. Poor Bruce. And *so* odd."

MAGOUCHE FIELDING, AN older friend, once asked Bruce directly: "Why can't you give Elizabeth a baby?"

Bruce replied awkwardly: "It's very complicated."

They had married with the intention of soon starting a family. "I'd simply *love* to have a little boy by him," Elizabeth had written. It was one reason for buying Ozleworth: "It was a nice place to bring up children because it's so safe. We fully expected to have children, and talked about whether to have two or four." Bruce had told Gertrude that they would grow up in the Catholic faith. By the end of 1967, Gertrude and Margharita were showing impatience for the moment when Elizabeth would be busy with "family responsibilities".

Elizabeth had been married a year and a half when she decided to submit herself for tests. They proved inconclusive. She described the treatment as "sloppy and unprofessional". She never saw the same doctor twice, received no report. "It was in the dark days of not telling you anything." The clinic wanted to test Bruce, but Elizabeth refused on the grounds that he was in the middle of exams. "He was never tested. So both of us spent the rest of our lives thinking it was oneself rather than the other."

The subject was very occasionally brought up. "Bruce was depressed that he didn't have children. It was so difficult to discuss because he always thought it reflected on him. He probably had a low sperm count. I felt it was my fault, some hormonal imbalance. At least we didn't blame each other. We did talk a little bit about adoption. But he said an adopted child always knows it's not with its real mother. Neither of us were maternal or paternal enough to take on someone else's child."

There seems little doubt that Bruce had entered marriage wanting children. "*Life is empty without children,*" he wrote in his notebook, adding a tick. He was good with children, able to see the world through their eyes. "I remember him best one Christmas when he tap-danced on the bubble wrap, making a tremendous amount of noise," wrote Elizabeth's niece, Alice. "He was showing us all how to pop them the fastest." Without children he could remain the child, but he was sensitive about his childless state. In 1982, Melvyn Bragg interviewed him for *The South Bank Show* in a programme devoted to *On the Black Hill*. It struck Bragg that "childlessness, being at the end of the line, even sterility" was a big theme in the book. "Sterility is carrying asceticism a long way, isn't it?" Uncharacteristically, Bruce was flummoxed. "I must say, I don't know how to reply. Maybe you've got me."

Chatwin's novel of childless twins shows empathy with a barren relationship. "Time in its healing circle had wiped away the pain and the anger, the shame and the sterility." But references in his notebooks suggest he blamed himself. In the Niger in 1972 he wrote: "Nearly became a Catholic. Childlessness. Fault."

Bruce aestheticised his predicament, converting it into something rarefied and power-enhancing. Positive references to infertility run through his notebooks. "There is a distinct connection between brain esp. in the male and infertility." Another entry quotes Francis Bacon: "The Noblest workes and Foundations have proceeded from childlesse Men." To which Bruce adds: "Low fertility and rising intelligence. The position of the shamanic personality."

Infertility came to be connected in Bruce's mind with the position of the shaman. In 1967 Bruce gave Lucie-Smith a copy of Andreas Lommel's *Shamanism—The Beginning of Art*. The sterile shaman of West Africa exerted for Bruce a particular fascination. "He's a sorcerer," says a boy in a draft of *The Viceroy of Ouidah*. "He can't make babies so he eats them."

He also linked infertility to the notion of escape: "Examine the possibility of sterility with bird . . . shed feathers, beating against a cage, internal fights and pecking in solitary confinement." This sentiment was poignantly expressed in relation to himself in a paragraph of *In Patagonia*. Trudging the unused path from Harberton to Viamonte, Bruce comes face to face with a lone guanaco, an animal related to the llama.

"He was a single male, his coat all muddied and his front gashed with scars. He had been in a fight and lost. Now he also was a sterile wanderer."

XVII.

∽

A Season in Hell

> *Sound scholarship*
> *Is one piece of luggage*
> *Too heavy for me*
> *To carry*
> *I am in a hurry*
> *And I travel light*
>
> —BC, NOTEBOOKS, MAURITANIA 1970

ONE DAY IN MARCH 1967, Bruce heard on Elizabeth's radio the summons of the dolorous notes of the trumpet found in Tutankhamen's tomb. The ancient sound, not heard for thousands of years, filled the Canongate flat. "I'm afraid he is itching to go away somewhere difficult and exotic and the US doesn't count at all," wrote Elizabeth. As Bruce said of Stevenson: "Samoa was the logical extension of a life in Edinburgh." In the event, he went not to Samoa or Egypt but to Czechoslovakia. He considered Mongolia and Afghanistan, but then settled, for his summer's excavation, on Zavist, 40 kilometres south of Prague.

He reached the massive earthen fortifications on 20 July. His destination was a wooded Celtic hill fort directly overlooking the River Moldava. Also on the Zavist excavation was a 23-year-old Italian, "who is my new friend," he wrote to Elizabeth.

Maurizio Tosi was four years younger than Bruce, but a great deal more worldly. He had studied in Rome, had dug in Afghanistan, had met Che Guevara in Cuba and had been sent by the Italian communists to Auschwitz for intense training in anti-fascism. But "my communism was in a raging crisis," says Tosi, who shared a room with Bruce at Zavist. In contrast, Bruce's "interest in politics was *zero*". Tosi forgot his troubles in women, "the top thought in my life", and already had a girlfriend at the camp, with whom he would make love in the lunch breaks.

After months pent up with archaeological minutiae, Bruce delighted in uncircumscribed narrative. "There is every reason why I should dislike Maurizio, but somehow I do not," he wrote to Elizabeth. "He is over six and a half feet tall and indecently fat. Despite the solid nature of Bohemian food he needs to be refilled every half-hour. In July he was awarded a doctorate at Rome University. His thesis, calculated to make me hate him, was on the close of the Indus Valley Civilisation and the coming of the Aryans. He got it all wrong, and used a number of inapplicable analogies about the movement of the Maya from Guatemala to Yucutan. Maurizio is never at a loss for some apparently brilliant remark about some obscure facet of Central European archaeology, but I fear that his knowledge is about as superficial as mine. He tells me he was once employed in smuggling microfilms from East to West Berlin. He is a man of many parts, an archaeologist of sorts, a smuggler, an International Socialist and also a self-styled great lover. Maurizio cannot talk about the stratigraphy of the Lower Quetta valley without finding two bulges that remind him of firm breasts.

"He bent double, which for him is no mean feat, to kiss the hand of a ferocious Slav lady archaeologist. She was somewhat affronted, but in general it must be said he enjoys considerable success. He is engaged to a girl in Andover, 'the Wessex bird', as he calls her. This is not to say that Maurizio doesn't have birds in any European town one cares to mention. The current object of his affections is Eva. 'Eva, the first woman, she gave herself utterly to me.' Eva is an enthusiastic, wide-hipped blonde with sparkling blue spectacles and buck teeth, who lives up the hill from Zavist with her refined but calculating mother, and I fear that Maurizio did not bargain for her as well. Mother and daughter work as a team, and they are determined to catch Herr Docktor Maurizio. Both have visions of a splendid Roman future, and Maurizio has built up such a baroque image of grandeur that it will be hard for him to dispel their illusions. He has already invited them to Rome. 'Supposing they really come,' he moans. 'How would I explain it to my family—and the Roman bird?' In the mean time Maurizio is eating them out of house and home—vast quantities of duck and dumplings, chocolate cake, red currant tarts and apricots. He sits on the sofa, and while mama presses her attentions and Eva ladles yet another spoonful of cherry jam down that ever open mouth, he contemplates himself in the mirror, occasionally inclining his head to admire that strange Roman profile. I cannot imagine how he will extract himself from the situation, especially as mama has specially rented a riverside cottage for the two lovers this weekend. Despite a lingering feeling that he may have made Eva pregnant, Maurizio faces the prospect of the final parting next week with equanimity. 'It is very simple,' he says. 'I shall burst into tears, and when I cry who can be angry?'"

Tosi remembers Chatwin's arrival at Zavist. "I noticed this guy was interested in people." Before the dig, they had dinner in a hotel, sitting on wooden benches while couples danced. "A young soldier, blond, reddish cheeks and a short, buttoned tunic was dancing primly with a girl and looking up so happily. Bruce said: 'It's extraordinary that someone can be happy with so little'."

Over the next week, Tosi observed Bruce in the field. "I could never foresee what was coming. He was doing nothing I expected. I spoke three or four languages and was involved in lots of political actions, but I could not compare with the wit and performing capacities and the culture, the knowledge that Bruce was able to express in a few minutes of conversation. That summer in Czechoslovakia, he was—or at least declared himself to be—an archaeologist. On the other hand, I cannot forget the sense of boredom he had any time we entered into the technicalities, the excavation, the survey work, the descriptive aspects of the site."

Tosi took him on his first visit to the site. "While strolling through the woods from the house to our excavations I went into the most detailed explanation of the fortification's lay-out, but he kept on pointing to the trees, giving them precise names, never responding to my attempts at professional involvement. The same applied when I showed him the trench and sections. Bruce was much more amused by the snakes. Zavist was full of snakes."

At the end of each day Bruce and Maurizio went into Prague. They explored the old city, the synagogue, the Jewish cemetery, Rabbi Loew's tomb, and they attended a wedding of yet another girlfriend of Maurizio's. When the week's dig was over, they parted: Maurizio for Afghanistan and East Iran; Bruce for Central Europe on a tour of museums in Hungary, Rumania, Bulgaria and Turkey—and to join Batey. In a restaurant somewhere, he scribbled on the back of an envelope: "I have never known an orchestra with a greater capacity to shock. We have been running through Lehár waltzes and whenever we hit a high note it is like crossing a humpback bridge, never fails to hit the wrong note." On another page he made a pencil sketch of Holwell Farm, as if he is explaining to someone at dinner the house in which he lived. "Cotswold cute" and "charming pink" he wrote underneath the drawing. *"Tout à fait tip-top noblesse d'Angleterre."* In the third week of September, he made his way home. "I'm in a horrid hot little room and I miss you," he wrote to Elizabeth.

WHILE BRUCE WAS away, Margharita had helped Elizabeth to decorate Holwell Farm. "I am full of admiration for the way she copes with everything," Bruce's mother wrote to Gertrude. For the exterior, Elizabeth had mixed a special ochre for the stucco using canisters of Winsor & Newton paint powder which the previous owner had left behind in the barn. In September, she took receipt of a double-boiler, another gift from Gertrude.

Bruce arrived home with several French cheeses and a Kelim carpet, and threw himself into a week of handiwork. He stippled the bathroom. He erected osier hurdles as a windbreak for the vegetable garden. He collected fresh water in milk churns. On 4 October, he wrote to Gertrude before going up to Edinburgh: "The whole place has taken a terrific turn for the better and is becoming simply beautiful inside. The kitchen is the most pleasant I have ever known and I think we will almost live in it. I am in the middle of painting the study which will be ready before we go. I once learned a very good technique for colouring walls. You paint them with flat white oil, and then put a very thin layer of coloured wax glaze. This gives the walls a slightly transparent look. We are doing the study in golden ochre which sounds horrible but I think you'll like it. The bathroom doors which I glazed green over grey blue are a great success. A painter friend of mine is seriously thinking of adopting the technique. The boiler at last works after its teething troubles and the whole place is remarkably warm and has dried out in a way I never thought it would."

BRUCE STARTED HIS second year at Edinburgh as the lone male in his course. The group of 41 first-year students had slimmed to seven: Bruce and six girls referred to by Piggott as "my foolish virgins".

Rowan Watson had abandoned his degree and Bruce did not seek another lodger. "We see mostly professors," wrote Elizabeth to Gertrude.

A blow was the departure of Charles Thomas to the chair at Leicester. No one was found to replace him to lecture in Dark Ages Archaeology and with his departure Bruce was stuck with Roman Britain.

London friends came on fleeting visits, but matters did not improve. "Bruce continues to be steeped in gloom," Elizabeth wrote in February 1968. "He says he is bored to tears here and doesn't like *anything* and so doesn't know what to do at all. I can't even make out if he likes archaeology now—he says the way you have to study it takes all the romance out of it and all archaeologists are stuck in their own little ruts and aren't interested in what the others are doing etc., etc. I think really it's this place—he hasn't anything to do except study."

As part of his second-year course, Bruce studied Fine Art under David Talbot Rice. What commended this course to Bruce was his tutor's friendship with Robert Byron, Talbot Rice's friend at Eton. It was Talbot Rice, after a visit to Constantinople in 1925, who planted in Byron an interest in Byzantine art. Together they had explored Mount Athos and collaborated in *The Birth of Western Painting*.

Inasmuch as anyone filled the gap left by Charles Thomas, it was Professor David Talbot Rice and his wife, the historian Tamara. "She is a big Russian version of Penelope Betjeman," Bruce wrote to Elizabeth, "and he beams."

Eager to hear scraps about Byron, Bruce was a frequent visitor to their house in Nelson Street. The Sunday lunches, served with mulled wine, provided him with a social beacon, while Tamara considered Bruce a breath of fresh air. "I can picture him, elegant, neat, clean, attractively turned out, hair brushed, very definite in his movements, no hesitancy: if he wanted a book from the book case, he was at it before you knew." She found him ambitious to distinguish himself, but reticent about his personal life—except for one or two vitriolic remarks about Sotheby's. "He wasn't a social climber, nor an intellectual climber. I always imagined he was lower middle-class. He was frightfully secretive over his parents. He said he came from Dursley, where his father was an engineer. He was so secretive I didn't even know where he lived." She got in touch with him through the Archaeology Department. "I couldn't see this meteor staying four years at Edinburgh. I kept saying to David: 'Will he last out?'"

TAMARA TALBOT RICE was a Lithuanian Jew who had spent the bulk of her life in exile. Her stories were not confined to Byron's wild shrieks and remorseless teasing, but ranged from Rasputin, whose coffin she had seen hijacked before her eyes in Sergevskaya Street, to Claude Monet with whom she used to sip honey-coloured tea, to her brother who had joined the Maquis. Tamara replaced Peter Wilson as Bruce's favourite subject for impersonation. "Tamara and Tamara and Tamara . . ."

Her childhood was one Bruce might have concocted for himself: the only daughter of a treasury official, she was brought up in St Petersburg and on two country estates. "Sometimes during Lent I was taken to a jeweller, generally Fabergé, to buy miniature Easter eggs to be worn as bracelets or necklace charms."

In 1918, she escaped from Russia on the last train using a false passport, reaching Stockholm in time for Christmas, pulled, so she claimed, behind reindeers under white skins in the snow. In Paris, she had worked in the fashion industry. At Oxford, she had known most of the Hypocrites Club, including Evelyn Waugh in the days when he was a cartoonist, and Robert Byron.

Five days before she died, Tamara considered the differences between Chatwin and Byron: "Robert I inherited from David. I *chose* Bruce as a friend. But I never had a deep personal affection for him. I think it was not possible. I could have it with Evelyn, who could be maddening, or with Robert, but not with Bruce. He was very self-contained." This self-containment, she felt, affected his work. "That's the difference between him and Robert, whom passion activated in the first place. Bruce had no passion. It was all cerebral."

In 1935, Tamara had accompanied Byron back to Russia for a Congress on Persian art. In the Hermitage they had seen displayed the same frozen excavations from the Altai, the same tattooed skin, which had so entranced Bruce. It turned out that on her family's estate of Volgovo on the middle reaches of the Volga "we had one or two nomadic burial mounds." Tamara, wearing Harrods boots and a sealskin fur coat, proceeded with her tutor to excavate these sites. "We dug up bits of horse harnesses, nothing exciting." But her tutor's tales of how the Scythians ransacked the Crimea in the fourth century and how the Great Wall of China was built against the nomads cultivated a fascination which resulted in her book *The Scythians*, dedicated "to those who lived at Volgovo", and continued to figure in her conversations with Bruce in Nelson Street. "He wanted to know: Where had the Ark begun? Had the Sarmattans been on Hadrian's Wall? When did metal stirrups start?" Exactly as her husband had pointed Byron in the direction of Byzantine art, so Tamara led Bruce to his subject. "It was first through me that he came to be interested in nomads."

IT MIGHT HAVE come to nothing without the paternalistic hand of Cary Welch, who in the winter of 1967 recommended Bruce to curate an exhibition devoted to the Nomadic Art of the Asian Steppes. Welch had collected this art—weapons, jewellery, horse-harnesses—from the age of 14 while still at boarding school with George Ortiz. He had persuaded the Asia House Gallery in New York to mount the first major exhibition to be called The Animal Style.

Welch never believed that Bruce would make a good academic, but once he had introduced him to Piggott and the decision was made he gave his full support. Recalling the excitement that Bruce had shown over the frozen herdsman, he put his name forward when he heard that the exhibition's principal curator, Emma Bunker, required an extra hand. "He was billed as a young scholar—and distant relative by marriage of Cary Welch—who, in spite of his captivating eccentricities was somewhat rational," says Bunker, a young academic in Buddhist studies from Denver.

The exhibition was not due to open until January 1970. Until that time Bruce was expected to use his Sotheby's training to contact museums and collectors and to gather the best examples of nomadic art, essentially portable objects worn by mounted herdsmen who wandered the steppes of Asia and Europe in the fifth and sixth centuries BC. Bruce embraced a project that reflected a variety of his interests. There was the prospect of a book to coincide with the exhibition. Furthermore, there was the incentive of income. Asia House would pay travel expenses to the areas for which Bruce would hold responsibility: Thule and Eskimo, North Russia and Finland. "From the moment he became involved," says Kasmin, "it marked the new Bruce."

That winter, on his way to Geneseo for Christmas with his in-laws, Bruce met Welch in Boston to discuss ideas. Welch agreed to loan several important bronze ornaments; so would Ortiz. In January, Bruce returned to Edinburgh with a noticeable spring in his step.

THE *événements* OF MAY 1968 passed him by. "What amused me was his tunnel vision," says George Melly. "He knew everything there was to know about Persian miniatures, but he'd never heard of the Muppets." While students erected barricades in Paris, Cambridge and Ohio, Bruce concentrated on the Asia House exhibition. "The prehistoric Animal Style of Central Asia now obsessed him," wrote Hugh Honour, who was then a series editor at Allen Lane, "and so well did he talk about it that Penguin was easily persuaded to commission him to write a book on the subject. Everyone who met him at that time was struck by him. He seemed a twentieth-century version of Robert Browning's *Waring*. And like Waring he would quietly slip away to no one knew where."

"I think he's probably going to spend the whole of Spring vacation-travelling," wrote Elizabeth. On 16 March, he departed for Helsinki's Kansallismuseo, "probably to be birched in the sauna at the expense of Asia House," he wrote to Welch. "I've never been able to make up my mind if I like the idea or not. Wouldn't it be awful if one suddenly found one was a physical masochist as well as everything else?" He had bought a bellows to take with him for what he conceived as "my Asia House tour". Also, "the largest *coco-de-mer* I have ever seen. Beautiful and obscene. We take it to bed."

In April, he was in France, Switzerland and Italy. He skied for four days with Ortiz in St Moritz, and afterwards drove with Elizabeth to Geneva to pick out some Siberian plaques from the Ortiz collection. They then embarked on a circuit of museums in Basle, Munich, Trento, Mantua, Ravenna and Turin.

Bruce consulted Tamara Talbot Rice at the embryonic stage. She confirmed what he suspected: by far the best stuff was in Leningrad. In 1930, Tamara had assisted with an exhibition of Persian art at Burlington House and its most striking exhibits had come from the Hermitage. "I told Bruce his exhibition couldn't be done without many important loans from Russia. He wanted me to come and help, but the money didn't materialise."

On 26 April, Elizabeth wrote: "Bruce's plans are still terribly vague; he only knows he wants to go to Russia and is waiting for the money to appear from somewhere." Piggott now came to the rescue. He invited Bruce to join him and Ruth Tringham on an official tour of archaeological museums in the Soviet Union.

It was a curious little group: Piggott, Ortiz, who had never dug in his life (described in Piggott's diary as "an odd young Bolivian millionaire") and Ruth Tringham, who had spent a year arranging the official invitation. "I did it all by letter. Bruce was not going to be part of it. Then before I knew it, Stuart included Bruce. And Bruce invited George Ortiz."

Relations between Bruce and Tringham, whom he described as "a lady Marxist archaeological student from Hampstead", were already stretched. It grated on her to find Bruce and Stuart Piggott so close. "I thought: 'What is this person doing here?' He knows nothing about European archaeology. He was treated as a post-graduate without any basis at all. I had a feeling he wanted an academic grounding to give him legitimacy. It got on my nerves." Moreover, the Chatwin van was causing Tringham problems. Its bottom dropped out before she had had it a year.

Piggott, too, was apprehensive about the group's composition, their different motives for wanting to visit Russia and the threats posed to his palate by a Soviet cuisine. "I now dread [the visit] and wake in the night thinking what hell it will be."

On 30 June, Piggott went to drinks at Robert Erskine's where he found Bruce and Andrew Batey. At eight the following morning, Batey drove them to Dover. At Ostend, they boarded a train for Warsaw, there intending to meet up with Ortiz and Tringham.

IT SEEMED TO Piggott that foreign travel was an escape for Bruce, "who is running away from himself by travelling." On 5 July, Piggott glimpsed the origins of Bruce's volatility. "Bruce talked a lot last night on the necessity of constant escape from Elizabeth's possessiveness, etc., etc. I can't make it out. 'Of course, she's sweet,' he said perfunctorily and then discussed how he could get a one-room flat on his own, somewhere to go and work. His travel passion is slightly maniac & could become actually so. And while he's highly intelligent he's not really a scholar and I would think won't make any real academic contribution to archaeology. But he might go crackers."

Bruce might have complained about Elizabeth's possessiveness, but he then sat down in his hotel room and dashed off a letter to his wife urging her to join him in Romania.

"Could you try and bring with you *my* compass which is somewhere in my room I think, and failing that can you buy a fairly good one? Can you also bring my copy of Parvan's *Dacia*, a small green book in *my* shelves and a map of Romania. I only hope you'll be able to come on the Transylvanian jaunt. Also remember to put the *tent* in the car + a *small* billycan for gas in case you run out . . . I think the best thing is to miss out Hungary if this is going to be difficult by taking the Yugoslav autobahn from Belgrade to Ljubljana."

His wife would get used to Bruce's hopelessly grandiose plans. "Usually he had these ideas halfway through a trip and decided he would like to have me along," says Elizabeth, who in this instance was expected to traipse across Eastern Europe at the drop of a hat, having taken care of visas and insurance. "I didn't get too worked up. The ideas were always amazingly impractical."

The following day Bruce changed his mind. He could be contacted in Athens.

On 9 July, one month before the Russian invasion of neighbouring Czechoslovakia, the party stood assembled in Warsaw. Tringham had come from an excavation near Prague, Ortiz from Paris. Bruce wrote to Elizabeth: "[Ortiz] may well be collected from the airport in a Rolls Royce . . . How can one explain his Bolivian nationality—as a fellow of Che Guevara?"

The trip was not an outstanding success. They spent a week in Leningrad seeing museums and drinking vodka with aggressive Russian archaeologists. Bruce wrote to Peter Levi: "Every plan was frustrated, and I'm afraid that most traditional Russian hospitality is a deep-seated desire to see foreigners drunk."

Bruce hated to lose possession of himself. Once at a restaurant he told Hodgkin: "I would never get drunk: it would be so awful not to be in control." This fear reflected itself in the short, clipped sentences of his prose. "Of all the talented brilliant writers," says Welch, "Bruce wrote the shortest sentences I've ever read. On one level he had great confidence; on another, he didn't." The play of these tensions, observed Francis Wyndham, gave his prose its power. "Reading Chatwin one is acutely conscious of authorial control—and therefore, simultaneously and intoxicatingly, of the alluring danger of *loss* of control, of things getting out of hand."

In Leningrad, things got out of hand. On 11 July, they attended what Piggott described as "an awful interminable evening" at the home of Vladimir Masson, head of the Leningrad Archaeological Institute. Tringham was sick in the bathroom while Bruce, with Masson slumped under it, stood on the table "reciting a Shakespeare sonnet for the benefit of his wife". He was crippled with a liver attack for days afterwards. "Liver pains and Animal Style are intertwined in my consciousness," he wrote to Joan Leigh Fermor.

Piggott regarded Bruce's version in *What Am I Doing Here* as "an incredibly variant text". (Bruce, for instance, shifts his recitation to Moscow, lengthens it from a sonnet to Orsino's opening speech from *Twelfth Night*, and directs it at Masson's sister.) "I think he lived in a fantasy world and was quite genuinely incapable of distinguishing fact from fiction. It wasn't a pretence."

In Leningrad the 58-year-old professor was at his most morose, loathing the food and unable to keep up with the three younger members. "Although Ruth is invaluable as an archaeological interpreter & Bruce very congenial & good about making arrangements etc., one has to remember they're both only 28 and don't tire and want to rest and really don't mind about food and comfort." He had also a financial concern. "Bruce is just so airy-fairy about finances that he lives on perpetual loans. Thank God I brought a lot!"

Leningrad disappointed Piggott on all levels. "I got very depressed and said so." The food was disgusting, the people dreary, frowsy and inefficient and the museums a letdown. At the Ethnographic Museum, "Bruce & George went all enthusiastic about objects of ethnographic art—very boring." After viewing the Scythian gold at the Hermitage, he wrote: "Nearly half way through the trip, hooray."

Ortiz, on the other hand, was swept off his feet by the Hermitage. He decided then and there that he wanted to be its Director. He offered to leave to the museum his collection of Greek bronzes if this could be effected. This sort of gesture was to the utilitarian Tringham an example of their ideological differences. "I thought of Bruce and George Ortiz as symbols of capitalist decadence." She disagreed with their interpretation of art in terms of beauty. "I argued that artefacts are things which have meaning only in context: they don't have any value for themselves." Bruce was angered by her refusal to allow something to be beautiful. "When one speculated on the character and beliefs of their makers, such inferences were frowned on as speculative, emotional and not scientific." Their arguments followed them on the Red Arrow to Moscow.

The Russian capital reinforced Piggott's disappointment. "Moscow is an incredibly dreary, fly-blown dump of a place—no wonder Leningrad is thought so marvellous." The museums were no better, nor the cuisine. "An unusually revolting snack in a crowded, shitty restaurant & to see the over-praised vulgarities of the Kremlin." On 20 July, after two days in Kiev, the tour was at an end.

"My summer was disastrous," Bruce wrote to Levi, without making mention of a mutual suicide pact proposed by Piggott.

PIGGOTT HAD GRUMBLED to Charles Thomas about his horror of growing old, his wish to be buried in a megalith. "There's nothing left to live for. I'll cut my throat and lie in Long Barrow." In Russia, he was tired, outpaced by three young people, disappointed. Confronted by the gruesome Scythian burial displays, Piggott's natural melancholy expressed itself in suicidal thoughts. He had already spoken to Tringham about committing suicide. "I was appalled," she says. Mindful of his predecessor's fate (Gordon Childe had taken a taxi to a sandstone cliff south of Sydney and simply walked off the edge), Piggott indulged in similar black fantasies.

He even wondered if Bruce and Elizabeth might want to join him. Bruce told her: "Stuart keeps wanting to have a suicide pact. 'Why don't we all three of us jump off a cliff or take pills or sniff gas?' " Elizabeth thought it was a joke. "We hadn't been married that long. Commit suicide—for what?" But Bruce was horrified. "He began to think that archaeology was something suicidal."

Bruce chose to take the proposal seriously. Piggott, he said, had suggested the idea more than once. Suicide lodged in Bruce's mind as a metaphor for Piggott's profession. He began to collect stories about archaeologists who had died in their own trenches, the result of a secret desire to be buried. "Most archaeologists interpret the things of the remote past in terms of their own projected suicide," he wrote in his notebook. And: "If an archaeologist has faith in his method he must use that method to its logical conclusion—and bury himself." By the time he returned to Edinburgh in October, he had built up in his mind the same contempt for archaeology as for the art world. "I began to feel with a certain amount of irreverence that I was entering a similar trap. All evidence had to be taken from inanimate objects. I decided what interested me most were those people who'd escaped the archaeological record, the nomads who'd trod lightly on the earth and didn't build pyramids." He had decided, in other words, to identify himself with the subjects of the Animal Style exhibition.

In September, Bruce went to New York to discuss the exhibition with "two supermale ladies". These were his Asia House collaborators, Emma Bunker and Ann Farkas. "Emma is fine but listens to not one word. Ann Farkas severe academic, but not unsympathetic." After "many parties", among them Andrew Batey's wedding in California, he arrived home on 10 October.

"He is dreading going back to Edinburgh," wrote Elizabeth, "but he really must."

Bruce had given up his Canongate flat in the summer. He moved into the Abercromby Hotel in the New Town. He plodded on, stuck in the rut of Ancient Britain. On 6 November, Elizabeth wrote: "Bruce gets more depressed every minute with Edinburgh." A fortnight later she drove up to collect him for Thanksgiving, not knowing that he had made up his mind to quit.

Just as Darwin at Edinburgh had shown no aptitude to be a doctor, so Chatwin discovered that his kind of intelligence was too manic for archaeology. He described his experience in the world of academics as his *"saison en enfer"*. His friend Christopher Gibbs wrote, "His mounting contempt for their lack of humility, their rigidity, the vulgarity of their deductions and their fear of intuition, blew him away from academe and the Athens of the North, and sent him into a nomad spin that was to last for a decade."

"Bruce's mind was as complex as an early civilisation," says Maurizio Tosi. "The earlier you go back, the larger the number of options." Had Wilson given him a full directorship, Bruce might have stayed at Sotheby's; had he arrived in Edinburgh two years later he might have become an archaeologist. It is Tosi's view that Bruce came into archaeology at just the wrong moment. It was bad luck he had lost Charles Thomas. It was even less fortunate that he started as a student before a new wind roared through the departments. "The environment he moved in then was very conservative." When, one year later, Tosi arrived in London to complete his MA, he could feel the changes which had started in America, where Archaeology was based in the Anthropology departments. By then, Thomas was injecting fresh ideas into the syllabus at Leicester. David Clarke had published the seminal *Analytical Archaeology*, inaugurating a new era at Cambridge, and in December 1969 there was a conference in London on the domestication and exploitation of plants and animals. "It was a grand opening to anthropology, working on both the dead and the living," says Tosi. "You could breathe the changes."

One of the embarrassed reasons Bruce cited for abandoning his degree was Piggott's refusal to let him complete it in three years instead of four. The sense was conveyed that Piggott did not wish to relinquish a brilliant student. This estimation Piggott confirmed to Penelope Betjeman, telling her that he counted Bruce as one of his best pupils and that the light went out of his life after Bruce had left. To Nash, Bruce hinted that his relationship with Piggott had begun to stifle him in the same way as had Wilson. Nash believed he had made this problem up. Ruth Tringham did not. "My impression is that both were much fonder of each other than they were of any women. In as much as either could have loved another person, they loved each other. My impression is that Stuart was in love with him."

Piggott died on 23 September 1996, aged 86. His diaries throw an invaluable light on Bruce's brief university career. They show that Piggott found Bruce to be an interesting and extraordinary young man utterly unlike the normal run of student, but that he felt sorry for Bruce rather than attracted to him.

22 October 1968: "I had Bruce to dinner on Saturday, but got bored over the avocado pears and felt so tired. B now staying at Abercromby Hotel up the road; madder I think. He and/or his marriage will crack up before long."

9 January 1969: "Absolutely no news of Bruce Chatwin. He came to me in a great state last term saying he was £6,000 in debt owing to buying the Glos. house, wouldn't take money from Elizabeth's family & simply had to take a job—offered one at £1,000 a year, one day a week, from Christie's. Shot off to London to investigate and hasn't been heard of since. I rang Holwell last night, but no reply. I suspect they are in America. Of course, he's mad—embarking on this degree without facing up to what his financial position over 4 years would be, and not realising that Elizabeth would not live in Edinburgh and is clearly opposed to the whole thing. I think he'll have to chuck the lot. 'Aye, folks are queer,' once again, and in both senses!"

29 April and Piggott had still not heard a word. "Really, what an odd young man. So bloody rude anyway to walk out without any proper explanation and not a word of thanks for all the considerable trouble I'd taken. I think the most charitable view is that he really *is* mentally unbalanced. A pity."

Finally, 26 May 1969: "Letter from Bruce admitting the idea of his becoming an academic archaeologist was a mistake and formally withdrawing. An odd but amusing episode, but clearly he would never settle down to anything approaching a sober routine life. What will happen *vis-à-vis* Elizabeth is anyone's guess. All very strange."

XVIII.

⟨≈⟩

That Wretched Book

Wild horses couldn't drag him back to Edinburgh,
so that's that.

—Elizabeth to her mother

At Holwell Farm, Elizabeth grew concerned. As soon as Bruce came home, he lost himself in the garden. "Bruce went mad and ordered about 20 things the other day: lots of trees and things like bamboo and gunnera." She had never seen him so unmoored. "He moved all the furniture around about ten times this weekend." He talked of buying a tiny flat in London.

With no degree to work for, he deflected his intellectual energies into the Asia House exhibition. For his $1,000 honorarium, he was expected to produce an essay on the Animal Style for the catalogue. He now immersed himself in this—despite provocation from Elizabeth's cats. Kittypuss had given birth to five kittens. The most annoying was Tigger. Elizabeth wrote, "If he can't get attention he does something bad like pushing all the books and newspapers off the table, or trying to extract the ribbon from the typewriter etc., etc."

Only breaking for Christmas in Geneseo, Bruce spent the winter in the downstairs study absorbed in his first sustained commissioned work. The essay became a vessel for the ideas that his two years at Edinburgh had stirred up. What he needed most at this stage he would not articulate until he had written several books. "What you really want," he told an Australian radio interviewer in 1983, "is someone who sees the point."

On 25 January, Elizabeth wrote to Gertrude: "He has now finished the catalogue introduction and it's very good." Bruce submitted it confidently.

———

"FOLLOWING THEIR PASSION for human urine, reindeer were attracted to human settlements." When Bruce's two fellow curators read his text, their worst fears were realised.

Entitled "The Nomadic Alternative", it was shot through with arcane folklore and anthropological speculation that would not fit benignly into the scholarly catalogue they had envisaged. Of particular concern was Bruce's emphasis on the role of the shaman in nomadic art: "Feared, sexually ambivalent, set aside from the 'normal' life of the tribe, he remains the hub of its creative activity, its cultural hero."

Ann Farkas, a Thracian scholar, says, "His essay had nothing to do with the exhibition or what we were trying to do. It was just about nomads. We read it and said to each other: 'This is horrible'."

Bruce's unconventional approach worried Emma Bunker. "We came from different angles. I came from a strictly academic background and I had not really travelled the world as he had. I expected him to have more footnotes. He was bored with academic nonsense. 'Those frilly-shirted fools,' he said."

As Farkas recalls, "things got pretty hot and heavy". With Bunker, she convened an urgent meeting with the Asia House director, Gordon Washburn, who shared their dismay. Appeals were made, and, as Bruce wrote to Welch, "other forms of torture are being greased and oiled for the intrepid English amateur who has dared plant his unwary feet on the hallowed ground of American scholarship." But he refused to alter what he had written. "He was unmoveable," says Farkas. "He just smiled and was charming." Washburn alluded to their unease in his foreword when the catalogue was published in 1970: "Mr. Chatwin, an anthropologist at heart, is inclined to find shamanism the most likely inspiration for the Animal Style . . . Mrs Bunker and Dr Farkas are less interested in unprovable hypothesis and more concerned with . . . exacting research."

Alone in their approval were Emma Bunker's children, ever after hopeful that "if only they could 'pee' in the snow, a reindeer would appear."

The exhibition was another year away, in another country. More immediately, Bruce wondered if there was not an English market for his essay, described by him later as "pretty pretentious, but not bad". On 20 January 1969, he wrote to Gertrude: "I am going up to town tomorrow in search of a publisher for a book based on the Asia House Introduction."

Lucie-Smith had directed him towards his own literary agent, Deborah Rogers. He says, "Bruce came to me and said he wanted to write, what could he do? I knew he would appeal enormously to Deborah." The meeting was effected by Kasmin, a mutual friend.

Over a Greek lunch in Charlotte Street, Bruce talked to Rogers about Mr Brady, a travelling typewriter salesman who kept a trunk in a hotel in Kingsway. "He seemed to belong to that nearly extinct species—the happy man." Periodically, Mr Brady would return from his travels around Africa to this room, pull out the black tin deed box and sift through his belongings, the assorted bric-a-brac of English middle-class life. "But each time he brought from Africa one new thing, and he threw out one old thing that had lost its meaning. 'I know it sounds silly,' he said, 'but they are my roots'." Rogers says, "I was hooked."

Bruce reported the result of their discussion to Welch. "At present I am focussing my attention and blandishments on Mr Maschler, who was the publishing genius behind Desmond Morris's *The Naked Ape* . . .".

On 23 January, Rogers sent Bruce's eight-page catalogue introduction to Tom Maschler, the chairman and publisher of Jonathan Cape. "Can he come and see you tomorrow? I am sure he is worth your spending half an hour with. I have a good feeling about him."

Maschler had published Joseph Heller's *Catch-22* and John Fowles's *The Collector*. He acted on infrequent but powerful hunches: "I've had this feeling a few times when I've *known*." Maschler had a similar reaction to Bruce, although he found the author more exceptional than his essay. "It was all right. It had a confidence, somewhere between research and experience, and was extremely professional and polished. But I do remember being pretty taken with this young man: he had an extraordinary assurance and an integrity. I was sure I was dealing with someone very special."

Maschler had commissioned few books ("20 in 40 years"), most recently *The Naked Ape*. As with Desmond Morris, he asked Bruce for a proposal. "I said to him—a trick I always play because it frees people—'I don't want a ten-page outline: do it in the form of a letter'."

On 24 February, Bruce delivered his open letter to Rogers. The book was to be general rather than specialist in tone and the question it would try to answer was: Why do men wander rather than sit still? He proposed to tackle the nomadic urge under nine headings. Chapter VII was to be called "The Compensations of Faith". Chapter IX, "The Nomadic Alternative", called into question "the whole basis for Civilisation and is concerned with the present and future as much as the past." The opening chapter was to address the question "Why Wander?" chiefly in terms of Bruce's own nomadic urge. "I have a compulsion to wander and a com-

pulsion to return—a homing instinct like a migrating bird." Rogers forwarded the "letter" to Maschler: "The idea is emerging with greater clarity as he progresses, despite the intentional looseness and preambly-ness
of the enclosed."

Maschler read the synopsis in his cottage above Llantony and was excited by its mammoth scope. He looked forward to the first chapters. "I
do just want to put into writing that I am convinced it will be an important book," he replied to Bruce. "Important in the way *The Naked Ape* was
important."

Maschler also sent Bruce's synopsis to Desmond Morris, who saw the
problem immediately. "What exactly is a nomad? It gets a little confusing
at times as I read his chapter summaries." It seemed to Morris that there
was a fundamental psychological difference between wandering away and
then back to a fixed base, on the one hand, and wandering from place to
place without a fixed base, on the other. "As I said in *The Naked Ape*, the
moment man became a hunter, he had to have somewhere *to come back
to* after the hunt was over. So a fixed base became natural for the species
and we lost our old ape-like nomadism."

Morris made the following suggestion. "Maybe the answer is to get
rid of the word nomad altogether and think in initially vaguer terms of
'HUMAN WANDERLUST'."

Bruce professed himself to Maschler delighted by Morris's comments.
"I'm sorry I didn't answer before, but my wife thought it was a bill and
kept it from me . . . I too have come to the same conclusion. The word
NOMAD must go." He had been reading "heavily" in the literature of animal behavior and the next week hoped to go to Le Mans. "I have a new
friend, a self-employed motor-bicycle ace, who follows a prescribed route
from Grand Prix to Grand Prix, and shows all the characteristics of a true
nomad."

Three days later he updated his thesis. "The first will be a Wandering
Beast chapter, preceded by an introduction. I estimate that the manuscript
should be ready to hack together by this time next year, that is providing
we don't decide to enlarge it with a section on the Lone American, who is
beginning to be a much more significant figure than I had imagined."

At the end of May, in the same week as he formally withdrew from
his degree course, Bruce signed a contract to write *The Nomadic Alternative*. He was paid an advance of £200 and Maschler conveyed his high
hopes to Deborah Rogers: "As I said before, I have a hunch; as you
said before, you have a hunch. Let's hope this lives up to both our
expectations."

———

BRUCE STRUGGLED TO write his nomad book for three years. A pattern emerged which would define his writing life: boundless enthusiasm dwindling into depression and inertia. To begin with, Elizabeth says, "he identified himself to the extent that he no longer dug in the vegetable garden. He didn't mind *me* gardening. That was all right because nomads had slaves who cultivated the oasis for them." His research took him back and forth from Holwell Farm to short visits among nomad tribes in Afghanistan, West Africa, Mauritania, Persia. But the deeper he researched, the more cumbersome grew the material and the harder he found to contain it.

He wanted to write a seminal work that restored the position of nomads to an important place in history and was a serious attempt to explain the origin of humanity. The pyramids we know, he said. Moses we don't. But the fact that Moses left few traces opened a limitless horizon to fill with every category of mirage. Anything that moved became worthy of his argument, from a hermaphrodite pharaoh to the musings of a tramp in St James's Square.

It took 14 years for him to be able to clarify his thesis: "The argument, roughly, was as follows: that in becoming human, man had acquired, together with his straight legs and striding walk, a migratory 'drive' or instinct to walk long distances through the seasons; that this 'drive' was inseparable from his central nervous system; and that, when warped in conditions of settlement, it found outlets in violence, greed, status-seeking or a mania for the new." The book had grown and grown. "And as it grew it became less intelligible to its author. It even contained a diatribe against the act of writing itself."

He would find himself stranded in "a nebulous no-man's land between scientific theory and autobiography". The resulting tome would cause him heartbreak. It would contain most of what he knew, but it was not *The Naked Ape*.

"It was so much a young man's book," he said, "with a tendency to air one's knowledge to the fullest extent and cram everything in. I finally consigned it to the dustbin because it was absolutely unreadable."

———

ONE REASON HIS book took so long was his ability to be distracted. Maschler did not know that *The Nomadic Alternative* was only one of several projects Bruce plotted at this time, all loosely linked to nomads. In February, for instance, he planned an anthology of shaman poetry with his neighbor at Holwell, the poet Charles Tomlinson. And on 21 March, Elizabeth wrote to her mother that Bruce's nomad project was temporarily on hold: "He's been distracted by another thing at the moment. He has got to know the whole cast of the English production of *Hair* and one night last week was at a party there talking to a theatrical agent who said they were looking for ideas for a really different, way-out musical so Bruce sits himself down at the typewriter last week and writes a scenario for a musical on Akhenaton, involving the Mitannians . . . who were semi-nomadic people from Iraq, the Hittites and of course the Egyptians. So he showed it to the agent who liked it . . . and so tomorrow they are drawing up a copyright. Goodness knows if it will ever come off, but Bruce is thrilled of course."

The inspiration for Bruce's musical was a 19-year-old Jamaican-born actor from *Hair*. Peter Straker had just split up with his long-term girlfriend and lived in Palmer's Green with his Jamaican Methodist parents. In the musical he played the part of Hud, the lead black boy. "I was carried in upside down on a pole dressed in the US flag, with no clothes on underneath. I'd slide off and sing. 'I'm a coloured spade.' Bruce thought I had the most marvellous voice."

Their paths crossed one afternoon as Straker was heading to the Shaftesbury Theatre. The *Evening Standard*'s Londoner's Diary, describing Bruce as "a bit of a scholar who knows a thing or two about Egypt", reported their encounter. " 'My God,' yelled out Mr Chatwyn [*sic*], 'You're the image of Akhenaton.' And without so much as a by-your-leave he dragged young Peter off round half the museums in London until he found a picture to support his theory. And sure enough the resemblance was uncanny."*

That night Bruce watched Straker's performance and the idea for a musical started to take shape. A complete lack of training was no obstacle. "In a moment of enthusiasm, or—rather—infatuated by a member of

---

* Bruce may have read of Ronald Firbank's infatuation for Evan Morgan, recorded by Ifan Kyrle Fletcher in his 1930 memoir. Firbank, finding in Morgan's features "an amazing resembling" to the mummy of Rameses, had hurried him off to the British Museum to see "his original". "His interest became almost an obsession. He came to believe that Evan Morgan was a reincarnation of Rameses, and must, therefore, be possessed of cosmic secrets."

the cast, I wrote a scenario for a musical one bright spring day," he wrote to James Ivory. "I'm a sucker for theatrical camp."

The outline is lost, but Straker remembers its drift. "Akhenaten was considered a visionary, a Christ figure. He was a hermaphrodite as well, which we liked the idea of." In Bruce's musical, the sun-worshipping Pharaoh would uproot his court from Thebes to the desert, getting away from old conventions. "Bruce had the idea of converting the theatre into a pyramid and having sand on the way in so you would get the feeling of desert and heat."

Bruce met with Galt McDermott, who had written the music for *Hair* and for the lyrics Straker approached John Tebelak, the author of *Godspell.* Bruce gave Straker his white jellaba, a gift from Gloria which he wore on stage, and during Straker's free day they would lunch at Le Casserole in the King's Road or Inigo Jones in Covent Garden. Straker found the relationship puzzling. "I don't know if we *had* an affair. My day-to-day life had nothing to do with Bruce."

The project soon petered out and with it the relationship. "His energy used to frighten me," says Straker. "I found him overpowering, not bullying, but larger than life. There came a point when I knew I was important to him and didn't want it. I used to laugh at him when he said he loved me."

One weekend Bruce invited Straker to Holwell to meet Elizabeth. "I was quite shocked at their relationship," says Straker. "I asked him about Elizabeth: 'How can you go on like this?' He said she liked the country and didn't like the city and she knew about that side of him."

Straker may well have been the impetus behind Bruce's need for a small flat in London. In April, he signed a short lease on a studio at 9 Kynance Mews, owned by an actor who played secondary roles in James Bond films. "Bruce has hardly been here at all as he's been preoccupied with his play, his book and selling things & getting the flat," Elizabeth wrote to Gertrude on 26 April. "B came down Thurs night with a rent-a-van and took some things up—including a double bed."

Kynance Mews was Bruce's London base for a year. He later shared it with Oliver Hoare, the carpets expert at Christie's, with a stipulation that he and Elizabeth had squatting rights once a week. Hoare's taste for kelim-covered benches and hessian cushions led to the flat's nickname, The Great Bed. That summer, Bruce lent Kynance Mews to Straker while he was abroad.

IN JUNE 1969, the nomad book supplied Bruce with an excuse to visit Afghanistan for the third and last time. He intended to follow the Silk Route with Peter Levi, who had been commissioned to write a book focussing on the Greek influence in the area. Levi originally had in mind a long *Childe Harold* kind of poem on Afghanistan, but he scaled down his ambition proposing instead "the kind of topographic or travel book that used to be written in the nineteenth century, only with sharper edges and more modern prose".

Collins agreed to pay him an advance of £250. "You can look at nomads and I can look at Greeks," Levi told Bruce.

Bruce, "a compass without a needle" as one friend called him at this time, fastened on to the poet. "He was then in the process of transforming himself from an archaeologist into a writer," says Levi, "and so far as any advice was called for, it was I who advised him to make the change."

They had renewed acquaintance on Bruce's vacations from Edinburgh. In Oxford to use the libraries, Bruce would meet up with Levi at Campion Hall. "One reason why we were friends," says Levi, "is that I never asked him questions. I just said: 'You do? You don't? Oh!' "

Their relationship was observed by Ian Watson, an academic living at Yarnton. "One had the impression Bruce didn't have anyone whom he trusted to tell him where to go. Peter helped him."

According to James Ivory, the thin and handsome Levi was for Bruce "a figure of glamour". Levi is aware that Bruce romanticised his life as a poet and Jesuit priest. "He thought it a wonderful idea to have all these pads all over the place: a room at Campion Hall; a room in Athens; a room in Eastbourne, where my mother lived. He wanted from me a way of life that was largely in his imagination. He thought my life was some kind of solution: I travelled about and I was a writer. That interested him for the first time while we were in Afghanistan. We talked about the problems of writing, about Russian poets like Osip Mandelstam. What I didn't know or notice was that Bruce was changing *himself*. You write in order to change yourself in my view. He was trying to remake his life and become a writer."

The two men met throughout the spring to plot their itinerary. Elizabeth walked with her cat in the Botanical Gardens while Bruce and Levi discussed the site of Ay Khanoum, a Hellenistic city which French archaeologists were then excavating on the Oxus. "Peter Levi is absolutely neat," wrote Elizabeth, "& I think Bruce will have a lovely time travelling with him."

Their plans were also observed by Maurizio Tosi, whom Bruce took down to Campion Hall. Tosi was in London to lecture on his exciting excavations at Seistan. In 1968, a year after digging with Bruce at Zavist, he had broken the hard soil with a pick and uncovered the Burnt City of Shahar-i-Sakhta in Eastern Iran, proof of an unknown civilisation between the Indus and Mesopotamia. Such a discovery Bruce might once have wished for himself, but it was evident to Tosi that archaeology was over for Bruce. "He spent one full day with me at the Institute of Archaeology to photograph the pot shards from Baluchistan which I had been studying. But it was very much like an elder brother helping the naïve dreams of his younger brother. His eyes were shining with excitement only when he spoke about the trip to Afghanistan which he and Peter Levi were to undertake that summer."

Before meeting Levi in Teheran on 17 June, Bruce flew to Cairo to earn the money which would finance the three-month journey. He concealed his mission from everyone, except Elizabeth. It was vital that nobody guessed the identity of his paymaster: Sotheby's rival, Christie's.

ONCE HE MOVED on, Bruce did not look back. "I've never felt a twinge of regret about Sotheby's," he wrote to Gertrude, "and every time I go back and see my poor ex-colleagues, I find they all want to do the same."

He was well aware of the unwritten rule that neither auction house poached staff from the other: these were rivals so bitter that Wilson could not tolerate mention of their name. "Christie's are crazy to have him work for them," Elizabeth wrote to Gertrude, but she felt alarm about Wilson's reaction. "He could do B a lot of harm." And indeed, says Elizabeth, "PCW did his nut" when news reached him that Christie's were flirting with his former protégé. What had soured their relationship prevented Wilson from tackling Bruce face to face. Instead, he invited Elizabeth to his London house and told her furiously: "We feel Bruce's knowledge is ours because he got it when he was at Sotheby's." Wilson offered to set Bruce up with capital to become a dealer, but Elizabeth refused on his behalf. "I said he would have made a lousy dealer. He was fine with other people's money, but useless with his own."

Elizabeth's allowance had cushioned him when he left Sotheby's. "It was a help, but you certainly couldn't live on it entirely," she says. Bruce had supported himself at Edinburgh by dealing, the junk shops providing a steady source of income. In one shop he had bought for £20 a chalcedony salt cellar. "He found the pair to it in the *Schatzkammer* in Vienna and the date is Burgundy, 1490!" Many of the objects had been collected by Scots seafarers, including a Maori sculpture, once belonging to Sarah Bernhardt, "for which he has already been offered more than twice what he paid". This rapid turnover upset Elizabeth. "I hate having him buy things & then sell them because it seems such a pity to let them go after we get attached to them . . . but it's a constant struggle, because people are always offering him huge sums for something he bought for £100 & it's a temptation."

After Edinburgh, where he had been on a student grant, Bruce's financial position forced him to reconsider Christie's offer. He agreed to work for them on a freelance basis—so long as his name did not appear on their books. On 25 January, Elizabeth wrote to Gertrude: "For goodness sake, don't tell ANYONE."

Bruce's retainer from Christie's amounted to £1,250 a year. This is what he lived on for the next two years, supplemented by the sale of various objects belonging to him or Elizabeth. The first part of his retainer was paid after a visit to Egypt and financed his journey to Afghanistan.

On 7 June, Bruce flew to Cairo with Christie's managing director, Guy Hannon. Their mission was to secure the sale of the contents of the Cairo Museum. The Egyptian government, anxious to raise hard currency to pay for the war with Israel, had decided to sell off some of its national treasures in order to buy a squadron of MiG fighter planes. They had approached Christie's with a list of tantalising objects. "The whole thing was too fraught for words," says Hannon, who took along Bruce because "he was reckoned to know more than anyone else".

They found Cairo tense and deserted. "Nobody was there because people thought the Israelis were going to drop bombs." Bruce and Hannon sat before a committee and together they ran through the list, providing their estimates. But the Egyptians had changed their mind. They no longer wished to sell their most important sculptures. "They wanted to sell us a huge number of stuffed ibis," says Hannon.

Surrounded in the Cairo Museum by the implacable face of the Pharaoh, a thought struck Bruce. "Where is the face of Moses, I said, amongst all this lot?" Every vestige of Rameses II was on view, down to his mummified fingernails, but nothing remained of the nomad who had gone out from the city and died in the desert. "And you have to ask that question in history: Who is a more important figure, Moses or Pharaoh? And you come to the conclusion: it's Moses." This sweeping question, as he prepared to join Levi in Afghanistan, became central to his thesis.

BRUCE AND LEVI landed in Kabul on 25 June, and dined with an English public school master who was hoping to be allowed to lead a team of undergraduates to the northern province of Badakhshan.

Among the missions to Kabul in 1841 was a Society for the Suppression of Vice among the Uzbeks. Rather in this vein, Peter Willey, a senior housemaster at Wellington College, had arrived from London to make a study for the Anti-Slavery Society. "They are, if the whole story bears credence, investigating the bond relationship between the growers of opium and Indian hemp and those who control the market," Bruce wrote in his journal. "This constitutes a master-slave relationship . . . Col Gregory has therefore provided funds and button microphones and miniature cameras. The expedition lives on corned beef."

The Willey Expedition seemed so ludicrous to Bruce that two years later he proposed it to the director James Ivory as a fit subject for cinematic treatment. "No spectacle, not even the Angel Gabriel on a trip, was more bizarre than one puffy public school master followed by three of the most exquisitely dressed and pretty and flirtatious boys, one with boots and marginally more masculine than the other two with handbags, as they picked their way delicately from the Ministry of the Interior to the Ministry of the Exterior to the Ministry of Education to the Ministry of Culture and finally when the Afghan government had made it abundantly clear that they didn't want to be investigated, least of all by an ex-British army major, the party dropped in on the PM to be shown the door, first of all quite politely and then really rather rudely . . . My Dear, it was funny, very funny."

Willey and his entourage haunted Bruce's third Afghan journey, hovering around Kabul, "because Kabul was where the Afghans said the expedition must remain and remain it did". Despite the criticism he heaped on the Anti-Slavery Society, his own expedition was not without its absurdities.

HIS EXPEDITION STARTED with a whipping. On 12 July, Bruce sent a postcard to Elizabeth from the British Embassy in Kabul. "British School in Teheran was populated by the most *awful* Cambridge archaeologists you can imagine. Breathing tomb fungus. We barged in on the Bala Hisar, a military fort, and both got lashed at by a very irate infantryman with his belt. Very uncomfortable but in fact quite funny."

Bruce and Levi were looking for pottery shards below the Bala Hisar, an imposing castle on the south of the Kabul river, when an enraged private soldier attacked them, unarmed except for his military belt. Levi dismissed the episode as an "odd little incident of fantasy" explained by midday heat. Bruce, in his journal, showed less composure. "A refreshing spot after a fiendish day. Poor P. He was wrong, obstinate and wrong. I warned and was right, triumphantly right."

Kabul, smelling of balsam poplars and petrol, held no more charm than before. Whenever they returned from an expedition, they heard the same donkey in the Embassy garden screeching with unsatisfied desire. At least Shah Jahan's marble pavilion, once offered to Bruce and Robert Erskine, had been restored among its mulberry trees.

From Kabul, they visited Bamiyan in the passes of the Hindu Kush. Bruce was looking for nomad tombs in the upper pastures. The highest point of his summer occurred early on in a valley behind Shar-i-Golgola. After walking 35 miles they came to a line of four nomadic burial mounds. "We looked and neither of us spoke, being unwilling to believe our eyes," Levi wrote in *The Light Garden of the Angel King*. "It was too good to be true, after so many enthusiastic conversations, that you only had to move an hour into the hills to come across unexcavated and uncharted burial mounds."

For Bruce, "the moment of sitting on the hot mounds was one of the rare occasions when poetry and life are mingled. *Plongé dans nature*. One has a desperate wish to communicate the almost mystical sensation, but finds oneself parched and impotent."

He turned to poetry to express his feelings. This was his legendary back of beyond, where the Animal Art of the Eurasian steppes had evolved. He was excited by his discussions with Levi and possibly by Basho and Marvell whose poems he carried in his rucksack. Higher up the same valley he watched a hawk chasing a lark over the rocks. He put the image into verse form.

A Crested lark
Caught in the wind
Lost a feather
The lark sang
On a smooth stone
The feather floated up
and was chased by a hawk.

His notebooks from now on contain frequent attempts at Levi's speciality.

"Afghanistan was the ideal place for these kinds of reflection," says Maurizio Tosi. In few other countries were the remains of the past so ubiquitous, mixing together civilisations arriving from distant corners with the Greeks, the Arabs, the Mongols. Tosi, having excavated there, well understood Bruce's fascination. "You stand in a barren countryside watching a group of camel- and horse-mounted nomads moving with all their stuff and flocks and behind them are still standing the most magnificent ruins of splendid buildings made by kings who ruled over farmers and craftsmen in large cities."

In the three months Bruce spent in Afghanistan he travelled almost everywhere on all kinds of vehicles and often on foot. Only in Patagonia and West Africa would he ever be such an intense traveller. "Peter told him about the joys of writing," says Tosi. "He came back and made up his mind to be a writer."

LEVI WAS GENEROUS about Bruce in *The Light Garden of the Angel King*. "It will be obvious from every page of this book that I was extremely fortunate in the travelling companion I did have, Bruce Chatwin. Most of our best observations and all the best jokes were his; it was he who was interested in nomads, he who told me to read Basho, he who had done all the right homework in my subjects as well as his own, who knew the names of flowers and who understood Islamic art history."

Bruce was less charitable. By the time of publication, in 1972, Peter Levi had fallen the way of Bruce's previous mentors. In a letter to Elizabeth, he claimed Levi's book "drove me wild with rage and I think I'd better not read it or I shall become apoplectic". A paragraph later, he added: "the thing that really infuriates me about the Afghan book is that all my remarks and observations are repeated verbatim as an integral part of his text."

Bruce began as a disciple, taking photographs for Levi's book. Yet he was an old Afghan hand. Levi's Hellenistic project soon irritated him, as did Levi. "Peter is being used by his neighbours as a spittoon. He declares that never will he again go on a bus. I can't imagine what alternative he has to suggest. It's perfectly all right to me. Behaving very stupidly. Says he goes to pictures to see the country." Bruce wondered how he could write poetry of any meaning with that attitude. He cautioned him about his behaviour towards officials. "Tell P he must not call the men at the ministry buggers, bastards, or anything else. If he believes they are, he will greet them accordingly . . . 'You've no sense of the practical,' I say." In August 1988, Bruce looked back on their trip without enthusiasm. "It was one of the more unpleasant experiences of my life. Peter always believes there's a pot of gold at the end of the rainbow. He kept picking up bits of pottery and saying they were from a great Greek temple."

Levi for his part was irritated by Bruce's habit of "playing at Napoleon". He was amused by Bruce's inability to set correctly a special altimeter he had bought in Holland. "It turned out he had us up Everest." And Bruce's one-upmanship sometimes tested his patience. At Kunduz, they found a watch in working order dated 1748 and afterwards wandered into the meat and vegetable markets. "I declared loftily but truthfully that all this was nothing to the fishmarket in Venice. Bruce turned out to be another enthusiast for that labyrinth of experiences, but infuriated me by saying, 'Aha, it was nothing to the fungus season in the market at Brno'."

Bruce's competitive spirit was strongest in his feelings towards Levi's book. "Peter says he was asked to write a book about Balkh. I countered by asking how on earth he could write a book about it when he'd been there for half a morning. He said it would take him a month to look up the necessary references."

The moment would come on their journey when Bruce became impatient to surpass his mentor.

BRUCE SUCCUMBED TO his usual sickness in Kabul. "Bruce had mild heat exhaustion and a sunstroke temperature," wrote Levi. "He sat dazed on his bed dressed in a long Arab gown, reading aloud fearsome sentences from the Royal Geographical Society's *Traveller's Guide to Health*, such as 'after collapse, death soon ensues'."

Levi meanwhile suffered from dysentery, refusing to eat "white food" like rice, milk or yoghurt.

In Kabul, an English hippie called Nigel joined them. Nigel, whom Bruce described as "small, elfin, mischievous, very queer and highly likeable", incarnated every fear the Willey Expedition entertained for Afghanistan. "Nigel has been approached by a young man who offers a complete armour of hashish," wrote Bruce. "Pectorals, body belts, cross over braces, necklaces, thigh packs, back packs, holding some 10 kilos in all. Costing not much more than $20 a kilo for high quality stuff. I am bored by the whole business."

Bruce felt Nigel was someone to be saved, not least from the clutches of the Anti-Slavery Society, still agitating to leave Kabul. He asked Levi whether they might hire him as an interpreter on their journey to Chagcheran in the north-west district of Ghor. " 'Can he come with us? We might save his soul.' I said, 'Oh?' 'Well, you see,' said Bruce, 'he was at Marlborough'."

They flew to the barren grazing grounds of Chagcheran, where Bruce had heard of a huge annual nomad fair. A week earlier there had been 1,000 tents. Now about 40 flapped in a dust storm, exciting Bruce, who had once slept beneath a jousting tent in Grosvenor Crescent Mews. "I am always moved by the sight of tents and I thought of the Field of the Cloth of Gold, the last gasp of a medieval chivalry that owed so much to the mounted cavalry of the Steppe."

The tents belonged to the Firuzkuhi, who came into Afghanistan with the first Turkish conquerors. Bruce's destination was their lost capital city, locked in the mountains of the Ghorat and identified as the modern village of Jam.

On 10 July, the three of them reached Shahrak in a bus, from there intending to ride to Jam. "Officer in charge is 23 and has offered us a room and use of his servant Jon-o, which means 'Soul-Ho!' One syrupy glance from our new soulmate makes me very nervous. He is so thin and angular one expects him to collapse in a disjointed heap. Deep, deep glance, rolling of eyes, and wide toothy smiles. In bazaar he has helped me stock up with provisions, carrying eggs in his turban . . ."

Not for the first time was Bruce unnerved by syrupy glances, but Levi is quite certain: "He didn't go to bed with any monkeys or goat-boys. He led the life of a Cistercian monk."

That night Bruce danced for his supper, "an ecstatic dance with 5 emphatic and suggestive thumps at the climax. An old man highly complimentary on my 'lady movements' and kept dragging me to my feet."

They set off on horseback for Jam, 14 hours away, Bruce perched in agony above some lilac tweed saddle bags which contained the horses' food. To his apoplectic mirth, Nigel and Levi had bought turbans. They looked to him "sensationally like crested pouter pigeons", Nigel bearing a resemblance to Lady Hester Stanhope. But the turbans saved their lives in the heat and Levi in his journal records that not long after mocking their appearance, Bruce talked about buying a black one.

Jam was famous for its apricot groves and its minaret of strawberry-coloured brick. This was situated in a shiny black gorge and rose into view

THAT WRETCHED BOOK *241*

at the apex of a chasm of nearly vertical cliffs. "One cannot adequately describe one's feelings of surprise and bewilderment at this marvel," Bruce wrote. Planted in a desolate, forlorn valley, the Minaret of Ghyath-ud-Din Muhammad, Sultan of Ghor for the last 40 years of the twelfth century, was, believed Bruce, one of the world's most audacious monuments. "It rears to the sky like some triple-tiered Moon Rocket and was built with exactly the same aspirations." Inside, a birch staircase swirled to the muezzin platform. Bruce climbed to the top where a few timbers stuck out like the frame of a worn-out umbrella. "High above me white vultures are spiralling in a thermal, and the crenellated turrets of the castle cling precariously to the peaks opposite. They were once adorned, we are told, by a pair of gold griffins, each the size of a camel. The permanence of the castle is due, perhaps, to the strength [of the mortar] for which Ghyath-ud-Din's father had a special recipe. Captives from Ghazni were forced to carry dried earth in sacks on their shoulders. They were beheaded and their bodies mixed in to form a paste. Charming . . . 'Nasty people,' says Peter as we take one last look at the minaret. 'Always cutting each other up. And horrible to their women'."

IT WAS PROBABLY in Jam that Bruce decided—without a word to his companion—to write a book on Afghanistan.

Levi had assumed Bruce to be researching his work on nomads. "Bruce has been reading Genesis & has been confirmed in his view of the essential role of vegetarianism in Paradise." Bruce's notebooks are clotted with conundrums for *The Nomadic Alternative*: "The main question is this. Is wandering—the urge to travel—an endoeomatic genetically inherited manifestation of a biological urge to explore or is it culturally dependent?" Occasionally a note of doubt creeps in. "I am afraid that I have conducted in truly nomadic fashion cavalier raids on specialised disciplines I have not even begun to master." Yet he never doubts the magnitude of his task. "Book must carry a new theory of motion as a mainspring of life."

At the time, Levi hardly suspected the scale of Bruce's ambition. Later, he would compare him to Casaubon in *Middlemarch*, always writing an important book that remained unpublished. "He was desperately competitive in a way I'd never have grasped. It was a pointless ambition, like a fire eating him out."

Bruce extolled the nomads for having left no traces. In the same breath he marvelled at the buildings he found in Jam and Balkh and Herat. Setting aside his obligations to Maschler, he would set down on his return to England an outline based on his three visits to be called *On the Silk Road.* Bruce's agent does not remember receiving his proposal and nothing came of it, but it reads not unlike Levi's proposal to Collins and matches many of Byron's aspirations in *The Road to Oxiana.* "The book would take the form of a travel diary with diversions to take in the aspect of the country, the mountains, trees, the crops and animals and birds; the travellers from the Buddhist pilgrims, who have passed through, the great conquerors; architecture, mostly Islamic, and art; the complicated ethnography; trade from ancient times to the present." Bruce would also provide illustrations. "Mostly the diaries will be used as a vehicle for my photographs."

One of Bruce's selling points was that nowhere else did there exist as at Jam such outstanding and visible examples of Islamic architecture. "Afghanistan is perhaps the last country where important Islamic monuments conspicuous above the ground can still elude the attention of scholars."

HE HAD EXPERIENCED the highpoints. From now on, the trip frustrated him. "I am in a mood of insufferable depression," he wrote in his notebook while waiting for permission to travel to Nuristan. "I feel I have achieved virtually nothing on this journey. No sense of a path travelled, just an aimless flailing around, a pointless dispiriting succession of visits to Kabul punctuated by occasional relief journeys into the hinterland. The peaks beyond seem far more exciting. Search for a Paradise which is elusive. Major Willey omnipresent . . . He has now been told [by the authorities] that he is suspicious."

In fact, the Willey Expedition had begun to inform the spirit of his own expedition with Peter Levi. When Levi was expelled from Greece three years later, Bruce wrote to Elizabeth: "PL is really about on the level of Major Willey."*

---

* When the Willey Expedition published its report two years later, Bruce sent a letter to *The Times* "in high dudgeon and irony—so high they won't publish it". The report registered its dismay at the effect of hashish on European hippies who were reduced to "begging like dogs" in "sun-drenched squares that reek of death and decay". Willey appealed to the United Nations to stop the twin evils of slavery and narcotics: "We are facing a sinister situation that is capable of infinite expansion with appalling consequences."

The hashed-out Nigel had proved to be one of Bruce's follies, useless both as interpreter and travelling companion. Bruce grew fed up when he was late for aeroplanes, and wanted nothing more to do with him. His anonymous photograph, taken by Bruce, appeared on the cover of Levi's book, but all mention of him is rinsed from the contents.

In this mood, Bruce started to miss Elizabeth. "There comes a point when this aggressive masculinity becomes a bore. One longs for the female." On the day he was belted at the Bala Hisar his mind had travelled back to his honeymoon. "I think of the New England coast, lobsters, pines, fog, clams and cranberry swamps." He wrote in his notebook: "The lone wandering man feels a definite need for his wife on his wandering."

On 21 July, he wrote to her: "So what I suggest is this . . . that we meet somewhere in Western rather than Central Asia on or around Aug 25." As always when he found himself "festering away in exotic climates I have a longing for CIVILIZATION with a capital C." He added: "I have realised several things on this trip. You know—they are very good for me. They act as purgatives. I am nearly 30 and instead of being fretted by it and imagining it not the case, I am pleased about it and have decided to act upon it." The trip had made him realise that above the rest:

"I am going to be a serious and *systematic* writer."

And: "I love you."

ELIZABETH ARRIVED IN early August. Bruce collected her from Kabul and they joined Levi at the Spinzar Hotel in Kunduz. "Anyone who thinks of bringing his wife on a journey like this should be warned that Elizabeth has unusual qualities," wrote Levi. The rugged conditions did not daunt her, not even when she had to be pulled by rope up a scree at 16,500 feet during a snow fall.

By the Kokcha River she immediately rescued a bedraggled quail which some children were pestering in a lane. She bought it for a shilling and carried it home in a hat. The bird, caught in the mountains, would eat only the tiniest crumbs. "Pinioned. Motionless. Lacking wing feathers and the feathers of the crown," noted Bruce. Elizabeth absorbed herself in the quail's recovery, taking it on the bus. " 'How are you?' I call to Elizabeth as we crash over the rocky road. 'The bird is drinking,' she calls back." The quail prompted memories of a pet chicken she kept as a child. "Look out!" Gertrude would cry as it swooped at the lunch table across the pedimented porch. When Levi suggested Elizabeth might let the bird go, Bruce warned: "Better a quail now than a lion-cub later."

In Kunduz, there was a brief parting of the ways. Peter Levi pressed on to Kabul while Bruce took Elizabeth and the quail on a lightning tour. Near Faizabad they heard the sound of camel bells. The Kuchi nomads were packing up their tents to go down to Sind for the winter. "The women and babies sat on camels at the rear," says Elizabeth. "There were men on nice horses shouting at goats and mastiffs to keep the leopards at bay."

In Herat, they stopped for a few days at the same hotel where Bruce had stayed with Erskine in 1963. "Elizabeth and I sat in the corner at dinner. Elizabeth said it's like being in disgrace at school. She laughed her infectious laugh. I laughed. The waiter laughed, though he couldn't understand what we found so funny." In its bell-shaped cage, the quail's calls sounded like clear water.

It was the first time since their honeymoon that they had been on an expedition in this close way together. As darkness fell one night beside the River Pech they lost their porters, but fires on the mountain indicated a village high up in the pines. In the dark, Elizabeth put a yellow hollyhock in her hair and kissed him. "She was so tired and exhausted and could hardly move."

Bruce was filled with admiration for his wife's physical courage. He took pleasure in her observations. Elizabeth, wearing a poncho and an Uzbek hat and carrying a fly whisk, was always pointing out things on their path. "Look, there's a tree toad, I think I saw his lip . . . Look, a nut! Look, there's a tiny, pretty fern in those rocks."

In Herat, they left an impression that remained fresh ten years later. On 25 March 1978, Elizabeth and Julia Hodgkin entered the shop of Hababullah, a turbaned dealer in a padded coat. Hodgkin recorded the incident in her diary.

"Ah! Chatwin, yes!" he exclaimed. "Incredibly enthusiastic to know, 'How *is* Chatwin?'"

XIX

Distractions

HOME IS A PERVERSION

—BC, NOTEBOOKS

"THAT WAS WHEN our marriage really worked," Bruce said of the Afghan journey. Bruce and Elizabeth travelled well together, and indeed he would tell many of his friends that he preferred to travel with Elizabeth than with anyone else. But they could not replicate this equilibrium at home. "He hates this place," she wrote to Gertrude.

The Chatwins came home to Holwell in October after staying a month with Millington-Drake on Patmos, "the most beautiful island in the Aegean." Bruce had smuggled out an Afghan bronze to finance the trip, while Elizabeth concealed in her bra a round Buddhist reliquary made of grey schist the size of a tennis ball.

The quail, which Elizabeth also carried home to Gloucestershire, was frightened by a dog and died. As consolation, Bruce bought Elizabeth a pair of painted quail, and for her birthday a grumpy grey African parrot which screeched whenever he approached. More animals arrived throughout the autumn. Elizabeth accepted from John Stefanidis a dog given to him by Peggy Guggenheim and recently recovered from meningitis. "Solomon Guggenheim" had never been in the country and scampered about like a wild thing, biting daisies. In November, Elizabeth also agreed to look after Penelope Betjeman's Arab gelding for a few months. Having no children, she channelled her energies into her animals and her husband.

Bruce was at the center of this menagerie. Despite his farm upbringing, he had no real sympathy for animals. In a diary he started at this time, he records how he took Solly—as he had become—to Wales with John Michell. "Lunch in Llandovery café. Proprietor enraged that I fed ham sandwich to dog. J. M. called it Marie-Antoinettish behaviour on my part." He left Solly in his room and when it was pointed out that it had no water, he said: "Well, he had a drink yesterday." Elizabeth's dogs sometimes drove him to fury. "He liked Io, but she disappeared down a hole when he was having his veins done." When one dog chewed a volume of Hart Crane's poetry, he told Tomlinson, whose book it was: "I could have slit its throat." He was most petulant about Elizabeth's cats—who repaid him in kind. Pumpkin, a furry ginger, loathed him. "He'd go around spraying everywhere when Bruce arrived, and used to stare at him," says Elizabeth.

The animals bore the brunt of Bruce's frustration at Holwell. "I hate cats, that's why Elizabeth has cats," he told the French journalist, Jean-François Fogel. "Maybe she is fond of them," suggested Fogel. "No! She has them because she knows I hate them." The hero of *The Viceroy of Ouidah* also hates his wife's orange cat: "When it miaowed he felt as if a scalpel were scouring the inside of his skull." Perhaps enacting Bruce's fantasy, da Silva kills it.

"I KNOW THAT our marriage is not typical and seems odd, but it works for us," Elizabeth told John Chanler. She rarely talked about her personal struggles. Once, driving to Greece with her younger brother Ollie, she said: "Bruce and I never discuss our relationship."

"Never?"

"No, we never do."

Ollie detected no animosity, "but I always felt it was a relationship I didn't envy".

Neither did the community in Ozleworth, which was united in thinking that Bruce treated his wife badly. Among them was the historian James Lees-Milne, who often walked with Bruce. "As Byron was hated by Lady Byron's friends, plenty of people would take up cudgels on Elizabeth's behalf without her encouraging them. She would never betray by a flicker of an eyelid that she thought she was being treated horribly, so we never presumed to treat her with sympathy."

The Chatwins' closest neighbours were Charles and Brenda Tomlinson. "When Elizabeth or Bruce were away, each one would come here to find out where the other was," says Brenda.

Many neighbours disliked Bruce and the feeling was mutual. The country set got up his nose much as Elizabeth's animals did. At one dinner party, a man asked him: "'What do you do?' 'I'm writing a book. What do *you* do?' '*Do?* What do ye mean *Do?* I hunt four times a week. How d'ye expect me to *do* anything?'"

He preferred to import his company from London, which could be exhausting for Elizabeth. "He was a marvellous guest but a terrible host. He was much too engrossed in talking. It wasn't much good telling stories to me. I was too sceptical. He needed another audience.

"He would never do placements. He'd get all his favourite people next to him, and then he'd simply leave the table and disappear because he had thought of something he wanted to write. He had awful manners in lots of ways. He'd push his plate away when he'd finished and he had a complete aversion to washing up." He did not wash up in 23 years of marriage. "Never, never, never."

He quickly became bored even by his own guests. "Last night we had Stephanidis and the Johnstons here for dinner, and Miranda and I got frantic with boredom half way through," he wrote to Elizabeth in India. "They arrived an hour late after the dinner was spoiled, and then batted on remorselessly about what Jeremy and Antonia, or Annabel and Clive were or were not doing with each other, stayed yacking till 1.30. God, the English are a bore. I have never felt such a yearning to be something else."

By Sunday, he had often sickened of whomever he had invited down for the weekend. He would take them for tea at the Tomlinsons and leave them there. "Every so often he'd appear out of the undergrowth with a guest," says Charles Tomlinson. "The most unexpected people turned up." Andrew Batey, James Ivory, an Afghan who needed a roof, the great-great-grandson of Wagner's mistress, the heir to a Dukedom who was a policeman . . .

"I can't stand those people," he told Tomlinson once.

"But Bruce, you brought them down here."

"Well, I can't stand them."

EVENTUALLY, BRUCE SETTLED down to write his book, dividing his time between Holwell and Kynance Mews with frequent dashes to Oxford. "I've never seen him so continuously cheerful before," wrote Elizabeth. "He reads piles and piles of books and writes away like mad . . . During the week he spends all day in the Bodleian or one of the other libraries in Oxford and says he's accomplishing a lot."

He was determined to finish his book by the end of his thirtieth year. "One's thirtieth year, you know, is make or break year," he wrote to Elizabeth. "I'm rather superstitious about it. Must be over by May or something awful might happen." In 1980, he told an interviewer: "Some fatuous person who had better be nameless said . . . you've got to publish your first book by the age of 30 if you're going to be a writer. That totally put me into a complex." But he was plagued by the restlessness he was trying to examine. "He liked either the tents of nomads or London drawing rooms," says Michell. "What he followed was spirit, and he found it in both places."

As if to mark his new life as a writer, Bruce began a diary: "12 Dec 1969. There's nothing like beginning a diary with an event." The event was a lunch party hosted by Ann Fleming ("faintly Ruritanian in appearance") for Noel Coward on the eve of his 70th birthday. "Coward was very senile in appearance and had bleary eyes, a puffy face and discoloured teeth. Dandruff on his coat in small scabs. But the brilliant smile was kind—and the mind undimmed. As I've had a major fixation about him since first hearing a squeaky record of "Stately Homes of England" in 1951, when I was eleven, I have waited exactly 18 years for today. It would have been terrible if I was too late. Happily not. Ann Fleming's partridge was coming down my nose, and my eyes watered with pleasure."

Coward aimed many of his remarks at his godson, Caspar Fleming. "Caspar was, as a child, indulged in the nose-picking his mother disapproved of. 'Why should you deprive the poor child of one of the greatest pleasures in life? I've been raking away since the cot and it's quite delicious afterwards. Messrs Fortnum & Mason could not provide . . .' as we went into lunch." Another of Coward's remarks, Bruce took to be directed at himself. "The best bit of theatrical advice I ever had—never let anything artistic stand in your way."

"I have always acted on this advice," Bruce wrote at the end of his life when he was secure in his identity as a writer and his style was, in his own words, "bleak" and "chiselled". But at the point of recording Coward's words he was still researching his first book. Not only was he open to artifice, but he was attracted to anything artistic, which perhaps explains why it was so hard for him to sit down and write.

That autumn he bought at Sotheby's a 1630 Mogul miniature of an Arctic tern, "the bird that has the longest migration of any species." As someone who preferred the image to live things, the austere painting transfixed him. He believed it to be the work of the great court painter Mansur from the menagerie of Emperor Jahanghir. After bidding for it in the Kervorkian sale in November, he walked to the London Library to read an account of the tern's migration patterns. On leaving the library, he was accosted by an elderly tramp who out of the blue likened himself to the bird then in Bruce's thoughts. In *The Songlines*, Bruce describes how he took the tramp out to lunch and questioned him about his involuntary compulsion to wander. He recalled his "immense surprise" at the tramp's reply: "It's like the tides was pulling you along the highway. I'm like the Arctic tern, guv'nor. That's a bird. A beautiful white bird what flies from the North Pole to the South Pole and back again."

Bruce's poles from now on consisted of the road and the writing desk.

BRUCE'S ATTEMPT AT the conventional diary form lasted two months:

DEC 12

John Michell and his girlfriend here. We talked of megaliths and the earliest astronomy. Elizabeth is off to Paris in the morning to see Hester Pickman on her way to India. We are going to the Prescelly mountains.

Hashish before going to bed. Light-headed.

DEC 15

Worked during the morning with interruptions on the book. Fluency is elusive. Reached an impasse with the first chapter. I think I have bitten off far more than I can chew. Elizabeth returned from Paris. Read some of Tom Wolfe's *Mid-Atlantic Man* which recalled vividly the suffocation of New York. Fine high clouds in the sky. Lurid sunset.

DEC 16

I have finally rearranged the first chapter and hope for God's sake that, third time lucky, it is final.

DEC 17

Worked in the morning and then drove to London in the snow. Went to Deborah's and met Robert Allen, very amiable boyish anthropological type writing a book called *The Useful Savage*. Party at Sheridan and Lindy's [Lord and Lady Dufferin]—everyone there. Twiggy, Justin de Villeneuve, Hockney, Peter Schlesinger, H. H. [Howard Hodgkin], the Knight and Olda [Desmond Fitz-Gerald, then married to Loulou de la Falaise], Gibbsie and Don McCullin the photographer, with whom I had a very instructive conversation; also Bob Silvers, Ed of *N. Y. Review of Books* here on a talent spotting tour, it seemed. Talked of Konrad Lorenz and the nonsense of ethologists. Jessica D-Home down here at Christmas. Cara Denman. G. O. [George Ortiz] very excitable but on good form.

DEC 18

Went to stay at Susanna and Nicky. To Patrick Woodcock, then shopping. Then to *Vogue*. Jill Weldon and B. Miller all very strange. I think they'll publish my photographs. Then to R. Allen, Peter Schlesinger to pick up a book. Huge and I'm afraid very bad canvasses. Then to Peter Levi on very good form. Very giggly. Back to dinner with the Duchess [Sally Westminster], her sister Diana, and Charles and Brenda.

DEC 19

Spent the morning clearing and organising my study and the latter part of the afternoon fiddling with the book. Less unhappy now than I was.

DEC 20–27

Blank over Christmas. Not my favourite time of the year. Drinks at Sally's on the Sunday. David Somerset smoother than ever—and very pleasant Gascoignes from Alderley. Spent the beginning of the week finishing—at last—the first chapter of the nomads. Arrival of my parents. CLC looking tired and in need of a holiday again—why he can't retire and treat his whole life as a holiday I can't imagine. Let him write a book, sail around the Horn—anything except to eke out his last active decade in a Birmingham solicitor's office. Adrian Chanler here and Hugh and we sat about in a lethargic state—drinking too much without enjoyment—eating too much with ill effects after.

Long walks alone up the valley which was cold and beautiful. Mist passing over a silvery sun. I am again feeling the pangs of restlessness, and am planning to go to Mauritania. The only country that nobody seems to have heard of. I know where it is, said Penelope [Betjeman]. It's in Eastern Europe and we all used to see it in '20s films. They wear white uniforms. "You're thinking of Ruritania"—and she was.

THE DIARY, LITTLE more than a catalogue of dinner parties, lasted only another month. "*Hate* confessional mode," he wrote in his notebooks.

BRUCE REACHED MAURITANIA in February, having come by way of New York where he had been to the opening of the Asia House exhibition. He travelled to Oualata to see the Nemadi tribe. "They are the greatest storytellers and they make a virtue of their sudden departures for the unknown," he wrote. It was one of three journeys he made specifically to investigate nomads on their migration routes. In April 1971, he stayed in Teheran with the Oxmantowns, who had been posted to Iran from Dahomey. In a borrowed Embassy Land Rover, he spent five days with the Qashgais on their spring migration. In January 1972, he returned to West Africa, travelling through Niger to Dahomey to see the Bororo Peuls, "a people obsessed by the horizons and their own beauty".

These trips were "cavalier raids". Most of this period was spent not in the saddle with nomads, but in libraries, writing about them. There was hardly time to merge with his subject, in each case little more than a week. Nor did he necessarily see nomads in their natural surrounds. The group of Nemadi had been forbidden to hunt their traditional wild oryx because of a drought. Bruce came upon them camped outside a town.

IT WAS THROUGH Alison Oxmantown in Teheran that Bruce met a British expert on nomads. Jeremy Swift was an economic anthropologist who had lived with nomad tribes in Africa, the Middle East and Mongolia. Where Bruce spent six days with the Qashgai and Bakhtiari, Swift spent six months—and another six months with the Tuareg in Mali.

Swift found Bruce extremely clever, funny, with "an enormous amount of knowledge about lots of arcane things", and well travelled. "Even then in the early 1970s he'd been to places that most people had never heard of." But he considered Bruce an artist, not an ethnographer. "I was studying nomads as a job. He was a wild romantic. Whenever he was near a nomad his imagination worked in overtime, jostling with Herodotus and Ibn Khaldun. He didn't spend much time with them. He wasn't a nomad in the sense that nomads would talk about being nomads. A real nomad would move to places that he or she knew about, would understand the space involved, would not go in search of sensations."

Bruce asked Swift odd and intelligent questions, but never tested his thesis, perhaps anticipating Swift's reaction. "Bruce's theory about people moving because movement is a natural condition is wrong. I've spent lots and lots of time with lots of groups. All say it's nice to move on: you don't have the quarrels you get in villages or cities, you go to pretty places, you get up in the cool mountains in summer and the plains in winter. But it's hell on wheels doing it, taking all your possessions and children. I remember the Bakhtiari women on the last bit of their migration, a high mountain pass through snow and a woman crying, sobbing with pain: '*Why* do we have to do this?' The prospect of Bruce offering a lift in his Land Rover would have delighted them. It meant they did *not* have to walk."

Like Desmond Morris, Swift objected to Bruce's definition of a nomad. "Nomads of today," Bruce wrote in his book, "are truck drivers, *gauchos, vaqueros, mafiosi,* commercial salesmen, shifting migrants, and those possessed of the samurai spirit, mercenaries and guerrilla heroes." Swift says, "He lumps together hunters, herders, gypsies. Everyone who moves is a nomad. In fact, what *separates* them is greater. Nomads move because their animals require fresh pasturing, not because of an innate neurosis. It doesn't mean movement is unimportant: it's enshrined in their way of life and they write songs about it—but it's secondary, something you do because your dependence on animals requires it. So many of them have said to me: 'If there was more pasture for our animals we would move less.' All over the world nomads *are* moving less and are not notably unhappy about it. Nomads have a strong sense of home and place. The notion of them moving around randomly is completely false."

Bruce's preference for classical authors over important nomad texts meant that his knowledge was tangential, says Swift. "Bruce knew a lot about nomad jewellery, but he didn't know a lot about nomad ethnography. He was much more widely read than me in a Victorian gentleman way, yet he doesn't seem to have read things central to his task—or to use them if he's read them. He talks about the Bororo—a good ethnographer would call them Wodaabe. Marguerite Dupire wrote two volumes on the Wodaabe, Derek Stenning another. Nomads are among the most studied people in the world. There is a huge corpus of ethnography. He doesn't cite any of it, apart from Fredrik Barth."

Swift likened Bruce's enterprise, the crux of which survived in *The Songlines,* to a brilliant attempt at an out-of-date form, a grand synthesis by an extraordinarily well-read amateur in the tradition of Francis Bacon, Gilbert White and Arnold Toynbee. "He wasn't cautious. That was one of the wonderful things about him. He would dramatically be plotting out several moves ahead, and you can't do that if you are a researcher. His method was not scientific. He was irritated by the caveats which scientists put around things. Scientists try to marshal evidence that disproves their hunch. Bruce fixes on a beautiful idea, a poetic idea, and marshals evidence to support his hunch. Sadly, that doesn't work. His canvas is too vast. He is trying to write something that is much closer to the history of mankind, but not having looked at the crucial literature he chases his tail. If you think of the eventually published result as a serious synthesis, it's futile. If you think of it as poetry, none of this matters."

BRUCE'S WILL TO realise himself in his nomad book is reminiscent of Balzac: "If I'm not a genius I'm done for." One of his favourite stories was Balzac's *"Le chef d'œuvre d'un inconnu"*, about an unknown painter at work for a long time on a great masterpiece. When the canvas is finally revealed, it consists of a few lines and one perfectly painted foot in the corner. "It's a very great story indeed," said Bruce.

In confident moments he thought of himself as Balzac's painter, an undiscovered artist engaged on a significant project. "I want it to glitter like a diamond," he wrote to Elizabeth in December 1970, and a month later. "As you know, to me this book is really important . . . There are parts I am pleased with and parts that are a mess. One cannot hurry something that can't be hurried. Am lurching through the last section quite rapidly now, next week will come to the Hero and the road of trials, followed by anarchists and modern revolutionaries, and then a concluding chapter where all the heavy guns are fired. Nerve required. I am quite unaware at the moment if I have gone off my head or whether the ideas are so novel, so outrageous, so shattering that no one will be able to put the book down . . . We shall see. *The Book must be done.*"

But whenever the end was in sight he wanted to start again. "Oh God, when will I get it done?" he wrote to her at the same period. "I've worked and worked for example 8 a.m. to 12 midnight yesterday . . . it is an endless drama of shuffling and reshuffling the component parts, turning passive verbs into active verbs etc." As Swift divined, what burdened him was the freedom with which he lavished the term "nomad". He wrote to Peter Levi: "Very interesting the use of the word 'nomad' as a term of abuse in the Sharon Tate murder case. 'A band of hate-oriented twentieth-century nomads' is about as bad a condemnation as one can get. I have written two chapters of my book. Then I decided they were too boring. So they will have to be rewritten. If only I didn't have an argument to follow. One always forgets what they're about."

In this way he picked at the book. Each journey resulted in another chunk of disparate material to incorporate. He grew thoroughly sick of it, until the day came when he confessed in his journal: "I must write that bloody book of mine in a sensible clear way. I opened the first page this afternoon rather like someone disposing of a letter bomb. It was horrible. Pretentious. But I still like 'The best travellers are illiterate and they do not bore us with reminiscences'."

This was the beginning.

BRUCE'S PREOCCUPATION WITH "that wretched book", as she came to call it, meant Elizabeth had to forge her own life. "Bruce never likes to plan anything at all, but I can't always sit around waiting to see what will happen," she wrote to Gertrude. "Besides, a lot of times he likes to go off by himself and I never know until after he's left whether he wants me to come too."

In September 1970, Elizabeth set off for India in a converted yellow grocery delivery van for which Margharita had made cushions and curtains. Her passengers were Beth Cuthbert, a schoolteacher, and the artist John Nankivell. Elizabeth's journey lasted eight months, taking in India, Afghanistan, Iran and Turkey, and was made at the instigation of Penelope Betjeman, who wished to investigate pagoda temples in the western Himalayas. Betjeman drove in a second Morris van with another artist, Elizabeth Simson.

Bruce was originally to be part of the group, but reneged. He needed, he said, to spend the summer in Greece working on his book. He also had misgivings about Betjeman, a close friend of Stuart Piggott. "Penelope seems to be very demanding and I'm afraid that eccentricity has an uncommon tendency to develop into egomania. This is perfectly all right as long as you don't have to travel with it."

As a compromise he agreed to meet Elizabeth in Istanbul and show her the city before the next stage of her journey, through Turkey in the footsteps of the Seljuks. From the Leigh Fermors' house in Kardamyli, he asked her to bring one winter suit, some cold weather clothes, gloves, rucksack, boots, new laces and socks. "Also you'd better bring my camera *en route*. I don't quite know what to do about money, but I believe I do get £1,000 on delivery of the manuscript."

In late September, Bruce was standing in Haghia Sophia when he heard a familiar voice: "Oh my dear, we've been raped." It was Betjeman—and Bruce was more or less the first person to whom she related an experience that thrilled her so much that her husband, the poet John Betjeman, sent her account of it out as a Christmas card.

Betjeman gave Bruce a graphic description of how she had lost contact with Elizabeth outside Trieste. Once over the Turkish border she had parked for the night in a cornfield near Edirne. She and Simson cooked dinner and then sat side by side in the front seat to read their books by the overhead light. Betjeman was engrossed in Robert Byron when the door was wrenched open by a Turkish soldier. He tried to drag Simson outside, but she grabbed the steering wheel. Betjeman, appalled, dropped *The Road to Oxiana* and shouted: "Elizabeth, Elizabeth, I will go. I'm too old to have a baby." In her beige tweeds she extricated herself from the van and moved to interpose herself, stroking the man's wrist and caressing his head. "Offer finally accepted as rescue came," wrote Bruce in his account to Paddy Leigh Fermor. "Not before the soldier had offered five Turkish lire, his week's pay, for the younger specimen." Left behind in the front seat, Simson started the engine. The soldier, eschewing Betjeman, hared off after the departing vehicle, but failed to catch up. Simson meanwhile flagged down a carload of Americans and they returned to the site to find Betjeman sitting in the cornfield, laughing hysterically. She had headed off into the field and, knowing a white face would show in the dark, had hidden with her head down in the corn. The Turkish infantryman had fled.

Bruce and Elizabeth stayed in the home of his old friend Guler Tunca. After five days, he decided to return to Holwell, complaining of toothache. He agreed to meet up with Elizabeth again in India once he had finished the book. "I make no promises as to the date." He would prevaricate throughout the autumn, making and breaking several more plans, to the annoyance of John Nankivell: "We spent our trip in a sense doomed by Bruce Chatwin because everywhere we were supposed to meet him he was never there."

BRUCE RECALLED HIS winter at Ozleworth in *On the Black Hill.* "The winter was hard. From January to April the snow never melted off the hill and the frozen leaves of foxgloves drooped like dead donkey's ears." He identified Amos's "gloomy house below the hill" with Holwell Farm. "It lay on a sunless slope and, at the snowmelt, streams of icy water came pouring through the cottage."

An American poet Loretta Anawalt, who visited Holwell at this time, came away feeling that she had been living "in a wet head of lettuce. Everything seemed damp and the air was redolent with the smell of wild onion."

To his chagrin, Bruce did not have Holwell to himself. Elizabeth, to cover running costs and to ensure that someone would look after her animals, had rented the farm to an American friend of Michell whom she had bumped into in a health food shop in Bath. Bruce described Linda Wroth as having "the wide staring intense eyes of the American intellectual initiate." They shared the house unhappily until the New Year. "Frankly, I thought she'd leave when I came," he wrote to Elizabeth. "She said 'I suppose it's your house isn't it?', but now she seems to have got used to the idea of my presence." He found her presence disconcerting. Brenda Tomlinson says: "She cooked an enormous bowl of brown rice and put it under her bed so that she could eat in her room without Bruce having to share her meal . . . Bruce would leave the washing up and she'd scream at him. Then Bruce would come down here. 'That woman has just screamed at me!' Then Linda would come down. 'That Bruce thinks I'm just going to wash up and clean for him!' "

As Elizabeth motored towards India, Bruce reported on life at Holwell in weekly bulletins to a chain of embassies. His teeth were better, a biopsy on the gums confirming the problem was not cancer. He had met some neighbours with horses. "I am going to exercise their hunters once or twice a week in Cirencester Park and have become quite horsey, stamping around the house in riding boots." In November, he celebrated Elizabeth's birthday in the garden. "The anniversary of your birth has been marked by a ceremonial planting—Holwell farm now has a *Salicetrium* and you can guess what that is till you return." One day he slipped his disc while lugging soil to the back of the house. "It has caught the nerve which leads to one's crutch and balls and I felt someone had given me the most almighty boot where it hurts most."

He exaggerated his injury to stay at home. He admitted to Elizabeth that her letters from Teheran and Kabul gave him "a slightly guilty complex". On 24 November, he wrote: "You must realise if I don't do this thing now it'll sit here for ever as I have a million other plans as well. I'm very sorry but there it is. I am going on and on until the first draft is available for Tom Maschler and have his opinion. Then I'll decide. I know the whole thing is very irritating for you especially with your companions— and incidentally Penelope is the last person I want to show me round Delhi and would put me off for ever." He cancelled one plan to meet her in Bombay for Christmas, another to meet in Delhi. "I don't know what

I can say about coming. I wish I did. I can't tell you how much I long to get away. But if I break the threads of concentration now, I'm honestly afraid that the whole thing will go down the drain." He knew himself: "The thing with me is that if I break the continuity it always goes to pot."

At Holwell, work on the book ground on with remorseless slowness. The house buzzed with legions of flies and a new addition: "long-eared bats that mysteriously secrete themselves into the bedroom and hover around at night after the flies. It's a curious sensation the noise of fluttering air, more mechanical than animal, and I could even hear the high-pitched screech."

By December, living with Linda Wroth became impossible. He thought her rude, disliked her boyfriends, "professional snivellers" who devoured his food and drink. "She really is quite awful. I can't stand her, and she's been making such a fearful scene because I'm here at all. When I suggested she GO and I STAY, there was no question of it." He did not know for how long they could endure under the same roof.

But there seemed no easy solution. He had given up Kynance Mews and his money situation was "terrible". Christie's had stopped paying him a retainer and by January he was overdrawn by £1,250. "We simply cannot go on asking my parents to fork up, as there will come a limit." He decided to sell his Greek kouros and Sarah Bernhardt's Maori sculpture. And he attempted some journalism, earning £200 from *Vogue* for an article on nomads. "Imagine my horror when *Vogue* proofs came back with the title changed to IT'S A NOMAD NOMAD NOMAD WORLD. Jesus, what horrors editors are." He complained to the magazine. "Either the title is changed or it's coming out, Thank you." But he lost the argument. "In spite of my screamings or I suppose because of them the *Vogue* article appeared with title . . . Lesson learned. Never write an article for the fashionable press after a hangover in two hours."

Hugh Chatwin remembers Bruce's agony when he came down to Stratford to discuss the article with their mother. All the notes he had made, all his travels, had petered out prematurely in an embarrassing piece of journalism. The book was "very nearly finished", he reported to Elizabeth, "but is in the most unholy mess. What do I do?" He began to feel ill: "I have caught worms and a terrific resurgence of ringworm, which must be from the cats." He developed a pain in his right intestine accompanied by a constant urge to pee. "I couldn't sit at the typewriter because of the agony in my stomach, coupled with really terrible nervous depressions." He worried if he was being poisoned. "Linda and I both have Holwell Farm stomach ache and we wonder if it could be anything to do with the well." He was having the water tested. "I am quite decided it isn't my fertile imaginations. It is quite definitely something biological in the water, local virus etc. God knows! But we really must find out." And he was fairly persuaded that the house was haunted. "Doors slam for no reason." He wrote to Elizabeth: "this is the nadir of our fortunes."

IN DECEMBER, BRUCE left Holwell. He cited Linda as the reason. "I am afraid I simply couldn't stand the atmosphere here one minute longer and one day filled up the car and fled. She infuriates me to the point of no return and has mercifully gone to Bath for the night which is why I have come today. However, she does look after the house well despite everything, though a sinister crack has appeared in the beam in the dining-room due to the jolting of her constant intercourse."

Bruce fled to Miranda Rothschild, a friend of Peter Levi. A tragic widow, she lived at Yarnton, a Jacobean manor house outside Oxford. Here Bruce and Miranda embarked on "an endless conversation".

Miranda, whose nickname was "Quail", was an attractive, faint-voiced rebel with boyish looks and a taste for adventure. The sister of the banker Jacob Rothschild, she had fallen for an Algerian revolutionary. They married, had a daughter, and then in 1964 he was assassinated in Tunis. "I found him in a charnel pit." She went to live in Athens, where she fell platonically in love with, among others, Peter Levi. She was sitting as usual in Flocca's tearoom, plunging her cake into a glass of icy water, when she looked up and saw "a beautiful-looking Jesuit, like an icon, thin as hell. We fell platonically head over heels." Levi could manage no more than "a mad flirtation", but he wished to help her. Miranda needed nationality papers for her daughter. Levi persuaded her to return to England and introduced her to his best friend, Ian Watson. To facilitate the passport, she and Watson married. They were living together at Yarnton when Bruce turned up.

"I was polishing Tudor glass and living on vodka and lime and baked beans," says Miranda. "I was jolly bored and Bruce arrives on the scene with Peter Levi. He looked gorgeous, thin, a wheaty, bronzy colour and cold blue eyes. He was every Jewish girl's dream and I was a plump, exceedingly neurotic widow with a name." Miranda galvanised Bruce's competitive streak. "Bruce felt if I had a girl I didn't want," says Peter Levi, "so should he."

Miranda left Watson in Yarnton and invited Bruce to stay at her mother's house in London. At 27 Blomfield Road, Bruce sat on an ottoman reading aloud his nomad book while she listened from a four-poster. "He read to me constantly, it was his whole burning self-expression. I was starved of it. I was enclosed. I'd always been a nomad. I was married to an Arab and before that I'd lived in a desert in Israel, south of Sodom—appropriately enough." She became a constructive audience in a period of self-doubt. "The main ingredient of our friendship was an intellectual passion. It was an attraction of opposites who had an idea in common. I'm listening and discussing and we love each other because of the nomad book. I'm part of the book."

Bruce and Miranda celebrated Christmas in Blomfield Road where they kissed in the woodshed. "It was like a first kiss, a bestowal. It had a mystic edge." Bruce wrote to tell Elizabeth that he was going to spend four days with Miranda in Paris. He was drawn to her boyish looks. "Miranda has found out she has no female hormones!! and is turning into a man—*imagine!*" In fact, says Ian Watson, she so much resembled a boy that a year later when travelling through Afghanistan, she excited the chief of police in Mazar-i-Sharif into such a state that he machine-gunned the bottom of her house, shouting: "Let him out! Let him out!"

Miranda was well aware of her androgynous attraction for Bruce and of the cachet of her pedigree. She found him an immensely talented but detached person whose emotional luggage had to be honed down to the single perfect accoutrement of a rucksack. "His ambivalence was his impetus. Sexually, Bruce was a polymorphous pervert. Think of the word 'charming'. Think of the word 'seduction'. Think of seduction as a driving force to conquer society, *Vogue*. He's out to seduce everybody, it doesn't matter if you are male, female, an ocelot or a tea cosy."

In Paris, Miranda seduced Bruce. "It was my fault. I invited it," she says. "I was love-lorn and I wanted something. But I didn't want *that*. He was lust personified. It had nothing to do with anything else." She describes an act of lovemaking of great speed and savagery, as if he wanted it to be over quickly. "It didn't leave any taste at all, and I was surprised. I was lacerated as if by a Bengal tiger." It never happened again. "And then came Akbar."

IN MARCH 1971, in response to an S.O.S. from Elizabeth, Bruce flew to Teheran to drive her back. Meanwhile, Gertrude had also received an urgent request. "It may sound very strange, so be prepared. I have brought with me a Pathan boy from Multan called Ghulam Akbar Khan." She asked Gertrude to write a letter to the American Consul in Istanbul saying she would vouch for him. "I guarantee he is absolutely honest as the day is long & very kind & thoughtful. He looks rather like a *gaucho* from the Argentine & is very athletic & strong."

It was a chance encounter with Bruce and Elizabeth that changed Ghulam Akbar's life. They had met him at the end of their Afghanistan trip with Peter Levi. Akbar had approached on his bicycle. He was 19 years old, from the Pakistan side of the border. His mother was dead.

He corresponded with Elizabeth, who had met him again while driving her van home through Pakistan. Akbar asked to join her. "He has decided to come back to England (or at least Europe) with us & is marvellous company & as nice as can be, but can't drive and speaks rather quaint English."

Akbar was not Elizabeth's sole passenger. There were in addition: Simon, a chess-playing hippy with no driver's licence, and three more quail. "They are supposed to sing, but don't like the travelling and hardly utter." Akbar, as a present for Bruce, had bought a hawk in a round cage that made the quail fearful. "He has to be supplied with little bits of raw meat all the time. I hope we never get out of reach of a butcher or the quail will be sacrificed." The hawk subsequently escaped through the van's sunroof.

Elizabeth had reason to be grateful for Akbar's presence. Outside a caviar port on the Caspian Sea, there was almost a repetition of the rape incident with Penelope Betjeman, whom she had left behind in India with the others. Elizabeth was walking on the bleak sand flats when an Iranian soldier approached with a bayonet. While Simon screamed hysterically that he had not got his shoes on, Akbar speaking his quaint English talked the soldier out of his purpose. "He did save my bacon."

On 7 April, the van arrived at the Oxmantowns' house in Teheran where Elizabeth hoped to find her husband. Having cabled Bruce, she had heard nothing since February. "I hope he'll be able to come to Teheran, but I suppose his back won't be well enough. I certainly hope he's turned the book in by now."

Bruce had arrived in Teheran a week earlier, on 29 March. This was the occasion when he borrowed an Embassy Land Rover and drove to Shiraz. "Saw the Qashgais on their spring migration, which was thrilling, and for five days filled a British Embassy Land Rover full of sheep, tribesmen, women suckling babies etc.," he wrote to Welch. He described in *The Songlines* how at Pasagadae the nomads glued their eyes to the way ahead. While Bruce could not help looking at the huge domed tents, designed by

the Paris firm of Jansen for the Shah's celebration of 2,000 years of monar-
chy in June, the nomads swept past without a glance, their eyes blinkered
to the horizon towards which they drove hundred upon hundred of separate herds.

Bruce returned to Teheran to greet Elizabeth. "He waited, impatiently
pacing around," says Alison Oxmantown, "looking out for her with all the
signs of one much in love and desperate to see her." There followed several discussions about Akbar. Bruce was concerned about the responsibility of taking an innocent Muslim to Europe. Alison felt Elizabeth had
picked him up as she would any stray and unhappy animal.

Alison had just given birth to a daughter, Alicia. "It was spring and
hot and Bruce walked up and down with our baby saying how it proved
the point that humans were meant to be on the move and that moving babies don't cry. Akbar, however, was dismayed that she was not being
breast-fed. He explained that even when he went to school and returned
from the long walk, his mother, now feeding smaller children, would
point him to a friendly sheep that he could suckle. We all thought of starting a coffee bar with sheep tied to the counter for a quick pint. When they
left I kissed him—he was very good looking—and Bruce said, very
sharply, that this would seduce him into the other world, which it did."

A week later, on 13 April, Bruce, Elizabeth and Akbar left Teheran,
dropping Akbar in Corfu to sort out his Italian visa. "Either the quails or
Akbar have to go," Bruce told Elizabeth as they continued on to Rome to
meet her parents. On 4 May in Rome, they received a desperate message
from Akbar. He had reached Genoa. "But with very truble. I spend three
days in Corfu. I next day get visa and reach to port but the ship was
gone." The Italian banks had refused to cash the cheque Elizabeth had
given him to cover expenses. He begged her to send money to the Pakistan
Embassy in Paris, the sole clue to his whereabouts.

Bruce turned up in a state at Miranda Rothschild's flat in the rue de
Grenelle. "He was having a breakdown," she says. "He was feeling so
guilty. 'Look Miranda, only you can do this. I know he wanted to get to
Paris to meet us. Will you please find him?' I took it on like an oath, out
of love. He told me the last time he saw Akbar he had long black hair and
was dressed in native costume. He now had to go back to Cold Comfort
Farm."

Miranda looked up the address of the Pakistan Embassy. "I began to
walk up and down the Champs Elysées to see if I could see a long-haired
Afghan. I looked for a couple of days, six-and-a-half hours at a time. I like
that kind of work. Suddenly I see this apparition, stinking of onions, tall,

slim with raggedy-cut hair in a pudding basin. I go straight up: 'You must be Akbar.' He'd had to sell his hair to get money for his passage. He hadn't eaten anything except onions for four days."

Akbar was living at a Youth Hostel at the Porte d'Ivry. Every day he had walked to the Pakistan Embassy hoping to find Bruce and Elizabeth, nine miles each way, carrying his suitcase since on the first day at the hostel someone had stolen his shaving things.

Miranda took Akbar back to the rue de Grenelle. Two weeks later Elizabeth visited. "Miranda is really being very good to him & making all sorts of efforts to get him a job and residence permit & so on," she wrote to Gertrude. Miranda's husband, already mistrustful of Bruce, was less than happy with Akbar, who struck him as "a good-looking idiot". Back at Holwell, Elizabeth soon became aware of tensions. "Rang up Miranda and Ian who were most weird on the telephone . . . Ian said the whole thing is hopeless—I don't know if he meant that in several ways or what. Apparently Akbar's presence has caused a lot of trouble."

Bruce expressed his concern to Welch: "Elizabeth's young Pakistani couldn't get into England and is now stuck in France, where he is adopted by the Rothschilds as their latest amusement and a lot of talk about the Lost Tribes of Israel. We are prevented from talking to him on the phone so jealously is he guarded. Very irresponsible performance on the part of everybody."

The story continued to unfold out of Bruce's orbit. "We became lovers," says Miranda. "He told me he was a virgin, I was his first love, proper poetic stuff, and he wrote letters saying I'm his moonlit gazelle. He was horribly persuasive. I'd only ever been called a sturdy little pony before." She had a yearning to see Afghanistan. She had wanted to accompany Levi on his trip with Bruce in 1969 and now returned with Akbar to the northwest frontier. "All my nomadism comes back. From a young earth mother with a small child I again became a wild tomboy, toting pistols on the frontier of Afghanistan with China. I wore native dress, slung with a pistol and cartridges. I rode wild stallions. My whole life changed."

Months later Miranda returned to Paris without Akbar. Ostracised, she passed her time in a bar opposite the Fontaine des Quatre Saisons. "*Sans cesse* from 10 a.m." At her divorce, Akbar's letters were read out in court. "Suddenly I get a letter from Bruce on blue paper, blue ink. *My dear Miranda, I want to see you more than anything else in the world. I want you to forgive me more than anything else in the world.* He comes to see me in Paris. He gives me a Mesopotamian duck-weight made of haematite. He'd affected my life to a tremendous extent. He owed me one."

ON 14 MAY 1971, Bruce stood in Aspall Church in Suffolk and watched Prince William of Gloucester unveil a sculpture to Raulin Guild. "You must try and imagine that some invisible power has carried him off as he was," Bruce had written to Raulin's sister Ivry. "Open, fair, free-minded and ruthlessly honest."

The ceremony put his own life in relief. By 30, he hoped to have finished *The Nomadic Alternative*, but the journey to Teheran had "quite broken my train of thought, and after one day I am already shaking with the malaise of settlement". He wrote to Welch from Holwell: "Oh to finish the book. I wrote the last sentence before I went away. Since when some ideas have evaporated and new ones have taken their place. Two, three perhaps four months of revision."

But in June, he could no longer tolerate Holwell. "The weather is so infinitely frightful that I have just decided to go to the South of France with my typewriter and E is going to follow later."

He spent the summer in the Basse Alpes, staying first in a remote hamlet owned by the artist Jeremy Fry. From Oppedette, he wrote to Elizabeth: "It's quite beautiful and completely unspoiled. Not a tourist in sight, and any amount of crumbling farm houses to buy, my dear. High up, plenty of air and wind. One wouldn't need a garden for the wild flowers are a treat, all wild briars and honeysuckle, my dear." He suggested Elizabeth "up-sticks" and join him in another month.

He lasted scarcely a fortnight on his own. The telephone had been cut off and he had no car. On 3 July he sent a telegram to James Ivory: DO COME BUT QUICK STOP HIRE CAR MARSEILLE. In a letter, he explained: "I do badly want to see you—for lots of reasons. Apart from the obvious one, I want to ask your advice."

LEVI, FIRMLY BASED in the poetic and spiritual worlds, now yielded to a mentor of worldlier inclinations, the American film director "Jungle Jim" Ivory.

Ivory was a friend of Welch who five years before had proposed a film set in India, featuring the Beatles. (Welch had written to John Lennon saying *Rain* was the best Indian music since the time of Akbar.) The location of the film, about the Mughals, was to be the Red Fort in Delhi.

"Also on the path of the Mughals would be a gang of international art dealer/thieves," Welch wrote to Bruce. "Maybe [Hewett] would even play in the *filum*!" Welch had discussed the project with Ivory, who was "wild" about it. "If the idea comes off, I see you in it too." There matters rested, but the prospect of making a film germinated in Bruce's mind.

Bruce had met Ivory in the autumn of 1969 at Hodgkin's house near Bath. Bruce stood in the late afternoon with his back to the wall, looking at Ivory and not saying anything. Ivory, then preparing to make his fourth feature-film, *Bombay Talkie*, found him entertaining company: "he really did make you laugh". In London, Ivory had visited Bruce's studio in Kynance Mews. "He lived like a bachelor. One understood he was married. Elizabeth was there in the background most of the time and sometimes she came forward and was important to him, but they were not the usual kind of couple. He never referred to her contemptuously. He spoke of her like a friend, like another boy or man. She wasn't a weight around his neck who would stop him having fun: she wasn't that kind of wife."

Ivory arrived in Oppedette and stayed a week. The bleak little house lay on a bare treeless hillside. They made a trip to St Tropez, drove to Menerbes in the hope of seeing Dora Maar climb up the hill, and visited Stephen Spender in the Alpillas. Ivory says, "He was tearing a motor car apart and his hands were covered in black oil." In the baking hothouse they slept on mattresses. "Then Bruce would say, 'I have to work now'. I would sit on a big chair out in the sun, but very soon I'd see him walking around, not working. And that seemed to be the pattern."

Bruce's aim in coming to France was, Elizabeth explained to Gertrude, "to try and finish getting the book organised and shortened." But whenever Bruce talked to Ivory about nomads, "my eyes would glaze over. He had a thousand shiny bits of weird and unrelated historical facts which he would scatter."

Bruce promised Ivory: "Never never never will I write anything longer than a few pages. Never—at least for a very long time—will I try anything that demands RESEARCH."

The advice Bruce sought from Ivory had nothing to do with his book, but with cinema. "I have in the rough a story, which doesn't really work as a novel because I have tried it. It is also a true story about someone I met by chance . . . Do you think there might be something in it for you?"

The story was "Rotting Fruit", about the Matisse collector from Miami, and became the first of several ideas which Bruce now pitched to "Jungle Jim" as possible subjects for a film.

Bruce's interest in film-making was, like his musical based on Akhenaton, his volume of shaman poetry, his book on Afghanistan, a nine-day wonder. "Perhaps I was too stupid to understand that Bruce was *serious* about his film ideas while seeming to play them down or make a joke of them," says Ivory. "It never occurred to me that he wasn't being entertaining in his letters with preposterous plots and characters. When I read all his letters together I see—too late—that Bruce might have been in earnest. I must have seemed a poor friend, letting him down all the time."

Bruce furnished Ivory with one idea after another, to be developed as soon as he had finished *The Nomadic Alternative*. All seem based on experiences in his own life: his encounter with Andrew Batey ("That Andrew story *is* fascinating. Maybe we could do something"); the Willey Expedition in Afghanistan ("That really is worth a filum"); and a project that foreshadows *Utz*: "Once I'm through I'll apply my febrile mind to the idea of the film about THINGS. Incidentally I have a splendidly macabre story about a compulsive collector of Cherry Blossom Boot Polish tins, set in North London between the wars, and ending with the most enigmatic death." He even conceived a plan to film his nomad book. "ACTION in film is to my mind the answer. I'm afraid film without fast action is for me nearly a non-film. To me it's the whole point of the medium. I am very keen to do something on the *pilgrimage* theme myself—the idea of *finding oneself* in movement. Any ideas?"

"Everything was fine," says Ivory, "but the thought of Elizabeth driving across France at that time to join him, as she said she would, and maybe walking in on us some morning made Bruce nervous. Eventually, reluctantly, I had to leave to join some American friends in Morocco." A wistful Bruce watched him go. "Perhaps I could go to Tangier too," Bruce wrote, "but . . . I am very very anxious about getting this book done. I know myself too well. Once in Morocco the footsteps lead to another horizon. I am a bum and I do not believe in work of any kind."

He nevertheless looked forward "to your acerbic comments on the riff-raff life in Tangier", in particular a character "known commonly as Ma Vidal, who owns some castle that sounds tasteless and hideous and is or is not normally for sale at a million dollars. All *meubles en matière plastique*."

Elizabeth arrived at the end of July. Bruce had asked her to come "with a car *plus* another typewriter as I suspect there will be typing to do, and the two large Oxford dictionaries and some money—enough money—mine if not yours, and also the *New Yorker* article about Chomsky which I left behind."

They spent August in a two-roomed house near St Michel l'Observatoire belonging to "a great expert on birdsong", who "periodically leaves for Patagonia or the Galapagos to record the dawn chorus". Yet again Bruce's attention flew to the person walking by the window, infinitely more interesting than the clutter on his desk. "Very unusual for a Frenchman to have an enthusiasm. The father was a famous old art collector called Henri-Pierre Roché who knew Picasso in the good old days of 1910 and wrote *Jules et Jim*." Bruce's landlord, Jean Claude Roché, provided another diversion. He had rigged up his nearby chateau as a studio to record birdsong that he sold commercially as cassettes. Requiring a voice to say the names in English, he asked Bruce.

Bruce's voice can be heard on the tapes enunciating "Cuckoo", "Arctic tern", "Whinchat" and so on, introducing the display and flight calls of 406 separate species.

XX

Deliverance

> *"Do you think love is the greatest emotion?"*
> *"Why, do you know a greater one?"*
> *"Yes. INTEREST."*
> —THOMAS MANN, *Dr Faustus,*
> QUOTED IN BC'S NOTEBOOK

ON 4 OCTOBER 1971, James Lees-Milne invited his neighbour to lunch. "Bruce came in like a whirlwind, talking affectedly about himself. He has no modesty." Bruce was then tackling his last chapter. To Lees-Milne, "Bruce is a young man of a different generation, Birmingham, very clever, bubbling with enthusiasms, still very young, feeling his way, not self-assured, and on the aggressive. I like him. It is a pity he is already losing his looks . . ."

They went for a rapid-striding walk with the dogs through the Foxholes woods. "Then he was enchanting, and all his preliminary social bombastic manner left him. He talked enthusiastically, that is what I like about him, sensibly, unaffectedly. I am certain that in another ten years he will have ceased to be bumptious. He said that he only felt happy in the wilderness, the natural wilderness of the world. Feels constricted in England, lonely at Holwell Farm, not surprising, and is very much conscious of today's lack of opportunity for exploration and getting away from the madding crowd." On the walk, Bruce told Lees-Milne how his mother had dressed him in her clothes when he was six. "In spite of this silly treatment he hates transvestitism, but [he] is inevitably homosexual . . . Said that homosexuality was nothing whatever to do with genes, or inheritance, but solely to upbringing and relations with one's parents. I don't altogether agree. He admitted it was odd how homos are on the whole more intelligent, certainly more sensitive than heteros . . . B has gone into this question in his Nomad book."

In *The Nomadic Alternative* Bruce pursues a line of anthropological self-justification. "The husband who wanders," he writes, "is far more likely to be surreptitiously unfaithful when at home." After Peter Straker, he went on to have several brief relationships. "I spend the weeks in Oxford now, heavily disguised as a skittish undergraduate, and, I confess, celebrating my thirtieth birthday with a skittish affair," he had written to James Ivory one year before. "Merton College, jasmine tea, shades of Max Beerbohm, red lacquer, ecclesiastical drag, mystical excesses of the Early Church Fathers combined with the intellectual mentality of Ronald Firbank. You get the picture? *Not serious*, very pretty."

Bruce once told a friend: "You'll never know how *complicated* it is to be bisexual." Elizabeth suspected about Straker and found out later about his moment with Miranda—"he eventually confessed"—but she did not know the extent of his infidelities. In none of them did he let himself go. Ivory who visited Holwell in the autumn of 1971 maintains that "strolling with him in a long upstairs hall with polished floorboards he privately told me he had given up homosexuality—that he didn't have those feelings anymore." Even if this was so, the tensions between Bruce and his wife mounted.

On 3 November, Lees-Milne was invited to Holwell for dinner. "[Bruce] was not very nice to Elizabeth, who cooked a delicious dinner; he was very abrupt and discontented; whereas when he came to tea with me the day before he was all charm. I have seldom met a human being who exudes so much sex appeal with so comparatively little niceness. What does this boy want? He is extremely restless. He hates living at Holwell, has to be continuously on the move . . . He has finished his nomad book, and I wonder how good it is. When the gilt has worn off his *jeunesse* how much substance will be left underneath?"

Lees-Milne records the occasion when he challenged Bruce. "Found myself lecturing him about treatment of his wife, but good naturedly. We laughed. He asks me frankly if I was glad I was married. Was able to say, yes, very. I don't think he is at all. He is going off for three months writing and will not tell his wife where he is going. I said that was cruel. He agreed."

By now, Elizabeth's family had become accustomed to finding one or other partner away. The marriage gave her father the impression of a weather cottage: "When one comes out, the other goes in." In January 1972, John Chanler and his wife Sheila came to stay. Elizabeth greeted them alone. "Every single time we stayed in that house, Bruce was not there," says Chanler. He and Sheila both understood her to be lonely. The vivacious girl they had known had grown introverted after seven years of marriage. And they could not help noticing her reduced circumstances. "She was literally pinching pennies," says Chanler. It upset him to discover that Bruce had sold some chairs and a table which Gertrude had sent from Meridian House. Elizabeth had taken to hiding valuables out of reach of her husband's "eye". She relied on a steady trickle of cheques from Gertrude to cover her bills. "I'm so broke I can only just eat nowadays," she wrote to her mother during John's visit. "Thank Heavens B is away as there is one less to feed & he likes to have proper meals anyway."

But she missed her husband: "Dear Max, well here I go again in hope one of these letters one day will reach you . . ."

ELIZABETH WAS UNLIKE most wives. "Love alters not when it alteration finds," she would say. Beyond the reverence and despite their problems there was a genuine *entente* that had given the couple their nickname: "the Chattys". Salman Rushdie says, "They were the only two people I know who were able to talk simultaneously, non-stop, for very long periods of time, about completely different subjects, while seemingly knowing exactly what the other was saying and not finding it a problem."

There was also a complicity. Jessie Wood, who shared a house with the Welches on the Greek island of Spetsae, says, "Elizabeth and Bruce were locked into a much more solid reality than many people realised." She and her husband Clem saw much of the Chatwins, who often stayed in their Paris apartment. "Bruce would never have done anything that he did if he hadn't had this feeling for Elizabeth. I mean, can you imagine Bruce with anyone else?"

Clem Wood from the dock at Spetsae once watched the spectacle of "the Chattys" leaping into the harbour. They were seeing Elizabeth's younger brother Ollie off on the Athens ferry, when, with no warning, the hydrofoil pulled away from the quay. "We jumped without a single word," says Elizabeth. "It was the only thing to do." Clem never forgot how the two of them hit the water together, in time, plunk—and then were arrested by the harbour master.

The *entente* was understood by Elizabeth's former flat-mate, Pattie Sullivan, who visited Bruce in one of his flats in London. "He could live like that because Elizabeth sat in the country with a warehouse of the stuff he'd acquired." Their existence reminded Sullivan of Philip Johnson's Glass House in Connecticut—"which is only possible because of a Victorian house up the road from which the food comes, the supply tent". In the same way, says Sullivan, "Elizabeth took care of things so that Bruce could appear on the stage of life in the way he wanted: 'I travel light, I have no possessions, I don't care about things, what are things to me?'"

IN OCTOBER, BRUCE sent *The Nomadic Alternative* to the typist. He was unsatisfied to the last. "I have just read some latest books on my line, and they show where I am wrong," he wrote to Ivory. "Whole tracts will have to be rewritten, though the main thesis doesn't change. I hope to give the thing in to the publisher in early Nov . . . In the end they'll probably turn the bloody thing down. It'll be interesting however to see which way the escape route runs."

In March 1970, one of the firm's readers had delivered a report on a sample chapter which Bruce had delivered to Maschler at Jonathan Cape. "Bruce Chatwyn [*sic*] is obviously a lively-minded and contentious young man, not afraid to take a swipe at all the ethnologists within reach and some out of it." The chapter was "all over the place, but I am inclined to think that it would be better to give him his head for the moment and let him do his own disciplining as he goes along . . . If he keeps his eye on the subject he may produce a rather good book."

Deborah Rogers recognised the untitled chapter to be "terribly raw". Careful not to say anything negative, she and Maschler agreed that Bruce should carry on. In early November 1972, Bruce arrived at Rogers's office in Goodge Street and delivered his manuscript with a great deal of fluster and apology.

Rogers waded conscientiously through it. "You've been waiting with such expectation, and you get this huge, unwieldy text. I remember the heart sinking." She found the writing leaden, the content plodding. "When you think of Bruce's prose as it became, the impeccable intellectual digestion—this was completely undigested. There was too much there." Unable to see a way to salvage the book, she nevertheless sent it to Cape.

Maschler read 50 or 60 pages. "They were terrible. They were completely sterile. They were a chore to read and I imagine a chore to write. Had he said: 'This is my book,' I would have rejected it." He delivered his verdict to Bruce face to face. "I was without hesitation able to say: 'Something's going wrong here and maybe you should not be doing this'." Maschler believed that Bruce, while shaken, had agreed with him. The project was suspended rather than rejected and Maschler did not ask for the £200 advance to be returned. "I remember Bruce saying as he left: 'I'll think about it.' I hoped I'd put him off." Not for another 15 years, until after he had left her agency, did Bruce tell Deborah Rogers how angered and upset he had been by the Maschler/Rogers response. But there was one writer at the time who observed the levelling effects of Maschler's words.

James Thackera, a New England novelist who had worked with Costa-Gavras, was writing film scripts in London. He and Bruce used to meet at Don Luigi's in the King's Road to discuss ideas. "I knew Bruce when it was still possible to know Bruce." Thackera had studied under Robert Lowell at Harvard and was writing a script on doubles. They talked about Lowell, Dostoevsky, Conrad. "He cared about me because I cared about writing." But Thackera observed his impenetrable solitude.

Once Thackera looked out of the window at Don Luigi's and saw Bruce walk by. "He was walking slightly stooped, not mincing but shuffling, with a look on his face, when he thought he wasn't being watched, of desolation." This fear is what most struck Thackera: "you felt he was terrorised". Bruce's expression reminded him of Wu Cheng Fu's definition of genius: "fear of vacuity".

BRUCE'S NEED TO write his book was not going to be extinguished by one disappointing response, although he conveyed his fatigue to the Leigh Fermors: "I have finished my book, but am so heartily dissatisfied with it, I hope it won't be published," he wrote on 30 November. "It's turned out to be the great unwriteable. But there's no point in letting it ruin one's life." He and Elizabeth were supposed to spend Christmas in Ireland. "But I have the most itchy feet and want to go to *Niger*—more nomads, the Bororo Peuls, the most beautiful people in the world, who wander alone in the savannah with long-horned white cattle and have some rather startling habits like a complete sex-reversal at certain seasons of the year. So I may be off."

To raise money for the journey to West Africa, he contemplated selling the Inca feathers that he and Elizabeth had bought with their wedding money. "Yesterday the phone rang from a friend asking whether I would accept $22,000 for it. You bet I bloody well would." The sale would contribute towards the cost of buying a flat in London. In a poignant letter to Gertrude, Elizabeth wrote: "At the moment there's no definite flat in sight, but it's better to have the cash ready when one does come. I'll be sad to lose the feathers though."

In early January, after spending a "rather disgruntled" Christmas at Holwell, Bruce flew to Niger. "I am at my lowest ebb at the minute, but will probably recover once the voyage starts."

For three months he travelled through Niger, Dahomey and Cameroon. On a ten-day camel ride to the mountains of Aïr, he tried to re-seed himself. "Feeling very Beau Geste and have grown neat military moustache to match," he wrote to Elizabeth. He reported its progress a fortnight later: "At the moment one might well have had a career in the movies in the age of Ronald Colman. It's sort of d'Artagnanesque."

One reason for coming to Niger was to make a short film about no-mads. "Bruce has been talking about nothing but filming," wrote Elizabeth. He had borrowed a 16mm camera from Erskine, who since their journey to Afghanistan had become well known on television. He presented a ten-minute item on works of art each week called "Collector's Piece", and a series of archaeological films called "The Glory that Remains" set on location. Taken with his example, Bruce planned to make a documentary about the market of Bermou in the Niger. "Most aesthetic market I've ever seen," he wrote to Elizabeth. "Tuareg, Bororo Peuls and Hausas, camels, cattle that might have come from Egyptian tomb paintings etc." As he told Ivory, he was excited by the concept of trade as "a language which prevents people from cutting each other's throats". But he had failed to take into account the demands of filmmaking. Not only was the equipment heavy to carry around without a car, but the film jammed and "people threw things at the camera when I pointed it at them". He wrote in his notebook:

"Jeudi, Tahoua, Niger

"Day of the market. Day of the film. Devoid of all human interest. Fingers tired from working the infernal machine, which didn't break down, as I feared. Exhausted return to *campement* where became embroiled in discussion, black racist farrago. Insulted right and left. Five bottles of beer presented to me unwillingly had the effect (when mixed with the sour milk of the market) of turning my stomach into a volcano."

In early February, he was back in Niamey from where he wrote again to Elizabeth. "Have just returned here after shooting the bloody film. I hated doing it—a blank day in my life. Can't remember anything at all."

It was not a complete waste. Out of the process had emerged the idea for a short story, "Milk". "I have started writing a long story—may even be a short novel. You know how I have an incurable fascination for French hotel/bordel keepers of a certain age in an ex-colonial situation. Well, I've been in on a most amazing series of encounters with one in Tahoua. Even held the fort while she had a *crise cardiaque* after sleeping with a Togolese bandleader (*L'Equipe Za-Za Bam-Bam et Ses Supremes Togolaises*). Much better than writing a travel piece because one can *lie*.

"*Second*—my moustache. It's beginning to curl up at the edges in a raffish, almost Blimpish way. I have to confess it is highly chic and for the first time in my life I feel I have got away from that awful pretty boy look and can envisage the possibility of growing old—if not with dignity at least with a certain style."

From Agades in north Niger, he cabled to Elizabeth not to sell the Peruvian feathers after all. "Don't know why I think it's the one thing we should keep."

HE ARRIVED BACK in March. "I have a moustache. I am thinner. I am crazy about Africa and the Africans," he wrote to Ivory. "Am about to send a letter to an African boy, who has just written 'I am very happy I have saved the money to write to you', also hoping that I am well and strong enough to do my job."

In London, he now supervised the decoration of a minuscule flat he had rented in Sloane Avenue, "a hideous one-room affair, shaped 'in the form of a pompadour wafer' to quote the estate agent." Bruce thought it more resembled the bridge of a second-class cruise ship of the 1930s. "The building was a famous call-girl warren before and after the war, and the whores are still there, mainly Hungarian, who drop their handbags in the lift and ask you 'Zahling, plis . . .' to pick them up. I am on the 9th floor with a panorama over London, which at that height doesn't remind me of London, so that's all right."

With Erskine's help he edited his nomad footage into a 25-minute documentary for Vaughan Films. He enjoyed the experience even less than the filming. "I always think I'm pretty disorganised but they are something else," he wrote to his parents. "I'd go in each day prepared to work on it and there'd be some hold up. I couldn't use the cutting room or my assistant was needed to pay court on some movie mogul. It's a terrible business. At least if you write, you are your own master."

Unfortunately, the only copy of Bruce's film vanished in the course of being hawked around European television companies. Erskine, who recorded the voice-over, remembered the result as "a bit wobbly", and Bruce told Ivory that "it's far too amateurish to be of any use".

By April, he was lapsing into gloom. "I have been mouldering as usual in the country. It all seems so prissy after Africa," he wrote to Ivory. "England is now little England with a vengeance, the world of boutiques and bitchery and little else." He was working again on "the bloody book" and "firmly believed it to be a load of humourless, egotistic, sententious rubbish".

On 25 July, Bruce abandoned London for America. "I'm sorry I left in such a precipitous hurry, but there we are. I usually do and I did," he wrote to his parents. "I was getting totally exasperated a. by the weather which had given me the worst chest and lung combination I have ever had . . . b. that film company was driving me nearly desperate." Before he left, Bruce had an interview at the *Sunday Times* and was made an offer, which he accepted, to work as arts consultant on the Sunday magazine. The job would start in November. Meantime he moved into Ivory's clapboard cabin in Oregon and began the formidable task of unscrambling his book. "In fact, I'm completely rewriting it," he told his parents. He had looked at the central argument and decided that "not even I could understand [it] let alone the poor reader." He had no idea how long the task would take. "I am simply going to sit here and finish it. I refuse to be budged. My book, whatever anyone may say, is far the most important thing I've ever attempted . . . So there we are."

Those who saw him during his American summer observed someone going against their own grain. He seemed to Loretta Anawalt a solitary, anti-social person "working very hard at creating an identity for himself". Before driving to his cabin, Bruce had agreed to meet Ivory at the Anawalts' home in Pullman, a small town in the wheat fields of Washington State in the Pacific Northwest. Bruce Anawalt, Loretta's husband, was a self-possessed Shakespearean scholar and an opposite to Bruce in every respect. His equanimity and his scepticism—"Bruce was weird"—made him a disconcerting presence.

"We were taking an outing to the town of Moscow," says Loretta. "We got to the highway and Bruce Chatwin said he wanted to get out and walk. 'But it's 8 miles!' we told him."

It was a hot day. The three watched "open-mouthed in astonishment" as Bruce, dressed in shorts and huge hiking boots, strode into the wheat fields and headed towards the railway tracks of the Union Pacific. "He was escaping us, just getting away, getting free of what was haunting him, impelled onto the tracks. I tell you, the man was spooked. He hadn't assembled himself from where he'd been, like his atoms were scattered."

Ivory tracked the figure of his friend thrashing in the most self-willed way through the wheat and over the irrigation ditches. "You felt this relentless pushing of himself to do this, some act of physical defiance, but it was unattractive. You felt sorry for him. You felt he was doing something wrong. Nobody would want to walk through that."

The wheat fields rose into hills, the landscape resembling the bottom of the ocean as if formed by the movement of water. "The hills are much loved by painters," says Anawalt. "They're like a sensuous feminine torso, rolling into hips and breasts, but Bruce walking into all that femininity seemed lost in it somehow."

To his three spectators, here was a person who wanted to be more than he was. Ivory felt Bruce brought this dislocated energy to bear on his nomad book. He was striving for gravity against his natural inclination to take flight. "It wasn't coming naturally to him. He had to work hard in certain areas. He created himself in a way. Maybe just to be taken seriously, that's what success was for him."

After driving for two days, they reached Ivory's cabin: a modest, comfortable house in the pine woods, next to a glorious lake. Bruce wrote to his parents, "There is a canoe and I can paddle up a river to look at beavers making dams and it's very warm for swimming." The place should have been conducive to work.

"The Book is coming on well," he assured Elizabeth. "I know what I'm doing instead of flailing around in a disorganised way with marvellous material and no sense of direction." Unconvinced, Elizabeth wrote to Gertrude: "I hope he'll get that wretched book done before he comes back. I'm sure it'll be very good, if only he could be satisfied with it himself." But in Oregon his diminishing confidence made it impossible to write. "He'd go off on these treks into the woods for hours and hours," says Ivory.

After ten days, they drove to San Francisco, staying on the way in Grant's Pass, where Bruce came face to face with Rod Calvert, a college friend of Ivory and a failed poet. Ivory had told Bruce stories about Calvert: how he had travelled, lived in France, New York, where he supported himself in odd jobs, but always The Writer. "He never got anything published," says Ivory. "He covered his walls with words like MATISSE because he liked their sound. That was as far as he got with a presentation of words in an artistic manner. Everything about him was presence and mental laziness, but he was a very funny man up to a point." The three of them spent the morning together. Ivory noticed that Bruce found it a gruesome experience to be confronted by Rod, who had been good-looking once in a similar way—blond, lithe, and rosy-cheeked—and was now dishevelled. "A young friend, spotty, about 16 came round so we could have a joint. They sat, this dull pathetic boy and Rod on the sofa and Bruce and I sat with them. Bruce was struck by the grotesqueness of the situation. Bruce could turn into Rod." Some years later Calvert was found dead in his rented apartment in Palm Springs, California, still unpublished.

After Ivory left him in San Francisco, Bruce stayed with another poet. Robert Duncan, "one of the most unpleasant people I have ever met, with a waxen witch-like face, hair tied in a pigtail and a pair of ludicrous white sideburns. He gassed on and on in a flat monotone and it was impossible to decide if the tone was hysterical or dead-pan". In a health food shop, where Bruce spent $50 on emetic food, he ran into a familiar face: "the dreaded Linda, who was buying her molasses and brown rice at the same time. Grown enormously fat she had, and she was with the Sufis." He found San Francisco "so unlike anything else in the US, it doesn't really bear thinking about. It's utterly lightweight and sugary with no sense of purpose or depth . . . This doesn't mean that one couldn't live here. In fact I think one could easily, preferably with something equally frivolous to do." Frivolity was not an option. Saying goodbye to Ivory, Bruce returned alone to the Lake of the Wood. For Ivory that was the end of their intimacy.

ON 14 SEPTEMBER, Bruce wrote to his wife, addressing her as "Dear Hurrubureth". He had been writing solidly, intended to stay until October when "a great hunk" would be done. He sounded cheerful. "I am writing fast, and then hitching the things up for the finer points of style later." In the course of his letter, he enthused about his forest walks. He might have been in the Forest of Arden or on the riverbanks in Stratford, playing *A Midsummer Night's Dream.* "I wandered along the Brown Mountain trail STARK NAKED for 15 miles without coming across a soul but deer and birds and that made me very happy."

Charlie Van, caretaker at Lake of the Woods, related to Ivory his encounter with a strange figure by Low Echo Camp. Van could not have been more surprised had he come face to face with a nudist off the stage of *Hair.*

"I saw this guy back in the woods a ways, hiking. And this son-of-a bitch was stark naked, except for his big hiking boots, going along like he was in a nudist colony and owned the place. I shouted Hey you! and he turned around. Most people, if you caught them like that, would have lit out, or maybe put their pants back on. Not him. He came over to me with this sort of sneer and asked me if he was on the right trail to Rainbow Lake. And you won't believe this, but he'd tied some flowers round his pecker.

"I figured he was a hippie except most of them can't talk, just grunt, but this one had a hoity-toity way of speaking. I told him if he didn't put his pants on I'd take him in and then he said, Oh he was a guest of Jimmy Ivory. I said, 'You still have to put your pants back on.' He fished them out of a little bag he was carrying and got into them. Good looking fella but sort of crazy look in his eyes just then; he reminded me of a little kid, when you say, 'No, you can't do that,' gritting his teeth. I didn't want to seem to be exceeding my authority, so I said, 'It's a hot one'."

Viewed through one lens, his nakedness was comic. Through another, disturbing—as if a drama begun in a typical vein of theatre was careening towards a breakdown. He had walked away from Sotheby's and Edinburgh claiming they were not what he wanted. He could not make the same claim for this book. In the image of him striding naked through the pine woods one senses the burden of his failed ambitions and those of his publisher. "I am convinced it will be an important book," Maschler had predicted. "Important in the way *The Naked Ape* was important." Bruce had not written *The Naked Ape*, but to even the most casual observer like Charlie Van he was coming disturbingly close to enacting it.

In *The Songlines*, which it became 15 years later, Bruce claimed he burned his nomad book. He did not. He threw it away and without his knowledge Margharita rescued the manuscript from the dustbin.

In one of the boxes containing the notebooks and texts which Bruce left in his will to the Bodleian Library in Oxford, there is the untitled green folder which contains *The Nomadic Alternative*.

It is easy to imagine the excitement with which Bruce's agent and publisher must have received this manuscript and how great their disappointment. It began:

"The best travellers are illiterate. Narratives of travel are pale compensations for the journey itself, and merely proclaim the traveller's inad-

equacy as a traveller. The best travellers do not pause to record their second-rate impressions, to be read third-hand. Their experience is primal.
Their minds are uncongealed by the written word.

"What follows is even more perverse than a written narrative of journey—a provisional account of an ill-advised and ill-prepared expedition
to discover the source of The Journey itself. Such an undertaking is a con-
tradiction in terms and foredoomed to disaster . . .

"And yet, in one sense, writing is a therapeutic exercise—a projection
of unfulfilled desires, a substitute for life unlived and actions not performed. And for inspiration I fall back on Baudelaire's proposal in the *Intimate Journals* for a 'study of the great malady, horror of one's home'. Few
are secure from the fury of this infection, this compulsion that beckons us
towards the unknown. To move exhilarates, to stay cripples. For in the
symbol of the Journey lies our principal dilemma. *Where* does happiness
lie? Why is Here so unbearable? Why is There so inviting? But why is
There more unbearable than Here? 'What is this strange madness,' Pe-
trarch complained to his young secretary, 'this mania to sleep each night
in a different bed . . .' "

Bruce's text is a dense conglomerate of portentous generalisations and
abstract theories. He throws into his thesis ideas about shamans, Che
Guevara, the tramp in St James's Square, the pyramids, the Qashgai, the
Nemadi, the gypsies, the Beast, culminating after 268 pages in a soaring
hymn to the spirit of the primitive nomad:

"The question is, 'Do you belong to MAN or the MACHINE?' With
each day more and more reply, 'We belong to MAN, and there's nothing
wrong with him.' There is no possibility for creating a New Man. To tam-
per with his genetics will not produce a New Man, but an adjunct of the
machine, and ally of the Devil. Man is an infant beside the Iguana and his
career a fleeting moment of evolutionary time. Yet he is an old man. His
nature does not significantly change. And he is kicking hard, greeting the
brutality of the machine with the sullen hostility of the pariah. The driving forces of history are the ways of the wandering savage."

As Bruce wrote of Raymond Dart: "The style alone suggests that
something is seriously wrong." Everything he wrote afterwards would be
a reaction against prose like this.

XXI.

⌘

The Journalist

PHONE HOPELESS COME ALGIERS
9 OCT STOP BRING DESERT SHOES ONE DRESS
AND NOT LESS THAN 250 POUNDS WILL REPAY
WILL GO CENTRAL SAHARA BRUCE
—Telegram to Elizabeth, 1973

AT EDINBURGH, BRUCE had turned down an offer from Mark Boxer to join the *Sunday Times*. The thought of going back to a world he had left behind, pigeonholed as an art expert, made him anxious. At the end of August he wrote to Elizabeth: "The idea of a job horrifies me. I am more doubtful about the thing than ever before." By 14 September, his reservations had intensified. "The more I cogitate it, the more I dread the *Sunday Times* business as being something I don't want to do. I have sent a host of letters from here about this and that, none of which gets a reply. I'm exasperated without having begun. One's independence is so fragile a thing."

IN THE SPRING of 1972, David Sylvester had resigned from the *Sunday Times* and the magazine began casting around for a new arts consultant. Francis Wyndham, a senior editor, said: "What about Bruce Chatwin?"

Wyndham—whom Bruce described as "a colossal inspiration to a whole generation of writers in England"—telephoned Holwell. He caught a dispirited Bruce bundling his manuscript into a suitcase about to depart for America. Bruce looked back on himself at this time as "penniless, depressed, a total failure . . . I felt that for writing creatively I'd somehow missed the boat."

The telephone call had nothing to do with his writing, rather with his photographs of Mauritanian roofs, doors and robes which Bruce had shown Sylvester. "Would I, he asked, like a small job as an adviser on the arts?"

Bruce met Wyndham to explore ideas with the magazine's new editor, Magnus Linklater. The 30-year-old Linklater thought Bruce's Mauritanian pictures "arty-farty".

Linklater had been appointed editor weeks before with a brief to curb the excesses of the colour supplement and to bring it within the orbit of the main paper. Under instructions from the editor, Harry Evans, "to go in and sort that lot out", he was alarmed to discover £70,000 of commissioned pieces and an art department running the roost. "The epitome of that was an eclipse of the moon which could only be photographed from a certain peak in Kenya. The photographer returned with an image completely black except for a sliver in the top right hand corner. David King ran it for two pages. The ad manager came up and said: 'I could have sold those pages for £5,000 and you ran two blank pages.' I suddenly thought: 'What the hell is this all about?' "

Linklater was wary, but he listened to Bruce whose journalism amounted to two articles for *Vogue*, another in the pipeline for *History Today* and a film on a market in Niger not yet transmitted. "Bruce talked brilliantly," says Wyndham, "but not journalistically and not like someone being interviewed for a job." He had no shortage of ideas: Madame Vionnet, the inventor of the bias cut; Eileen Gray, the designer of the chromium chair; Theodor Strehlow, an Australian anthropologist who had grown up with the Aborigines; a Greek who had amassed a priceless collection of Leftist art in Russia. "I rather feebly said, 'OK'," says Linklater. He hired him on a retainer of £2,000 a year.

Whatever Bruce's qualms as he entered the hessian and black leather vestibule in Gray's Inn Road and rose to the fourth floor, they soon vanished. Days later Elizabeth was writing to Gertrude: "The *Sunday Times* things look as though they're going to be just for him."

Bruce's three years on the paper were the final stage of his apprenticeship as a writer. Sotheby's had introduced him to a network of contacts and taught him to see and to remember. Edinburgh had provided a measure of academic base. After three years of tussling with his nomad book, the magazine gave him a deadline and an audience. "Journalism does help you a lot in the opening stages, as long as you set your own journalist standards and don't kow-tow to the fashion of editors," Bruce said. "Examine the great journalists of the past, like Stephen Crane. If you're thinking about a wide readership you have to have clarity at all costs. It's a very, very good training."

Bruce joined the magazine when it was still at its height. Dubbed "Thomson's Folly" on its launch, the colour supplement had become, in the words of Philip Norman, "Fleet Street's most profitable as well as its most fashionable publication", with a readership of one and a half million. For a while there was nothing like it.

Fiercely independent from the main paper, the small editorial team considered no subject too ambitious or too trivial. They did what they wanted and held themselves accountable to no one. "What I liked about journalism is that you studied for an exam you never took," says Roger Law, who worked in the art department. "We were quite cliquey and utterly irresponsible." Norman, a young reporter, recalled that anything was allowed, except the word "shit" and pubic hair in photographs. "The feeling as one sat in that fourth floor office," wrote Norman, "was of appraising and evaluating all Mankind." In his 1995 novel, *Everyone's Gone to the Moon*, Norman parodies a typical edition. The cover features a flat-chested model with legs like "articulated pipe-cleaners", while inside pictures of starving famine victims mix with advertisements for double cream interspersed by long articles printed in "lovely chaste type" in book length paragraphs: "Anthony Burgess on Mickey Mouse . . . V. S. Naipaul on the hard-up princes of Rajasthan . . . Cartier-Bresson in Bali . . ." There are theme issues on such topics as "What did Christ really look like?" or "the Steins" (based on a theory held by David Sylvester that every important person in civilisation has or had a name ending in Stein). In Norman's novel, the magazine's editor describes the Stein idea as "us at our adventurous eclectic best". He sums up the magazine's philosophy: "If a thing's worth doing, it's worth doing to absolute bloody excess."

The magazine was best regarded for its photojournalism. Bruce was much impressed by a profile of General Giap, photographed by Don McCullin and written by James Fox. He took the author to lunch and swore him to secrecy: "I don't want anyone to know this. The reason I went into journalism is that I wanted to compete with you."

Fox and McCullin comprised one of half a dozen photographer-writer teams who globe-trotted for weeks at a time. Fox once spent three months in Zaire at the *Sunday Times'* expense. Instead of returning at the appointed date, he sent word that he wanted to go to the Ituri forests, there spending six more weeks.

Bruce had sympathy for this attitude. One of his first suggestions was a round-the-world trip. In the next three years he would file from Paris, New York, Moscow, Marseille, Algeria, Peru.

THERE WAS A saying at the *Sunday Times*: "Whoever runs the flat-plan runs the magazine." Wyndham's imprimatur was important, but so was the approbation of Michael Rand, the silent art director, who together with King and his assistant Roger Law laid out the pages. This trio were a law unto themselves and naturally suspicious of writers. "It was like belonging to a Masonic lodge," says King, at the time a member of the Socialist Workers' Party. Law remembers the moment when Bruce won over all three. "I was introduced to what looked like an upper class toff with strange blue eyes. He had this travel essay by Mandelstam, *Journey to Armenia*, and he read it aloud to the art department. That was it: we were in love with Bruce. I ended up reading poems by Mandelstam."

Bruce's Russian taste coincided with David King's, the arts editor. King was a talented designer and collector of Russian photomontage posters "which pack onto a sheet of paper all the enthusiasm of the Red Revolution". Trained by the Central-European George Lois, King designed covers that combined a Russian constructivism with American nous: a tiny button mushroom to illustrate the post-war era, with the headline, "Every day from now on is a kind of bonus."

King had an eye to crop a photograph so as to transform it. "The reason we all stuck to David," says Law, "is because he'd take your picture, crop it and it would look good on the page. Bruce was interested in the visual side more than other writers. They hit it off like a house on fire."

King was responsible for laying out Bruce's posthumous book of photographs in 1993. "Bruce was one of the most visually aware people I've met. With a professional photographer, you decide what you want to photograph and normally you shoot around it, using 100-odd photographs of one image. Bruce never did that: he shot one picture, then another. You never got a sequence, or a choice." Bruce's images, shot with a Leica, a separate light-meter and only one lens, were, to King, "unbearably inquisitive" of their subject. "He loved wood and corrugated tin—art without artists. And he wasn't afraid to shoot pictures in the sun."

When he arrived in November, Bruce did not expect to have to write anything. He envisaged a sedentary job in the mould of Sylvester, his magisterial predecessor, who advised on whether, say, the new Alma

Tadema exhibition was worth covering. In this role, his first responsibility was to organise "One Million Years of Art", a six-part pictorial series encompassing nothing less than the history of art and the latest of several projects which its creators self-mockingly code-named "the wankers". Conceived in the bath by the magazine's former editor, Godfrey Smith, the debut "wanker"—"1,000 Makers of the Twentieth Century"—had attracted 60,000 new readers. Pressure was put on Linklater to suggest likeminded schemes for boosting circulation.

Bruce's project, hurriedly assembled in the spring of 1973, was inspired by the 1937 book of a little-known Ohio professor and discovered by Michael Rand on his shelves at home: *An Illustrated Handbook of Art History* by Frank J. Roos Junior. Rand floated the idea of expanding this into a visual dictionary. Linklater agreed. "I desperately needed another promotable series. I envisaged a prosaic guide, leading the readers through artistic masterpieces from the Renaissance onwards." This is not what he got.

Linklater was on holiday when Bruce buckled down in Holwell to compile the illustrations. He asked Lucie-Smith to assist him. "I was there to provide the bread and butter, and to remind him he had to have Giotto," says Lucie-Smith. In the event, Bruce seized the project as an opportunity to make a manifesto. "One Million Years of Art" was a display case for his own taste, uniting the collector of curiosities, the Sotheby's expert, the journalist.

The series ran for six weeks during the summer of 1973. It opened with a photograph of stone implements used by African nomads and incorporated many favourite Chatwin objects. Dotted among the "thousand examples of man's art from primitive times to the 1970s" were stamp-sized photographs of a felt appliqué saddle-bag from the Altai, a Seghers landscape and a photograph, taken by Bruce, of an Afghan lorry. "Bruce injected his own distinction into the choice, heavily influenced by Ludwig Goldscheider's *Art without Epoch*," says Lucie-Smith. "The Afghan lorry is pure Goldscheider." This lorry, carrying the Japanese contraceptives, was one of four images Bruce supplied to challenge our idea of what constituted art. ("We have frequently by-passed the obvious masterpieces in favour of curiosities—and even the obviously bad," he warned readers.) Relying on provocative juxtapositions, he managed to squeeze into the series his own photographs of a tray laden with fish, and of a Mauritanian door (later the hardback cover for *What Am I Doing Here*). At Holwell, the gardener was surprised to recognise Exhibit 417: the Peruvian papagayo feathers. Bruce elucidated for *Sunday Times* readers how ancient Peruvians had discovered long before Rothko that "blocks of pure colour floating one above the other produced a mood of anxious calm".

On 26 August, he explained in a short post-script the philosophy behind his selection: "Our aim has been to break down the compartments of period and place into which art history is too often divided and if this series has encouraged even a few people to widen their visual horizons then it will have achieved its aims."

Linklater, hugely embarrassed, fielded the wrath of the marketing department. "It was completely *not* what I had in mind. A million years! I just wanted it from 1342. It was a typical example of the hijacking of the magazine by the nexus. It did not put on a single extra copy."

The Chatwin series confirmed Harry Evans's judgement that the magazine was self-indulgent, mired in triviality, out of touch. "They've lost all regard for what the ordinary reader wants," rants the editor in *Everyone's Gone to the Moon*. The editor was a Northerner, like Evans, who thought Alma Tadema was a woman and Leni Riefenstahl a man ("like Lenny Bruce") and whose ideal series was a look at the seeding of readers' window-boxes. Linklater had placed himself in a dangerous position. By promoting a series like "One Million Years of Art," he was not carrying out his editor's express wishes.

BRUCE WAS IDEAL for the role of arts consultant, but thanks to Wyndham this was not the role he fulfilled. With Wyndham's encouragement, he went to Paris to investigate a pair of *grandes dames*, relics of the 1920s fashion world. Madeleine Vionnet had freed women, including Bruce's Aunts Jane and Gracey, from the tyranny of the corset (*"le corset, c'est une chose orthopédique"*). She had designed her dresses to be worn as "a second, more seductive skin". Bruce met Vionnet—"96-years-old but alert and mischievous"—in her salon in the Place Antoine-Arnauld, unchanged since she decorated it in 1929. He responded to the aluminium grilles and mirror glass. "The interior is as clean-cut and unsentimental as Mme Vionnet herself . . . Like a Vionnet dress, this is spareness achieved expensively."

Sonia Delaunay came to Paris from Russia in 1905 and lived "in a bedroom which is something between a room in an expensive clinic and a monk's cell". Accepted as a leading abstract painter before the Great War, she was preferred by Bruce for her clothes and literary acquaintances. She had designed patchwork dresses with bright geometric shapes to be worn in Bugattis and was a friend of the globe-trotting poet Blaise Cendrars. "The greatest poet of our age," she flatly told Bruce, who quoted Cendrars for his epigraph in *In Patagonia*.

Bruce enthused to Wyndham about these two elderly pioneers on his return to Gray's Inn Road. "There was never any mention that I was going to have to write anything. I said, 'Now we must find a writer,' and he looked at me and said: 'But you're writing this'." Bruce's eyes lit up, says Wyndham. "He wasn't confident—he didn't see himself as a journalist. But he reacted with great excitement."

BRUCE WAS FORTUNATE to have Wyndham and not someone younger and competitive as his immediate boss. Wyndham had first heard of Bruce as the boy with the golden eye from Sotheby's. Millington-Drake, referring to him as "Chatwina", had warned Wyndham how "some people think he's too big for his boots". Christopher Gibbs made him appear even less enticing. When Bruce looked at a painting, said Gibbs, it was quite different to the way anyone else looked at a painting. "I said: 'What happens when Bruce looks at a painting?' Gibbs said, 'It sort of falls off the wall.' If anything I *didn't* want to meet him."

Bruce's life had followed a cycle in which he set out in one direction after another to discover his talent, only to go to pieces. Under Wyndham's guidance, he found his *métier*. "Words—I didn't feel about them till the *Sunday Times*," he told Colin Thubron. "I think it was something bashed out of me in my education." Wyndham became the most enduring of Bruce's mentors. On 20 October 1977, almost five years after joining the magazine, Bruce wrote to him from Italy: "I spent my solitary lunch thinking of the enormous amount I owe to you."

IN *Everyone's Gone to the Moon*, Wyndham is caricatured as the brilliant journalist Evelyn Strachey: "a man of about 40 with a large balding head and the close-set eyes and drooping mouth of some inbred minor prince . . . He wore unfashionable charcoal trousers, pulled high around his bulky waist, and a white, short-sleeved shirt of some archaic porous Aertex-like material. His right hand was turned palm downwards, holding a lit cigarette. His left rested on his hip." Strachey on form was "the best there is".

In his profiles of the singer P. J. Proby or of the broadcaster and presenter of *This Is Your Life*, Eamon Andrews, Wyndham elevated trivia to high art. The effect of his deadpan prose was lethal. Lax about his own writing talent, he was not lazy at editing. He liked to match serious writers with apparently frivolous subjects and to cause tension by playing disparate pieces one against another—Don McCullin's war photographs, for example, with Bruce's article on Paris couture. Trained on *Queen* magazine, he sought in every edition "a good mix". This, the antithesis of a theme issue like "One Million Years of Art," ideally consisted of "something serious, something shocking, something hysterically funny, something beautiful". Bruce's books are extensions of this formula, juxtaposing *Insight*-style investigation with profiles, art, fashion—all written under the influence of what Norman describes as Wyndham's "barbed observation and limpidly cool technique".

ON 14 NOVEMBER, a fortnight after Bruce started work, Elizabeth reported to her mother. "He seems quite happy at the moment, but one never knows how long that will last." He had spent the previous three years engaged with abstract theories. It unblocked him to step on a plane to Paris with a photographer and then to spend only two hours with someone during which time everything took on significance. Required to deliver 2,000 words by a fixed date, he told Simon Sainsbury: "It suddenly gave me the discipline." Since 1969, he had been locked in to what he thought writing should be, engaging himself with the origins of mankind. The exercise of profiling two elderly French ladies he found comparatively easy. "It was no more difficult than writing papers in Edinburgh," says Elizabeth. Oliver Hoare, complimenting him on one of his articles, was impressed at the modesty of his reaction. "His basic attitude was: if he could do it, anyone could." He told Hoare: "It's simple to write. You just get down to it."

Wyndham pronounced Bruce's pieces on Vionnet and Delaunay exemplary. "If I did advise, it was *against* a certain preciousness and *for* crispness. Also, it's so important to get *how* the person speaks, rather than what he says, the way they talk." But Bruce required the minimum of editing. "It happens to so many people. They misunderstand their own talent: they slave away at something that is a mistake and suddenly they find through chance that they *have* a talent and it really is easy. That's why his pieces were so fresh. They were very accomplished, didn't need changing and they weren't imitative of other journalists. I didn't ever have to teach him how to write. What I felt I did do, which was not difficult, was to encourage him."

GIVEN THE GREEN light to suggest stories, Bruce did not stop. "Little did he know what we were used to," says Wyndham. "No one had an idea. He came in and had *rows* of ideas." Rarely was he more ebullient than when coming back to tell Wyndham about a story he had researched. "I thought he was marvellous, a great big treat."

The fashion editor Meriel McCooey shared an office with Wyndham. Bruce would walk straight across to Wyndham's desk emitting high-pitched shrieks. "It was always an entrance. You could have put a proscenium arch in front of him." He dressed in a blue shirt to match his eyes, dark navy blue jackets and a Little Lord Fauntleroy coat. "He had a thing about little boy clothes." But when he laughed out of control, she wondered, sometimes, if there was not a touch of insanity. "At times he looked like the cover of *Mad*."

The photographer Eve Arnold accompanied Bruce on two assignments. "There are people who are camera-loved and people whom the camera couldn't care about. He was one of the camera-loved. He was always on and he loved the attention. If you took the features apart, there was not one great feature: he was too boyish-looking for real elegance or style. His attraction lay in the mobility of his face, the absolute rubber quality as it moved back and forth."

Roger Law left the magazine to create the puppets for the satirical television series *Spitting Image*. This is how he would have satirised Bruce in the autumn of 1972: "You'd have starey blue eyes and floppy fair hair and the manic animation of a storyteller and it would fit into the category of our 'Talk Bollocks' slot—like Jonathan Miller as a cabbie breaking off to lecture you on The State of Man. It was a very intense, frenetic performance. You had to keep out of spittle's way. You never retaliated because you knew how vulnerable he was. When he wanted to tell you about Butch Cassidy and what you really wanted was a beer and it's nine degrees below and you're on the corner of a Manhattan street, you still listened. He always came up with something—an image, a story, which you wouldn't forget for a while. Making images that stop people so they remember is what we're all about."

After his initial guardedness, Linklater warmed to Bruce. "Editors have few pleasures. One of them is hearing the stories journalists bring back. Viscerally, Bruce was a real journalist. He didn't play fast and loose with the facts and he had an instinct for what made a story: something that no one has written about which is new and intriguing but not completely out of touch. All Bruce's stories had a recognition factor: Butch Cassidy, The Wolf Boy, like Mowgli; the Woman in the Desert, in the line of Thor Heyerdahl. But you got the impression that what mattered to him, more than writing itself, was sitting down and telling you about the story he was doing or about to do or had done. The bushfire of his imagination leapt over unproductive ground and inconvenient bits of territory to the next bit. That was the reason he was such good company—he was so stimulated by his own stories."

As highly as Linklater rated Bruce the feature-writer, he never altogether relaxed in his company. "There was a slight one-upmanship in the way he talked, a sort of snobbery in the names he dropped. You always felt with Bruce he'd produce things which revealed he had a greater depth of awareness than you in the things you knew about."

BRUCE BECAME ONE of the magazine's star reporters. "We soon forgot about the arts and under Francis's guidance I took on every kind of article." He wrote a dozen features over the next three years and in his last months gathered together most of these, with some tampering, in *What Am I Doing Here*. With two exceptions, they were articles he suggested himself—discussed and commissioned at lunches with Wyndham and the art department in the Progressive Working Men's Club, a café in Farringdon Road.

Bruce mostly pitched ideas to take him abroad. "The *Sunday Times* still hasn't decided whether his round-the-world scheme is too expensive or not," Elizabeth wrote to Gertrude at the end of December 1972. But in January he was sent to Russia.

David King's preoccupation with Soviet political art resulted in Bruce flying to Moscow to meet a collector of banned Leftist art who worked as a minor functionary at the Canadian Embassy. Bruce's Sotheby's friend, Tilo von Watzdorf, who had spent a week in Russia seeking Constructivist works to auction, was responsible for the idea. Watzdorf had met the 61-year-old George Costakis, known as "the mad Greek who buys hideous pictures". For 26 years Costakis had stubbornly tracked down abstract canvases by artists like Tatlin and Malevich, officially ignored since 1932. Watsdorf described the extraordinary collection to his friend—"who went off like a shot".

Bruce was attracted to characters like Costakis, who reflected facets of himself and to whom, through his contacts, he had access. Nor were they necessarily talented, eccentric or famous. One of his best articles was motivated by sympathy for a young outsider who had suffered a nervous breakdown. In August 1973, Bruce read of an immigrant Algerian, a 36-year-old sewage worker called Salah Bougrine who had without warning gone beserk in Marseille and fatally stabbed a bus-driver. With Don McCullin, Bruce travelled to France to understand the pressures that had driven Bougrine to leave behind wife and family and, finally, go mad. He visited a squalid *bidonville* and crossed into Algeria to meet Bougrine's father, a shepherd in a yellow headcloth on a chalk-white hillside. Bruce's sympathy for Bougrine, the demented exile, and his undisguised contempt for the fleshy-nosed protagonists of French racism received a warm welcome from Algeria's ambassador in London. "I was deeply moved by the compassion and great understanding with which you have written on this subject," wrote Lakhdar Brahimi, after the article was published in January 1974. Inviting him to dinner, he told Bruce how much his conclusions had dismayed the French Embassy. "I fear I intended that," Bruce wrote in his notebook. "But then I did come back from Marseille angry."

Each time he came back with a story, Wyndham "encouraged, criticised, edited". One cannot underestimate his influence. With Levi, Bruce had discussed Russian and English poets. With Wyndham, he discussed fiction. "I had assumed Bruce to be as knowledgeable about writing as he was about art. He wasn't. One of the things that excited me about our friendship was that he hadn't read any of the classics, or very little. So it was exciting when he did suddenly read *Madame Bovary* or Hemingway's short stories, which seemed to him as revolutionary as when they came out in the 1920s."

In Our Time struck Bruce as a total innovation of form. Typically, he compared Hemingway's prose to the visual arts. He told David Plante, to whom he gave a first edition, that this was the moment literature became Cubist. "I'm always seeing things in terms of images," he said. "I could never, for example, do an interior monologue." He was impressed by how Hemingway was able to evoke the emotion without providing the emotion, how he created a tension in his prose and dialogue that drove the reader to the next sentence. "Gertrude Stein says to Hemingway about some early things he has written: 'Ernest, comments are not literature.' Bruce understood that," says Plante. "He described." Bruce told Jean-François Fogel: "Hemingway's interesting even when he's bad."

Bruce raised Flaubert and Hemingway to the shelf that housed Mandelstam and Robert Byron. He studied them with microscopic attention. As slavishly as he had imitated *The Road to Oxiana,* he pared his prose in conscious imitation. "No whiches, thats and whos," he put in his notebook while reading *The Sun Also Rises.*

At this time he also discovered Ernst Jünger's *On the Marble Cliffs.* In June 1974, the magazine published Bruce's interview with the German aesthete, soldier and botanist who had recorded in his extensive diaries the Nazi occupation of Paris. Jünger, a member of the German High Command, noted with the dispassion of a trained beetle-collector how looting soldiers destroyed musical instruments yet spared mirrors, and how in a Wagner concert the trombones suddenly fell silent because the starving musicians had no breath left.

Bruce at this time had "an unlimited and obsessional regard" for Jünger's work, says the critic John Russell. "More than once when we met he went back and back to *On the Marble Cliffs.* I put this down to his interest in extreme cruelty and the ways in which it could be inflicted."

Bruce continued to be fascinated by Jünger to the end of his life. Wanting to write another essay on him, he squeezed his German publisher for fresh information. "In those days I was a kind of Jünger expert," says Michael Krüger. "The mystery about him has never been solved, even now. Here was a man in the middle of occupied Paris with bombers flying overhead and he's standing on the roof with champagne in his hand making little remarks. Bruce was deeply affected and involved by this coolness: how, in the middle of the biggest possible chaos, is it possible not to move, not to run away, not to accept all kinds of moral commitment? He would ring me up. 'Did you see Jünger? What is he doing? Was he a Nazi?' Always the question of immorality came up. Is it important for our notion of a writer if he has a moral life or not? Does the experience of immorality bring you to a deeper understanding of mankind? It was the same for Montherlant, the same for Lorenz—he was deeply interested. You came to the conclusion there must be something doubtful about Bruce's own life which produced this interest."

Collaborators exerted a powerful attraction for Bruce, who respected no political agenda and whose Jacobite ancestors, the Arbuthnots, had ended up as German mercenaries. "The rumours were true," the narrator writes in *Utz.* "He had collaborated. He had given information . . . to protect, even to hide, a number of his Jewish friends." Bruce admired the Italian writer Malaparte, author of *Kaputt,* who, before he turned, had worked for Mussolini; also, the circle of French writers hovering around Jünger: Montherlant, Drieu la Rochelle, Paul Morand. "He was interested in borders, where things were always changing, not one thing nor another," says Elizabeth. One journalistic project he discussed with Hans Magnus Enzensberger was a walk around Berlin.

Bruce, who was himself often mistaken for a German, chastises Jünger—just as he chastises Robert Louis Stevenson and T. E. Lawrence—for those same characteristics that he himself possessed. "His eyes are a particularly cold shade of blue. He has a light cackling laugh and drifts off when he is not the centre of attention." Bruce observes Jünger's "frozen, brilliantly-coloured style", comparing it to "the prose equivalent of an art nouveau object in glass". He attacks Jünger's style for the faults which critics later detected in Bruce's work. "He writes a hard, lucid prose. Much of it leaves the reader with an impression of the author's imperturbable self-regard, of dandyism, of cold-bloodedness, and finally, of banality . . . the diary is the perfect form for a man who combines such acute powers of observation with an anaesthetised sensibility."

The two writers overlap in other respects: a taste for "obscure allusions and philosophical speculation" combined with a "spirit of higher curiosity" which induces Jünger, for example, to watch the execution of a deserter. Jünger observed his pain in a distancing, enamelled light. "No one but a man of Jünger's composure could describe the appearance of a bullet hole through his chest as if he were describing his nipple." No one, perhaps, but Bruce.

"Bruce absolutely nailed him," said Stephen Spender, who had interviewed Jünger at the end of the war. "He was an excellent journalist in the best sense. He saw *through* people."

Alongside the absolute confidence of the cataloguer, he brought to his journalism the knowledge of what to leave out. He was able to suggest, to supply just enough data but no more. He knew the magic of a name and of the specific detail that gives authenticity and conviction. "An observed detail has a resonance—a branching truth—that no generalisation can match," wrote John Updike. In his writing as in his conversation Bruce had an eye for what makes a person or an object leap into relief. "We would probably all notice it to some degree," says Freddy Eberstadt, an American psychologist who knew Bruce in New York, "but he would focus on the thing which casts that person in a vivid light, like the way their hair was dyed. It was too apt to be a caricature or cartoon. It was not a Proustian or Joycean talent; more like a Daumier or a Toulouse Lautrec." He knew, too, what to leave out in his images. His short sentences delight in abbreviations. An old gentleman in Moscow "owned a wing strut of the glider Letalin"; a Prussian Junker on the Volga was a proud ex-aviator who balanced his Leica on the stump of his arm. A long list of Guggenheim descendants ends with Iris Love, "an irrepressible archaeologist who excavated the right index finger of the Venus de Milo".

Bruce's profiles do not observe the conventions of the normal interview. His subjects say little, perhaps because he renders them mute. Nor is he shy to voice disappointment. With Sonia Delaunay, he tells us, "conversation is not easy." Gaston Lefferre, the Mayor of Marseille, says even less. "In interview, he gives out virtually nothing: there is little point in repeating what he said." The same goes for Mrs Gandhi ("the interview was a bitter disappointment") as well as Ernst Jünger. "In answer to questions, he simply recited an excerpt from the diary . . ." But Bruce with his fount of knowledge elicits more. "Since I had an interest in Montherlant, I was able to draw Jünger out a little further." For Bruce, Jünger produces a photocopy of his friend Montherlant's spattered blood on his suicide note.

This sort of name-dropping and one-upmanship irritated older journalists. On the *Sunday Times*, his manner came to represent everything Linklater had been appointed to flush out. Cyril Connolly, for one, did not warm to him—nor he to Connolly. "He was," wrote Bruce, "extremely nasty to me. The dreaded Widow Orwell first introduced me to him, saying: 'You two must get to know each other. You're both so interested in . . . er . . . the truth.' 'Oh?' said Connolly, 'and what particular aspect of the truth are you interested in?'. . ."

But younger colleagues rated him above senior writers on the magazine like V. S. Naipaul: "Personally, I would swap every Naipaul in the world for Bruce Chatwin, a Linklater discovery whose work I first read in the Magazine," wrote Philip Norman. "While a Naipaul winces by an hotel pool, Chatwin is out, speaking in local dialects, translating hieroglyphics and riding the pampas on horseback without a saddle." James Fox, who became a friend, also admired Bruce's style. "He had the ruthlessness to get where he wanted to, but he managed to combine this calculatedly with just enough good manners for it not to be offensive." And unlike other journalists, Bruce immediately became part of the circle of those he wrote about. "He infiltrated, was accepted as an equal."

ONE OF HIS subjects was André Malraux. In the winter of 1973, over a lunch meeting at the Working Men's Club, Bruce suggested a profile of the reclusive French writer. He believed the author of *Le Musée Imaginaire* to be "one of the most original minds of our time".

They had met before. On 12 February 1970, on his way to Mauritania, Bruce had dined in Paris with Jessie Wood, the daughter of Malraux's late companion Louise de Vilmorin. "Malraux was there and was obviously deeply upset, both by the political state of France and the death of Jessie's mother—but what a fascination it was to hear someone who knew Stalin, Ho and the General well."

Malraux told stories. Afterwards, Bruce wrote them down:

"1. He and de Gaulle showing Kruschev round Versailles and somehow the simple severe parquet de Versailles is mentioned. Kruschev interposes and says that they have the same in Russia but theirs is inlaid with ebony. The General in an aside to Malraux: *Cet homme commence à m'ennuyer.*

2. A meeting of the Kremlin:
Stalin says—holding his vodka—toasting his comrades—welcoming them—cajoling them.
Comrade Patagoskin, c'est le Ministre de Communications—et si les communications ne marchent pas (here he breaks his glass in his fingers) *Comrade Patagoskin sera perdu.*"

OTHER SUBJECTS DISCUSSED that night were the political origins of the Mongol Empire (they agreed, "a very, very difficult problem") and Hemingway (*"un fou qui a la folie de simplicité"*).

Three years later, Bruce entreated Jessie Wood to arrange an interview. "One rule I made," she says, "is that I never, never asked Monsieur de Malraux to see people. People were always calling up. It's something I never did for any of my children who were journalists." Nevertheless, on Bruce's behalf she asked Malraux, and he agreed.

One cold afternoon, Bruce, the Woods and the photographer, Eve

Arnold, drove in a battered Simca to Jessie's family house at Verrières-le-Buisson, 20 minutes from Paris. In the Salon Bleu, Bruce sat talking with Malraux, in French, for four hours. The lights were not turned on and as the afternoon progressed they went on speaking in the half-light, Malraux sitting among the framed doodles of cats he had drawn during his cabinet meetings with de Gaulle. He was frail, propping up his chin with trembling hands. "Since I found him sad, I only took one photograph," says Eve Arnold. The rest of the time she listened. "Bruce flicking out his tongue—with his green biro racing across the page—had such dynamic force. The range of things they talked about was incredible." The English gentleman, how there was no such thing in France and this was too bad; Afghanistan; the Mughal Empire; de Gaulle and T. E. Lawrence.

"In Lawrence's career and personality Malraux seems to have recognised elements that coincided with his own." Bruce responded similarly to the elderly French writer, "a talented aesthete who transformed himself into a great man". Bruce was able to understand Malraux's incarnations better than anyone: archaeologist, aesthete, art smuggler, adventurer, "compulsive traveller and talker". The meeting had elements of the archetypal Borges story in which a young man encounters an elderly stranger who turns out to be his older self, his *fait accompli*. Bruce did see in the Frenchman a version of himself. "Malraux is alone. He can have no followers. He never allowed himself the luxury of a final political or religious creed, and is too restless for the discipline of academic life. He is unclassifiable, which in a world of -isms and -ologies is also unforgivable." In Bruce's final question there is an urgent need for reassurance about the landmines ahead: "And what of the prospects for an adventurer today?"

Bruce was euphoric. The afternoon was so much more than he had anticipated. Malraux had been quite open. "He was totally enchanted by Bruce," says Jessie. "He called me up afterwards. There was a bond between these adventuresome spirits. He saw all Bruce's fantasies and originality."

THE GERMAN WRITER and polemicist Hans Magnus Enzensberger was another who understood Bruce's penchant for "adventurers of the mind" (and for such "doubtful figures" as Malraux and Jünger) as an aspect of his flight from Englishness. "*What Am I Doing Here* is a title which can do without the question mark," he wrote in a review for the *Times*

Literary Supplement, "the summary of someone who never found a definite place for himself, a man forever on the move, both in terms of space and social context." In these pieces, most of them written for the *Sunday Times*, Bruce began to close the gap between journalism and literature. "Chatwin's meticulous sense of the metier made him steer clear of the pitfalls of the commission. Not for him the know-all attitude, the jaded taste and the flashiness of the reportage. Here is the uncommon spectacle of a writer using the press on his own terms, using the tools and opportunities of journalism to the advantage of literature. This gives a rare freshness even to the most ephemeral pages."

Bruce specialized in returns and departures, taking what he needed and moving on. His Malraux profile was published in June 1974. By then his interest in journalism was waning. He worked on a retainer until October 1975, although in the last year he took advantage of the *laissez-faire* spirit to award himself an unofficial sabbatical while he researched what was to become his first published book. Thereafter he would accept commissions if they took him to places he hankered to visit: Capri, the Volga, Nepal, Hong Kong, India. In 1978, three years after he had left the *Sunday Times*, he wrote a profile of Mrs Gandhi for the magazine. This and "One Million Years of Art" were the only assignments he did not choose himself. His experience of writing the Gandhi piece, commissioned at Wyndham's suggestion, affirmed his decision to leave the magazine for a larger, more enduring project. "I do not want to *have* to make bread and butter doing journalism, because ultimately it corrodes," he wrote to Elizabeth. Where the experience of meeting Malraux had inspired him, Mrs Gandhi produced in Bruce a seesaw of emotions: "I go through alternative phases of 'Love Indira' or 'Hate Indira'." He came to know her as "that nightmaring lady". But this was not his first impression.

Eve Arnold was again the photographer. She flew out a week after Bruce. She found him "passionately in love" with Mrs Gandhi. She was like Joan of Arc, he said. He wanted to protect her. Nobody had prepared him for her "most marvellous sense of the ridiculous"—a quality she shared with Malraux. The two of them had been sitting in a circuit house when she turned to Bruce and said: " 'Bruce, you have no idea how tiring it is to be a goddess,' and then she said, 'Have you got any more of those cashew nuts?' After that I really started to love her."

Eve Arnold watched Bruce at work. "From the beginning Bruce considered himself a writer," she says. "If you dared say 'journalist' he'd go into orbit with anger. He kept insisting to Mrs Gandhi he needed more time with her. When she said 'Why?' he insisted he was a *writer*, his piece should be lasting. She was not very gracious about it, but she did knuckle under."

Arnold was amused to read the finished piece. Bruce had not changed the facts, but she could not help noticing his tendency to become the protagonist. In a hotel near Assam, Mrs Gandhi had offered her bed to Arnold "because it makes me tired to watch you work". In Bruce's account, Mrs Gandhi, solicitous for his grazed forehead, asks instead if *he* needs a rest. "Not the case at all," says Arnold. Nor did he have any compunction about pinching Arnold's story. In his profile, he tells Mrs Gandhi about a wolf child he had been to see in Sultanpur. The boy had been found, playing with wolf cubs, in the forest. He ate chickens alive, including entrails, and was unable to speak, emitting a noise between a growl and a howl.

Interested, Mrs Gandhi says: "Well, Sanjay didn't speak until he was six . . ."

Sensing her vulnerability (her son Sanjay had just been arrested) Bruce brushes her hand and murmurs, "Don't worry." Gradually, he writes, Mrs Gandhi picks up the conversation and he is amazed to hear her say "Thatcher". Then she says to him: "How that woman wants to be PM! When she came here to Delhi she was so nervous. I felt like telling her, 'If you want to be PM that badly, you'll never make it'."

These words had been said to Eve Arnold while Bruce was in Sultanpur. Knowing Arnold was syndicated and Bruce was not, Mrs Gandhi had requested Arnold sit next to her on the plane. "She asked me 'What's your next assignment?' 'Mrs Thatcher,' I laughed. I told Bruce later what she'd said . . . He was a sponge. He absorbed everything around him and transmuted it into something all his own. He was faithful to the story line. He just found it made a better story if he was the No. 1. Normally, you edit out something. Bruce edited himself in."

IN THE VILLAGE of Azamgarh, two hours from Benares, Arnold and Bruce fell in with an Indian journalist who was starting out on *India Today*. If Malraux had presented to Bruce a future image, Sunil Sethi was his younger self. He called him "the 23-yr-old whizz-kid of Indian journalism".

"I was sitting outside the hotel," says Sethi, "eating this terribly spartan lunch when up drove a rickety white Ambassador car in a swirl of dust and out fell these two pink people. It was so incongruous. One was a very small lady with long white hair piled high in a grandmotherly way. The other was a very silly-looking, pink Englishman.

"I said, 'Can I help?'

"He said, 'We're looking for some water, actually. This lady's very sick. She is Eve Arnold.'

"I said, 'Oh, yes, I remember seeing your wonderful pictures of Joan Crawford.' He just looked at me, his eyes growing wider and wider."

The hotel was full. Sethi gave up his room for Arnold while he and Bruce slept on the roof. They were blown about by a sandstorm, but this bothered neither of them. "We hit it off immediately. We just couldn't stop talking," says Sethi. "Furbank's biography of Forster was out and we talked about that and who could write about India. I said: 'Listen, Forster got it right'." Sethi was impressed by Bruce's range of knowledge. "He didn't have a magpie mind. It was a classic nineteenth-century dilettante mind in the best sense. Conversations were made up of allusions, bits and pieces that came up not from a meat grinder but from some endless private jigsaw. He was always connecting, always playing with the truth in interesting ways. It was a personal joust."

Leaving Arnold to recuperate, they went back to Benares. Down one street Bruce pulled Sethi back. "Come here! Look at this!" Sethi supposed he had found a temple. "But it was just four chimney-sweep faces lit by sparks from the staves of iron they had thrust into the fire. Charcoal-blackened iron-smiths, barely visible through a crumbling arch, amid the mad raucous colours of an Indian bazaar. It was always like that: 'Let's find out, let's look at the view again, let's look at the papers'."

Sethi, wrote Bruce, was "an exhilarating companion". He became one of a few with whom Bruce chose to talk personally. "He was very, very insecure about confidences," says Sethi. "But I was much younger and I was out of context to his whole world. Distance made it a very abiding relationship. It wouldn't have lasted if we'd lived together in the same society."

Bruce appealed to the younger journalist to assist him in his endeavour. He told him: "Now you've got to help me figure this Mrs Gandhi out."

BRUCE TRAVELLED FOR two months, from Cape Cormorin to the Himalayas. He then settled down in Spain to structure a long article. "A bitch to write—about a bitch," he wrote to his parents. "I went very sympathetic to anyone who attempted to govern the ungovernable, but in the end couldn't dredge up one particle of sympathy for the woman . . . Even in the villains you can usually find something—but Mrs G is the essence of bathos." He wrote to Welch how on the desk of her Assistant Private Secretary he had found a manual for ventriloquists called *Mimicry and Mono-acting*. "She's far worse than you'd ever imagine. I was prepared to allow her at least a dimension of greatness, but all you find is a lying, scheming bitch. If she were really evil, that would be something. If she were really Indian, that also would be something . . . She charmed me at first, I have to admit. But I couldn't stomach the pettiness of the lies. Her enemy Charan Singh summed her up when he said: 'Mrs Gandhi is incapable of telling the truth, even by mistake'."

THE *Sunday Times* had foreseen a different piece. "They hated it," said Wyndham. "They wanted a foreign correspondent's profile. I met Brian Moynihan at the lift. 'They hate it, they hate it'."

In grand disdain, Bruce wrote to Sethi about the rows. "The copy came back scrawled all over: WELL? IS SHE COMING BACK OR ISN'T SHE? or WHAT IS THE POLITICAL SCENE? That kind of thing, with a request that I rewrite.

"But why should I? Print or don't print, but don't bother me . . . Preferably, don't print, because anyway I don't like writing about people I don't like."

On 26 July 1978 he wrote with more news. "The Wolf Boy article comes out next week in the *Sunday Times* Magazine. Of course they were much more pleased with that one than Mrs G. My slight rows over Mrs G (which I don't want talked about) were concerned with the fact that I wrote down only what *I* saw, not what other people say." As for the *Sunday Times*, "the whole thing seems to be on its last legs. Do you wonder in an organisation where Old Etonians have to trim their accents to Yorkshire when they go *upstairs* to the Editor, to cockney when they go *downstairs* to the print rooms?"

On 12 September, Bruce wrote to Elizabeth: "I bet they've chopped up the Mrs Gandhi piece: the sub-editor *manque le moindre étincelle d'intélligence et de goût et d'humeur*. I really am NOT going to write for them again."

Bruce wrote to Sethi, "Resolution of the month: Never to write for newspapers." As an awful warning and everything he wished neither of them to become, he held up the example of another journalist on the *Sunday Times*, Cyril Connolly. "I've really gone *off* him," Bruce had written to Elizabeth after reading an article which "was silly egocentric drivel, but that is what goes down . . ." He considered Connolly "a rotten novelist" and was unable to read *The Rock Pool*. "However, *The Unquiet Grave* is a book I return to again and again, so brilliant yet so terribly indicative of the pitfalls of English literary life."

Under the heading "Quotation of the Month" he typed out for Sethi a cautionary Connolly paragraph. "The more books we read, the sooner we perceive that the true function of the writer is to produce a masterpiece and that no other task is of any consequence . . . All excursions into journalism, broadcasting, propaganda and writing of films, however grandiose, are doomed to disappointment."

Given Sethi's "unbearable curiosity" and his capacity to arrange characters on a written page, he should attempt at least one lasting masterpiece. "In a world where millions of hot-air-laden pages are printed annually, it becomes a duty to go, see and condense for future readers at some unseen date." He offered the following, hard-earned advice: "I am not suggesting you walk out of *India Today*, but feel you have reached a point where journalism had taught you the necessary art of condensation and the technique of story-hunting, but as such had nothing to offer you."

Bruce also furnished Sethi with the reading list he might have wished for himself at that age. He slays the lions who had written about India. "India is the land of the short story. It will never have its *War and Peace*. Mr Scott's opus is a tragic bore; Mrs Jabberwallah [*sic*] can't write; R. K. Narayan isn't good enough and Mr Naipaul is a pontificator . . . I like *Passage to India*, but believe that E. M. F. is a poor model, as Somerset Maugham is a lethal one. Forgive me for suggesting you go on a course of Chekhov, Isaac Babel, Maupassant, Flaubert (especially *Un Coeur Simple*), Ivan Bunin (whom I'll get for you), Turgenev, and among the Americans early Sherwood Anderson, early Hemingway, and Carson McCullers, especially *The Ballad of the Sad Café*.

"I wouldn't take too much notice of this: it does reveal my inability to come to terms with English literature in general, excepting of course the Elizabethans and the outsiders. But we have nothing in the C19th or C20th to beat the narrative drive of someone like Poe.

"My latest passion is Racine, though heaven knows where it's going to lead. But the past week has gone writing an introduction to another passion, the prose of Osip Mandelstam, the most important writer to be snuffed out by Stalin . . ."

"Don't leave it too late," he urged Sethi. "I've left it far too late."

XXII.

⟨⟨⟨⟨⟩

"Gone to Patagonia"

Don Bruce, he talked a lot, bastante.

—Señora Eberhadt, Puerto Natales

Magnus Linklater has no recollection of the telegram Bruce claimed to have sent the *Sunday Times*: gone to patagonia for four months. The telegram most likely took the form of a letter to Wyndham.

The letter arrived on Wyndham's desk in December 1974, postmarked Lima: "I have done what I threatened / I suddenly got fed up with N. Y. and ran away to South America / I have been staying with a cousin in Lima for the past week and am going tonight to Buenos Aires. I intend to spend Christmas in the middle of Patagonia / I am doing a story there for myself, something I have always wanted to write up."

The story "could be marvellous, but I'll have to do it in my own way". It related to Charles Milward and to the piece of brontosaurus skin thrown out in the move from Brown's Green to Stratford in 1961. Bruce had not stopped thinking of Patagonia: the safest place in the event of nuclear war, the place where he planned to escape from school, the habitat of several tribes he had studied for *The Nomadic Alternative*. The lectures at Edinburgh he most responded to were Charles Thomas's on the Welsh in Chubut and on Charles Darwin's shocked reaction to the Yaghans of Tierra del Fuego. A meeting in December 1972 with the Irish designer and architect Eileen Gray had rekindled Bruce's "childhood infatuation"—after visiting Gray, he wrote to thank her for "the most enjoyable Sunday afternoon I have spent in years". Gray, then 93, had on the wall of her Paris apartment two maps of Patagonia that she had painted in gouache. Bruce said: "That's one of the places I've always wanted to go to." It was Gray's ambition too: if she were young again she would try to see Cape Horn. *"Allez-y pour moi,"* she said.

When he finally set out, Elizabeth had had no idea he was making plans. "But that wasn't the only time that I didn't know what was going on in his head." One day in September 1974, Bruce was in the bath at

Holwell, chatting to Elizabeth, when Gertrude rang up to say that Bobby was ill and she had taken him to hospital. "Bruce had a funny sixth sense about lots of things," says Elizabeth. "He said: 'If you want to see your father alive, get on a plane tomorrow morning.' He took me to the airport." On 1 October, shortly after he had seen Elizabeth, Bobby had a stroke and died.

Bruce flew out for the funeral and stayed on in Gertrude's apartment in Fifth Avenue. He had $3,500 expenses from the *Sunday Times* in his pocket and was supposed to be writing a story on the Guggenheim family. But he felt at the end of his tether with the paper—"anyone would be after a short while".

Wyndham was also in New York. He and David King were drinking in the bar of the Chelsea Hotel when Bruce appeared, dressed like a Boy Scout in khaki shorts, rucksack on his back. "He said: 'I'm off to Patagonia. Tell Magnus I'll get in touch.' Then he left." Wyndham and King had another drink and an hour later, from a cab going down Broadway, they saw him striding along, talking to himself, and people looking back in a surprised fashion. "I had this feeling he would walk and walk until he reached Patagonia."

The literary agent Gillon Aitken had also met him in New York. He says, "The only subject on his mind was Milward's story. He kept talking about Patagonia—and he talked so much about it that I said: 'You must stop talking about it, you must go, go, go'." On 2 November, "on the spur of the moment," Bruce made a break for it.

HE FLEW FIRST TO Lima, in order to talk to Milward's daughter. Monica Barnett was a former journalist who had started to put together Milward's sea stories with the idea of publication. She was reluctant to turn Bruce loose on her father's papers, among them a 258-page journal of his life at sea. While permitting him to make rough notes, she insisted that he did not remove this manuscript from the house.

After Bruce's visit, Monica rang up Margharita and was enthusiastic about her charming, unconventional second cousin. Margharita passed on the news to Elizabeth. "She said that Bruce was a fascinating young man & that I must be very proud of him. I am!"

Bruce was riveted by Milward's journal and the contents of his letter book, interleaved with photographs and postcards from Birmingham. "Charles Milward's life strangely compacted into the mythic present," he

Bruce's marriage to Elizabeth Chanler in the private chapel at Geneseo, 21 August 1965. He never demonstrated his "eye" better than in his choice of a wife. They were known as the Chattys. [Courtesy of Elizabeth Chatwin]

"No man can wander without a base." Holwell Farm, Wotton-under-Edge, was the Chatwins' home from 1966 to 1981. Bruce thought it was haunted. [EC]

The sitting room at Homer End. "Elizabeth took care of things so that Bruce could appear on the stage of life in the way he wanted," observed her former flatmate, Pattie Sullivan: "' I travel light, I have no possessions, what are things to me?'" Above the fireplace are the Inca feathers Bruce and Elizabeth bought with their wedding money. [Paul Yule]

Elizabeth on a bus in Afghanistan, 1969. "That was when our marriage really worked," said Bruce, who was full of admiration for his wife's physical courage on a difficult journey. [EC]

Bruce on his third visit to Afghanistan in 1969. The people responded warmly to him: "an Afghan truck driver greatly admired my ears". [Chris Rundle]

Gulem Akbar Khan in 1969. A chance meeting with Bruce and Elizabeth in Multan changed this young Pathan's life. [EC]

Bruce photographed by James Ivory in the Oregon desert, 1972. The film was not developed until 1998. Ivory says: "When I study the photograph, his image springs out at me and suggests there was a man there I might not have known as well as I thought . . . a male version of those romantic nineteenth-century European ladies who travelled to the East to paint watercolours and were captured by sheikhs and kept in a harem for 1001 nights." [James Ivory]

Bruce aged 34, with the Welsh community in Gaiman. In Patagonia he ruffled many feathers, but he discovered himself as a writer. [EC]

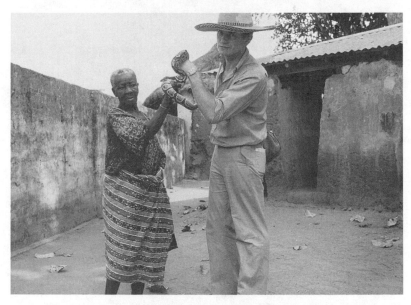

Bruce at the Python Temple in Ouidah, 1976. At Sotheby's he had briefly kept a python as a pet. [John Kasmin]

A postcard to his parents from Ouidah in 1972, picturing Bruce with a moustache, which he called "d'Artagnanesque". [EC]

Bruce was drawn to men from ordinary backgrounds who set themselves up royally on remote shores. Francisco de Souza landed in Ouidah penniless from Brazil and became the richest man on the Slave Coast. [PY]

The eighth Viceroy of Ouidah, Honoré de Souza (*left*), with his chamberlain Norberto de Souza in 1998. They are reacting to questions about Bruce's novel, *The Viceroy of Ouidah*. [PY]

Bruce looking for descendants of de Souza in Benin in 1976. [JK]

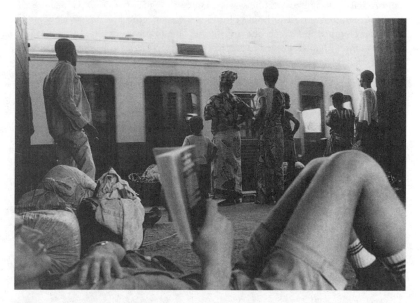

Bruce reading Huysmans at Parakou station in Benin, 1976. Two weeks later he was caught in a coup. [JK]

Bruce needed gurus and had a talent for going straight to the fountainhead. *Clockwise from left:* 1. Stuart Piggott, Bruce's professor of archaeology at Edinburgh University. [Thames & Hudson Ltd] 2. Francis Wyndham, Bruce's editor at the *Sunday Times*. It was Wyndham who first encouraged him to write. [Times Newspapers] 3. The Australian anthropologist Theodor Strehlow (*c.*1936) lived with the Aranda Aboriginals until he was 14. Bruce thought his *Songs of Central Australia* one of the most important books of the twentieth century. [Kath Strehlow] 4. The palaeontologist Bob Brain at the Swartkrans cave in Johannesburg. His book *The Hunters or the Hunted?* proved to Bruce's satisfaction that man was not predatory in his origins. [PY]

wrote in his notebook, and to Elizabeth: "I like my cousins enormously. Monica Barnett is exactly like Aunt Grace to look at. The diary of Charlie Milward is fantastic, even if it could never be printed in its present form. The story of the wreck, of Louis de Rougemont, of Indian massacres, of life at sea on the Cape Horners is exactly like something out of Conrad. Am going to Buenos Aires tonight."

Bruce arrived in Argentina on 12 December at one of the more unstable moments in its history. "It was like the latter days of the Roman Empire," he told ABC radio. Perón had returned a year before, triggering a massacre at the airport, and had died shortly after. The Montonero guerrillas had begun their assault on the enfeebled government of his widow Isabella. The revolutionary atmosphere did not impair Bruce's ability to gather contacts for his journey south, but he felt the tension. At dinner with the Braun-Menendez family, who had done a great deal to develop Patagonia in the late nineteenth century, a window slammed. "In all their minds this was an attack." That winter, one of their cousins had been fatally wounded in the stomach during a kidnap attempt.

Based at the Hotel Lancaster, Bruce responded to Jorge Luis Borges's "almost endless city", its wide cobbled streets, its wedding-cake architecture, its bookshops. "Buenos Aires is utterly bizarre," he wrote to Elizabeth, "a combination of Paris and Madrid shorn of historical depth, with hallucinating *avenidas* flanked with lime trees, where not even the humblest housewife need forego the architectural aspirations of Marie-Antoinette. I have been mixing with Anglo-Argentines who have lost command of English and all knowledge of home and with some of the crustier Argentines who speak it far better than I do."

Among the latter was "my best friend here", a 22-year-old writer, Jorge Torre Zavaleta, "who is absolutely enchanting and of a culture and sensitivity that has died out in Europe". Bruce had met Jorge in a red brick chateau in Calle Zenteno belonging to Jorge's uncle, a former Argentinian foreign secretary. Jorge entered the library to find Bruce sitting in jeans on a red damask chair, legs apart, and talking about his project "as if he was in love". At lunch, they sat beneath the striking portrait of a cowboy. Painted on leather in 1842 by a French artist called Monvoisin, it showed a recumbent *gaucho* in a cap and red chemise, holding a *maté* gourd to his bared chest. Bruce was taken by the dark face frothed with a black moustache and excitedly described the *gaucho* as an odalisque. Jorge had plenty of times sat beneath the same figure without it striking him in this way. Since that moment, he has only been able to see the *gaucho* as an odalisque. "Good observation is a kind of invention."

Jorge was a friend and reader to the blind Borges. He was trying to give up law and pursue a career as a writer against the wishes of his family. Bruce stood at a similar crossroads. Jorge invited him to the Jockey Club where they talked about books. "He spoke very little Spanish," says Jorge, "and not with a good accent either, but I felt he had done a lot of homework." Bruce's excitement frankly mystified his host. Patagonia, to Jorge as to most *porteños*, was "a back alley where different cultures swirled about and rather a boring place". It was fine for Scots and Germans, but Argentinians preferred to visit Scotland and Germany. "To me, Patagonia was just emptiness."

Bruce heard the same sentiment expressed at the Braun-Menendez's house in Punta Arenas. "Here am I inundated with Patagonian literature and I hear from across the table in Spanish heavily larded with a German accent, 'I doubt if there are five books on Patagonia'."

No one did more to overturn this perception than Bruce did. Over the next three and a half months he discovered Patagonia as a subject, and himself as a writer.

PATAGONIA IS NOT a precise region on the map. It is a vast, vague territory that encompasses 900,000 square kilometres of Argentina and Chile. The area is most effectively defined by its soil. You know you are in Patagonia when you see *rodados patagonicos*, the basalt pebbles left behind by glaciers, and *jarilla*, the low bush that is its dominant flora. Patagonia may also be described by its climate. The wind which blows with terrific force from October to March made Antoine de Saint-Exupéry's plane fly backward instead of forward.

Travellers from Darwin onwards noted how this bleakness seized the imagination. Patagonia's nothingness forces the mind in on itself. The stern Welsh pioneer, John Murray Thomas, trekking inland in July 1877, wrote in his fading pencil: "Last night dreamt of Harriett that we were in the bedroom. Had a nice kiss. Hardly a night passes but that I see her in my dreams."

In Patagonia, the isolation makes it easy to exaggerate the person you are: drinkers drink; the devout pray; the lonely grow lonelier, sometimes fatally. In Punta Arenas, Tom Jones was one of Charles Milward's successors as British Consul. In his 1961 memoir *A Patagonian Panorama*, he wrote: "Whether it is the dreary and crude climate of Patagonia or the lonely life in the camp after the day's work or remorse after a bout of hard drinking, I cannot say, but I have known, some very intimately, well over 20 people who have committed suicide." Bruce would be moved most by the dreamers and adventurers whose dreams had failed them.

The first sheep farmers arrived from the Falkland Islands in the late 1870s, but the temptation among their descendants to cling to the culture their forbears left behind remains fierce. Patagonia spans two nations; a good many of its inhabitants pass a life likewise divided, rebuilding the environment they have escaped. The more remote the valley, the more faithful the recreation of an original homeland. In Gaiman, the Welsh preserve their language and their hymns. In Rio Pico, the Germans plant lupins and cherry trees. In Sarmiento, the Boers continue to dry their biltong (of *guanaco*). Bruce wrote in his journal, "The further one gets from the great centres of civilisation, the more prevalent become the fanciful reconstructions of the world of Madame du Barry."

Patagonia is one of those fertile territories of fantasy, like the Galapagos, which has scarcely advanced from its early maps showing blue unicorns, red centaurs and giants. It still likes to think of itself as a land of giants. "Not those giants referred to by Hernando de Magellanes," wrote Tom Jones, "but those men and women, many of them British, who made this vast, bleak and windswept land, prosperous and habitable for civilised people." Today, it remains scattered both with dinosaur bones and living relics who live 60 kilometres from the nearest pavement and talk of "leagues" and "chappies" and "t'other side". Everyone seems seven foot high, an oddball. Dreams proliferate. "Patagonia is different from anywhere else," says Teresita Braun-Menendez, of the family with whom Bruce had dined in Buenos Aires. "That loneliness, that grandiosity. Anything can happen."

BRUCE HAD COME to Argentina with a fixed idea. "I always try and decide what I want and then I will try and find it," he told the broadcaster, Melvyn Bragg. He was keen to retrieve from his abandoned nomad book the idea of the Journey as Metaphor, in particular Lord Raglan's paradigm of the young hero who sets off on a voyage and does battle with a monster. Such journeys are the meat and drink of our earliest stories, Bruce told the Argentinian journalist Uki Goni—an "absolute constant, a universal in literature". He wanted to write a spoof of this form. Where Jason had sought the Golden Fleece, Bruce would seek the animal in his grand-mother's cabinet. Wishing to make it more of a spoof, he even harboured the notion of calling his book: "A Piece of Brontosaurus".

The spoof was a protective device, concealing a desire to continue his serious exploration into wandering and exile. "Tierra del Fuego was the last place man had wandered to on foot," he told Goni. "There is some way in which Patagonia is the ultimate symbol of restlessness for the human condition." He intended to grapple with his theme not in the abstract terms which had suffocated his nomad book, but in concrete stories.

"Your fascination is people?" asked Goni.

"Yes, in the end. It took rather a long time to discover that."

The people Bruce would meet in Patagonia were often rootless story-tellers like himself. "My temperament is definitely towards the fantastic," he told Goni. "The whole of this journey was like a pursuit—not only for this ridiculous piece of skin, which was a sort of fantastical enough quest anyway, but then as it developed it became chasing one story or one set of characters after another." It was, he said, "the most jaw-dropping experience because everywhere you'd turn up, there, sure enough, was this somewhat eccentric personality who had this fantastic story . . . At every place I came to it wasn't a question of hunting for the story it was a question of the story coming at you . . . I also think the wind had something possibly to do with it."

ON 18 DECEMBER, he took the overnight bus to Bahia Blanca and at 8 a.m. reached the small town of Cabildo. His destination was "El Chimango", the *estancia* of David Bridges. Bridges was the son of Lucas Bridges, who had written one of Bruce's favourite books, *Uttermost Part of the Earth*. His grandfather, the first missionary to Tierra del Fuego, personified Bruce's childhood fantasy to the abandoned orphan. Found on a bridge wearing clothes marked with a "T" and christened Thomas Bridges, he was at the age of 19 put in charge of a mission on Keppel Island and from 1887 he lived on the Beagle Channel at Harberton in a green and white house pre-fabricated in Devon. "His lack of roots in England forced him to establish new roots in Tierra del Fuego." One reason for visiting David Bridges was to establish contact with Bridges's relations in the far south.

Bridges picked up Bruce outside the chemist in Cabildo and drove him to the house he was building half an hour away. The brick bungalow lay on a hill, roofless, with a sweeping view over charlock fields to the Sierra de los Vascos. Bridges showed Bruce round the farm. He had worked on the maps of his father's book and shared his blunt suspicion of travellers. "I think explorers rather than missionaries ought to be put in the cook-pot," he says. He nevertheless found Bruce "distinctly positive" as a person.

Bruce's book on Patagonia would upset many of the people who lived there. Bridges is not one of them: "If you haven't ruffled any feathers you certainly haven't written anything worth writing." In the book, Bruce gives Bridges the name of Bill Philips. "I asked him to disguise me, although he didn't put enough damn camouflage. No one likes being discovered. No one likes looking at their own passport photograph, but I found it accurate. It's not flattering, but it's the truth." Bridges confirms the accuracy of other portraits. "I thought he was being extremely discreet down south and therefore you could think it was someone else's passport. I've never known an author yet who's left a happy stream behind him. Some get on their high horse, and what they get on their horse about is as ridiculous as a fish on the roof. They have illusions about themselves that a photographer hasn't."

"MY BUSINESS WAS TO record what people said," Bruce wrote of his time in Patagonia. The author would be the thinnest presence. "I'm not interested in the traveller," he told ABC radio. "I'm interested in what the traveller sees."

He described his odyssey to Colin Thubron in photographic terms. "I was . . . determined to see myself as a sort of literary Cartier-Bresson going SNAP, like that. It was supposed to be a take each time." The comparison is instructive. Cartier-Bresson is popularly defined by his notion of the "decisive moment", an instant when everything in the picture is in balance. Bruce sought the same reverberating image. He wrote quick snapshots of ordinary people among whom he passed a very short time: stay longer and the picture would fog. Few guessed what he was up to. (In the Residential Ritz hotel in Punta Arenas, Bruce wrote down his profession as *estanciero*, or farmer.) This, partly, is why many of his subjects resented him. Not telling them that the camera was rolling, he caught them unawares and condensed their lives into a few vivid details. The portraits were not untrue, rather an encapsulation and the effect was to heighten and intensify. In the process, some felt, he had made off with their intimate moments and preserved them behind the glass of his prose for strangers to look at.

Nowhere was this resentment more acutely felt than in the community of Chubut.

IN 1865, A boat-load of Welsh settlers landed on a beach near what is now Puerto Madryn. They had come to the desert to be free of England. Today, the name Bruce Chatwin conjures up everything the original emigrants had sailed to leave behind.

On 22 December, Bruce walked along the beach among the seals. "I am feeling tired and fat and old, cannot bear to look down to see the rings of fat that have been added to my waist over the last few weeks . . . I must unburden myself and go where the tourists are not." On Christmas Eve, travelling by bus, he reached the village of Gaiman, 20 miles inland.

Gaiman's schoolteacher was Albina Zampini. Her father was a Jones who had arrived in 1886. She took pity on Bruce and invited him to a Christmas Eve party at the house of her sister, Vally Pugh. "Poor chap, he didn't have any presents so I gave him a linen handkerchief. He was eating *turron*, a hard candy, which he said reminded him of the mylodon. The main subject on his mind was that giant sloth."

Albina introduced Bruce to Enrique Fernandez, a young musician, who became his guide. In the book, Bruce calls him "Anselmo" and writes that when he played Chopin "you could imagine you were in the presence of a genius". Enrique died of AIDS in May 1990, but a photograph kept by his mother shows a young man of 26 in a brown jersey with both hands on the piano. He has a long nose and a moustache. Bruce told at least two people that he seduced Enrique, although his notebook makes no reference to this.

On Christmas Day, Enrique took Bruce to the smallholding belonging to his friend Edmundo Williams. Edmundo and his brother Geralt showed Bruce the contents of the adobe house, a collection of Welsh relics which Bruce photographed, and afterwards Geralt drove him to church in a 1958 Dodge.

Edmundo took intense exception to the few lines Bruce wrote about him. It is not too much to say that they changed his life. His resentment illustrates a sentiment widely held: whereas V. S. Naipaul insulted the important, powerful people when he wrote about Argentina (in *The Return of Eva Perón*), Bruce upset the little people, those who could not answer back.

Bruce called Edmundo "Euan" and suggested, subtly, that because he was single he was other things too. This infuriated Edmundo. He had received this stranger politely. He knew nothing about appearing in a book and suddenly, two years later, other strangers start coming to his door asking personal questions he does not want to answer. Through his fleeting appearance in *In Patagonia*, people have assumed an intimate knowledge of him he was rarely prepared to give anyone. It was Edmundo's link with Enrique which was especially damaging and misleading, as the book recasts Edmundo in a role Bruce, off the record, later acknowledged as his own. He wrote to a friend: "What I took OUT of that story was the head falling backwards at the end of the mazurka . . . and lifting him off the piano stool into the bedroom."

Bruce's Patagonian notebooks contain few personal revelations or confessions of the sort he is adept at chiselling out of others. He told Uki Goni: "There are some people who go through the day and just write up what they've seen in the evening and I've tried that, but it's absolutely no good. It goes dead on you. So what my diaries are is just constant notes. I'll always have it in my pocket and just scribble down what's happened that minute and how it's struck me, fragments of conversation." But the fragments, the confessions are never his own. *He* is teasingly absent.

On 4 January 1975, he arrived in Rio Pico. This village of German and Boer descendants is as remote as you get in Patagonia, 78 kilometres down a dirt road which comes to a halt near the Chilean border. The desolation draws from Bruce the remark: "Who would bomb Patagonia?"

He met in Rio Pico a Ukrainian nurse whose legs had been amputated. Alma Arbusova de Riasniansky is another example of Bruce seeing what he wanted to see. He changes her name, which protects her and also heightens his snapshot. He describes her shelves of Russian authors and says that the words Mandelstam and Akhmatova "rolled off her tongue". In fact, Alma reads Conan Doyle and Agatha Christie. She has not heard of Osip Mandelstam.

But in this snapshot he does not give us the full picture. When they meet she inveighed against homosexuality. Bruce quotes her as saying: "England in full decadence tolerating homosexuality." In handwriting so small it is barely legible, he adds: "longing to tell/dare not". Even at the end of the remotest road in Patagonia, he is unable to confess to his diary without betraying the anxiety that someone is looking over his shoulder. He still, at 34, resists the label of homosexual.

BRUCE HAD SPENT four days in Gaiman, the longest he lingered any-where in Patagonia. On 29 December he headed further inland, reaching Esquel at the foot of the Andes. For the next three weeks he zigzagged from the cordillera to the pampas, "spending nights in the grass, in caves, in peons' huts, and sometimes between the linen sheets of an old-fash-ioned English *estancia*. On my back I carried a small leather rucksack con-taining a sleeping bag, a few clothes . . . and half a bottle of Vintage Krug to drink at the worst possible moment."

This tantalising digest is typical. Paul Theroux, who reached only as far as Esquel, is not alone in wanting to know: "How had he travelled from here to there? How had he met this or that person? Life was never so neat as Bruce made out."

His notebooks and letters provide some details. "Dying of tiredness," he wrote to Elizabeth. "Have just walked 150 odd miles. Am another 150 from the nearest lettuce and at least 89 from the nearest canned vegetable. It will take many years to recover from roast lamb." There are frequent ref-erences in his notebook to his stomach. "Difficulties of Patagonia. I want a salad. Cannot face any more meat. Dust in your eyes. Feeling rather weak of hunger . . . Have an overwhelming desire to eat canned peaches."

He took trains and buses and hitched rides where he could, and walked a lot, as when he trekked from Harberton to Viamonte. "Basically, God is kind to people who walk on foot." Once, beyond Rio Pico, he rode a horse but fell off, injuring his hand, and had to visit the clinic named after the Ukrainian nurse. He often found himself abandoned to the road-side. "Tourists always wave at the hitchhiker walking in the other direc-tion; going in the same direction, tight-lipped they pretend he does not exist." On 18 January, near Lago Posada, he managed to thumb a ride only for the lorry to break down.

"Day of disasters—wrecked my plans. Certainly well said that the in-ternal combustion engine is the modern replacement of the Devil.

"Good subject for a story—the young *camionero* crushed by his own lorry—the one thing he loved.

"19th Sunday.

"How to describe the immense boredom, the inertia of waiting for the lorry to recover. We had another puncture last night coming too fast down the *barranca* . . ."

At last he gets a lift with a depressed gendarme who reminds him that "the tragedy of the semi-educated has yet to be written". The gendarme turns out to be another storyteller. He believes the Vikings marched deep into the Brazilian jungle and that the Incas were in contact with the Martians. "How else to explain their intelligence?"

Sometimes he slept in the open, sometimes in cheap hotels, and wherever he could in the *estancias* of those he wrote about. At Viamonte in Tierra del Fuego, he is remembered by Bridges's cousin Adrian Goodall as "the chap who brought his own cereal" (Elizabeth's muesli). *Estancias* like Viamonte reminded him of the headmaster's house in an English boarding school.

Usually, he arrived unannounced. "He felt he was welcome anywhere," says Elizabeth. "He couldn't imagine not being welcome." This attitude caused friction further south. At Despedida, he appeared without warning while Jacqueline de las Carreras's husband was shearing. "He was very arrogant, very sure of himself, very narcissistic," she says. "He didn't speak any Spanish and he didn't make any effort to be understood. He was very 'Me, myself and I'm the Queen of England'." He appalled Nita Starling, a 60-ish spinster who looked after the garden, by asking if she would wash his clothes. She refused.

Bruce would reserve his prickliest comments for Natalie Goodall, who lived at Harberton, Lucas Bridges's old house. He telephoned to say he had been given her name by David Bridges. "N. G. sounded quite gratuitously nasty on the telephone—hope she drowns." Nor did their relationship mend when he reached Harberton. "The question of payment to Natalie Goodall rubs one completely up the wrong way by suggesting you are just another bum in search of a bed. Some maybe, but . . ."

ON 21 JANUARY, in the small village of Baja Caracolles, Bruce wrote to Elizabeth. He was stranded in the middle of nowhere, but he had arrived.

"Dearest E.

I have begun letters I don't know how many times and then abandoned them. Now I am stuck, for 3 days at least, because the justice of the peace, to whom I confided some of my things, has run off with the key.

Writing this in the archetypal Patagonian scene, a *boliche* or roadman's hotel at a crossroads of insignificant importance with roads leading all directions apparently to nowhere. A long mint green bar with blue green walls and a picture of a glacier, the view from the window a line of lombardy poplars tilted about 20 degrees from the wind and beyond the rolling grey pampas (the grass is bleached yellow, but it has black roots, like a dyed blonde) with clouds rushing across it and a howling wind.

On no previous journey am I conscious of having done more. Patagonia is as I expected but more so, inspiring violent outbursts of love and hate. Physically it is magnificent, a series of graded steps or *barrancas* which are the cliff lines of prehistoric seas and unusually full of fossilised oyster shells 10" diam. In the east you suddenly confront the great wall of the *cordillera* with bright turquoise lakes (some are milky white and others a pale jade green) with unbelievable colours to the rocks (in the pre-*cordillera*). Sometimes it seems that the Almighty has been playing at making Neapolitan ice cream. Imagine climbing (as I did) a cliff face 2000 feet high alternatively striped vanilla, strawberry and pistachio in bands of 100 feet or more. Imagine an upland lake where the rock face on one side is bright purple, the other bright green, with cracked orange mud and a white rim. You have to be a geologist to appreciate it. Then I know of no place that you are so aware of prehistoric animals. They sometimes seem more alive than the living. Everybody talks of pleisiosaurus, or ichtyosaurus. I met an old gentleman who was born in Lithuania who found a dinosaur the other day and didn't think much of it. He thought much more of the fact he had a pilot's licence, at the age of 85 being probably the oldest solo flyer in the world. When he was younger he tried to be a bird man.

I have been caught in the lost beast fervour and 2 days ago scaled an appalling cliff to the bed of an ancient lake . . . and there discovered to my inexpressible delight a collection of fragments of the carapace of the glyptodon. The glyptodon has if anything replaced the mylodon in my affections—there are about 6 whole ones in the Museum of La Plata—an enormous armadillo up to 9–10 feet long, each scale of its armour looking like a Japanese chrysanthemum. The entertaining fact about my discovery, and one that no archaeologist will believe, is that in the middle of one scatter of bones were 2 obsidian knives quite definitely man-made. Now Man is often thought to have done away with the Glyptodon, but there is no evidence of his having done so.

Not an Indian in sight. Sometimes you see a hawkish profile that seems to be a Tehuelche i.e. old Patagonian, but the colonisers did a very thorough job, and this gives the whole land its haunted quality.

Animal life is not extraordinary, except for the *guanaco* which I love. The young are called *chulengos* and have the finest fur, a sort of mangy brown and white. There is a very rare deer called a Huemuel and the

Puma (which is commoner than you would think but difficult to see). Otherwise *pinchi* the small armadillo, hares everywhere, and a most beguiling skunk, very small, black with white stripes; far from spraying me one came and took a crust from my hand.

Birds are wonderful. Condors in the *cordillera*, a black and white vulture, a beautiful grey harrier (also amazingly tame), and the black-necked swan which has my prize for the best bird in the world. On the mud flats are flamingos—these are a kind of orange colour—the Patagonian goose inappropriately called an *abutarda*, and every kind of duck.

You would think from the fact that the landscape is so uniform and the occupation (sheep-farming) also, that the people would be correspondingly dull. But I have sung "Hark the Herald Angels Sing" in Welsh in a remote chapel on Christmas Day, have eaten lemon curd tartlets with an old Scot who has never been to Scotland but has made his own bagpipes and wears the kilt to dinner. I have stayed with a Swiss ex-diva who married a Swedish trucker who lives in the remotest of all Patagonian valleys, decorating her house with murals of the lake of Geneva. I have dined with a man who knew Butch Cassidy and other members of the Black Jack Gang, I have drunk to the memory of Ludwig of Bavaria with a German whose house and style of life belongs rather to the world of the Brothers Grimm. I have discussed the poetics of Mandelstam with a Ukrainian doctor missing both legs. I have seen Charlie Milward's *estancia* and lodged with the peons drinking maté till 3 a.m. (*Maté* incidentally is a drink for which I also have a love/hate relationship.) I have visited a poet-hermit who lived according to Thoreau and the Georgics. I have listened to the wild outpourings of the Patagonian archaeologist, who claims the existence of a. the Patagonian unicorn b. a protohominid in Tierra del Fuego (*Fuego pithicus patensis*) 80 cm high.

There is a fantastic amount of stuff for a book—from the Anarchist (Yes, Bakunin-inspired) Rebellion of 1920, to the hunting of the Black Jack Gang, Cassidy etc., the temporary kingdom of Patagonia, the lost city of the Caesars, the travels of Musters, the hunting of Indians etc. Everything I need . . ." There is no better précis of *In Patagonia*.

THE PRIMARY STORY remained Charles Milward and the sloth skin. As he followed its tracks south, Bruce found Milward's story more compelling than he had anticipated. In Lima, he had learned from Monica that her mother Isabelle, before she married Charles Milward, had been raped by an English *estanciero*. On 27 January, Bruce reached the *estancia* of La Colmena, south of San Julian. He had telephoned from the station, "seven leagues away", mentioned Bridges and said he was on his way in a taxi. Jack Frazer and his Danish wife Ingebord chatted to Bruce for an hour. That night he stayed in the manager's house and he left early the next morning "without saying goodbye, let alone a thank you".

The Frazers, Bruce wrote, "live in a world of perfect lawns, a little whisky, white trellises, zinnias, sweet peas, greenhouse cucumbers, cucumber sandwiches." He found Frazer "pink, quite amusing, with a mouth turned down at the corners". Monica believed that it was Jack's father who had raped her mother, Isabelle.

She had sailed from Glasgow just before the outbreak of the First World War. She was the daughter of a Scottish steelworker, 26, tall, slender with an 18-inch waist—and deeply religious. She had been hired as a governess to a Scots family in Patagonia. One night, according to Monica, her employer took his wife in to town for her third confinement. "Mother remained on the farm and apparently he made an excuse to return without his wife and once there, attacked my mother in a particularly brutal way, breaking down the door of her room into which she had barricaded herself. He took her by force after a bitter struggle.

"That night she left the farm—I never knew how, but doubt that it was on horseback as, so far as I know, she never rode a horse in her life— and made her way across several hundred miles to the nearest British Consulate, which was in Punta Arenas. And there, as was her right as a British subject, she asked for help. The Consul was Charles Milward."

Isabelle, pregnant and in dire straits, worked as Milward's housekeeper until she was able to sail home. She gave birth to a son and in 1916 she returned to Punta Arenas and married Milward.

PUNTA ARENAS AT the time of Milward's shipwreck in 1898 was known as Sandy Point and had the air of a British colony. Until the opening of the Panama Canal in 1912, workers were paid in English currency. A casual leaf through the *Magellan Times*, "the farthest south British newspaper", conjures up glimpses of their lifestyle in advertisements for Egyptian cigarettes, Ford cars ("the car of the camp"), and Robertson's dip ("a sure scab-killer").

And then a new notice: "C. A. Milward—engineer, boilermaker and ship repairers". Milward was forever looking to improve his lot at the end of the world. He first considered placing vast billboards along the Magellan Straits. Then he bought a foundry with a German partner whose nationality at the time was not a problem. Milward cut a respectable if not grand figure in Punta Arenas. He was a founder of the International Rifle Shooting Association and prominent in the Fire Brigade. From 1903, he also acted as both British and German Consul. But something in his nature led him to believe he could always ride two horses. "He was German Vice-Consul as well as English. No wonder Winston Churchill and Lord Fisher thought he was a German agent," Bruce wrote to his father. The appearance at his house in Calle España, in bizarre circumstances, of a young Scottish woman in a distressed state did not enhance his standing.

On 10 February, Bruce wrote to Elizabeth: "I have been hurtling around Punta Arenas in search of the ghost of Charlie Milward. Fascinating place. For example, parked on a beach with a rash of tin shacks almost on top of it is the *Kabenga*, the boat that took Stanley up the Congo. There is a concrete replica of the Parthenon which is the Gymnasium. There are little octagonal summer houses that could be Turkish. My menu of last night was as follows: *Loco de mer mayonnaise* (Abalone)/*Jambon Cru de la Terre de Feu*/*Pejerrey à la planche*/*Latuna nature* (prickly pear)."

Punta Arenas was a town to Bruce's taste and in atmosphere rather like Victoria, British Columbia, visited by him the previous year. The houses of the English, mansions in the style of Sunningdale, lay up the hill, while the palaces of the Braun-Menendez family were hidden off the main square behind cypresses and monkey-puzzles that were lashed by a perpetual hurricane. "These houses were imported piece by piece from France and still look as though they have been miraculously dislodged from the Bois de Boulogne. I dined with the Brauns last night among their palms, their Cordoba leather, their aseptic marble goddesses . . ."

He found his cousin's front door overlooking Calle España, not far from the still-existing foundry, behind a green gate cast with the letter "M." "Captain Milward's house, which I mistook for the Anglican church, is a towered, crenellated building with overtones of Edgbaston, Birmingham, now turned into a claustrophobic Chilean middle-class home." Modelled on his father's vicarage of St Clements and painted in a hideous dark brown, it was nicknamed "the chocolate castle". In the garden there was an octagonal summerhouse and a crazy-paving path bordered with London Pride and Sweet William.

Bruce spoke to his cousin's friends and detractors. Francisco Campos Menendez, "a foppish man with an English accent", told how during the First World War Milward would go and see the harbourmaster very early in the morning to demand the expulsion of the *Dresden* and one day received a jug of cold water poured on his head. Bruce met a woman who had worked for the Milwards. "Said they were *dreadful*. He . . . put her on a bread and water diet for a week for breaking a bottle of brandy. She was 14 at the time." She found Mrs Milward "really common", her husband "not much better".

Bruce detected a whiff of scandal hanging about Milward's later years. He seems to have been ostracised by the "true Britisher" element of Punta Arenas. This stemmed in part from gossip surrounding his marriage, in part from his close links with the German community. On 25 February 1915, Milward was replaced after 13 years as British consul. He was given a Landsdowne gold watch for his services, but his obituary in the *Magellan Times* hinted at strenuous opposition in the British community. "When the war broke out . . . his position became a difficult one." His fortune drained away. The Panama Canal had opened, fewer ships required his foundry. Meanwhile, his German partner had run up debts. Alongside Royal Ventua toothpaste and an undertaker offering a stock of zinc-lined coffins, Milward's advertisements grew smaller and smaller.

Milward died in his bed in the early hours of 6 December 1928. The British Legion cancelled a picnic. He was buried in the local cemetery facing the low outline of Tierra del Fuego across the choppy straits where 30 years before he had been shipwrecked.

Today, the graves in the English sector are in a sorry state, vandalised or choked by lupins and pansies. It takes a while to find Milward's. The wind blows a bush of white snowberries over the grey headstone of his brother Arthur, known as "Old Mother Milward". Charles's name is hard to decipher. On the slab of muddy white marble stands an empty mayonnaise jar.

IN PUNTA ARENAS, Bruce befriended an Australian girl ten years his junior. Judith Jesser and her companion Paul were precursors of those who would descend on the country clutching tattered paperback copies of *In Patagonia*. Jesser, in a letter to her mother, wrote of Bruce: "We met this Eng journalist and author Charles Bruce Chatwin, who is writing a number of articles for the London *Times* plus gathering information for a book he is writing. He is rather an eccentric type of chap, who is in his middle 30s but still looks like the typical private school English boy with big feet and blond hair that he parts down the centre, and he has a very pronounced Oxford accent. He is married to an Elizabeth née Chanler, whose father was apparently in charge of the Intelligence section at Pearl Harbor when the Japanese bombed it, and hence was not held in esteem for some period after. This Bruce is interesting to listen to and since we have been on the mainland we keep meeting each other."

Bruce saw a lot of Jesser. Later, they travelled on the same boat to Chiloe, an island off the Chilean coast. "He never stopped talking," she says—about Elizabeth, about Butch Cassidy, about how Chilean communists, as soon as they got into power, killed off the stud merino rams for food.

On 11 March, a cloudless day, Bruce chartered a plane to fly over Desolation Island. He wanted to look down on the spot where Milward's ship had sunk. Scared of flying on his own, he asked Jesser and Paul to come along. "He found us. He was frightened. Would we please go with him?"

Two days later, Jesser witnessed a more unsettling episode. The three of them took the bus to an old fort with a museum in Fuerte Bulnes, south of Punta Arenas. They started walking back along the beach. Bruce's talking now got out of hand. Without warning, they stumbled into what seemed to be a military establishment with a dug-out and camouflage. "He was walking along, chatter, chatter, chatter and I said: 'I'm not pleased with this, this doesn't feel right'." Bruce insisted there was nothing to worry about. "Then all of a sudden we were arrested," says Jesser. "We were put in this little wooden building while ten to 15 really young interns stood around training machine guns on us." A nervous young officer came and asked what they were doing. Jesser looked to Bruce, the oldest of the party, to quieten him down. She was unprepared for what happened next.

"Bruce was really naïve. He started to ask these questions which were not pertinent to the situation, like 'How many people are there in this establishment?'" The tension was deepening by the minute when Paul noticed the officer wore an Alpinist badge and indicated that he too was a climber. The situation eased, but Jesser was surprised at Bruce for having misjudged it. "I thought he was bloody dumb."

They flew with Bruce to Puerto Natales, from where it was a short journey further north to the *"cueva del milodon"*. She and Paul slept in a hut while Bruce stayed in a hotel. On visiting his room, she found, open on his bed her missing copy of D. H. Lawrence's *Kangaroo*.

IN 1895, A man called Eberhard discovered the hide of a strange animal at the back of a cave on his land. One evening in March, Bruce arrived at the nearby *estancia* of Eberhard's grandson. "On a wet and windy night a complete stranger, muttering strange gibberish about the mylodon, was taken in, fed, bedded and entertained by the most hospitable household in Magellanes," he wrote in the guest book. When he explained why he had come, Eberhard replied in English: "So . . . you are of the family of the robber."

The animal skin had measured four feet by two and its discovery prompted a widespread belief that "a great mysterious quadruped" might still be extant. Scientists in London, La Plata and Berlin clamoured for evidence. One of Milward's money-making schemes was to dynamite Eberhard's cave for lucrative scraps. He sold one consignment of skin, claws and bones to the British Museum for £400; and, of course, he sent a tuft to Bruce's grandmother as her wedding present. "It all went," says Señora Eberhard. "Nothing's left. Only a mountain of shit."

Bruce spent the night at the Eberhards' and in the morning walked the four miles to the cave. It lies in a spectacular setting, gawping over Last Hope Sound from a cliff of pebbly conglomerate. Bands of white *margarita silvestri* border the path and the air smells of camphor and clover. Seen from the back wall through a frieze of southern beech, the black mountains patched with snow rise from the bay. The cave mouth is 200 yards wide, 30 metres high and a whole village could fit inside. The visitor's imagination is depressed only by the life-sized fibreglass effigy at the entrance, resembling a shaggy, small-eared horse standing on its hind legs.

This cave provided the emotional focus of Bruce's pilgrimage. He wrote in *In Patagonia*: "I tried to picture the cave with sloths in it, but I could not erase the fanged monster I associate with a blacked-out bedroom in wartime England."

Milward's wedding gift was not a piece of "monster". The mylodon was a herbivorous ground sloth three metres long with thick skin and powerful claws with which it grubbed for insects. It frequented the cave between 11,500 and 8,000 BC to take advantage of the salt-lick and did not have the most sophisticated digestive system. "The floor was covered with turds, sloth turds, outsize black leathery turds, full of ill-digested grass, that looked as if they had been shat that week."

Bruce emerged with some coarse, wiry strands of reddish hair. He had his Fleece. On 5 April, he walked into the Barnetts' house in Lima carrying a ball of fossilised mylodon dung which he plonked on the tea-table. "The dung was odourless," says Monica's husband. "But Bruce was still slightly whiffy."

XXIII.

⌇

I Don't Know What You'll Make of It

*I recall that on the 31st August last you telephoned to
say that you were now writing books and that your
first story would be published on 21st September, and
I am wondering, please, what monies you are
expecting from this source. At the present time the
Bank's only security for your account is the guarantee
of Mr C. L. Chatwin for £500 (unsupported) and
a life policy surrender value £87.*
—LLOYD'S BANK, BIRMINGHAM, TO BC,
7 OCTOBER 1977

ELIZABETH AND HER mother joined Bruce in Lima. He had set off for
Patagonia with a rucksack and a little duffel bag. "When we met him five
months later in Peru he was in a small room and the walls were lined on
at least three sides with stacked up books that he'd picked up. And he'd
left a lot of stuff in Buenos Aires and he had to go back and pick *that* up."
Together they toured Peru in the Barnetts' camper van. On 5 May, he arrived in New York, impatient to start writing.

Unwilling to work at Holwell, he rented a house on a private island
off the Connecticut coast. Fisher's Island was an enclave of Waspdom,
"stuffy as all hell", but he found the "dreamlike surrealist atmosphere"
agreeable.

Stone Cottage belonged to a family of mattress makers and was the
gatehouse to their "Norman castle". It had a conical tower, gabled windows smothered in ivy and lay at the tip of the eight-mile island on a
promontory surrounded by wind and sea "and flights of ferocious sea-
gulls". Elizabeth bicycled up and down to fetch groceries in her basket
while he arranged his notes.

A number of eccentric writers had borrowed the gatehouse, named after a turn-of-the-century Tolkien called Stone who had created an imaginary language for his novel *Islandia*. "It is slightly like a set for a Hitchcock movie," Bruce wrote in one of the very rare letters he sent from Stone Cottage. He apologised to his parents for the silence: "I'm sorry I'm so hopeless at writing. When you pore over the typewriter all day, it's the last thing you want to do."

On 25 August, he was able to tell them he had completed half the book. "There is a 3-inch pile of manuscript, much of which will have to be scrapped when I come to the revision. The island has been well worth while."

He was reluctant to return to London until he had finished, but could no longer fend off the *Sunday Times*. He had written to Francis Wyndham: "I don't want to receive any official *S. T.* correspondence in the Argentine." To justify his $3,500 advance from the magazine, Bruce now submitted two profiles: on the Guggenheim family and on Maria Reiche, a German expert on the Nazca Lines whom he had visited with Elizabeth and her mother in Peru. He also planned a third article. "I am going to the West to Utah to do an article for the *Sunday Times*," he wrote to his parents. This was on Butch Cassidy and the Sundance Kid, whose tracks he had occasionally crossed or followed in Patagonia. The pair were thought to have been killed in Bolivia, "but Cassidy's sister, now in her 90s in Utah, says her brother spent the '20s as a country gentleman in Ireland and returned to Utah for burial. This is the case of the Hero that never dies."

The magazine never published the Butch Cassidy article. On 27 October, Elizabeth wrote to Gertrude that "all Bruce's editors are being removed". On the 24th, Linklater returned from lunch to discover a notice on the board: he had been replaced by Hunter Davies. At Linklater's hastily assembled leaving party that night, Meriel McCooey yelled at a white-faced Harry Evans: "*You*! I mean *you*! William fucking Randolph Hearst! Do you know what you've *done*?" In a subdued voice, Michael Rand spoke for many, including for the absent Bruce, when he turned to the art assistant Roger Law and said: "The party's over, boys."

The sensibilities of the new editor were confirmed after Davies visited Linklater at his Islington home. That Sunday's edition of the magazine had carried photographs by Leni Riefenstahl of a Sudanese tribe. "I'm sure you'll want to change the magazine," said Linklater, "but I hope you won't abandon the tradition of marvellous photographs." According to Linklater, Davies replied: "Quite frankly, Magnus, most people who picked up the magazine on Sunday would have said to themselves: 'Bloody hell, not another load of black tits'."

Bruce had come back on the *Queen Elizabeth II* in mid-September. He was "not quite sure of his own position," Elizabeth wrote to Gertrude, "but won't be able to work under the new regime, so it has all come to an end . . . It's too bad really, but it's been a nice few years for him & as usual he had most things his own way."

His position very soon clarified itself. One of Davies's first acts was to stop Bruce's retainer. "Looking at the stuff he'd done, I really thought it was purple prose, self-indulgent, poncy stuff which personally I didn't like. I wrote him a letter. 'Very sorry, your contract's not renewed'."

It did not matter. Bruce incorporated the Butch Cassidy material into his first draft. In November, he rented a cottage in Bonnieux in the Luberon to complete it.

"THE FATAL THING is ever to tell anyone about what you're really writing till it's done because a) you don't do it and b) you get people vaguely worked up about it and they try to tell you what to do." Bruce had spent several years unable to make his thesis into a publishable book. He did not want, as he told the Argentinian journalist Uki Goni, another "rotten experience". This time he kept silent until he was finished. Friends, agent, publisher understood him to be still embroiled with nomads. He stayed in France all winter, all spring, writing and rewriting and reshaping until it was finished.

Robert Byron presented *The Road to Oxiana* as a diary, encouraging readers to think that it had been dashed off on the hoof. In fact, it took three years to write. Likewise, Bruce gave the illusion he had gone to Patagonia for four months and then produced a book. But he took with him a body of knowledge he had cultivated for years.

Although *In Patagonia* was an overnight success, it had been an arduous apprenticeship. His confidence was fragile. He once told Elizabeth: "I wish I could write really well." When she assured him, "You're really good," he said: "No, I'm not really good." But once he started writing he wanted to be in the front rank. "He knew he wasn't top notch and it bothered him," says Elizabeth. Peter Adam, who would lend him books from his library says, "You would not catch him talking about Tolkien or Iris Murdoch. He went always up the ladder and somehow that's how he

wanted to be seen: Hermann Broch, Elias Canetti, Thomas Mann." His
Italian publisher, Roberto Calasso, says: "He had a huge ambition. But
not more than any other writer." He reminded Calasso of Italo Calvino:
unless you try to do something apparently impossible, you cannot be a
first rank writer.

Bruce had a knack for simile because he had seen and remembered so
many things, but this was the only part of writing that came easily: he
willed himself to be a writer. He perfected his style by dint of sheer concentration and focus, typing out his drafts again and again, and reading
them aloud to be sure they were lucid. His friend Christopher Gibbs
likened the relentless winnowing and culling to his previous life as a collector. "Like old lacquer applied and rubbed away, applied and rubbed
away a hundred times more, that texture, so admired in the Orient in former times, is found again in Chatwin's prose."

He was a highly visual writer. "Writing is the painting of the voice,"
he wrote in his notebook. "The more it resembles it, the better it is." He
sought in his prose the abstraction he admired in Sung dynasty painters,
of flattened forms suspended in space with no suggestion of depth. Writing of Mu Chu'ih, he singled out "his splashed ink technique, the quick
dots and dashes, the incisive stabs of the brush, the swirls he used to
achieve running water or ruffled feathers, the long patient stroke with
which he brought a branch quiveringly alive." He observed this empty,
jettisoned effect in certain Cistercian monasteries or in Cézanne's last
work, in which, he wrote, "the essence of Mont Saint-Victoire is captured
in a few strokes of watercolour. What is not appreciated is that this empty
space is not empty but full; and to realise this 'fullness' requires the most
single-minded discipline. Either the work must be perfect or it is
nothing."

It is hard, reading him, to escape another link: between the elegantly
starved-down style he aimed for and the asceticism of the Moorish nomad
who "whittles his possessions down to a minimum". The dominant colour
of the nomad is blue, he wrote; their dominant art-form patchwork. "A
much darned and patched piece of blue cloth is often far more expensive
to buy than a new piece, because patchwork carries the imprint of human
associations." The desert nomads wove together their fragments to create
the modern effect of Bruce's Peruvian feathers. "They build their shacks,
palisades, doorways and furniture with anything that comes to mind—
scrap metal, abandoned cars, packing cases, sacking, old advertisement
hoardings—the components foraged at random but fitted together with

an unerring eye that still exemplifies the desert sensibility. The result is curiously like a Schwitters collage or a Russian Constructivist 'assemblage'."

Bruce's prose has this fragmented quality. "He didn't have the intellectual organisation to write a conventional book," says Lucie-Smith. "With the exceptions of *On the Black Hill* and *Utz*, everything consists of fragments, all shattered and brought back together." Gregor von Rezzori was aware of the labour involved: "One of his obvious virtues was discipline. Which was also the cause of his well-concealed exhaustion."

IN THE FIRST days of August 1976, Bruce arrived at Deborah Rogers's office with a 350-page typescript. It was no longer titled *A Piece of Brontosaurus* but *At the end: a journey to Patagonia*. Five years had passed since he had delivered *The Nomadic Alternative*. "With that book, you felt he had been crushed by the weight," says Rogers. "When Bruce came in with his new manuscript there was this buoyancy. 'I don't know what you'll make of it,' he said."

On 6 August, Rogers sent the typescript on to Tom Maschler. "As one might expect, the book is extraordinary, and like nothing else—a law unto itself. But I think it is also quite wonderful, though does need some work."

Bruce had told Maschler nothing. "It arrives. I have no inkling that this is anything other than the nomad book. And then I read this thing." Maschler describes the experience as "one of the ten most exciting events" in his publishing career: "to read this book which I have commissioned, which bears no relation to what I had commissioned". He judged the manuscript needed "very little editing—it was magnificent and almost ready to publish". But he believed improvements could be made and passed it to one of the Cape editors, Susannah Clapp. In her report five days later, Clapp shared Maschler's enthusiasm, adding a caveat. "This *is* very extraordinary—and a possible problem." While struck by "the very high quality of the writing" Clapp did not feel always impelled through the 350 pages. It seemed a series of exquisite cameos without a central drive. "If I weren't so impressed by the matching of informativeness with intelligent description, I would say a sad no. As it is, I don't feel able to dismiss it—particularly since this may mean saying goodbye to someone who may well have other good books to come. But I don't think it's on as it stands."

Clapp played a crucial role in reducing the text. "All the qualities one associates with his style were there from the beginning," she says. "A teasing hovering between fact and fiction; a combination of a very spare syntax and short simple sentences, with a rich flamboyant vocabulary, lots of arcane words, lots of peculiarities and a non-chronological, rather elliptical structure. The question in editing the book was to try and maintain that structure he called Cubist—in other words, lots of small pictures tilting away and toward each other to create this strange, angular portrait, and yet at the same time to introduce a sense of progression and drive." She and Bruce went through the book, cutting and rearranging. "Bruce was very responsive," says Clapp. "He would often decide on the spot to take something out. Quite alarmingly he would strike through a whole page and sometimes he would decide just as quickly to add—and he would come back with another ten pages in his haversack because something else had occurred to him. We reduced it by about a quarter to a third of its normal length."

Bruce, who knew how to take advice, said he learnt a lot from Clapp. Eventually, she left Cape for the *London Review of Books*, but she would do preliminary work on his next book and also edit *Utz*.

ON 26 AUGUST, Bruce wrote to a friend: "To my immense relief Jonathan Cape have taken my book on Patagonia." Under the terms drawn up eight years earlier, Maschler agreed to pay an advance of £600. The publication date was set for 13 October 1977, with an initial print-run of 4,000 copies. He pressed advance copies on influential critics and editors like George Steiner and Jack Lambert, and on publication day sent a telegram to Bruce at Millington-Drake's home near Siena: I KNOW THAT IN PATAGONIA WILL BE A SUCCESS.

BRUCE NEVER LIKED to be on hand for publication. "I'm chicken about reviews," he told ABC radio. A fortnight later, a sheaf of them arrived from his publisher. Maschler's "hunch" had paid off. "It is rare indeed for me to be able to say that the reviews reflect my own feelings about a book I admire as much as I do yours and yet this is the case."

Paul Theroux wrote in *The Times*: "He has fulfilled the desire of all

BRUCE CHATWIN

real travellers, of having found a place that is far and strange and seldom
visited like the Land where the Jumblies Live." Theroux chose it as his
Book of the Year. So did Jack Lambert in the *Sunday Times*. "Dreams,
those who remember them tell me, are surrealistically clear; so are the
weird scenes Mr Chatwin swiftly, often curtly, conjures up."

Several authors sent letters. Graham Greene wrote to say that *In
Patagonia* was "one of my favourite travel books". Harold Beaven appreciated the pressure of reading and experience pushing behind every line.
"It's an athlete's book: taut, tough, elegant; not a travelogue exactly, nor a
scholarly foray exactly, but an interpenetration of both, so skilfully fili-
greed that the travel becomes part of the research as the research part of
the quest in a continuous, yet sporadic, movement." In Greece, Paddy
Leigh Fermor did not want to let the sun go down "without writing to say
what a marvellous book it is". He thought it "splendidly original", merely
wished "you had let it off the leash a bit more, to luxuriate and ramify".
The sections were "*too* short", so that he felt "a bit like a child being
rushed through a picture gallery and always lagging behind, longing to
dwell". He offered this advice: "I think out of avoiding sloppiness you
sometimes give things you are worried by and things that leave you cold
the same deadpan or poker-faced treatment." He urged Bruce next time
to "let it rip".

Few showed greater enthusiasm than the French writer, and Patagonian Consul in France, Jean Raspail. He wrote "in a state of emotion" after finishing the book, bringing news of an award. "The Patagonian
consulaté which represents in France the government of H. M. Orélie-
Antoine I, King of Patagonia and Araucania in 1863, has decided to award
you the first great prize of Patagonian literature."

Most surprised were Bruce's colleagues from the art-world, for whom
the news that he had written a book had somewhat the same impact as
hearing that he was to be married. "I was astonished," says Richard
Timewell. "I would never have thought of it." This reaction was shared by
Hewett, Muensterberger, Nash and Erskine. "I was extremely surprised
and quite frankly jealous," says Lucie-Smith. "Why can't *I* write like that?"

There were some dissonant voices. On Christmas Day, 1977, James
Lees-Milne "dipped into Bruce Chatwin's *Patagonia* which has had unde-
servedly rave reviews. No form to the book, a random selection of unpleasant incidents. What a ghastly country it must be." Steiner, writing to
Maschler, also expressed reservations. "My problem with it is simply this:
the highly mannered style, the off-beat and wry brevities, the archness of
personal valour and the carefully-paced eruditions (bitten off self-depre-

catingly)—all this is that *New Yorker* formula which I have been seeing from the inside these past twelve years!"

By and large, these views were exceptional. The book's success was summed up in a note from Wyndham: "Perhaps none of them *quite* get the hang of what you are doing, but as they say in *Vogue*, 'everyone' is talking about it!"

BRUCE LIKED TO adopt an insouciant attitude to reviews. "Don't flap too much about the critics," he wrote to the artist Keith Milow, "and never try to please them and don't ever complain about them. It isn't worth it. The function of the artist is to work for (a) himself (b) to leave something memorable for the future, to shore up the ruins. Fuck the rest of them!" Yet in the very next sentence he confessed "to a sneaking pleasure at a card I got yesterday from Jan Morris saying that my description of the Welsh in Patagonia actually moved him/her to tears."

One aspect of *In Patagonia's* reception did vex the author. Most critics united in calling his "peculiarly dotty book" a travel book. He wrote to Welch that while the critics had been very complimentary, "the FORM of the book seems to have puzzled them (as I suspect it did the publisher). There's a lot of talk of 'unclassifiable prose', 'a mosaic', 'a tapestry', a 'jigsaw', a 'collage' etc. but no one has seen that it is a modern WONDER VOYAGE: the Piece of Brontosaurus is the essential ingredient of the quest."

The sale of his American rights for $5,000 provided an excuse "to do a bit of explaining". On 1 December 1977, he drafted a letter to Rogers, requesting that the book be taken out of the travel category. He wanted the blurb on the American edition to convey four points, in his opinion the key to understanding the book:

1. Patagonia was the farthest place to which man walked from his place of origins. "It is therefore a symbol of his restlessness. From its discovery it had the effect on the imagination something like the Moon, but in my opinion more powerful."

2. The form described in the *Daily Telegraph* as "wildly unorthodox" was in fact as old as literature itself: "the hunt for a strange animal in a remote land".

3. He preferred to leave the reader with the choice of two journeys: one to Patagonia in 1975, the other "a symbolic voyage which is a meditation on restlessness and exile".

4. "All the stories were chosen with the purpose of illustrating some particular aspect of wandering and/or of exile: i.e. what happens when you get stuck. The whole should be an illustration of the myth of Cain and Abel."

But the question of categorization continued to trouble him.

BRUCE'S FIRST BOOK is the literary equivalent of his grandmother's cabinet, a collection of stories gathered with a singular eye. For all his insistence that he followed a traditional form, most readers disagreed. Among booksellers it inaugurated a category: "the new non-fiction".

Its literary influences are nevertheless easy to discern. An earlier choice of title, "Journey to Patagonia", acknowledges the debt to Osip Mandelstam, whose *Journey to Armenia* he had read aloud to the *Sunday Times* art department. Mandelstam, he wrote to Sethi, "in poetry, but more so in prose, is one of my gods". In his introduction to it, he called Mandelstam's laconic, elliptical travel book "among the outstanding masterpieces of the twentieth century" and its author "the shaman and seer of his time".

On 14 April 1979, Mandelstam's translator, Clarence Brown, wrote to ask "with a certain trepidation" whether Bruce was aware "that the spirit of OM seems to peep out from behind this or that phrase or stroke of portraiture or landscape". Bruce replied by return. "For what it's worth—and at the risk of being a bore—I'd like to put it on record that you are surely the finest translator out of Russian alive; that you have a most finely-tuned ear for the cadence of a sentence; that your literal translations of M's poems are far better than the work of the versifiers, and, lastly that you are TOO MODEST. In an ideal world you would be appointed *generalissimo* in charge of vetting all translations from the Russian; one only has to think of the horrors of the so-called Oxford Chekhov . . .

"Of course *Journey to Armenia* was the biggest single ingredient—more so even than met the eye. Perhaps too much so—'skull-white cabbages etc.' . . . But one bit of plagiarism was quite unintentional (though indicative of the degree to which I had steeped myself in the *Journey*). Not until after I had passed the final proofs did I realise I had lifted 'the accordion of his forehead' straight. I rang up the copy-editor in a panic. She said it was too late and, besides, all writers were cribbers."

Bruce admitted to cribbing from other Russians. Brown's translation of Mandelstam's *The Noise of Time* had led him to "discover" writers like Isaac Babel ("Soon afterwards I started to write"). He had "immersed" himself at the time of writing in the literature of Turgenev and Chekhov: the way Anglo-Argentinians clung to their estates in order to enjoy a life in town was exactly the story of *The Cherry Orchard.*

It appeared to Welch, who read the book "VERY VERY slowly because each phrase is so provocative and enjoyable", that Bruce's style in its combination of flamboyance and austerity owed something to Eastern influences. "Particularly I like it because it has the qualities I find in Mughal pictures: extraordinary portraiture, very deep and psychological, superb technically, with all sorts of enrichments." Bruce was delighted at the connection: "The Babur-Nama has influenced me greatly in what I write. With the possible exception of Isaac Babel, I know of no writer capable of such economic portraits of people. What I love is the clear, staccato line with a fantastical flourish at the end . . . Such directness in Babur. Such awesome GAPS."

Then there were the Americans: Edmund Wilson's travel journals, *Black Brown Red and Olive,* Gaylord Simpson's *Attending Marvels,* and, of course, Hemingway's short stories. Along with *Journey to Armenia,* Bruce had carried *In Our Time* in his rucksack.

MARTHA GELLHORN, TO her infinite regret, was once married to Ernest Hemingway. Possibly because of this connection, Bruce sought her out on the pretext of gathering information about Mandelstam's widow Nadezhda, whom he wanted to meet in Moscow. (Gellhorn recommended Bruce take her marmalade, cheap pens, writing paper, scent, American thrillers and pills for an ulcer that she only suffered each spring.) "I think he wanted to survey the landscape," she said. "I was very surprised by this fey creature bouncing in and chatting. He promised to take me to a rugby game and never did."

Apart from the structure of their sentences, their careful repetitions, Bruce shared with Hemingway the same "wonderful memory". Also, said Gellhorn, a vision of themselves as adventurers. "When you're daydreaming as a child you're always Joan of Arc or Richard Coeur de Lion: that's one of the pleasures of childhood. But it's supposed to change." She felt that Bruce had not grown up. "If you and I go on a journey it's hell and we get dysentery and it's misery. If he goes, because he's an ad-

venturer to himself first, these amazing things happen." She contrasted
him with Paul Theroux. "Anything Theroux wrote about, he did. He
doesn't make it heroic. He made it the way it was—which you'd pay
money *not* to do."

Both Bruce and Hemingway were "*mythomanes*", said Gellhorn.
"They are not conscious liars. They invent to increase everything about
themselves and their lives and *believe* it. They believe everything they say."

BRUCE IN AN early draft had opened *In Patagonia* with the description
of the *"mythomane"* Louis de Rougemont, a visionary charlatan who first
met Captain Milward at a banquet in New Zealand, successfully predicted
Milward's shipwreck, and ended his days on stage leading a show called
The Greatest Liar on Earth.

In his journal Milward describes his surprise at meeting de Rougemont again in London: "He spent many hours a day, for a long time,
studying in the British Museum and reading all manner of interesting adventures there. I once asked him how he dared to annex an albatross story
and make it into a pelican story, to which he replied: 'Well, you see, zer
vas no albatross zer and zer vas pelican.' 'But it's not true,' I said. 'No,' was
his only excuse, 'but it does come in so very well just zer'."

The temptation to seek comparisons between Bruce and de Rougemont, a star who was "booed off the stage in Brisbane", is not frustrated
by the author. "I once made the experiment of counting up the lies in the
book I wrote about Patagonia," he told Michael Ignatieff. "It wasn't, in
fact, too bad: there weren't too many." The book did, however, ruffle
feathers in Patagonia.

First there was a confusion over the mix of genres. Just as Patagonia is
not a place with an exact border so Bruce's book did not fall into an easy
category. Was it travel writing? Was it historical fiction? Was it reportage?
And was it true?

Though he changed most names, Bruce left a trail of offended people
in the Welsh community. Unused to scrutiny, they judged what he wrote
with a nineteenth-century Methodist eye. They found it hard to conceive
that their characters were so transparent that they could be reduced to a
few vivid details by a stranger they had met for an hour. He had pinned
them down as specimens, like Ernst Jünger skewering his beetles. In
Gaiman, Geralt Williams compares the shock of reading about himself to

the first time he heard his voice: "When someone tape-records your voice, you don't recognise it as yours."

Unlike the subjects of Cartier-Bresson's *Tete-à-Tete* portraits, Bruce had not sought Geralt's permission. As a result Geralt felt diminished. He had not had an easy life in the desert. Bruce had described his difficulties with a twentieth-century eye, passing swiftly through his life and refusing to dwell on it. He had snatched the intimacy Borges writes of: "that kernel of myself that I have saved, somehow".

"He wrote in a *mañera sobradera,* an English way of looking at things when they were the Empire," says Luned Roberts de Gonzalez. "*Condescending* would be the word." He was too slick, too sharp, made people more interesting than they were, did not catch the spirit, says Albina Zampini. She prefers a book like Wilfrid Blunt's *Of Flowers and a Village.* "Now *that* I enjoyed immensely."

The problem is exacerbated by the world-wide success of *In Patagonia.* Few complete histories exist of the region. Most books concentrate on one aspect: the Welsh, the Anarchists, the early travellers. Bruce cherry-picked the lot and with his connecting gaze integrated them into a single narrative that has become, for foreign visitors, their favourite guide-book. "We should write something on the English who come here with *In Patagonia,*" says Luned's son, Fabio. "It's their bible."

THIS POPULARITY FUELS the resentment of local historians. Best-known is the Argentine, Oswaldo Beyer. In Buenos Aires, Bruce consulted the left-wing Beyer about the Anarchist uprising in the 1920s. He had read Beyer's *La Patagonia Tragica* which, "on a cursory glance" he wrote in his diary, "seemed to me to be the hysterical, doubtless justified, ravings of a poor lawyer, driven to dementia by the greed and drunkenness that surrounded him—the work of a man with a persecution mania".

In February 1994, Beyer published a ringing attack on Bruce. *In Patagonia,* he wrote, was the key to understanding Europe's arrogance, always treating Beyer's part of the world with a colonial attitude. He felt guilty whenever he saw a copy in a window. He had furnished Bruce with a bibliography and photocopies of various articles, while at the same time wondering "how he was going to read these because it seemed to me his knowledge of Spanish was very deficient". This explained to Beyer various, unspecified "errors of interpretation". And he accused Bruce, who had only spent "three weeks in Santa Cruz and Chubut", of passing off other people's material on the anarchist Antonio Soto "as if it was the product of his own investigation".

Most deeply upsetting to Beyer was the wealth he imagined Bruce had accrued. "He made a fortune from this book," he declared. "He sold the rights in Germany for $300,000 dollars, in America for double that, the same as in England, without counting the rest of the world."

Beyer's reaction explains why it was impossible for many years to find *In Patagonia* in Buenos Aires. As Bruce wrote to Jorge Torre Zavaleta, who reviewed it in *La Nacion* : "I have always been a bit mystified about the book's reception in the Argentine, particularly since the Spanish translation seems to have sunk without trace."

In Punta Arenas, Bruce had also consulted the Chilean historian, Mateo Martinic, author of 23 books on Patagonia "for the moment". Bruce found Martinic to be a chauvinistic patriot with a mechanical intellect, "a politician tooth and nail, but one whose attitudes do not lead him to the extremes of either party". Martinic, who admits to a "strict" historical vision, dislikes *In Patagonia* for its sensationalism. He takes Bruce to task for exaggerating the killing of Indians and for reducing Patagonia to five or six precious stories without reflecting "in the best way" the contribution made by the British. But the author was not, he concedes, writing a history. "The problem is not Chatwin," he says, "but those who read Chatwin and think it *is* the bible."

THE BOOK MARTINIC most recommends is *A Patagonian Panorama* by Tom Jones, the one-time British Consul in Punta Arenas. Jones's daughter, Daphne Hobbs, is Bruce's most vociferous critic.

She does not possess a copy of *In Patagonia*. "I would not sully my shelves," she says. But she still, 20 years later, writes regular letters to the *Buenos Aires Herald* against a book which "whilst containing some elements of truth was much exaggerated and in some instance pure lies". One section angered her sister so much that she consulted a lawyer, only to be advised that you cannot libel the dead.

In Chapter 85, Bruce adapted a story from Captain Milward's journal about Daphne Hobbs's father-in-law. In the journal, Milward describes how he visited his friend Ernest Hobbs on his *estancia* on Tierra del Fuego and noticed a human skull "set up on the wall of the pigsty". The skull belonged to an Ona Indian, part of a group who had fled after killing two Chilean sailors. This Ona had been shot by "tame" Indians working for Hobbs, Milward writes: "Hobbs, of course, took no part in the killing and he simply reported that his tame Indians had got foul of some wild ones and that the wild ones had got the worst of it."

Bruce ratchets this encounter up a notch. He recasts it in direct speech, makes Hobbs reluctant to tell Milward what really happened and invents a second meeting in which Hobbs effectively admits to instigating the attack. This tampering understandably incenses Daphne Hobbs. "That conversation never took place. It was a pure lie." Speaking without proof but with conviction, she would "put my hand in the fire" to defend her father-in-law from a charge of Indian killing.

Bruce obviously embroidered the scene. But one must question why he did not change Hobbs's name as he protected identities elsewhere—unless he was persuaded that Hobbs had connived at the murder. This is a hard claim to verify. British farmers did have a hand in Indian killing in Tierra del Fuego, as Jones acknowledges in *A Patagonian Panorama*. "Many were murdered and a bad page of Patagonian history was recorded when one or two farmers paid one pound per head to Indian killers, a few of them British, for those liquidated; proof of accomplishment was the production of the Indian's ears." This does not mean Hobbs was among the Indian killers. Neither does it mean he was not. Bridges worked with Hobbs for many years on *Estancia* Baker and does not consider it impossible. "I'm quite sure that Ernest possibly did most of the things that are attributed to him—good and bad. Unfortunately, that is the way life works."

BRUCE HAD NO scruples about rattling family skeletons, or about reshaping even his own cousins' lives and natures, their names or their appearances. Charles Chatwin, who all his life had suppressed mention of his grandfather's embezzlement, was mortified to read, in the book's sole footnote, an account of the scandal surrounding Robert Harding Milward's imprisonment. Charles asked his son to remove the paragraph in future editions. After Bruce agreed to this, he wrote to say that he felt the rest of the book "a worthy recognition of a lot of endeavour & hard work put in by you, and . . . to my mind, completely free of any padding".

More distressed were Charles Milward's daughters, Monica and Lala.

They had looked forward to the book's publication, but "feelings ran high" after it appeared. According to Monica's husband, John Barnett, "they were spitting tin-tacks!"

On 28 November 1977, Monica wrote to Bruce expressing her "shocked horror—yes, horror" over a paragraph "full of conjecture and half-truths" which she felt had impugned the honour of both her parents. The paragraph dealt with her mother's rape. ("One night the whisky-soaked proprietor went for her and laid her down. She ran from the house, saddled a horse and rode through the snow to Punta Arenas.") By "raking up her bitter shame", Bruce had given an impression of Isabelle, "never Bella!", as a "rather cheap adventuress" preying on the soft heart of a lonely old man.

Lala objected deeply to his depiction of their father. "One of the things that drove me out of my mind was that he called my father 'Charley'. He was never called that. He was 'Charles' or 'Captain Milward'. He described my father as tall, having startling blue eyes and black mutton chops, with sailor's hat at a rakish angle. He was short and red-headed and bald by the time he was 30, and always wore a black tie. And he was not this sickly old man. He died very suddenly of a heart attack."

Monica could not understand her cousin's motives. "Surely it cannot be resentment of us?" she wrote to Bruce. "To my knowledge, not one of my Mother's family, children or grandchildren has ever harmed you in any way. We had never even heard of you until you turned up on our doorsteps. You were received with great kindness by my sister and her husband and later by my husband and myself. We welcomed you in our home, first alone and later with your wife and mother-in-law, who were with us over a period of several weeks. I allowed you free access to my Father's papers, although I never dreamed that you were copying portions of my father's 'Journal' with the intention of inserting them in full in your book . . . but I understand now why you insisted on staying on, shut up in your room upstairs while we were in the process of moving house."

She accused Bruce of embezzling the material she had hoped to use in her own book. "Maybe your memory is hazy, but when I gave you access to my Father's papers, I never gave you permission to photograph the 'Journal'—quite the contrary, I sought to make sure that it didn't leave the house." She asked him to imagine her surprise on finding "a receipt for 197 pages of photocopying dated 30 April". He had, she wrote, "lifted" sections "virtually word for word from my Father's 'Journal'—which is our one inheritance from him".

Bruce apologised at once. "If I am in the wrong, then I am deeply in the wrong. But I recall the matter differently." He agreed to remove the offending paragraph, change "Bella" to "Belle" and to credit Monica fulsomely in future. But Monica and Lala never forgave him. He became in Lala's words: "the cousin of whom I am not proud."

THERE ARE ERRORS of fact in the book which had he known about he would have corrected. Several may be attributed to his poor Spanish. (In the Sialesian Museum in Punta Arenas, for instance, he writes down the wrong name for the murdered priest: Father Pistone instead of Father Juan Silvestro.) Other mistakes seem the result of his haste. (Patagonia is generally understood to begin not at the banks of the Rio Negro, but 120 kilometres north at the Rio Colorado.) But there are strikingly few cases of mere invention. Bruce told the Argentinian critic Christian Kupchik: "Everything that is in the book happened, although of course in another order." The "lies" he admits to Michael Ignatieff are examples of his romanticism, as when he describes Señora Eberhard's ordinary stainless steel chair as being "by Mies van der Rohe" or makes the Ukrainian nurse in Rio Pico a devotee of his beloved Osip Mandelstam instead of Agatha Christie. These are tiny artisitic devices. "He is not writing a government report," says Wyndham. Nor a tourist brochure.

Jean-François Fogel says of *In Patagonia*: "No one goes on such a journey." People who read it wanting to find out something about Patagonia are left behind. The uniqueness of the landscape hardly comes into view. The book is largely about interiors which are elsewheres. "With little exaggeration," wrote the German critic, Manfred Pfister, "there are no Patagonian Patagonians, at least not in Chatwin's Patagonia." The structure is of a journey constantly interrupted, zigzagging among texts and through time. As a master fabulist Bruce has absorbed the rules and contrived something original out of them. He mixes and plays with literary forms, entering Drake's cabin with the same flamboyant ease as he enters an *estancia*, or the mind of a *guanaco*. "Once you read his interpretations you can't forget easily," says Guillermo Alvarez, for 20 years a geologist in Patagonia. "I always saw *guanacos* and they followed me. I thought they were *guanacos*, nothing more. Then I read Chatwin and I saw *guanacos* in a different way. Now I wonder: 'What does the *guanaco* think of me?' He motivates me to think, to want to know more, to be more observant. This is his power. Once you read him, you want to know: 'Is this true?'"

Generally speaking, Bruce does not subtract from the truth so much as add to it. He tells not a half-truth, but a truth-and-a-half. His achievement is not to depict Patagonia as it is, but to create a landscape called Patagonia—a new way of looking, a new aspect of the world. And in the process he reinvented himself.

◌⟋∾

XXIV

"Kicked by Amazon"

"How much did it [In Patagonia] *change you?"*
"It enabled me to go on writing books."
—BC, AUSTRALIA, 1984

BRUCE DEVOTED A chapter of *In Patagonia* to the story of a 33-year-old French lawyer, Orélie-Antoine de Tounens, who came to be first constitutional monarch of the Araucanian Indians. Bruce traced the present claimant, Philippe Boiry, to a public relations firm in the rue Poissonnière in Paris. Other pseudo-royals in his address book were the claimant to the Aztec throne and the King of Crete. He would also be amused by a musician, Melvin Lyman, who in 1969 declared that he was God.

Bruce was told about Lyman by an excited Welch who had visited "the divinity" in a fortress of six dilapidated houses in the Fort Hill district of Boston. In January 1970, Welch's intriguing report of the drug-taking Sufi guitar-player ("the music was mostly Hank Williamsish") attracted Bruce to Boston. He came upon Lyman's followers noisily eating popcorn and watching the Super Bowl. Lyman, or "Christ" as Bruce called him, sat like a movie mogul in the plushest armchair. "He operated several remote control switches, and while an enterprising insurance company proposes life policies for Hippies at special rates (higher), he turns round so that I can see his face . . . He is a mixture of boyishness and decrepitude. He has lost his teeth."

The interview was very short.

" 'What's your name?'

" 'Bruce.'

" 'What's your sign, Bruce?'

" 'Taurus.'

" 'You're a liar, Bruce. *He's* Taurus. Look at him!'

"The bodyguard stood close by. He was small and dark and hairy. 'You're not the same as him, Bruce'."

In his own words, Bruce took "a clinical interest in Messiahs". The story of a man who rose from humble origins to assume superhuman powers would be the subject of his second book.

ON 21 SEPTEMBER 1976, Bruce wrote to the writer Gerald Brenan outlining a fresh project. "Some years ago I went to a place called Ouidah on the slave coast of Dahomey and met members of a family called de Souza, now totally black. The original de Souza was a Portuguese peasant, who went to Bahia, became captain of the Portuguese fort on the slave coast and successively the leading slave-dealer, the Viceroy of the King, and one of the richest men in Africa. At one point he had 83 slave ships and two frigates built in the Philadelphia dockyard, but he could never leave his slave *barracoon* and his hundred odd black women in Ouidah. The family went mulatto and are now *feticheurs* [*sic*]. A de Souza is high priest of the Python Fetish, which Richard Burton saw on his Embassy to Dahomey in the 1860s. At that time it was in decline but, since independence, has taken a new lease of life. Tom Maschler of Cape's says I should go and try and chronicle the gradual blackening of the family."

Bruce had carried the story around with him a long time. As a boy he had read Burton and Skertchley and had memorised the etchings of King Ghézo's Amazons, bloodthirsty women who carried Winchesters slung across their backs. ("They were mostly elderly and all of them hideous," wrote Burton. "The officers were decidedly chosen for the size of their bottoms.") In addition, the fate of his murdered uncle must have quickened an interest in West Africa. Humphrey Chatwin's seed necklace in his grandmother's cabinet was strung on that coastline.

He also picked up isolated bits of information about Dahomey from his friends Brendan and Alison Oxmantown. In November 1965, Bruce had celebrated the Oxmantowns' departure for Cotonou. Brendan was quick to detect similarities with Papa Doc's Haiti: at his suggestion, the hotel sequences of *The Comedians* were filmed in Cotonou's Hotel de la Plage. Brendan reported to Bruce on an extraordinary colloquium held in 1966, part of a cultural exchange between Ouidah, the old slave town, and Bahia in Brazil, where a great proportion of the slaves had settled. "Do descend if in need of a little French colonial decadence after caravanserai-ing around the Sahara," he urged Bruce. "It's kind of different from your normal sphere of converts, convicts and patriarchs and incense in the snow."

Bruce arrived in Ouidah in February 1972, after his not terribly successful filming of the nomad market in Niger, and by then the Oxman-towns had departed for Teheran. He peered into the Python Temple. He spent a week "wandering among the peeling ochreous mud walls and clanking armadillo corrugated-iron roofs". He attended the sacrifice of a cow and behind a wall in the Quartier Brésil he found his story.

An old black lady showed him into a room containing an ebony four-poster bed. On a table stood a bottle of Gordon's gin, "half open and a glass of gin poured out in case he woke up", and in an alcove a plaster statue of St Francis, "the saint of holy wanderers", guarded a tombstone. The words on the grey marble slab read: FRANCISCO FELIX DE SOUZA.

"And then the old lady rolled back the bed sheets and you looked through, down—because the mattress was only sort of half there—at the most amazing sight. A mass of blood and feathers and sacrifices . . ."

De Souza, known as Cha Cha, had died in this bed in 1849 at the age of 95. A painting over the door showed a hook-nosed white man in a red scarf and tasselled cap who resembled Garibaldi. He was called Cha Cha because he was always in a hurry. The old lady was one of his descendants.

IN OUIDAH, the dead are not regarded as dead. Their presence is ven-erated by the sacrifice of living animals. Few today are more venerated than Francisco de Souza. His relatives, all black, still proudly celebrate their white ancestor's birthday. Every 4 October, more than 200 de Souzas gather from along the coast and congregate in his house for a 48-hour binge. They drink gin, sing songs sprinkled with Portuguese (although the language of the country is French) and shuffle to the beat of square drums, their faces concealed behind carnival masks of pharaohs, lions and cream-skinned princesses. The man who has worn the Viceroy's sash and tasselled cap since 1995 is Honoré de Souza, called Cha Cha VIII, a cheer-ful businessman who has the aluminium concession for Togo. For two days, his courtyard fills with the noise of ripping chicken flesh and the smell of singeing feathers.

The source of the first Cha Cha's riches and the nature of his com-merce—viz. the sale of their own countrymen—does not disturb Fran-cisco de Souza's descendants. "He had to earn a living," one of them says. "Slaves were the commodity then. Today it's rice." In 1988, the 200th an-niversary of de Souza's supposed arrival in Ouidah, the family's leader dis-tributed a pamphlet enjoining them to take seriously their responsibility and to promote the prestigious name of the founder. "Wake up! Our ancestors call us! Let us be true to the spirit of Dom Felix, the nobility of his origin, the exemplary life he led, his work."

Bruce discovered that de Souza's origins were not so noble: his mother was a Brazilian Indian and almost all that is known of his father is that he was Portuguese. Nor were de Souza's life and work exemplary. He was, however, lucky. He profited from a dramatic upturn in the fortunes of the Brazilian tobacco trade. The Portuguese in Brazil refused to smoke to-bacco from the lowest leaves of the plant. The merchants around Bahia experimented by dipping the leaves into cane molasses which, besides be-ing reasonably pleasant tasting, also added weight. The sweetened pipe to-bacco, known as *soca*, found an unexpected market in West Africa. The Kings of Dahomey and their families became addicted, preferring *soca* to all other brands of tobacco—even to the cowrie shells which they used as currency. Pierre Verger, an expert on the slave trade between Brazil and West Africa and the authority on whom Bruce depended, wrote: *"le tabac est le produit qu'ils estiment le plus et sans lequel ils ne peuvent vivre."* The Kings had few commodities with which to finance their craving, but they could offer an erratic supply of slaves.

In 1750, Bahia was sending 15 ships a year to Ouidah. A manifest records 2,000 rolls of the syrupy-smelling tobacco one way, 700 negroes the other—to work on the sugar and tobacco plantations in Bahia and in the gold mines of Minas Gerais. According to Hugh Thomas, slaves from Ouidah were prized by the Portuguese who thought they had "a magic nose for knowing where gold deposits were". In about 1788 a penniless de Souza disembarked from one of these ships.

He had come looking for work in the slave factory in Ouidah and had either been hounded out of Brazil for a political crime or deported for forgery. In any event, in Ouidah he prospered. "After staging a palace rev-olution in which he deposed one king of Dahomey for another," Bruce wrote in *What Am I Doing Here*, "he set about reorganising the Dahomean army—with its corps of Amazon warriors—as the most efficient military machine in Africa." In 1821 King Ghézo, whom he had rescued from prison, gave de Souza the title of Viceroy and with it a virtual monopoly of the slave traffic. But there was one punishing condition: he could never leave Ouidah. "Prince de Joinville, a son of Louis Philippe, came to call and described fantastic displays of opulence—silver services, gaming sa-loons, billiard saloons—and the *chacha* himself wandering about distract-edly in a dirty kaftan."

The spectacle of a black family taking inordinate pride in their de-scent from a white—or white-ish—slaver was irresistible to Bruce. He sent a photograph of himself sporting a Cha Cha moustache to his parents: "This town, an old slaving port, is one of the most fascinating places I've ever been in . . . Fascinating material for a book."

BRUCE WAS ONCE more in Ouidah in December 1976, while waiting for the final proofs of *In Patagonia*. He planned to spend three months in West Africa and Brazil researching a straightforward biography of de Souza. He invited the art dealer John Kasmin to accompany him on the African part of the journey.

They landed in Cotonou, Yoruba for "mouth of the river of death", on 21 December. Dahomey was now the Marxist Republic of Benin. A curfew began at 11 p.m. and officials of President Kérékou were suspicious of foreigners unless they were from North Korea, the country's closest ally. They travelled in constant fear of expulsion.

They had arrived in a stiff sea wind in the traditional season for warfare and slave collecting. In Porto Novo, they visited the pathetic museum and its retired director, Clement de Cruz. "After many askings we find our chap and enter his house," Kasmin wrote in his diary. "A room Howard Hodgkin would love, a little round table and four 1940 chairs, and that's all. What a chat—in semi-intelligible (to me) French from this very opinionated, and I suppose, intellectual savant of culturation, tradition, extended families etc., but he is helpful to Bruce who relishes this stream of vapid profundities."

On 23 December, they proceeded to Ouidah, two hours along the coast. Bruce was pleased to find the same guide as he had in 1972, "a young, honey-coloured mulatto with a flat and friendly face, a curly moustache and a set of dazzling teeth". Sebastian de Souza was a direct descendant of Cha Cha.

In the garden of the Portuguese fort, sitting beside the last governor's burnt-out Citroën DS, Bruce and Kasmin consumed "a stylish lunch": a bottle of William Lawson whisky and a tin of Malassol caviar, a parting gift from the sculptor Anthony Caro. They visited the Python Temple and the compound of the voodoo chief priest, the Hounon Dagbo. "This Dagbo refuses to shake B's hand," Kasmin wrote in his diary, "which embarrasses B who, stepping backward, trod on the bare toes of a stout lady joining the party."

Bruce and Kasmin walked the red track from the Viceroy's house, under the yellow berries of the Auction Tree, and three miles through plantations to the sea. At a conservative estimate, two million men and women filed along this route between 1640 to 1870. Canoes rowed them through the choppy shark water to de Souza's ships. Bruce and Kasmin looked at the straight line of white breakers and absorbed the incredible fact of how the intoxicated rulers of Dahomey bartered their people for Birmingham rifles and roll after roll of tobacco. On every cargo, de Souza took a percentage.

Christmas Day found Bruce and Kasmin 120 miles north in Abomey, the former royal capital. They explored the low thatched halls of the nondescript palace and imagined the mud walls hung with hooks bearing human heads, "as thick as they can lie one by another". The kings of Dahomey, practitioners of human as well as of animal sacrifice, hunted their victims in season, like pheasants. The army's crack troops were the tall soldier-women who fought with a ferocity, according to one witness, A. B. Ellis, "that most resembled the blind rage of beasts". Skertchley and Burton, whose texts Bruce used for reference, described them as Amazons. Skertchley elaborated in details that Bruce would remember. "Whenever a woman becomes unsexed, either by the force of circumstances or depravity, she invariably exhibits a superlativeness of evil . . . What spectacle is more calculated to inspire horror than a savage and brutal woman in a passion?" The Amazons beheaded their prisoners, out of sight, in the palace compound, where they poured the blood into pools three feet square and set miniature canoes afloat on it. Sometimes they mixed the blood with gold dust and sea-foam and patted it into the walls. "Pretty nasty feeling of blood and slaughter hangs here," wrote Kasmin, "but, as B says, it is all colour eventually."

Forbidden to take photographs, Bruce could not resist sketching the palace's grisliest attraction: two thrones mounted on human skulls. The taller, five feet high and carved from a kapok tree, belonged to the Viceroy's pox-scarred patron, King Ghézo. It stood beneath an open black umbrella, bolted into four cracked, nicotine-coloured craniums. Next to it, embellished by two skulls, was the stool belonging to Ghézo's mother, Princess Agontimé. According to Dahomey tradition, Ghézo's half-brother Adandozan, whom he usurped, had sold her to Bahia as a slave.

Their visit concluded in an audience with the present king, in a simple room adjoining the museum. Kasmin describes Ghézo's grandson as "an ancient gent in many robes and skirts and spectacles". His throne was a 1930s office chair covered in green leatherette and for the interview a bare-bosomed lady held a decorated umbrella over his head. "We launched into an exchange that most nearly resembled those recorded last century. The king declaiming and telling stories via the interpreter—occasional newcomers crawling in and kissing the floor and rubbing dirt on their foreheads as in olden days. A delight. He was in full control and displaying a clear memory, this grandson of the great Ghézo. The story was of de Souza, the first Cha Cha, and his search for Ghézo's mother who had been sold into slavery. B was most turned on and saw his book quickening."

Bruce wrote: "A man came in and kissed the concrete floor. The King went on with the story. He came to the end and we paid a thousand francs. He told another story and we paid a little less. He could go on all day. He liked telling stories. He liked getting paid for them. There was not much left for a king to do."

Upon payment, King Sagbadjou, who claimed to have been born the year of Richard Burton's visit in 1863, told Bruce what he knew of the Brazilian. "He was a tall man," he said, "bigger than the two of you together. My grandfather lifted him over the prison wall. My grandfather, you see, was even bigger than de Souza."

Ghézo's half brother King Adandozan had incarcerated de Souza after an argument, dunking him periodically in vats of indigo to dye his fair skin. Ghézo, hating the man who had sold his mother into captivity, discerned in de Souza a useful ally. Once he had lifted him over the wall they made a blood pact. Years later, de Souza repaid the favour. He earned his title of Viceroy after rescuing Ghézo from prison.

"The story is wonderful, already forming in my mind, but I've hardly touched on it yet," Bruce wrote to Elizabeth. "I think it will have to be written in the high style of *Salammbô*." He extended his usual invitation. "If you liked and could afford it you could come out in Feb for 3 weeks—fare to Cotonou £320. I will have lodging in Pto Novo hopefully, but it is hot and sticky and I'll be working. x x x B."

FOR ANOTHER FORTNIGHT, Bruce toured the north. He and Kasmin visited a game park and entered Togo where a barman asked: *"Êtes-vous aventuriers?"* Kasmin wrote: "B. is delighted." Bruce, meanwhile, wrote to Elizabeth that travelling with Kasmin was "quite exhausting, because one could never tell when he would begin one of his British sense-of-fair-play outbursts." In Ouidah, they were allowed to witness a ceremony for the initiation of novices. The God of War was paraded, according to Kasmin, "on the shoulders of a boss-eyed tough who looked like Dudley Moore". Without warning, state officials rushed in, interrupted the dance, and took Bruce and Kasmin angrily aside. It was forbidden to photograph such events: they must hand over the film, or go to the police. "The dance continued, but B and the chief priest defended our position & after a nervous period of noisy discussion we were allowed to leave & with the film too. We got out of town fast. Who had forgotten to tell us that photography is not allowed in Benin without a permit from the Tourist Bureau? I was v. indignant, but B oiled the people as he always does. Were I alone I would have been arrested many times."

ON 7 JANUARY Kasmin flew home to London. Bruce told Elizabeth: "One or two near scrapes, but he was an excellent fellow traveller and we both enjoyed our little tour." Kasmin was nevertheless aware that he had left behind a companion who was "quite disconsolate" about what form his book would take.

The original plan, to write a biography of Felix de Souza, was floundering in the poverty of documentary material. In Benin, no archives survived for the de Souzas. The last Portuguese governor, in 1961, had burned down the fort in Ouidah, destroying all records since 1725. In a bid to delve more history out of the slaving families, Bruce crossed the border into Nigeria.

He spent a week in Ibadan, staying with Keith Nicholson Price, a friend of Gerald Brenan. Bruce arrived out of the *harmattan* covered in a fine, white powder and looking prematurely grey. He wore jeans, a multipocketed jacket and carried a large leather shoulder bag, producing from it a two-year-old letter of introduction.

Price is one of several who wanted to hold on to the experience of meeting Bruce, to fix it in their journal. Afterwards he wrote a record of Bruce's visit. He described a character who bustled with energy: "his self-discipline, his inner tension and sense of hurry, his insensitivity and self-ishness . . . were a kind of blinkering in his reactions to the outside world. He had work to do and perhaps he knew instinctively he would have very little time in which to do it."

After dinner on the second night, they talked about writing. "His first book *In Patagonia* was about to be published and he felt extremely sensitive about it. He doubted the confidence that his publishers had shown in him. Also Paul Theroux's *The Old Patagonian Express* had just been published and was selling well. Bruce greatly admired the work and considered it 'a truly brilliant book . . . I'm sure its success will affect my sales and if that happens any future books of mine will be affected and so will my income and my only real loves, travelling and writing'."

Next morning Bruce was up and away before seven, having instructed Price's steward to prepare an early breakfast. He returned late. With every day Price noticed a growing reticence "which seemed to come from fatigue and an increasing frustration".

Bruce had pinned much on a meeting with Pierre Verger, then teaching at Ibadan. Verger was typical of the experts whose insights he commandeered. Bruce did not so much appropriate their work as popularise it. He knew how to repackage the esoteric, make it palatable for a broad market. Like Bob Brain in the cave at Swartkrans, or Mateo Martinic in Patagonia, or Theodor Strehlow later in Australia, Verger had devoted 20 or 30 years of investigation to his subject when Bruce appeared out of the blue, bubbling over with contagious enthusiasm, trying to find out everything he knew. "Bruce always went straight to the fountain-head," says Paddy Leigh Fermor. "He found the best authority he could and asked hundreds of questions and then he would come back the second best informed man on that particular subject in the world possibly."

Verger had been working on the cultural links between Bahia and Africa since 1946. His exhaustively researched *Flux et Reflux de la traite des Nègres entre le Golfe de Bénin et Bahia de Todos os Santos, du XVII au XIX siècle* was Bruce's primary source on de Souza.

Verger was an autodidact. Born in Paris in 1902 of prosperous Belgian parents, he had begun working in his family printing business and knew the painful process of transforming himself from a dandy into a scholar. Drawn, in the words of the anthropologist John Ryle, to "the allure of otherness embodied in non-European peoples" Verger escaped first through photography (from the 1930s he was the front-line photographer of *Life* magazine in Algeria, Cuba and Mauritania); and then through the meticulous documentation of the slave trade and religious practice in north-eastern Brazil and West Africa. Initiated into the voodoo priesthood in Dahomey, he was a "babalao" or father of secrets.

He was cynical, and what he liked about African and Brazilian religions was that morally they were cynical too. Their witchcraft was based on malice, which he saw as corresponding to his deeply morose view of

346   BRUCE CHATWIN

human nature while at the same time giving rein to a sensuous delight in the world.

Bruce had hoped that Verger would energise his quest for de Souza, but their brief meeting was not a success. He wrote to Elizabeth, "I met the famous Afro-Brazilian scholar of encyclopaedic knowledge but little practical use. Tight with information. A fantastical old queen, having a tiff with his Yoruba boyfriend." Verger, who once called scholars "colourless parrots", may have felt the same towards Bruce. He thought *The Viceroy of Ouidah* "OK—but why did he have to change the names?"

Bruce's failure to charm Verger into revealing his secrets depressed him. "After the meal, which Bruce had only picked at, he slumped onto his usual chair looking ill and exhausted. His face was ashen and there were dark rings around his worried eyes. 'Wish I hadn't started this,' he mumbled. He had been trying to interview some of the Brazilian families of West Africa—the de Souzas, the Mendozas and de Silvas—to obtain more memoirs of their slave-trading ancestors." Price was not surprised. "Their reserved and suspicious manner would deter the most hardened investigator."

One day, when Bruce was out, Price heard a chant of "thief, thief" in the street and looked out to see "a mob of about a hundred" harassing a young girl who was being dragged along by two men. Apparently, she had stolen a loaf of bread. "Her bodice had been ripped and from the look of her small exposed breasts she was no more than 13 years old."

Price watched her disappear into the police barracks opposite. He thought no more about the incident until the next morning when he found Bruce up and about, correcting his notes.

"What was that noise?" Bruce asked. "That screaming? I couldn't sleep at all." Price had heard nothing.

Bruce's bedroom window faced the police barracks. That evening Bruce stormed into Price's sitting room.

"It's started again."

"What's started again?"

"That screaming. Can't concentrate with that noise, it's so distracting."

Leaving Bruce in the house, Price went across to the barracks, where he knew the lieutenant on duty. He asked what was going on. The policeman grinned. "A thief . . . The boys are having some fun."

He had a writer staying, Price told the policeman. The screaming was a distraction.

"I was hoping that the mention of the close proximity of a writer might have some effect on him. The lieutenant was unimpressed.

" 'Try and stop them,' he said and shuffled some papers on his desk. 'You want her?' he asked without looking up. 'Want a bit of fun?'

"A short piercing scream came down the corridor.

" 'Fun? Doesn't sound like she's enjoying it much.'

" 'She's young, a learner. You want her?' I nodded and he tossed me a key."

By the time Price arrived the girl was alone, half-naked on the floor and seemingly asleep. "She was a pitiful sight." Angrily, he kicked the boarded window and the boards fell away. "She was as light as a feather. I lifted her and placed her outside the window. Her wrap fell off completely and I noticed blood on her thin legs." Price in a whisper urged her to leave. After first falling to her knees she crawled away.

When he returned, Bruce went white. "You're mad."

"I agree. But she got away and now you can write."

"You shouldn't have interfered," said Bruce.

Before returning to Benin, Bruce shook Price's hand and promised to send him a signed copy of *In Patagonia*. "This is something I would have treasured, but it never arrived." Price's last words were: "Just take care. The current regime think that every white man is a mercenary intent on killing the president." Bruce laughed. "I'll be fine."

ON 14 JANUARY, by the light of a guttering lamp, Bruce wrote a rambling letter to Elizabeth from Porto Novo, Benin's capital. He had rented a room in Sebastian de Souza's family house, "in a street lined with Portuguese houses built by creole nabobs who returned from Bahia in the 1850s. It is infernally sticky and I have to confess the whole of this part of the trip is something of a trial."

Cha Cha's story still eluded him. Verger had impressed on him the absence of records. Bruce had taken this as a cue to switch genres from a biography to fiction. "I've been reading some Balzac and think the only way to treat de S is to write a straight Balzacian account of the family, beginning with a description of the place and then switching back to him and writing through to the present. Quite a mouthful."

He had changed his mind about Elizabeth joining him. "Frankly I don't now see any point in your coming out because it isn't a joyride and the only way is to get it over as soon as I can." He concluded: "Going with Sebastian de Souza to a football match in Togo and will write from there again with more news."

Hours after finishing this letter his research was cut short in a dramatic fashion.

ON SUNDAY 16 January 1977, Kasmin dined with Maschler and updated him on the progress of the "Dahomey book." The publisher saw "a big future for B". Kasmin had just finished writing these words in his diary when the telephone rang. There had been a coup in Benin.

Not until the 21st did Kasmin hear from Bruce. "Woken at 7.30 this morning by Bruce calling from Abidjan. He escaped from Cotonou yesterday and related his experiences during the mysterious coup of last Sunday. Was arrested, roughed up and locked up with hundreds of other Europeans and some blacks. Some shootings, much brutality and chaos . . . His story of hiding in a de Souza closet and then at the Gendarmerie, a mercenary type being brought in with gun and dressed in camouflaged combat suit who transpired to be the French Ambassador, found while out on a partridge shoot; and the Amazon who kicked him for being slow at undressing on command. Poor B. was worried whether he was wearing underpants or not."

Kasmin was not the only person Bruce telephoned from Abidjan. A week after the coup, the *Sunday Times* interviewed an anonymous "refugee" who claimed while in detention to have been assaulted and deprived of food and water. The report, written by James Fox, his former colleague on the magazine, described "a French scholar who wishes to remain anonymous in the hope of continuing work in Benin". It added this detail: "The mercenaries even had time to hold 'a drinks party' in a thatched chalet in the grounds of the Hotel de la Croix du Sud . . ." Then what the "refugee" called a "witch-hunt" for foreigners took place. Stripped to their underpants, the informant and 600 others were told variously that they would be held incommunicado for five days, tried by a military tribunal, or "shot at five a.m. the next morning".

The coup had begun late, at 7.30 a.m. and had lasted five hours. People who heard the initial explosions mistook the noise. "I heard boom boom and told my mother there's going to be a lot of rain," says Latif de Silva. The members of the coup comprised a hundred or so Africans, Belgians and French, sponsored by exiled Beninois wishing to overthrow Kérékou's Marxist state. From a training camp in Morocco they flew to Gabon, picking up arms in France-Ville. The pilot radioed ahead to Cotonou: his DC8 was bringing personnel for a festival.

But someone had betrayed them. In Cotonou, the army were waiting. And Bruce, on his way to the football match in Togo, was caught in the crossfire.

THE STORY GREW in the retelling. The first version bears little resemblance to the last, published in *Granta* as a "story"—a word, wrote Bruce, "intended to alert the reader to the fact that however closely the narrative may fit the facts, the fictional process has been at work". In the gap between the two versions is found the clue to Bruce's storytelling process. The inflations, distortions, confabulations are all there.

His initial account of the coup is written in his diary. It starts in Porto Novo, just after he has finished his letter to Elizabeth. "Sunday morning began with me under the mosquito net in the bedroom in Sebastian de Souza's yard." Sebastian appears, dressed in brown, elegant for the football match in Togo. The two of them walk to the autogare in Porto Novo and squash into the back of a crowded Peugeot 405. On the coast road to Cotonou, they notice people waving from cars. The driver, thinking a wheel might be coming off, stops the car.

"*C'est la guerre à Cotonou,*" he is told.

"I knew it," Sebastian says. "I knew it would happen." He has been longing for Kérékou's "yapping police state" to collapse. The others in the car are delighted too. They about-turn and drive back to Porto Novo, rejoining Sebastian's anxious wife. They sit down on her leatherette chairs and listen to Kérékou broadcasting on the radio. Mercenaries have landed at Cotonou airport in a DC8. "*L'heure est grave.*" All citizens are urged to block the roads and go with guns to secure the airport. The speech would play several times that day to the background of spliced applause bought in from the BBC.

Possibly, this is the moment when, as he told Kasmin, Bruce hides in Sebastian de Souza's closet. "Trembling voices" he writes. Sebastian is taken off to the Douanes. Bruce waits a short time before "gingerly" stepping outside.

In the street, a waving crowd shouts: "*Mercenaires, mercenaires.*" He is wearing khaki shorts with patch pockets ("the badge of a mercenary"). He finds a gendarme who bundles him into a van—"For your own protection". He is taken to the gendarmerie and later marched at gunpoint to the Centre de Recherches where he finds the French Counsellor and a doctor friend in hunting rig. Both men had been seized from the bush with a booty of dead birds and their ancient twelve-bore shotguns. Bruce seems to find the details more ridiculous than dire. "Looked absolutely mercenary, dressed for *la chasse*, dressed to kill."

Later, they are joined by three Swiss birdwatchers captured with precision binoculars and a long lens camera, the size and shape of a mortar.

By afternoon, the talk is of mercenaries retreating towards the marshes of Ouidah. Bruce and his companions are ordered into a police vehicle and driven to Cotonou. At the Camp Ghézo, they join a cheerful crowd of between 300 and 400 blacks and whites, all down to their underpants. They are herded into a shed, made to strip. "Separated from all my possessions including pack. Thought I didn't have on underpants. Sent into a corner and sat down. After 5 minutes asked to redress and I clung to my bag desperately."

There is no mention in his notes of the brutal "Amazon" he told Kasmin about on the telephone. Nor does Kasmin recollect seeing on their journey any female soldiers.

After being stripped—he is wearing "pink and white boxer shorts from Brooks Brothers"—Bruce is ordered back aboard the truck and taken to the Sûreté Nationale and made to sit in a waiting room. Questioned at last by an amiable policeman, who complains of his ruined weekend, he is led before the commandant, a man with thin red eyes and white woolly hair. When Bruce tells him he is a tourist, the commandant says: "*Leur cas est plus compliqué.*"

These are the words Bruce writes next: "Foreign prints: 'Kicked by Amazon'". It is not clear what they describe. In his journal, nothing much happens at this point. At 9 p.m. he is placed in a room with a wobbly fan where he passes the night. But in his *Granta* article, published seven years later, there appears at this point a fearsome woman in the mould of Ghézo's warriors: "I stood like a schoolboy, in the corner, until a female sergeant took me away for fingerprinting. She was a very large sergeant. My head was throbbing: and when I tried to manoeuvre my little finger onto the inkpad, she bent it back double; I yelled 'Ayee!', and her boot slammed down on my sandalled foot." (One cannot but be reminded of how, a few days earlier, he had trodden on a woman's toes in Ouidah.)

Then to what do the words "Foreign prints: 'Kicked by Amazon'" refer? Was Bruce assaulted? Or was he projecting himself into a scene from a print which a moment before he has seen hanging on the commandant's wall: a print that illustrated, say, the pages of his Skertchley or Burton? As Kasmin says of Bruce on their Benin trip: "His model *was* Burton." If so, it is a paradigm of how his imagination worked: to escape an uncomfortable situation by seizing on a piece of art and, as in a Borges story, incorporating himself into it.

Kasmin is not alone in observing how Bruce was able to go on adding to his stories. "He's got so many role models and heroes and he's endlessly confusing and conflating them. He got a naughty, giggly pleasure out of it." As Piggott noted too, he was "genuinely incapable" of distinguishing fact from fantasy.

A year later the story has metamorphosed further. Bruce told James Lees-Milne on a walk from Badminton to Holwell of certain "hair-raising experiences" which had occurred on this journey. Lees-Milne put their conversation into his diary. "In one little country—I forget which he was arrested for some misdemeanour, passport not visa-ed, and beaten up. He was hit in the face, stripped of all his clothes—what a pretty sight to be sure—and humiliated in public. 'How awful!' I said. 'Well,' he replied. 'I must confess to having rather enjoyed it.' 'Then you are a masochist, I surmise.' 'Just a bit,' he answered."

Few friends were told about the "gang-rape", nor did Bruce ever write it down. This story may owe less to Skertchley or Burton than to Rimbaud (who was gang-raped in the Paris commune) or T. E. Lawrence (who alleged a similar assault by Turkish soldiers). According to Elizabeth, the incident took place "a few days after he left Benin". Bruce's journal merely reports how the coup peters out. Detained overnight, he is hauled up before an apologetic police tribunal in the early afternoon on the following day. "Actually made them laugh and got out." He moves into the Hotel de Plage, where *The Comedians* had been filmed, and three days later flies to Abidjan in the Côte D'Ivoire.

In Bruce's version to Elizabeth, he was raped here. "He was waiting to go to Brazil. He got a room in some cheap hotel and couldn't lock the door and soldiers came in to demand money and raped him. That's what he told me. He could barely say it. 'I didn't do anything. There were several of them'."

If true, terrible. Yet a suspicion persists that the true rape victim was not Bruce but a thin-legged, 13-year-old girl in Ibadan, whose screams he had heard from his bedroom.

XXV.

∽

Brazil

I want to forget. I want to sleep with Negroes
and Negresses and Indians
and Indian women, animals and plants.

—BC NOTEBOOKS

FROM ABIDJAN, BRUCE flew to Monrovia to catch the KLM flight to
Rio. As day dawned he engaged a young Englishman seated in the row behind in lengthy conversation about how narrowly he had escaped death.
He betrayed no sign that he might have been assaulted by soldiers. He
seemed to Nigel Acheson "very comfortable, not at all frightened". His
chief concern was that in the chaos of his departure from Benin, his bags
had been directed to Egypt. "Will walk off the plane with nothing but the
clothes I stand in," he wrote in his notebook.

Acheson was returning to Rio to a teaching position at the Cultura
Inglesa and became Bruce's host and guide during his two months in
Brazil. He had intriguing South American connections: his family had
worked in Iqique during Chile's nitrate boom. Their story of sudden decline and humiliating suburban decay predictably captivated Bruce. The
grandfather who was put on a boat with £100 in his pocket; the grandmother who continued to wear her Worth dresses until they were thread-
bare; the sad end in Cheltenham, polishing the brass plates on the steps
at night to keep up the pretence they still had servants. Bruce encouraged
Acheson to write down the story. Overawed by his display of erudition
and "utterly charmed" by him, Acheson offered Bruce a mattress in his
spartan apartment at 194 Rua Assis Brasil.

Bruce loved Brazil's atmosphere of public sensuality. With nothing
much to do until his luggage reappeared, he frequented Copacabana. His
Brazilian notebook immediately registers his excitement. It shows him
susceptible to "the cat-like figures" on the beach, bronze bodies anointed
with oil, mulattos with "corkscrew curls tumbling in cascades". After

meeting a Mr Willis from Minneapolis playing in the sea, Bruce wrote: "I prey to the most unreasoning desire." He was powerless to resist. He had enjoyed adventures on previous travels, but in a sporadic way, and usually with black women whose "African rumps" he found "infinitely alluring". ("A tight black bottom I could never resist," he told Gregor von Rezzori.) In Brazil he became an avid sexual tourist and a hemisphere away from his wife and family, he talked in an intimate way to his younger host.

One night he described a homosexual encounter which had taken place with a boy at Marlborough after a rugby match. "He surprised himself," says Acheson. "He said he had never spoken so openly." Bruce said he had no time for gay politics, or the gay community, and he abhorred the word "gay". "I'd much rather be called a bugger," and he roared with laughter.

In common with his Viceroy, whose "solitary wanderings" set him apart and who longed to "unburden his load", Bruce's confessions suggest a liberating mortification, like the tears that save de Souza from his violent impulses. In Brazil, with Acheson as the foil, he launched into a world of homosexual promiscuity that flowered four months later into his first grand passion.

He quickly tired of kicking his heels in Rio. He found its people "cowed and lacking in personality", he wrote to Wyndham. His purpose in coming to Brazil was to visit the north where de Souza had lived before sailing to Ouidah. Five years before Bruce had written in his notebook: "I want more than anything to go to Bahia." Bruce, who spoke little Portuguese, asked Acheson if he would consider accompanying him as interpreter. They arrived in Bahia shortly before carnival, after a 32-hour bus trip.

They shared a room in a cheap, rat-infested hotel near the Pelhourinho, the old slave quarter. Acheson was amused by Bruce's military-style shorts and by the sack of bran he carried in his backpack, "like horsefood". He helped Bruce to make calls to writers and historians who could enlighten him on the slave trade. "He was ablaze at the connections between Bahia and West Africa." Soon they were joined from Rio by Acheson's partner, Fernando. They explored the city and its surrounds together, sometimes following the needs of Bruce's research. The landscape was strikingly reminiscent of the coast near Ouidah, paths of red earth leading through plantations and here and there among the trees a tobacco planter's crumbling home. "The architecture is wonderful," Bruce wrote to Kasmin. "18th century rococo with genuinely Chinese overtones

brought direct from Macão, whose towns look like the willow pattern."
They visited a cigar factory, a Germanic fortress of stained cement. They
saw the sticky, man-high cane fields that had sweetened the tobacco for
the Kings of Dahomey. And one night in a fetish house overlooking the
sleepy river town of Cachoeira they witnessed a ceremony of candomblé
that differed little from the voodoo rituals in Ouidah. Candomblé, writes
John Ryle, is "a world where women and homosexuals are privileged,
where the doubly disadvantaged can be given high status". Bruce described it in a letter to Kasmin: "the 'daughters of the god' trance-dancing
in colossal white lace crinolines and the boys—girlie boys—in silver and
lace all shuddering as the Shango (the god) hit them between the shoulder blades and one boy twisting and whirling off the platform his silver
thunderbolts glittering down the mountain and coming back up again
and collapsing into the arms of the 'mother'—a middle-aged white lady
with spectacles, hair in a scarf and the air of a bank manager's secretary."

The Viceroy of Ouidah would celebrate this sexual abandon—Ama-
zonian, uninhibited, challenging, feral: "Her shoulders shuddered at the
first roll of drums. Then she spun around. She pirouetted. She strutted.
Her arms pumped the air, her feet kicked the dust. Sweat poured from her
breasts and a musky perfume gusted into the Brazilian's face: not once did
she let her gaze fall away from him.

"The drummers stopped.

"She stood before him, on tiptoe, swaying her hips and languidly laying out her tongue. Her arms beckoned. She bent at the knees. Then she
arched her spine and bent over backwards till the back of her head
brushed the ground." One senses in his dancer the frenzied expression of
long-withheld sensuality.

Bahia during carnival was "searing with sexuality" says Acheson.
"Bruce cruised around and often went off on his own to make conquests."
Once, returning to the hotel, Acheson and Fernando had to wait downstairs because their room was occupied. A paragraph in Bruce's notebook
records an encounter. "He came in off the street—same still Africa look.
Hard belly-bones, eyes not watching and watchful. Moustache. '*Transar,*'
he said. Lay on bed, removing pants—mouth soft. Flat chest smooth. The
curl of hair on belly like warts compacted. Go on to clamp down any
show of affection."

Bruce's Viceroy shows this fierce detachment on coming to Bahia:
"His green eyes made him famous in the quarter. Whenever he flashed
them along a crowded alley, someone was sure to stop. With partners of

either sex, he performed the mechanics of love in planked rooms. They left him with the sensation of having brushed with death. None came back a second time."

Bruce used the "patchiness" of his material as his excuse for recasting de Souza as a bi-sexual wanderer. He attributes to his fictional creation his own impulses, desires and abhorrence of domesticity. De Souza's Bahia phase is the time in which he puts away his masks and becomes fully himself.

"The lineaments of his face fell into their final form.

"His right eyebrow, hitched higher than the left, gave him the air of a man amazed to find himself in a madhouse. A moustache curled round the sides of his mouth, which was moist and sensuous. For years he had pinched back his lips, partly to look manly, partly to stop them cracking in the heat: now he let them hang loose, as if to show that everything was permitted."

Like the Viceroy, Bruce identifies with strangers and craves their simple lives and pleasures—"yet he could never join them." Acheson comments on Bruce's attraction to muscular young black men and *marmelucos*, or mulattoes, whom he admired for their "marvellous" flat chests. "What he had a horror of was domesticity. One boy invited Bruce to his tiny place. Bruce described with a shudder a meal he'd prepared, the mundaneness. 'I don't want *that*'."

To Kasmin, Bruce wrote from Bahia: "I have to say Brazil is very fascination [*sic*]." He down-played his enjoyment to Elizabeth: "I am heartily sick of it," he wrote on the same day. "Full of folklore, bad art, intellectuals in search of Atlantis and smart folks who go to *candomblé* in jangling earrings. I am staying with the missionaries of the British Church and when got down I retire [to] the graveyard where I read while marble personifications of sleep mourn our English gentlemen, victims of yellow fever." He planned to see Elizabeth in Lisbon in April. "Perhaps we could meet in the Hotel Seite Aix in Cintra—the most beautiful-looking hotel in the world." But he could not promise this until "the wretched proof comes".

His page proofs of *In Patagonia*, for which he had been waiting since December, had been mislaid in the Brazilian post. "Everything's gone wrong! Where was it we were hexed?" he asked Kasmin. "Somewhere I have it in my mind you said we'd been hexed. Well, not only the arrest, the visa withdrawn, the traveller's cheques stolen, the bronchitis (from the Beach Hotel of Cotonou), the bags sent to Cairo instead of Rio, the ten day pointless wait, now Tom's proof of *Patagonia* has got lost in the post between Rio and Bahia just when I have to go off north."

Two days later, the proofs arrived. He wrote to the copy-editor to say the hex had been "unstuck for me by a gypsy *cabocha* or fortune-teller who prophesied, after a certain amount of greasing, that it would arrive to-day—which it did".

The title was still not resolved. Bruce revealed to Acheson the same insecurity over his work as he had with Nicholson Price in Nigeria. "He asked advice about the title. He couldn't bear the idea of 'Journey to Patagonia'." This self-doubt increased along with his frustrations over his new book. Even with Acheson to translate, he was not finding fresh or relevant material. The problem, as in Ouidah, was the absence of archives: all documents on slavery had been lost in a large fire in December 1890. Traces of Francisco de Souza were hard to come by. In Ouidah, he wrote, "the de Souzas are convinced they still have a fortune in Bahia." One trouble was that in Bahia Souza was a name as common as Smith. (There are 27 pages of de Souzas in the Bahia telephone directory.) "In the *souzala* or old slave quarter the blacks are all de Souzas! But then everyone is a de Souza or has de Souza cousins in Brazil." He was further hampered by the lack of a tradition of oral history. He was able to find information on de Souza's banker, who made his first fortune from salt-dried beef and died in a colossal palace. But about Francisco de Souza, his family and fortunes and the house in which he grew up, nothing. "None of the black de Souzas are aware of the big House in Brazil from which de Souza was expelled as a boy and which he reconstructed in Africa."

AFTER CORRECTING HIS proofs, Bruce decided to head north through the cactus scrub of the *sertão* to San Luis de Marañon. His purpose, he told Kasmin, was to investigate the fate of Ghézo's mother, Princess Agontimé, "who was sold into slavery and was got back by de Souza". The story as told to Bruce in Benin was that when Cha Cha became Viceroy he promised Ghézo he would find his mother and bring her home. For a while, the famous slave princess Agontimé supplanted the Viceroy as the focus of Bruce's research.

The Brazilian north yielded little. Acheson had returned with Fernando to Rio. Without a sympathetic companion Bruce succumbed to the lassitude, "the terror of Brazilian life", which he saw afflicting everyone around him. "What to make of a town in which the bookshop offers: Isaac Deutscher's *Life of Trotsky. The Theatre of Meyerhold. The Life of André Malraux. The Forbidden Loves of Oscar Wilde* and not a single Brazilian novel." In Picos, a truck-stop town in Piaui, the poorest province in Brazil, he stayed in the Charm Hotel, from the facade of which the letter "C" had dropped off. In Crato, where moths covered the walls of his room "like flint arrowheads", he wrote: "Got down by the heat. Would find it impossible to write a sentence here." Steady reference was made to "the boredom of waits". The aimlessness weighed on him. "The boredom is infectious; that is the trouble." One day while waiting for a boat in Alcantara he wrote: "Terrible fear my talent has deserted me. This the most unlively journal."

He uncovered no new fact about Princess Agontimé. Cha Cha, forbidden himself to leave Ouidah, had despatched an emissary to retrieve the royal slave, but Ghézo's mother was never found. The only possible source of news as to where she may have ended her days was with Verger. Once in San Luis de Marañon, it had puzzled Verger to record certain voodoo expressions he had not heard before. In Abomey he made enquiries and was told that this was the secret language of the King's court: only someone belonging to the royal family could know such expressions.

On a hot day in Recife, in a dark house stuffed with books, Bruce called on the historian, Gilberto Freyre. He must have hoped that this meeting with the author of two important works on Brazilian slaves would be more fruitful than his encounter with Verger two months before. It was not. Freyre had the air of a *grand seigneur* and there was something "vaguely second-rate" about his dress. "Interesting up to a point," Bruce wrote. "An intellectual sponge perhaps." He departed empty-handed.

As Bruce left Freyre's house, he was arrested for the second time that year. He asked a tidily dressed old man "with a big wart on his hand" for directions and had begun to walk down a track leading through a cane field to a wood when a Volkswagen drew up.

"The Director wishes to speak with you."

"Director of what?"

"The Prison."

Bruce was driven into an open prison and forced to wait. The prisoners had numbers on their clothes. He felt hot and angry. Presently, the Director returned from lunch, an enormous man with shiny black hair. He inspected Bruce's rucksack, his passport. He leafed through his notebook and read a description of a church painting that troubled him. Bruce claimed in *The Songlines* that "the Brazilian secret police" took what he had written to be a description, in code, of their own work on political prisoners—and filched the notebook.

The notebook, of course, survives. Alongside his account of his arrest is a description of the paintings. They were rather like his Aunt Jane's watercolours of pierced and naked men. In a Recife church he had described a San Sebastian "with a neat arrow-head thrusting out of his ear and beautiful loin cloth whipping in the wind tied with a golden sash". In more vivid torment was the negro slave Christ in the church of São Francisco in Ouro Preto. Narrow-waisted, yet with "voluminous curves of the body" the negro Christ had his "throat cut like a meat-knife slit" so that the apple wood showed through. The Director felt he understood. According to Bruce, "I am a hippie or a missionary. A priest. The most dangerous of all. What was I doing? I explain."

But the Director remained suspicious.

"How could you know Dr Gilberto Freyre?"

"Phone him up."

"No."

Again, the Director opened the passport. Burkina Faso. A Marxist state. What was Bruce doing sniffing round a prison, he asked?

"I didn't know it existed."

It couldn't have happened in a worse month. Didn't he see the notice? Bruce replied that he was talking to an old man.

"When did you learn Portuguese?"

"In Brazil."

"In five weeks?"

"Yes!"

The Director told Bruce this was impossible. His vocabulary was remarkable. "You must be very clever Mr C., but I assure you it's no use being clever with us."

THE STORY EXAGGERATED Bruce's mastery of Portuguese. Towards the end of March he returned to Acheson's flat in Rio. He remained in Brazil another week before flying to join Elizabeth in Europe, but in this time he embarked on an affair with the barman at the Othon Palace Hotel in Copacabana. One day he went for a drink with Acheson in the outside bar where they met João, wearing a green jacket. "He was not an educated Brazilian and didn't speak English," says Acheson. "Bruce had a go at Portuguese. They were chalk and cheese, but he was clearly smitten. He asked if he could use the flat to invite João back there while I was teaching."

The brief relationship, despite language difficulties, touched Bruce more deeply than he expected. A year later the image of the young man was still on his mind. He had asked Acheson to give João a present. Acheson had taken him a box of chocolates left over from Christmas. "I'm not entirely sure I approve of feeding João with Black Magic, unless he was going to the gym as he promised," Bruce wrote. "To my eternal regret there has been a six-month silence now. My replies in Portuguese were quite inadequate, both in literary and emotional content, to this kind of thing:

'Tenho pensado muito em voce de dia de noite a toda hora nao me esquece I do my love my beautiful, tenho vontade de te abracer te beijar sentir o seu corpe que tanto bem me faz. Quando esta frio eu penso em sair de casa a sua procure para me esquentar aquecer meu corpo com o seu calor, mas logo me lembre que e impossivel te encontrar pois voce esta tao longe de mim.' *

—which for rhythm and poetic expression could almost come out of the *Song of Songs*.

Ah! the geographical impossibility of passion!"

AFTER THREE AND a half months in Africa and Brazil, he had landed in Lisbon on 6 April. He found the city sad, communist posters everywhere. "One with sub-machine guns, hoe and spanner. Curious that they should have chosen the emblem of Cain." He visited the Gulbenkian Museum, but was depressed by the works of art enclosed in a bunker of concrete. "Anything less suitable for showing off French furniture hard to imagine." He missed João.

He took a train to Spain, to spend Easter with Elizabeth and Gertrude

* "I have been thinking of you a lot, day and night, all the time—don't forget me *I do my love my beautiful*, I really want to hug you, kiss you, feel your body that makes me feel so good. When it's cold I think about going out to look for you so that you can warm me, warm my body with your heat, but suddenly I remember that it's impossible to meet you because you are such a long way from me."

in Guadeloupe. It was on this journey that he committed to his notebook one of his most naked moments. He is transported without warning to the wrenching farewells of his childhood. "In train beside the Tagus. Yesterday feeling disembodied from the flight and now to tears, for one of the only times in my life, from separation from J. My father always to be departing."

He was nearly 37 and, like his Viceroy, he could no longer hide.

XXVI.

⚭

New York

The Greeks have the idea that there were limits
to the range of human behaviour and, if anyone
had the hubris to go beyond those limits, he
was struck down by fate. Well, one would agree.
—BC to Michael Ignatieff

Two months after returning to England, Bruce fell helplessly in love with a 27-year-old Australian stockbroker. He met Donald Richards on 25 June 1977, at Paul and Penny Levy's wedding in Oxfordshire. Among the guests was the artist Keith Milow. He introduced Bruce to a handsome Australian covered in hay. "We'd been rolling in the golden cornfield adjacent to the party," says Milow. "Something clicked between them which I was not prepared for."

Millington-Drake, who would entertain Bruce and Donald on Patmos, described their meeting as "the big break in Bruce's life". Before, he had had passing affairs with men. "This was the first time he'd committed his life to a man. Bruce was infatuated with him."

Donald had fled Brisbane where his father worked for a company making asbestos roofing material. Like Bruce, he was a boy from the suburbs who had managed to remake himself. Where Bruce was an extrovert, Donald was socially reticent but, unlike Bruce, uninhibitedly gay. "He was a sexy, whorey, homosexual who jumped into bed immediately and was terrific," says Peter Adam. "It was the one area where he was very secure."

Donald used his sexuality to advance modest cultural ambitions. At Queensland University, the poet Val Vallis had introduced him to opera. "He was an elegant creature, the nearest thing to a well-bred cat. His movements were gracious without being effeminate, but he wasn't ruggedly masculine either."

He was much brighter than people gave him credit for in London and

New York. He won a Queen's Medal and a first in History and Government, but his soft-spoken manner could camouflage his intelligence. "There is absolutely no way round the fact that he was a bore," says Bruce's doctor, Patrick Woodcock. "He was Mr Cliché. 'There's nothing like the English strawberry . . . Fred Astaire, you know, really was the most marvellous dancer.' If you didn't want to go to bed with him it was a difficult evening."

Deeply insecure on many levels, Donald had a talent for making useful people fall in love with him. "Donald certainly made use of his sexuality, many people did that," says Adam. "But he had more to follow up. If he had an interesting social life it was also because he was good-looking, intelligent, young, from abroad." After arriving in England on a scholarship, he reported back to a friend in Australia, Clinton Tweedie, how in London he lived with an aristocrat, "Sebastian Sackville-West". In fact his lover was Sebastian Walker, the children's book publisher, for whom Donald wrote two books: *Know Your Dogs* ("Like the evolution of the human race, the evolution of the dog has been a long and puzzling process") and *Know Your Cats* ("Cats have personalities, just as humans do. In many cases their natures develop according to the kind of household they live in and the amount of care and attention their owners give them"). Donald lived with Walker in Alwyne Place in Canonbury. There was even a mock wedding. But he was not faithful.

Donald's predilections, sharpened by amyl nitrite, are suggested by Tweedie, a modern art collector from Brisbane. In 1983, Donald had moved to a small flat in Covent Garden. That summer he invited Tweedie to use it while he was away. Finding the place "lousy with bed bugs", Tweedie summoned Westminster Council to come and spray it. Two burly cockneys arrived one morning at 7 a.m. They took up the rugs and then lifted the bed to reveal, neatly stacked, a cache of 15 dildos "in all shapes, lengths and colours", three lengths of rope, a beaded corset and a Polaroid of Donald bent over a Le Corbusier chair "with a smile on his face and impaled on an enormous dildo held by a black hand". Tweedie hastily packed the objects into a Cathay Pacific travel bag.

Donald's allure for Bruce was his exuberant libido. "Bruce saw Donald as a challenge," says Milow, "very wild and sexual and hard to keep up with." He was heavy browed, possessed of "unbelievable eyes with black edges to them," according to Elizabeth. Adam understood the chemistry. "Bruce quite liked tarty men and he justified them if they could also read Rilke and know that Kafka wasn't a deodorant."

From 1977 to 1982, Donald acted as his sexual mentor. The gay world was a territory to be mastered in the same way as Sotheby's, Edinburgh or Patagonia.

THE AFFAIR CONTINUED behind Sebastian Walker's back. Bruce once asked Peter Eyre to go with him to a Berlioz concert. "Donald was there with Sebby and Bruce wanted to watch him." Such furtiveness tinged the relationship with farce. Bill Katz, the New York dealer, recalled how he saw Donald drop Walker at a railway station—"and two minutes later Bruce appeared, as if out of a bad movie".

Linklater once met Bruce unexpectedly in a bar with Donald. "Bruce was looking incredibly woofterish and I'm not sure he didn't have eye make-up. He was uncharacteristically reticent and unfriendly. He was in a completely different compartment and I wasn't supposed to be there."

The affair surprised Kasmin. "In no way when we were in Africa did Bruce disguise the fact he was partial to black bottoms. My impression was that he had adventures from time to time, usually when on a trip. But he never seemed to be *driven* by sex at all, less than most." Kasmin's back bedroom at 8 Gloucester Gate was one of Bruce's billets in the late 1970s. Kasmin once returned home after a night flight to be met by a sheepish Bruce. "It's slightly embarrassing. Could you take a short walk round the block? I can't explain—*it's too complex.*" Kasmin understood there to be someone in Bruce's room. He dumped his bag in the hall and went for a walk. "I was pretty pissed off. But that's how I knew Donald was the real thing."

Hodgkin was especially interested to hear of Bruce's infatuation. That year the married artist had fallen in love with a much younger man. Bruce had proved unsympathetic. "I can't think the H. H. situation is all that painful," he wrote to Welch. "The trouble is that it got out of hand. In the English 'art world' his became the most publicised private life of the century, and he didn't know how to handle it. When everyone else over-dramatizes your life, it inevitably becomes more dramatic." Bruce, who had once told Hodgkin "it would be so awful not to be in control", soon found himself embroiled in a more or less identical drama.

If Donald loved Bruce, it was a love that could accommodate a mul-titude of partners. By keeping out of reach, he generated in Bruce unfa-miliar pangs of jealousy and longing. "Talked to D. R. in morning," reads a rare reference in his notebook. "Bitter sweet phone call. Less obtainable than ever—was at Oxford exploring the bisexuality of under-graduates."

Upon learning that Hodgkin had become involved in a triangle with Walker and Donald, Bruce attacked him at a party. "What the hell are you doing sleeping with Donald and Sebby?" Hodgkin says, "I was full of tears. Bruce in one of his many borrowed voices said: 'Don't be so lachrymose!'"

Hodgkin sensed that Donald was flattered by Bruce's love yet found it awkward. This is borne out by a breezy letter from Donald, by now an opera buff, after a visit to see *Carmen* at the Edinburgh Festival. His letter to Bruce, the only one to survive, is shot through with the stock observations which animate the text of *Know Your Cats*. "I do love the borders (tho I remember your bad times in this town!) . . . I do apologise for not writing; but I have been paralysed since returning from NY—with work, swollen glands (I think I've contracted mumps from Jaimie Astor), a venereal scare (all OK!), ennui . . . I long to see you, so I can relax, and tell you *everything*. Rest assured I do look forward to *that*. Meanwhile take care, and keep writing, with my love x x x x D."

Bruce behaved as if stricken by Donald, but Hodgkin questions the depth of his feelings. "He'd come out. But it wasn't real, more like a garnish to his identity. And it didn't save him from sentimentality. When he talked about being in love with Donald, it wasn't about that: it was about Donald being in love with him. I don't think Bruce ever passionately loved anybody."

BRUCE INDICATED HIS painful situation to Sunil Sethi. "Such a monumental depression that I couldn't drag myself out of bed in the morning for fear of what frightful things the day had in store. I *think* I gave you to understand I was going back in such haste to see someone. This is not my usual practice: usually I delay departure for England (*Le tombeau vert*) until the last possible moment. However, when the someone met me at the airport, I knew that something was seriously wrong (frightening how people can change in a month), and for three weeks the wrongness built up in a crocodile of misery, while I battled at my typewriter with that beastly woman who had ruined my journey to India [Mrs Gandhi]." A month later, Bruce revealed that the someone "is Australian". "The fact is," he wrote, "I have left England feeling exceptionally bruised, bruised not the least by some of my closest friends, who use my obvious discomfiture to turn it into heartless gossip. There is something horribly claustrophobic about my country and yet . . . I cannot get used to the life of exile."

Flying to Boston that December, Bruce wrote in his notebook: "England more depressing than ever. The spirit of meanness and envy. Idiotic posturing. I am terrified in England of allowing myself to get drawn into an old-fashioned nostalgic conservatism. That kind of attitude would lead to an intellectual hardening of the arteries which already I see in many of my contemporaries."

To escape the "heartless gossip", Bruce took Donald abroad. One weekend they stayed with the fashion designer Loulou de la Falaise near Fontainebleau. "We shared an ecstasy pill," says la Falaise. "Bruce started winding forget-me-nots through Donald's hair and we said: 'Now listen, *enough* of that Lady Chatterley stuff!' He'd come to us because we were 'family' and less critical."

Their most frequent destination was New York, where Bruce had access to his mother-in-law's apartment on East 79 Street. Bruce had no reservations about implicating his wife. In June 1978 Elizabeth wrote to Gertrude with a request: "Two friends of ours called Sebastian Walker & Donald Richards want to know if they can stay in the apt . . . They could go in the double. They are really nice—great help to me as they're opera fans & go to everything so I can always have company. They tell me when things are worth going to & & get me tickets. Just what I've always wanted. Sebastian is an editor at Chatto & Windus & Donald is a stockbroker & I'm sure you'd like them if you met them."

Whatever Elizabeth suspected of her husband's activities, she did not let on. She was used to people falling in love with him, or wanting to possess him, and had taught herself not to be threatened. "He was constantly gyrating on his own axis, to cause a sensation, to find a sensation. That's what made him so exciting, but you couldn't get close to him. People thought they did. Half the time he tried to get away." Given his secrecy, she could not easily untangle the nature of his affairs. Further, she chose not to. "It didn't worry me. It was just: 'Oh, here we go again.' I always felt he was going to come back. There was no point in confronting him. He didn't like show downs at all. Occasionally, I *would* wonder why on earth we'd come back from somewhere having had a very nice time and he'd simply drop out of sight. He didn't tell me, but I worked out that he'd gone off to see Donald."

Gertrude allowed Bruce free run of the apartment when she was at Geneseo. She was less aware than Elizabeth about what Bruce got up to in New York. Hodgkin, expecting to find Bruce installed alone, once surprised Mrs Chanler in her sitting-room. "She was sitting with a *comme il faut* young man," says Hodgkin, "very expensive clothes, brilliant, doctorate—and black. And he was in New York because, says Mrs Chanler leaning forward, he's Bruce's friend. 'That's how we met, isn't it?' To me, she said: 'I suppose you're looking for Bruce?' I asked, 'Where is he?' The black man replied: "He's out running round the park trying to keep Old Father Time at bay'."

Bruce's excursions with Donald Richards to New York coincided with a point at which the gay world became the chic scene: universal, glamorous, freewheeling and not so underground. He felt free to introduce his lover to old friends as well as to new.

In December 1980, Bruce took Donald to a dinner given for him by Freddy Eberstadt. Bruce had suggested the guests. His marriage had put him in touch with high society in New York, but it was not the sort of society that appealed to Elizabeth. That night they included the opera director Robert Wilson, Kynaston MacShine from the Museum of Modern Art, Keith Milow, Edward Albee, Jerzy Kosinski, Diana Vreeland and Gloria Vanderbilt. There was also there Pam Bell, an Australian poet whom Bruce had met in London. "The people were so grand you weren't introduced," she says. "'What was your name again?' I said to Jerzy Kosinski. You looked down a long line of tuberoses and there was Gloria Vanderbilt with diamonds literally from one tit to another. She looked like she'd robbed the burial mound at Ur." Bell thought Bruce that evening was at his most manic. "He had on a dinner jacket and bow-tie and jeans and high-heeled yellow boots. Every now and then he threw his knees up to his chin and collapsed in hyena laughter. His face was a Halloween mask: ugly, hysterical, grotesque."

Bruce's behaviour could be explained by his infatuation. "He was arse over tea-kettle about Donald," says Eberstadt. "If one had ever seen a passionate relationship, this was it. He talked constantly about Donald in terms I could not understand. 'Don't you think he's so amusing and bright?' while all you'd heard Donald say was 'Shut the door'. The Donald he talked about and the Donald I could see across the room seemed to have nothing to do with one another—and this from the most perceptive talker you're likely to come across in a lifetime. But he knew Donald, and I did not and I guess we were both happy with that situation."

Baldly apparent to Eberstadt was the fact that Donald did not reciprocate. "At the far side of the room he was cruising Robert Wilson."

Donald continued in flamboyant pursuit of Wilson at a benefit gala where John Richardson, Picasso's biographer, was also present. "Bruce stood back watching Donald operate. I remember him commentating with masochistic glee: "Isn't he *hateful*? Now just watch him for a moment. He's after Robert Wilson. He's rubbing up against him. It hasn't worked, my dear. Poor Donald is looking so stricken. Isn't he vile? But I am *absolutely obsessed*'." Bruce discussed his passion with strange detachment, says Richardson, as if it were a rather interesting symptom. "It was curious that the only person with whom he could become obsessed was an incredibly third-rate character who behaved unbelievably badly."

George Steiner in an essay on Ernst Jünger describes the German writer's "terrible detachment" as the focus of the dandy who masters experience by elegance: "The dandy confronts the sum of life, but keeps it at gauntlet's length." Something of this pose is hinted at in Bruce's journal entry for Tuesday 17 February 1979. "DR easing up gradually. He looked congealed with a kind of terror at the sight of Kynaston's apartment, but began to thaw when we went to the Chelsea Hotel . . ." The entry comes from a time when there were few boundaries left. "Next day worked in the morning: but at 12.30 we went to see Robert Mapplethorpe."

IN HIS ESSAY for the Asia House exhibition in 1970, Bruce cited Diogenes's deprecation of city life and wrote of how, locked within a city's walls, men "committed every outrage against one another as if this were the sole object of their coming together".

Mapplethorpe's studio, wrote his biographer Patricia Morrisroe, was a port of call for men with every perversion. "They dressed up as women, SS troopers and pigs. One wore baby clothes and a bonnet, drank from a bottle and defecated into his diaper." Another liked having initials carved into his skin.

Bruce was photographed on one of his visits to Mapplethorpe's studio loft on Bond Street. In 1983, he repaid the compliment by contributing an introduction to *Body and Eyes*, Mapplethorpe's book of portraits of the female body-builder Lisa Lyon. The novelist Edmund White judges Bruce's introduction as "by far the best essay ever written on Mapplethorpe", but it reveals no less of its author. In 1974, Bruce had held up Cartier-Bresson as one of the models for *In Patagonia*. He was now evolving a new aesthetic for his second book: the exotic and sadistic history of a slave-trader. He found one aspect of it on the walls of Mapplethorpe's studio.

Bruce observed "a black bedroom behind a white wire-netting cage and, ranged around, the paraphernalia of an irreverent perversity: a scorpion in a case, a bronze of Mephistopheles and a much smaller bronze of the Devil with his toasting fork." Here Mapplethorpe took his "haunting portraits of men women and a series of 'sex pictures' that froze—in more or less liturgical poses—the intimate activities of the so-called 'leather scene'." Bruce is as incisive about Mapplethorpe as he was about Jünger. "His vision is cold and sharp. He is fascinated by the satanic, and confronts his night-biased world with the elegant and melancholic stance of the dandy. His eye for a face is the eye of a novelist in search of a character; his eye for a body that of a classical sculptor in search of an 'ideal'. His sitters—whether celebrities or pick-ups, beautiful girls or his black friends—seem mesmerised not by the lens but by his presence, and temporarily transported into a dream world."

The photographer told him: "I really don't know how I take these pictures," but Bruce, who lit his prose in the same way, understood Mapplethorpe's techniques. Mapplethorpe's effect was achieved not by contact but by detachment, seeing with the clarity of first impressions and avoiding the mess of intimacy. "Except for a few close friends, Robert rarely took pictures of the same sitter twice—an hour or two of intimacy, an inimitable image, and that was all."

"Talk about birds of a feather!" says John Richardson, who knew them both. "Mapplethorpe was a shoddy version of Bruce."

That Mapplethorpe should have photographed him is a sign of Bruce's effect, also of their complicity. "I, too, was photographed by Robert," says Adam, who was one of Bruce's lovers during this period. "But Bruce was one of the few people Robert took with his clothes on. To use Mapplethorpe as a society photographer does seem to be a little bit far-fetched."

Possibly this was the occasion when Mapplethorpe suggested to Bruce he might like to meet his brilliant writer friend, Edmund White. Mapplethorpe telephoned White, who lived nearby. Bruce walked around, rang the bell. White wrote down what happened next: "Maybe it was the excitement of druggy, sexy New York before AIDS, or of the Mapplethorpe connection, but seconds after he'd come into my apartment we started fooling around with each other."

Many of Bruce's partners at this period had the attributes of Edmund White: good-looking, interesting and famous. Even if Bruce was not as guilt-free as White or Keith Milow or Sam Wagstaff, he knew how to pick. These artistic, highly intelligent people were different from old-fashioned intellectual homosexuals like Forster and Auden who could only sleep with the lower orders. "Now you went to bed with your own kind," says Adam. "By pushing back the limits, homosexuals . . . experienced an exhilaration, a joy few people know," he wrote in his autobiography *Not Drowning but Waving*. "They had arrived at a point where society would have been free of the hypocrisy of sexual guilt it had carried for centuries." Without this feeling of real joy and liberation Bruce would not have travelled down this road. "Maybe by joining in that dance of death," says Adam, "he thought to conquer his terrible guilt feeling."

Anonymous sex was also seductive. Mapplethorpe's "night-biased world" was based on S & M clubs like the Anvil or the Mineshaft, a two-storey warehouse in the meat-packing district on the corner of Little Twelfth and Washington Streets. Here Bruce could enter a sex department store where everything in the world was available. People were tied up and beaten; there were baths where they were pissed on. Muscular men jangled about in chains wearing nothing but leather jockstraps, caps and masks; or lay back in slings, waiting to be fist-fucked, their legs up, taking poppers, eyes rolled back, moaning. And everywhere huge pots of Crisco lard.

The Mineshaft, a former slaughterhouse, was not to everyone's taste. Donald once took along Sebastian Walker who confessed afterwards how repelled he was by the degree of promiscuity and "the image of people lying in rows on their stomach waiting to be buggered and an awful lot of blood around".

Bruce left so many crossed-trails, it is hard to gauge how much he participated in, or enjoyed, Mapplethorpe's hard-core world. He spoke to a female friend of going to the Anvil, "sticking your prick through a hole in the door, what fun it was—but maybe he was trying to *épater*, to shock us." A black teacher, Louis Grant, told Welch that "Bruce was behaving badly" in New York: "He was not doing things right, something was going wrong." Given the emotional triangle of which he was a part, it is likely he was exposed to Walker's conflicting attitudes. Richardson could not picture him as a whole-hearted participant. "I used to go a lot to baths in the Village: the Eagle's Nest, the Spike, the Ramrod. They came and went. I was the old hand. I never saw Bruce in any. I didn't have the feeling Bruce was an habitué." Richardson once took Bruce to a leather bar for blacks. "He was too grand for them. It's no good being sort of la-di-da. He stuck out in any company, whether in a gay bar or drawing room by playing the star bit."

Bruce was unforthcoming with Richardson as with everyone else about his sex life. "I never felt he was nearly as much a cruiser or sexually-obsessed person as most of my gang. But I think Bruce had a lot to hide. I think he liked danger. I always assumed he liked being violated in some way and preferably by brigands, gypsies, South American cowboys. It was part of his nomad pattern, to go off into the desert and get raped by Afghan brigands. It's something Lady Hester Stanhope-ish. It wasn't so much the sex as the sauce it came in, some Afghan chieftain draped in a cartridge belt."

One of Bruce's notes for his Viceroy reads: "As if to purge himself in blood, he worked in the abattoir." He told Ben Gannon, an Australian television producer: "You know Donald experimented with everything in New York and so did I." Donald, certainly, participated. He was the relatively anonymous subject of a Mapplethorpe study in which two black hands are photographed gripping an erect penis. Likewise, the hero of Blaise Cendrars's *Moravagine* "experiences a sensual pleasure in plunging at last into the most anonymous abyss of human poverty. Nothing discouraged or disgusted him, not even the enervating promiscuity of the poor folks who took [him] in."

THE AUTHOR GITA Mehta saw Bruce in London and New York and New Delhi over this period. "The whole point of promiscuity is that you avoid big emotions, you don't trail any weed." In India, Mehta was with a gay friend when Bruce dropped in. " 'Have we met?' he asked my friend, who replied, 'Oh, we had a raging affair five years ago.' Bruce's promiscuity probably was escapist," she says. "He found his danger in his solitariness. *In Patagonia* was about the danger of travelling alone."

Bruce's tendency to view himself as a separate self gave him enormous freedom to misbehave. Promiscuity provided release for a streak of masochism. Bruce's notebooks make frequent mention of "the pleasures of pain". David Sulzberger once drove with him and Elizabeth to Clouds Hill, T. E. Lawrence's cottage in Dorset. "Bruce was aware that comparisons were being made. He was very silent. He loved it. I found it very sinister: tiny, *faux*-monastic, sadomasochistic." Bruce later gave the National Trust pamphlet on Clouds Hill to Loulou de la Falaise's husband, Thadée. "He was fascinated by this lodging, thought it quite wonderful," says Thadée. "He pointed to the leather couch in the photograph: 'That's where he was whipped!' He wasn't interested enough in people to have a proper sexual relationship. He had this masochistic fantasy of being overpowered and abused by bandits." The Australian novelist Murray Bail, who would become one of Bruce's most intimate correspondents, was conscious of this strain when he visited Bruce in England. On 24 October 1987, Bail wrote in his notebook: "He told of a Russian he'd met in Prague. Dark ex-monk who after being harsh with women would slash his face with a razor, his face criss-crossed multiplying the torment."

As Ivory observed, a part of Bruce responded to the idea of being violated. "Always with Bruce there was this playing-with-fire thing, seeing how far you could go. He did all these things which are dangerous: he did literally go to the edge in various treks he made to remote villages. That also was a testing of himself." Sometimes he trekked too far. "Bruce was doll-like," says Magouche Fielding, "also devilish. I was worried he'd get murdered."

One night in July 1978, the collector Paul Walter, another of Mapplethorpe's subjects, was walking with a friend through the gay quarter of Barcelona when he came upon a dazed Bruce in a rough area near the port. He was alone and dishevelled, wearing a white linen suit and a white shirt practically unbuttoned. "He was all in white," says Walter, "except there was a trail of blood on his shirt." Walter's first thought was that Bruce had been beaten up. "He didn't look like he was in trouble, but he looked like he may have been." Walter waited for Bruce to recognise him, give a signal. But he walked on.

In conversation with Arkady in *The Songlines*, Bruce described a visit to the Nemadi in Mauritania with the authority of one who has lived among the tribe. In fact, he was with the Nemadi only two or three days. One of the tribe was an old woman who smiled at him. He told Arkady: "I live with that old woman's smile." The sentiment may be honest, but one cannot help feeling a little duped. It is the same with Bruce's nightlife. It would be more in character for him not to participate—and then to turn the story into something fantastic, suggesting the reverse.

He told Muensterberger just how much he enjoyed playing the role of voyeur. In becoming a writer, he had legitimised that impulse. At a party in London in the early 1980s the photographer, Russell Dexter, was screwing Nureyev, who was leaning out of the window, when suddenly both men became aware of someone standing behind them in the doorway, watching. It was Bruce.

BRUCE'S SEXUAL AWAKENING through Donald Richards coincided with the emergence of his literary fame.

In June 1978, the 38-year-old Bruce was working unhappily in Spain on *The Viceroy of Ouidah*. "On Monday, stuck in bed at 10 a.m. on a bright sunny morning, Tom Maschler my publisher rang to say that *In Patagonia* had won the Hawthornden Prize for imaginative literature (previous winners include Evelyn Waugh and Dom Moraes!). So I stopped mooning and pulled myself together."

In England, the book had sold nearly 6,000 copies in hardback. But its publication in America one month after winning the Hawthornden eclipsed even Maschler's expectations. Bruce's editor at Summit Press, Jim Silberman, had bought American rights for $5,000 after reading Theroux's review in *The Times*.

One after another the critics stood up.

"*In Patagonia* takes travelling back to its magic roots," wrote Alasdair Reid in the *New Yorker*. "We must look with enormous anticipation to wherever Mr Chatwin goes for us next." In the *Detroit News* James Vesely wrote that Bruce was "the kind of fellow Noel Coward had in mind when he wrote his song about mad dogs and Englishmen who go out in the midday sun." In the *New York Review of Books*, Sybille Bedford began her review: "*In Patagonia* is one of the most exhilarating travel books I have read. Chatwin has a young and individual voice and yet writes in the tradition of the traveler scholar or the traveler poet—one of the *vrais voyageurs* of Baudelaire's lines, *ceux-la seuls qui partent / Pour partir, coeurs legers semblables aux ballons*." The *New York Times Book Review* carried two reviews within a fortnight. The first, by Ted Morgan, believed Bruce's book the equal of Graham Greene's *Journey without Maps*; Somerset Maugham's *The Gentleman in the Parlour* and Paul Theroux's *Great Railway Bazaar*. Hilton Kramer, in the same newspaper, judged *In Patagonia* "a little masterpiece of travel, history and adventure". Kramer was not the first critic to be left "most curious" about the author.

BRUCE HAD RENTED a house near Ronda. "Reviews from U.S. to burn the eyes out," he wrote to Elizabeth in Holwell. "Doesn't mean to say they won't come up with a stinker, but mentioned in the same breath as *Gulliver's Travels, Out of Africa, Eothen, Monasteries of the Levant*, Kipling's *Letters of Travel* etc. People lose all sense of proportion." There was even a *Rolling Stone* cartoon showing the author wandering about Patagonia with a cup of tea in his hand and a bowler hat. "The one that did go really to my heart was a Robert Taylor *(Boston Globe)*: 'It celebrates the recovery of something inspiring memory, as if Proust could in fact taste his madeleine'—*ENFIN* somebody's got the point."

He said to his mother: "Who knows? I might even make some money."

Most astonishing was the response of Elizabeth's cousin, Chanler Chapman. Writing from his hospital bed in Rhineback, New York, Chanler warned Gertrude: "my mother's namesake, your concupiscent, luminous, spangled daughter, Elizabeth, will have trouble with Bruce Chatwin. This electric conversational account of the greatest most terrifying wasteland in the world is a 5 alarm message from Orion's Belt . . . It compels belief. The man writes the way he looks in the snapshot on the jacket blurb. Bruce Chatwin is suddenly & conclusively shown to be a writer on the same ultimate level of excellence as John Livingstone Lowes in *Road to Xanadu.*"

The plaudits continued as the sales passed 20,000 in hardback. In December 1978, *In Patagonia* was chosen by the *New York Times Book Review* staff as their book of the year. And in May 1979 Bruce flew to New York to receive another prize: the E. M. Forster Award, presented by the American Academy of Arts and Letters. "Ushered into a colossal cocktail with the faces of every book-jacket exposed behind their martinis," he wrote in his journal. "All the sacred cows hauled out for the lunch." In the room were Elizabeth Hardwick, Derek Walcott, Joseph Brodsky, Allen Ginsberg, I. B. Singer, Susan Sontag, Kurt Vonnegut and Caroline Blackwood. "Barbara Tuchmann gave me my prize. *In Patagonia* apparently . . . put me 'in company with the great travel writers' . . . Very curious my new literary life."

Bruce embraced it giddily. "After *In Patagonia,* he became an overnight sensation," says Eberstadt. Just how much so was signified by an interview with William Shawn at the *New Yorker*. "The BIG NEWS is this," Bruce wrote to Elizabeth, "when Mr Chatwin was finally, after a positively Byzantine series of manoeuvres, ushered into Mr Shawn's pure, intellectually Bauhaus office he rose and said it was nice to meet a *New Yorker* writer who had never written for the *New Yorker*. The upshot was a commission to do my Chekhovian trip through Eastern Europe directly I finish Mr de S. plus as many thousand dollars as I need."

His new sense of worth revealed itself in his changing attitude towards writers previously admired, like Paul Theroux whose enthusiastic review of *In Patagonia* had contributed to its American publication. Two years earlier, he had praised Theroux. Now, in a letter to Sethi, he was less sure. "Paul Theroux's *The Old Patagonian Express* (such a cheat the title!) although it's a success commercially is not good. He happens to be a friend of mine, though, and if I can't quite stomach what he does, he is one of the more lively spirits around London. In November we gave a combined talk to the Royal Geographical Society, which completely bewildered types like Lord Hunt, as we took the audience breathlessly through a literary excursion to the Antipodes."

Theroux gave an account of that evening in *Granta 44*. "In it, I suggested that he was something of a mythomaniac and had a screaming laugh and bizarre conceits that provoked him to such behaviour as monologuing to the mountaineers Lord Hunt and Chris Bonington about great climbs he had made."

Bruce also appeared with Theroux on BBC2's *Book Programme* with Jan Morris "in her/his twinset and pearls. Going back to London in the taxi she/he said: 'I was so interested by what you said about the dangers of travel. You see, having travelled all over the world, both as a male and as a female, I can safely say it's far safer to travel as a female'."

Bruce was not part of an intellectual cabal in London, but in New York he infiltrated several. "New York was important for him," says Elisabeth Sifton, who became his American editor. "He made deep friendships and his artistic life regenerated." He mixed with Susan Sontag, Lisa Lyon, Jasper Johns, Bill Katz, Loulou de la Falaise, Barbara Epstein, Robert Hughes, Hans Magnus Enzensberger. "He seemed to know people in all sorts of spheres, from the ultra rich to the chic," says Enzensberger who first met him with Hughes at the home of a Brooklyn heiress. "The three of us erupted in conversation. Bruce had such a lot of éclat. He was very brilliant, very good-looking, very stylish, but also something of an alien. Millionaire ladies were impressed to be his inferior in some way. He managed them very well, with a sort of hauteur. He was almost French in his stance. He had something then of the dandy which never disappeared. But when he got outside in the street, I sensed a sea-change. He was very simple, not interested in this any more. It was clear he belonged to us, he was an intellectual."

The critic John Russell says: "When he was in New York his presence had a real (not a sham) glitter, as if he wanted not so much to charm as to subjugate everyone he met. He also dressed down to a degree that had a dandyism in reverse—unusual at that time—and would appear at some fashionable lunch in a collar-less shirt (no tie, of course). He got away with it."

He enjoyed his success. "He was vulnerable to incredible wealth and aristocracy," says Rushdie. "He was vulnerable to old ladies who were vulnerable to him. He had a wonderful array of international battle-axes. Wherever he would turn up there would be some fantastically tough old lady who would want to spend all her time with him and he with her. He multiplied himself all the time and that's another way of saying perhaps he stretched himself too thin." He became a walker for Diana Vreeland, the doyenne of the fashion world whose demented extravagance he understood ("Pink is the navy blue of India"). He ate with Susan Sontag in Chinatown. "He was the only person whom I could invite to eat a *hakka*—fried intestines and toe-nails". And he met Jackie Onassis.

"CALLED AT 10.40 5th to pick up J. O." Confirmation of Bruce's glamorous status was his friendship with Onassis, about whom he spoke at length, alluding to shared intimacies. "He met Jackie two or three times," says Katz, "but she did say she was charmed by him."

One evening in December 1978, Bruce arrived at Onassis's apartment to escort her to a dinner party. "Was it John [her son] who came down in the lift in a vaguely bike-boy's jacket? Thin, washed and face enigmatic— beautiful distant smile, tight hips in blue jeans on the way for forbidden pleasures." Upstairs, he cast his eyes around the apartment: exquisite eighteenth-century French chair, straw mat on floor, lacquer table piled with magazines, an album which said "Jack 1962" on the spine. "She came in: in black gold pyjama pants, looking wonderful. The whisper is conspiratorial not affected. The whisper of a naughty child egging you on to do something mildly wicked."

Bruce told Kenneth Rose how "mucking out a barn in Wales he recalled that it was exactly a week since he had been having a drink with Jackie Onassis". Her effect on him can be seen in a letter he wrote not long afterwards to Elizabeth:

"Dear Maxine

An impossible piece of paper to write on. Life in New York highly social. Dinner parties every night. Escorting Mrs Onassis to the opera next Thursday. Met her again with the John Russells, and my God she's fly. Far more subtle than any American woman I've ever met. A man called Charles Rosen, who has a reputation for being THE CLEVEREST MAN IN AMERICA, was pontificating about the poet Aretino, and since nobody reacted or contradicted him, turned his discourse into a lecture. He was halfway through when she turned on him with her puppy-like eyes, smiled and said: 'Yes, of course, you can see it *all* in the Titian portrait'."

Old friends shrank from the new Bruce. "He had changed," says Tilo von Watzdorf. Erskine remembered how he came back from America and said: "I've just met the most wonderful person in my life. She's so wonderful, I can't tell you how wonderful." It struck Erskine the tone was one of snobbery. "Or had he found merit in someone previously deemed to be spurious? I was a bit sad. I felt I'd slightly lost out with Bruce. I stopped seeing him when he was much too busy being lionised by *glitterati*. I thought: 'He's in another room now and it's not a room I terribly like being in'."

Erskine was not alone in feeling neglected. Welch had introduced Bruce to Onassis, but Bruce now avoided the Welchs when he came to America. Welch wrote to him, "All our encounters of the past few years have been useless: too many people about. Neither of us at his best under mob conditions." Edith Welch felt Bruce had turned away from them in favour of Mapplethorpe's razzle-dazzle world. His childhood and Marlborough friend Guy Norton saw him at a restaurant in London: "I said to Bruce 'How are you?' and he dismissed me. I wasn't surprised. I'd heard from friends in the Midlands how he didn't want to be reminded he belonged to that circle."

Peter Adam thought that Bruce had become "swamped" by his own silliness. "He was aware—how could he not be?—that he was special. It was a tragedy that he diluted his currency with this silliness, being impressed by people, running after the famous, Nureyev, Jackie Onassis. Why want to be a Truman Capote when you could be a Büchner?"

THE BRUCE CHATWIN of the New York years is one aspect of his life that many close friends, even his wife, could hardly have anticipated. Their puzzlement runs parallel to those who worked with him at Sotheby's and were frankly astonished to discover that he had become a writer. Having immersed himself in that world he was equally capable of rejecting, or denying it.

James Ivory was a close friend for two years in the decade before Manhattan. In 1972, he took a photograph of Bruce on their drive through Washington State to Oregon, and in a way that image was frozen because it was not developed until 1998. When Ivory had the film processed and looked at the spirit of his friend 26 years on, and already ten years dead, he reflected that he might have misjudged Bruce.

"Bruce loved to have people caress and fondle him (in private). I think he found sex personally very self-affirmative, and as natural and easy as eating. He seemed to be without hang-ups, or guilt. But when I study the photograph I took of him in the Oregon desert, his image springs out at me and suggests there was a man there I might not have known as well as I thought. He must have had a more dangerous, a more self-destructive kind of sex drive than I guessed. I can't help thinking of the trip he told me about that he made to Russia in order to run down some modern paintings, and how, when he went to view this secret collection, its keeper, big and brawny, once Bruce was inside proceeded to lock the door. Not to keep the KGB out, Bruce said laughing, but in order to passionately throw him down on the floor, where he raped the daylights out of him. A true story or a heavily fantasised one, embellished for dining out? But why should it not have been true? I think he must have experienced, and not just fantasised about, such encounters in the nomad lands he loved to explore. His readiness, his eagerness, in prim Western societies to have someone unbutton his flies, must have had more violent developments in the much wilder, far-off Oriental places he trudged through—not looking very different from the rosy-faced, overgrown schoolboy in the photograph I took. He must have been a sexual magnet in those lands; he must have seemed easy prey: a male version of those romantic nineteenth-century European ladies who travelled to the East to paint watercolours and were captured by sheikhs and kept in a harem for 1001 nights. Is this possibility part of Bruce Chatwin's image and legend?"

XXVII.

༄

Oh, mais c'est du Flaubert!

> *He felt a slight pain in his chest. The pain came and*
> *went in twinges below his heart. It was not serious.*
> *This particular pain came when he was in England.*
> *It was his English pain. He greeted it as an old*
> *friend. It was the pain that told him to head south.*
> —From BC's unpublished story,
>   "November"

THE CHANGES IN his life may be reflected in Bruce's fictionalised life of de Souza: a generous man engaged in an abominable traffic, a reluctant exile who fought his natural good impulses to conduct his low life. "I wanted to show in the book how the fate of the slave trader is really rather the same as the fate of someone who might be an executive of Shell or a mining company, who's originally a good man who gets bound up in the impossible economic system and then is actually dragged down by it."

The changes also colour the difficult composition of *The Viceroy of Ouidah*. Bruce was tormented by the question of *where* to write his book. From now until the end of his life he was in search of what he described to Kasmin as "this mythical beast 'the place to write in'".

He had written to Kasmin from Bahia: "I think I'll sit out the summer at the farm because *this* will need a lot of other men's books if it's to be anything—though I'm still taken with the story." The prospect of Gloucestershire, however, filled him with dread. "As you know I find it very hard to work there," he wrote to Elizabeth from Benin. He wrote to Kasmin of "the state of hysteria that comes over me at Holwell Farm", and in a letter to Acheson explained how, "wherever I go, particularly in deserts, the image of that misty Gloucestershire valley passes before my eyes. But one should never go near it, except to recharge the IDEA of it once every two or three years."

Once asked what he did in the country, Bruce said: "I just pace up and down and stand against the wall and I do this," and he banged his head against a wall. One evening in London he had a sad encounter. "At the end of the Burlington Arcade a thin black boy in a black leather jacket was beating his white crash helmet with his head still in it against the lamp-post. Then he hit his fist against the trashcan, bruising his knuckles. I asked what was the matter. He smiled sheepishly, wriggled, shuddered and said 'Oh, I'm so fed up!' I asked if I could help, but he said, 'You can't do nothing.'

"Coming back 5 minutes later across Piccadilly, police cars with hooting sirens were roaring up in the street. He had lobbed a brick through the jeweller's window. A man with white hands was removing a diamond and enamel necklace off its grey velour neck stand. A couple from Chicago said: 'He probably comes from Chicago. The blacks in Chicago carry on like that.'

"He had run off . . ."

Bruce felt a natural sympathy for the boy. He, too, had exhausted the alternatives. He was boxed in. Nothing in the end could relieve him, except the writing.

"THOSE OF US who presume to write books would appear to fall into two categories," Bruce wrote in an article for *House and Garden*. "The ones who 'dig in' and the ones who move. There are those like myself who are paralysed by 'home', for whom home is synonymous with writer's block and who believe . . . that all will be well if only they were somewhere else."

He would complete his second book in other people's houses. "Bruce was very good at borrowing places to stay," says Kasmin.

In May 1977, he rented Maschler's cottage above Llantony. "It's not far from Penelope [Betjeman] and he has bought a tiny Fiat for £500 to get around in, as it's pretty remote," wrote Elizabeth. "But it's only an hour and ½ from here so we can get together when he needs a break." No sooner was he installed than it began to rain. The downpour continued through June and July. The cottage leaked, the structure for the book eluded him. "The whole of last summer is like a bad dream to me," he wrote to Elizabeth.

In October, Elizabeth drove him to Italy where he moved into a wing of Millington-Drake's villa at Poggio al Pozzo. All was well to start with.

"Flat is exactly what I wanted," he wrote to Kasmin, "within bicycling distance of Siena on a south-facing hillside. Hope to recover from my summer of infinite frustrations." The bare stone villa stood on a hilltop overlooking the oak- and pine-hills of Chianti. When Kasmin visited at Christmas he found it warm but short of windows and armchairs, with no "cosy reading corners".

Millington-Drake charged Bruce £25 a week. He was by now accustomed to his guest: "He was a cuckoo, though he thought of himself as a nomad. When he came to stay, he settled in and made his nest in whatever part of the house he had been assigned; then, when it suited him, he would move on to another nest in someone else's house. He expected to be fed. 'What's for lunch?' he'd cry as he breezed in at half-past twelve. Occasionally, he would contribute a couple of bottles of champagne or, as a great treat, some wild rice. Then there was the telephone bill. He telephoned continually to his agent, his friends, to a young man he'd fallen in love with in Brazil. At the end of a visit he would offer 10,000 lire (about £4) saying he hadn't used the 'phone much."

Bruce resumed work at Poggio in a brighter mood. "This is better than the Welsh Mountains," he wrote to Wyndham. "Bare hills, bright light and most of the English gone back for the winter. I cycle to Siena for groceries and speak to shopkeepers in an incoherent mixture of Spanish, Portuguese and Latin: they smile breezily and ask if I want peanuts." Meanwhile, he was writing about the Dahomean coup. "Have written four bad pages and will reduce them to a single line. So it goes."

He had started out confidently: "I know exactly what to do with the book: write it in one long stretch without even the favour of chapters," he wrote to Elizabeth. "Balzac's *Eugénie Grandet* gave me the idea. You begin in the present in the present tense and you flash back into the past and then write through to the present.

"I am beginning with the family celebrating their annual commemorative mass in the Church in Ouidah and retiring for the dinner in Sigbomey which means the Big House or Casa Grande in Fon . . . The scene is then set for his life and what a life! Cattle drover turned man drover who ends up the prisoner of the King of D and dies of *rage* at being trapped when all he wants to do is get *out* of Africa and retire to Bahia."

Bruce's talent was to dig up extraordinary facts and link them. "He was an intellectual gibbon who swung from connection to connection with incredible ease," said a friend. His imagination, oddly, faltered at pure invention. He could enlarge and colour and improve his stories, but he could not make them up from scratch. After toiling a month on de

Souza, he reached an impasse. "I had thought of giving it up when I was kicked out of Benin last winter," he wrote to Welch. "Then thought that was weak-kneed and so I go on. I am in no position to judge how it will turn out." He felt distracted by thoughts of João and, lately, of Donald. By December, rumours had reached Maschler. "Kas mentioned to me on the telephone today that you were a little depressed about progress on the new book and perhaps a little lonely as well? I don't know how I can help except to tell you that my confidence in you is absolutely supreme. As I never cease to tell you *In Patagonia* is one of the best first books we've published for many a year and it's no more than a beginning for you. That, I realise of course, only makes it the harder to follow in a way."

In January, Bruce showed him the first 107 pages. Maschler was encouraging: "At its best . . . *The Merchant of Ouidah* goes way beyond *In Patagonia* in its qualities. And that's quite something. I know you can get it right . . . When you are at the end we can *really* talk about structure." He enclosed a £100 bill for Bruce's expenses at his cottage in Wales. "Sorry it's so much, but as you will see most of it is your telephone conversations!"

"YOU'VE GOT TO steal wherever you can," Bruce told James Fox, when Fox was having difficulty with the composition of *White Mischief.* "You must go down to the London Library and look at the beginning of all the great books. No white knuckles. Don't sit there gripping the rails in terror. Plunge in."

After *In Patagonia* Bruce embraced a new set of authors. Attempting a more classical structure, he looked away from Mandelstam and Hemingway towards French writers—Balzac, Flaubert and Racine.

"We used to read Racine out loud together," said Millington-Drake, who felt that Bruce had switched his ability to find antiques "to one of finding unusual characters".

His neighbour Charles Tomlinson was responsible for much of his French (and other) reading. Tomlinson had pressed on him the notebooks of Philippe Jacottet and Raymond Radiguet's *Le Bal du Comte d'Orgel* ("Of course, that's the great book, you know," Bruce told him later). But Bruce was most excited by Racine. "The greatest master of psychological realism in the world is Racine," he told an interviewer in Australia, "and in a Racine play the characters are always doomed from the moment they open their mouths and yet they are still permitted the liberty by the author of hope and they are still permitted the illusion themselves that things are going to turn out differently from what they do and that sets off an essential tension in a story."

In the summer of 1978 Bruce saw an open air production of *Phèdre* in Paris with Peter Eyre. "He liked the purity and discipline of Racine, the tight mechanism of the plot, the way the characters express themselves by what they do rather than by what they say," says Eyre. "I remember him saying that Racine's vocabulary was a hundred times more compact than Shakespeare's. He told me that in writing this book he was trying to apply the same classical discipline."

Bruce's admiration for Racine was quite soon unlimited. "I am *very* serious about *Bajazet*," he wrote to Jonathan Miller, after studying the play for its prison atmosphere. "I believe there's some way that Racine can be made to work for a non-French audience through being declaimed/intoned in the bravura passages with the help of music." His enthusiasm would result, some years later, in a comical interview with a French journalist who asked him, when promoting *The Viceroy of Ouidah* in Paris, what he thought of Racine. "As an Englishman who comes from Stratford and thinks Racine's infinitely better than Shakespeare, I was off." After an interval, the lady interrupted in a puzzled, anguished voice: "Mais *Racines*?" She meant Alex Haley's *Roots*.

NEXT TO RACINE, he admired Flaubert. One year into his book, Bruce wrote to Milow: "the Flaubertian *conte* is progressing *pero muy lentamente*. I might just manage to finish its hundred or so pages by the end of the year. What I had estimated at three months will be at least six, but that's the usual story. Yet imagine the *Chartreuse de Parme* being written in eleven weeks [actually, 53 days] and packed off to the publisher without need of corrections! On the subject of Flaubert, read *Un coeur simple*, in French, or at least with a French text in hand. Best thing written in the 19th century—and ours?"

"Un coeur simple" is the first story of *Trois Contes*. Heartbreakingly unsentimental, it has the sweep of a Russian novel in miniature: an entire life hastened and condensed into 40 pages. Flaubert gave his Félicité a heart so pure that even after half a century she had nothing to confess. Bruce, by contrast, had chosen a man with everything to confess. He sought for *The Viceroy of Ouidah* the same pace, control and tone as Flaubert, but he found the technical problems colossal: "how to string so

many disparate facts and ideas into the life of one man, *and* carry the reader sailing from page to page." He wanted his book, like *Trois Contes*, to be extremely small. "I doubt if it'll print up to much more than a hundred pages. But then I've never liked long books myself, so I don't see why I should try and write them myself. Unless you're Tolstoy, most of the 'great books' of the world should have been cut in half."

When Bruce gave him his novel to read in typescript, Wyndham compared it to *Salammbô* and *"Hérodias"* in *Trois Contes*. "It's a sadistic book in a way. There's a heartlessness." Writers like Colin Thubron wonder if this very quality that makes his books so powerful is, in the end, what holds him back and makes him fall short of his models. "His lack of heart is arguably a fault," says Thubron, "but it is hard to see how his virtues could have co-existed. Maybe his extraordinary qualities depended on there being no heart."

Bruce's fascination was for visual surface, and in the process finding the inner by describing the outer. "At all costs stay dead pan," he wrote to Bill Buford, the editor of *Granta*. The composer Kevin Volans says, "Bruce felt art and composition of the late twentieth century should be 'pure description'. I told him what Morton Feldman once said to me: 'In the twentieth century there is no such thing as background. *Everything* must be foreground.' Bruce understood this. The author should not get in the way. His description should be totally direct. There must be no secondary material, nothing between him and the object. He was the Matisse of writers." He once said: "A trick I learned, when writing something tragic and claustrophobic, is to write it from the outside as if you are just present at a *tableau vivant*."

Thubron says, "What was underneath the surface spoke through the patina and he would in many ways leave that to happen without delving. Stylistically he was neutral—there were very few value judgements or value adjectives. But underneath he was moral. There was a tension between the mental passion, the intense intellectual involvement with what he was doing, and the coolness of the prose." The effect, to Thubron, was of a cold dawn light. It reminded Sybille Bedford of a shipwreck by Watteau, and Bob Brain of a photograph of the *Kasluk*: a ship squashed in tinsel ice, lit from the back, everything gleaming for that moment, everything in silhouette with a corona around it, transformed by an icy radiance. "It was a style honed to survive," says Thubron.

Flaubert offered a style, also a look. Bruce crafted each page to resemble the pages of his French master. He was concerned with the integrity, even the visual effect of the paragraphing. "His one sentence paragraphs are very like Flaubert," says Wyndham. He took infinite pains over the cover, the print. To Jonathan Cape's designer he conveyed his preference for Bembo, smallish, lots of leading and small Roman numerals for the chapter openings. "He despised what English books looked like," says Wyndham, to whom he gave a first edition of *Trois Contes*. "He loved the chaste white covers of the French."

And he resorted to visual aids to break out of an impasse: "One quite useful technique—which I used for the fantastic compression necessary for *The Viceroy*—is to get a board with a huge sheet of graph paper, divided into squares. You then write the 'synopsis' sections on little cards and pin them on with drawing pins. You then have a flexible way of setting out the story with the possibility of change."

Sunil Sethi stayed with Bruce while *The Viceroy of Ouidah* was being written. "His pens were always Mont Blanc; his notebook was always a *moleskine* from a place in Paris that no longer exists. His complexity comes out of this great fastidiousness. For Bruce to sit down was a great achievement. He was the mother of all grasshoppers. And he was only sitting down when he found the right book and a very comfortable chair, or he was reading his day's work to you." To ensure the clarity of each sentence, Bruce read out his books. Sethi says, "They have been read aloud, every word—sometimes to the point of high self-consciousness. The point was to see when you were getting bored." When correcting the French proofs, Bruce stayed in Paris with Loulou de la Falaise. One night she and her husband lay in bed, kept awake by Bruce. He was reading his proofs aloud in the bath.

"Oh, mais c'est du Flaubert!"

To TRY TO finish the book, Bruce rented a house in Ronda for five months: "an exquisite neo-Classical pavilion restored by an Argentine architect who has run out of money." He wrote in longhand on 20 yellow legal pads, refilling his Mont Blanc from two bottles of Asprey's brown ink. But progress was slow. "Ow! the strains of composition and of keeping up the momentum," he wrote to Wyndham. "How to eliminate the longueurs without eliminating the sense. Will *never* tackle a historical subject again." The days were hot and lethargic and his self-doubt was "in full flood". He wrote to Sethi: "Five hours of work and I'm exhausted. I will the words to come, but they won't; don't like what I've already done: feel like burning the manuscript.

"I get up at sunrise at eight; over coffee I sit out on a semi-circular ter-race, contemplate the mountains opposite, and the hideous glazed pottery busts of a nymph and the Infant Bacchus on the arched portico: then set-tle down to work. Four-and-a-half hours brings me to 12.30 and letter-writing time if I am to catch the post which closes at 2. I leave the house at 1, bounce down the mountain in my little Fiat and zigzag up the other side of Ronda, which perches on the top of a sheer cliff and looks like an iced cake. I unlock the aluminium PO Box, usually empty and hurtle to the market, which also closes at 2. Twice I have had a fight with the local *condessa* (a Southern Rhodesian called Faffie) as to who shall have the last lettuce. Then to a bar in a side street which has magnificent *tapas* (*hors d'oeuvres*) which I make into lunch. The other day I had a raw clam and was violently sick in the middle of the night. The proprietor is a fantasti-cal red-haired queen, with draperies of white flesh hanging from his up-per arms. I have seen him smile once, when the bar was full of soldiers.

"Then usually I go for a swim at the pool of a friend called Magouche [Fielding]. She is an old friend, magnificent, stylish, the daughter of a U.S. Admiral: her name was once Agnes MacGruder, that is, until she worked for Edgar Snow's 'Support Mao' campaign in New York in the '40s, met the painter Arshile Gorky and married him.

"She still lives off the contents of the studio, is haunted by Gorky's suicide and quarrels frantically with all but one of her four daughters. One of these is married to the son of Stephen Spender, lives in Tuscany and is the most dangerous gossip I know (though I love her) . . .

"So the afternoon is usually spent bellyaching about Magouche's chil-dren. Then I look in on two peasants who keep the house, Curro and In-carna, who keep me in onions, raspberries, cucumbers. They live in a spotless white house shaded by walnut trees in the bottom of the valley. Then I try to work for another three hours, but can rarely get much done other than prepare notes for the next day.

"After that cook dinner. Last night disgusting experiment with spices bought in Morocco. Then read Flaubert, Racine or Turgenev if I'm up to it: Maupassant or Babel if my eyes start to flutter."

When he got the American reviews of *In Patagonia*—"I have a huge batch of them"—he bounced across the valley to share his literary success with Magouche and Xan Fielding six miles away. That summer Xan was engaged in writing a book on the winds. Bruce disrupted his concentra-tion on a more or less daily basis. "Bruce would appear, unfortunately, al-ways as we were sitting down to lunch," said Magouche, "with little nuggets about some female saint in medieval France who had theories on wind. You would hear him as he approached the house. He had crossed Ronda, picked up his post—this simply stuffed with prizes—and he couldn't resist putting it on the table and reading it out. Then he would talk. Everything he was thinking, doing, being, feeling. Xan would go off to his study and pull his hair. 'I can't stand it. Either we've got to go or Bruce has got to come at a different time.' When I asked Bruce not to turn up to lunch every day he was awfully sweet. But he wouldn't have understood. He did see himself as a sort of present to mankind. He'd come with such nice ribbons and wrapping and heaven knows what goodies inside, yet you never did unwrap it."

By September, the tension was apparent even to Bruce. "Apparently when I came up with some more 'Wind' information, he took offence and thought I was trying to patronise him. Also resents my friendship with Magouche. I've tried my best to like him . . ." A week later, he was able to report: "Xannikins has gone off to climb in the Pyrenees and so everyone is much more relaxed. He is an area of LOW PRESSURE."

Magouche, whom he had first met with the Leigh Fermors in Greece, had introduced Bruce to Ronda in 1974. They would go on lengthy walks. "Bruce had been up every peak in the valley. When I walked with him I would say: 'I can't go on if you talk, I'm going to stumble.' It was, after all, interesting." She observed his contradictions. She knew him to be very generous—especially with his time ("I never heard him say, 'I can't do this'."); also a total sponge. "He was sensitive about other people, but not in relation to himself. I was once cross with Xan and walked out of the room with some horrid quip and Bruce reprimanded me: 'That was hard to take.' He didn't like arguments."

Sometimes on their walks they had discussions about Elizabeth. "She was very good at accepting his terms," says Magouche. "I knew he was slightly miserable. Things were going badly. In as much as he could, he did love her. But there was a crystal core. As Beatrice Lillie said, a diamond is a cute but cold stone."

DURING THE LAST stages of the writing of *The Viceroy of Ouidah*, Bruce stayed with David Plante, the American novelist. Plante, a painstaking diarist, lived outside Cortona. He wrote about Bruce's visit at length:

"Bruce came in his small car, the back seat piled with books from the London Library, to stay ten days or so and then be off with the same burst with which he arrived. Without commenting on the house, as if he had been here many times and was totally at ease, he immediately set his type-writer on a small, wooden, paint-spattered table in the midst of bags of cement and stacks of bricks in one of the downstairs, unfinished rooms and began to work on his novel about the slave trade in Dahomey. He makes corrections in brown ink, then, he said, he always types the novel over from the beginning. After a few hours, the floor was covered with sheets of paper on which he's made his corrections, and when he left the table with the new typescript he left the pages on the floor. I picked them up. He did this day after day.

"Stephanie was staying with me, and I at first wondered if they would get on. What they had in common, they discovered, was black women— Stephanie from her experiences in prison in America and Bruce from Africa. They talked about the feel and the taste and the smell of the skin of black women, the bigger the women the better. Bruce kept laughing, short, high-pitched, abrupt laughs and saying, 'Wonderful, quite wonderful'.

"I never know if I should believe Bruce or not.

"When I am alone with him he loves men, when he is with Stephanie he loves huge black women, and when he is with others—?

"Sometimes he went off on his own to walk through the valleys and chestnut-covered hills. He wore khaki shorts and knee socks, and asked me, standing in the doorway, if I thought he dressed all right. He in fact looked very beautiful against the green hills across the valley. I hadn't thought that there was a right and a wrong way to dress for a walk in the Umbrian countryside. (Only later did I find out he wore knee socks to cover his varicose veins.)

"Once, he cooked supper—walked to the hamlet of San Leo and bought a chicken and lemons, and stuffed the chicken with lemons cut in half, a dish he had learned to prepare in, I think, North Africa. While he prepared in the kitchen, talking all the while about his novel, I, trying to pay attention both to what he was doing and what he was saying, picked up whatever he dropped. He has the ability to act rapidly and to talk rapidly at the same time, as if he were two people, one all motion, the other all talk, and sometimes one distracts the other, but mostly, amaz-ingly, they converge. At moments he would stop as if the acting and talk-ing parts of himself suddenly divided and left him wondering what he was doing and where he was, and he'd say, 'It's really all too much, all too much,' and then go on as before. The chicken stuffed with lemons was delicious.

"He gave me the typescript of the novel to read. I suggested he cut a few metaphors and similes, one, in the middle of a paragraph jammed with them, comparing the motion an oar makes in the water to Arabic script. He said, 'Yes, yes, of course.'

"When we were alone, Stephanie out painting, I listened to Bruce talk about where he will live. I said, 'I think you should make up your mind that you won't live in any one place.' He said, 'Yes, you're probably right. I couldn't bear having a house of my own—as I can't bear the house I have with Elizabeth in Gloucestershire—because of all the problems: the roof, the plumbing, the land.'

"We talked about Flaubert . . .

"He didn't say where he was off to when he left—as I imagine he hadn't to the last people with whom he was staying . . ."

BRUCE'S DELIBERATIONS ABOUT where to live touched on what, to Kasmin, was his biggest problem: "He never knew where to be. It was always somewhere else."

He wrote in his notebook in Brazil: "A house is only useful to me if it is somewhere I can write in." Sulzberger had properties in Paris and London, both useful to Bruce. "He had a form of writer's cramp which made it difficult for him to sit at his own desk and write. It was a lot easier to go to someone else's space and camp there, but without someone else in it—and he was slightly resentful if you turned up. He was practically allergic to the presence of others while he was writing."

At the same time, he hankered after his own space. "Everyone, in some way or other, is territorial and there's no point in having a place that isn't one's own," he wrote to John Pawson. He was ever looking to buy himself a bolt-hole in the Vaucluse or Spain (in 1976, for instance, finding a "little dream house" in Alhaurin-el-Grande: "I think we'd better buy it," he wrote to Gerald Brenan). Smallness was a pre-requisite. "Every time I saw in the countryside a one-room house with a window," says Sulzberger, "I thought: 'That's a Bruce Chatwin house'." While walking with Loulou de la Falaise on the edge of Fontainebleau, Bruce spotted a tool shed. "This is the *perfect* place for writing in!" In 1986, on the brink of buying land "somewhere in the Mediterranean", he outlined his ideal house to Pawson: "I need a courtyard, a flat roof with walls like a room open to the sky, 2 bedrooms (1 a library-cum-bedroom) and a living-room-cum kitchen with an open fire. All simplicity itself like that Portuguese architecture from the Alentejo. So you can think about it."

He could not stay anywhere long before "the *malaise* of settlement" crept upon him. Even his favorite places soon bored him. In August 1970, he wrote to Elizabeth from Patmos: "As one gets older, one realises that there are some places that suit one, and others that emphatically do not. One can only find out by experience. Paris and this place are two of them." Yet a month later he was glad to leave. "Patmos is the most enervating place—bar Edinburgh—I have ever spent any time on. One was really ready for the Revelation. Beautiful though it is—the wind howls or it blisters in the sun—those pinnacles of jagged rock finally pierce through to the subconscious. Smart English girls of brittle conversation burst into tears after a week. No food or water, but above all that terrible feeling of not being able to get off which is psychologically devastating. If I hadn't had something to do I would have gone mad."

He went maddest in England.

THE STRAIN OF living at Holwell meant that Bruce and Elizabeth were often apart. When alone, Bruce expressed his admiration for her gritty independence and was loyal to the concept of their marriage. Gillian Walker asked him on one of his numerous visits to New York: "Bruce, where's Elizabeth?"

"I think she's in Afghanistan."

"But Bruce, there's a *war* in Afghanistan."

"I don't think that would bother Elizabeth!"

Meeting Elizabeth in this period, Walker found her friend's stoicism poignant. "She never *ever* said: 'This is a really sticky wicket'."

Bruce still needed his wife's unconditional love. Soon after Paul Walter saw him in distress in his white suit, he telephoned Elizabeth from Barcelona seven times in the course of one day. "He never told me what had made him frantic. It was a cry for help and attention." Elizabeth dropped everything, drove out.

As late as 1979 Bruce was defending the integrity of their relationship to Sontag. "Is this a marriage?" Sontag asked him. "Really?" He replied: "Oh, yes. Absolutely. You bet." Sontag assumed this was true. "What was more interesting, he wanted me to think it was true."

On his only visit to the Welchs' new home in New Hampshire, he held up Nigel Nicolson's *Portrait of a Marriage*. "This," he said, "was an ideal marriage." The model couple were Harold Nicolson and Vita Sackville-West, whose unconventional marriage accommodated bi-sexual affairs.

In Italy, Beatrice von Rezzori asked Bruce: "Who is your best friend?" He replied, "Well, I guess it's Elizabeth. She's my best friend." There still existed a physical bond. The Rezzoris testified to the Chatwins' closeness, as did Kasmin. In 1979, Fox arrived at Holwell on his Kamazaki Z900, "a very quiet motorbike", and caught Bruce and Elizabeth kissing. "I just stopped in front of the kitchen window and saw this long and touching embrace between the couple, which was incredibly surprising because I had never conceived of such tenderness between them."

Hand in hand with the tenderness went a hurtful neglect. "He never told people he was married, I was the guilty secret off in the countryside," says Elizabeth. "He projected some sort of image to these people and he didn't want to behave differently if I was around."

Because they did not see much of Elizabeth, there were those among Bruce's friends who thought she must be difficult or boring or that, like Mary in *On the Black Hill,* "she carried her devotion to the point of eccentricity". He gave out several versions of his life with her. He did not know what he wanted and his frustration came out, like a child, in mean outbursts. "He could be wantonly dismissive," says Sethi. "It was a constant whine. Sometimes he was so vicious, I'd be angry. Once I did nearly hit him."

Bruce pulled a lot of faces, but he never pinpointed what was wrong. Whatever it was at that moment, it would change. "There was always something wrong with Elizabeth," says his friend Sarah Giles. "But there was always something wrong with everybody unless they were icons: Wyndham, Lisa Lyon, Sontag—they were people not on his doorstep."

His frustration could erupt in unnecessary cruelty. James Fox retains "a vivid image" of walking with Bruce, Elizabeth and others from the *Sunday Times* to a lunch haunt. Elizabeth, who had her dog with her, was not allowed to bring Solly into the pub. "Bruce turns round and tells her to go away, which shocks everyone," says Fox. "They can't understand the relationship." To Francis Wyndham, the dog offered a good explanation for Bruce's behaviour to his wife: "She insisted on Bruce staying with us here (it was vaguely a 'working lunch'), while she happily took the dog home." Meriel McCooey, however, standing on the corner by the hairdresser, overheard the exchange. "I didn't say anything, but I thought: 'That's horrible.' Elizabeth went without a word. I couldn't understand why she didn't thump him."

Erskine, one of Bruce's oldest friends, cringed to observe his petulance. After *In Patagonia* was published, Erskine was invited to a lunch party in the garden at Holwell. "It was such a nice day, everybody having a good time, when it was curtailed by a horrendous piece of bad temper. Suddenly, Bruce got into one of his semi-hysterical moods and made jokes about his wedding: 'Oh, I can't tell you what it was like!' He dashed inside and produced the wedding pictures. 'Look at this, look at this.' Elizabeth kept grabbing back the precious album. Then Bruce would rip it out of her hands and find another photograph. I very much took her side. It was one of the most embarrassing moments of my life."

Bruce included Elizabeth less and less in his plans when he was writing *The Viceroy of Ouidah*. His letters from Spain reveal an irritable detachment. He made no claim on Elizabeth when she sought advice over whether to sell Holwell because he hated it so much. "I simply can't begin to advise you about the farm from here, because . . . I have no idea whether you have had any conversation at all with your boneheaded family financial experts on the pros and cons . . . Financially, that is, if you want to stay in England, it would be better to have more land and less house, rather than *vice versa*." He was more concerned about his own predicament. "My urgent requirement is a small base which I do not have to get into hock with mortgages." He was furious at his inability to act. This rage found its way undigested onto the page. In a crazed fit, the Viceroy killed his wife's cat and left her soon after: "The strain of living with her told on his nerves . . . He took to sleeping rough, hoping to recover his equilibrium under the stars."

Writing to Kasmin from Ronda, he confirmed the direction his life had taken: "I left England in a particularly bruised condition. I long to live there, but in a situation that doesn't get on top of me. You are right: the answer is to live alone."

BRUCE RETURNED TO England on 31 October 1978. He had been five months in Spain, during which time he had seen Elizabeth twice. They met at supper at Badminton where she had gone for a charity concert given by Los Paraguayos—"the ugliest little men you've ever seen," she wrote to Gertrude. Bruce installed himself in Holwell, but complained of the cold. "B says we are definitely coming for Xmas. He can't leave till he's written a good first draft of his book, but it should be done by then. He's working on it all the time. Basically it's finished, but parts are still rough in his opinion."

In November, he found a one-room "cubby-hole" in Albany, a former maid's room which he sublet from Christopher Gibbs. No sooner had he arranged for a builder to convert it, than on 9 December he flew to America. In February, he wrote to Elizabeth from New York where he had seen Jackie Onassis, Robert Mapplethorpe, Donald Richards. "I have to say that I would like to spend about five months of the year in New York rather than London." He was keen, he said, to go to Australia "as soon as possible".

BRUCE'S ACTIONS WOULD have caused most people to leave him, but Elizabeth did not. For 15 years, she had accepted his terms. "He did what he wanted to do and didn't take her wishes into account," says David Nash. "But he had great respect and didn't want to hurt her." In April 1980 she reached the end of a road.

The occasion was the Badminton horse trials, one of the most spectacular outdoor events in England, and for Elizabeth, who had been forced to make her own life in the country, an important fixture.

"Bruce didn't come down very often and then he came down with David Nash," she says. "I was really cross he'd suddenly descended on me the one weekend I was occupied and expected me to drop everything. He was completely unsympathetic about other people's arrangements: he was never there unless it suited him and he'd turn up regardless of what plans I'd made. I said, 'You can't come to dinner because that would make thirteen, but come with us to lunch.' I'd arranged to go with the Fergussons to Badminton and they left with military precision. I told him: 'We do have to leave on the dot'."

Elizabeth waited. Bruce and David did not arrive. "There I was, with an extra lunch for two people, and they didn't come. They went on their own."

The breaking point had its origins in a loudspeaker announcement. Nash was standing beside Bruce at a jump when over the tannoy they heard: "Lucinda Prior-Palmer has withdrawn, having refused the faggot pile for the third time." Both men got the giggles. "Bruce was in high spirits after that," says Nash. "We went home to Holwell and Elizabeth was cross with us because we hadn't met up. There was lots of friction, not about horses, but to do with who wanted what kind of life."

For the first time Elizabeth took a stand. "I chucked him out."

Furious, she wrote a letter to The Tower, near Brecon, where Bruce had gone to stay with George and Diana Melly. "I told him: 'You can't take advantage like that. I don't want to see you for a while. Make your-self scarce'."

Bruce told her the letter was "sententious". On 29 April 1980, he wrote to Sethi in Delhi: "I fear that our relations are going from bad to worse. The trouble with living separate lives, as we have done for so long, is that you end up with totally different conceptions of life—to the extent that when you do try and make arrangements together, they end in disaster.

"Last week-end I tried to show willing and put on my best tweed suit for the Badminton Horse Trials: the result was terrible. We have since had an exchange of letters that hint of separation/divorce.

"A dreadful worry: what to do?

"Must go now. I have to lunch with my US publisher who is the key to my present existence."

Two days later, on 1 May, a snowstorm covered the Ozleworth valley. After living there for 14 years, Elizabeth decided the time had come to sell Holwell Farm.

XXVIII

Border Country

Rimbaud, like so many whose minds are occupied
with cosmic visions, had no inhibitions where money
was concerned and he saw no reason why he should
not sponge off his friends.
—ENID STARKIE, *Rimbaud*

ON THE DAY *The Viceroy of Ouidah* came out, Maschler sent a telegram to Bruce at Albany: NO LIVING WRITER'S WORK MEANS MORE TO ME THAN YOURS STOP EVERY GOOD WISH ON PUBLICATION DAY TOM.

Many years later he expressed reservations. "If he hadn't written *In Patagonia*, I'd have thought it wonderful. But it's a poor man's *In Patagonia*. What he's trying to do is to go further and in the process of attempting to be richer he's going the other way." Clapp, who worked with Bruce on the manuscript, felt it had been "written by someone who was having difficulty writing. I saw the panic on his face as we tried to tease it to life. It was extremely tight. Its denseness and its harshness reflected its subject matter." A year later Bruce asked his American editor what she thought of the book. "I danced around," Elisabeth Sifton says. "I said I thought it was beautiful, but cold and repellent." "But it's *meant* to be," he said. Sybille Bedford thought it contained "too much excruciating leprosy". Rushdie, too, felt "it exoticised the material in a way that isn't successful". Critics agreed. The novel, wrote Bruce, appeared to the "bemusement of reviewers, some of whom found its cruelties and baroque prose unstomachable". In West Africa, King Nema of Elmina told Bruce, who was with Werner Herzog then filming the novel: "Well, sir . . . you have written a very round-about book."

The novel had many good reviews, but overall the reception was one of rather qualified rapture, a feeling that his fascination with the grotesque had run away with him. "I didn't quite pull it off," Bruce told Martin Wilkinson while loading wood into a shed in Shropshire, "but it was probably the best book I'll write." Final hardback sales were 4,938, fewer than for his first book, while sales in America barely exceeded 7,000, a third of the sale of *In Patagonia.** Georges Borchardt, Bruce's New York agent, articulated the American response in a letter to Rogers: "It's very good, but I think it needs something to explain to the reader exactly what it is. Specifically, is it all fiction or how much of it is actually based on research etc.?" At Summit, Silberman had paid $20,000 for the American rights. In May 1982, he remaindered 8,980 hardback copies. "Readers," he says, "couldn't connect it with his first book, which made them very uncomfortable."

No one would ignore the novel more pointedly than the judges of the Whitbread who, as if *The Viceroy of Ouidah* had never been, awarded their First Novel prize to Bruce's next book.

The disappointing response accounted for the direction Bruce now took. Edmund White wrote: "I had the distinct impression that Bruce had been frightened by the failure of his extravagant, hyper-exotic Viceroy (after all, he lived by his pen) and rather cynically, and shrewdly retreated into the Hardy-like solidity of *On the Black Hill* for his next sortie."

THROUGHOUT 1980, AS his relationship with Elizabeth continued to disintegrate, Bruce assembled material for his new book—"on a pair of Welsh hill farmers, identical twins who have slept in their mother's bed for the past 43 years. Marvellous subject, but do I have the *poetic* talent for it?"

Each of Bruce's books is a reaction against the one before. Where *The Viceroy of Ouidah* luxuriates in cruelty, distance, wealth, *On the Black Hill* withdraws into a tender, static world and explores the unchanging grind of agricultural existence. Where the action of *The Viceroy of Ouidah* takes place in the real time of a Racine play, *On the Black Hill* unfolds over a century.

In choosing the Welsh border, Bruce returned to the area he loved best. "No man can wander in fact without a base," he said in 1984. "You have to have a sort of magic circle to which you belong. It's not necessarily where you were born or where you were brought up. It's somewhere

---

* In British paperback *The Viceroy of Ouidah*—for which Maschler had paid a £2,500 advance—has sold 91,135, compared with 114,689 for *Utz*, 245,953 for *In Patagonia*, 313,791 for *On the Black Hill* and 355,992 for *The Songlines*.

you identify with, to which you always happen to go back. This area of the Welsh border I regard as one of the emotional centres of my life . . . It's what Proust calls the soil on which I still may build."

Banished from Holwell Farm and with Elizabeth no longer there to react against, Bruce looked homewards: to a place not unlike the small-holding outside Birmingham where he had grown up. "He was in exile from everywhere," says Elizabeth. "Except the Black Mountains. It was the only place he went back and back and back to."

Wales was a constant, a sanctuary from the extremes and excesses of New York. Bruce was conceived in Wales. He went there as a child. Here he had courted Elizabeth. His family's scent was everywhere.

There had been a tradition of holidaying in Wales going back to the time of his great-grandparents. Julius Alfred Chatwin, the architect, liked sketching in the Welsh mountains and fishing for trout in small Welsh streams and every summer he took a house for six weeks at Barmouth. Bruce's grandparents, Leslie and Isobel, would bicycle to the Llantony Valley, the closest place to south-west Birmingham for wild walking. And in 1930, Charles Chatwin came on the first of his five visits to Llantony, that Easter taking his sister Barbara on the pillion of his motorbike. "Bruce would hear about Wales from the word go. When he was about seven and Hugh three, I took the boys to Rhyadder in a small open car and all three of us slept in the back." Two years later, Charles drove Bruce to Mount Snowdon in the farm van. "For the first night we drove up the miners' tracks in the lower regions of Snowdon, and slept under the mountain. The next day we walked to the top."

In early Marlborough days, Margharita took Bruce and Hugh for short holidays with the Anderson family. They stayed on a hill behind a sandy beach south of Criccieth Harbour. Bruce immediately took off with Gavin Anderson and walked to Black Rock, several miles away. They returned after dark to find a hue and cry. "We were confined to our room the next day," says Anderson.

On another day the two boys were stopped by the local police for smashing pebble-filled bottles against a wall. "Bruce was master of the situation, did all the talking." They were taken home in the police car and received another dressing down.

In Bruce's second year at Marlborough he bicycled to Llantony from school as part of a summer camp. The 95-mile ride took him over the Gospel Pass into the secluded valley that he came to think of as "my home base".

MARLBOROUGH HAD BOUGHT a farmhouse at Capel-y-ffin, four miles above Llantony Abbey. The money was supplied by an old farmer who arrived in the Bursar's office one day, unannounced, and admitted to having charged the college "a penny a pound too much for butter" over fifty years. He presented a cheque for £869 16s 19d and walked out.

In buying Castle Farm, the headmaster hoped to realise a wish for boys "to fend for themselves in some distant and preferably uncivilised place. Their activities should involve a good deal of sustained physical effort and their comfort should depend largely on their own exertions."

In July 1955, Bruce bicycled to the valley with five Marlburians. After an early morning dip in a tub on the mountain side, they worked solidly to restore the building: they made new window frames, new furniture and wove curtains, some of the material provided by Margharita. Bruce in his report is described as "quite immature, but sensible and a good worker".

Out of that trip is preserved Bruce's first effort at travel writing, aged 15.

"We set off at 9.45 for Castle Farm having been delayed somewhat by Noel [Parker] taking hours to wash his feet and climed [*sic*] up the hill to the pass. We charged down Hay Hill and went straight on to Glasbury where we stopped to buy some ice-cream . . . We arrived in Rhyadder and were very thirsty and so invested in ice-cream (better!) and more 'pop' at a café where a very heavily made-up and extremely ugly give served us." He slept out under canvas ("I discovered that I had been sleeping on the eggs"). "The rest of the journey was more or less uneventful except for Hay Hill, the inevitable Hay Hill, and arrived back just in time for supper."

Hay Hill rises out of the Black Mountains and is visible as far as Malvern. The ridge narrows along Offa's Dyke into the escarpment known in the novel as the Black Hill.

IN DECEMBER 1979, Bruce rode towards it in the back of a cart driven by Penelope Betjeman, who lived in a remote cottage above Hay-on-Wye.

"I remember Penelope Betjeman—who was a sort of mother to me—saying, 'You really ought to come here because the stories are just as good as all those things in Patagonia you write about'."

Betjeman, then aged 70, is the Philippa of his Welsh novel: "She was a short and very courageous woman with laugh wrinkles at the edge of her slaty eyes, and silver hair cut in a fringe. She spent several months of each year riding alone round India on a bicycle." Born in the Cavalry barracks at Aldershot, she was the daughter of the commander-in-chief of the army in India. Bruce had met her when still at Sotheby's and he saw her intermittently at Edinburgh. She was bossy, buxom and stubborn and her honesty came without any dressing of tact. "If there was a spot on your nose, she would tell you," says Elizabeth. Bruce venerated her eccentricities and saw the deeper spirituality. She in her turn understood Bruce and fed off his enthusiasms. "I think she was the only real loss in his life and he always missed her," Elizabeth wrote to a friend after Betjeman's death. "The loss," Bruce wrote to the same person, "is hardly bearable."

Betjeman, like Elizabeth a practising Catholic, had learned to tolerate John Betjeman's love affairs, but she was unable to live with him. She was a natural adviser to Elizabeth, whom she called "Chatters". It was through Betjeman that Elizabeth had first discovered India. From the 1970s they organised trekking tours in the Western Himalayas. Bruce, always resourceful in meeting his needs, was especially good at finding all-accepting mother figures, and Betjeman cushioned him after his separation from Elizabeth.

Betjeman had no telephone at New House ("thank God"), but kept in touch with neighbours by calling on them unannounced in a horse and trap. One afternoon, she took Bruce to meet "my boys": Jonathan and George Howells, two bachelor brothers in their sixties, who lived on the eastern side of the Black Mountains in a white farmhouse also called New House. "The story she told of them (and which captured my imagination) was that sometime before the War their mother, seeing them to show no signs of interest in the opposite sex, had sent them to the fair at Hay-on-Wye to meet some young ladies. They came back with crestfallen faces, never having seen girls in short skirts before. This put them off forever."

Bruce had a natural sympathy for people cut off, nursing loss and hurt. Jonathan and George would become the Lewis and Benjamin Jones of *On the Black Hill* who, after one abortive venture into it, shrank from the world and went into a retreat which lasted a lifetime.

BRUCE AND BETJEMAN arrived at a white farmhouse tucked out of sight below the Black Hill. It had a slate roof and window frames painted green.

"Two or three hours' walking will carry me to as strange a country as I expect ever to see," wrote the nineteenth-century American author Henry Thoreau in *Walking*. "A single farmhouse which I had not seen before is sometimes as good as the dominions of the King of Dahomey." They found the brothers working the blackthorn hedges with a curly, dark-haired boy in sunglasses. Their great-nephew, Vivian, "a boy of really incredible good looks", stood to inherit the farm.

"How are you, my boys?" cried Betjeman.

Jonathan winked at Vivian. "She calls us 'my boys', but we're older than she is."

Invited inside for tea, bread and jam, Bruce entered a parlour in which nothing had changed since the war. "It was a squint at the nineteenth century," he said later. The small room was dominated by a William IV piano with broken strings. There was an oak settee with brass studs, a side of bacon hitched up to the rafters, and on the wall a photograph of their parents' wedding in Dorstone in 1907. The room smelled of resin from the pine logs and a "musty masculine smell". There was no bathroom and the brothers washed in a tin tub.

Vivian, who would ride up on his motorbike from Dorstone, was suspicious of Bruce. "Bruce sat with his back to the piano and said he was a writer. He didn't say he was going to write about *them*."

The brothers impressed Bruce. His notes say that they wore identical Wellington boots scrubbed of mud; that they both had on their father's flannel shirts, fastened at the neck with a copper stud. Their waistcoats and jackets were woven from the same thick brown tweed, and their chocolate corduroy trousers came from a measure-yourself company in Harrogate. The only difference was in their hats. George in his "best" with trilby hat and suit looked "exactly like the picture of James Joyce in Paris".

George was younger by a year, and smaller. His baldness emphasised the birthmark on his forehead, and half his teeth were gone. But a serene smile gave him an "air of saintly *detachment*".

Jonathan, the boss, was the less quizzical. Straight-backed, pronounced veins in his temple, he could not breathe properly following a bicycle accident which, says Vivian, "put his nose all over the place". The brothers talked freely, about their past. They were born in the nearby house and moved to New House in the 1920s. "They went to no school, learned everything from their mother in the house, to read and write, but did go to Sunday School in the Chapel on Sundays," wrote Bruce. "In the days of their father they had two teams of shire horses and a cob. Their grandmother, born in the 1840s, remembered working oxen to the plough which was far slower and was liable to attacks of fly which made them mad."

The only person they saw day to day was their great nephew. "They wouldn't say a bad word against anyone," says Vivian. "But if ever they had a bad dealing they would never deal with that person again." They were generous in other ways. Vivian sometimes turned up with his blonde girl-friend on the back of his Yamaha. "When Sue's grandpa died, they over-heard her saying she couldn't afford a hat so they went into the kitchen and came back with 50 pound notes and put them on the table. 'Buy a hand-bag as well'." Bruce in his novel would convey the brothers' gentleness and their father's hardness.

George Edgar Howells was the model for Amos in *On the Black Hill.* As a young man, he had rented 13 ewes. By the end of the Depression, he owned a flock of 300. He would buy sheep at the auctions in Brecon and take them back on the train to Hay and drive them up over the bluff. A cantankerous know-all, his pleasure was to sit of an evening at table and carpenter frames for his prints. Two of these, "Divided Affection" and "Wait a Minute", were hung on the wall, their frames chiselled out of beams taken from the big hall in Glasbury. George had died in 1958. At the top of a narrow staircase his bedroom stood untouched, his boxes of shoes not opened.

Their mother, Mary Ann, was a Radnorshire girl who had worked in London as a maid and also for a vicar in Snodhill Court, four miles away, from whom she had bought the piano. She collected silver and green wil-low china and was "honest as a dye". She lived to be 90 and the brothers had looked after her in her failing years.

Jonathan and George were the eldest of four children. They had al-ways lived together, separating once, for a six-month period of convales-cence, when Jonathan was 15 and his horse took off and the end of the shaft pierced his leg. "People used to say they're an old married couple," says Vivian. Bruce was intrigued to learn that they slept upstairs in the same bedroom, a room with two beds, a sloping roof and a window look-ing up to the hill.

The farm consisted of 298 acres with 400 wool sheep and 26 cows. This was the Howells' world and they had rarely left it. If they ventured out, it was most usually to Hay twelve miles away. Neither brother drove, but George piloted the tractor in to Hay on Fridays, parking in the Co-op yard while he did the shopping.

On Mondays, as children, they had gone on bicycling tours dressed in blue serge suits, caps and bicycle clips. They had once been to Stow-on-the-Wold, but never abroad and never to London. "I doubt whether they had seen the sea," says Vivian. The one obsession they had was for aeroplanes. "We never went in a bus, we never went in a train, oh, no no, but we went in a plane," they told Bruce. "And then I discovered that in fact that they had gone for their 75th birthday in a light aircraft as a sort of joy ride and . . . had a huge scrap book which dealt with every air crash, nearly, of the twentieth century." It was this conversation, Bruce said, "which is what really prompted me to write the book." The novel "is about people who are forcibly settled, as it were, but yet they wander in their imagination."

BRUCE INSTALLED HIMSELF in the area. One Sunday, he walked alone across the Cefn Hill. The snow was deeper than he expected and he fell through to his knees. Inky clouds banked up behind Lord Hereford's Knob, but as he looked back into England the fields were green. "The two brothers were mucking out the cowshed onto the dung pile. They seem incapable of doing anything apart . . . They showed me the granary and stable that they built in 1937. I had asked whether hired labour used to sleep there, but they never had a hand, only their brother and sister." Sitting on the settee, they discussed the world. They kept in touch with events from the television on the piano and knew all about how Yugoslavia was divided.

Bruce drew a plan of the interior in his notebook and promised to visit again. "Tacit agreement that I shall satisfy their craving for knowledge about the outside world and they will provide me with something of theirs."

The Howells always seemed pleased to be interrupted by Bruce. "My uncles loved talking about the past." Vivian was not so content to have his work disrupted. "And then Bruce started turning up. He tried to haul bales, but he was a waste of time, he just didn't know how to do it. Then he wants to learn to hedge, he says. But he'd do bugger all except talk. A hedge we'd do in a week took a month to do. He used to drive me round the bend, to tell the truth, because I couldn't get on and do anything."

It surprised Vivian to learn that Bruce had grown up on a farm. "He came back in the spring and Uncle Johnny put him on a tractor, a little 414 International, and taught him to drive—but Bruce couldn't brake. We used to keep cattle in the Pikes [a nearby farm], eight to ten months old. I'd grab the bullock by the nose and Uncle Johnny'd pour in a bottle of mineral bullets. 'Can I have a go?' said Bruce. He got his arm round the neck and the bullock took off, dragging him round the shed. He didn't give no impression he'd been on a farm before.

"I used to say to my uncles after he'd gone, 'Why's he asking these questions for?' "

THE HOWELLS' FARM reminded Bruce of his own remote upbringing at Brown's Green. In *On the Black Hill* he gave a version of what might have been. The novel is about two brothers who do *not* wander, who do *not* marry, who complete each other in a way Bruce himself seemed to have longed for. It explored what would have happened if he had never left home.

Even with Elizabeth to anchor him he was, as Hodgkin observed, "terribly lonely". "I used to think it was the loneliness of someone doing what he did and I would think it was something we had in common, but it wasn't that. He was dead lonely and he took it with him into the desert. It was the one thing Elizabeth couldn't do anything about."

Nor could Hugh. Climbing with his brother among the sheep above Castle Farm in the 1960s Bruce had said to him: "I am Abel, the shepherd, the free spirit, the keeper of high ground and birdsong. Who are you?" The question dumbfounded Hugh. "I shut up. I wasn't supposed to say anything." Hugh had become a surveyor for the City firm of Weatherall, Green & Smith: he was a settler. He worked in the company for 20 years. Like Bruce, Wilfred Thesiger had a brother who lived a regimented life. Brian Thesiger joined the regular army.

On the Black Hill began as a short story about the two bachelor brothers. "I started out writing a few paragraphs and then, suddenly, I wrote that the brothers were identical twins," he told Bragg on the South Bank Show. "I don't know why I wrote it, but it just occurred to me that they might be. And having written that line, which is a separate paragraph to itself, I suddenly realised that this was a novel and not a short story and that what I'd done sort of predicated a book of 450 pages instead of 30."

He may have got the idea of twins from the Greenway family who lived a mile from Betjeman at Wernagavenny and whose telephone ensured that Bruce returned repeatedly. "I always go over to Olive to use the telephone," said John Betjeman. Bruce likewise. "He would go for a walk in the morning to clear his head at 10 a.m. and come for coffee," says Olive. Bustling in and out of her kitchen were Olive's 26-year-old twin sons: Russell, a builder, and Colin a carpenter.

At Marlborough, Bruce had known three sets of twins. In Dahomey, he discovered that twins were not regarded like ordinary men but considered gods (when visiting the Porto Novo museum with Kasmin he saw wooden effigies to Ho Ho, the sacred deity of twins, to be carried at all times by the survivor if one dies). As a child, Bruce had told stories to his imaginary friend, Tommy. He never, one suspects, altogether abandoned Tommy. "He'd galvanise himself into the activity of writing with early morning yells," says Matthew Spender, one of Bruce's hosts in Italy. "You'd hear cackles, laughs, cries of pleasure and encouragement. 'Now, now.' He was talking to himself as if he was outside and he had to boss himself around. 'Now what we're going to do is this . . . No, that's *quite* wrong.' You'd wander out of your bedroom thinking there were visitors for breakfast and no, it was Bruce getting up."

Out of the same compulsion, Bruce would invent an intimate, inviolable Other. "The novel is between Bruce and Bruce," says Jonathan Hope. "He would have loved to have had an identical twin."

The twins Lewis and Benjamin, though the most fully realised, are not the first "doubles" to appear in Bruce's work: in *The Viceroy of Ouidah*, the Viceroy becomes a blood brother of the king of Abomey, while his favourite twin daughters are sent back to Bahia, finding work as prostitutes. Bruce was attracted to the erotic possibilities of twins. He was delighted when his Finnish publishers proposed to change *On the Black Hill* to *Erototammatomatt*—"which of course was the title I'd been looking for all the time!"—and communicated this to Sontag, who wrote to him: "I look forward with the greatest impatience to 'the novel about the incestuous brothers' as it was referred to by John Richardson the other night." Edmund White recorded that the first oral sketches of *On the Black Hill* and *The Songlines* "were pretty gay, whereas the final versions were dully normal". Bruce's notebooks contain hints—"Novel is of *incest* . . . Twins—one queer, the other not"—as well as this paragraph: "Though the pleasure Jonathan takes in being embraced by Lewis puts him into raptures, he prefers to follow, not to walk side by side, to tread in his footprints, to gulp of air knowing it to be the gulp he had exhaled, to sing on and in the same trajectory—to do everything in imitation—to put his head on the rumpled pillow." Bruce toned down the incestuous element, but the device of twins allowed him to explore an intense male relationship which John Updike, in the *New Yorker*, would interpret as "a homosexual marriage".

So the short story became a novel he had to research. "I had to get all the twins literature out." He read Musil ("a twin has 25 times less chance of being famous") and Gogol's "The Nose" ("to be pursued by oneself") and he discovered Elvis Presley was a twin.

As ever, Bruce needed to test his theories on a pre-eminent authority. "Some of the details," he assured ABC radio, "were checked for me by the greatest expert in the world on twins." He described to Wyndham, to whom he dedicated the novel, how "when I went on to read the psychoanalytic literature on twins, the only book that really impressed was by a Professor Zazzo, written, I think in the '40s. Last January, I went to lunch with the translator of *The Viceroy* in Paris, and there, on his desk, was *Météores* [by Michel Tournier]. 'Funny,' I said, 'I'm writing a book about twins.' 'Funny,' he said, 'my wife is a psychiatrist who works with the leading expert on twins, one Professor Zazzo.' We rang for an appointment. The professor was in his eighties. Utterly charming! I apologized for disturbing him. My questions were those of a novelist. I wanted to make sure my story held together. 'But Monsieur,' he replied, 'I have 1,200 case histories on twins, and if I had your talents, I would be Balzac.' He then put me right on a number of points, and mentioned Tournier. It seemed that Tournier had also been obsessed by his book and had checked his plot with Zazzo, as I did mine."

Zazzo showed Bruce his card-indexes, his questionnaires. Some of his findings were exciting. "For example, you have situations whereby identical twins are separated: one is brought up in Germany and is raised as a Nazi and the other one is taken to America and raised as a Jew and they both marry a red-headed girl called Betty and they have an underground workshop and they both collect ship models and have pug dogs." This, said Bruce, implied not only a telepathetic signalling over long distance, but a strong genetic bias towards behaviour. "Much more interesting to my mind was the fact that when twins are stuck together they will resemble each other very, very little by the end." The weaker twin, Zazzo revealed, would sometimes be given the opportunity to redress the balance and be six inches taller and shave six months before. "He told me of a story which he had encountered among French country boys in the '30s which was exactly the period I was dealing with. He said there was a case whereby the younger twin was first shaving on his own. And he looked in a mirror with a cut throat razor and had the sensation that he was cutting his own brother's throat, which is of course an incredibly powerful image. It was one that I couldn't resist using in the book."

Another coincidence struck Zazzo, that Bruce's own name Chatwin ended with the syllable "twin".

BRUCE CONSIDERED VARIOUS titles for the novel: *Two by Two, The Young Men, Mr and Mr Jones* and *The Vision and The Rock*. If New House Farm inspired the farm which he calls The Vision, the model for the Rock was a grey stone smallholding called Coed Major reached high up on the hillside through a chaos of battered hawthorn bushes. "Before the War, the Barn (as Coed Major was called) was famous for being a place where local farmers could dump their illegitimates. It was a place of wild female energies."

Coed Major was owned by "a great local character"—called Joe Philips, or Joe the Barn. He lived there with a much younger woman, Jean the Barn. Unlike the situation of his first two books, where he parachuted in and out, Bruce forged genuine and empathetic connections with the people of the Black Mountains.

He rode over to Coed Major with Betjeman shortly after their visit to the Howells brothers. On a blowy morning in January, they picked their way through the bright bracken on to the exposed saddle of land. "The dogs howled as we dismounted and a procession of geese and ducks flew off among the wreckage of red tractors and pullets." Over a rough stone wall a lichenous figure moved through the mud in gun boots.

Joe the Barn was a cheerful man in his eighties. He had sandy eyes in a weather-beaten face and a turned-up nose "like an imp". A single brown incisor poked from his lower jaw and when he opened his mouth a strange smell came out of it, "the smell of something ancient". He was a scrap merchant, rumoured to be a sheep thief. "How be you?" he asked Betjeman.

He showed them into the house. One end of the barn had fallen down and the other end blown open. "How they survived the cold I can't tell," wrote Bruce. The tables and chairs were covered with the greenish white smears of fowl droppings. A woman was mucking out the first room: "the mysterious Jean".

Joe shared the Barn with Jean whom he treated as both his wife and daughter, and with his chickens. Jean was about 40, with flashing eyes that caught the sun. She wore a brown jumper, a greasy corduroy hat and a shirt which had been torn and patched together "like a broken spider's web". On the table was a bucket of chicken mash—"which I suspect she ate".

Jean had the Howells' gentleness. Incredibly shy, her round and pale blue eyes were always cast down. "She would say something and flinch a look at her hands, all covered with fowl droppings but somehow purple." Her arms, legs and even her back, she said, were covered with sores. When Penelope told her she should see a doctor, Jean replied, wringing her hands: "It's not for we to go to the doctor."

She lived for Joe and for her animals. Betjeman asked if she ever ate rabbits or hares. "No, I just let 'em live, let 'em love. Let the hares live, and the rabbits live and the foxes, I won't harm 'em."

Joe sat at the oilcloth-covered table and told Bruce he recognised him. "He thinks he saw me before as a little lad in Capel-y-ffin."

WHEN BRUCE RETURNED to the Barn on 17 January he discovered Joe had been taken to Bronllys Hospital with a stroke.

Jean told him how she had got up in the night to put more coal in the fire and found Joe fallen off the settee where he slept. He had caught his head on the box with the chickens in it.

"I hope 'e comes back—we've been together all our lives."

Distraught, she offered Bruce a cup of tea. "Do please. I promised you a cup a tea when you came last week with lady what's a't yer call her?" The kettle was found, hung on a hook over the fire. She served Bruce watery tea.

Without Joe, she had to look after the animals on her own. It was hard work, starting at seven to feed his dogs with meal and old bread. She didn't know how she would manage.

"And now I 'ope he comes back. How I hope so. We was together all our lives like—together."

Bruce and Betjeman visited Joe in Bronllys Hospital later the same day. They found him thin and frail and clean. "When they scrubbed him all the stuffing went out of him," wrote Bruce. An eye opened, rolled up. Seeing Betjeman, he said simply: "And 'ows you?"

His left leg was paralysed and he was incontinent. His one thought was for his animals. Whenever Bruce visited, he enquired how they were and added a message for Jean: "Tell 'er to keep on feeding—and you if you go there, chuck 'em a bit of hay and a fist of oats . . . the dogs won't bite you," and he pulled his lips so tight that they went back over the yellow incisor and a tear came over the ridges under his eyes. Bruce watched, amazed. "He started to cry whenever the animals were mentioned, but not a shred for Jean."

Bruce went the next day, walking up through the snow. "Again to see Jean the Barn to tell her how Joe was getting along. She thought last night he'd gone because at three in the morning all the dogs which are kept in rough corrugated iron sheds started howling. The room was so full of smoke that you could hardly see your forearm: the soot from the chimney had fallen into the grate and the fire was belching clouds of blacky-yellow smoke. Outside, a pale gold sunset as the sun went down behind the hill, but inside the filth was indescribable and I smelt all over of coke fumes for four hours or more with eyes smarting that I could hardly read.

"I took her a 28lb bag of rolled oats which she said she needed for the ponies and after humping it on my back for three miles through the drifts was a little exhausted . . . She is determined to stay on in the Barn, even if Joe doesn't come back [and] says that if she can get through January she can get through. I was quite impressed to find she knows the hour and the day of the month very exactly."

Bruce took it upon himself to watch out for Jean. He braved the howling dogs and the ammoniacal smells of the chicken droppings to help with odd jobs. He showed more practical skill than Vivian Howells would have imagined likely. A door from the kitchen led directly into a barn so full of muck that the cattle bumped their backs on the roof beams. He dug that out for Jean. He unblocked her chimney. When a ram was lost, he went out with a shovel and scooped away the impacted snow until they found him. He staggered under bundles of bracken through the snow-drifts and helped with the foddering and feeding.

" 'All animals, no matter what it is, you got to feed 'em.'

" 'You too, Jean,' I said.

"And her face creased up like an old oriental woman and she laughed and laughed."

Slowly, he won her confidence.

One day after he had brought Jean a cake, Bruce walked into Olive Greenway's kitchen. "Olive says the talk in Crasswell is that Jean has a fancy-man, ME!" Without doubt, he felt a great bond for her. Jean's energies and innocence put him in mind of a Celtic wood spirit. She was a convincing argument against Lorenz. "Damn the Marxist interpretation of history. Damn Darwinism and the survival of the fittest." Here was the example of a woman "who has been made to suffer any kind of indignity and who comes across with a basic standard of behaviour which we as a species can retain." She was, he wrote, "a heroine of our time".

Speaking to Bragg about Jean and Joe and the Howells brothers, he said: "I don't see these people as strange. I wanted to take these people as the centre of a circle and see the rest of our century as somehow abnormal."

BRUCE, IN THE opinion of his friend Loulou de la Falaise, was a *pique-assiette*, "someone who eats off another's plate". He lived in at least seven places while writing *On the Black Hill*, half of these located within miles of the brothers' farm. His hosts along the border country included Betjeman, Maschler, the Wilkinson family near Clunton and further south, George and Diana Melly in their tower at Scethrog, "a lovely place to work, the only distraction being a view of a white farmhouse through a slit window". Bruce made each of his hosts feel they enjoyed a special relationship with him. When Maschler told George Melly that Bruce had written *On the Black Hill* at his cottage there was nearly an argument: "What do you mean?" said an indignant Melly, "he wrote it at *my* house!"

How did he progress from sitting next to someone at a dinner party to moving into their house for several months? Diana Melly had first met Bruce in 1973 and not registered him. The rest of the party had gone to hear George Melly play at Ronnie Scott's, all except Bruce. "To listen to somebody else performing was not for him"—or as Elizabeth's sister-in-law Carole Chanler phrased it: "It was a question of hiring a band, or Bruce." Melly came across Bruce next in 1978 when he was borrowing Maschler's cottage to write *The Viceroy of Ouidah*. John Wells's wife Teresa was staying at The Tower and telephoned Bruce, who walked over for tea. His attraction for Melly would be more than that of a charming guest who sang for his supper. "It was not just a matter of being entertained by him, or thinking that he was eccentric." She felt connected to him. "He was very childish and needed looking after," she says. "That appeals to people.

It certainly appealed to me." In March 1980, Melly had lost her son from an overdose. She was receptive to a letter from Bruce asking if he could come and stay (and also if she could arrange for Francis Wyndham—with whom she was editing Jean Rhys's letters—to be there too). "For me Bruce filled a bit of the void. I became a mother-figure. He suited the bill at that moment and that's when we became close friends. He didn't put himself out to please or entertain. Like a child, he took everything." One day in July he took her to Tenby. They crawled on their hands and knees to see what stepping stones would have looked like to the twins as small children.

He began actually writing the book in the stable flat at Cwm Hall, the home of Martin and Stella Wilkinson. Bruce turned up at the end of October 1980 in a 2CV with a mountain bike on the roof. The flat, said Stella, "was just austere enough for him to feel comfortable and comfortable enough for him to feel austere". Above his desk, he pinned a nineteenth-century Methodist print, "The Broad and Narrow Way". Haunted by this image, one of the twins Benjamin Jones "believed, seriously, the road to Hell was the road to Hereford whereas the road to Heaven led up to the Radnor Hills".

One day Bruce returned, excited, from a bounding walk on a hill above the farm known also as the Black Hill. He had a title. "I'm going to call it *On the Black Hill*," he told Martin.

In his room over the stables, he fell into a routine. He came to the main house for breakfast at 8.30, made toast, scurried back. "I could hear his brain going clickety-click round the corner and him talking to himself," says Stella. He worked hard till 9 p.m. when supper was ready. Every now and then he played the great chef. In December 1980, he celebrated the arrival of Stella's mother Chiquita Astor (whose Argentinian family owned the Monvoisin *gaucho* so admired by Bruce). "He made a turkey stuffed with chocolate and peanut sauce and a mad spice no one's ever used before or since from Jersey City. Everyone was full of admiration," says Martin. "Next day on a high because of the success, he decided to go for a *poulet à l'ail*. There was a lot of talk about how the Winter Queen had had it for breakfast. But instead of putting in 30 cloves of garlic, he put in 30 whole garlic. It was completely inedible. There was rather an embarrassing silence about that and he didn't quite admit he'd got it wrong."

When he put his heart into it, he had the energy to transform any non-event into an event. "He had an incredibly strong character and it penetrated the bricks and the mortar," says Stella. He changed the atmosphere of a chill February picnic by producing a bottle of 1964 Lafite. "He was in ecstasies, holding up his glass," says Martin. "And somehow he convinced everyone that it was a warm day and we were having a picnic in summer."

Much though Stella loved her guest, she deplored his manners. "He was happy to use up your chattel, but couldn't accept responsibility for the kitchen of life. He lived two winters with me and I saw him for three meals a day and he did not once lift his plate from the kitchen table to the kitchen sink."

His hosts could pay dearly for his visits. There was not just the telephone bill. While staying with Matthew and Maro Spender in Tuscany, Bruce noticed a roasting spit that Spender had just bought.

"Now I have to go and see Grischa [von Rezzori] and I have to take a present. That will do fine."

"OK, but you'll have to reimburse us," said Spender.

"How much?"

"70,000 lire."

"Well, I'm not going to give you money. I'll send you some of our tweed. No, I'll do better than that. I'll have it made into a Norfolk jacket. You'll just have to give me your measurements." Two years later the garment arrived, woven from Elizabeth's wool, with a huge bill. "It was three times more than I've ever spent on a jacket," says Spender.

He was needy. "I might be working in the garden and he'd shout from the tower. 'Is there any coffee?'" says Melly. He could not bear to part with energy other than in writing and talking. "Anything was a pressure to Bruce," says Sarah Giles, who had let him use her mews house in London when writing *The Viceroy of Ouidah*. "If you'd say 'Are you going to be home to let the window cleaner in?' he'd have a minor heart attack because that would become a commitment." Ideas came first. "He could wake you in middle of the night with a poem, he never knocked," says Kasmin. Nor was he self-conscious about bodily functions: "He never shut the door when taking a shit. He'd walk in and take a crap while you were shaving." One morning he surprised Giles in her bath at Buckingham Mews. "Bruce walked in to go to the bathroom. 'Oh my dear, it's absolutely appalling. I ate a filthy fish dish last night.' And down came his trousers and plop. I've never met anyone who's done that, ever."

His solipsism attracted comment. "When someone else at the dinner table talked about a subject other than the one Bruce was obsessed with, he might open his already half buttoned shirt and examine his chest," wrote Plante. "He had, it appeared, an odd lack of self-consciousness that allowed him to do in public what people only do in private as if no one round him could be aware that he, in the middle of a dinner party, was probing his bare chest. If addressed, he'd look at the people sitting around the same table as if not quite sure who they were."

At The Cwm, Stella Wilkinson was occupied with her two children. "It was like having *three* small children. He demanded attention. He was heroically selfish, but not purely self-indulgent or egocentric." His insatiable curiosity came first, his need for flattery second.

One of Stella's children told her: "I love Bruce, mum, except when he gets up and claps his hands and shouts." When he imitated a camp Brazilian dwarf, Alice and Matthew thought it freaky. "He was awkward with my children," says Martin. "They disturbed him because of their frank emotional nature. They used to send him up a lot, calling him Bruce Quack-Win."

Bruce worked steadily and well at The Cwm, but longed for a hot climate. "Bruce rings up once in a while and seems fine, except when it's raining and then he can't stand anything," wrote Elizabeth to her mother. He decided to spend April 1981 in Yaddo, "a sort of 'monastery' for writers" on the edge of the racecourse at Saratoga Springs. "I went first to New York for a week of the usual round of varied pleasures—all ultimately the same," he wrote to the Wilkinsons. "Then to an island called St Maarten, the wreck of somewhere really rather beautiful, wrecked in the sense that it was absolutely overrun by Yanks." In St Maarten, he made a thrilling discovery: "WIND-SURFING. I have to say that I really do want to be 17 all over again, and become a professional windsurfer. I am not bad. I stay up in Force 3-4 winds. I can bounce the board a bit over the wave-crests, but I shall never be good."

His second discovery in St Maarten related to his Welsh novel. "It was far easier to conjure up Jean the Barn and the rest of them when separated by 5,000 miles of sea. Why, I can't say. I think it's because the story stands a chance of being a circular whole when you can't get at any more material. If I am thinking, what colour are those clouds, or what are the twins up to, the story rapidly gets out of shape, becomes instead of circular—pear-shaped."

Bill Katz had invited Bruce to the Caribbean. On a misty day Bruce walked up a volcano. Just for a moment the fog lifted and Katz saw a figure at the top of the crater. "He was in Wales. He was acting these things out, hugging himself." They stayed a fortnight in Jasper Johns's house. Bruce windsurfed in the afternoons and wrote in the mornings. "It was a strange scene," says Katz. "He'd have all his books in front of him open at special pages. He'd find a *Moby Dick* and look at a page until some phrase set him off and he'd type. Then he'd look for another page." After lunch Katz would hear screams. "He was on the 'phone to Elizabeth, like out of a horrible comedy. He liked everything to be a scene, to be important enough for a scene. Every day they'd have 40 minutes, bickering."

After his host departed, Bruce moved into the guesthouse. This was scheduled for demolition. He was reluctant to leave. It would take dynamite to prise him out of St Maarten.

AS BRUCE'S FAME grew, so did the number of people prepared to offer him a perch. At his house in Lucca, Hugh Honour began an anecdote: "When Bruce Chatwin was here last year . . ." Before he could finish, Stephen Spender interrupted with: "I wonder how many other friends of his, and in how many other different parts of the world, are saying that at this very moment."

A favourite hideaway was a medieval signalling tower near Florence, owned by another of Bruce's father figures, Gregor von Rezzori. "His strategy was exquisite for a writer," said Rezzori, author of *Memoirs of an Anti-Semite*. "He would pay with anecdotes and by being there. He was a born guest, as writers should be."

Rezzori lived close to the tower with his elegant wife Beatrice. In *Anecdotage*, he recorded Bruce's arrival: "He climbed out of a white 2CV to whose roof he'd strapped a surfboard . . . I could see his adolescent's head before me, sharp as a new—minted coin. A stable currency. Sun-bright. BC the 'Golden Boy'. The alert always slightly crooked smile. The piercing gaze above it. The unquenchable curiosity in the sea-blue eyes (which once had gazed themselves blind on too much art). The calculating machine behind the peasant brow . . . No one would have thought this belated youth capable of writing anything more than his own name. And yet he was virtually glowing with promise. I went to meet him . . . and I thought I was never like this. Never so all-of-a-piece." Rezzori felt for Bruce "an indulgence tinged with tender melancholy". Clearer than many, the older man saw through Bruce's snobbish, irritating, shifty side. "Bruce Chatwin the writer in his glass-clear fragility was utterly vulnerable. Which explains his restlessness and his antiseptically pure poetic sense."

Bruce's room on the third floor looked south-east over the oak and chestnuts towards Rezzori's homeland, the Bukovina. It had painted striped walls, a Neapolitan inlaid chest and a French *faux-bambou* bed over which was hung a Lebanese mother-of-pearl relief of the Last Supper. It was, Bruce wrote, "a place where I have always worked clear-headedly and well in winter and summer by day or night and the places you work well in are the places you love most."

The Rezzoris had a maid, Giuliana, who reported on his progress. "One morning she went to the tower to straighten up and returned distraught. 'How many people are staying in the tower?' Just Signor Chatwin. Why? She had overheard an entire assortment of voices: men, women, children. It was Bruce writing. Reading aloud the many-voiced chaos at a country fair in Wales."

PERHAPS WITH THE excruciatingly slow writing of *The Viceroy of Ouidah*, Bruce had earned his wings. The new manuscript was completed quickly, by the end of 1981. Clapp having left Cape, Bruce required a working editor. He found one in Elisabeth Sifton, his new American publisher.

He had decided to part company with Jim Silberman at Summit. He was unhappy at the failure of *The Viceroy of Ouidah*; upset, too, by what he interpreted as Silberman's reluctance to release *In Patagonia* as a mass market paperback. ("Bruce was conveniently naïve about how contracts worked," says Rogers.) He arranged a meeting with Sifton, the editor-in-chief at the Viking Press.

Sifton had been at Radcliffe with Elizabeth and had read both of Bruce's books. "He came to my office. On a ledge behind the sofa was a copy of Mandelstam's collected prose: I'd bought it ten days earlier. Bruce was explaining to me how, when he came to New York, he needed someone to talk to in publishing—and suddenly he sees the book. 'OH! You're reading *this*.' He patted it. 'Ah, well, then. You know the hand of the master.' That was the magical moment," says Sifton. "He trusted me."

He telephoned Rogers: "I've fallen in love, I've fallen in love and whatever you say to me I'm leaving Jim Silberman."

In March 1982, Bruce spent a week in Sifton's office and they went through the text. "We sat side by side and he said it all aloud to make sure it was rhythmically and acoustically correct." He told her how much he had ingested from Mandelstam, Hemingway, Flaubert. "You know where I got *that*!' he said of the market scene. He had taken it from *Madame Bovary*, but changed the man's lisp. He once told me there were two kinds of reading: for pure pleasure and for plunder. But his penetrating reading was both pleasurable and studious. He wanted to know: how did Flaubert achieve the effect, how did he set it up? He was interested in the technical problems of fiction: how, bluntly, does one crank the narrative through time." Sifton, who later edited *The Songlines*, was impressed by Bruce's intelligence and integrity. He responded to her detailed queries. "Here you had this problem. Here is my solution—or does it present new problems?" He paid immense attention to every detail, line by line, relishing the editorial process. "Not that he needed it," says Sifton. "He was a very fierce editor of his own work. He needed the companionship."

Maschler marketed *On the Black Hill* as Bruce's fictional debut. "I think it an outstanding first novel by one of the most talented young writers we have taken on since I joined the company in 1960," he enthused to a Cape rep. "With this book we could win the Booker Prize for the second year running."

Maschler planned a first print-run of 10,000, changing publication date so as to comply with Booker deadline of 30 September. Excitement mounted with news that the South Bank Show intended to start their autumn season with a documentary on the novel.

The first reader to respond to *On the Black Hill* was Charles Chatwin. This time he did not ask his son to remove any paragraph. "I like OTBH," he wrote from Stratford on 11 August. "You have continued your brief style of giving a picture of a person or an occasion in the minimum of words. And, like you, I like all the characters (except the Collector!!)." He had made a couple of small notations on the proof copy which he thought Bruce "might care to consider in, say, a paperback edition". He had not heard of a "Law Society Annual"—"The books would almost certainly, in that era, be 'Law reports' or 'leather-bound law reports'." And a bombardier would get a Military Medal.

As publication approached, Bruce readied himself for departure. A memo alerted Cape's publicity department: "Bruce will be in Siberia on publication day."

THE DECISION TO root his fiction in a chastened, familiar setting won his widest audience to date. Within five years, the novel would be an English A-level text. For Rushdie, it would be Bruce's best: "a really beautiful book where all the energy goes into the people and the situation and not just the creation of Fabergé eggs of sentences." James Lees-Milne confessed surprise in his diary: "Reluctantly I began Bruce Chatwin's novel *On the Black Hill*; reluctantly because I did not think his first much-acclaimed book on Patagonia good. This novel is excellent. Bruce has identified himself with these strange Welsh border folk with their rough, reclusive ways. His keen observation of their manners and their landscape, and descriptions of nature & flowers are matter of fact, and yet very poetic."

In early October, Elizabeth wrote to Gertrude about the reviews. "Some good, some raving, some not so good. He 1st pretends he doesn't care, but he really does & wants to know everything each one says. If they were really all bad I think he'd give up & do something else."

There was relief that the slave coast had given way to the landscape of Hardy, Kilvert and D. H. Lawrence. In its evocation of place and season, wrote *The Times* critic, the novel "signals the arrival of a major novelist who has come home to find his roots here, his truth in this soil". Auberon Waugh, while mispelling his name Chatwyn, said his was the first novel in two years of reviewing on the *Daily Mail* "which begins to merit the accolade of 'masterpiece', and it does not make the tiniest concession to anything which has happened to the English novel since Hardy". The *Sunday Telegraph* approved of the vivid narrative. "The writing throughout is often a poet's."

Paul Bailey, however, delivered a damning verdict in the *Evening Standard*, declaring it a "curiously coarse-grained book" populated by cardboard cutouts. "Bruce Chatwin is a very clever man who has decided in *On the Black Hill* to write about very simple people. It was not a wise decision . . . The writing is rife with cliché. 'He was like a man possessed' occurs twice within eight pages. Most surprising of all from this lapsed stylist is the monstrosity that first appears on page 120 when an NCO's eyes 'had narrowed to a pair of dangerous slits'. Eyes that narrow to slits are the property of Cartland & Co." The author's recourse to cliché indicated the larger failure. "At no point does he ever bring Lewis and Benjamin to imaginative life. He plods wearily through their mainly uneventful history without capturing its uniqueness. *On the Black Hill* has the quality of an earnest documentary at its best. At its worst it suggests Mary Webb on a very off day."

Bailey's review rankled, but it summarised a view that *On the Black Hill* was conventional, lightweight, carpentered to win the approval of an English literary establishment. In his book *Doubles*, the critic Karl Miller christened Bruce's literary landscape, a place of deliberately strange people, Chatwinshire. He was suspicious of Bruce's large lexicon, the "general herbaceousness" of the writing and the prevailing purple of its vegetative life ("Convolvulus continually threatens to smother the phlox"). This was "the jewelled prose of the upper-class English traveller, carried to the threshold of burlesque—and maybe across it, to produce a variety of Camp and a latter-day Wildean largesse." The result was "a more accomplished and decorative book than it is an interesting one. It is a *tour de force* of doorstep exoticism which . . . fails."

The novel did not appear on the Booker shortlist, but there was a consolation. On 9 November, Rushdie sent a telegram of congratulation: WHITBREAD JUDGES OBVIOUSLY HAVE EXCELLENT TASTE. *On the Black Hill* had won the First Novel prize.

THE AWARD EASED Bruce's anxieties over the book's status. Since the summer, he had worried that anyone tempted to seek out the models for his characters would find them. Betjeman had given his manuscript "WITHOUT MY PERMISSION" to a friend in Cusop, "one of the local gentry, and a bluestocking to boot!" The friend, wrote Bruce, "managed to get almost everything wrong; and though she professed to have loved the book, have wept real tears etc., was full of fatuous suggestions as to how, in her view, it could be improved and was determined to identify every character in the novel with someone she knew."

Bruce was sufficiently stung to produce a three-page vindication of his work to Graham C. Greene, Jonathan Cape's managing director. "I want to make it clear at the outset that *On the Black Hill* is not a *roman à clef*, not some kind of faction, but a work of the imagination that has its own structure and operates accordingly. True, it is set in the Black Mountains or, preferably, the Radnor Hills. The town of Rhulen could be either Hay-on-Wye, or Kington, or Knighton, or Clun. There is indeed a Black Hill on the eastern scarp of the Black Mountains, but there is another one, overshadowing the house, in Shropshire, where I began the first draft of the book.

"I have used the Border Country, (which I have known since the age of six); the eternal feud between the two farms; and the motif of twins (for whom there is no possibility of an advance) as vehicles for a sustained meditation on the concept of Cyclical, as opposed to Linear, Time. But I have done an immense amount of research, in life and from old newspapers, to root the story in actuality."

Anxious to defend the book as a work of fiction, he catalogued the most sensitive elements. The Howells' farmhouse kitchen, he coolly agreed, "does in some way resemble that of The Vision (Chap I); but then it is hardly different from *any* border farmhouse from before the War. The Howells brothers are not twins. They were not involved in the First War. Their mother was an ordinary Welsh farmer's daughter from Radnorshire. Both their parents survived till well after the Second World War. They have not lived in the house all their lives. They have one sister. Also a younger brother, who, in turn has a son called Vivian, a dashing dark-haired boy who stands to inherit their 300 acres, but has not to my knowledge yet done so."

Bruce argued that the Howells' situation was "so tangential to the story of Lewis and Benjamin in the book that one needn't worry about it". He closed his letter with this reiteration: The Vision "is, I repeat, a creation".

As quick as he was to explain to his publishers that his novel was not based on anyone in life, further from home he felt free to tell an Australian interviewer: "There's very, very little I've invented in that book, but on the other hand there's a whole series of combinations to put it together in a continual story."

Bruce was, as Updike well observed, "a demon researcher". He could never have invented his world without having first collected his characters. He tells a different kind of truth in his notebook, a thread of Hereford-shire folklore about the Old Lady of Black Hill: "You meet her in the mist and she deliberately misdirects you."

BRUCE NEED NOT have worried: he had disguised his characters well enough. Neither brother read the book and when in 1987 Vivian took Jonathan Howells to a screening of the film version in Dorstone, the elder brother refused to believe it had anything to do with him. "I said 'That's you, Uncle Johnny,' but he wouldn't have it was him," says Vivian. "He thought it was the Gore boys down in Grosmond, ten miles away."

George Howells did not live to see Andrew Grieve's film. Early one morning, four days before their wedding in 1987, Vivian's new fiancée sat bolt up in bed and said: "He's died."

Jonathan could not live at New House without his brother. He moved to a house in Michaelchurch. He died on Boxing Day, 1991.

Joe the Barn never recovered from his stroke. Following his death, Jean left Coed Major in bitter circumstances. Bruce fought her corner, but without success. She had no title to the Barn and was forced to move across the valley into a caravan with two white fan-tailed pigeons. The twentieth century has continued to wash over and not pulverise her. She is not aware that Bruce wrote a book, nor that there exists a film. She does not watch television because it makes her head "funny". Mrs Lewis at The Bull's Head once offered her a drink, but she did not accept. She has been to Gloucester once, and once to Abergavenny and sometimes to Hay for the fair, "but people trod on me toes".

XXIX

ᕲᜡᕒ

A Judicial Separation

He thought Jasper was talented, adorable. He was
quite besotted.
—JOHN KASMIN

THREE MONTHS AFTER Elizabeth ejected Bruce from Holwell, in July 1980, they met in London. Later, on the train to Newport, he wrote in his notebook: "Lunch with Elizabeth. Poignant. Sad. We discussed our lives in the past tense."

"He minded terribly that everything had gone wrong," says Wyndham.

In Elizabeth's words, their separation had become a *fait accompli* without any discussion whatever. "He thought he was permanently banned, but he didn't tell me that's how he had understood it." As a Catholic, she refused to divorce him. "I didn't want a divorce unless he wanted it and unless one had someone else in mind. Penelope was longing for me to find someone else. She kept saying: 'If you meet anyone wonderful, you'll go off.' But there was no one I wanted to go off *with*."

They had met to discuss the sale of Holwell, their house since 1966. The farm was too large for Elizabeth to manage on her own. She was, she wrote to her mother, "frantically looking" for a house with enough land on which to graze her sheep. "Bruce is v. busy writing and says he has so many projects for the next 10 years that he can't really think about it so I must just go ahead and find what suits me." Elizabeth never spoke directly about the troubled marriage to Gertrude. Nor did Bruce tell his parents. "Father mentioned something about them being separated," says Hugh, "but they didn't seem more or less separated than they had been before."

In September 1981, she bought Homer End, a wooden schoolhouse in a valley south of Oxford. Pattie Sullivan asked why she was moving. "Because I hope it being closer to London, Bruce will spend more time there," said Elizabeth.

———

SHE SENT BRUCE a photograph of the view ("there is a gap through which you can see the Downs miles away"). At first he wanted nothing to do with the new house, or "The End" as he called it. "E. seems to think she wants to buy a 'thirties house somewhere near Henley-on-Thames," he wrote to Martin Wilkinson. "Sounds as though one needs it like a hole in the head, but there's no accounting for taste. As for me, I've got the itchy feet again, so I suppose it doesn't really matter." Despite himself, he brightened when he saw the house. Light, with wooden floors and large sliding windows, it was built in the style of the farm in Sweden where he had stayed the summer when he was 14.

Bruce helped Elizabeth move in. He bought a picnic on the first day and spent the week stripping the wallpaper, relining the walls and painting the little sitting room. "It's much better if something doesn't belong to him," wrote Elizabeth. But she found the move stressful: "I erupted in terrible boils." Bruce wrote to his parents: "Spent a week re-papering Homer End—which, I have to say, is extremely glamorous, if something of a threat to my writing." He, too, was tense. He feared Elizabeth might create difficulties over their belongings: she had paid for most of them. He coveted the painting of the tern that flew from one pole to another. "It was a symbol to himself, for himself," says Elizabeth, who allowed him to take the bird. "He was so completely overwhelmed that he changed tack a bit. And then he disappeared and I hardly saw him for ages."

They agreed on a judicial separation, relieving him of liability for her taxes. He spelled out the virtues of the arrangement to Wilkinson seven years later: "Of course, you must do what Elizabeth and I did: go and see a lawyer and separate out *les biens* of a marriage. Don't get divorced, just get a separation. It's so lucky that's what I did with Elizabeth, because then we found each other again." The Birmingham solicitor in Bruce urged him to do things correctly, lending a caution to his actions which allowed him to maintain a thread, however tenuous, to Elizabeth. "He was mad about a judicial separation. He wanted everybody to have one. I wasn't married, but he wanted me to get married so as to get a separation," says Francis Wyndham. "It was made for him. It meant his home wasn't his. Then he started being at home a lot, because he could do what he did with everyone else."

Early in September, Wyndham received their change of address card.

"As from 10th September 1981, Mr & Mrs C. B. Chatwin will be at Homer End."

ELIZABETH GAVE BRUCE $50,000 from the sale of Holwell to buy his own place. Ideally, he would have stayed put at Albany, but Gibbs wanted back his cubby-hole. Bruce betrayed a compromising naïveté in pressing Albany's secretary for an alternative flat. "Some of what you say," wrote Col Chetwynd-Talbot, "is quite honestly, best forgotten. In telling me that Christopher Gibbs has lent you his top room for two years, you convict him of a breach of his lease . . . On page 2 you urge me to connive in others breaking their leases!"

In November, he found a place. "I realised, battling through the traffic to the West End that the one thing I need London for is to be in walking distance of the London Library," he wrote to his mother from the Rezzoris' tower in Donnini. "I said to myself, 'If I can't have Albany, then what I want is a one-room attic in Eaton Place'; and there, in the *Sunday Times* next day, it was! It's actually quite a large room, at least twice the size of the whole of Albany, but so hideously cut up, messed up, and hideously decorated that no one apparently wanted it." The flat had three big windows facing south over the rooftops and cost £31,000 for a 53-year lease. "It represents the limit of my attachment to London, and I pray the whole thing doesn't fall through. Much prefer one nice room to a lot of dreary ones."

He bought the lease on the Eaton Place attic in January, in the same month as he delivered his manuscript of *On the Black Hill*. At the age of 41, he was able to use the money Elizabeth had given him, plus his Cape advance of £7,500 and the prospect of a $50,000 advance from Viking in America to buy his first home.

While the builders renovated the flat and Elisabeth Sifton read the manuscript, Bruce flew to Kenya with Donald. For ten hot mindless days they snorkelled and windsurfed off Lamu. "The trouble with it here," Bruce wrote to his parents, "is that either the wind blows 5 knots or 20—and I need 10. I always seem to get catapulted forward and end up in the sea about 15 feet ahead of the board—but, *one day* I'm going to overtake Hugh in his ocean racer."

After Lamu, he hired a Land Rover and took Donald up-country to look at game. They camped in sight of Mount Kenya and in the night were woken by something munching in the long grass outside their hut. "Coughing of a leopard, scream of baboon," Bruce wrote. One evening in Baringo, six Turkana boys with "superb torsos and fine dandified faces" entered the corrugated iron restaurant. The leader was naked to the waist, in a pink loincloth, and carried a phallic-headed acacia club. "As D. & I sat down he beckoned No 3 to sit beside him and embracing him, played a while, slapping his long-fingered hand on his arse. No 2 came across the room to the bar and flexed his buttocks standing so that the knots and pleats of his loincloth fell away from his leg. We had never seen such a display of male sexuality."

Donald's enjoyment of Kenya was diminished by Bruce's "total self-absorption" and their quarrel over the loss of one of Bruce's notebooks. "Travelling with Bruce was hell because he forgets everything," Donald told Patrick Woodcock. "You know what the silly cunt did? He had all these notes and he left them on top of the Land Rover and drove off and the whole thing was wasted." By the time he saw Woodcock a week later, Bruce had whipped up a more colourful version. "Every minute was EX-TRAORDINARY. There were my notes on top of the Land Rover and a family of monkeys came along and they were so beautiful and I watched them and there were too many of them for me to stop them."

In April, Hodgkin received a postcard from Bruce in Kenya. "He wrote something to the effect that until you've screwed inside a tent with lions roaring outside, you've never lived. I told this to a friend in New York who said: 'Poor Bruce. Poor Donald'." It was to be their last journey together.

ONCE HE HAD installed Elizabeth in Homer End, Bruce rarely saw her. He wrote her one letter in three years, about money. But he regularly communicated by telephone, ringing up at any hour from all over the world.

In April, he was in New York, irritating Gertrude for the first time ("I do think he might have called me up. I kept wondering when he would arrive. Anne B said she met him on the street one day. I thought he was going to stay here"). In May, he rang from Italy, where he was promoting *The Viceroy of Ouidah*. He had been interviewed by Italo Calvino and appeared on television to inveigh against the Falklands War. "I suggested that no encouragement should be given to either belligerent by the Common Market Community. Next day Italy refused to renew economic sanctions—for which of course I was roundly castigated by the British Embassy. Someone even suggested I should be put in the Tower of London." In July, he was in Millington-Drake's house in Greece. "Bruce is in Patmos for a few weeks & I don't know where after that," wrote Elizabeth. "Now he has his flat he seems quite content with London and goes down to Wales the rest of the time. He can't bear my animals so he only comes down here when he wants a book or piece of furniture for the flat."

Elizabeth, meanwhile, needed to earn money. She continued to lead treks to India with Betjeman and in August 1982 she began work at Toad Hall, a garden centre near Marlow. She earned £45 for a three-day week, working on the counter. "I have to man the till (which I told them I can do, but of course I never have before)." For the first time, she acknowledged to Gertrude that Bruce was not the person she had married and her situation was less than ideal. "But don't say anything if you run into him in N.Y. He's changed a great deal in the past year and I can't predict what his reaction might be."

She could no longer conceal her pain from friends. She spent that Christmas in Suffolk with Anne Thomson, whom she had known from Sotheby's. "I've got to get used to the fact my marriage is at an end," she said. Thomson was heartbroken to see Elizabeth in such a reduced state. "You wanted to say to her: 'Get him out of your system.' Any other woman would have caved in or shot Bruce or shot herself."

A letter from a friend from before her marriage called to a spirit that seemed to have died: "I'm so sorry to hear about Bruce. I think for years you have been going through this anguish with him and I can understand how bitter you must be feeling. Listen, Elizabeth—don't lose heart. If you really do care for him—FIGHT—but be subtle about it. I personally think (I may be wrong) that all these years he took you for granted and walked all over you and he still does. Perhaps he feels that he can have his fling and that you will still welcome him back with open arms when he needs you. You must be a little tough—I'm telling you it pays. What is all this talk about old people's home etc!! Look—all my time in London I admired you because you were so clever and at the same time so gentle and charming. Lots of men loved you. You must look around and be a little more forthcoming (in the sense of giving something of yourself instead of being a closed book) to men around you . . . Just don't dry up—Elizabeth. You are bright and loveable. Just exploit your qualities. No man is worth pining for when he exploits you. Let BRUCE feel what he is losing, if he loses you."

Donald had never seriously threatened Elizabeth. But that summer when Bruce was visiting Millington-Drake in Patmos, what she had most feared finally overtook her.

BRUCE AND JASPER CONRAN met in a restaurant in Greece. "I was with a girlfriend," says Conran. "We'd gone down to the port for dinner and somehow we all came round a table. It transpired Bruce knew everybody—my family, Paul Kasmin. When we got back to London he got my phone number from Paul and he rang me up."

Conran was 22, already a successful couturier. The son of the novelist Shirley and the designer Terence, he had studied at the Parson's School of Design in New York where he had been taken up by Mapplethorpe's patron, Sam Wagstaff. In London at the end of the 1970s, he had offices in Great Marlborough Street. He designed two collections of women's clothes a year and among his clientele was the Princess of Wales. "Bruce loved that," says Paul Kasmin, Jasper's best friend. "Both were on the up. They knew the same people and had a lot in common. Jasper very much liked Bruce's style, his information and energy."

Bruce had known Paul Kasmin through childhood and corrected his essays when staying in Gloucester Terrace. On his return from Greece, he stayed with him at Kasmin's cottage in Devon. "Before going to sleep he talked about a friend of mine he'd met. He started off timidly asking about Jasper and continued next day. 'It would be *so* nice if we saw more of each other. Couldn't you arrange a dinner with your friend from Greece?' My father hated the whole thing. It was the worst thing that had ever happened. Jasper was like a surrogate son to him."

Jasper was 20 years younger than Bruce, but he was more intellectually matched to him than was Donald. "I felt in the role of Zeus to Ganymede," Bruce told Leigh Fermor, "whirling him off like an eagle."

He invited Jasper to his newly refurbished flat. "Bruce was pretty straightforward. He made the lunge."

Sybille Bedford, a guest of Bruce's at this time, felt the magnetism that must have overwhelmed the 22-year-old. She recalled Jasper as a small, jockey-like creature who catapulted into the room and collapsed on the floor. "Bruce didn't turn a hair." After dinner, Jasper drove her home in a large open Mercedes, playing *Don Giovanni*. "Thank you for a dazzling evening," she wrote to Bruce. "I'm still trying to find a way of describing your habitat to myself. You have achieved an essence of simplicity, order, *raffinement* and security that must be Carthusian. I think of the *Trois Con-*

tes, the sensuous food and the Montrachet—and there was that return in that extraordinary car drenched in Mozart. Dear Bruce, thank you indeed."

"I was in love," says Jasper. "It was very much my first love. There was nobody like him. He was gorgeous and knew it. To be clever, witty and bright is a devastating combination."

And Bruce responded. Fox watched Bruce in amazement standing in the drive at the Mellys' house in Wales, anxious and jittery, waiting for Jasper to arrive. "It was the first time I'd seen this side of him." Friends commented on the pride Bruce took in Jasper. "He was slightly fatherly: he wanted to teach him things," says Honour. They travelled to Greece, Venice, Donnini, Bali. "They were very much a couple," said Millington-Drake. "Before, there was never a 'we'," says Sarah Giles. "With Jasper it was totally 'we'. 'We're going to run around the park now'." Staying with the Rezzoris for New Year with Jasper, Bruce appeared dressed in a toga with his eyes made up. It was the first time Rezzori had seen Bruce looking like a homosexual and not a Boy Scout.

"It was the closest thing I knew to Bruce being in love," says Paul Kasmin, "but he was very much on to the next thing." Barely had he started his relationship with Jasper than he took off to Australia for four months. He may have been infatuated, but it was not going to change the way he lived or worked. And there was another reason for him to go abroad. He had just come out of St Thomas's Hospital after an operation. He convalesced with Diana Melly at her London home in St Lawrence Terrace. "It was something genital," she says. "It was mysterious, painful and embarrassing and he did not want to talk about it."

XXX

Australia

Shanghai! Montevideo! Alice Springs!
Do you know that places only yield up their secrets,
their most profound mysteries, to those who are
just passing through?
— *The Moor's Last Sigh*, SALMAN RUSHDIE

IN HIS GRANDMOTHER'S cabinet there was a Victorian walker's compass and next to it a pocket sun-dial with the names of cities written on the rim: Boston, Easter Island, Buenos Ayres, Ochotsk, Tartary, and—on the dial just below the needle—Botany Bay.

After the success of *On the Black Hill*, Bruce confessed to Elizabeth "my tremendous difficulty dreaming up what to do next." He wrote to his parents: "With so many 'cooked-up' books knocking around, I don't really believe in writing unless one *has* to." In December 1982, he gathered up the card index of *The Nomadic Alternative* and flew to Sydney. Elizabeth expressed her relief to Gertrude: "I'm glad he's finally gone as he's had a fixation about it for years. He'll either love it or hate it, but he might find a vehicle for the nomads or it'll finish him off."

He had long wanted to visit Australia. His cousin Bickerton Milward had worked as an engineer in the Broken Hill gold rush; Donald was Australian, as were Bruce's friends Robyn Davidson and Pam Bell. And through the work of the Australian anthropologist Theodor Strehlow he had developed a romantic notion of Aboriginals. "I am turning towards both the idea and actuality of Australia with something like the fervour of a first love affair," Bruce wrote to Robyn Ravlich, a producer for ABC radio.

In the course of two visits he made in 1983 and 1984 to Central Australia he would find, at last, a people on whom he could graft his 15-year-old theory. The journeys would result in his fourth book, *The Songlines*.

He landed in Sydney on 19 December, slipping effortlessly into the embrace Australians extend to outsiders. For the next month, he passed "a mindless time with lots of exercise and lots of sun". Still fragile after the operation, he wanted to recuperate as far as possible from England.

His time in Australia coincided with a wave of acclaim in America for *On the Black Hill*. John Updike in the *New Yorker* and John Leonard in the *New York Times* both reviewed it at length. "The reviews such as I've seen are not simply favourable; they understand what's going on," Bruce wrote to Elizabeth. "Robert Towers on the *front* page of the *New York Times* completely got the hang, but the one that pleased me most was the man in *Time*, and the concept of the 'still centre'." Wyndham cabled news of another positive notice in the *New York Review of Books* by V. S. Pritchett. "Good for Sir Victor!" Bruce wrote back. "*On the BH* is also, I may say, no 4 on the *Sydney Morning Herald's* hardback best-seller list." In April, he learned it had won the James Tait Black prize for the best novel of 1981.

The reception encouraged Bruce to shed the inhibitions he felt in England about discussing his work. In Australia, he would agree to half a dozen radio interviews, one of them overheard by the Nobel Laureate, Patrick White, who had read of the trouncing given to *On the Black Hill* by "the evil Pearl Barley" as he called Paul Bailey. He telephoned to request a meeting and Bruce recorded their conversation:

" 'Can I speak to Bruce Chatwin? It's Patrick White here.'

" 'I'm he.'

" 'I was thinking of you the other day. I thought of going to Patagonia—to die there. What are you doing this extended weekend?'

" 'Going to Adelaide.'

" 'A pity. We could have met.'

" 'Can I call you when I get back?'

" 'You could have done, if I could have remembered my phone number. Here try this'."

While their eventual meeting, at a restaurant in Sydney, was not a success, Bruce told the ABC that he was "constantly being jolted into serious and moving conversations". As in Patagonia, his appetite was whetted at every turn by the incongruities that immigration had made possible: in a fibreboard house in the outskirts of Sydney, a former concierge to Brigitte Bardot in Saint-Tropez ("*agréable, MAIS* . . ."); or later on, a policeman on an Aboriginal reservation whose favourite book was the *Ethics* of Spinoza. "You wouldn't find *that* in a Manchester constabulary." He told his interviewer: "I'd like to *live* in Australia."

Bruce's literary success did not dazzle his Australian hosts, who regarded him with a kindly, sardonic eye. "A lot of people didn't know who he was or care or were particularly impressed," says Ben Gannon, a television producer at whose beach house Bruce stayed in Bondi. "He quite liked that, although he did also like to perform."

He responded physically to the sun and the surf. Sobered by his operation, he took an excessive interest in his health and appearance. He worked out at City Gym in Williams Street. He ran along Bondi beach, swam laps at the Bondi Iceberg Pool, windsurfed. He ate healthily, mixing goat's yoghurt and fruit in a blender. "We've got to get the fruits going," he would say in the morning, wielding a knife. There was vanity in his body consciousness, also the element of "keeping Old Father Time at bay". People in England looked like slugs, he told the ABC: in Australia, the women were "beautiful, resilient and resourceful".

So far as Elizabeth and his parents knew, he was staying on the waterfront at Darling Point with Penelope Tree. "She, as you may know, was once the most photographed model in the world: but has now decided that she can't bear either England or the US and has settled here."

More often, Bruce lodged elsewhere. His anonymity in Sydney allowed him to live life on several levels. To Wyndham and Rogers, he gave his address as 11 Gaerloch Avenue, the tiny downstairs room in Gannon's 1950s beach house.

Bruce had met Gannon in London eight months before at a production of Racine's *Bérénice*. As Gannon was leaving the theatre, "on the other side of the foyer Donald and Bruce were deciding whether to have dinner and you could tell the relationship was really rocky. Then Bruce came up without Donald and said 'Let's go out to dinner'."

Gannon went back to Eaton Place, sitting on a chest while Bruce produced a bottle of warm, very good champagne. "I was completely entranced by him as anyone was first meeting Bruce. He talked fanatically of Racine, the flat. He was flirtatious and sweet. I ended up staying the night in this uncomfortable broom cupboard. I have the feeling he picked me out. He was the active partner and so was I. So it was unsatisfactory, but because it was Bruce it was rather funny and it didn't matter, which was unusual."

Bruce had not yet met Jasper and was still too preoccupied with Donald Richards to take on anything more than a casual encounter. The relationship had ground both of them down. "Bruce by now wasn't in love with Donald," says Gannon, "but he felt guilty. He'd introduced him to something and Donald didn't have any follow-through when Bruce was gone. There were a lot of arguments. 'Donald's being so *difficult*. I had to give him all this *money*'." Finally kicked out by Sebastian Walker, Donald had moved into the Covent Garden flat. But he had no job and when that autumn he decided to return to Australia, it was Bruce who paid his fare. "It was absolutely impossible to have him moping around, penniless and frustrated," he wrote to Diana Melly.

The end was played out in Australia over that New Year. Penelope Tree joined Bruce and Donald at a house in Byron's Bay on the coast north of Sydney. "We were on a roof and a huge fog descended," says Tree. "Bruce was sitting on one deck chair and Donald was next to him in another and you thought: 'How the hell did they get together?' " On New Year's Day they entered the rainforest. "We spent a lot of time taking mushrooms. Everything was dripping and undulating and moving and sinister. Bruce looked up, trying to find the sky, and said: 'God, this is the most depressing place I've ever been. I feel so claustrophobic.' Suddenly, I looked around at all these writhing vines and black rocks—and he was right."

Tree had known Bruce since the 1970s. She had never seen him in such low spirits. "He was so curious about everything—everything except feeling," she says. "He did feel—as in that New Year—but you could tell he put a tremendous lid on it, and that's what made feelings so unpleasant."

His depression and restlessness infected everyone.

"JAN 2, 1983—B back from Queensland," Gannon wrote in his diary. Bruce stayed a further three weeks in Gaerloch Avenue. After a swim and a yoghurt, he would make a stab at working. "You'd hear a constant clattering from his little Olivetti," says Gannon. His thirst for diversion exhausted Bruce's host. "He talked a lot and most of the time it was fascinating, but sometimes you'd want a bit of a break because generally it was all about Bruce." There was little work done. "The sky is so blue, the sea is so blue, and the surfers so unbelievably elegant," Bruce reported to Rogers, "that the room in which I have been trying to write has not seen much actual writing."

On 12 January, he wrote to his parents: "Well, I must say, I'm feeling extremely revived. I seem to have recovered totally in the sun and wide open spaces . . . But so far, I've really done nothing, except recuperate, read books, windsurf and go to aerobics class in the gym with Penelope Tree."

At night, he cruised Oxford Street. "When he was here he'd go to clubs and saunas and pick up people," says Gannon. "It was a liberated time. Bruce was more free and easy here than he could have been in London. He didn't bring anyone home, but he used to go out on the prowl."

One of the clubs he frequented was Ken's Karate Klub. Modelled on the bath houses of New York and San Francisco, this "sex on premises venue" was designed in imitation of a fantasy Roman baths. Horned satyrs and concrete putti (from a garden supply shop) stood guard over the entrance to the steam room where, shielded by steam and bathed in marine lights, visitors reclined on a columned platform.

"Once you're in here the real world does not exist; you've no idea whether it's morning or evening," says the manager, a German Buddhist who came to Sydney in the early 1980s. It delighted Herr Becker to arrive from Stuttgart in this unrestricted country where no one required him to carry an identity card. Clubs like Patches, Kings' Steam and The Roman Baths provided a respite from the world outside. "If you're a relationship person, you wouldn't enjoy it. There's no courting, no getting to know you and you don't have to see them after. It's a very practical and unromantic approach to life."

Bruce never struck Gannon as being in any way embarrassed, ashamed or unhappy about his homosexuality. "Nor was he a conventional homosexual. He talked about Elizabeth all the time and she was frequently mentioned in conversation as his wife."

On 12 January, Bruce wrote to Elizabeth: "This, I must say, is the country to settle in. You've no idea how beautiful the land is, and the climate, just on the fringe of the arid and wet zones . . . Of course, on one level, it's a complete Cloud-cuckoo-land, really very far away from the rest of the world; and it's going through a recession; but if anywhere has an underlying optimism this is it. I think really a combination of things like the Malvinas (as I now persist in calling them) and Paul Bailey's snarky review have made me feel so irreversibly un-English that I really had better start doing something about it . . . I have an idea—yes. A relatively outlandish one, that will take me to Broome in the Far North West, or rather to a place called Beagle Bay. I have a card index of the old nomad book to plunder—but God knows what'll happen."

At the end of January, he cleared out of town with his rucksack to pursue his idea. "I am hoping that the concept of the new book will begin to germinate, however blank I feel about it at present," he told his parents.

HE HAD IN mind to write a "sustained meditation on the desert", intending to establish himself "in the most abstract desert I could think of" and sift through his card index: "I thought I would go to the hottest part, Marble Bar, and sit in a hotel," he said on ABC radio. "But I never got to Marble Bar."

His first stop was Adelaide where he intended to meet the widow of Theodor Strehlow whose work on Aborigines, he claimed, was "indeed perhaps the reason for my being here in Australia".

Strehlow was an embattled autodidact who had suffered a cardiac arrest at his desk in 1978, four months after selling colour photographs of secret initiation ceremonies to *Stern* magazine (subsequently published in Australia) and four hours before the official launching of the Strehlow Research Foundation to commemorate his life's work. His father had been a Lutheran pastor at the Hermannsburg mission outside Alice Springs and Strehlow had grown up among the Aranda, an insider. Like Verger, he called himself *inkata*, or ceremonial chief. For 40 years, between 1932 and 1972, Strehlow collected from Aranda groups some 1,800 objects, many of them sacred, and so the source of the controversy which may have led to his death. He also collected, wrote down and recorded Aboriginal songs, "ancient and traditional poems, intoned according to old and customary modes," and in 1972 he published *Songs of Central Australia*. It was this difficult book, long-ignored and virtually impossible to buy, which moved Bruce to contact his widow Kath Strehlow.

"When Bruce introduced himself on the phone, my words to him were: 'Let me say hello to the first man in the world who's read it'."

A profile of Strehlow was one of the ideas Bruce had proposed to the *Sunday Times* magazine in 1972. Strehlow was a figure after Bruce's heart—"he'd grown up speaking Aranda, Classical Greek, German and English—in that order". Bruce had closely read Strehlow's *Aranda Traditions* and it scandalised him to learn that this, too, was out of print. "It is a twentieth-century lynchpin: you only have to look at the work of Lévi-Strauss to realise this," he told Kath, convinced of Strehlow's impact on *Pensée Sauvage*. He confided to another friend that Strehlow "was a real homespun *genius*: examples of which, as we know, are in short supply. His *Songs of Central Australia*—wildly eccentric as it is—is not simply some kind of ethnographical tract, but perhaps the only book in the world—the only real attempt since the *Poetics* of Aristotle to define what song (and with song *all* language) is. He arrives at his conclusion in a crabby way. He must also have been impossible. But nonetheless VERY great." He wrote to Kath: "Sometimes, when reading *Songs of Central Australia*, I feel I'm reading Heidegger or Wittgenstein."

On 28 January, Bruce arrived at Kath's chaotic house in the Prospect suburb of Adelaide. She showed him the specially built cabinet which housed the artefacts willed by Strehlow to her for safekeeping. "Things never seen by whites before—now pasted up with brown paper," wrote Bruce. "The horror of anyone looking. The pricelessness of the information." Stored in the cabinet were sacred poles covered with feathers, feather boots to disguise footprints and black engraved stones, oval in shape, which represented a man's external soul as well as the title deed to his territory. These stones or *tjuringas* were wrapped up in leaves or paper bark and hidden in caves, or carried round by their owners in a bag or suitcase. They did not properly belong in a suburban house in Da Costa Avenue. Thomas Keneally says: "The great tragedy is for a human to lose his *tjuringa*." Without a *tjuringa*, you could not attend to your ceremonial life with vigour. You were deprived of vital contact with your land, your identity, your ancestor. Kath Strehlow's cabinet was a Pandora's box of untended ancestral voices.

These *tjuringas* were the subject of a ferocious debate. Strehlow's enemies accused him of wrongly assuming that he was the last anthropologist to see the Aboriginals in their native habitat. At the end of his career his political focus came unstuck. He found himself in the untenable position of attacking modern Aboriginals, implying they were not Aboriginal enough and not worthy of maintaining their land because their culture had degenerated. The collection, Strehlow argued, was bequeathed him by concerned Aranda elders. "The collection was his to decide what to do with," says Gary Stoll, a Lutheran pastor whom Bruce visited at Hermannsburg. Stoll once asked Strehlow if the elders had given any instructions about what to do with the collection if he became too old. Strehlow replied: "I was told that if at the end of my life I could find a totally trustworthy white person, I was to pass it onto them."

"If not?"

Strehlow hesitated. "They did say if I couldn't find a totally trustworthy white person, I was supposed to destroy it."

He left the collection in the care of Kath, his second wife, until their baby son Carl came of age, but this deepened the injury felt by a younger generation of Aborigines. For them the artefacts were elements of a sacred male domain: it was considered a gross violation for a woman to possess or to view them.

Bruce did not yet appreciate what he had stepped into. His concern was to find out what he could about songlines and to buy a copy of *Songs of Central Australia*. Kath sold him an unbound proof. "I put a map in the back so he could see where the songlines were." She also produced her husband's daybooks and diaries for Bruce to read. The next couple of hours defined Bruce's next four years. "I sat down, only for a morning," he said, "and I suddenly realised everything that I rather hoped these songlines would be, just *were*."

A "SONGLINE" IS the term popularised by Bruce for "*tjuringa* line" or "dreaming track". It is not translatable in any sense. It is at once a map, a long narrative poem, and the foundation of an Aboriginal's religious and traditional life. For an outsider, the songline's sacred truth is inaccessible, its mechanism fantastically complex. It is secret and there are penalties for those who transgress in the manner Strehlow did.

But to a writer like Bruce, searching for the essence of "wandering", how attractive: to imagine that the meaning of a country could be established by the stories written across its landscape. Strehlow, by making accessible this landscape, revitalised Bruce's thinking. He found in Strehlow's work a structure on which to hang not only his nomad theories, but more or less everything else in his notebooks: quotations, meditations, sketches, telephone conversations, encounters which had taken place all over the world whether in an Afghan bazaar, a Sudanese desert or a New York drawing room. Later that year Bruce would appear in a television discussion with Borges. The programme was prefaced by Borges's parable of a lost man who discovers himself on his deathbed: "A man set out on a quest to discover the world. Through the years he populates a space with images of provinces, kingdoms, mountains, bays, ships, islands, fish, rooms, instruments, heavenly bodies, horses and people. A little before his death, he discovers that this patient labyrinth of lines traces the image of his face."

Strehlow was overwhelmed by the beauty of the songlines as an idea as well as baffled by their complexity. He compared his attempt at understanding them to opening a door in a secret palace and entering "a labyrinth of countless corridors and passages". To Bruce, the whole notion of the tracks of ancestors seemed a "vastly grander" conception to any-thing man had hitherto constructed: "The pyramids are little mud pies in comparison."

Through Kath, Bruce became a fellow of the Strehlow Foundation. His uncritical rediscovery of the author of *Songs of Central Australia* even-tually led to the charge that he did not tackle the ethical issues thrown up by Strehlow, but repeated his errors.

"If there is one criticism I have of Bruce," says the anthropologist Geoff Bagshaw, "it's that he rightly appreciated the scholarship of Strehlow's work, but fell enslaved to the myth which resided in Strehlow's head. Aborigines would say: 'If you want to understand our culture today, don't go to white writers, we're perfectly capable.' It's a Dances-with-Wolves syndrome, that you need a white guy to mediate and render Abo-rigines intelligible.

"Bruce is part of a uniquely English tradition of men in rumpled white shirts at the far-flung corners of the world. I'm not saying he didn't have some understanding, but *The Songlines* is the fictionalisation of a re-ality that in part was filtered through his understanding of Strehlow and presented as solid fact."

BRUCE FLEW TO Alice Springs to study Strehlow's book *in situ* and to test his theory. "I wanted to find out how it *worked*." He spent February in Central Australia. He would return to Alice one year later, for a further month. His visits to the interior amounted, in total, to nine weeks.

As it had in Patagonia, Bruce's brief foray caused resentment. His abil-ity to encapsulate infuriated the white experts whose hard-earned knowl-edge he relied on. One of these was Jenny Green, who has worked with Aboriginal women from the settlement of Utopia since 1975 and compiled a dictionary of Alyawarr, one of the main Aboriginal languages spoken by several thousand people in the Utopia area. After 24 years, Green still ap-proaches the deep stem of the songlines with a humility, respect and ten-tativeness that she found absent in Bruce's endeavour. "None of us would dare to do it or presume to. I'm getting to the point of trying to translate a few lines of song. Even then I can't work out where words begin."

But Bruce felt he had no choice. He did not speak the language, and although his interest in Aboriginal culture was authentic it was not a sin-gular passion. "When you confronted any Australian ethnologist they would throw up their hands in horror and say, 'Oh, you need 20 or 30 years before you understand this.' Of course, I don't have that amount of time."

His sources were the anthropologists and lawyers who had spent the necessary time with the Aborigines. Many were involved in the Land Rights movement and based in Alice Springs. Strehlow, for them, was not a name to bandy about with uncritical fascination. Not only was his research considered outdated (he had researched *Songs of Central Australia* when Aboriginals were nomadic, but by 1983 the Aranda community was settled and politicised), but his collection of sacred *tjuringas* remained an enormously contentious issue. Bruce landed in Alice Springs at a moment when the political struggle for land rights was judged more important than any anthropological study. His anachronistic, point-blank questions angered those involved in the practicalities of land title, housing, health, while he found "the White Land Council heavies . . . ludicrous in their pretensions and self-deceit."

"Bruce offended quite a lot of people who thought he was behaving inappropriately," says Toly Sawenko, then a consultant to the Aboriginal land rights body of the Central Land Council. "He would come into the café where the Land Rights people congregated and fire questions at the top of his voice. 'And in Aboriginal law who actually *holds* this knowledge?' He was unaware he was breaking the code: that their job was not to disseminate Aboriginal culture. But he was being Bruce. His brain was in curiosity-overdrive all the time."

Alice Springs was a political town and Sawenko's colleagues were maddened by Bruce's lack of interest in the political issues. Moreover, they found his ethics questionable. They assumed a writer's ethics were the same as an anthropologist's (i.e. letting the people who you are research-ing know up front) and did not forgive the novelist's lapses. Geoff Bagshaw, whom Bruce met at the Aboriginal community of Haasts Bluff, feels that Bruce was in promiscuous pursuit of knowledge, but lacked the wisdom to manage it. "He reflects the reaction of a cult without secrets. There is something intolerable in the West about secret knowledge. Every-thing has to be transparent." Aboriginal society is, by definition, a secret society. Even to gain a rudimentary knowledge you have to pay your dues in a profound way, prove that you are a worthy and appropriate person. "There was an absolute obligation on Chatwin to demonstrate his respect for the people he dealt with," says Phillip Toyne, the lawyer in charge of negotiating the hand-back of Ayer's Rock to the Pitjantjatjara people. "They had very little to gain and much to lose by giving information." Bruce, it was widely believed in Alice Springs, did not pay his dues. Instead, he plundered Aboriginal culture as Charlie Milward the Sailor had plundered the cave in Last Hope Sound.

And yet people did compromise themselves. They did talk to him.

BEFORE BRUCE LEFT London, the Australian writer Robyn Davidson had given him a list of friends she had made in Alice Springs when writing her camel-odyssey *Tracks*. These contacts provided him with the two central characters in *The Songlines*. The first was Toly Sawenko, who resembles the charismatic Arkady Volchok who opens the novel: "He had a flattish face and a gentle smile . . . only when you came up close did you realise how big his bones were." Sawenko happened to be engaged in mapping sacred sites for the Aboriginal Land Council, and was using Strehlow's map as an important reference. Once again Bruce had found the perfect guide. He was to make Sawenko, along with himself, the protagonists of what was to become the final version of his nomad book.

Bruce represented himself as writing a serious academic study. He asked permission to accompany Sawenko on a site-mapping exercise. Sawenko, ever correct, sought authority from the Chairman of the Land Council, who agreed on condition Bruce took with him no camera, no notebook. "Fine," said Bruce. Although the narrator of *The Songlines* is forever producing one, Sawenko is adamant: "I never saw a notebook on our journey."

On 8 February, Sawenko gathered his maps and swags and drove the English visitor up the Stuart Highway. He talked expansively as Bruce sat, rather subdued, beside him and only occasionally asked a question.

They camped the first night in the truckstop town of Ti-Tree and in the morning collected several Aborigines from the settlement of Stirling. They then drove to Osborne Creek, where they camped a second night, returning next day to Alice Springs. The whole journey took three days.

Bruce could not possibly have realised at the time that he was going to make Sawenko his central character, nor that his book would be a novel. He still wanted to write a serious book on nomads, but once again what he wanted most eluded him. As he prepared to take the plunge, he panicked and suddenly found more congenial subjects in those who had helped him on to the diving board. They pointed him back to the personal—which is what gives *The Songlines* its pulse. It is a book about nomads, yet nomads are supplanted by a host of other characters.

Bruce would base the central character of *The Songlines* on a man about whom he knew surprisingly little. Toly—short for Anatoly Sawenko—was the Australian-born son of a Ukrainian immigrant whose grandfather was born somewhere on the Black Sea. In 1918, the government seized his land and his family never saw him again. Sawenko's father was forced at a young age onto the road. He learned how to survive with the gypsies; from them he learned to play the accordion and to make honey vodka. He married before the war and had a son whom he called Anatole. He served with the Russians in the Second World War, in a regiment that ran out of ammunition. The commander abandoned the troops, leaving orders to defend their position. Sawenko and his fellow soldiers fled the approaching tanks but were eventually captured by the Germans. Allowed into a cornfield to shit, he and two others escaped. At midnight, his companions judged it safe to stand up and were shot: all day the Germans had been waiting. He waited in the corn until they had left and with a bribe of honey vodka bought himself new papers. As a dispossessed Pole, he was interned in a civilian camp where he met a 17-year-old girl, also from the Ukraine. He married her, supposing it improbable that he would see his wife and son again, and by a stroke of fortune was offered a passage to Australia. A second Anatole was conceived on the voyage to Melbourne. This was Toly.

In 1975, Toly's mother returned alone to the Ukraine, while her husband remained in Melbourne. On her visit she established contact with his pre-war family. She met his original wife who had also remarried, to a fanatical and resentful patriot. And she met the first Anatole, a worker in a chemical factory. He wanted to know about his father. He imagined him to be immensely rich, having seen the napkins and tea towel in her suitcase. She returned to Australia with photographs and a crude 45 rpm record cut in a shopping precinct. In Melbourne, Toly's father listened to the voice saying: "I'm your son, how are you?" It was the only time Toly saw his father cry.

In 1976, Toly's father made his reluctant pilgrimage home. He was terrified. The KGB interrogated him about his war record and turned up at a banquet for him under the trees in the back yard of his home. Everyone wanted presents. After six weeks he was emotionally exhausted. He cut short his journey and on his return kissed the earth of Australia.

Toly grew up speaking Russian. He taught his father enough English for him to read the *Melbourne Age* and graduated with a first in literature from Melbourne's La Trobe University. He first came to Haasts Bluff to visit Phillip Toyne, a friend from university who was agitating for Aborigines to have their own legal representation. "It was like going to another country inside your own," says Sawenko. He remained in Central Australia as a schoolteacher, first in Papunya and then in a settlement east of Alice where he lived in a caravan with Jenny Green. Jenny worked with the women, Sawenko taught and dispensed medicines. "Eighty per cent of the children couldn't hear me. I spent a lot of time treating perforated ear drums." The name of the settlement, Utopia, may have inspired Bruce to recast Sawenko in his book as "Arkady".

Sawenko had left Utopia by the time Bruce arrived in Alice. Unlike the Arkady figure who comes of age on a trip to Europe, Sawenko had only ever been abroad to New Zealand, where it rained all the time. During this trip he was contacted by the Central Australian Land Council: he was so good with people, would he consider acting as an intermediary, going to Aboriginal communities in order to help with the preparation of land claims? He began mapping sites for Aborigines who had been forcibly removed from the desert in the 1920s and 1930s. For six months he ferried people from their settlements back to their original lands in the remote country west of Tennant Creek. It amazed him to see how much the elders and their children remembered. "There were kids who had never seen the country, but had been taught the song." He marvelled at how they learnt to orient themselves in featureless country, getting a precise fix by vegetation or a slight rise in the contour of the landscape. "Any tree was a neon sign. No bit of country was insignificant in their eyes. There were just degrees of significance."

Sawenko's next job, upon which he had embarked shortly before Bruce arrived in Central Australia, was to advise on a railway line planned from Alice Springs to Darwin. He was to ensure that the proposed Alice-Darwin link avoided sacred sites. "My purpose was to identify who owned the country in the area where the railway people wanted to go and identify the areas that needed protecting. They'd say: 'You can't put the railway there, because it would damage this sacred site.' But they were factoring into their heads where in their vision of the landscape they would find it acceptable." Some sites were too important to talk about until threatened with a bulldozer, home to forces which if not ritually controlled would unleash themselves at a level of apocalypse. In Utopia, the engineer, Des Smith, wanted to lay the railway track between two hills. Out of the question, said the nervous Aborigines. Smith told Sawenko: "If I can't go through that ridge, I want to know why." The Aborigines explained. The gap was a Maggot Dreaming: if someone violated their sanctuary, bush fly maggots would come out of the ground and destroy everything. Sawenko was struck by how quickly the engineer accepted their world view.

This was the sort of story that delighted Bruce, and Sawenko had lots of them. "At last! I've found the right formula for the book," Bruce wrote to Elizabeth. "It's to be called, simply, OF THE NOMADS—*A Discourse*. And it takes the form of about six excursions into the outback with a semi-imaginary character called Sergei during which the narrator and he have long conversations. Sergei is incredibly well-informed, sympathetic but extremely wary of generalisations—and is always ready to put the spoke into an argument. The narrator is a relentless talker/arguer. I've done two chapters and it really seems to work in that it gives me the necessary flexibility. Needless to say the models for such an enterprise are Plato's *Symposium* and *The Apology*. But so what? I've never seen anything like it in modern literature, a complete hybrid between fiction and philosophy: so here goes . . . if only I can get this one off my mind, it will be an enormous relief and I might start living a relatively normal life thereafter."

AT TI-TREE they had camped beside the tin shack of a brusque and likeable ex-seaman called Jack Clancy. Once prominent in the union movement, Clancy remained a Communist (he had given Sawenko a copy of Lenin's speeches in Russian). Clancy had a withered arm, but was "tough as nails", says Sawenko. "He treated Bruce like a toffee-nosed Pom."

In *The Songlines*, their encounter constitutes a seven-page interlude. Apart from changing Clancy's name to Hanlon. Bruce transcribes the incident as it occurs.

" 'So you're a writer, eh?' Hanlon said to me.

" 'Of sorts.'

" 'Ever do an honest day's work in your life?' "

Sawenko says: "Clancy gave Bruce a real confrontation. But he was lonely for stimulating company. Bruce picked up on his vulnerability. When we left Clancy said to him, 'There's a caravan out there—if you want to write books'."

Clancy died in 1997. Today his tin shed is deserted, eaten by white ants, and the light pushes through a smashed window. No one has stolen his communist library, his collected Auden, nor the stove on which he slapped steaks for Bruce and Sawenko; outside, his derelict Chevrolet still pokes out of the tall grass.

Fifteen years on, Bruce's tracks are a bit derelict too, but they may be traced. Little of what occurs in his "novel" is invented. Mostly, it is modified reportage. The character of Arkady is at best an embellished version of Sawenko. So are the male and female characters that Bruce meets on his journey. The reader might be able to recognise the real-life characters, but none of them can recognise the narrator. If there is anyone who is truly fictionalised in this cast, it is the novel's all-seeing narrator: the "I" named Bruce.

THOSE WHO MET Bruce while he was researching *The Songlines* noted a discrepancy between the Bruce they met and the Bruce in the book.

"He places himself not only in the centre of every situation and scene, but reflects himself in the most positive and self-serving way," says Phillip Toyne. "He's sensitive, insightful and full of cosmic observations."

This was not how Toyne remembered Bruce. Having read and admired *In Patagonia* he provided Bruce with information. Toyne nonetheless grew irritated at the way Bruce behaved then. "He wanted to find out as much as he could on a super-accelerated fast-track basis, but he didn't like to be told there were limits on his right of access to things that he would have to be here years to truthfully acquire. It's disingenuous for him to say that he's not interested in sacred knowledge because songlines *are* sacred knowledge. The very issue of songlines is as sensitive as you get with Aborigine people, who don't readily talk."

In *The Songlines* Toyne is spread over two characters: the host of a barbecue and Kidder, the gym bore: a rich city interloper "good-looking in a sourish way", who flies his own plane and who shames his lifelong friend Arkady into saying, behind Kidder's back, savage and bitchy things about him. "The shrill upward note on which he ended his sentences gave each of his statements, however dogmatic, a tentative and questionable bias. He would have made an excellent policeman."

Bruce's resentment grew out of a barbecue held in Toyne's garden in Alice Springs. "He wrote spitefully of me because I was bitterly resentful of the fact he gatecrashed my party," says Toyne. "I specifically told him it was inappropriate. He was desperate to meet Pat Dodson, who was avoiding him. He just turned up and Pat, lucky for Bruce, was too polite to leave."

Named Father Flynn in the book, Dodson is an important Aboriginal leader. Of mixed Aboriginal and Irish descent, he was a Catholic priest in Broome before exchanging the cloth for Land Rights. In 1983, he was Director of the Central Land Council and one of the authorities whose brains Bruce was eager to pick. Together with Strehlow and Sawenko, Dodson was pivotal to Bruce's enterprise, someone who might articulate the songlines from an Aboriginal's perspective.

Toyne's barbecue is a centerpiece in *The Songlines* and Bruce wrote about it as if he were a welcome guest. Not only did he gatecrash, after being advised by Toyne, twice, not to come, but he monopolised the principal guest.

"A good deal of indignation brewed up in P. T.", Bruce wrote in his notebook. Speaking to him by the fire, Toyne told Bruce the cautionary tale of an American anthropologist who had recorded secret songs from the western desert for a company in America specialising in ethnographic music. On behalf of two distressed Aborigines, Toyne brought an injunction against the record distributors, who returned all 300 copies. Toyne took the records back to the community, built a huge bonfire and ceremonially burnt the lot.

Bruce tried to explain his own project, how it differed. "Lost P. T. in the process. I was extremely jittery and didn't put my point clearly enough—but eventually did arouse the interest of Pat D. He was it seemed interested by the nomadic hypothesis."

Bruce had been aware of Dodson appraising him. "Could only see the bumps of his face in the firelight and a huge beard and long legs. An immensely strong brooding silent presence." The reason Dodson had already declined to speak to Bruce, had consistently refused to see him, was that, like Pierre Verger in Ibadan, he was tired of being cornered by outsiders.

Dodson may now be dismissive of Bruce, but that night he did speak to him. Their conversation by the fire lasted into the small hours while everyone else peeled off or fell asleep around them. "We all went to bed and still it went on and on," says Phillip Toyne's then wife. Gradually, skillfully, Bruce drew Dodson out until he would be able to weigh Father Flynn's voice with all the sacred knowledge required to explain a songline.

They discussed Christ and the Devil; they discussed the Old Testament and New; and it is apparent from Bruce's notes that they discussed the tracks of the ancestors. "P. D. explained how if the track from A to B went across others' land the people of point A would have to ask their permission before singing the song." The former priest told Bruce, giving him his leitmotif: "In theory the whole of Australia resembled spaghetti." Whether Bruce pushed Dodson to go further, to say things he should not have said is unclear. But the spectacle of Bruce the unwanted guest, stealing secrets at the fire is what makes his host of that night so annoyed even now. "He gives readers the impression it's his knowledge and it's not," says

Toyne. "The book would collapse if he didn't have access to other people's insights. He got his real information from Pat Dodson and Strehlow. What he wrote was not a novel, it was a barely-veiled diary. It's a cheap escape to say: 'it's a work of fiction and therefore I can do what I like'."

THE CAMOUFLAGE OF fiction *did* allow Bruce to do what he liked. Asked on ABC radio whether the Bruce who narrates the book is the same Bruce who writes it, he hesitated: "Whether it happened to me there and then is another thing which I keep rather close to my chest."

There are moments when the two Bruces are not the same at all. Bruce the author, for instance, was terrified of snakes. Bruce the narrator is fearless, with a Hemingwayesque bravado that allows him to arrive in any country speaking the language and knowing the local customs.

Bruce and Sawenko camped the second night at Osborne Bore. As Sawenko went off to fetch water, Bruce asked nervously: "Are there snakes?"

"Nothing's going to bother you," said Toly. "Tuck your mosquito net under the swag, don't think about it."

Their two Aboriginal companions sensed Bruce's concern. If he was afraid of snakes, they said, the best thing was to tie up the corners of the swag to little sticks so it would be six inches off the ground. "They did it for him," says Sawenko, "and then they curled up flat on the ground. Bruce said, 'What are they doing?' I told him: 'They're fine, they're not going to think about snakes. But if you're going to think about snakes, it's worth everything for your peace of mind'."

In *The Songlines*, by contrast, the sight of a snake-trail in the sand plunges Bruce's companions into hysterics. The men get twitchy, Arkady so fearful that he decides to sleep on the roof of the vehicle. But "Bruce" is unfazed.

"For myself, I rigged up a 'snake-proof' groundsheet to sleep on, tying each corner to a bush, so its edges were a foot from the ground. Then I began to cook supper."

Upon rereading the passage, Sawenko says: "How impressed people must have been. The reader feels inadequate."

The Songlines is as much about nomads as it is about Bruce inventing himself as his best, most achieved character: intrepid and practical traveller, humble sage, sharp-witted inquisitor. This was Chatwin as he liked to see himself, a Hemingway hero full of deep feeling yet economical with words. But as Jenny Green says: "He murdered people with talk."

The same kinds of reinvention takes place with Bruce's sexuality. For the first time in his books, he is a sexually-alive observer.

THERE IS A curious probing heterosexuality that surfaces in *The Songlines*. Separated from Elizabeth, new female friendships sprang up, all of which carried the charge of romantic possibility.

"So what was it, I wondered, about these Australian women? Why were they so strong and satisfied, and so many of the men so drained?"

Robyn Davidson saw Bruce in Sydney on his return from Alice Springs in March. "I know he had infatuations. He thought Australian women marvellous: 'They can do anything: fix trucks, fly aeroplanes, talk about any book you've ever read'." Davidson was an archetype of this kind of strength: highly intelligent, competent, unusual. One night she and Bruce hugged each other goodnight. "It was not asexual. Having thought he was homosexual, I then revised my opinion: he simply chose to withdraw from it rather than was naturally repelled by it. He had a very complicated sexuality: he refused to be categorised or sewn up. Women weren't cut out of it at all, but men were probably simpler for him."

Two of Bruce's "infatuations" were Davidson's friends in Alice Springs: Sawenko's former girlfriend, Jenny Green, whom Bruce met while walking along the road at Ti-Tree (Green, he told Davidson, was "the most beautiful woman he had ever seen"); and Petronella Vaarzon-Morel, an anthropologist who had worked with Sawenko on Walbiri land claims. In the novel, Arkady's wife Marion is a hybrid of these two women, but mostly she evolves out of Bruce's attraction to Petronella.

"In Alice Springs he had this frisson," says Davidson. "He told me it was very hard to leave."

Bruce introduced himself to Petronella in the middle of February, at the end of his first visit to Alice Springs. He knocked on the door of her house on Winnecke Avenue while she was mowing the lawn. She was dressed in shorts, her long blonde hair in a scarf to keep the grass and dirt away. She invited him into the house that she shared with the sociologist Pam Nathan, who was a twin.

"How remarkable," said Bruce. "I've just finished a book on twins."

Petronella was Dutch, from a family of Amsterdam artists. Her father had lived in Haiti and the South Pole. Her ex-husband had become a Sufi in Morocco after coming out as a homosexual.

Petronella had watched her husband struggle painfully with his homosexuality. "To have this dissonance in your soul is a wretched thing. It sends off tremors which are debilitating and motivating as well. Which is not to say he didn't give in to it and enjoy it when it happened. But all the time it was a struggle more complex than guilt, worrying each aspect of your life."

Bruce walked and talked with Petronella during his second week in Alice Springs. They had a genuine rapport. "It felt like a long conversation lasting days," she says. "I felt he had a warm and generous heart. He leaned towards the goodness of people. Even though a lot of what he wrote in *The Songlines* was shallow, he still had the ability to touch base with things that were genuine." She was excited by what she understood to be his spiritual guest. He spoke of his interest in nomads in terms of the great religions of the world, of prophets who disappeared into the desert to have visions. Bruce was keen to hear from Petronella of her experiences with the Walbiri and Kaytej. She had worked with Aborigines for a long time and Bruce, watching her at ease with them, found exhilarating their acceptance of this blonde-haired woman. It is possible he supposed that intimacy with her would lead to an intimacy with their culture.

Bruce was staying at the Melenka Lodge, a back-packers' hostel. One night he took her for dinner to the Alice Hotel, a smart 1950s establishment with a cricket pitch on the roof. "Bruce waltzed in, commanding. He was very big. He filled up spaces. He didn't tone things down." That night he tried to seduce her. "He made it clear he found me attractive and said he'd been writing another novel, about a romance. After dinner he said: 'Come back with me.' I said No, I'd walk him. He tried to persuade me. He almost pleaded. 'This is so important to me. I need to know certain things.' Of course, I was tempted because I was attracted to Bruce, but it was clear to me it was much more about himself. There was a sense in which he was intoxicated by the place, the things he had found out, and I was part of it."

Next day, Petronella saw him off on the bus to Broome. "I remember him embracing me, jumping on to the bus." Months later, he wrote to her: "*Never* have I caught a bus in such a DIZZYING way." He was coming back to Australia, hoping to see her. "I'm writing something very odd, which although set under a gum tree somewhere in the MacDonnells has nothing much to do with Central Australia. No, that is wrong, it has everything and nothing to do with Central Australia and I need desperately to know certain things." He had used the same phrase as they walked home in Alice Springs.

When he had no reply, he wrote again. Where was she, why hadn't he heard from her, what was going on? Unknown to Bruce, Petronella had moved to Bloomington to take a master's degree at Indiana University. The card did not reach her for another four years. On 17 September 1988 she sent him a letter: "I have wanted to write to you, but didn't know if you'd remember me. I have just come in from a trip out bush, suffused by a sense of magic and life that is the gift of the desert in bloom. And on re-reading your letter I am reminded of the wonder in you, that so struck me on our first meeting." Since that time Bruce had stood out for her "as a source of inspiration". She ended: "I'm reminded of the words of Rainer Maria Rilke: 'That at bottom the only courage that is demanded of us: to have courage for the most strange, the most singular and the most inexplicable that we may encounter.' I'm glad to have met you." Bruce was too ill to reply.

Their paths would not cross again, yet Bruce had never forgotten Petronella. After his second visit to Australia, in March 1984, Bagshaw wrote to her. "Bruce Chatwin has come and gone. He asked to be fondly remembered to you. If you ask me, I think you've quite taken his fancy."

In *The Songlines* Petronella is Marian, the inaccessible, idealised and elusive lover of Arkady who dresses in a skimpy, flower-printed dress and takes showers in the desert. "Then she strolled back, silhouetted against the sunlight, glistening wet all over, the wet dress flattened out over her breasts and hips and her hair hanging loose in golden snakes. It was no exaggeration to say she looked like a Piero madonna, the slight awkwardness of her movements made her that much more attractive." At the end of the book, she marries Arkady. "They were two people made in heaven for each other. They had been helplessly in love since the day they met, yet had gradually crept into their shells, glancing away, deliberately, in despair, as if it were too good, never to be, until suddenly the reticence and the anguish had melted."

BRUCE RETURNED TO Sydney on 5 March. A very different person knocked at Penelope Tree's door in Darling Point. He flung his backpack onto the dining room table and said: "I don't care what you are doing, you're just going to sit down and listen to what happened to me." He then launched into an account of his adventures over the previous weeks. "It was like seeing one gigantic light bulb above his head," says Tree. "I'd never seen him so excited or turned on. He'd not only been out in the wilderness, but he'd come back with a great idea. He talked for maybe two and a half hours and for the time he was speaking he made me understand the concept of songlines. He had it; he definitely had it, and he loved Australia because of that."

The Bat Cave

"Tous les anglais sont homosexuels."

"Oui, tous."

"Sauf que toi, mon chéri."

—BC NOTEBOOKS, NIGER 1972

THE URGENT NEED to make discoveries about himself which he communicated on Petronella's doorstep soon dissolved. Two weeks after leaving her in Alice Springs, he picked up a boy in King's Cross and,
according to Gannon's diary, spent the night out. Three days later he flew
to Bali to meet Jasper Conran. Bruce had not involved him in his plans
and during this time appears to have been unreachable.

Their fortnight together in Indonesia seems to have deepened Bruce's
feelings for Jasper. There were friends he had made in Australia who were
shaken by how much he loved the young man. At the same time it appeared that Bruce had refused to accept that he was supposed to be having a relationship. "It must have had the feeling of being chilling to the
other person," said Wyndham, "but Bruce wouldn't play that role."

It was when he was with Jasper in Bali that Bruce entered the next
phase of his illness. In the Bali Hyatt, they ran into Kynaston MacShine
from the Museum of Modern Art in New York. "You got the feeling that
Bruce was making Jasper pay the bills and at moments Jasper wasn't too
happy about that," says MacShine, who hired a car for the three of them
to tour around in. They looked for Indian textiles and in Barbadoor
parked outside a bat cave. According to MacShine, Bruce did not enter
the cave. "He didn't walk in. He didn't take a torchlight into a dark area.
He didn't get involved." But three years later, when searching for the origin of his illness, Bruce dug up the memory of the bat cave in Barbadoor.

On 6 April, he flew back alone to Sydney with what he described to
Rogers as "hideous food poisoning". He had a high fever, with night
sweats, and was bleeding. He recovered after a week, but already he felt an

inkling that his food poisoning was something more. "He had an idea he wouldn't make old bones, a presentiment," says Jasper. "I once asked him: 'Why are you so intense?' Bruce said: 'I *have* to be'."

Bruce later told Elizabeth that on his return to Australia from Java, he picked up a copy of *Time* magazine. Inside, there was a photograph of him taken by Paul Kasmin and an article on the "gay plague". He had the same response to the article as to Gertrude's telephone call about Bobby. "His instant reaction was always right," she says. "He knew he was in for it."

He wrote to Petronella's empty home in Alice Springs, explaining his illness: "I am terribly sorry for sloping off without warning and not coming back—as I fully intended. The truth was I got hideously ill in Java, with amoebas and all that—so ill, in fact, that for a moment they thought I had cholera. And though I did go back to Sydney for a week or two, I was in a considerably *lowered* condition."

In this condition, feeling "flat, dried-out, alienated," he telephoned Elizabeth.

AT A POINT when matters stood far from clear between him and Elizabeth, Bruce once telephoned the Levys in Long Hanborough, at whose marriage he had first met Donald. "He wanted to stay on his way to Wales," says Paul. "He was keen to get to Penelope Betjeman, but not willing to go off into the night." The Levys gave him pyjamas and a toothbrush and came in to his room to check all was well. Bruce, already in bed, appealed to them with a whisper. "I know this is an odd request, *but could you tuck me up?*"

Just as his books were reactions to each other, so each of his *personae* needed to play off against themselves. Without Elizabeth, he was liberated. Liberated, he was lonely. Lonely, he was a little boy who had to be tucked up.

On his second visit to Australia he drove to Ayer's Rock with Salman Rushdie.

"You know, I've been very unhappy lately."

"Really?"

"Yes, I've been very unhappy and for a long time I couldn't work out why and then I suddenly realised it was because I'd missed my wife. I sent her a telegram to meet me in Katmandu and she sent a telegram back to say she would."

This was the first time Rushdie had heard Bruce talk about Elizabeth. "He was definitely missing her," says Robyn Davidson. "He constructed this story that he was semi-estranged and wanted to see her. I was surprised by the way he talked about her: with tremendous respect and affection. I got the idea of this very special relationship that wasn't necessarily sexual or was; but certainly was a deep affection of souls. When I first met her I thought, as everyone else did: 'How is it possible, these two completely unmatched people, and why?' And in a quarter of an hour I moved from being dumbfounded at this ultimate mismatch into seeing she was the only sort of wife he *could* have had. She's so real. He'd surround himself with all sorts of people and she'd be the constant. I think he absolutely loved her."

The way they got back together did not in fact begin with a judicious exchange of cables but a telephone call. Elizabeth received his call in Homer End. "He rings up. 'I've been offered by *Esquire* to go anywhere I want. Where do you think?' We discussed Japan, the South Pacific Islands, Nepal. He said he wanted to go to the mountains. So I said Nepal. I'd never been there."

He paid for his air fare to Katmandu by reading *In Patagonia* in six installments for ABC radio. In the middle of April, Murray Bail drove him to the Blue Mountains outside Sydney. "I wanted to show him a world class view, seeing he had seen everything in the world. I stepped back for him to admire the view, as you do up there. He looked at it for a second and then turned to me: 'What's the date today? Next week I'll be at the base camp of Everest'."

XXXII.

⌒⊶⊸⊷

An Hour with Bruce Chatwin

Everyone—especially those approaching 35—has
an idea that kills him in the end.

—BC, AUSTRALIAN NOTEBOOKS

THEIR MONTH IN the Himalayas marked the beginning of Bruce's rapprochement with Elizabeth. "We walked off and on for about 20 days," she wrote to Gertrude. "We did see wonderful birds and animals and even what could be Yeti tracks!" Accompanied by three sherpas, a cook and three dzos ("which are a cross between a cow and a yak"), they climbed to 15,500 feet. "It was the most relaxing holiday I think I've ever had."

By returning to Elizabeth, Bruce would be able to write *The Songlines*. The next four years would be a dash to finish it against his gathering awareness that he was dying. He determined to complete the book before his illness was named and he incited everything in his character to work at double speed. "That book was an obsession too great for him, a monkey he carried around on his back," says Rushdie. "His illness did him a favour, got him free of it. Otherwise, he would have gone on writing it for ten years."

Bruce returned from Nepal recovered from his "blood poisoning", but with an unexplained lump on his hand. He fell sick again after his second visit to Australia in 1984. "He's having a bad time with some horrid skin virus which attacks his face & his gums," Elizabeth wrote to Gertrude. "I think it may be getting better now, but he's not cheerful & says the book isn't going well either."

From childhood Bruce had been prone to bronchial colds. These new symptoms put a chill in his heart. Nin Dutton drove him from Adelaide to Brisbane and recalled how, on the last leg of their four-day journey, he fell into a fearful melancholy. "He wouldn't utter and he grumped and so I said, 'Stop the car, I can't stand it. Let's play some music.' He suddenly announced his mother was ill, which I didn't believe for a moment." The illness was his.

Rushdie says, "He never allowed himself to be afraid in the company of his friends, but I saw it a few times in his face. He was so afraid of dying, he couldn't speak his death sentence. He was in a state of great fear, shaking with terror." Rushdie noted how, at the moment he became scared, Bruce went back to Elizabeth, abandoning homosexual activity and reconstructing the facade of family life. "He said to me he'd fallen in love with his wife. I felt it was genuine. How could it not be?"

Elizabeth shared Bruce's foreboding. "From the early 1980s I had the recurring feeling, not necessarily to do with our separation, that we didn't have very long. It was no more definite than that and it could have been either of us."

Bruce's presentiment of his mortality may explain his pressing desire to locate *for himself* the equivalent of an Aboriginal songline.

"I COME FROM the middle of England," he said on a BBC programme. The people there might appear to be the most sedentary and entrenched in the British Isles, "but if you scratch their skin underneath you'll find they're burning wanderers". On his return from Nepal, in June 1983, Bruce made a pilgrimage to Sheffield, Baslow and Stratford in order to reclaim parts of his childhood identity and the tracks he had followed with his grandfather. "I made the experiment of re-covering our walk to the Eagle Stone to tread a path I had not trodden for 40 years," he wrote in his notebook. "But when I came onto the moor, I was *lost.*"

All his life he had longed for connection, yet he disliked ritual and ceremony and he rejected his own duties towards wife, family, territory. There was no way he could possess for himself the coherent identity he perceived in Strehlow's Aborigines because something in him insisted upon a perpetual unravelling of horizons, a continual reshaping of self. He would have to create for himself a fully-realised written version of it, and, typically, he now combined the search for his own beginnings in Derbyshire with his investigations in Australia and the very origins of the species. "To understand human nature, you have to know the circumstances under which we became our species."

When in Kenya in 1982, Bruce had written to his parents of an encounter with Richard Leakey. "A few years ago he excavated the skull of a hominid—a near-man—dating from 1.5 million years together with his stone tools, and evidence of his camp-site. Leakey is a Kenyan MP, and even in the half talk we had—in between his visit to the Prime Minister and his work as head of the National Museum—I felt that we saw eye to eye on an astonishing number of points. The fact that he picked up on so many of the same references as I did with the nomad book encourages me to take it up again."

It was in the course of his research that Bruce's attention was drawn to a newly published book by the director of the Transvaal Museum, the palaeontologist and naturalist Bob Brain. "Bruce telephoned to say he had read *The Hunters or the Hunted?* and wanted to come and talk."

ONCE WE WERE all nomads. Nomadic existence was peaceful. That is what Brain had proved at the Swartkrans cave, working at "the point where man becomes man". His new book provided Bruce with the last piece of his puzzle. It had the same impact on him as *Songs of Central Australia.*

In January 1984, Bruce escaped the gloom of a Welsh winter and paused in South Africa on his way back to Australia. On 2 February, he discovered with Brain the charred antelope bone. He was moved to write to Gertrude for the first time in several years: "As Lib may have told you, I came to talk to a man who wrote a book about the Earliest Man, and I've had perhaps the most stimulating discussions in my life. Prof. Brain has, for the past 20 years, been excavating a cave near Johannesburg in which you find at the lower level (Date: around 2 million years) a situation in which the ancestors of Man were literally dragged there and eaten by an extinct giant cat called *dinofelis.* Then in the upper level, Man (the First) suddenly takes control and the Beast is banished.

"The only way to inhabit a cave, which is also inhabited by predators, is to deter them with fire. And though archaeologists have been hunting for fire in Prehistoric Africa for 30 years now, the earliest hearth they could find was only 70,000 years old. On the one day I visited Brain's cave, at Swartkrans, I remembered how nice it would be to discover the human use of fire in the cave. Half an hour later, we excavated a bit of blackened bone. Brain, who is a most undemonstrative man, said: 'That bone is remarkably suggestive!'—which indeed it was. It turns out I was present at the uncovering of a human hearth, probably dated around 1,200,000 years old. The earliest by 700,000 years."

The most stimulating discussions in my life. The substance of their discussion would become a vital component of *The Songlines.* "The Beast is the heart of the book," Bruce told Thubron.

Brain had stuck patiently to his task and had been rewarded. He represented everything that Bruce would like to have been but by temperament could not be. Moved by Brain's modesty, the scale of his achievement, Bruce sent a postcard to Wyndham. Brain "should be given a Nobel Prize on the spot".

SOMETHING IN BRUCE loosened in the presence of Brain, "a man of infinite gentleness and patience". In the resonance of their findings, Bruce slipped into a reflective mood. He gathered in the strands of his life.

He was meant to be writing a travel article to pay for his detour. He had flown to South Africa with Kasmin. They spent February visiting Botswana, Zimbabwe and Namibia. In the Kalahari he bought a footstool for Jasper, but his thoughts kept returning to his childhood. One night he dreamed fondly of his parents, dancing in the moonlight in evening dress. Beside the Zambesi, "which appeared to be blowing back upstream," he sat on a log and looked at what was once a District Commissioner's house with its mosquito screen and terraced gardens gone to seed. "To think that I in my schoolboy dreams, pictured such a place as the place in which I would spend my life, in khaki shorts, with Shakespeare and Shelley, dreaming of a leafy Warwickshire which no longer existed."

These thoughts ran concurrently with his struggle to synthesise the mysteries offered up by Strehlow and Brain. "Black mood. Cross with all the world," he wrote in his notebook on Mount Omei. His alternating introspection and compulsive theorising began to create fissures between him and Kasmin.

The *Observer* had commissioned Bruce to write "My Kind of Town". "It was a question of finding a town which rapidly *could* become his favourite town," says Kasmin. Bruce had looked at the map and selected Molepole in Botswana, apparently the largest village in Africa. Kasmin's diary for 8 February records their arrival. "At the little hotel we shared a big hall with 40 or so solemn and abstemious blacks, conference of southern schoolteachers . . . Molepole was enormous but no centre at all . . . The highway is tarmac super new. Plenty of cars—Toyota land cruisers, BMW, Merc, Rovers etc. Not a single typically African jalopy."

"It was so deeply unlovable we had to find another town," says Kasmin. With their options narrowed, Bruce chose Luderitz, within striking distance on the coast of Namibia.

Luderitz turned out to be a nondescript mining town. "There's a lot of friction between us," Kasmin wrote on 26 February. "His way of swapping 'facts' with ill-informed members of the public irritates me. He has so many diverse opinions & theories about realpolitick—goodness knows how he adds them up in any consistent pattern. At this relatively low point (in relationship) I brood on his driving—frequently vague so the car wanders to the verge, and then his use of the mirror—at each glance he is riveted by his own image & adjusts his facial expression while we wobble again . . . somehow we get into no real trouble."

Bruce was irritating his loyal friend, he was dreaming of his parents, he was unable to hammer out a structure, he was ill with a mysterious virus. He alluded to his difficulties in an ABC interview a few weeks later in Adelaide. "There is a point at which my African research and my Australian research tie up and I am damned if I know how I'm going to put them down on to paper." He had "vague ideas floating in my head and I can't formulate them at the moment". His search for the point at which all these ideas converged would, he suspected, "drive me mad".

HOLED UP IN the Mellys' medieval tower on the Usk, he had written to Bail: "Australia, I find, even on the most superficial level, is extremely difficult to describe." Ever since leaving Australia in April 1983, Bruce had longed to make another foray into the desert near Alice Springs. "Aboriginal Australia was—and still is—one of the world's most astonishing phenomena—the anthropologists and linguists are still only scratching the surface."

One reason for his return was to spend more time on an Aboriginal reservation. On 14 January 1984, he wrote to Petronella: "What do you think the chances of being able to arrange a trip up to Kintore? I missed the chance of going out of sheer stupidity and regret it." Receiving no answer, he wrote to Lydia Livingstone, a friend in Sydney. "Thinking of you often if not always. And now, next week, I take the first leg of my return journey *towards* you—if somewhat obliquely—just to Johannesburg and the Kalahari desert—then on March 2 to Sydney."

An invitation to the Adelaide Writers' Festival was his excuse to go back. "They wrote to me the other day, and said that 'since I fit into no known category' they are going to programme 'An Hour with Bruce Chatwin'. Lord save us! What shall I say?"

Bruce viewed the literary world through the same prism as he had viewed Sotheby's and Edinburgh. There were times when he was curious and eager to learn from it, for he had come late to writing and this made him vulnerable to flattery: he once told Emma Tennant "George Steiner *adores* my book—and mummy loves yours". Yet he shrank from the pack. "I agree with you about the London literati," he wrote to Bail. "The only possible use I can think of for a spaceship would be to take them out of our orbit—but then more would grow! . . . The review of [Thomas Bernhard's] *Concrete* by some arse was enough to bring one to the passport-burning stage. But then England, unlike Ireland, Scotland or Wales, is an utterly barbarian country." About the only prejudice Enzensberger found in Bruce was "his sincere disgust of England". He professed to hate the London publishing scene and coped with it either by disappearing or by celebrating its absurdities. "There have been some frightfully funny incidents here," he told Bail. "The best is that Virago Press were about to publish an astonishing new 'find', a novel by a young Pakistani girl called Rahita Khan or something like it, with some quite sexy scenes between Pakistani girls and white boys: all very suitable to bring 'literature' to Britain's Asiatic community, all set for a big promotion etc., when it was discovered that Rahita Khan was an Anglican clergyman in Brighton called the Rev. Toby Forward! Great?"

However good he was at promoting the public *persona* of Bruce Chatwin, he was a private person. In his literary life, as elsewhere, he ran away from his growing reputation even as he was attracted to it. "I'm fed up with being a *soi-disant* 'writer'," he wrote to a friend in Adelaide. "It's my experience that the moment one starts being a writer, everything dries up."

In October 1983, he had appeared on BBC television with Borges and Mario Vargas Llosa in a discussion about South American literature. He wrote, "Llosa and I share some of the same ground, in that we have both written about a Brazilian village called Uaua: we were even there in the same month. I thought it'd be rather a good thing to chat about the dreariness of Uaua: but he thought otherwise, and the moment the cameras were turned on him, he turned from being lively and entertaining into the WRITER-AS-PUBLIC-FIGURE. Of course, we both dutifully held our tongues when the Magus of BA appeared, and any attempt to have a chat thereafter was drowned in a flow of beautiful 17th-century English and beautiful Castilian verse." As Borges waited to come on stage, he over-heard Bruce extolling him on the monitor: "You can't go anywhere with-out packing a Borges. It's like taking your toothbrush." Borges responded: "How unhygienic."

Bruce was relieved to discover that his friend Salman Rushdie had also been invited to the Adelaide Festival.

Rushdie says, "I fitted into his compartment 'My literary life'." He had first met Bruce in Cambridge at a dinner for George Steiner. Upon learning that Bruce had come from Scotland, Steiner asked if he had been with John Updike at the Edinburgh Literary Festival. Confronted with a *bona fide* European intellectual, Bruce reached for his Man of Action hat. "I said (realising my *fantastic* error before I actually said it): 'No, I've been doing something much more atavistic. Shooting stags!'—which, I'm afraid, was true. It had the most terrible effect; and I'm sure that no mat-ter what I say and do, he'll look on me, in his heart of hearts, as a mur-derer. Be that as it may, I've shot stags since I was a boy. And though I say it, I'm a good clean shot—when it comes to stags, and nothing else."

This was not quite true. The good clean shot was delivered by his friend David Heathcoat-Amory at Glenfernate. At the critical moment, with the stag in range, Bruce had refused to take the rifle and pushed it away. "No, I'd like *you* to shoot it," he told his companion.

When Rushdie learned of Bruce's plan to revisit Alice Springs, he asked if he might travel with him. "I said to Bruce: 'What would make it worth while for me to go all the way to Australia is if I were able to come with you into the centre and look around a bit.' I thought it would be a wonderful short-cut into the reality of that, to me, completely unknown world." Bruce was willing and they arranged to spend a week together in Central Australia after the Festival was over.

Bruce arrived from Africa on 4 March and for a hectic week he min-gled with Thomas Keneally, Angela Carter, D. M. Thomas. He dined with Kath Strehlow. He planned with Nin Dutton a drive from Adelaide to Brisbane in order to see more of the outback. And he introduced Rushdie to Geoff Bagshaw, whom Bruce had met in a caravan in Haasts Bluff a year before reading *Midnight's Children*. Bagshaw, an old friend of Petronella, afterwards wrote to her. "Bruce, Salman Rushdie and I had a very pleasant lunch in a sunshine-bathed park the other day. As you would expect Rushdie is a very interesting man." It was from Bagshaw that Bruce learned that Petronella had moved to America.

The poet Pam Bell, who had seen Bruce last in New York, met him in one of the large tents. "He was wandering around in that caged-tiger sort of way, an animal on the prowl, restless." Bruce had just watched Vladimir Ashkenazy rehearse Beethoven. "He was excited because Ashkenazy had told the violinist that Beethoven was in love at the time with a woman called Teresa and she must imagine, in playing, the word Teresa, Teresa, Teresa."

At the end of the week, Bruce and Rushdie flew to Alice Springs. "As the plane took off I looked down and I saw this incredibly moving landscape, like the moon with atmosphere," says Rushdie. "By the time we landed in Alice Springs, I was really excited." There Bruce introduced him to the characters who would reappear, without much disguise, in *The Songlines:* Sawenko, Jenny Green, Phillip Toyne. "One of the strange things about being introduced to Alice Springs by Bruce is that when I got to know these people a bit they drew me aside. 'We weren't really sure about you because you came with Chatwin.' They were suspicious of him: they were left-wing—and Bruce was a friend of Kath Strehlow."

Bruce also introduced Rushdie, by telephone, to the friend who had originally put him in touch with these people: Robyn Davidson. "Having never before read her book," says Rushdie, "my view until this trip was why travel across the desert on a camel when you can fly?" He changed his mind after he found *Tracks* "mellowing in a rack" in an ethnic bookshop. Bruce insisted that, since Rushdie had enjoyed the book, he should meet Davidson when he went to Sydney. The introduction was to have far-reaching consequences. "He left his wife for my friend the 'camel lady' Robyn Davidson," Bruce wrote to Nin Dutton. "All my fault—or so I was told!"

Bruce and Rushdie rented a four-wheel drive and drove to Ayer's Rock. Bruce disliked cars as he disliked planes. "The spirit of generosity already threatened by the horse, evaporated entirely with the motor car," he wrote in his Patagonia notebook. Nor was he a reliable driver. As with Kasmin in Africa, Bruce's thoughts on the way to Ayer's Rock concentrated anywhere but on the road ahead. "I was looking out of the window at Australia and Bruce was in Russia with Costakis," says Rushdie. "He talked unceasingly from dawn to dusk, a relentless name-dropping." In the middle of the red wilderness, they paused to look at a dingo on the road. "Bruce, meanwhile, was talking about the Aga Khan and Diana Phipps. I finally cracked. 'Bruce, is there anybody you know who's not famous?' He got incredibly upset and began to bluster and scream: it wasn't his fault and he wasn't a snob, it was because he'd worked at Sotheby's."

There were a lot of funny stories, too. "I remember quite often the car being in some danger because of the amount of laughter around. There are people who exist through what they say and Bruce was one of those. I've never met anyone so much more talkative than me, so that was reassuring. I thought: 'At least I'm not in the gold medal position of chat.' It was a non-stop monologue with interruptions from me. There's a poem written by some comic writer called *The Rime of the Wedding Guest*, which is designed to be read simultaneously with *The Ancient Mariner*. And this wedding guest says, 'Oh, Mariner, oh, incredibly interesting, uh-huh, uh-huh, albatross, well, I really have to . . .' I was like that, going uh-huh a lot while Bruce went into his non-stop spiel."

At Ayer's Rock, they stayed in the Inland Motel. Bruce, who claimed that it always rained when he was in the desert, woke Rushdie from a siesta, dragging him outside to see a vision: the sky black with thunder and the huge rock a waterfall, rivulets cascading down.

Ayer's Rock was in the process of being handed back to the Aborigines, thanks in part to Phillip Toyne. Bruce climbed the peak, although he considered it blasphemous to do so. "Bruce's degree of fitness was extraordinary," says Rushdie. "He rocketed ahead." Bruce was to say later: "The craziest thing I think I have ever done in my life was to take part in a race with the Swiss basketball team down Ayer's Rock, a real running race. How I got to the bottom I do not know, but I was second." Rushdie, evidently, lagged far behind. "I don't remember any basketball team."

On the drive back to Alice Springs, Bruce continued talking, using his friend as a sounding board to test his theory of the songlines. "His thesis is nutty," says Rushdie, "but in a funny way it doesn't matter because it has poetic truth, a mystical validation." While he responded to the metaphor, Rushdie distrusted Bruce's anthropological accuracy. "Bruce's vision is that this is a continuous song disgorged while walking through a landscape whose creation it describes; if you walk at 6 m.p.h., the song will describe what you see. If you think about this for five minutes, it's the longest song ever, much longer than *The Iliad*. It's true, the song tells of the creation myth in a few verses, but it doesn't create an exact relationship. He was trying to make it more exact than it is. I asked him, 'What happens when the stories cross? Is there a grid?' He didn't have the answer."

Three years later, Thubron detected the same uncertainty. "I asked him what happened at the point where a person's map gave out, his *tjuringa*, and he met another territory and wanted to go through it? He said, 'I don't know,' and something to the effect that he didn't know too much. There was a slight inflection in his voice, a slight tickle. Bruce could get a bit angry or intolerant if you didn't believe him."

Rushdie warned Bruce, "They're all going to hate it." But Bruce insisted: "This is the book I want to write." While dining with Jenny Green in Alice Springs, his flash temper seemed to turn on Rushdie. "S. R. kept audience spellbound with knowledge of other novels. Is he so bookish that he can't now look on the surface of life?" Phillip Toyne had a different experience of the meal. "Rushdie was completely eclipsed by Bruce, who rendered him speechless." There is something telling about this collision of memories. Either Bruce did not realise how much he talked; or he was dealing with his anxieties by talking. Perhaps both.

Bruce's frustration about getting to the heart of the mystery intensified once Rushdie had departed for Sydney. "I still cannot fathom out the relation of site to track," he wrote in his notebooks. "Still my question is not answered; always objections." Revisiting the Hermannsburg mission outside Alice Springs, he had called on Pastor Gary Stoll, who had worked closely with Strehlow. He had met Stoll on his first visit, found him "one of the most intelligent and expert people on the Aboriginal scene". But when Bruce asked him "the gist of my principal problem, whether or not a man could actually visit his own conceptive site," Stoll was unable to help. "He agreed the only person who could really have sorted out the question of the 'dreamings' was [Strehlow] himself." But the secret had returned to its source.

Bruce was unable to ask Petronella for help, but he was fortunate while at the Adelaide Festival to have met Rob Novak, who ran the store in Kintore. On 18 March, at Novak's invitation, Bruce arrived at the settlement with a permit to stay two weeks.

The small, dark-haired Novak, who had heard Bruce speak at the Festival, was interested in literature. At Kintore he kept a good stock of novels by Milan Kundera, Flannery O'Connor and Robert Walser. In *The Songlines*, Kintore is renamed Cullen and Novak is Rolf, always to be found in his store with his head over Proust.

For a fortnight, Bruce lived in a three-room caravan. He impressed the community with his practical skills. One day he fixed a bit of flapping iron above the health-care shelter; another day he changed a flat tyre while on a kangaroo hunt. But he did not appear to Novak to communicate in a meaningful way with the Aborigines. "He had no Pintupi and their English is not very good. I didn't see him talking at any length to any Aborigine." This, says Novak, was an insuperable barrier. "In his book there are no Aborigines laughing. They laugh the whole time."

In such a short time in Kintore, it was easy for Bruce to gather a wrong impression. Daphne Williams sold Aboriginal paintings at the Papunya Tula Artists co-operative in Alice Springs. Her salary was paid for by the Aboriginal community, her profits ploughed back into it. One day she turned up at Kintore to collect a painting from Tommy Lowry. Bruce followed her around. He was, she says, "highly disruptive" of her work, talking across the Aboriginal artist as he explained the dreaming. "Tommy was telling the story of two men chewing tobacco which made them pass a lot of *gumpu* and formed a lake. When Bruce asked me what *gumpu* meant, I said, 'P-I-S-S if you must know.' I told him off." In *The Songlines*, Daphne is caricatured as Mrs Houston, an exploitative and very determined woman: "Mrs Houston worked her lips. You could almost hear her mental calculation: a white gallery . . . a white abstraction . . . White on White . . . Malevich . . . New York." But Bruce had got it wrong, says Novak. Williams, could not in any respect be compared to the dealers of his Sotheby's days: she had devoted many years to helping Aboriginal artists, not exploiting them.

Bruce was not an initiate like Strehlow and could never hope to be. Before he left Central Australia for the last time, he met a man who was. On his return from Kintore he agreed to a Sunday morning book-signing at the Connoisseur bookshop in Alice Springs. To drum up an audience, Carol Davies, the owner, advertised in the local press. "What she meant by advertising," says Rushdie, "was a small ad in between a sale of fertiliser and how to get your tractor repaired." Only one person turned up: the local historian, Dick Kimber.

Kimber asked Bruce to sign a copy of *In Patagonia*. "I thought he was a sad, lonely, lost man. It was as though he was playing a role." With striking blue eyes and a light tan, Bruce reminded Kimber of Peter O'Toole. "He wanted to be Lawrence of Arabia, but to me he was never getting into the part." They left the bookshop together, walking in the direction of Todd Mall. It was a bleak day, with grey scuddy skies. As they walked, Bruce talked of Strehlow. He admitted that he had needed "a bottle of red" to get through his book, but the answer was "all in the songs".

Kimber, who had been through an initiation ceremony, told Bruce: "I'm not wishing to disillusion you. It's only *part* of the answer."

Bruce stopped near Flynn Church. "He said, '*Surely*, I've got it now.' It was like I'd hit him," says Kimber.

From Alice Springs Bruce flew to Adelaide to join Nin Dutton. They drove through Broken Hill, the mining town where Bickerton Milward had hoped to make his fortune, to Boona, staying the night with Pam

Bell. She listened to Bruce talk of the Aborigines. "He knew the mystery was there and he didn't understand it," said Bell. "In *The Songlines*, he was desperately trying to go to the centre. It was the most important thing for him and he realised halfway through he wasn't going to be able to do it. He was excluded. You have to *earn* mystery. It's only lovers who get there."

XXXIII

ᗧᗣᗣᗣ

A Sincere Fumbling

*It is ironic that my book which is a passionate
defence of movement should involve its author in
years of limpet-like existence.*
—BC TO JOHN PAWSON, 1986

"I'M LONGING TO see you," Jasper wrote from Marrakesh in March. His postcard showed the wedding ceremony of the Ait Haddidu. He had bought a house near Regent's Park and gutted it. He wanted Bruce to move in with him. "This is my studio," he said, showing Diana Melly around. "And this is where Bruce could write." Bruce's influence was present in the bare floorboards, the white walls; and in Eileen Gray's map of Argentinian Patagonia, the pair of the map of Chilean Patagonia that he had given to Elizabeth. Bruce was there a lot over the next two years, but he did not share Jasper's dream.

"I do think Bruce was very happy with Jasper," says Melly, who would have them to stay at the Tower in Scethrog. "The problem came over who was who. Bruce was much older than Jasper and you would have expected him to be more fatherly, more mature. But Bruce was never a father figure. He was always disappearing."

"He just didn't want to be cornered," says Jasper. "He had these different worlds which he compartmentalised. I don't think Bruce thought of himself as one thing or the other. The fact that he married Elizabeth knowing what a great part of his sexuality was, and with people saying 'Ah, we know what *you're* about', made him more fundamentally non-committal. Which, at the end, is exactly what was wrong with my relationship. There was nobody like him, so witty, so sharp, so bright, but there were aspects of him, finally, I couldn't deal with. Bruce did not treat me very nicely. I was young and along comes this glamorous creature who's fantastic. It was very much my first love, but he would up sticks and bugger off at the drop of a hat. In Australia, he didn't ring me and didn't write, and ignored me. While he was there he had affairs with other people. I found out and he told me it was true and I'd had enough. It was more than I could take on a daily basis. I couldn't structure my life. I'd just moved into a house. I wanted a proper life. I wanted him to move in with me. As far as I knew, Bruce had split up from Elizabeth. I didn't know this was a situation that was on-going. I never knew otherwise until he was ill. And I can tell you, I was appalled. I had to come to terms with the fact that he had deceived me as well."

One day Ivry had lunch with Bruce and Elizabeth in Oxford. "When I got him alone I said: 'Bruce, what's all this about you and Jasper Conran?' Bruce said: 'Nothing has changed, Ivry. I meant it, *nothing* has changed'."

"Probably there was nobody Bruce loved more than himself," says Jasper, who would refuse to read *The Songlines* because he felt Bruce had left him to go to Australia. "And nothing meant more to him than his own written word."

BRUCE'S INITIAL IDEA for *The Songlines* was to write it in the form of a letter to his Italian publisher, Roberto Calasso. "He was tortured by the fact he had no structure. He thought of putting everything in a letter to me from a totally unknown place in the middle of nowhere." The book was to have been called *Letter from Marble Bar*.

The next idea was to cast the book as a Platonic dialogue. "The novel, if such it be, consists of the narrator (myself) and a Russian immigrant to Melbourne (based loosely on someone I met) having a long, drawn-out conversation in the shade of a mulga tree." This evolved from his 1983 journey with Toly Sawenko.

But again the book changed shape after his visit to Swartkrans with Brain. When *Of the Nomads* was replaced as a title by *The Prince of Darkness is a Gentleman*, Maschler tentatively enquired, "I assume it *is* the book we talked about! i.e. in shorthand AFRICA." Bruce was guarded: "Should we say it's longer than anything I've attempted before. It is, I suppose, a novel: though of a very strange kind; but as I have the most unbelievable difficulty slotting all the bits in, I'd really rather not talk about it."

His battle to structure his book lasted until July 1986. "The book is not just an 'Australian' enterprise," he wrote to Nin Dutton, "but sets down a lot of crackpot ideas that have been going round my head for 20 years."

BRUCE RETURNED FROM his second Australian visit in April 1984. He found Mrs Thatcher's England in a "soupy pre-Fascist condition". He wrote to Bail: "Without wanting to sound unpatriotic, I now find that a week in my country is as much as I can stomach. It used to be two months, but now, like the dwindling pound, it gets whittled down and down and down . . ."

That summer he lent Bail his Eaton Place attic while he tried to work in Homer End. "I'm only capable of functioning away from all the hulla-baloo . . . My impulse is to sell up and go away somewhere rather primi-tive—or at least isolated from the literary 'buzz' that nags at me with the insistence of a pneumatic drill in a neighbouring street. The answer is this: that no amount of comfort, padding, recognition etc., is, in any way, a compensation for having one's head and time free. And London is such an abominable trap!"

He was also ill. On 20 November 1984, Elizabeth wrote to Gertrude: "Bruce is well, but has a nasty virus on his face which looks like chicken pox. He's apparently had it for a couple of years, but it didn't show up much. The only treatment is to have some incredibly cold nitrogen put on it which sort of burns off the spots." In his run-down state, he developed bronchitis.

As winter approached, he did not find it any easier to concentrate at Homer End, "this promenade-deck-of-the-Queen-Mary house of ours". The house was light, with a sweeping view, but he was easily distracted, not least by Elizabeth's cats. "This a.m. there was an unfortunate inci-dent," Elizabeth wrote to Gertrude. "I usually get down 1st & check the kitchen for corpses and remains, but today missed a nasty pile of some-thing they sicked up & Bruce sat on it. It was on his chair . . ."

He poured out his heart to Kasmin: "This peripatetic existence of mine must stop. I must have *mon bureau, mes fauteuils, mon jardin* (as Flaubert writes in a letter)—somewhere in a relatively good climate, which means the Mediterranean (*pas des bêtes!*), and I must have it soon. God knows how I'll raise the cash, if it means the sale of my London flat + my art then *tant pis pour eux*!"

He spent Christmas at Homer End, then packed up his books, his notes, his scuba suit and his surfboard and departed by car for the Mani. He had been quite ill, Elizabeth told Gertrude, "and needed clearance from the Doctor before setting off on his long drive to Greece".

He had found "the most beautiful place you can imagine": a self-service flat set in an abundance of silvery-green olives within the sound of the sea at Kardamyli. He arrived at the Hotel Theano on 1 January 1985.

Bruce's seclusion in Greece lasted seven months while he ground out a first draft. Elizabeth and Margharita would join him for several weeks in January. For the rest of the time, he worked alone. One of his few correspondents was Murray Bail. "I've put a block on being available from London, and that includes the post," Bruce wrote. "I have a room with a view of olives, cypresses, a bay. I work till 3; then walk in the hills; then read; then sleep. Not bad. Costs next to nothing. I go on with the book and have reached such a stage, I simply daren't look back."

Bruce described Bail to Nin Dutton as "a really good egg!" They had enjoyed each other's company immediately and he grew to depend on the younger writer for advice, especially about Australia. They became literary intimates. "What am I reading here?" wrote Bruce on 1 March 1985. "I have the Sinyavsky, in French (*Bonne Nuit*), but cannot finish it . . . Otherwise, three novels of Svevo, who I'd never read before; *The Idiot*, which I last read in the Sahara; Michel Tournier, who is obviously inventive, but I now think is far too kitsch; *Dialogues* of Plato, to see how you express ideas in dialogue (The answer is, 'I don't') plus the usual array of technical and scientific stuff."

Drawn to Bail's quiet wit, Bruce found himself in the unusual position of trusting another writer. In his letters to him, he entered into the equivalent of a Platonic dialogue.

Bail had visited Bruce at Homer End in August. Bruce read to him the Swartkrans section, after which Bail wrote in his diary: "It's ambitious, difficult. Felt it was written too smoothly, lightly." Bail told him of his misgivings. He suggested that if something was impossible to prove then the tone had to be searching. Bruce was immediately grateful for his uncompromising reaction. "I feel I must reply at once to say how much I value your comments about not making the book so easy . . . I know exactly what you mean and have, anyway, embarked on a different track."

It was from Bail that Bruce learned of the publication of another book on songlines, Charles Mountford's *Nomads of the Desert*. "A disaster with the Australian book—in that another, by accident, had cannibalised it—temporarily," he wrote to Penelope Tree. Bruce was alarmed at Mountford's fate. The Aboriginals had decided that he had broken Aborigine law by reproducing secret ceremonial material. "The entire edition was pulped," wrote Bail.

Chosen as an intimate, Bail found himself fielding Bruce's worries and frustrations. "He spent so much time imagining himself that people do have trouble adding his parts up, and so did he," says Bail. "It troubled and confused him. He never seemed at one. He's a construct, a bowerbird—as is anyone who's a good mimic. The original Cubist, all surfaces in different directions, including from behind."

Few understood Bruce's aesthetic better. "It was an aesthetic of removal." It struck Bail from their discussions on art how many of the paintings and photographs Bruce admired had no people in them: Malevich's white canvasses; the cloud scenes of Turner and Constable; the spotted bare landscapes of Fred Williams, whose work would appear on the paperback cover of *The Songlines*; the grey abstracts of the Australian Ian Fairweather (on whom Bail had written a monograph). "They were emptied of characters and references." Bruce's admiration for austerity and plainness pervaded the arts. He urged Bail to visit the unfinished Cistercian Abbey at Le Thoronet in the Var. "Everything had been removed," says Bail. "It was plain, immaterial and resonant because of the emptiness. It summed him up."

Bail stayed in Eaton Place during the summer of 1984: "It was like being in a space-capsule, secretive, on the top looking down, everything hidden away. If you swung a cat, you would smash its head four times, straight off." The flat was so small that the person to occupy it before Bail, while making love to a famous model, had electrocuted himself in the single deadly light socket. "*To gain extra purchase*, he put his foot against a plug in the wall," Bruce told Bail with glee.

Hugh Honour wrote of Eaton Place: "Although Bruce's mind might seem to have been a *Schatzkammer* filled to bursting with a miscellany of impressions which flowed out impetuously in his conversation, his apartment in London belied this. Hardly more than a box-room converted into a tiny bed-sitting room . . . he called it 'a place to hang a hat'. Spartan in its spareness—polished wood floor, no carpets or rugs, a built-in bunk for bed, and very little furniture apart from his Empire sofa and two plywood tables by Aalto—the surroundings he created for himself and for the objects he loved were no less rigorously pared down than was his prose."

This spareness was a deceptive camouflage. John Pawson, the architect whom Bruce employed to convert the flat, noticed that the cupboards were stuffed with Russian gold forks and Fortnum's Gunpowder teas. "I got into frightful trouble by saying he wasn't living as simply as he was professing."

Bail sat on a Napoleonic steel folding-bed. "It was elegant, but would he have bought it if he hadn't known Marshal Ney had lugged it to Moscow? Draped over the bed was Freud's shawl. 'Not only that . . .' said Bruce. I waited for the punch line. 'This is the *very* shawl Freud had around his shoulder when he fled Nazi Europe and arrived in Charing Cross.' Everything needed a myth. It made them more exclusive." But the campaign bed had nothing to do with Ney: Bruce had bought it in Paris. As for the "shawl"—a thin, pale indigo bedspread, hand-woven with West African symbols—this had belonged to his Kynance Mews landlord. "He had some connection to Freud's sister," says Elizabeth. "Bruce loved it because it was African. It got more and more interesting the longer he had it. "Maybe Freud had laid it on his couch for people to lie on . . .' "

Into this confined space Bruce hung an eighteenth-century Swedish chandelier. "It was very handsome, but conventional," says Hodgkin, "and he talked about it in the most marvellous way. 'You can see it comes from the north and it's snow and it's ice and I'm lighting it just for you.' The wax dropped plop, plop, plop, onto the floor. 'Bruce, Bruce, shouldn't we put something down?' Bruce was totally impervious. 'What are you *talking* about?'"

In the same breath as he rhapsodised about Malevich and Fairweather, Bruce singled out to Bail an unlikely canvas by a nineteenth-century Australian artist as one of his favourite examples of Australian art. In Adelaide, he had stood transported before Tom Roberts's 1891 narrative work *A Breakaway!* The painting depicts a young horseman in an arid landscape stretching from his saddle to control a stampede of drought-stricken sheep. Bail saw this competing tension at work in Bruce. "He was very awkward about a number of things. He could not bring himself to be natural. He had a smooth attractive surface, but he was split, rather like his books, between fact and imagination. It was very hard to determine his true shape."

The Cistercian emptiness he strove for was aesthetic rather than spiritual. "He was not at all a moralist," said Rezzori. "His morality was totally aesthetic—built of the best inks, but not with blood." He once told Hodgkin: "I want you to read this." It was a short story, based on something by Poe. "But why?" said Hodgkin. "I think you're quite beady about these sort of things," replied Bruce. Hodgkin says: "It was the same expression that he used when he showed me an Indian painting—to test whether it was genuine or fake. He was very concerned about his own writing being as good as possible. He had a sort of artistic morality."

It was a state he achieved most satisfactorily in his prose, where he could shuffle the contents and subtract and subtract until he had wrought the clarity and resonance of Le Thoronet. Naturally his impulse was towards the baroque of his conversation and storytelling. He had to labour for his simplicity, discarding the ornate by first verbally sculpting the story, word by word, version after version, often, as he admitted, to the "intense irritation" of his audience. Krüger, his German publisher, remembers how Bruce told him about *On the Black Hill* in Lindos, the waves coming in and Bruce talking very quickly, like a machine. "I've never met anyone who talked so quickly. It was psychotic, not making an end, and, whenever interrupted, zigzagging back. It was a kind of sickness." When *In Patagonia* was published, Bruce told Hodgkin: "Oh, you don't need to read it." He had already spoken it. "He had told it word for word, telling me on walks." It was the same with *Utz*. One night in New York he called on Sontag. "For an hour he told me *Utz*, non-stop. Then the book came out. There was virtually nothing new. Bruce didn't relinquish control; there was no letting go. What went in is what he originally wanted it to be."

"His instinct was always to pare down," Bail says. "He liked a plain, firmly based simplicity of style: Turgenev, Flaubert, Edmund Wilson. He wanted to be a clean, clear writer and introduce ideas that were original. That stuffed him up as a novelist. He always researched his novels too much, except *In Patagonia* where he's not presenting a theory. He has a plainness of language, which is good, but it's a teacher's language rather than free-floating. He stands behind the lectern, putting an extra distance between himself and the reader. He can't tell a story without giving a lecture on twins or nomads. But he's not a novelist: he couldn't imagine them. And he couldn't go the full distance of research in understanding his subject. So he could make two readers unhappy." This, for Bail, was the problem with *The Songlines*. "He took risks with it, which I admired, but the book is split between fact and imagination and the imagination part comes off second-best."

Bruce longed for Bail to look over his text. He planned to go to India in the New Year. "It would be terrific if you were there too," he wrote. "In fact, I cannot imagine anything in the world I'd like more."

BRUCE'S ROOM IN the Hotel Theano was a convenient five-minute walk from the home of Paddy and Joan Leigh Fermor. Their low arcaded house of red-streaked limestone was perched on a steep cliff opposite the waterless island of Merope. Magouche Fielding had introduced Bruce to the Leigh Fermors in 1970. That August, Bruce had stayed with them when writing the first draft of *The Nomadic Alternative.* "The whole Taygetus range plunges straight down into the sea and eagles float in thermals above the house," he had written to Elizabeth. Then he brimmed with hope for an early completion of his book. "I really do think it will/or can be ready in its first draft by *November* (early)." That was fifteen years before.

At the end of most days Bruce walked through the olive groves down to their house in a hollow surrounded by "pencil thin" cypresses. Leigh Fermor was Bruce's last guru.

Leigh Fermor was a man of action and of knowledge to a degree that Bruce envied. As a child, he lived at the vicarage in Ipsden near Homer End. He was the son of an absentee father, a geologist in India. He had known Peter Wilson before the war, when Wilson lived in Maids of Honour Row ("where he played the accordion"). He had met a drunk Robert Byron in The Nest nightclub. His war career had inspired a film (based on his capture of the German commander in Crete, General Kreipe). He spoke Latin, Greek and Romanian (Bruce, he said, reminded him of the Romanian proverb: "a child with too many motivations remains with his navel string uncut"). And he knew almost as much about nomads as Bruce.

A dedicated wanderer, Leigh Fermor had written a classic book based on a walk through pre-war Europe. In 1933, at the age of 18, he had set off on foot from London to Constantinople, returning four years later. He had taken with him the canvas rucksack "weathered and faded by Macedonian suns" which Robert Byron and David Talbot Rice had carried to Mount Athos in 1927.

A Time of Gifts had come out the same year as *In Patagonia.* While Leigh Fermor felt Bruce should "let it rip", Bruce believed the other should prune. "Paddy and Bruce are a very different type of creature," says Sybille Bedford, "but they are both grandees of style and erudition. In both a toughness goes with a certain sybaritic quality."

Leigh Fermor was then working on the second volume of his walk to

Constantinople. He found Bruce "one of the most extraordinary people one has ever met. Very, very extraordinary, highly gifted, rare person." He was impressed by his wide and accurate knowledge, by his energy and diligence. "Bruce was a very punctilious note-taker—'I must just make a note'—when something cropped up in conversation. He had tremendous filing cabinets and a card system. The amount of prep he'd done was fantastic. I'd just read in Jordanese about the costumes of the court of Attila. I said to Bruce: 'Do you know what the women of Genghis Khan wore in the evening?' 'Yes,' he said, 'I do. They wore the skins of field-mice sewn together. Probably the jumping jerboa that jumped around in the Asian steppes. There was a good example of this in Katanda a few years ago where there dug up a Khan woman, a leader of Huns who'd been kept intact by preserving her in a patchwork jerkin made of these skins.' I was dazzled. I was astonished by the idea of Huns wearing a garment of field-mice, that was quite enough for me, but he knew everything. He knew more about the Europe of Philip II than Braudel."

Writing after Bruce's death, Leigh Fermor described the quality of his friend's erudition. "Abstruse art-forms and movements of thought, history, geology, anthropology and all their kindred sciences were absorbed like breathing . . . There was always John Donne or Rimbaud to think or to write about, palaeontological riddles to brood over, speculation on the influence of Simonides of Ceos on the memory techniques of counter-Reformation Jesuits in China, and the earliest whereabouts of Mankind."

Bruce was competitive with the older man. "He did like to get things right," says Leigh Fermor. "He was talking about elephants moving across those Central Desert prairies. I said, 'Bruce, it's not pronounced *mahoot*, its *mahout*.' A flicker of vexation would go over his face if one corrected him. But he did occasionally cap me. About seven years before he came to stay, I couldn't resist it, I swam across the Hellespont. It took me a long time, nearly three hours. Joan was there with a boat, shouting, 'Come on, get a move on.' Bruce said: 'I haven't swum across the Hellespont, but I have swum across the Bosphorus, which is a bit wider and the current a bit stronger.' I said, 'Anyone with you?' 'Yes, there was a very nice *caique* following me with three Turkish princesses'."

Invariably, if there was an audience of four or five, Bruce would get carried away. "He loved parties, to which he contributed a great deal. In our village taverna one night there was a certain amount of drinking. Bruce got up on the table and did a dance, like a solitary dervish, with a demonic expression on his face. One thing Caspar Fleming noticed, and I saw what he meant: Bruce sometimes opened his mouth in such a way that it went, 'clackety-clackety-clack,' rather like a ventriloquist's dummy. Sometimes he'd get so excited that he'd go into a kind of tailspin and end up with a sort of 'pop' in mid-air, very curious and difficult to describe."

He was at his most rewarding when alone on a long walk with nobody else to dazzle. "He had rather a harlequin quality, very light on his feet, up and away, eyes sparkling. Wherever he went, he was off like a bullet to the horizon, learning everything at tremendous speed." Leigh Fermor wrote of him surging across the headlands and the canyons "as though he were in seven-league boots, only stopping to identify a momentarily puzzling flower or some rare hawk flickering high overhead . . . Bruce was interested in everything."

"UP BEHIND KARDAMYLI, there is a first line of hills with little villages dotted about, and then a line of snowy mountains," Bruce wrote to Diana Melly. "I usually break off at 2 and go walking with Paddy."

He was a living illustration of his own "crackpot theory" that the human frame was designed for a day's march. He once received from Redmond O'Hanlon a postcard of an emaciated, Giacometti figure with the inscription: "*Après* a short walk with Bruce." He believed that walking "is not simply therapeutic for oneself, but is a poetic activity that can cure the world of its ills". Plante found a clue to his restlessness in Thoreau's *Walking*. "To saunter, [Thoreau] thinks, could mean to be *sans terre*, without land or home, but to be equally at home everywhere. Bruce did have a home with his wife Elizabeth but his restlessness was such that she herself accepted his feeling that he was *sans terre*." In medieval times children would shout, "There goes a Sainte Terre, a saunterer, a Holy Lander" of someone asking for charity under pretext of going to the Holy Land. Plante believed that Bruce in his wandering "was looking for the Holy Land, looking at least for the small objects that remained of its former habitation as evidence of something deep in humanity that might be humanity's saving grace".

One day while exploring the limestone gorges with Leigh Fermor, Bruce came across the tiny ruined church of St Nicholas in Chora. "I hadn't seen it for donkeys' years," says Leigh Fermor, "a tenth century Byzantine church on a headland two miles up a mountain, surrounded by oaks and olives and full of bats." The dust-coloured interior, painted with blue and yellow frescoes, was no more spacious than Bruce's London flat and contained a marble, three-legged stool from a pre-Christian shrine.

Bruce said of the Greeks that they reserved all the best building sites for God. He loved the building and its views over the Messinian headland to Venetico, the Venetian isle. "We'd often go and have picnics there," says Joan Leigh Fermor. "One always thought of it as Bruce's place."

On his walks he resembled the Old Testament scholar in *On the Black Hill*, "a hollow-chested figure with white hair blowing about like cotton-grass, striding over the heather and shouting to himself so loudly that he frightened off the sheep". Bail was struck by how much he looked at the ground; also by how someone of such taste could, at the same time, be so utilitarian. "He was a fearless pisser. He'd stop and piss right in front of you while talking. He used to fart very freely, too." Kasmin was not alone in trying to keep up. "He always walked ahead of everyone, talking to himself and to you and you could never quite hear what he was saying." An entry in his notebook reads: "Nothing can be more irritating than walking long distances with someone who cannot keep up."

Leigh Fermor was an exception. Wanting to learn from him, Bruce reined himself to walk side by side. On one of their walks, Leigh Fermor told him the Latin expression *solvitur ambulando*—it is solved by walking—"and immediately Bruce whipped out his notebook. Everything was useful to him. He piled it into a great sack and when alone winnowed and used it when most apposite, which is what a writer should do."

Bruce sewed many of their conversations into *The Songlines*. "Compression is what's needed," he wrote from India. "And when talking of compression, how's this for the thud of nomad horsemen into one line (I mentioned it on one of our walks)? Juvaini in his *History of the World Conqueror* reports this unconscious hexameter from the mouth of a refugee from Bokhara after the sack of Genghis: *'Amdand u khandand u sokhtand u kushtand u burdand u raftand'* [They came, they sapped, they burned, they slew, they trussed up their loot and were gone.] Juvaini, quoted by Yule in his edition of Marco Polo, says that the essence of all his book is contained in this one line."

Bruce, like Leigh Fermor, hated the classification of travel writer. "He was a writer who happened to travel. He was writing to prove or further some idea, like the songlines." Leigh Fermor could tell what a burden the novel had become from their discussions in Joan's kitchen where Bruce took turns to cook dinner. "One always had the idea he was going to devote his life to a really tremendous book on nomadism which didn't see the light of day. He would like to have unravelled everything about humanity. He was engaged in a sincere fumbling. It was an imaginative peregrination, taking a Nijinsky leap into history. *The Songlines* covered a lot of the ground. He wrote it all out at Kardamyli—and he suddenly tore it in half: he wasn't happy about the narrative in Australia."

One afternoon Leigh Fermor visited Bruce. "The room was total chaos, like the leaves of Vallombrosa. He was elated. He had thrown the pages everywhere. 'I've suddenly seen the light. I know how to write this book'."

He had decided to change its shape a third time after a long telephone conversation with Sifton. "He had a powerful argument he wanted to make about the origins of human culture," she says. "But whenever he tried to make it, the result read like a pseudo-academic ex-poet who wished to be a social scientist. I discouraged him from the sequential. I thought it ought to be intuitive and poetic rather than logical. I said: "Instead of considering the notebooks as a problem, why not consider them as part of the solution? Why don't you just use them?"

He did indeed incorporate his notebooks into the text. "His *moleskines* came to the rescue," says Leigh Fermor. "They gave it a kind of keel."

XXXIV.

୬୦୩୬୭

There Is a God

And I will be a monk on Mount Athos.
— *The Station*, ROBERT BYRON

FIVE MONTHS OF sun and wind restored him. There was no visible sign
at Kardamyli that he was ill. He was a picture of fitness, windsurfing
across the bay in an elegant wet-suit. He was still Gregor von Rezzori's
" 'Golden Boy' . . . In his eyes the Aegean, the wind of a long road in his
close-cropped blond hair."

In May, a week after his 45th birthday, Bruce set out to fulfil a boy-
hood ambition: to visit Mount Athos. He had wanted to see the Holy
Mountain since reading *The Station* at school. Robert Byron's account of
his 1927 visit with Talbot Rice was a eulogy to this sacred, all-male enclave:
"To anyone who has sojourned beneath the Holy Mountain, there cannot
but have come an intensification of his impulse to indefinable, un-
analysable emotion." Byron was atheist; the monastic republic had been
dedicated to Orthodoxy since the ninth century. And yet, wrote Lees-
Milne, "his entrenched aesthetic principles responded to the mystical
abracadabra of the Orthodox Church's ritual."

Cary Welch in 1953 had hired a *caique*, stopping off at each monastery
to listen to the services. "After two hours of chanting suddenly this thing
occurred, of short duration, but astounding. Two monks achieved a mystical soaring height, like Couperin's Third Tenebrae Service." Welch recalled that sound when in 1964 he had a vision of St Francis. "I was in bed
one morning in Channing Street. It was a classic trite flash of light. I felt
my brain and heart joined and I was amplified ten times. There was a lot
of chirping of birds and a wonderful sense of innocence and paradise."
The vision was Giotto's fresco of St Francis with the birds.

Of his friends, Lees-Milne and the artist Derek Hill were annual pilgrims. Bruce importuned both to take him. Lees-Milne records in August,
1980: "No, Bruce, I said, you can't. Was I fear rather bossy. Would not let
him open roof of car. Bruce asked me if I had known Robert Byron. Able

to say, yes . . . He admired Robert's writing, but says the strained jokiness of that generation embarrasses him."

Next, Bruce asked Hill, who had visited Mount Athos 15 times. Hill was a friend of the Abbot at Chilandari monastery, who could facilitate their permits. Finally in 1985 Hill agreed to accompany Bruce. "I was slightly apprehensive because he was a great complainer. I thought he'd find the monks smelly or the beds hard or that the loos stank. But it was a revelation to him and it altered his life too late."

Bruce and Hill arrived at the frontier village of Ouranoupolis, the Gate of Heaven, on 21 May. They bought provisions for four days and the following morning joined a group of noisy German tourists on the boat to Daphne. The wind blew offshore and the waves glittered as they headed towards the faint grey outline of the mountain.

A FORTNIGHT BEFORE his visit to Athos, Bruce wrote to Bail: "Athos is obviously another atavistic wonder."

Bruce did not impress friends as religious. "There was never, not a word talked about God," says Leigh Fermor, reflecting on their conversations over five months. "I'd always assumed he was agnostic or atheist. Religion was understood to be a corollary to his attitude to life. Everything had a physical or natural explanation." Bruce once told Charles Tomlinson: "What we want is not more belief, it's more scepticism." He wrote: "My whole life has been a search for the miraculous: yet at the first faint flavour of the uncanny, I tend to turn rational and scientific."

As a 15-year-old, Bruce had made a journey to Rome to visit the Pope. Before his wedding, he took religious instruction from Father Murray. "Nearly became a Catholic," he wrote in his notebook. Then, just before they were married, the priest at Geneseo gave Elizabeth the leaflet explaining why she should not marry a non-Catholic. "That put Bruce off forever," says Elizabeth. Thereafter, his religious faith became subsumed in his nomadic theory: he believed that movement made religion redundant and only when people settled did they need it. "Some form of religion is the brain's system of putting a brake upon change," is an entry from his Benin notebook in 1972. "Religion is a travel guide for settlers." The nearest thing he had to religion was his theory of restlessness. Just as he was a nomad *de luxe*, so he was an ascetic *de luxe*. His London apartments were decorated with religious artefacts to resemble a Greek cell, but his response to organised religion was dictated by aesthetic consideration.

"He turned it into a costume drama," says Elizabeth, who had never abandoned Catholicism and went to church once a week. "When I wanted to buy an old priory, he said: 'I can walk around in robes'."

Since his illness in Java there were signs of a sea-change. One entry in his journal reads: "The search for nomads is a quest for God." Another, "religion is a technique for arriving at the moment of death at the right time." In April 1983, while recuperating with Elizabeth in Nepal, his thoughts had turned to a man's *athos* "in the Greek sense of abode or dwelling place—the root of all his behaviour for good or bad, his character, everything that pertained to him".

ON THE BOAT, as the balconies came into view on the girth of the mountain, Bruce remembered, and jotted down, an anecdote about an Athonite priest: "Paddy [Leigh Fermor] says that one story about Fr N tells of how some grand French people found the old hermit in his cell and were surprised to be asked in perfect French 'Where do you live in Paris?'

" *'Faubourg St Honoré.'*

" *'A quel numéro?'*

" *'Tel et tel.'*

" *'Ah!'* says he, *'à deux portes de mon bottier'* [bootmaker]."

They landed in Daphne at 4 p.m. and had lunch with Father Mitrophan, "who says he allows his chest to get wet with rain in winter and never has a cold". Even now, one suspects, part of the appeal was the abbot's worldliness, not his lack of it.

In the days ahead, Bruce met several who retained a stylish engagement with what they had left behind. On the path next day, walking towards Caryes, he spoke with a Greek American novice who wanted to talk about Hampstead, knew all about the Grand Duchess Ella. Another pilgrim was a Serbian cavalry colonel, a royalist who complained about the *"battements du coeur"* and "had written a book on the iniquities of Winston Churchill". At Chilandari Bruce came face to face with a young man from his own background. Father Damian was "a sweet freckle-faced novice" who had been born in, of all places, Barnt Green and apprenticed at the Milward needle factory in Redditch, "an experience which gave him his monastic vocation." It was Father Damian who showed him round the chapels.

"Bruce got up at 5.30 every morning and went to services," says Derek

Hill. Deeply preoccupied with Aboriginal songlines, Bruce was suscepti-ble to the incantations which had so moved Welch. The Kyrie eleison, chanted hundreds of times, cast a spell. During one service at Chilandari, Bruce turned on a group of noisy tourists. "I made a scene, demanding hushes at once and interrupting the service."

He responded to his physical surroundings: the bees in the magnolia, the Russian icons, "the nose-pink hermitage" of St Basil. One afternoon after his usual *maté* (mistaken by the cook for hashish), he walked to the monastery of Stavronikita once painted by Edward Lear. After St Basil's, this was Derek Hill's favourite place in Athos. Bruce entered through an arch of grapes carved from wood, but round about there grew grapes that tasted of strawberries. "The most beautiful sight of all was an iron cross on a rock by the sea." Whether moved by the rich liturgical worship, or the tradition of mystical prayer or the unbroken continuity with the past, he then wrote: "There must be a God."

Beyond this entry in his journal, Bruce was silent and he felt the de-sire to be consoled by silence. "He didn't talk about it, but I knew by his whole bearing it had affected him," says Hill. "I think it hit him like a bomb."

Hill had known Bruce for 20 years. He had no doubt that as Bruce looked down on that iron cross in the waves he had a spiritual experience that unfroze something in him. "All he could say was: 'I had no idea.' He took it very seriously," says Elizabeth.

On 8 June, Elizabeth wrote to Gertrude. "Mt Athos was a great suc-cess. He loved it and was totally captivated, so I'm really glad he went. Derek did a pencil portrait of B. which he is giving us. It's just done on a piece of stiff card like you put in an envelope with photos. Anyhow it's quite good, except for the mouth & D. says that is the classic remark about a portrait. But I think he can change it."

XXXV.

❧

India

I'm completely out of touch, which is,
as you know, the way I like to be.
—BC TO DEBORAH ROGERS

HE HAD BEEN away seven months when, in July 1985, he returned
home across the Channel. "Catarrh started in the Pas-de-Calais," he wrote
to Rogers.

It was an important homecoming. Elizabeth held her breath. "He settled right down with his books, shifting from room to room: the library,
the living room, the small living room. After he had been here for a bit he
had 50 books by his bedside. He said: 'It's not possible', and I said: 'It is.
There are 50 books'—all things he was reading concurrently. Then he said
he wanted to work in the kitchen. I said, 'No', because that's where I had
the radio on and the cats."

His cold worsened through the autumn. "I went wind-surfing on a
crummy little reservoir near Oxford, and my hand was white and numb
after ten minutes," he told Leigh Fermor. "But what I miss most are the
mountains! The country round here is tolerably attractive, immaculately
kept: but then you keep running up against the cooling towers of the
Didcot power-station; the antennae of Greenham Common; the nuclear installations at Harwell—all of which give me the feelings of
claustrophobia."

How was he going to finish the book in these inhospitable conditions?
Fearing a lung collapse, he accepted a commission from the *New York
Times* to write an article on the American botanist Joseph Rock, who had
lived in Yunnan. The paper agreed to "stump up" flights for him and Elizabeth to Hong Kong and China. He decided to winter with her afterwards in Katmandu.

In early December, Elizabeth came from Yunnan to Nepal ahead of
him to arrange the house, but in Katmandu a disaster greeted her. "The
house we were promised: an Englishman's house with servants and sofas,

in the country etc fell through," Bruce wrote to his parents. "E was then offered a *cottage orné*, in a garden admittedly right in the heart of the city, not far from the Royal Palace. She had to furnish it etc, which all cost money; and when I arrived from Hong Kong, I had, I have to say, misgivings . . ." The house was empty except for two foam rubber mattresses. "My biggest worry," wrote Elizabeth, "is that it may prove to be rather noisy here for B. It varies from day to day, but sometimes it's pretty bad, hammering from new buildings nearby, awful Hindi movie music blaring at top level, hooting motorcycles & cars & other times shrieking children . . ." That was not all. "The house, it turned out, was sitting in a pool of pollution," wrote Bruce, "plus the fact that over the wall was the city shit-house, plus the fact that they burned the shit and other refuse at night so that the fumes would settle in our throats. All I can say is that it brought back a kind of bronchial misery I associate with Stirling Road in the winter of '47." Still searching for its origins in something benign, he was set on locating his illness in his childhood tendency for flu.

Elizabeth had also caught bronchitis—"which for her is very unusual". They became iller and iller until Kasmin, who had joined them in Nepal for Christmas, insisted that they abandon Katmandu and fly at once to India.

"To Benares (because the planes to Delhi were full) where we sat by the Burning Ghats and inhaled a different kind of smell," Bruce wrote to his parents. "You literally stand within, say, 15 feet, of half a dozen burning corpses: and after you get used to the smell—though I with my cold, could hardly smell a thing—it all seems perfectly natural and harmonious. We then drove to Delhi along the Grand Trunk Road (all planes and trains booked) in a taxi. I hoped to show Kas the Martinière, which is an enormous 'French' 18th-century chateau, now a boy's school, but since the fog was such that we couldn't see the bonnet of the car, there seemed little point. On to Delhi where we stayed with my pal, Sunil Sethi . . . now the editor of the *Indian Mail*. He has a new and beautiful wife: all very soignée."

Sethi was aware of Bruce's routine from Ronda. In Sethi's Delhi apartment, Bruce began bashing on the typewriter at 8 a.m.—at 12.30 lunch, "simply cooked rice and dal or kedgeree with a slight flavouring of cumin—sick people's food"; at 3 p.m. a huge, brisk wander.

"He had this whole thing athletes and politicians have about keeping yourself fit, the tightening of your body before you really tighten your mind. He was obsessed by a Gandhian diet of frugality. Indira Gandhi was like that. She said to him: 'You know the trick is to change your underpants three times a day and drink gallons of lime water. Eventually you phase yourself out.'

"Like her, he believed that minimum food is good for the body. He hated heavy sauces—it was the same with art or books, he was awfully particular. He was on a constant search, as if for an elixir, for the final preservative of youth. He couldn't pass a mirror without looking for crow's feet. And there was an element of parody. His search for shampoos! He was always talking about herbal Indian cures and trying out shampoos and I'd say, 'You foolish man, you've hardly got any hair left'."

In Delhi, Kasmin left them and they were joined by Murray and Margaret Bail. Bruce had looked forward to this meeting for a year.

JUST AS HE preferred to think of Eaton Place as empty, so Bruce liked to think of himself as someone who travelled light, with only a brown leather rucksack. Made for him by a saddler in Cirencester, this was a copy of a rucksack belonging to the French actor Jean-Louis Barrault, whom Bruce had sat next to on a plane.

But travelling with Bruce in India, says Bail, was "like travelling with Garbo". Bruce's luggage included 40 kilos excess baggage in books. There was also the typewriter, the card index, the champagne, the muesli, the pills, the hats, the boots, the grey suits, the pyjamas. "His amount of luggage was really colossal," says Bail. "We needed a driver."

On the platform at the British-built station, Bruce was entranced by the rivets, girders and steam-engines still in operation from the Raj. "The railway station reminded him of home. He was at home and not at home." Bail was mildly surprised to look down from his bunk on the train to Jodhpur to see "Bruce's bum in the moonlight: he was getting into his pyjamas, like at boarding school."

When he arrived at Jodhpur, Bruce wrote a note to "Bapji", the Maharaja of Jodhpur whom he had met with James Ivory at the Cannes Film Festival in 1969. "The palace in Jodhpur is the last *great* ruler's palace to be built anywhere," he wrote to his parents. "At least as large as Buckingham Palace and completed, finally, in 1949. My friend H. H. (or Bapji), a totally wonderful character, replied to my note at once, saying he was overcome with his 40th birthday celebrations. Would we come for a drink now? This minute? Which we did: to find him also entertaining a real lunatic, the Belgian ambassador to Iran." Bruce now enlisted the Maharajah's help to find a place where he and Murray might peacefully work. "I said I was looking for somewhere to write, and Bapji immediately proposed a cottage in a mango orchard laid out by his grandparents at a place called Ranakpur, about 75 miles away."

The simple green hunting lodge at Ranakpur sounded more wonderful than it was. "The first stab at this mythical beast, 'the place to write in', was a dud," Bruce wrote to Kasmin. The climate was dry, but the swimming pool empty and every day tourists staying in one of Bapji's hotels were liable to swoop on the place for lunch. "The servants would slope around in shorts and cook too much and haunt us for leftovers," says Margaret Bail.

Nor was there anywhere for Bruce to spread his books. He and Bail sat at card-tables under the trees, ten yards apart, and from time to time Bruce read out Arkady's dialogue for correction. "He'd call out, 'Does this sound Australian enough?' or 'Does this sound right to you?' and I'd say, 'No, no, no, that's not crude enough'." Bruce was grateful for his adjustments. "Murray was a great help with Australianisms," he wrote to Kasmin. "What one can't help feeling is the degree to which English has been Americanised, compared to 'Australian'. I've always thought that Australian writing, on a page, looks a little archaic: now I'm beginning to realize why."

One day Bruce came to Bail's room in some agitation. "He said he couldn't describe the songline. I said 'Why don't you break ranks and do diagrams, like Stendhal in his autobiography?'"

Four months before he delivered his manuscript, Bruce was still unable to articulate its central image.

After a fortnight the Bails departed for Udaipur. "I cried when Elizabeth and I said goodbye," says Margaret Bail. When she had first met Bruce, in Sydney, she had thought him "the most charming man I'd ever met", but it irritated her the way both husbands had left their wives to make the travel arrangements, "do all the practical things", while they sat under trees. "I think all writers are shits."

Murray Bail remarked on the difficulty Bruce experienced in saying goodbye. "I said, 'We'll see each other soon.' But Bruce had to switch to an object. He examined a glass ball he held in his hand and decided to comment on the facets of light on it. 'Have a look at this *extraordinary* bit of glass I've found'."

A century before, Bruce's great-grandfather, Julius Alfred, had designed a palace of glass for an Indian Maharaja. Bruce was delighted with the turn of events that now supplied him with his own version of a Maharaja's palace. Though not glass, it reflected everything which until this point he had been unable to take in.

At Bapji Jodhpur's three-day birthday party ("the maharanee choked solid with diamonds and emeralds; all the courtiers in whirligig Rajasthani turbans and real white jodhpurs") Bruce met Manvendra Singh, a "total charmer" who was to provide his Shangri-la.

A mixture of courtier and landowner, Singh was almost the same age as Bruce, yet, he wrote to Bail, "he represents the male world of my father in his absolute fairness and tireless, unostentatious work for others". To Diana Melly, he wrote: "He is the 'identical twin' likeness to my father."

In a letter to his father, Bruce explained how he secured his writer's paradise: "I did my usual babble [to Singh] about finding a place to write in, and he said, 'I think I have the place'. He had, too. Although he lives four days a week in town, he has his family fort, a building going back to the sixteenth century, around a courtyard with neem trees and a lawn, its outer walls lapped by a lake with little islands, temples on them etc. The rooms we occupy are a self-contained flat, blue-washed, with nineteenth-century Anglo-Indian furniture, photos of maharajas, and a never-ending procession of birds. The country is flattish, and almost semi-desert; and since there was no monsoon last year, the situation is quite grim. But the lake, which is filled from a canal, is one of the only tanks in the region, and the stopping off place for all the migrants on their way to or from Siberia. Almost within arm's reach are ducks, spoonbills, egrets, storks, cranes, herons, bee-eaters, a dazzling kingfisher which sits in the nearest tree. Each morning brings something new. Tea arrives with the sun. Siesta. Walk. More work. Then in the evening you hear the muezzin being called from the Mosque, and incredible bangings and trumpeting from the Krishna Temple, then silence.

"I have the most charming study to work in, and work I do."

Bruce and Elizabeth spent two months as guests in the wing of the red fort at Rohet. "One is so well looked after, and above all, CALM," he wrote to Sethi. He conveyed to Kasmin a life of Arcadian languor: "A cool blue study overlooking the garden. A saloon with ancestral portraits. Bedroom giving out onto the terrace. Unbelievably beautiful girls who come with hot water, with real coffee, with papayas, with a mango milkshake. In short, I'm really feeling quite contented. The cold and cough has been hard to shake off. A dry cough always is. But thanks to an ayurvedic cough preparation, it really does seem to be on the wane. Today was Republic

Day, with Mrs Chatwin on hand to present the prize to the volleyball team, and sweeties to 500 schoolchildren." He wrote to Melly: "I've not seen her happier or more cheerful in 20 years (the time we've been married!). I even think she is coming round to the fact that those houses, and that particular way of life, are as bad for her as for me."

Waited on hand and foot, he slowly recovered his health. "I adore it here. Lunch yesterday, for example, consisted of a light little bustard curry, a puree of peas, another of aubergine and coriander, yoghurt, and a kind of wholemeal bread the size of a potato and baked in ashes. A sadhu with a knotted beard down to his kneecaps has occupied the shrine a stone's throw from my balcony; and after a few puffs of his ganja I found myself reciting, in Sanskrit, some stanzas of the *Bhagavad Gita*. I work away for eight hours at a stretch, go for cycle rides in the cool of the evening, and come back to Proust."

Not only did he enjoy his immobility, but his spirits continued to mend. "Well, I have to say the Fort is a real piece of luck," he wrote to the Bails a month later. "We couldn't be happier here. There is just enough going on, either in the courtyard or by the lake, to arouse and interest, and not too much to distract me . . . E. is off to Bombay to see her friends for a week: but I refuse to budge. It is ironic that this book of mine, which is a passionate defence of wandering, as opposed to sedentary habits, should involve its author in a more or less limpet-like existence . . . As for my own 'Awful Mess,' I've now got to the critical stage in which there is a sudden shift from Australia, in order to answer Pascal's assertion about the man sitting quietly in a room. If it comes off, then I'm on the downward stretch."

Here Elizabeth came to the rescue. One day at Homer End she had produced a huge loose-leaf folder bulging with pages: the manuscript of the nomad book that Margharita had rescued. Bruce believed he had thrown this away. "He started mining it," says Elizabeth.

Taking a hammer to the manuscript, Bruce reduced *The Nomadic Alternative* to a narrative rubble. *The Songlines* would be, in part, the story of his fieldwork. Borrowing the patchwork structure from two commonplace books—Cyril Connolly's *Palinurus: The Unquiet Grave* and Edith Sitwell's anthology, *Planet and Glow-Worm*—Bruce reworked his fictionalised journey in Australia into a collage of quotation and diary. "I've had a terrible time with the 'Australian' book: have torn up 3 successive drafts: only to find . . . that the only way is the 'cut-up' method," he wrote to Calasso, the intended recipient of *Letter from Marble Bar*. He told Leigh

Fermor: "I've decided the only thing to do is to let it run its own course and shove everything in . . . I've been casting back over my old notebooks, and have managed to find a place for things like this:

DJANG, CAMEROON

There are two hotels in Djang: the *Hotel Windsor* and, on the opposite side of the street, the *Hotel Anti-Windsor*

Or:

GORÉE, SENEGAL

On the terrace of the restaurant a fat French bourgeois couple are guzzling their *fruits-de-mer*. Their dachshund, leashed to the woman's chair, keeps jumping up in the hope of being fed.
—*Taisez-vous, Romeo! C'est l'entracte*"

Had he not been ill, Bruce may never have decided on this bold "experiment", but it was the only way through what amounted to a 17-year writer's block.

ON 6 MARCH 1986, the Chatwins left Rohet. "Elizabeth has to get back to her lambing," he wrote to Nin Dutton. "The past week has really been too hot. It would be fine if I didn't have something critical to do. But it's too hot to take exercise, and the mind starts to go soggy too. So I'm taking her to Delhi and then going for the rest of the month and most of April to a guest-house we've heard of not far from Simla."

Bruce completed his first draft of *The Songlines* at The Retreat at Bhimtal, a bungalow beside a lake in the mountainous region near the Nepalese border. He described it to Kasmin: "Old English tea plantation now run as a hotel guest house by Czech adventurer type, ex-inhabitant of Punta Arenas in Chile, refugee from Germany in the 1930s for having thrown a knife at Hitler." He had the house to himself, with a veranda and a *rosa banksiae* clambering over it and a view of wheatfields. The only other person he saw was a holy man. "On the mountain above lives a charming sadhu, the father of the Forest, whose business it is to protect the trees," he wrote to Elizabeth. "Old Smetacek has gone to Germany for four months. Sounds an incredible character . . . This is Jim Corbett country and as I'm writing about man-eaters I appear to have landed in the right spot. Below the sadhu's cave there is a leopard lair, but the animal is supposed to be very friendly."

On 10 April, Bruce wrote another contented letter. "It's still very nice here, but the heat increases each day with hot dusty winds coming from the plain. I've done some very good work. The cut-up method does actually solve the problem. I've just been writing the tramp and the Arctic tern." He planned to celebrate the final chapter with a trek. He had hired three porters, bought the provisions and saddled up, when he was shocked to read, in the *Times of India*, a leader headed "Journey to the Beginning".

"What was this? *Betjeman? . . . Field-Marshal Lord Chetwode? . . . dismounted from her pony on the Jalori pass? . . . and had gone to sleep for ever?* The paragraph was a most sensitive piece of prose, but I could not finish it. The porter found me wetting the newspaper with tears. I had to go to her."

At the news of Penelope Betjeman's death, while leading a trek in the Western Himalayas, Bruce dropped everything. He paid off his porters, gave them the provisions and as fast as he could made his way to Kulu for the funeral. He had known Betjeman for 20 years. She was a close friend of Elizabeth and had supported both through the rockiest time of their marriage. In Wales, she had become "a sort of mother to me". Once at a children's party in the Black Mountains she sent Bruce into her woods to imitate the fire-breathing New House dragon. "You're meant to be a dragon, not a wolf," she had told him crossly when she came upon him growling behind a tree.

He approached her pyre in a bushy glade below Khanag. "Felt dazed," he wrote. "Chestnuts in first leaf. The pyre built over the stream. Remains of her padded parka in the charcoal. Little white flecks of charred bone. Threw on a couple of violets. Warm hazy sun. Mild headache."

On 24 April, he described her funeral to Leigh Fermor: "Yesterday morning, her friend Kranti Singh and I carried her ashes in a small brass pot to a rock in the middle of the River Beas which was carved all over, in Tibetan, with the Buddhist mantra, O the flower of the lotus. He tipped some into a whirlpool and I then threw the pot with the remainder into the white water. The flowers—wild tulips, clematis, and a sprig of English oak-leaves (from the Botanical gardens in Manali) vanished at once into the foam.

"The doctor, who was with her on the trek, gave 'heart-attack' as the cause of death: but the word 'attack' is far too strong for what happened. If ever there was a 'natural death', this was it. All morning she was in the best of spirits—although people in the party said she was already beginning to dread going back to England. Around 10, she called in on her favourite Pahari temple. The priest, who knows her, welcomed her to join in the pujas. She received the blessing and then rode on towards a place called Khanag. There she dismounted to rest, laughed (and scolded) at her pony which had strayed into a wheat field, and was talking her head off to her Tibetan porter when her head tilted sideways and the talking stopped.

"Although it's nowhere finished, I had—only two days before—been writing the final chapters of the book: of how Aborigines, when they feel death close, will make a kind of pilgrimage (sometimes a distance of thousands of miles) back to their 'conception site', their 'centre', the place where they belong. In the middle of nowhere in the desert I was taken to see three very old Aborigines, happily waiting to die on three metal bedsteads, side by side in the shade of an ironwood tree."

Only to Elizabeth did he describe what happened to him as he walked from Betjeman's pyre. As he sat, pausing for breath at the top of the Jalori pass, an old sadhu sitting outside a shrine had asked to tell his fortune. "The man looked at his palm and blanched, would not say anything," says Elizabeth. "Bruce said he got a terrible intimation of mortality." When he had first arrived at Bhimtal, he had effortlessly jogged around the lake. By end of his visit the run winded him.

XXXVI

ᕗᕟᕟᕟᕗ

An AI Medical Curiosity

> *You may know the characters are absolutely doomed*
> *to some fate, but the characters themselves must be*
> *allowed to hope.*
> —BC TO NS

HOMER END. THE name has the ring of a long voyage over, of cliffs in sight. One hot day in early August 1986, Elizabeth drove Bruce to Reading. "On the way back B had a horrible attack when he started to go blue & was just gasping," she wrote to Gertrude.

Since his return home in May, he had suffered from night sweats and asthma. More recently, he had developed a hoarse voice and noticed "some vague skin lumps". He wondered if he had picked up an Indian amoeba from the drinking water in Rohet, if he had an "allergy to dust", or if it might be something to do with the iron-oxide in the paint, specially ordered from Sweden, with which Robyn Davidson and Hugh, two weeks before, had decorated the house.

This condition worsened by the day. "He can only go for little slow walks & is always cold & sits wrapped up with a heater on all the time," Elizabeth wrote. "He's very weak & looks awful & sleeps a lot. He's only got a tiny bit more of the book to do."

The last third of the manuscript was the "common-place book" of quotations, meditations and vignettes. "I put this into shape on sweltering summer days, wrapped in shawls, shivering with cold in front of the kitchen stove. It was a race for time." Early in August, 17 years and three months after signing the initial contract, Bruce finished his book, "which to all the publishers' distaste I insist on calling a novel". He had a new title *The Songlines*, but was still not happy with what he judged to be an "incoherent first draft". It was, he told Colin Thubron, "the first draft of the last gasp". But his attitude was: "I'm going to finish the book because I said I would do so and I'm a trouper and then I'll have time to be ill."

Too weak to work with her on the book in New York, he telephoned

Elisabeth Sifton at Viking. "The first thing he said on the phone was 'Elisabeth, I'm dying'." It was very presumptuous, but could she come to Zurich? "Mark up what you think and meet me there." On 16 August, he flew to Switzerland, taking his watercolours. Before Sifton arrived he intended to go up into the mountains to paint, "thinking that a combination of mountain air and walks would revive me, and that first rate medicine was always at hand," he wrote to Bail. "Fat chance! The next thing I knew, on my first day in Zurich, was that I could hardly walk along the street."

On 18 August, he was admitted to a clinic in Mühlebachstrase, anaemic and dehydrated. "He was in a considerably reduced state," the Swiss doctor wrote in his report. "Weight 66.0 kilos, constantly coughing and with acute diarrhoea." On 20 August, Bruce was X-rayed and serological tests were performed for Malaria parasites, Bilharziosis, Brucella, Treponema pallida, Listeria, Toxoplasma. Dr Keller, unable to determine the cause of the anaemia, recommended a diet of poached fish.

Bruce had booked Elisabeth Sifton into his hotel, The Opera. "Part of me was in despair," she says. "A lot of the manuscript was in chaos. The notebooks were not in the right place. They were not well-proportioned. We made a plan to meet every morning and discuss the book until he was too tired. But our meetings degenerated into long conversations about life and I couldn't get him to focus. He was distracted by his terrors. Propped on pillows he would tell me stories with his eyes blazing, full of vim and roaring with laughter. 'My dear, I've had this *amazing* dream.' And then he'd be too weak to move. He didn't finish off a single page—as he had done in my presence with *On the Black Hill.* He'd look at my marks and say, 'Yes, yes, next point'."

She was with him five days. In a Swiss vegetarian restaurant he nearly fainted. She walked him up the hill to the clinic. "One day he gave me, wrapped up, a stool specimen, which I was to carry to the doctor. 'It's not AIDS or anything,' he said, reassuring me'." After five days, another concern became her foremost one. "He wasn't telling anyone he was so ill. I was the only person who knew. He told me: 'Now I must get well, you can go now.' I refused to leave until he telephoned Elizabeth."

In Homer End, Elizabeth was growing nervous. "Nothing from Bruce . . ." she wrote to Gertrude on 26 August. "Don't know if I should worry or not, but of course I do."

Elizabeth flew out on 1 September. She found Bruce in his hotel bed, unable to move. "One minute he was freezing cold, the next he had terrible sweats. He needed endless towels to dry him off. He could not make red corpuscles and was dying right there and then." He had thought of going to the desert to die. He had tried to arrange visas for Mauritania and Mali, had managed to sit upright in a booth for a photograph. He wanted to curl up in the corner like a dog, he said. On 5 September he returned to the clinic, running a temperature of 39°C. "The doctor did endless tests and finally called me into his office by myself."

Dr Keller had received the results of the lab tests. While there was no evidence of a chronic infectious disease, the findings suggested "a severe immunodeficiency syndrome". The tests were negative, except one, highlighted in a yellow marker. "*HTLV-III-Virus-Antikörper / HIV positive!*"

"Did you have any idea?"

"No," said Elizabeth.

"But didn't you mind?" said Dr Keller. "Your husband having all these affairs?"

"I'd have minded more if he'd gone off with a woman. These people were never a threat."

Dr Keller then informed Bruce, who had already guessed. The doctor urgently recommended that he return to England and go to a hospital there.

Elizabeth contacted her GP to arrange for an ambulance to meet them at Heathrow. "We barely got him out of the plane. He couldn't stand properly and was catatonic." On 12 September, 3.34 p.m., Bruce was admitted to the John Warin emergency ward in Oxford's Churchill Hospital. He was identified simply as "an HIV positive 46-year-old travel writer". From this day on, he would be forced to submit to the unsparing taxonomy of the medical profession.

Elizabeth did not stay the night. Neighbours came to fetch her while efforts were made to rehydrate Bruce. On 14 September, during a blood transfusion, his temperature reached 40.3°C. "Had rigours during the transfusion which ceased once it had stopped," read the report. His urine was black and he was described as poorly. "The fact is I very nearly croaked," he told Murray Bail. "I was not expected to live through the night. It was not unpleasant. I was hallucinating like mad and was convinced that the view from my window—a car park, a wall and the tops of some trees—were an enormous painting by Paolo Veronese. Can we ever escape 'Art'?'?"

He described a "definite glimpse of the Pearly Gates" to Matthew Spencer. His vision combined features of an early Byzantine Christ Pantocrator on Mount Athos with Renaissance frescoes near Poggio a Caiano. A great number of people were engaged in some banquet or ritual festivity. "As he approached its surface, he felt an incredible excitement, as if at last he could pass through the shield of mere appearances of which paintings are made. What textures! The clothes! The velvet, the long sleeves, the pearls like little white planets, each an individual all-engrossing other world!

"As I stretched out my hand to touch, he said, the figures began to move, to beckon me to join them. He took the hand of a man standing there and walked with him into the painting."

"He was a taste man to the end," says Bail.

Another vision was described in literary terms. "I saw green-capped schoolboys leaving school, an infinite library of books which turned into a library of primroses and a troupe of glass horses which galloped off in a shatter. It was like something from Borges' *El Aleph*."

Less pleasant was the hallucination Bruce outlined to Colin Thubron. He was sliding down an ice tunnel, as if through a gigantic gut, "and the whole thing was cracking crkk crkk crkk as I slide rather slowly down the ice and at the bottom there were a whole series of icicles like stalactites which when I hit them ripppped me apart and I remember my whole shoulder coming off and I was dismembered . . . One's organs absolutely scattered all over the place . . . There was definitely a feeling that this was death and I was definitely dying."

THE JOHN WARIN WARD for infectious diseases treated meningitis, pneumonia, traveller's diarrhoea, cellulitis, amoebic liver abscesses from India: everything caused by germs.

The first doctor to examine him was the ward registrar, Richard Bull, who understood Bruce's name to be Charles Chatwin. Acutely confused, with "the occasional inappropriate response", Bruce told Bull of his "sense of mortality" while dispersing Penelope Betjeman's ashes in India. He looked, wrote Bull, "very unwell": his voice was hoarse, his legs were numb and his face was covered in red spots and ulcerating skin lumps.

Though not uncooperative, there was a piecemeal quality to the way Bruce offered up his medical history. Over the next two days, Bull established that he had travelled widely since 1962, including to the Middle East, Afghanistan, India, America, Haiti, South America, Australia, Dahomey, Togo, Cameroon, Kenya; that he had been "bisexual since youth"; that a possible contact for HIV was an Australian whom he had known between 1978 and 1981. There are in his answers traces of a man in despair, seeking an explanation for his illness. On 14 September, he gave an alternative explanation. The record puts it: "NB Experienced 'gang rape' in Benin (W Africa) in 1978".

He described this experience to another of his doctors, David Warrell, professor of tropical medicine and infectious diseases at Oxford University. Warrell considered the rape story implausible. In October 1988, Bruce would tell his French doctor, André Le Fesvre, that he believed he had contracted HIV from an Australian in Australia, while to Francis Wyndham he said that he had traced the lineage to Mapplethorpe's lover in New York, Sam Wagstaff.

On 14 September, Bull discussed the diagnosis with Bruce and Elizabeth. "She knows her own risk and is thinking about a blood test. Patient told he is seropositive, has pre-AIDS but true AIDS not yet certain." Bruce would cling to that uncertainty.

Over the next five weeks he was examined by a number of specialists. It confused him to have to repeat the symptoms. He was unaccustomed to reciting a reliable narrative about himself. But "the self is all I can think of," he wrote to Bail. By 23 September he had refined his diagnosis, telling one doctor that he had 'fungus in his blood', which has caused 'this wasting disease' ". On the same day, he was seen by a clinical photographer. "Quite anxious for his identity to be concealed, so we covered his eyes."

In 1986, AIDS was a phenomenon that had been known for barely five years. Its clinical management was in its infancy. At that time an AIDS patient was expected to live between three and five years.

"Statistically, one would most likely at that stage in the west have caught it through homosexuals," says David Warrell, who took over as Bruce's doctor in November 1987. In the popular mind, AIDS was the new Black Death and perceived as a homosexual disease. In this alarmist climate rumour and misinformation proliferated. Bruce was in the throes of the disease at a time when society's anxieties about it were at their peak. "When it became known he had died from AIDS, Margharita had friends in Stratford who wouldn't speak to her," says Elizabeth. "There was so much ignorance. We were all ignorant. One knew it was caught from sex, but there were also rumours that it was caught from sitting on the toilet or kissing or drinking." In a letter he wrote to the *London Review of Books*, Bruce warned: "One point cannot be emphasised too strongly. An infected person must never use anyone else's toothbrush or an electric razor." No one was more afraid of this "gay *Götterdämmerung*", as Bruce called it, than Bruce himself. "The word 'AIDS' is one of the cruellest and silliest neologisms of our time. 'Aid' means help, succour, comfort—yet with a hissing sibilant tacked onto the end it becomes a nightmare. It should never be used in front of patients." This was the nearest he came to a public admission of his illness.

He hated the name, and the idea of such an ugly label being applied to himself was unbearable. He had spent his life escaping from definition only to succumb to an illness that defined him and would lump him in popular conception with notorious homosexuals like Liberace, Rock Hudson and Robert Mapplethorpe. "AIDS is especially terrible for people like Bruce," says Lucie-Smith. "It's not merely that you know you're going to die, but all the layers of pretence get stripped away."

IN THE MONTHS ahead, Bruce denied his HIV status to his closest relatives and most of his friends. "In hospital he talked about pythons because nobody wanted to mention the word," says James Fox. "It was so fierce, the way he surrounded himself in a smoke of different colours, that one didn't dare speculate." Bruce told Sunil Sethi, after his friend Sheridan Dufferin died of AIDS: "Everyone thinks I've got it too, but it's not true." Eve Arnold heard how Bruce had appeared at a Cork Street gallery opening screaming at Kasmin, so that everyone could hear. "You son of a bitch, telling everyone I had AIDS. It's not true, not true. You were my friend and you betrayed me!" Even Millington-Drake, who died of AIDS in 1994, was convinced until very late on that Bruce was telling him the truth: "I really didn't believe he did have AIDS, but a tropical disease." For Millington-Drake, the matter was easily explained: "He was afraid of admitting he was going to die. And it was a great deal to do with protecting his parents and Elizabeth's parents."

"To me it was all very simple," says Hugh Chatwin. "He would not let down his father."

In Zurich when he first received his diagnosis, Bruce had asked Elizabeth to keep the news from his family. "He minded terribly," she says. "He always thought he could tell his mother, but not his father. 'I don't want him to think badly of me.' He hoped he could hold out until they had found a cure."

Consequently, Charles, Margharita and Hugh remained in ignorance of Bruce's illness and sexuality until his last months. "As far as his sexuality went our parents didn't know him at all," says Hugh. "They would have recognised his tendency to be a little camp and they had pillow talk about his dressing up, but they were protected from Jasper, etc. None of his liaisons came anywhere near this household. They didn't know because I didn't know."

And there was Elizabeth to consider. "People think the reason he didn't face up to AIDS is Elizabeth," says Francis Wyndham. "But she didn't care if the whole world knew. It wasn't to save her face. The way Elizabeth played it was: 'I'll just do what Bruce wants'."

Elizabeth's complicity was endorsed by a friend, a Thai woman who wrote from Bangkok on 30 September. "I always do admire your courage and wisdom. Now you are doing the right thing again in not telling his parents. You always sacrifice for him & we all know how much you love him. I think he appreciates it now."

BRUCE'S CONCEALMENT OF the HIV virus was encouraged by the presence of an unknown fungal infection. "It was an unusual presentation," says Dr Bent Juel-Jensen, the consultant physician in charge of the ward. "Bruce was admitted with HIV, but we were puzzled because there were none of the manifestations you would expect in somebody who was HIV. In this country, you usually have the *Pneumocystic carini* organism. Bruce was riddled with a rare fungus. I'd never seen a case before." Bruce latched onto this fungus.

On 15 September his doctors had suspected the presence of Kaposi's sarcoma, one of the commoner dermatological manifestations of AIDS. But subsequent biopsy reports failed to mention this again for another 17 months. Efforts concentrated on diagnosing the fungus that had infiltrated his liver, spleen, bone marrow, lungs and skin. On 26 September, the culture was taken and sent to the Radcliffe laboratory where it was identified as *Penicillium marneffei*, a mould fungus that is a natural pathogen of the bamboo rat in South Asia. This fungus is now known to be an AIDS-defining illness, but in 1986, as Bull wrote in his report to Dr Juel-Jensen, it "has previously only been reported in Thai and Chinese farmers."

China was the one country Bruce had forgotten to include in his list of travels. In November 1985, on his way to Nepal, he and Elizabeth had visited Yunnan in south-west China. Near the Thai border they had stayed in a village hut at 7,000 feet. He remembered, now, that he had become sick after eating a "black egg" at a peasant feast. A harvest was in progress. The air was dry and dusty and he remembered the thrashing of wheat. "He had probably breathed in the spoor," says Juel-Jensen. "It was just bad luck that his body defences didn't measure up. It probably wouldn't do you or me any harm, only if you're immune deficient."

Needing to feel he suffered from something special and unwilling to address the fact he had contracted a "homosexual" disease, Bruce had to understand his illness as this bone fungus. There was enough absence of information at the time to allow him to do this. The truth was he had both. He would not have attracted the fungus had he not first contracted HIV.

Juel-Jensen put Bruce on a prophylactic anti-fungal drug, Ketoconazole. "He made a remarkable recovery for a while. For all of us it was a question of suck it and see. There is always a possibility that the patient will survive. There is a world of difference between a possibility and a probability . . . but none of us had any experience and little literature."

THE DISCOVERY OF "an extremely rare (i.e. no white man has it) fungus of the bone marrow" cheered Bruce. "For Bruce it was wonderful: he could make a story," says Elizabeth. The fungus reinforced his sense of uniqueness: "an Aı medical curiosity," he wrote to Bail. "It was like collecting a very great object," says Robert Erskine. It was also treatable. "It must have been a colossal relief to pin his symptoms on an innocent curable disease," says David Warrell. "He didn't want to accept that the underlying HIV was the problem. It was a sort of secret. There was a great deal of denial, or at least of unwarranted optimism that he could conquer it."

Bruce quickly metabolised his illness into something rich and strange. "He didn't want to be defined as homosexual; what he wanted to be was extraordinary, the odd one out," says Jonathan Hope. "The fungus fitted into his pursuit for eclectic esoteric knowledge." He told Matthew Spender: "My dear, it's a very rare mushroom in the bone marrow which I got from eating a slice of raw Cantonese whale." He told Loulou de la Falaise he had eaten a rotten thousand-year-old Chinese egg. "He told me his disease came from bat's faeces," says George Ortiz. By describing and redescribing the *Penicillium marneffei*, he constructed an illness, particular to himself, that he could live with. "None of us was allowed to say

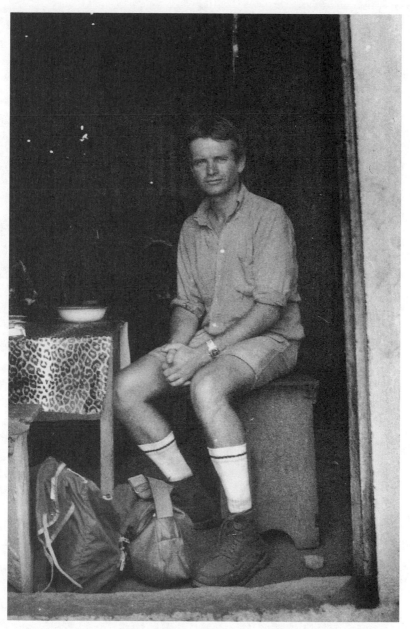

Bruce eating gruel for breakfast in Ouidah, 1976. He wrote in his notebook: "I have never felt any real attachment to home and I fail to produce the normal emotive response whenever the word is mentioned – except when travelling . . ." [JK]

Bruce wrote his books anywhere but home. *Clockwise from left:* 1. James Ivory. Bruce stayed in his clapboard cabin in Oregon while he grappled with his first, aborted, book, *The Nomadic Alternative*. [PY] 2. Penelope Betjeman invited Bruce to stay in her remote cottage on the Welsh border. [Topham] 3. Paddy Leigh Fermor was his host in Greece. Bruce envied his breadth of knowledge and experience. [PY] 4. Bruce with Diana Melly, wife of George Melly. He wrote in their tower in Scethrog. [Diana Melly]

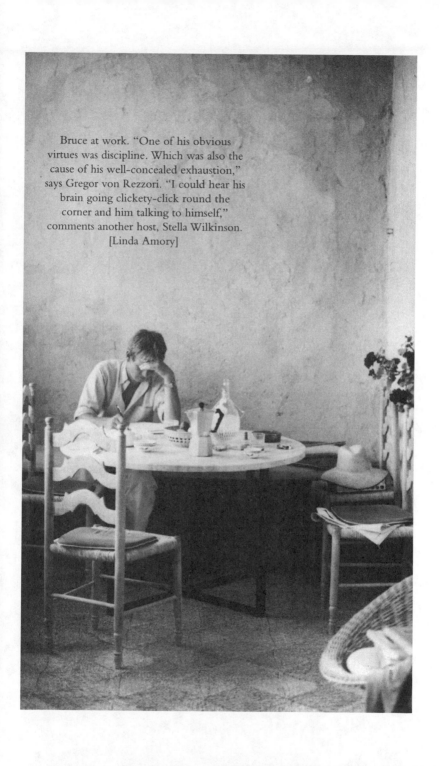

Bruce at work. "One of his obvious virtues was discipline. Which was also the cause of his well-concealed exhaustion," says Gregor von Rezzori. "I could hear his brain going clickety-click round the corner and him talking to himself," comments another host, Stella Wilkinson. [Linda Amory]

Bruce had a brief affair with Teddy Millington-Drake while at Sotheby's. "Bruce envied him his ease with his sexuality," says Ted Lucie-Smith. Bruce often wrote in his homes in Patmos and Tuscany. [Diana di Carcaci]

Donald Richards, an Australian stock-broker and author of *Know Your Cats*. Between 1977 and 1982 he introduced Bruce to the gay scene in New York. [Powerhouse Museum, Sydney, Australia]

Bruce spent New Year 1984 with Jasper Conran at a house in Tuscany. *Left to right*: the playwright John Guare, Gregor von Rezzori, Bruce, Kasmin, Beatrice Monti, Rezzori's wife. *Seated*: Guare's wife, Adele Chatfield-Taylor, director of the American school in Rome, Jasper Conran. [JK]

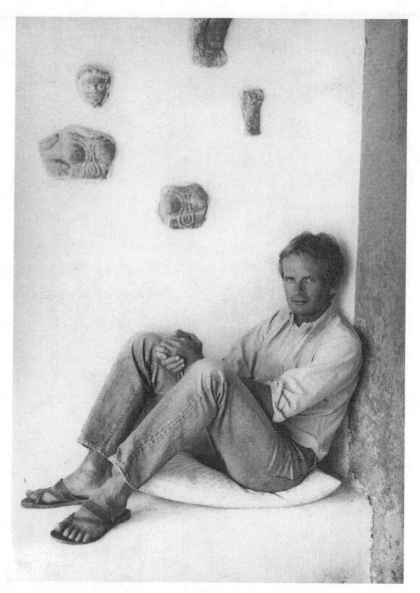

Bruce at Donnini in 1981. "He was amazing to look at," says Susan Sontag. "There are few people in this world who have the kind of looks which enchant and enthral. Your stomach just drops to your knees, your heart skips a beat, you're not prepared for it. I saw it in Jack Kennedy. And Bruce had it. It isn't just beauty, it's a glow, something in the eyes. And it works on both sexes." [Jerry Bauer]

Bruce at the Swartkrans cave, 2 February 1984, on the day "the world's earliest hearth" was discovered. [Bob Brain]

Bruce and Werner Herzog after a marathon 48-hour conversation in Melbourne. "He was the ultimate storyteller, one of the truly great writers of our time," says Herzog. [Werner Herzog]

"Arkady", who made a three day trip with Bruce in Alice Springs in 1983. Toly Sawenko became the unwitting model for the central character of *The Songlines*. [PY]

Bruce the nomad, Africa 1984: "My life at present is the way I like it. *Perpetuum mobile.*" [JK]

Bruce and Elizabeth on the road to Delhi in 1985. "Elizabeth and I have not had an easy marriage, but it survives everything because neither of us have loved anyone else." Bruce was very susceptible to illness. On this trip they both came down with bronchitis. [JK]

Bruce with monks on Mount Athos, May 1985. "The search for nomads is a search for God." In his last months, he converted to the Greek Orthodox Church. [EC]

Bruce is buried in an unmarked grave on the Peloponnese, beside a tenth-century Byzantine chapel dedicated to St Nicholas in Chora. He admired the Greeks because, he said, they reserved the best building sites for God. [PY]

AIDS," says Salman Rushdie. "For all those years we had to talk about funguses. He was trying to make things go away by not saying them."

On 13 October he wrote a letter to Gertrude, "the first one I have written since the 'collapse'. Trust me to pick up a disease never recorded among Europeans. The fungus that has attacked my bone marrow has been recorded among ten Chinese peasants (China is presumably where I got it), a few Thais and a killer whale cast up on the shores of Arabia. The great test comes when we find out whether I can go on producing red blood cells on my own.

"That is the worst of the news! Otherwise things are very cheery. Your eldest daughter has become a *real* nurse."

Elizabeth prepared his food at Homer End and took it to the Churchill. By the end of October he was eating well and walking unaided around the garden. He had responded well to a series of blood transfusions and the course of Ketoconazole. He was not coughing, had no headache. On 21 October, after six weeks in hospital, he was discharged.

Charles and Margharita waited to greet him at Homer End. According to his instructions, Elizabeth had told them nothing of his HIV status. "The tensions were horrendous because we couldn't tell them anything. It was terribly hard keeping it from them because you knew there wasn't any hope, but you could not say that to them." They helped Elizabeth to look after him and drove Bruce to Oxford for a weekly check-up. "Charles continues to make a good recovery," Bull reported to Juel-Jensen on 3 December. "Weight risen to 74 kg from 62 kg and apart from *Mullusculum contagiosum* on his face there are no abnormal stigmata. He is keen to go to the south of France for the English winter."

Jasper Conran's mother, Shirley, had offered him her house in Seillans above Cannes. Anxious to escape Homer End, the winter, his parents, Bruce accepted.

"IN THE SUMMER, obviously a prey to my malady, I turned arsonist and destroyed heaps of old notebooks, card indexes, correspondence."

In mid-December, on the eve of his departure with Elizabeth on the train to Nice, Bruce wrote a long letter to Cary Welch. Among the correspondence he had nearly chucked on to the fire was a bundle of letters from Welch, dating back to 1966. Rereading them, Bruce was reminded of how much the two friends had fallen out of touch. The lack of contact with someone with whom he had once been close gave Bruce the distance to simplify the harrowing past six months into a polished account of his illness, diagnosis and hopes for recovery. As long as he could tell stories about it, his illness might go away. Bruce's letter also alerted Welch to his next project, which would take as its subject a collector very much like Welch.

My illness was a dramatic episode. I have always known—from a fortune-teller or from my own instinctive promptings?—that I would be terribly ill in middle-age, and would recover. All summer, while I was putting the final touches to the book, I was obviously sickening, but preferred to put it out of my mind—even though, on a sweltering summer day, I'd be wrapped in shawls beside the Aga scribbling onto a yellow pad. I imagined I'd recover if only I could reach some mountain pastures, and so gaily set off for Switzerland: only to find, next morning, that I couldn't drag myself a hundred yards down the sidewalk. Obviously, something was seriously wrong. Thinking I was prey to some Indian amoeba, I consulted a specialist in tropical medicine, who took one look at my blood count, and, next day, said amiably: 'I cannot understand why you're alive. You have no red blood corpuscles left.' He failed to make a diagnosis, having run through a complete set of tests; and Elizabeth came to fetch me home in a definitely dying condition. I have a vague recollection of being wheeled to the plane; another, of the ambulance at London airport and then a blank. By the time I got to Oxford I was not expected to last the night. I did incidentally have the 'dark night experience', followed by the Pearly Gates. In my delirium I had visions of being in a colourful and vaguely medieval court where women offered me grapes on tazzas. At one point I called to Elizabeth, 'Where's King Arthur? He was here a minute ago.'

Anyway, although I was on life support, they still couldn't find the cause until, on the fourth day, the young immunologist rushed into my room and said 'Have you, in the past five years, been in a bats' cave? We think you've got a fungus of the bone marrow, which starts off growing on bat shit.' Yes. I had been in bat caves, in Java and in Australia. But when they grew the fungus, as one grows a culture for yoghurt, it was not mine after all. The most expert mycologists were consulted: samples were flown to the US, and the answer, which finally emerged, was that I had, indeed, a fungus of the marrow, but one which was known only from the corpse of a killer-whale cast up on the shores of Arabia and from ten healthy Chinese peasants, all of whom had died. Had I been consorting with killer-whales? Or with Chinese peasants? 'Peasants,' I said decisively. Indeed, we had. Last

December we were in Western Yunnan, following the traces of the Austro-American botanist, Joseph Rock, whose book *The Kingdom of the Na-Khi* was admired by Ezra Pound. We went to peasant feasts, slept in peasant houses, inhaled the dust of peasant winnowing; and it must be in Yunnan that I inhaled the particles of fungal dust, which set the malady in motion. I lost half my weight; came out in lumps and scabs, and looked entirely like the miniature of Akbar's courtier in the Bodleian whose name I've forgotten. I had a fearsome drug administered on the drip constantly for six weeks. I had blood transfusions, and in the end I made a rather startling recovery: at least, one which my doctors did not expect. It'll mean a change in one's life, though. Apparently, one can't ever quite get rid of a fungus like this, so I shall be on pills indefinitely; will have to report from time to time, and *not* alas go travelling into dangerously exotic places. The last stipulation I fully intend to ignore. In the meantime, rather than face the sodden gloom of an English winter, we are setting out for Grasse where we have borrowed a flat and where I hope to bash out my tale of the Czechoslovakian porcelain collector.

~~~~~~

XXXVII

The Harlequin

MICHAEL IGNATIEFF: *Where in your work is the*
division between fiction and non-fiction?
—BC: *I don't think there is one.*

"WHY DON'T YOU write a short story about that man in Prague?" As
Bruce lay miserable in his sickbed, Elizabeth produced a letter he had sent
her from Czechoslovakia in the summer of 1967, when Bruce was still an
archaeology student. The letter resurrected his journey through the museums of Central Europe as he made his way to the excavation site near
Prague, but most of the letter was devoted to his friend on the Zavist dig,
the "self-styled great lover" Maurizio Tosi.

Every evening for a week the two young archaeologists would take the
tram into Prague. It was a year before the Russian invasion. "Prague is one
of the most curious places in the world," Bruce wrote. "The whole place
is utterly bourgeois and obviously always was. Communism sits on it in a
most uneasy way, and I would have said cannot last long. It is virtually impossible to meet a single Communist. Even in the trains and buses they
joke about it. Some of the younger generation might be communist but
would not dream of owning up to the fact. It must be one of the few
places in the world where one can hear the American position in Vietnam
actually defended . . . I had a long lecture from a man on the excavation
who could only be described as a peasant on the merits of Eton and how
England was an education to the world."

In love Maurizio Tosi behaved with the theatrical detachment that
Bruce would later grant Utz. "A succession of Merry Widows and Countess Mitzis passed through his bed . . . The secret of his attraction to the
divas was his technique—you could call it a trick—of applying the stiff
bristles of the moustache to the lady's throat . . ." What begins as a funeral
in *Utz* is taken from one of Tosi's finest performances: as the best man to
his Moravian girlfriend.

On their second afternoon at the site, Tosi was telephoned by Lea, a former lover. She was in Prague. Tosi made an excuse to his girlfriend at the camp and that evening climbed aboard the tram with Bruce.

The Moravian bird, [Bruce wrote] had come to Prague to get married. The bridegroom was an ineffectual young German from Magdeburg with a fall-away chin and pointed shoes. She had known him for three years. 'And to think,' exclaimed the outraged Maurizio, 'that when she was making love to me on the Linear Pottery site at Bylany, she knew him all the time. It confirms my opinion of the faithlessness of women. How could she give herself to the dirty German?' Anyway for the time being she apparently could and would and the reason for her contacting Maurizio was that he should be best man at the wedding. He at once changed tack and agreed with alacrity, and also insisted that I come too as a witness. The time of the wedding was eight-thirty in the morning on the next day at the church of St Ignatz. 'Don't you understand?' he said, 'she is only marrying him because she is pregnant. I shall play the part of the faithful and wronged friend and in two years I shall have her.' I think that Maurizio may have miscalculated again because the two seemed absolutely devoted and stood in the foyer of the hotel kissing and fondling each other to the fury of the headwaiter, who finally told them to desist.

So the next morning quarter past eight found Maurizio and I in archaeological clothes, carnations in our buttonholes, on the steps of the baroque church of St Ignatz in Charles Square. One old woman was desultorily cleaning the aisle and another prayed loudly and devotedly in the chapel of the Holy Sepulchre, a real rock-cut tomb with a plastic Christ looming over the boulders which were rather unsuitably planted with gladioli and gloxinias. An untidy man appeared and was under the impression that I was the organist. When I protested, he shrugged and said he would play himself. This he did on two chords only and to this cacophony the bride arrived in a large Tatra saloon accompanied by her parents and the bridegroom's mother, a solid German hausfrau in a crinkled pale blue suit. The bride's mother was a good-looking woman evidently in a savage temper, and her father a mild-mannered little Czech who squinted through his spectacles. Maurizio bent double and kissed the ladies' hands to their evident surprise. The bride must have been wearing her grandmother's wedding dress, and the bridegroom's shoes were more pointed than ever. And so this comic little procession made its way up the aisle to the thump-thump of the organ, and came to rest inside the pink marble altar rails where the priest was waiting. St Ignatz is a vast building, about the same size as Bath Abbey with astonishing pink and white plaster decoration and angels and saints dripping from every cornice. The grey marble pillars rippled like the waters of an oil-covered sea, and the organist thump-thumped while the ceremony proceeded in an undertone. I winked at the mother who winked back and began to look more cheerful. And finally the organ stopped while the priest gave a short address. On either side of the altarpiece St Peter exhorted and St Paul comforted while St Ignatius was wafted up to heaven in a rosy sunset and above supercilious cherubs pouted on plaster clouds, and for a moment there was peace. Then the organ thumpthumped again, and never was an aisle so long. By nine-ten the seven of us were in the Hotel Miramar in a corner of the cocktail lounge drinking the happy couple's health with a Hungarian wine that tore to my liver. In the corner by the deserted bandstand was a stuffed bear which a cleaning woman dusted as she cleared up the squalid mess of the night before. And that was the most curious wedding I have ever been to.

This exuberant letter would be the embryo for the novel Bruce completed in his convalescence. "I had thought I'd use that time to read and re-read all the great Russian novels," he wrote to Cary Welch. "Instead, hardly able to hold a pen, I launched forth on my story: a tale of Marxist Czechoslovakia conceived in the spirit and style of the Rococo." In contrast to *The Songlines, Utz* would be light, tight, short, decorative—about a man who collects and sits still.

THE BRUCE WHO wrote *Utz* was not a Bruce in flight. From his bed in the south of France, with Elizabeth at his side, he turned back to a world he knew.

In 1967, one year after his resignation from Sotheby's, he asked Kate Foster, in the porcelain department, whom she could recommend to see in Prague. She suggested the name of Dr Rudolph Just, a businessman and passionate collector of glass, silver and Meissen.

Over tea on the Sotheby's roof, Foster explained to Bruce why he might find Just interesting. A year before, Sotheby's having agreed to give her study-leave, Foster had driven to Prague for the purpose of acquiring German, the language of most ceramics catalogues. On 30 June 1966, at 10.30 am, Dr Just had led her into his two-room flat in the Jewish quarter. "He was a small man, rather colourless, thin-featured, who undeniably lived off his nerves a lot. He explained to me that when his wife died, the authorities came along and said: 'This is two rooms and you're on your own, you'll have to be moved.' They had listed his entire collection and he lived in permanent fear. The Communist Party HQ was round the corner. He was sure his flat was bugged." In order to stay on in his apartment, Just had married his housekeeper, Lida. "He was very nice to her. She was plainly dressed and kept in the background. She was in the room when I arrived, then went off and sat in the kitchen."

The flat comprised the kitchen, a bedroom and a large sitting room sub-divided into an eating area and an ante-room. "He was afraid of people looking in," says Foster. "The flat was quite dark and stultifying, yet it was vibrant because every single thing meant something to him."

Foster drank tea from a Meissen cup. "He wanted to know what his stuff was worth. He had a voracious appetite to know what was happening in the glass, porcelain, political and cultural world. He was starved of knowledge. I represented for him the available current information in the West." Later, she drove Just in her white Triumph Herald to a hilly region outside the city and told him what he wanted to know. Meanwhile, she inspected his remarkable collection. "He had some money in Switzerland and this enabled him to buy."

The walls were hung with eighteenth-century engravings and Bohemian canvases of 1860 and in among the paintings were plates. There were glass-fronted bookcases, the shelves lined with old textiles as both setting and protection, and every surface was covered with little objects: Roman glass, Züricher gold glass, Augustus Rex vases, Augsburg and Nuremburg silver, Meissen dwarves and a few very rare Meissen figurines of the earliest possible period, *c.*1720. "He had on the whole off-beat things, but it was all classy stuff: definitely a scholarly collection."

Just wrote to Foster. "You know that I do not collect any more . . . but a short time ago I acquired an extraordinarily interesting historical, and very early Kreussen Tankard, *c.*1620. I am far more interested in objects which pose not easily resolved problems than in those which everyone knows, and most wish to possess, only because they are desirable and cost a lot of money."

To his delight, Foster was able to confirm that Just's collection had some of the best examples of its type she had seen. He gave her a ceremonial handle from an eighteenth-century mining officer's staff and the following day took her to lunch with his friend, Dr Hrazky, the director of the Jewish museum. "The menu said 'crap' instead of 'carp'. We spoke in German, but both men knew what that meant."

Their farcical meal, in a fish restaurant now vanished, would find its way into Bruce's novel. "Under the heading CRAP DISHES, the list contained 'Crap soup with paprika', 'Stuffed crap', 'Crap cooked in beer', 'Fried crap', 'Crap balls', 'Crap *à la juive*' " . . .

NO NOTEBOOK RECORD survives of Bruce's "four-hour encounter" with Just: he may have burned it. According to Elizabeth, Bruce saw Just's apartment, they walked round Prague and then Just said: "I'm going to a brothel." And that was that.

The novel opens with Utz's funeral in 1974, transformed from the wedding Bruce had attended with Maurizio Tosi. The nebulous narrating "I" is a writer engaged on a work on the psychopathology of the compulsive collector. He has come to Prague to write a magazine piece on Emperor Rudolf II's passion for collecting exotica. Exactly as Bruce had done that summer, he pauses on his journey south to see the *Kunstkammer* or "cabinet of curiosities" assembled by Emperor Rudolf's uncle. The amalgam of curios is taken from collections visited on Bruce's way to Prague, in Aix, Bonn, Nuremburg and Vienna. "Rudolf's treasures—his mandragoras, his basilisk, his bezoar stone, his unicorn cup, his gold mounted *coco-de-mer*, his *homunculus* in alcohol, his nails from Noah's Ark and the phial of dust from which God created Adam—had long ago vanished from Prague."

Knowing no one in Prague, he has asked a friend for contacts. "My friend the historian" urges him to see Kaspar Joachim Utz, "the Rudolf of our time", and, exactly as Foster had done, gives him "an outline of the facts as he knew them".

They make contact, eat a fish lunch with Utz's colleague, Dr Orlik, an expert in the woolly mammoth, and finally the narrator is led back to Utz's flat.

The tiny apartment was an elaborate version of 198 West Heath Road in Birmingham. Bruce converts his grandmother's Victorian cabinet into Utz's plate-glass shelves. "The shelves were backed with mirror, so that you had the illusion of entering an enfilade of glittering chambers, a 'dream palace' multiplied to infinity, through which human forms flitted like insubstantial shadows." His father's white christening mug, the Bruce china, are elevated into the most priceless porcelain in the world, a miscellany conjured from Bruce's recollection of notable objects at Sotheby's. The star of the collection (sold at Sotheby's on 25 June 1963 for £9,000), was the masked Harlequin: "the arch improviser, the zany trickster, master of the volteface . . . Mr Chameleon himself".

WITH COLD WAR PRAGUE as his backdrop, Bruce's hero is someone who tries to accommodate an oppressive and hateful regime by retreating into a child's world of possessions. But in the end there is no private space. This place of refuge becomes not an escape, rather the point of contact between himself and the authorities. He can enjoy his collection provided it stays where it is—and he leaves it to the State.

Halfway through writing *Utz*, Bruce set out to explain its theme to Colin Thubron. "This was a man who'd ruined his life by clinging onto his enormously wonderful collection of Meissen figurines through the horrors of the Second World War and the early years of Stalinism. The whole thing had trapped him because he could never leave the collection and it ruined his life. On the other hand, as compensation he managed to shrink his horizons down to the world of *commedia dell'arte* figures, so he lived the life of Harlequin and Pulcinella and they were his real friends and *blocked* out the horrors of the Novotny and Gotchok regimes."

A year before his death, with the novel complete, Bruce was still trying to articulate what the story was about. Upset by a proposed blurb, he responded with a list of the ideas that had not been put across:

"No idea of the illusionist city of Prague.

"No idea of the 'private' world of Utz's little figures as a strategy for blocking out the horrors of the 20th century; that the porcelains were real, the horrors so much flim-flam.

"No indication of the technique which allows the reader an insight into the fictional process (and how a story-teller sets about it).

"One of the principal themes of the book is that Old Europe *survives*.

"Marta [Utz's maid] epitomises the fact that the techniques of political indoctrination fail and are bound to fail.

"No idea that Utz identifies himself as Harlequin, the Trickster, and runs his own private *commedia*—outwitting everyone until, finally, he finds his Columbine.

"No idea of the Jewish element—Utz is 1/4 Jewish—or of the somewhat subversive notion that the collecting of images, i.e. art-collecting, is inimical to Jehovah—which is why the Jews have always been so good at it.

"Art collecting = idol-worship = blasphemy against the created world of God."

In the novel, when asked whether art collecting is idolatry, Utz replies:

"Ja! Ja! . . . Because it is forbidden . . . ! Because it is sinful . . . ! Because it is dangerous . . . !"

IN 1967, RUDOLPH Just's contortions to build and maintain his collection reminded Bruce, then in revolt from the art world, of his friends Cary Welch and George Ortiz.

"I am Utz," agrees Ortiz. "I am a victim of my collection. I've collected with an obsession that has eaten away my innards. Here am I, a Bolivian collecting non-French art, paying in non-French money and because of French patrimony law, I cannot take my works out of France."

Nevertheless, the Ortiz collection of antiquities has been exhibited at the Royal Academy, in Berlin and also at the Hermitage (which Ortiz first saw with Bruce in 1968). "My whole collection was made with no preconceived intellectual approach. It was purely visceral, emotional, intuitive. My gift is to be able to appreciate, sense, perceive the ethos that great artists have put in their creations. That is why I can see a work of art and I will know nothing about it and it hits me in the guts and later on I learn it's the essence of that culture. It's a gift I have in the same way as a Mozart, a Bach, a Cézanne, but," says Ortiz, "it's also a handicap."

Does Ortiz agree with Bruce's argument that works of art take the life out of those who collect them? "Completely. I can't perceive people. I can only perceive objects."

His obsession is "a visceral need" for the pursuit of truth. "Great art gives lots of hope. It's not just a collection. It's a message. Why do people looking through vitrines have a smile on their face? Bruce knew of this search after purity and was influenced and impressed by it. The basis of our friendship was my admiration for his taste. We had the same understanding of works of art. Bruce at one point wanted me to go against collecting. He said he had liberated himself of objects, they didn't mean anything. It was a lot of crap."

Bruce teased Ortiz that the he had based the story of *Utz* on him. "I *hate* Meissen. He knew I hated Meissen. That's why I hate *Utz*."

THE NAME UTZ may have derived from an American friend of Peter Levi, a poet from Baton Rouge called Steve Utz, pronounced like "butts".

Utz lived in Cambridge with a girlfriend whose uncle had assassinated Senator Long and whose father had driven the getaway car. Bruce had also met another Utz: Charles Tomlinson's German translator, Joaquim Utz.

But Utz was also Bruce, who never transcended his ambivalence about the art world. It continued to haunt him. In western Patagonia, remote from any museum or gallery, he had written in his notebook, "a man's relation to things as a surrogate for other contacts is fascinating". In 1979, he proposed to the *New Yorker* a story set in Eastern Europe, "on the bourgeoisie behind the Iron Curtain". More recently in Australia, he had brooded on the fate of Theodor Strehlow, whose collection of 1,200 Aboriginal artefacts had poisoned his life—and threatened the health of his widow. "I'm riveted by the affair of Kath Strehlow and the Aboriginal collection," he wrote to a friend, as if—perhaps—he had lacked the courage when in Australia to take on his true subject, which was Strehlow. Kath Strehlow is in no doubt of the deep impression "the affair" left on Bruce: "I think he got the idea of *Utz* from the Strehlow collection. Bruce saw that these objects had a life of their own, were weighted with other people's stories and burdens and troubles."

A fortnight after seeing her cabinet of sacred *tjuringas*, he was in Alice Springs. One of his conversations with Petronella Vaarzon-Morel concerned a man in Prague who was ruled by his possessions. "It was ticking over in his mind."

DR JUST DIED in the mid-1970s, but the fate of his collection remained a mystery. In 1982, Bruce visited Prague's National Museum of Decorative Arts to ask about the Meissen. It was closed, but a woman came downstairs, took him into the street and asked him if *he* knew where it was. When museum staff went to Just's apartment it was empty. Kate Foster never heard of any part of his collection reappearing.

At the end of July 1987, with two-thirds of his "Hoffmann-like tale" complete, Bruce and Elizabeth drove to Prague in his 2CV. "My legs . . . are still liable to go lilac and blue in the cold," he wrote to Nin Dutton, but he looked and felt much better. On his visa he described himself as "farmer".

As *Utz*'s narrator found upon his return to Prague, "it was a city at the end of its tether". In Prague they met Barbara Epstein, editor of the *New York Review of Books*. "The Czechs were totally cut off from the west," says

Epstein. "You'd go into a bookshop—and no Kafka. [Václav] Havel was in prison and there was a funny feeling of not wanting to get into trouble. It was very delicate who you saw."

"Bruce loved to imagine we were being followed," says Elizabeth.

One night they had dinner with the novelist Ivan Klima who was working as a window-cleaner and messenger boy. Proud of his status as a writer, Klima told Bruce that people were touchingly nice when they gave him messages.

Elizabeth took Bruce to several of the places described in *Utz*. They attended another wedding with a pregnant bride. They visited Rabbi Loew's house-like grave. They walked in the Jewish cemetery where he had walked with Maurizio, through the forest of dark-pink stones. And they visited No 5 Siroka, a pale building with tall bay windows which overlooked the cemetery.*

Bruce's notebook for the week is spare in detail: "Smells of dustbins . . . posters for holidays in USSR . . . lights in a ballet school . . . crumpled sycamore leaves . . . childishness of art collecting." What stood out from the drabness were the galvanised dustbins that the Prague municipality every day emptied onto a mountain of rubbish visible from the city. Bruce had noticed these great grey bins in Dr Just's former foyer. "That's what gave him the idea for what might have happened to the collection," says Elizabeth.

At the Yalta hotel, they were woken up every night at three in the morning by huge rubbish lorries. In his notebook, Bruce compares the double-action leverage to "a praying mantis devouring its mate. Double gulp. The masher inside. The flashing orange light. Lift dustbin up. Tipped it into maw."

In the novel, Bruce raises the possibility that into that maw Utz had tipped his Meissen.

"I'M UNIMPRESSED WITH the new," Bruce told Michael Ignatieff in an interview for *Granta* in 1987. "Most advances in literature strike me as being advances into a *cul-de-sac*." In *Utz*, Bruce rescued his own past. He also recovered a culture like Dr Orlik's permafrosted mammoths. On dis-

---

* Bruce takes part of his description of Utz's flat from one of the bedrooms in the Chanlers' New York apartment at 1 E84, a whole floor which Gertrude bought after the sale of Meridian House in 1966.

play in Utz's cabinets during the Cold War is the history of Middle Europe—before it was swept away "by revolution and the tramp of armies".

The novel is a catalogue of the recondite, the arcane, the forgotten. On Eastern Europe he had consulted Hans Magnus Enzensberger. "In *Utz* one element I recognised is the old patterns which have been put into deep-freeze and somehow survived: partly frayed, partly shopworn and impoverished, but still there." *Utz* is a short novel, yet Bruce scatters names into it like seed: Cellini, Montezuma, Noah, Tycho Brahé, Kepler, Arcimboldo, Marx, Stalin, the brothers Grimm, Rothschild, Kropotkin, Goering, Titian, Klement Gottwald, Picasso, Matisse, Mies van der Rohe, Horace Walpole, Johannes Böttger, Marie Antoinette, Buddha, Chekhov, Charlie Chaplin, Stefan Zweig, Marco Polo, Kublai Khan, Basilius Velentinus, Nebuchadnezzar, Baudelaire, even Tweedledee and Tweedledum.

Bruce himself pokes fun at this roll-call in the book—"names that meant not much more to Utz than a list of railway stations from Ventimiglia to Bari". But to some it was pedantry at the expense of meaning, an intellectual shorthand "worthy of a television quiz". After *Utz* was shortlisted for the Booker Prize, the satirical magazine *Private Eye* ran their "Annual Cut-Out-'n'-Keep Guide" to the front-runners. This included *Tutsi-Frutsi* by Bruce Hatpin: "Wry, evocative, sensitive account of a Viennese ice-cream collector who fills his cavernous flat in Marxist Prague with hundreds of different flavoured ice-creams. One day he wakes up and finds that they have all melted. As the *Daily Telegraph* commented: "*Tutsi-Frutsi* is a wry, evocative novella in which ice-cream collecting is used as a paradigm for man's insatiable urge to eternalise the transient.' Checkwin is of course best known for his award-winning cult novel *Tramlines*, which shows how the ancient Incas invented trams. An insatiable nomad, he lives in Notting Hill like everybody else."

In Prague, the reception was different. Bruce spent a short time in Czechoslovakia (two weeks in three visits over 20 years), but he presented an authentic picture recognisable to Central Europeans. They trusted him, submitting to his world and to his knowledge. At Prague University, Dr Martin Hilsky lectures in English literature, with a special interest in the portrayal of the new Czech Republic in foreign literatures. "I would say that *Utz* is certainly the best book, and the only book that captures the essence of Prague, by an English writer. He has penetrated into the atmosphere of the city. You can follow the geography. I didn't notice one mistake." Of the scores of books written at the time about Eastern Europe, including novels by John Updike and Philip Roth, so many seemed to Hilsky overtly political. "It's a journalistic platitude to say you need your enemy. What I really admired about Chatwin is that he did not make Utz a hero. His portrait of a Czech intellectual is very sensitive. He says the Czech propensity to bend before a superior power is not a sign of weakness. I thought that brilliant. There are many people like Utz, who survived Hitler and Stalin, yet who are not morally inferior."

When he first read *Utz*, in 1989, Hilsky became suspicious of his reaction. "I said to myself: 'You like Bruce Chatwin's book so much that you do not realise it is self-flattery. It is a myth you like too much.' It is honest to doubt your feeling, but I have come out with the feeling that, yes, it is a great book 100 per cent."

LATE ON IN *Utz* the reader is surprised to learn that Marta, the quiet woman who serves as Utz's housekeeper and whom we first meet scrubbing potatoes on a Meissen dish, is his wife. To many, the Chatwin marriage had this covert quality. As with Utz, Bruce's affirmation of his married life was belated.

Both *Utz* and *The Songlines* end with scenes of reconciliation. Marta, the carpenter's daughter who loves her ganders, harks back to Jean the Barn, but in her capacity for a "spontaneous overflow of healthy animal spirits" there are deep traces of Elizabeth—as there are of Bruce in Utz. Every April, Utz would leave Prague for Vichy: "By April . . . he felt acute claustrophobia, from having spent the winter months in close proximity to the adoring Marta . . . Before leaving, he would make a resolution never, ever, to return." After a month away, "he would then bolt for home like a man pursued by demons". Elizabeth shared with Marta an endurance, a patience and Cordelia's unasking love. In all of Utz's affairs, the regular flow of sopranos through his bed, "there was never a hint of reproach on her part. Nor on his the least acknowledgement that she had ever been inconvenienced."

In *Love Undetectable*, Andrew Sullivan, an HIV-positive and openly homosexual writer, asks what can be purchased from the horror of AIDS: "Plagues and wars do this to people. They force them to ask more fundamental questions of who they are and what they want . . . Out of cathartic necessity and loss and endurance comes, at least for a while, a desire to turn these things into something constructive, to appease the trauma by some tangible residue that can give meaning and dignity to what has happened."

Bruce's insistence on Utz's romantic and redemptive gesture, "outwitting everyone until, finally, he finds his Columbine," is fuelled by the same desire for a second chance: to spend what was left of the light on something constructive. Near the end of the novel, Utz and Marta marry. "And from that hour they passed their days in passionate adoration of each other."

In the darkest days of their separation, when Elizabeth was selling Holwell, Pattie Sullivan had acted as a messenger between them. "When I was involved in these transactions, I had a sense Bruce cared about Elizabeth and that in the end they would be reconciled." Bruce's illness enabled that reconciliation. His "eye" had singled Elizabeth out, but possessing her he had travelled away from her: ill, he was forced to see that perhaps he had been travelling to find what had been there, within his reach, all along.

"Bruce was a bit shaky," says Barbara Epstein, watching him with Elizabeth in Prague. "But Elizabeth just let it be. They were very close at that point." Elizabeth felt it too. "We were certainly closer than we had been for a long time."

"Elizabeth is being marvellous," Bruce wrote to Nin Dutton after his discharge from the Churchill. Just as she had eleven years before on Fisher's Island, she created the conditions for him to write in the south of France. "Have been giving B large doses of VTC," she wrote to Gertrude, "& it seems to have had a fantastic effect on his legs which are working much more normally." One night Hugh Honour stayed with the Chatwins in Seillans. It moved Honour to see the way they behaved towards each other. "Elizabeth exuded this atmosphere: 'Here we are, this is another tough journey we're on, a trek in the Himalayas, Bruce has slipped down, but soon he'll be better'."

Passing through London that summer, the Chatwins dined with the Erskines. Robert and Lindy Erskine, too, were affected by the "loving, very genuine look of compassion" Bruce gave Elizabeth. Erskine says: "I remember Bruce sitting in this chair saying: 'This disease is awful, but it has enabled me to rediscover my wife,' and he said this with a passion that surprised me. It was almost as though the whole thing had been put off since their early marriage. He indicated there had been a coolness and it was now patched up. One can be cynical and say he fell in love with his nurse. But I thought that was real, real, real. It *wasn't* someone saying: 'I'm terribly fond of my nurse because she looks after me so well.' And it was so surprising because Bruce didn't speak of his feelings, didn't let on."

Other friends detected Bruce's desire to begin again. "When he was very ill, he came in a wheelchair to lunch," says Emma Tennant. "We put a special table on the ground floor. I said: 'Elizabeth is looking terrific and I'm not quite sure what she makes me think of.' Bruce said: 'She looks American. *Now can you see what I saw?*'"

Cary and Edith Welch, who had sailed with the Chatwins on their honeymoon, saw them in Curzon Street where the Welches had rented a flat. "Elizabeth was trying to help Bruce and he looked up at her with such love and devotion: it was quite an uplifting aura," says Edith. "The whole thing was happy, even though he was being wheeled in and out."

This sense that Bruce had broken through to another shore and had accepted that he was part of a couple, was recognised by his German publisher, Michael Krüger. In December 1987, Bruce travelled with Elizabeth to Munich. They went with Krüger to the Franziskaner beer hall. Krüger had last encountered Bruce on Lindos with Kasmin and Rezzori. "After Greece, when he was the most beautiful looking gentleman in the world, he looked pale and funny. His skin was dry and his hands had changed totally." This was the first occasion Krüger had met Elizabeth. "Suddenly, I knew she existed. After that, she was always in the picture." It seemed to Krüger that Bruce's illness had prematurely delivered him into the kind of happiness that comes with being old. In Greece, it had looked as if Bruce might never grow up at all, but suddenly, in a few months, he had moved from adolescence to slippered contemplation. "This illness meant a deletion of sexuality, of hunger," says Krüger. "This barrier was gone and he could meet her in a very different way. No more running away or making his words a curtain. I had the impression of an old couple sitting there. After all the battle of life they would be together. For the first time I had the idea that he was a husband and Elizabeth was his wife. I had the impression of a wonderful couple like Ovid's Philomena and Baucis."

In one of his last letters, Bruce wrote to Gertrude: "Elizabeth and I have not had an easy marriage, but it survives everything because neither of us have loved anyone else."

A Cosmic Book

"Are you a traveller by profession?"

"Absolutely not."

"What are you by profession?"

"I suppose I'm a writer, so-called."

—BC INTERVIEWED ON ABC RADIO

The Songlines WAS published on 25 June 1987. It was his testament and he dedicated it to Elizabeth.

A week before publication, he slipped back into England to fulfil the publicity schedule arranged by Jonathan Cape. In the construction of the Chatwin legend, Bruce could be a reliable labourer. On 9 April he had written to Nin Dutton: "One thing is certain, I must be out of England when the book comes out in June. I hate all the publishing hoo-haa and, as I've discovered to my cost, you can't give one interview without opening the floodgates . . ." Between 17 June and 22 June, however, he submitted to 14 newspaper and television interviews. "He was brisk about promotion and understood what a best-selling author has to do," says Shirley Conran, who had the chance to observe Bruce on his author tour in New York and Toronto. "Somehow Bruce came across as unworldly. He was *very* worldly. It was not part of his personality, but his background." Shirley was conscious, too, of his tough business side. "Most authors can't read their royalty statements. He could."

Within Jonathan Cape, there had been confusion over how to market the book. Bruce was adamant: he did not wish to be regarded as a travel-writer. If *The Songlines* was marketed as a travel-book, it would be slotted in the travel section beside "the Cyclades Islands on $5 a day". On the other hand, "in literature it would be beside Chaucer". *The Songlines* was fiction. ("A lot of this is fiction, a lot of this is made up," he told Thubron, who was one of his interviewers. "But it's made up in order to make a story real.") He had explained his position in a broadcast interview to

512   BRUCE CHATWIN

ABC in Australia. "Look at the greatest novel of the nineteenth century, *Madame Bovary*. Every incident is a compilation of various things. Flaubert researched and researched. Very little is *invented*. The borderline between fiction and non-fiction is to my mind extremely arbitrary, and invented by publishers."

When *The Songlines* was shortlisted for the Thomas Cook Travel Award, Bruce issued a statement: "The journey it describes is an invented journey, it is not a travel book in the generally accepted sense. To avoid any possible confusion, I must ask to withdraw it from the shortlist." Tom Maschler, writing to Gillon Aitken, Bruce's new agent, was glad of the attention: "Not many authors write books which are candidates simultaneously for non-fiction and fiction awards!"

The Songlines TRANSFORMED him, as John Ryle wrote, "from a cult writer to a bestseller". Most newspapers singled the book out, illustrating their review with the photograph of a younger, healthy-looking Bruce. Reports of a mysterious Chinese fungal infection gave him allure. While losing none of his back-packer appeal, he strode into the realm of literary respectability.

If his publishers had fretted over the genre, critics and readers welcomed a misfit who dodged the usual categories. His harlequin tricks annoyed some, who complained that he had set up an intellectual apparatus he could not support, and had failed to give the Aborigines their due voice. Many more cheered the violation of a conventional novel structure and the sheer scale of his ambition. The American author Shirley Hazzard wrote to him: "Reading your *Songlines* again, I thought it one of those works destined to alter the plane of thought from which an important theme has long been surveyed and discussed. Things can never again be quite the same as they were ante-B.C."

Bruce's ebullience, his obsessional vitality, his very intense intellectual involvement combine in *The Songlines* to produce, in Colin Thubron's words, "his most considerable book, and the one most central to his personality and interests". It may not succeed on its original terms, but what it does achieve, as fiction, is to allow the world into the songlines. "I can't say I believe the songlines *literally*," says Thubron. "Maybe any third-year anthropology student could shoot it to bits, but what's wonderful is the passion with which Bruce approaches it, his love of it, the way he writes it, the imagery, so that it involves you while you are in it, you inhabit it."

Thomas Keneally had watched Bruce and Rushdie check out of their hotel in Adelaide to go to Alice Springs. "I thought at the time this dotty Brit is going to go crazy out there and this Indian prince is going to be a bit more ambiguous about it." Keneally judges *The Songlines* to be "a cosmic book", although he found an overripe sentimentality in Arkady's marriage to Marian. (As did several others, Keneally shrank from the figure of Marian striding around the outback in soaked rags.) "Australians were raised to think that at the heart of Australia there was a dead heart. Australia is not European-sensibility friendly and it took a mad desert freak like Chatwin, a sort of literary T. E. Lawrence, to go to places like that. To realise that far from Australia having a dead heart, there was a map, there had always been a map. It's a dangerous thing to say, but I think he did Aboriginal Australia a service. If there were ten books I had to set every Ozzie to read not for the sake of nationalism but for the sake of coming to terms with who we are on earth, *The Songlines* would be one of them." Keneally responded to Bruce's hopefulness. "The evidence in the cave meant we had not crushed each other's skulls at every conceivable opportunity over food, women, whatever, but we were in fact the ones who were preyed upon by a sabre-tooth tiger. I don't know how scientifically reliable it was, but I was willing to take it as a hopeful fable for human kind, a fortifying myth."

The hybrid form was welcomed by Hans Magnus Enzensberger. "To my mind it's at the interstices of genres where the most interesting things happen," he says. "Chatwin's transgression is much more important than any avant-garde fumbling. He has elements of pretension, but these also have to do with freeing himself from very rigorous ideas of literature in England, where the mere fact that you write a book about a collector in Prague sounds pretentious. In psychological terms, Chatwin suffers from *Beziehungswahn*—a delirium of establishing connections. In *In Patagonia* somehow everything connects in a seemingly mad way, but in *The Songlines*, he took on more than he could integrate. In this escape from English culture, he had perhaps a penchant for rather obscure thinkers. I remember once we talked about Spengler. That is something which here in Germany one would consider not merely old hat, but lacking in any rigour, an intellectual indecency. He had a weak spot for such people. That in *The Songlines* disturbed me a little, but it was perhaps his overreaction to insularity. Once he had decided he wouldn't be restricted by the English, he became rather defenceless. He gave up his philosophy, which is empiricist, but he didn't have antibodies. Hence the freshness of Spengler. For him, Spengler wasn't stale at all."

Robert Hughes, who himself challenged the academic establishment with his own magisterial picture of early colonial Australia in *The Fatal Shore*, applauded Bruce's transgression. "I don't think it matters in the least, as long as you grant that some of it is made up. Passages in *The Songlines* are extraordinarily beautiful. Bruce caught Australian generosity—'Have a steak and stay forever'—with perfect truth. Turgenev couldn't have done it."

In Australia, the book represented for many critics "the rapacity of Empire". Christopher Pearson judged that Bruce did for the Aborigines what Robert Hughes had done for the convicts. "*The Songlines* is a work of arcadian sentimentality, a tremendous misuse of poetic licence," and he quoted Stewart Harris: "If there is one person more damaging to the position of the Aboriginal Australian than the racist, it is the person who idealises them and romanticises them." Ruth Brown bridled at Bruce's colonial attitude and political naïveté. "Chatwin may have helped to put Aborigines on the map in Britain, but it is a map superficially exquisite and tasteful like a Mont Blanc pen, and as unrelated to everyday life." Nor was Patrick White impressed. "One wonders where truth ends and fiction begins," he wrote to Maschler. "I happen to know he was driven round the outback by Nin Dutton who turns into a tough guy of Cossack descent in the book. Some of the questions from other writers are interesting. Much of it is plain boring."

IN ALICE SPRINGS, Bruce's inability to penetrate Aboriginal culture disappointed those who had helped him, that is to say those who were most profoundly involved. "I got into trouble for telling everyone to tell him everything because he'll write a beautiful book," says Robyn Davidson. She resented the way he paid back those with whom he had had run-ins, such as Phillip Toyne and Daphne Williams. It was the first and only time she had seen a spiteful side to Bruce. "Maybe he wrote that out of the fact he was just scratching the surface and he *was* excluded. He found it very difficult as an idea that there were some things you couldn't know. He felt that information should be free, that knowledge is out there for everybody. That's not so. In Aborigine society, information is a currency."

Toyne says, "Many people who had nothing to do with Chatwin thought *The Songlines* was a great book, but it doesn't go far enough to take on the true liberation of fictional writing. I think he has made a global reputation for himself literally by standing on the heads, shoulders, fingers and hands of people."

The most obvious example is Toly Sawenko. "I was completely floored by *The Songlines*. I had no inkling before during or after that Bruce had chosen to write a book about his adventures in Alice Springs. I had one postcard from Paris of a Picasso. After the book came out I never heard from him again. He didn't send a copy."

Since 1987, Sawenko has had to endure a stream of back-packers knocking at his door. The appeal of Bruce's mystical endeavour was not limited to middle-class white Australians for whom the book provided a window into Aboriginal culture. The back-packers arrive from all over the world. "Their attitude is: 'Here's a character a bit like me, more knowledgeable but with enough physical description to hang a mind adventure on. Let's take a metaphysical journey'." And so they want to meet Arkady. "What was only a three-day journey has become an unauthorised biography. Bruce doesn't do anything to make the reader think this is a created character. He says of the narrator, this is Bruce who grew up in Sheffield. He's just paying lip-service to the notion of fiction because the characters are so recognisable. It's an occupational hazard for all fiction that writers are going to be basing their characters on real people. My question is: what kind of relationship should writers have with real people?"

Not only for himself does Sawenko regret that Bruce was not open about his intentions. By basing his text so largely on Strehlow, Bruce risked committing, in Aborigine eyes, the same transgressions. "Bruce hadn't sorted the protocols through. He hadn't sat down with any Aborigine. He gets his information second-hand and repeats it." Sawenko believes that Bruce missed a tremendous opportunity by not posing his conceptual questions directly to the people he was writing about. "Aboriginal people are capable of dealing with the world in a philosophical way. The problem is, he just wasn't there long enough, he didn't get involved at any depth. That was anathema to Bruce. He came with an interesting set of questions and I admire him for posing the challenge to himself, but he didn't really carry it off, and how could he? There was never any way he was going to get it right considering the whirlwind time and baggage he brought with him. He would have needed to get to know some Aboriginal people, which he just didn't do. He uses me as a convenient artifice, but it's still a white man speculating over how interesting Aboriginal culture is."

Petronella, too, felt Bruce's understanding could have been richer, more careful, given what he was capable of. "He has wonderful moments where he captures certain facets of people's characters, but he doesn't grant the Aborigines any voice at all. He reproduces the white-fella-as-boss colonial relation. The fallacy that they are going off into the netherlands because of an urge to walk is based on a misunderstanding that people wander aimlessly. But the people's knowledge of the country is *precise*. They have a terrain which they regard as home. Bruce regarded their land as a kind of non-home. He didn't deal with nomadism as a true concept. He's dealing with the flight of prophets into the desert for visions and how this reflects on him."

Bruce's failure to reach the source results in what Jenny Green calls "an interesting absence of song". This absence, says Davidson, is the key. "One of the things he doesn't describe is the journey of a dreaming, because it's the one thing he couldn't see. He wanted it to be what he had read in Strehlow, but when he went there, it wasn't, and he had to make it up."

When pressed to describe the central image of his book, Bruce said: "It's a low, rather beautiful 'aaaahh'."

WHILE BRUCE'S POLITICAL naïveté exposed him to attacks from those working closely with the Aboriginals, even critics like Toyne had to concede that his popularising of the songlines introduced many white middle-class Australians to the culture of the country they lived in. Murray Bail admits, "A lot of people hadn't heard of the songlines—including myself."

For Mario Vargas Llosa, a novelist Bruce openly admired, it did not matter whether the songlines were strictly accurate or a charming literary fraud. "Because to pass off fiction as reality, or to inject fiction into reality, is one of the most demanding and imperishable of human enterprises— and the dearest ambition of any storyteller." Reading *The Songlines* on a visit to Australia in the belief that it was an anthropological work, Vargas Llosa was reminded of Borges.

In England, the book enjoyed a swift popular success. Cape had paid an advance of £20,000 and initially printed 10,000 copies. Hardback sales eventually reached 20,779. In July, it became number one on the *Sunday Times* best-seller list and was among the titles chosen for the Queen's summer reading.

Ostensibly, Bruce had completed his opus and unloaded what

Rushdie called "the burden he's been carrying all his writer's life", but he had trouble relinquishing it fully and even tinkered with the text in foreign editions, in the French edition omitting the marriage between Arkady and Marian. His dissatisfaction stemmed from his sense that the book had gone to press before it was ready. "There are masses of details I'd like to have checked, but *physically* could not," he wrote to Nin Dutton. He had written the last third of the book, he impressed on Welch, "in semi-hallucination". Handwritten messages in signed copies of the book conveyed a sense that he had needed more time, had not reached the heights he had aimed at. To Hugh Honour: "Remember—this is only the first draft!" To Harry Marshall: "a sequence of non-sequiturs". There was an awareness that his illness, even as it had sapped his physical strength, had imposed the necessary deadline. "All in all *The Songlines* is a pretty odd production," he wrote to Charles and Brenda Tomlinson. "The fact that I wrote the last chapter just before what was all but the last gasp gives it a very rough quality—to say the least! But I have an idea that what's written is written, with all the glaring defects: and if I'd tried to deliver everything I had in mind, the result might be even more incoherent than it is."

Maschler, then in the throes of selling Jonathan Cape, Chatto & Windus and The Bodley Head to Random House, did not share Bruce's anxiety. This was the book he had envisaged in 1968. "You called what I have 'a draft'," he wrote on first receiving the manuscript. "If that is what it is, then it's the most perfect draft I've ever read as a publisher."

"Bruce Chatwin's *Songlines* is recommended by many; is top of the poll," wrote Lees-Milne in his diary on 1 December. "I must I suppose read it. But shall probably be irritated. Saw him in London Library last week. He came up to me in the reading room. Somewhat changed. Those fallen angel looks have withered. Rather spotty and poor complexion, but upright and active since severe illness. Poor Bruce. I said to him, 'You are having a well-deserved swimgloat'."

XXXIX.

⌘

My Inexplicable Fever

> *Nothing resembles a person as much as*
> *the way he dies.*
> —Gabriel García Márquez,
> *Love in the Time of Cholera*

AT THE SAME time as *The Songlines* topped the best-seller list, Bruce's doctors in Oxford thought they were dealing with two different people. He had submitted his yellow fever specimens with his first name, Charles. "I apologise that some of his 'stickers' have Charles, which is his first name, on it, and not Bruce. It is one and the same person," wrote Juel-Jensen to the pathologist. The mix-up was consistent with the confusion Bruce's doctors had in dealing with his illness. Richard Bull thought it likely he had developed full-blown AIDS. He had written to Juel-Jensen on 27 February 1987: "His overall prognosis remains unknown as there is very little experience in this infection, but one can only presume that his disseminated fungal infection in the presence of HIV would constitute the criteria for a diagnosis of AIDS." Juel-Jensen was more hopeful. In April, he had put Bruce on a new anti-viral drug, AZT, which worked, for a while, a miraculous effect. "He has no side effects so far from his pills. He can walk ten miles and climb a mountain of 1500 feet without any problems," Juel-Jensen reported in July. "I feel at present pretty optimistic and I think it is a good idea that he should go off to France where he can write in peace. He has been more productive recently than for many a year."

HIS "REMARKABLE" IMPROVEMENT (which can now be recognised as characteristic of AIDS), Bruce attributed to a combination of the AZT and a change of climate.

Like Stevenson and Rimbaud a century before, Bruce chose to convalesce in the south of France. From December 1986, he based himself
when abroad at the Chateau de Seillans. The house, an eleventh-century
fort, was built by hunters at the edge of a 60-foot cliff so they might sleep
with their back to it and know that no animal would climb up. In the
nineteenth century, the house was occupied by the Comtesse de Savigny,
who built a perfume factory in the hills behind. It was to perfume that
Shirley Conran compared Bruce's charm on their first meeting, "like a
wonderful cloud of Miss Dior". She says, "I reeled away, drunk on it."

Shirley, a best-selling author and divorced wife of the restaurateur Terence Conran, had known Bruce before he was involved with her son.
They had met at an Author-of-the-Year party at Hatchards in the late
1970s. "Suddenly this fair-headed chap was at my elbow and I said 'What
do you think is the best way to see a country?' 'By boot.' My first impression was that he was a Yorkshireman or Lancastrian and he'd said 'By
boat'." She describes Bruce, to whom she bore a resemblance, as "the older
brother I never dreamed of having . . . Bruce and I would talk in half sentences, like the Queen when discussing racehorses—no one else could understand." While she never experienced the pain of falling in love with
him, she did observe others whom Bruce held in his thrall, including her
son. "A lot of people were in love with Bruce and I'm sorry for all of them.
I saw the misery it brought. We have all loved people and left them, but
when Bruce danced on to the next he had the ability to leave them feeling empty and bereft in a way I doubt they ever recovered from. He'd
wander carelessly in and out of someone's life in an afternoon and they'd
be dazzled for the rest of their lives." It was not only, she says, that he did
not want exclusivity. "There was a dark side of him that wasn't a scalp-
hunter but was amoral. His wanting to externalise his personal frustration
onto others was the result of some misery, some fury with himself. He did
not know himself and did not care to know himself too closely. He was
like Ariel: in this world but not of it."

Shirley was an equal and firm friend to Elizabeth. "Elizabeth can seem
fierce because she's so shy and modest. Her gruff voice and short-sighted
scowl of condescension put people off, but it is the smokescreen of a remarkably knowledgeable and erudite woman who is a woman of action
just as Bruce was a man of action. I admire Elizabeth's adventurousness,
her generosity, her morality, her kindness. She has a beautiful nature. She
always bows into the shadows when Bruce takes centre stage. In fact, Elizabeth is the person most like Bruce I've met."

The way the Chatwins quarrelled very happily reminded Shirley "of my two young children in the back of my sports car. 'You said you'd get it.' 'I didn't. I said I'd get it if I was passing and I didn't pass.' Bickering was an important part of their child-like relationship."

Shirley says: "When I think of Bruce I think of integrity." To some, then, it appeared bizarre that he should choose the house of his lover's mother in which to convalesce. Here again he showed an ability to render normal the extraordinary, and *vice versa*. ("I could see the oddness of the situation, but it didn't bother me," says Elizabeth.) One note he left for Shirley reads like an instruction he might write to a housekeeper. She should take care in closing the front door. The white umbrella was a house gift. The champagne in the fridge was to be drunk. The plastic cushion was for the chair on the terrace—"Jasper thought it horribly vulgar, but it did for the convalescent."

THE HUGE SOUTH-FACING terrace looked over the tops of the village houses to the mountains. This was where he wrote *Utz* sitting on a Provençal cushion. He would return to it repeatedly until his death.

Bruce worked well at Seillans, but he over-estimated his strength. He "gets carried away by feeling good and then overdoes it," Elizabeth wrote to Gertrude on 27 February. Whenever he felt strong enough, he wanted to leave the terrace behind and travel.

In February, he drove to Milan to see Roberto Calasso, his Italian publisher. Once on the move, his alertness to detail was restored. In Calasso's visitors' book, he wrote down a conversation overheard in a Nice restaurant. The audience were two sisters who "would appear to share a remote ancestry with the piranha fish". The speaker was a stout pharmacist who wore six rings. "Over coffee, he said the following:

> " *Je vais vous raconter l'histoire d'un homme qui est parti pour son voyage de noces avec sa nouvelle femme, et, pendant le voyage, elle était tuée, meutriée par quelqu'un. Et lui, pour oublier ses tristes souvenirs est parti pour* . . . and at this point one expected the words *'Tahiti' or la Nouvelle Caledonie* . . . but no! . . . *'il est parti pour la Bélgique où il est devenue président d'une societé de fabrication du chocolat* . . . *de la laiterie* . . . *et même les produits chimiques'.* "

IN MARCH, HE was anxious to visit North Ghana where Werner Herzog was filming *The Viceroy of Ouidah*. "This poses problems of a new nature when it comes to protecting him adequately," wrote a worried Juel-Jensen, who saw him in Oxford on his way to Accra. In response to Bruce's request for a wheelchair, Herzog had cabled back: "A wheelchair will get you nowhere in terrain where I am shooting. I will give you four hammockeers and a sunshade bearer." Bruce seemed to be emulating his Viceroy.

After ten days in Ghana, he embarked on a course of AZT. By May, his dry skin had improved. He no longer had an overwhelming feeling of tiredness. Elizabeth gave him some weights to exercise his arms and chest. "He's really awfully well except for his feet which are still rather numb & stiff."

His travels accelerated over the summer with the publication of *The Songlines*. On 4 July, he drove with Elizabeth, via Vichy, to Bayreuth to watch Herzog's production of *Lohengrin*. "Then to Prague & the Tatra Mountains with our camping gear. Then he gets flown to the Edinburgh Festival for 3 days." From Prague, Bruce wrote to George Ortiz: "I *am* sorry I never made it to Geneva: our arrangements in July got a bit out of hand. Now they are even worse: Prague, Budapest, Vienna, Rome, London, New York, Toronto—all in the space of a month. The Chatwin yo-yo is functioning again." He plotted to Murray Bail the itinerary after Canada: "Then . . . ? Madrid? Perhaps! . . . Vague plans may mature for an Australian winter (ours) but I'm not sure . . . We're off on a world tour—I hope!"

As his last piece of publicity for *The Songlines*, Bruce had agreed to take part in the Toronto Harbourfront Reading Series. He arrived from New York on 15 September, committed to two engagements: an on-stage interview and a half-hour reading. The founder of this celebrated event was the Canadian poet Greg Gatenby. "At 2 p.m., the publicist rang to say that just before going on Chatwin had vomited in the dressing room and asked to be rushed back to his hotel, cancelling all other interviews." Gatenby did not meet Bruce until the following night, at dinner before his reading. "We sat outside at Spinnaker's restaurant. It was a sunny day and he looked a picture of health, like an aerobics commercial. My first instant thought was, 'This is Stephen Spender 60 years ago,' but my next thought was that this son of a bitch primadonna was perfectly healthy, not sick at all.

"I said to him: 'Have you travelled much in Canada?'

" 'No.'

" 'Permit me to ask. Is there any place in the world you haven't been to, but would like to?'

" 'No. Actually, there *is* one place. The Canadian Arctic'."

Gatenby and Margaret Atwood had been approached to start a Writer-in-Residence programme in Baffin Island. "We thought it might be good publicity and talked about him going up there. Nobody goes to Baffin Island without a guide, because the polar bears there stalk people. It's where the American astronauts went to train for the moon. It conjures up everything to do with the north: horrendous storms, three to four days' supply of food, terrible beauty. At the idea of the north, Chatwin's eyes lit up. 'Are you serious?' I then wrote to him in France: great news, I've got it approved, you can go any time you want. I received back a handwritten note. He was now so ill, paralysed in both legs. He could not travel."

BRUCE BLAMED HIS collapse in Toronto on a punishing publicity schedule. He apologised to Gatenby: "There's something about a book tour—which pray God I never do again!—that stews one up into a fever." But back in Oxford his "febrile illness" did not respond to treatment. Dr Juel-Jensen retired from the Churchill Hospital in November. He worried in his last report that Bruce's P24 antigen was positive again. "I fear that all is not well."

His doctor's concern did not deter Bruce from spending a fortnight in the West Indies with Elizabeth. "We went first to an island called Ile des Saintes, off Guadeloupe, which is peopled by a very strange clan of *mestizo* Indian-negro-Breton fishermen," he wrote to Bail. "Nothing happened to interrupt our days of sleeping or taking a boat to the coral reefs *except* for the ludicrous incident when squatting in the bush I inadvertently let my balls brush against a plant which is *the* toxic plant of the West Indies. And since we were on our way to Mass, the agony of standing in church was indescribable."

He cited this incident to his new doctor, David Warrell, on his return to the Churchill in early February 1988. He had explosive diarrhoea, no appetite and complained about pains in his spleen. "A bad bout of flu", he told Bail. But the fungicide was killing his flora and making him sicker. On 12 March, he was taken off Ketoconazole. Two weeks later, the fungus returned with new virulence, this time for good. Seventeen months after the possibility was first raised, a skin biopsy indicated that the spots on his face were "highly suspicious of *Kaposi sarcoma*". On 29 April, one of the specialists in the John Warin ward described him as a "very nice 47-year-old travel writer with AIDS". It had taken 20 months to establish once and for all what the clinic had initially suspected.

As A WRITER who had, metaphorically, found love not just with Elizabeth but with a readership, Bruce could not bear to risk parting with something so hard won.

"Suppose that I were now to reveal that I have AIDS, full-blown AIDS, and have been ill during most of the course of what I have related. I would lose you. I would lose you to knowledge, to fear and to metaphor. Such a revelation would result in the sacrifice of the alchemy of my art, of artistic 'control' over the setting as well as the content of your imagination. A double sacrifice of my elocution: to the unspeakable (death) and the over-spoken (AIDS)." Gillian Rose in *Love's Work* understood what it costs an artist to speak about AIDS: one runs the same risk of losing one's reader as one would one's lover. Writing about a terminal illness is, suggests Rose, like breaking your contract with your reader. But Rose, a philosopher at Warwick University who died of ovarian cancer in 1995, was by nature an artist intent on transforming her "shrieks" into "shouts of joy". She *had* to abandon equivocation and risk losing her readers, "otherwise I die deadly, but this way, by this work, I may die forward into the intensified *agon* of living." But for Bruce, the unclassifiable harlequin, to speak meant quite literally to sacrifice the "alchemy" of his art. He could not, like Rose, write his way through his illness; rather, he equivocated to the end, unconsciously asserting his rights to the intimacy that Gabriel García Márquez speaks of in *Love in the Time of Cholera*: "the sacred right of the sick to die in peace along with the secret of their illness".

Many of Bruce's readers would be disappointed to learn that he had actively denied his illness, even to himself. They might have wished for him the courage of Gillian Rose, to speak about the impasses, the limitations and the cruelties of a peremptory death. He had developed a powerful thesis for travel and so they expected him to be a fearless strider everywhere, or at the very least to provide them with an original, clear report from his visit to what Bruce himself called "the scene of the Grim Reaper". ("I've been on the scene of the Grim Reaper, and I can tell you it wasn't too bad," he told an interviewer.) It frustrated them that he had not responded to the huge idea of living with death as another journey. Instead of pushing to the limits, he had retreated. "If you read into what he writes something which has an impact on your own moral life, why shouldn't it have an impact on *his* moral life?" says Sean Baumann, an eminent South African psychiatrist. Baumann had worked in the community around Bruce's Black Hill and was himself a twin. "He should have said he was dying."

Bruce's "moral" life was, no doubt, impinged upon by his illness. His abiding ambivalence about his sexuality and his fear about dying of AIDS, inextricably linked anyway, are bound up in the same energies which drove him to travel and to write—a case, perhaps, of a deficiency on one side of the balance producing the fruit of the other. If, in fact, the Beast which stalked him all his life grew out of this fear, there is pathos that he never engaged or resolved his ambivalence. Yet it seems reductive to say his Beast was purely sexual.

"He *was* ashamed," says Peter Adam, speaking from experience. "Part of it, the outward sign, was his homosexuality, but there was the much wider thing of not knowing how to belong. He was deeply aware of his non-commitment."

Bruce's ambivalence, his suppression of not the truth so much as any enquiry into the truth, is what makes him the writer, the journey-maker and the storyteller that he is, wholly unwilling to be categorised by anyone. But some think he might have written better novels, been a greater man if he had, confronted with death, been less of a "Bruce".

Duncan Fallowell argues that it is Bruce's very fear that clips his wings, prevents him from being a writer in the way of his models. "AIDS and the prowling death gave Chatwin the opportunity to write an extraordinary book—his character, which gave us the books we have, meant that he couldn't take that opportunity." Speaking as a gay activist, Fallowell voiced the harshest objections to Bruce's management of his illness. "Hypocrisy, lies, distortion, deceit, threats, self-disgust, cooking the facts and shame—all these may make life more interesting, but they're no good when trying to cope with AIDS and all are exemplified in the case of the writer Bruce Chatwin, the most important AIDS casualty in the arts to date." This was written after Bruce's death, on World AIDS Day, and Fallowell, while among the more vociferous voices, was not alone in his punishing verdict. Peter Adam also wished Bruce had come out openly. "A great man had," says Adam, "the writer Jean-Paul Aaron: '*Mon SIDA à moi*,' he said on *Apostrophes*. If Bruce had not been such a moral coward he could have come to terms with his dying much better, and his living. Why prolong the prejudices?" But Adam also remembers how slow England was to wake up to AIDS. At that time in England, very few well-known people had AIDS, or, if they had, it was a secret disease more so than in France or America. "With AIDS came also the big lie," Adam wrote in his autobiography, *Not Drowning but Waving*. "Sons would not tell their mothers, husbands protected their wives from the truth—the list of people who died became longer . . . it was usually the most brilliant, the most shining, the most hopeful who left us." Adam and Fallowell felt that the gay community needed an articulate spokesman. They felt that as a public figure, and writer of proven worth, Bruce had a responsibility to lead the way. On 26 October, the day after Bruce's spectral face had appeared on BBC television's coverage of the Booker Prize, Tony Parsons requested an interview for the *Sunday Times*: "Seeing someone as special and precious as Chatwin with AIDS would perhaps bring home the enormity and horror of the disease to the millions who read the *Sunday Times* and—maybe—inspire a little more understanding and compassion than sufferers have received so far."

But do people who are not dying have a right to judge those who are? It is unlikely that Bruce would have told another how they should exercise their own free will.

Colin Thubron defends Bruce's decision. "Ideally, I would have liked him to have spoken publicly, but he didn't and why should he? His reasons were respectable. It wasn't anybody else's business. It was his own affair. Simply because AIDS has become politicised is not enough. And with nobody knowing what your personal affections are, it's somewhat presumptuous. The AIDS riposte would be that people should not feel ashamed of it anyway—but that's all very well if your wife is alive or your middle-class elderly parents. I don't think it's anyone's place to put the well-being of all those dying from AIDS before a number of people who would feel deeply ashamed of it."

The novelist and biographer Sybille Bedford also supports Bruce's non-committal stance: "I think it's entirely private. It would have been distasteful for him to have been an example of the brave AIDS sufferer. Aldous Huxley died of cancer: he didn't tell anyone, even his son. He just carried on as long as he could with enormous courage. It builds a wall around you, or let us say some screens. It's very bad for your profession. People whisper in corners."

Despite all his efforts not to be English, Bruce would die a quintessentially English death: abroad, clothed in secrets ("his impenetrable aura of concealment," Adam called it), holding out, deflecting to the end and not without a profound sense of shame and regret. "My life isn't as it should be," he told Adam, remembering with envy the gypsy boy on his horse whom he had watched as a child.

Bruce was not a clichéd self-hating homosexual. He met interesting people through sex. According to James Ivory, he found sex "as natural and easy as eating". He even fell in love. But he was not at ease with his sexuality (a word he mocked). "There was a kind of guilt thing about his homosexuality, as if he had not quite come to terms with it," wrote Adam in *Not Drowning but Waving*. As his HIV developed into AIDS, Bruce associated his homosexuality with what was happening to his body. "He had a great self-disgust and guilt," says Wyndham. From his hospital bed in Oxford, Bruce whispered bitterly to Wyndham: "I've never spoken to you about sex before, but sex is madness."

"At this point, the idea of homosexuality was repulsive to him," says the composer Kevin Volans. "He associated homosexuality with disease." To expect him to be a spokesman for homosexuals was to ask him to step outside his character and serve a political agenda from which, by temperament, he was estranged.

"He is famously criticised for the way he dealt with AIDS," says Wyndham. "His evasion may not be politically correct or crowd-pleasing, but I think he was dealing with it in a wonderful and very heroic way. He assented to it being a kind of secret in order to protect Elizabeth, his parents, the Chanlers, Jasper. He turned it into a Bruce."

The Songlines HAD made Bruce a public figure. "My book," he wrote to Cary Welch on 22 February, "has brought me a host of new friends from 'every quarter'. But the latest is a simply astonishing person. He is called Kevin Volans, an Anglo South-African composer—and composer of genius—who has gone into the field in Africa rather as Brahms or Dvořák went looking for folk-songs. He has filled his head with the sounds of the veldt, with Zulu chant, the shepherds' pipes echoing across the valleys of Lesotho—and without in any way being 'ethnic' he has produced an entirely new modern music that also makes me think of Schubert. He is the favourite composer of the Kronos Quartet, who, it would appear are the best string quartet in America for modern music. Unfortunately, their record of Kevin's work entitled *White Man Sleeps*, which is a huge hit in the US, omits the 4th movement which is so utterly transporting that one gasps with wonder. Anyway this is to me one of the really nice things that's happened to me."

The Kronos Quartet wished to commission a new theatre score: Volans, composer in residence at Queen's University, Belfast, had suggested *The Songlines*. Volans sent Bruce his narrative piece, *Hunting: gathering*. Bruce responded at once. "It was music I had never heard before, or could have imagined," he wrote. "It derived from nothing and no one." He left a message on Volans's answer-machine. "I've listened to your tape. I think your music's wonderful and you must come straight away."

Volans travelled nervously to Homer End. "I was convinced he thought I'd be some South African hunk in a bush jacket and I was terribly aware that I wouldn't fulfil that expectation. I arrived. Elizabeth took me upstairs. The first thing he said was: 'Elizabeth, fetch Kevin some champagne'. There were then three minutes of awkwardness, because he was adjusting to the way I didn't look."

Later Bruce said: "I then realised you looked exactly the way you should look."

By the end of the three minutes, Volans had fallen in love. "I sat there like Scheherazade at the foot of his bed while he told me stories. There was literally nothing I wouldn't have done. I adored him. He was one of those people who did have the key to the world."

On the day after Volans left, Bruce would telephone him: "Since your massage, I've got the feeling back in my leg—so you see, I can't live without you."

"I feel the same," replied Volans.

"Enough said."

But after their first series of talks both realised that *The Songlines* was not suitable for a theatre piece.

"In the morning," says Volans, "I went through to his room and he told me, 'But I know *exactly* what we can do: Rimbaud.' Bruce considered Rimbaud's *Une Saison en enfer* a western Songline: he had written about going to the desert *before* he went there. Bruce told me about Rimbaud's death scene and phoned Michael Ignatieff. 'I want this book from Paris.' He didn't waste time. Ever."

Volans, who had lived in Africa, expressed his "perfect empathy" for the idea. On his return to Belfast, he set immediately to work on the libretto with Roger Clarke, a poet whose work Bruce admired. The opera was first performed at the Almeida in London, in July 1993, as *The Man with the Wind in His Heels*.

Bruce had already been considering an operatic project at the time of Volans's visit. In one of his remissions, he approached Peter Eyre to write an opera based on the salon of Florence Gould in wartime Paris. Gould was an elderly biddy in the tradition of Madame Vionnet: a soprano at the Opera Comique, a collector of Impressionists and porcelain, and during the occupation of France an extravagant hostess to several in Jünger's collaborator circles whom she entertained at the Hotel Bristol. "The opera would begin in English and end up in French," says Eyre, who scratched his head at Bruce's behaviour. "I went with him to 'Mario's' round the corner to have lunch and he insisted on paying. I said afterwards to Valerie Wade: 'Something must be wrong with Bruce. I've never seen him pay'."

Bruce began to puzzle friends in other small ways. In his letter to Cary Welch about Volans, he mentioned his interest in the astonishing revival of Orthodoxy in Russia. "I didn't know if you know, but I now think of myself as Orthodox and will be going back at some point to Athos to stay with my Serbian friends at the monastery of Chilandari." A week later he wrote to Nin Dutton of other goings-on. "The first news is that I finished and edited a new book: the title *Utz. Tout court*! Anyhow, it seems to have caught the imagination of the publisher because we're suddenly inundated with money which we don't really want. My temperament tells me to give it away: but that's not so easy. And it's certainly a change from being on the breadline."

Two of his books—*On the Black Hill* and *The Viceroy of Ouidah*—had just been adapted for film.* His new agent, Gillon Aitken, had at this point also secured an advance of £100,000 for *Utz* as well as for a collection of journalism to be titled after the question posed by Rimbaud in the Ethiopian desert: "What am I doing here?"

After 20 years of struggling to make a living, Bruce was in a better financial position than he had ever been. He had a sense of new-found wealth; also of new-found health. "Still convinced that he is making a unique recovery," read his medical report.

WHAT ALSO SURPRISED friends about his illness was the way he became more himself. A new strain of sweetness entered his observations—an enjoyment of simple pleasures.

---

* Herzog was not the only film-maker interested in *The Viceroy of Ouidah*. In August 1985, David Bowie tried to buy the film rights.

Propped up in bed in the Churchill, he registered in his notebook an uncomplicated satisfaction with life. "Last night Sister Patterson came in and gave me one of her 'healing touch' massages. She really does make me believe in the 'laying on' of hands. Afterwards I felt completely relaxed . . . After she massaged my hands, she flicks her own as if she were casting out demons . . . This time the oil smelled of something I knew perfectly well, lemony. But I was so perfectly happy I forgot to ask her."

Once he had finished *Utz*, he threw himself into editing his journalism. He helped me—by no means a close friend—with my first novel. He understood immediately how to make it better and asked me to dedicate it to him. In his notebook he alluded to future projects. He wanted to write a book on healing. In hospital, he read a small-printed Bible from which he marked passages that seemed consistent with his pilgrimage, including a verse from Saint Mark: "And he ordained twelve that they should be with him, and that he might send them forth to paradise. And to have power to heal sicknesses and to cast out devils." Thrilled by the description of the Boanerges as "the sons of thunder", he wrote: "That's it. Now I know where to start. The title can be everything."

"The Sons of Thunder" was not his only idea for a book. "There are so many things I want to do," he told Elizabeth. An essay on Jünger; an introduction to *Songs of Central Australia*; another to Ivan Bunin's *Dark Avenues*. Like Ravel, he felt he had only just begun. He spoke to Volans of a triptych of stories after Flaubert's *Trois Contes*, "one set in Ireland in the days of Irish kings". To Michael Oppitz he spoke of plans for a novel on the anthropologist Joseph Rock. He told Barbara Bailey of an idea for a novel set in a South African village, exploring the gossip and jealousies. "He was coming out to do it," says Bailey. "It was on his schedule."

None of these projects materialised, but he did begin work on a novel. The idea had been with him since he met Elizabeth's family in the 1960s. The story once again reflected his sympathy for old people. On 29 February, he wrote to Nin Dutton: "I've started something new: which will probably fail, utterly, for being too ambitious. I have a scene in which an utterly beguiling American woman in her early '70s—courageous to the point of camping alone in Wyoming—takes her picnic lunch into Central Park and is mugged by a black kid. That's how it appears to be, except that she soon has her attacker sitting beside her, using *her* knife not his to cut up the chicken, and there follows a long animated discussion in which he refuses $50 but accepts $10." The incident was based on one of Gertrude's friends in Rock Creek Park, Washington. "I hope you will like her as a character because I have called her Ninette and have hauled in a bit of you. The whole book is way into the future and may take years to write."

The scene was from his "Russian novel". He had talked about this to Tom Maschler who wrote to him: "Perhaps this will be . . . the 'international' novel (Russian, France, etc) you have spoken of. If you recall, that is the book which I told you would be an enormous commercial breakthrough in addition to being great literature."

On a walk through Central Park in 1981, Bruce had discussed the plot with his American editor Elisabeth Sifton. The novel would weave in three cities—Paris, Moscow and New York/Washington ("he surely didn't want London"). More significantly, it appeared to be Bruce's attempt to fictionalise his wife's Jamesian family. Late in the day, he was going to turn his gleeful, transforming gaze on his wife: he was taking Elizabeth for his subject, not as a Czech servant girl but as an American aristocrat and, in the process, attempting to celebrate what, originally, had drawn them together.

The novel, entitled *Lydia Livingstone*, was intended first and foremost as a love story. To write it, he planned to move to Paris and learn Russian. When Rushdie pointed out, "There *are* some love stories in Russian literature," Bruce was unperturbed: "Oh yes, but they're *quite* different."

Bruce told Elizabeth that the novel was partly based on Louise de Vilmorin's daughter, Helena, who had imported to New York at great expense and with extreme difficulty a Russian artist with whom she had fallen madly in love. He arrived with his mother and other hangers-on and she was suddenly saddled with an enormous contingent. Lydia Livingstone was the name of a young film agent Bruce had met on his first visit to Sydney. On 4 June 1983 he had written to her: "both Mr [James] Fox and I agreed that the best thing in Australia is Lydia Livingstone."

There is no doubt in Rushdie's mind that Bruce's Russian novel would have enriched his reputation, and that the breakthrough would have come about through his willingness to write, at last, about love. "He was a warm person, but wrote a cold prose," says Rushdie. "I can't fault his technical decision not to talk about himself. He made the decision to keep the whole side of his sexual and emotional being out of his work. In the complete works of Bruce Chatwin there is not a loving fuck. But find the thing that is missing in a writer's work and that is the answer to the writer. The answer to the riddle of Bruce was the absence of love in his work and that incredibly important aspect of human life he'd put a curtain round. I hoped that one day if he would drop that curtain and admit what he was like and write from his whole self then we would have a colossal novel."

For Rushdie, what was missing in Bruce's writing was the admission of Bruce's own real nature. "The thing that he concealed from all of us and that he kept in compartments, essentially his sexuality, is concealed completely. That's the creature at the perimeter prowling around. All this fantastic entertainment and language and originality and erudition and display is a kind of hedge against not letting in the truth. The writing might have become astonishing if he had."

IN HIS LAST months, Bruce began to reveal a person who was a great deal warmer and more emotional than his prose suggested. Peter Adam once accused him of not showing his heart in his books. Bruce shrugged it off with a smile, saying: "The heart *is* there, come on look for it. It is not with the best sentiments that we write the best literature."

He certainly gave the promise of heart. He was, as Hodgkin says, "someone people fell in love with immediately. In a way that is the most important—and, finally, creative thing about him." Rosy Hall, who met him at a Chanler family wedding in 1986, wrote to Bruce's mother-in-law: "I can honestly say he truly exceeded all my expectations. Adjectives cannot describe him completely. I can truthfully say he captivated my heart and my soul."

He buoyed people up, was a thoughtful and loyal friend. "He knew how to piss on friendships and drive you into the ground, but he was there in the end," says Sethi. "He never let a friendship die, he knew how to keep it." In 1971 Tilo von Watzdorf's father died in a train crash. "I learned at Sotheby's and went home," he says. "Bruce stayed with me from afternoon till late at night. He was better than family. I wouldn't have wanted to have been with anyone else."

He could be generous. He knew what to give and thought about his gifts. He gave to Emma Tennant a pair of gold lion-head earrings from Mycenae, 3,000 BC. He gave to Anne Thomson Elizabeth David cooking-pots. "My best presents have come from Bruce," she says. "He only liked the best." In Sydney, Pam Bell received, out of the blue, a box of lapsang souchong from Paris. "He made me feel that for some minutes he had cared about me. People very often say they have thought of you. With Bruce you really did believe it."

He could be generous with his time. Self-absorbed, he was still able to think carefully about other people's work in progress. He helped James Fox with the structure of *White Mischief.* "He said: 'You're going to come down and we're going to talk about it." He encouraged Bill Buford in his first book *Among the Thugs*. "Can I take a strong personal interest in the manuscript? . . . I think there are ways of slightly toughening up the syntax and vocabulary. I could show you what I mean when we meet." When Patrick Woodcock came out of hospital, he telephoned him to say he was going to bring supper. Woodcock says, "He brought enough food for 25."

Hodgkin says, "One of the things which puzzles me looking back is how much I loved him. I find it very hard to see why. He was seriously cold." Yet to call him cold-hearted or snobbish or narcissistic—all of which he appeared on the surface—is to watch him fall between the floorboards. His good qualities outweighed the bad. No matter how irritating Bruce could be, there was something touching and fresh about him. His friends might bitch and mock, but they adored him. "He was a source of more pleasure and more amusement and provocation than any friend I've ever had," says David Sulzberger.

There are signs that Bruce at the end of his life was finding it in himself to reciprocate. He was beginning to unite the bits of his universe and break down those compartments that had been useful to him in living his life. It was noticeable, for instance, how eager he was to introduce his friends not only to each other but, for the first time, to his wife and family. "He was a great pigeon-holer until the end," said John Hewett. "Then he let his guard down and everyone was introduced. One was amazed at how much affection he felt. You had to go through a shower of knives before. Now he was incredibly sweet."

Friends like Stella Wilkinson were affected by the surfacing of a vulnerability that may always have existed but had not always revealed itself. "You put his shoes on him and it was as if he appreciated it, as if at last he was letting you touch him. You may not have thought you liked him, but when he was dying you realised, in fact, you loved him."

One night Robyn Davidson was staying at Homer End, "a bloody mess" after the end of her relationship with Rushdie. "Bruce showed me his little Inuit seal and I said it was one of the most enchanting things I had seen. When he came to say goodnight he put the seal in my hand, curled my fingers over it and said, 'You can play with it tonight'."

BRUCE SPENT MARCH and April in and out of the Churchill. He was permanently on the telephone, explaining his illness as "an impossibly rare bone disease" or "undiagnosed malaria", and summoning friends to his bedside. Though his behaviour was growing odder, it did so gradually enough for most of them not to notice. They took his actions at face value: it was Bruce a little louder, a little brighter, a little more Bruce-like. But there were others who recognised the cause of his frequent illness and erratic behaviour. Lees-Milne had suspected a year before. "Feb 4th, 1987. Pat Trevor-Roper told me that Sheridan Dufferin and Bruce Chatwin and Ian MacCallum all have AIDS; that they might seem to recover from some mild ailment, only to get another, but when a serious attack of pneumonia or such assailed them, then they would go under. Very terrible. Derek Hill, now rather proprietary of Bruce, denies it in his case, and tells Pat that Bruce caught a mysterious and rare disease from bathing in the South Seas too close to a whale, or some such nonsense."

Bruce's refusal to make a public statement fuelled the speculation. There had been a period, after his collapse in Switzerland, when he spoke openly about his illness to a select group including Francis Wyndham and Christopher Gibbs. In his last year, a need to confess without risk did lead him to tell several others, like the young Australian gallery-owner Rebecca Hossack, but these confidants tended to be people he did not know well. By contrast, he was unable to speak privately to his family or to those with whom he might be in daily contact. "He never admitted it to me," says Shirley Conran. "I thought it was polite to accept whatever he said, but I knew it didn't add up. I thought it was sad he didn't come out and say: 'I'm dying of this thing.' In a way, he *didn't* think he was dying, and I'm glad it came as a surprise."

The force of his denial persuaded a majority that his illness was what he claimed it to be. But it launched him into an elaborate game of charades, the fear of which showed in his features. His terror was apparent to Jane Abdy, to whom, aged 19, he had confessed his first love in Cornwall. "I was in Ebury Street in a taxi when I saw Bruce in a loden coat. I was about to lower the window when I saw this incredible expression on his face, as if he'd seen the statue of Commendatore in *Don Giovanni* rising up to take him down to hell. If I'd said anything he wouldn't have heard. He was absorbed in his own horror."

People who loved him did what they always did with Bruce and did not ask questions. In his presence, they behaved as though everything was normal. But on centre stage, the illness which he could not bear to name was ravaging him. Gregor von Rezzori, who had called him the Golden Boy, now described Bruce's "sapphire-blue visionary's eyes glittering fanatically in a boyish Anglo-Saxon head that had already become a skull.

(It was poignant how his youthful curls had thinned. Damp with fever like the down on the skull of a new-hatched chick)".

IN FACT, BY the end of February the fungus had infected Bruce's brain and he was suffering from a toxic brain syndrome which began to manifest itself in hypomania. It impaired his ability to think and act rationally while sparing his verbal fluency and his ability to beguile. His non-stop talk, his grandiose schemes, his unrestrained buying sprees, threw those around him into turmoil.

At the same time, his hypomania made him a concentrate of himself: someone funny, private, romantic, persuasive who believed fiercely in his own stories. A full-blown self.

"Dear Gertrude, I need your help. I'd prefer to tell you the details in person, but I have indeed been hammered over the past two years and I hope I have been hammered by God. The fact is that I made the leap into Faith."

On 6 May 1988 Bruce wrote a long letter to Gertrude in which he appears to be trying to fulfil every expectation she may have had of a son-in-law. He reiterated his love for Elizabeth and spoke of their joint finances and plans for the future. Much of the content was fantastical.

"If ever I had a regret, it is that I could not have become a monk—an idea which kept occurring to me in the *cauchemar* of Sotheby's . . . God willing, it seems possible that I could become a lay brother. This does not mean that I would cease to write. I have been gifted with the pen and will continue to the best of my ability. I have been doing very well. My income for this tax year from April the first is around $600,000. But I want *none* of it for myself. If I were alone in the world I would hope to give it away to the sick. I do have responsibilities: to Elizabeth, to my parents and to Hugh. I have devoted certain royalties to *my* charity, The Radcliffe Memorial Trust, which is run by the man who saved my life. But I must be prevented from giving too much away.

"It does seem that my inexplicable fever was malaria: the temperature returned to normal nine hours after taking anti-malarial pills. You can imagine what $3^{1}/2$ months of raging fever has done to the system. But I don't regret a second of it.

"My grey matter functioned perfectly and I took a number of most rational decisions. I am entirely concerned with the matter of healing . . . I hope to divide my life into four parts: a. religious instruction b. learning about disease c. learning to heal d. the rest of the time free to give my un-divided attention to Elizabeth and the house. A tall order, but with God's help not impossible."

He could not do this work, he told his mother-in-law, if he was fet-tered to possessions. "I have envied and grasped at possessions, but they are very bad for me. I want to be free of them." He wished to give Eliza-beth all he had in the form of a trust. "I have never known the extent of her capital, but I believe I would increase her existing assets by at least twice if all mine were totted up." The real difficulty was to get her to spend money on herself. "She said it is in her Iselin blood. She is retentive of possessions, whereas I have always thought that by giving or dispersing, you attract more."

In his final paragraph he asked Gertrude to buy Elizabeth a horse. "I have been very worried that she is over-exhausting herself and might make herself ill: a. by the strain of looking after me (not easy!) b. by the house, the cooking and the garden. c. most exhausting of all by the sheep. She loves the sheep but, literally, they tear her apart. I think she needs a horse instead and stabling when she goes to India or with me to the sun. It's wonderful riding country all around and the field is big enough for a horse and a donkey."

Gertrude, who wondered if he was suffering from "manic depression", showed the letter to her eldest son John. "Ma, I have very carefully read Bruce's letter twice. I am glad he has come to some sort of conclusion as to what he is going to do, but obviously some of it is a pure fantasy. His marriage to Lib is a fantasy . . . If they had a true marriage it is not his money, or her money, but our money. It belongs to both of them." John did not consider "the horse routine" a good idea at all. "I don't think Lib really wants to get into that kind of life and she does love her sheep."

On 17 May, Bruce returned to the subject of the horse. "The horse! Obviously she has to be an Arab mare, not perhaps up to competition standard, but breedable." He suggested to Gertrude that they both went Dutch on the purchase and upkeep ("with the proviso of "a 'safety-net' so that the horse doesn't have to be sold for 'economic reasons' "). Otherwise, he was on the mend. "I get better by the day . . . The nerves should heal entirely within five years."

Eleven days after writing this, Bruce was back in the Churchill for an emergency blood transfusion. He had lost the feeling in his legs, which he referred to as "my little boys". He was frightened they were not there, wanted to see them. "Profound loss of walking ability," noted his report. From now on he would be "wheelchair dependent". He had believed that walking was a way to cure ills. The refusal of his "unruly boys" to respond to his call brought home to him that at last he was no longer the spry, youthful explorer. He told Elizabeth: "If I can't walk I can't write."

Rimbaud had written a century before: "I am entirely paralysed." Over the summer, Bruce increasingly identified with the hero of Volans's opera: the Rimbaud of the piercing blue eyes, the gang rape in the Paris commune, the flight to Africa, the religious conversion, the poet who "makes himself a seer by a long, gigantic and rational derangement of all the senses". But as the opera progressed, Volans noticed that the correspondences were growing more and more uncomfortable. "Bruce wanted *Aida* as he got sicker. 'We must have camels and sand dunes.' Later on, he decided he was the only person who could play the role of Rimbaud. I had to invent reasons he wouldn't like—six week rehearsals etc.—without saying the obvious one. He couldn't sing."

Anxious to perform in that role, Bruce was not, however, limited to it. He became in his brother's words "one of his own characters": the Viceroy of Ouidah, scribbling "incoherent prophecies", and more obviously, the compulsive collector of the novel he had just finished. Unable to collect stories, Bruce replaced writing with buying. "He went from a nomad possessing nothing to Utz," says Volans. "He wanted everything."

BRUCE DESCRIBED *Utz* AS "a kind of Middle European fairy-story— with some savage digs at the art business!"

By 1988, he had more or less relinquished "anything artistic", apart from a few tiny, exquisite objects stored in a cardboard box. "I called it his Box of Treasures," says Elizabeth. "He'd come back and get them out on the table and literally play with them, arranging them as if they were chess pieces. There were eight or nine of them and from time to time something came and went." The cardboard box operated as the black tin deed box of Bruce's Mr Brady, the typewriter salesman who, whenever he returned to London from Africa brought one new thing for the box. "He spread out the old things on the bunk. He threw away the old one that had lost its meaning." Rushdie likened the Box of Treasures to "a tuck-box of goodies" under his bed. "When you were privileged, he'd get it out. What I liked about his attitude was the idea of beauty completely separate from ownership. These things were a transient population. You never owned them. They were for you to look after for a time and let go."

The objects were simple, sacred and small, what might be painted on a postage stamp or held in the palm or fit into his knapsack. "What I've kept are funny things which are more or less abstract in quality," he told ABC. An Eskimo seal-toggle of walrus ivory; a white shell nose ornament from the Solomon Islands; a Celtic iron cross; an Ainu knife; a jade long-life symbol; a wooden funerary mask from Buenos Aires province; a Ngoro red lacquer snuff box from Japan with the black showing through. Holding up the latter, Bruce told Kevin Volans: "If you want to know what encapsulates what I am and everything I believe in, it's this."

The objects had cost hundreds, not thousands of pounds. In 30 years of dealing, the most Bruce paid was £4,000: for a small oil painting from the Danish Kunstkammer called *The Ambassadors*. This was a portrait of Poq and Qiperoq, who in 1724 became the first two Greenlanders to leave their country voluntarily.

In the last year of his life, Bruce began the process of dispersing the box's contents among friends. To Christopher Gibbs, an Egyptian gaming piece of green-blue faience; to Kevin Volans, a circular sixteenth-century brown lacquer box which had belonged to Herrigel, author of *Zen and the Art of Archery*; to George Ortiz, the haematite gold weight from the Spencer Churchill collection. "It was a pure object, possibly from a meteorite," says Ortiz. "It was a gesture of coming back to earth."

Mr Brady, too, gave the impression that he was free of things. "But he knew that nobody is free of things." In the same breath, Bruce replaced his Box of Treasures with an alternative collection. Conceived in honour of Elizabeth, the Homer Collection would be Bruce's memorial to his wife and to his taste with the considerable sums he supposed he had earned through his writing. He told John Pawson, for instance, of a £13 million advance on a film script.

AT THE END of June, Gertrude received a letter written in what seemed to be a child's hand. "I have been buying your daughter the beginnings of an art collection which I hope will be wonderful. In New York we bought the wax model for Giovanni da Bologna's Neptune which has to be one of the most beautiful small sculptures in existence. We are making arrangements to give it to the Bargello in Florence with the use of it in our life-times. We also bought an incredible German drawing of the mid-fifteenth century."

Bruce drew the idea of the Homer Collection from the collections of George Pitt-Rivers, Gertrude's father Irwin Laughlin, and George Ortiz.

His ambition did not surprise John Hewett, who at Sotheby's had introduced him to Pitt-Rivers and Ortiz. "Really, what came out was what had been there all along." Hewett had never taken seriously Bruce's denunciations of acquisition. Nor had Cary Welch: "Oh for the open road with nothing but a backpack, but how nice to have some castle to return to crammed with El Grecos. Suddenly, in great haste, he was putting together the very thing he'd teased us about."

Bruce's desire to build a collection modelled on the museum at Farnham explains his latent rage against those, like Peter Wilson and John Hewett, whom he accused of destroying such monuments. Discharged from the Churchill on 14 June, Bruce began his eerie transformation into Utz. An early purchase was the wax bozzetto of Neptune, bought from Mrs Blumke in Madison Avenue. The dark amber figure, with one arm missing, stood only a few inches high. According to Welch, "this was a study by a Flemish artist which had been offered around for years". Bruce, convinced the fragile figure was unique, wrote a cheque for $70,000.

He was uninhibited by normal constraints of wealth. "Our accountant said he could spend £100,000 on the collection," says Elizabeth. "Bruce added noughts on and told everyone he had millions. You couldn't persuade him. He had more money than he'd ever had in his life, but he had lost track of what he did have." It was a sad paradox that just when he did have money, it came at the moment he was least able to handle it sensibly. For a period, he spent this sum every day.*

BRUCE AMASSED THE Homer Collection in a burst of shopping sprees to London during June and July. One of his first excursions was witnessed by Volans, who had interrupted their Rimbaud project to write, as a curtain-raiser to the opera, a 26-minute string quartet called *The Songlines*. Volans intended to hire a piano, but Bruce, deciding this was inadequate, bought him a Bosendorfer upright for £13,000. "We pulled up at Bosendorfer in Wigmore Street and he gave me five minutes to choose," says Volans. "Then we went on to Cork Street."

Volans watched how the dealers in Cork Street fell over Bruce. "His eye was not out of control. He knew exactly what he wanted: he was im-

---

* Robert Mapplethorpe collapsed into a pathological form of collecting at the end and was wheeled to auctions. The same was true of Loulou de la Falaise's step-father. "He didn't have a penny and went round buying jewels and my mother had to take them back."

mensely precise. 'I want that Japanese lacquer box I saw, the one made for export.' He would write cheques out for £100,000 and no one would question. The prices were breathtaking." In brisk succession, Bruce bought a Bronze Age arm band for £65,000, an Etruscan head for £150,000, a jade prehistoric English cutting knife, a flint Norwegian hand-axe and an Aleutian Islands hat. He could not sit waiting for the objects to be wrapped. They were shoved into plastic bags and attached to the back of his wheelchair.

Like this, with objects worth a quarter of a million pounds dangling from the handles, Volans pushed Bruce up Bond Street towards the Burlington Arcade. They called in on Christopher Gibbs, where Bruce purchased an expensive chair. "It had started raining," says Volans. "Christopher ran across the road and bought some plastic macs. At Piccadilly, Bruce shouted 'Stop! stop!' to the cars. We teetered on the pavement in pouring rain with these valuable items in plastic bags and Bruce holding up his hand, saying 'Stop all cars!', very angry with me when I wouldn't push him. His mind was soaring. He was really enjoying himself."

Safely across Piccadilly, Bruce plunged even deeper into his pocket. He wrote out cheques to dealers in Jermyn Street for an Assyrian quartz duck and a bolt of eighteenth-century silk to cover the chairs in the dining room. Only at Spink's did staff declare their unease—over a Tibetan tiger rug which he wanted to take away. Thwarted, Bruce appealed to the chairman with whom, 20 years before, he had shared Grosvenor Crescent Mews. "Of course, Anthony will give me credit. He's known me all my life." He left with the rug.

On another expedition he crossed Duke Street and called at Artemis where Adrian Eales worked, a former Sotheby's colleague who had bought Holwell Farm from Elizabeth. Bruce specifically asked for an engraving, *The Melancholy of Michelangelo*, by the sixteenth-century artist Giorgio Ghisi. This weird and whimsical study showed a pensive figure on the edge of a huge pond surrounded by sea-monsters, lions and birds. By rare chance, Eales had the print in stock. The price: £20,000.

"He felt so clever to have found it," says Eales. "He told me it was for Elizabeth. He was now getting so much money from his royalties that he wanted to give her really special things. He was extremely plausible."

Bruce had to have the engraving *immediately*. He asked Eales to send it to the Ritz.

His expedition with Volans and Gibbs had also ended at the Ritz, where he had rented a room for the afternoon: "Seventy pounds. *Very* rea-

sonable!" There was a flurry of telephone calls and more dealers turned
up, including Oliver Hoare who had shared Bruce's flat in Kynance Mews.
"I had two lines from Prince Baysunghur, the son of Tamberlaine. The
page was a metre wide, with some of the most beautiful Islamic script
from the early fifteenth century. It was £45,000, a big purchase. 'I always
wanted that,' said Bruce. It was the same old panache. He had his Bologna
modello with him, pointed to it. 'Bring it here, it's the most miraculous
thing.' He'd insured it for £600,000. I said, 'What do you mean?' If it had
a wick on top you could light it and use it as a candle."

At the end of the afternoon, Bruce turned to Christopher Gibbs with
an ebullient eye. "Tomorrow, musical instruments, women's clothes and
incunables!"

THE HOMER COLLECTION was not to contain anything warlike and
for this reason Bruce returned the Bronze Age arm band. The objects had
to be of enormous beauty with a spiritual edge and to reflect every religion, from Inca to Islam, as though making real his "One Million Years of
Art" series for the *Sunday Times* magazine.

Many of his purchases celebrated the leap Bruce had himself made,
only recently, into the Christian faith.

One of Bruce's hallucinations, following his collapse in Zurich was of
the Christos Pantokrator. He described his vision to a figure who became
important for him in these months: Kallistos Ware, a Bishop of the Greek
Orthodox Church living in Oxford. "He felt he was lying in the middle
of the church in the Serbian monastery of Chilandari during a vigil service. There were candles and lamps and monks were singing." His vision
had brought back to Bruce his experience on Mount Athos, convinced
him of its authenticity.

His short visit to this centre of monasticism, Bruce told Ware, had
marked a turning point in his life. "I think Bruce felt when he went to
Athos: this is the truth," says Ware. "While there he seemed a different
person, transformed, marked by total happiness." As a result, Bruce had
decided to become a member of the Orthodox Church. "This was not a
passing fancy but a clear and firm intention, a hope, an objective during
his illness."

There are 2,000-3,000 lay English members of the Greek Orthodox
Church. The usual practice is to receive people by baptism. Ware receives
four or five converts a year. "His plan was to go to the Holy Mountain to

be baptised there. For him, it was definite that he must be received there, because his whole conversion to Orthodoxy was bound up with Athos. I remember thinking, looking at him, that getting him there was going to be a complex business, with little boats and a jetty. I did say to Elizabeth: 'Does he understand what he's doing? Does it represent his considered judgement?' She said, 'Yes.' Obviously, had he been in good health I would have wanted to talk to him much more thoroughly. I would have been interested in his motivation; how he saw his future life as an Orthodox; why he really wanted to be one. It would have meant going to divine liturgy in principle every Sunday, keeping different feasts, and going to a spiritual father for confession.

"Normally, when someone becomes Orthodox I do ask them to make a confession of their whole life. I feel if people are making fresh start they would start with a fresh slate. He never himself said, 'I have AIDS.' To me this wasn't important, why he was ill. The view of the church is: all sins can be forgiven. What matters is not our own worthiness but our desire. Nothing on his part would have constituted an obstacle. What sort of Orthodox he would have been, that's another question. I wouldn't have thought his parish priest would have had an easy task."

Ware received Bruce several times over the summer and arranged for Father Mitrophon to meet him on the shore of Mount Athos in September. Meanwhile above his hospital bed, Bruce kept a prayer written by David Jones: "MAY THE BLESSED ARCHANGEL MICHAEL DEFEND US IN BATTLE LEST WE PERISH IN TERRIBLE JUDGEMENT."

HAND IN HAND with his conversion to the Greek Orthodox faith and the hasty assembling of the Homer Collection went Bruce's urgent desire to find the origins of his illness. "In a Bruce-like way, he latched onto AIDS as something he was going to find a cure for," says Francis Wyndham.

At the end of July, friends of Bruce around the globe received a curious circular asking for contributions to "The Radcliffe Medical Foundation—'Expanding the Frontiers of Medicine'". Headed by a list of patrons who included Lord Goodman, the Duke of Marlborough, and the Bishop of Oxford, the letter was signed by Bruce. "I would like to think of this letter as an endless chain. If you have friends or relations who you think would be interested, I would gladly send it to them."

In the manner of a Victorian explorer, he sought funds to mount an expedition into an isolated community of central Africa, unspecified but most probably the Sahel in Eastern Chad, where he hoped to locate the origins of the HIV virus and so produce a vaccine.

"We live in a time of new viruses: a time of Pandora's Box," his circular began. "Climatic change is the motor of evolution, and the sweeping changes in climate that have affected many parts of Africa offer ideal conditions for a virus that may have been stable over many thousands of years to burst its bounds, and set off to colonize the world.

"The most pressing medical problem since tuberculosis is HIV (Human Immuno-deficiency Virus), vulgarly known as AIDS. The word AIDS should never be used by the medical profession, since it plays into the hands of the gutter press, and causes panic and despair: in France, not even M. Le Pen could do much with 'le SIDA'. There is, in fact, no cause for panic. HIV is not a late twentieth-century *Götterdämmerung:* it is another African virus . . .

"As you probably know the virus constantly mutates and there seems little hope at present of preparing a vaccine. Excellent results have been achieved by the laboratories in describing the virus; but in the future we shall have to look elsewhere. The stable form of the primordial HIV must exist in Africa, and we intend to find it. The pessimists will say it is like looking for the proverbial needle in a haystack. The problem may be simpler: that of the archaeologist who knows where to dig."

The man in charge of the expedition to the Sahel was to be Bruce's doctor at the Churchill, David Warrell. "He is one of the finest clinical physicians in this country. He has spent many years in the Far East, working in the field to advance the study of cerebral malaria. He is a world authority on snake-bite; but he has recently returned to Oxford to lead a team of researchers into HIV."

On his retirement in November, Juel-Jensen had handed Bruce over to Warrell as a special category patient. Although he received his treatment on the National Health, Bruce behaved like a private patient. "Bruce was the most demanding patient I've ever had in a way," says Warrell. "He commandeered the whole system. The force of his personality held you in a room talking to him. He had ideas about almost everything. At first I was dazzled by the diversity—as anyone was for the first time on meeting him or reading his books. As he went on I noticed a repetition, a paucity of originality, a recycling of concepts again and again. This was the only real evidence that he was 'mildly demented' in the medical sense."

Bruce was anxious to share with Warrell his theory of HIV. He wrote in his last notebook: "Any 'new' species—a man, a swallow or HIV virus must begin its career in a very limited core area—before bursting out on the world." Man had emerged from Africa. Why not HIV?

Warrell listened, fascinated. "One had to explain how such a devastating virus remained quiet for many years. The anthropological side of Bruce was intrigued by the idea of an isolated community which suddenly made contact with the outside world. He thought it was a palaeontological problem."

Warrell agreed that an "archaeological logic" pointed to Africa. Although he judged Bruce's scientific evidence thin, he was drawn in. "Bruce was a non-scientist with a very active mind trying to be constructive to save himself. His imagination was not limited by any scientific discipline. He made me feel very clay-footed and conventional. There is this idea of a creative step or jump one has to make for a discovery. I was aware I didn't have it and he might. Central to his relationship with me was a mystical feeling that this knowledge might enable us to defeat the disease."

Bruce knew the perfect man to help them track down the "primordial" virus: the palaeontologist Bob Brain. He interested Warrell in Brain's work and described the day on which Brain and he had discovered man's first hearth at Swartkrans. "All of us who came into contact with Bruce felt that sort of magic might touch us," says Warrell. "I tried to fit Bruce's design into some scientific structure. I thought: 'It's bad for mankind if I don't'."

Excited, Bruce telephoned Brain in Pretoria and invited him to move to Oxford where, funded by the Radcliffe Medical Foundation, he might start work on the epidemiology of the AIDS virus. "He thought that the distribution of the virus in Central Africa could be traced to racial groupings and this could go back a long time in human history," says Brain. "I couldn't think of any conceivable handle for this theory." He declined.

Not put off, Bruce plunged into the composition of his fund-raising letter. "I couldn't restrain him from writing it in my name," says Warrell. The letter went out on 25 July. Over the next few days, Bruce kept in close touch with Warrell. "I don't normally give patients my telephone number, but one was very vulnerable to his enhanced expectations. He used to ring me often at home to give revised estimates, upping the numbers. 'I think I've recalculated the sum of money.' The profits from some projected book mentioned the figure of £20 million. That was worrying. It was clear evidence that he was demented."

"BEING BRUCE, HE could see the funny side," says Elizabeth, but to her distress works of art continued to pile up at Homer End. A piece of the Red Fort, a portable twelfth-century altar from Lausanne, a Han tortoise ink-well, a £70,000 icon of Saint Paraskevi wearing a glowing tomato-coloured robe. "They were for me; he knew I would never spend money on things like that; wonderful, wonderful things, but I couldn't keep them." Art worth over a million pounds at one point filled the dining room to bursting point, paid for with post-dated cheques. Bruce could never have hoped to honour these cheques. Behind his back Elizabeth started to return what he had bought even as it was delivered. Unwilling to involve Charles Chatwin, Elizabeth asked Robert Erskine to help. "We set up an arrangement to catch these things," Erskine says. " 'Look, you'll get them back, he's not going to last long, so please let him have them'." Elizabeth also called upon Hugh Chatwin.* On 30 July, an exhausted Elizabeth flew to America to stay with Gertrude, leaving Bruce in the care of his brother for a fortnight. Once she was gone everything began to unravel.

On the eve of Elizabeth's departure Hugh collected Bruce from Homer End and drove him to Stratford for the weekend to be nursed by his parents. Within three minutes of swinging out of the drive at Homer End, Bruce confessed to his brother. "Hugh, before I go completely mad, there's something I must tell you. I have taken some risks in my time, but this time . . ." He told Hugh about "a priest called Donald" in New York. "He wouldn't mention the word AIDS. He referred to it as HIV. I was stunned." Hugh insists that he had not seen this coming. "Juel-Jensen had told us in 1986 that Bruce was HIV. We knew it could develop into AIDS, but until that moment I had gone along satisfied and hoping because he had had what seemed to be a total remission. He blew up into a proper size. Having done it once, he could do it again."

Hugh did not tell his parents what he had learned. As the weekend went on, it became apparent to him that Charles and Margharita would have difficulty handling Bruce for the two weeks Elizabeth was away. "I could see he was going to cause them trouble. We were all worried. On

* While most of the dealers involved behaved with exemplary patience, some did not and insisted on banking the cheques.

Sunday, Bruce said he had to go to London 'to finish his business'. I decided I'd better sleuth him."

Hugh drove his brother to the Portobello Hotel in Notting Hill Gate where Bruce had booked a room. The brothers shared this room for the rest of the week. "It was the first time we'd been at such close quarters since making models at Brown's Green." Hugh judged the situation grave enough to request three weeks' leave. "I was there to look, listen and find out what was wrong. I knew from Elizabeth something was wrong, but as a surveyor you try and find out what the truth is before you arrive at any opinion."

Bruce's first appointment on Monday was at the National Gallery. He dressed in khaki drill slacks and a short herringbone coat and instructed Hugh to wheel him up the steps. "He brought with him an enamel snuff box which he had identified as coming from a painting by David," says Hugh. Bruce outlined to the perplexed Director, Neil McGregor, his plans for the National Gallery to put on an exhibition of actual objects found in paintings and to embark on a comprehensive purchase of Russian icons. He also formulated the idea of creating a little room in the National Gallery to house the Homer Collection.

In the course of that week, Bruce embarked on a second buying spree. Their outings followed the itinerary established with Volans, now preoccupied with the Rimbaud opera. He bought a collection of 1920s Fortuny dresses, a medieval wall-hanging, some silver, a Cézanne watercolour—the last he painted of Mont Saint-Victoire and nearly all white—and a lump of amber with a fly in it. "I took that back a month later," says Hugh. "I was sweeping up after what he'd arranged to buy with Kevin, but he was in control. Nobody could stop him. He was using his clout and taste to do it: 'I'm getting my royalties, I've got my money coming in'." And so Bruce assembled his collection, in the words of his psychiatric report, "without any appropriate consideration or bargaining".

Sometimes he managed to escape Hugh's surveillance. Francis Wyndham was walking down Westbourne Grove when a taxi stopped. "There was Bruce, frightfully skeletal. 'I'm going to the Portobello Hotel!' He was on the loose in his wheelchair. The driver looked worried."

That evening Wyndham turned up at the Portobello Hotel with David King. "Traders kept on arriving—like something out of the Arabian Nights. There was one man, one almost saw him in a turban, whose wares tumbled out onto the bed and something priceless rolled away and we were on all fours clambering for it." Another dealer produced photographs of enormous gold lions in a restricted area of China: Bruce undertook to fund their removal at once. "Bruce kept on ringing up room service; he showed us a beaded Chanel suit he had bought for Elizabeth, like chain mail; he said Hugh was a genius. Then Robert Erskine came in. None of us gave the game away: he lifted us up into this realm of fantasy with the power of his storytelling and his sweetness. It was deeply disturbing and upsetting. He just wanted to get beautiful, rare things and put them in a museum. He was very happy."

For Robert Erskine, the spectacle was too painful. "For the first time Bruce's 'eye' had gone."

Bruce's final destination on Friday was Rebecca Hossack's gallery of Australian art. "He said I made him remember his time in Australia. He kept coming because he said there was energy in my smile." Over the summer Bruce had grown to be a regular visitor at her new gallery. Impressed by a still life on show, he had wanted the artist to paint the backdrop for the Rimbaud opera. In June, he saw Hossack's Aboriginal exhibition. He took to turning up three times a week. "I'd be sitting there late at night in a track suit and a car would draw up with Bruce and his brother. He'd sit in his wheelchair and hold court. On one of his last visits, he said: 'You know I'm HIV positive, but we've worked out a cure. It's terribly exciting and it involves the blood of a Nubian slave.' I don't have much sense of humour and I took it literally and thought, Well, that's interesting."

All week, he had been high on his need to achieve his collection, but on the Friday evening, "he crumpled and went frail," says Hugh. "He said: 'I'm done, done, done'." Hugh lifted Bruce into his Jaguar and drove him to Oxford. Halfway down the M40 he turned to his brother and said: "I think we might go to hospital."

BRUCE WAS KEPT in Room 9 on the John Warin ward. Five days later, on 10 August, Nurse Patterson found on her patient's report in red ink: "Not to leave the ward under any circumstances. To be sectioned if necessary."

Bruce's plans had been getting progressively grander. In the Churchill, his mind started racing again. He wanted to buy the Duchess of Windsor's clothes. He wanted to buy Elizabeth a Bugatti for £2 million. He wanted to found a city and to develop underwater tourism. "It was a burlesque," says Kevin Volans. "He was terribly excited about being made an

Oxford don because of his incredible theory of archaeological virology. He said they were wrong to call it that: it was historical virology: he'd invented the notion." He had solutions for ending the Cold War. "He was going to write to Gorbachev and go and see him and stop all this nonsense, sort it out, and he, Bruce, was going to get the Nobel Peace Prize." John Pawson, the architect who had converted Bruce's London apartment, was having an early morning swim at a hotel near Dallas when Bruce telephoned: he had been appointed Minister of Architecture, he wanted Pawson to be his paid advisor, would send a car to collect him from the airport and which flight would he be taking? "There was an incredible enthusiasm. He was always quite convincing. One had to prick oneself to say that isn't going to happen, but one wanted to will it." Paddy Leigh Fermor was about to leave for Bulgaria when Bruce called. "He wanted me to meet him on Mount Athos and join the Orthodox Church and act as his sponsor." A helicopter would fly Bruce, Leigh Fermor and Volans to the Holy Mountain. There Bruce intended to become a priest. He told June Bedford he had already decided on his religious name: Father James. "He did see himself as a priest," says Hugh.

Many of the proposals announced by telephone sprang from an urge to heal others. "Aren't all true healers—from the prehistoric shaman on—all 'thundermen'?" he wrote in his notebook. Not his least ambitious plan evolved from an idea planted by Hugh: to construct field-hospitals out of castor bricks and parachute them into trouble spots.

"It was an idea to keep him amused," says Hugh. "I'm involved with Crisis Action Hospitals. I told him of the Natural Resources Group, a company in the north of England that was making plastics and closed-cell rigid foam blocks out of vegetable oils like soya, castor, desert weed, rape, palm oil." The company had sold artificial rubber sheeting to India and was negotiating to build a factory in China.

Bruce leapt on the possibilities held out by Hugh's castor-brick hospital with all the enthusiasm of their great-grandfather who had once seen a future for the leather tyre. He believed he had a perfect troublespot for such a hospital: Afghanistan, the site of his earliest expeditions. Through the Aga Khan's wife he was put in touch with Prince Saddhruddin, who had at the UN a specific responsibility for Afghanistan. "The last words I spoke to Bruce," says Hugh, "were to arrange for a pile of 50p coins to put in a pay-phone by his bed to ring up Saddhruddin Aga Khan."

THE REPORT Nurse Patterson found was based on the patient profile from the ward psychiatrist. "Mr Chatwin is, of course, a man of great intelligence and ability who has led a most unusual and interesting life. On at least a couple of occasions he has been under considerable personal stress. I am told that 'living on his nerves' is a fundamental part of his personality." However, Bruce's pressing speech, his grandiose ideas, his variety of "inappropriate associations" suggested that "he is suffering from mania as a complication of his HIV infection." If the patient remained unwilling to take medication voluntarily, the psychiatrist advised David Warrell, "I think there would be an argument for your signing a three-day order under Section 5 of the Mental Health Act."

ON THE SAME day, Juel-Jensen telephoned Hugh Chatwin with a request that he go immediately to the Radcliffe. There Hugh was informed that the reasoning side of Bruce's brain had shrunk. The doctors wished to give him a drug to control the mania, for which they needed the family's consent. In Elizabeth's absence, Hugh signed the paper. He then told his father, who took over.

Charles Chatwin was acquainted with the drill. He had lived with the spectre of his grandfather's gross debts and he had experience of his mother certifying lunatics. He swiftly arranged through Wragge & Co. for the Court of Protection to appoint a receiver. Bruce was put on lithium and his chequebook taken away. David Warrell was asked to sign an order restraining his patient. "As doctor in charge I had to say from a medical point of view he was temporarily not responsible. I felt very uneasy and Bruce was absolutely furious when he discovered. It was the episode that precipitated my losing his confidence."

Elizabeth came back from America on 15 August, and went straight to Bruce in hospital. He was muttering that the doctors had told him part of his brain was dead. Confined forcibly to the ward, he had violent mood swings, was demanding and irritable. He seized Kevin Volans's arm. "You must save me. You must get me out of here. They all think I'm mad. I'm not. They can't keep up. I'm simply thinking too fast for them."

"The saddest thing," says Shirley Conran, "is that Bruce was well enough to know that what he was most terrified of was happening to him: his brain had been affected."

Slowly the lithium worked its effect.

One day Bruce decided he wanted back his wax Neptune. As part of a ploy for getting such works of art out of the house, Elizabeth had suggested they should be carried to London to be photographed. When she asked Vic Pearson to retrieve the tiny figure from his warehouse, he could not find it. One of the keystones of the Homer Collection had disappeared. (It was never found.) The news crushed Bruce. Miserable, he told Elizabeth: "It's symptomatic of everything."

His wild behaviour predictably found its way into the gossip columns. On 6 September, *Today* broke the following story: TOP AUTHOR CHATWIN FALLS VICTIM TO AIDS. "To the horror of his charming wife Elizabeth and the total shock of close friends like Jasper Conran, author Bruce Chatwin has become Britain's first outstanding talent to succumb to the full force of AIDS."

For Charles and Margharita, the gossip that this story generated realised their worst fears. Charles contacted Hugh. "I want to know: are you holding something back from me? Can you tell me whether this story is true?" Hugh told him it was. "He didn't say anything. Professional men don't show their reaction."

Bruce had at last confessed to his brother, but he still had declined to tell his parents. His aunt Barbara, a deaconess in the Church of England supported his decision. As soon as Elizabeth landed in England, Bruce insisted that she drive him to see his father's sister in Pershore. On 16 August he was taken on a day outing. He demanded the two of them be left alone. "I thought how lovely to want to see me," said Barbara Chatwin. Unable to sit, Bruce was laid out flat on a rug on the grass. "I sat on a garden chair looking down at him and he started to talk. 'There's something I want to tell you.' And I sat and listened and it wasn't until after he'd gone that I realised he'd found a clergyman in order to make a confession. I suddenly realised: 'I'm sure he knows he's dying'."

Barbara Chatwin felt it best that her nephew protect his parents from the truth: she, like Charles, had lived through the scandal of Robert Harding Milward. But she had underestimated her brother. Bruce had gone to great pains to conceal something which, in the end, his father—if not Margharita—might have been equipped to handle. During the war as a naval commander, Charles had presided over a court martial on board the *Cynthia*. On the day before his own death in 1996, he told Hugh: "I'm sorry to say we had to part company with the ship's carpenter. He was caught interfering with young sailors on board."

"Bruce had worried about Father," says Hugh. "He thought his mother would understand and that his father wouldn't. It was actually the other way round." Margharita suffered the more visibly. "It was an awful, terrible sorrow," says Hugh. "It was total pain."

THE STORY IN *Today* was kept from the person it most concerned. Efforts to divert Bruce concentrated on the imminent publication of *Utz*. Tom Maschler, who had taken a four-month sabbatical, was moved to make his warmest commendation to date. "Let me put it in writing," he wrote to Bruce. "The first pages of *Utz* are the most perfect Bruce Chatwin that I have ever read at an early stage. Come to that, they may be the most perfect Bruce Chatwin, period. This book will be a little gem." He had finished reading the corrected manuscript before going on leave. "I've said it before, and I'll say it again, there is simply no writer in England for whose work I have a greater passion than yours. This statement is made with all my heart."

Utz was published on 22 September and seemed everything that *The Songlines* was not: in place of a sprawling, philosophical treatise on movement which roamed the globe, he had written a compact, old European love story whose drama concentrated on the objects in a single room. "Each book of his seems to set out to contradict the expectations aroused by its immediate predecessor," wrote John Lanchester in the *London Review of Books*. Peter Conrad in the *Observer* saw "tantalising" links with the last book. "The timeless space of Aboriginal dreaming resembles the illusions of Prague, a labyrinth where you can wander back through history." Several reviewers perceived in the author the fragile and masked Harlequin, seldom what he seemed, forever pivoting on his base of gilded foam. For Robert Stone in the *New York Times Book Review*, the novel represented Chatwin "at his most erudite and evocative", but he found the author's world "a stern, unforgiving place; the worst crime there is obviousness, followed in order of gravity by complaining and scrupulosity."

Most British critics echoed Philip Howard in *The Times*: "This shiny little novel is not just about pretty little porcelain figurines, but about dirty great issues of life and creativity." The British edition of *Utz* outsold *The Songlines* in hardback. Final hardback sales were 21,745 and in early October it was shortlisted for the Booker Prize and later for the Whitbread.

Also on the Booker shortlist of six was Salman Rushdie's *The Satanic*

Verses. "Bruce always used to deride the Booker and along comes *Utz* and gets itself onto the shortlist," says Rushdie. "He suddenly became keen on a literary image in which he'd never been interested before. Two days before the prize-giving he rang me up. 'Salman, I've come to a decision. If I win the Booker, I'm going to say I'm going to share it with you and if you win you say the same thing about me. I think that would be very good.' I stalled. I said: 'Let's just think about it'." Both of their books lost to Peter Carey's *Oscar and Lucinda.*

Bruce had refused any promotional work because of his illness. Yet the extent of his deterioration was broadcast on 25 October, the evening of the Booker Prize award. As his sole piece of publicity, Bruce had agreed to appear on BBC television to discuss his novel. His interview at Homer End was more revealing than he can have intended. With bright, sunken eyes, he spoke of how Marta's love had triumphed over Utz's collection. Love had won over art, which "always lets us down". But almost for the first time, people were not listening to Bruce's words. They were taking in his scooped features, his sticky-lipped enunciation, his lank ashen hair.

Bruce would not be able to retract or hide from his effect on viewers. Had he been healthy he would never have permitted the indignity of that brief appearance. It confirmed to friends like Simon Sainsbury what they had suspected all summer. "To me it was very sad. Here was this brilliant man off his head."

XL

Fallen Angel

> . . . *possession* by the *Beast*
>
> —BC, NOTEBOOKS, 1971

HE FELT NO pain, only weakness. The nerves had gone. He blamed it all on a nurse infecting him with refrigerated blood "thereby completely screwing up the nerves in my hands and legs". In October, no longer satisfied with the way he was being treated at the Churchill, Bruce sought the help of a doctor in Paris. "The promise of a special cure brought those who could afford it to the French hospitals in droves," wrote Peter Adam in *Not Drowning but Waving.* "Every day a new pill seemed to be found, some costing a fortune, or not available on the market." Bruce had established contact with André le Fesvre through the Aga Khan's wife, whose hairdresser le Fesvre had reputedly cured of AIDS. On 11 October, Bruce and Elizabeth visited the le Fesvre clinic at 7 rue Washington. They stayed in Paris for a week of tests, Bruce receiving two blood transfusions and a course of calf serum that, for a month, restored him.

Le Fesvre had read Bruce's books. He found the Englishman *"un homme tellement seduisant".* They had areas of interest in common: le Fesvre's two chief fascinations were Patagonia and the Sahara.

Paris was the European city most affected by AIDS, in part perhaps because of France's ties to former African colonies like the Chad and Benin. Le Fesvre had not himself worked in Africa, but he believed, from talking to French military doctors in the region, that over time certain nomadic tribes in isolated parts came to develop an immunity to AIDS, while still exhibiting symptoms of the HIV virus. On their journeys south through Uganda and the Congo basin they came into contact with other tribes who were not immune—and so the infection spread: Cuban soldiers operating in Angola took the virus back to the Caribbean, from where it crossed to America. "We spoke a lot about my thesis," says le Fesvre. "It is not verified, but the epidemic appears to have become established along the routes of the nomads." He believed that those nomads carried the disease and although they themselves did not come down with it, they passed it on. Le Fesvre's explanation had for Bruce the power of a parable: the very people in whom he had located the key to a model existence were the carriers of his death.

Bruce's last brief remission was abetted by his excitement at le Fesvre's theory of the immunity to AIDS among West African nomads. However, this was not the case. As Dr Michael Elmore-Meegan, a British immunologist working with nomadic tribes in East Africa, says: "There is simply no information that would imply or indicate any resistance in any nomadic population. The only group that has demonstrated possible genetic resistance is a small group of Nairobi prostitutes."

On 24 October Elizabeth wrote to Kath Strehlow: "He seems better and cheerier so I'm very hopeful." Even Bruce's doctors in Oxford, not overly enthusiastic to release him to the embrace of alternative therapy, detected an improvement when he returned to the John Warin ward at the end of October. "Surprisingly well and cheerful. Can now do up buttons," read his report on 1 November. He went back to le Fesvre's clinic on 6 November for four more days of treatment and on 18 November was discharged from the Churchill. Two days later, Bruce and Elizabeth flew to Seillans, intending to spend the next month there. "It will be just as easy to continue with Bruce's treatment there as here," Elizabeth wrote to Gertrude. "Everyone who's seen him is delighted with how much better he looks and seems."

ON 20 NOVEMBER Bruce left England for the last time. He had continued to see "streams of people"—including Cary Welch, George Ortiz and Kath Strehlow—before he left. He wrote in Kath's copy of *The Songlines* "with love beyond the grave" and seemed quite unaffected when she sobbed. He sat in his wheelchair and listened to Nin Dutton's daughter Tisi sing his favourite Brahms odes: *"Von ewiger Liebe," "Die Mainacht," "Sapphische Ode".* One of his pilgrimages was to Ivry Freyberg at Munstead. He sat in the Orangery "and suddenly gazed straight at me for about ten minutes without stopping, as though he wanted to etch me in his mind". He told Ivry: "I never forgot the moment I first saw you at Marlborough in a green suede hat. You epitomised everything I thought mattered. You epitomised London glamour." His last words to her before Elizabeth drove him off in the car were: "I will win, I'm going to win. I'm going to win."

Michael Ignatieff found him "incorrigibly stylish" on his last visit to Homer End. Bruce had on a pair of high-altitude sun-goggles, bought for his next trip to the Himalayas. He lay on the grass outside the newly-painted house, wrapped in blankets, "and talked in a faint whisper, full of cackles and laughter like some majestic and unrepentant monarch in exile, like one of the fantastic and touching figures in his own fiction, staring up in the bright, blue sky, while the white clouds scudded across his black glasses."

To all he spoke of future plans: after Christmas he would visit San Francisco, then Australia, then Russia. "In January, I'm going to swim with the dolphins," he told Pattie Sullivan who saw the Chatwins off at Heathrow with a gift he had requested, a pair of Brooks Brothers flannel pyjamas. His emaciated appearance shocked Sullivan as everyone else. His face was a white triangle of pain. Moving with difficulty in his wheelchair, he could scarcely complete a gesture.

One person reluctant to see him in this state was Jasper Conran. After Bruce's collapse in Switzerland Jasper had visited him in the Churchill Hospital. Bruce, terrified he might have infected Jasper, wanted him to have a blood test. When Bruce was discharged in October 1986 there was a reconciliatory meeting at Homer End with Elizabeth present, following which the Chatwins attended Jasper's 27th birthday party. But Bruce's behaviour exasperated Jasper, whose hurt had grown stronger than his love, his humiliation deepened by the fact Bruce had returned to Elizabeth. Bruce, who wanted both Jasper and Elizabeth in his life at that moment, did not hear Jasper's complaints that he was acting inconsiderately, or understand his intractable anger. He reported back to Elizabeth of "hysterical screaming fits" in restaurants. Despite being many times asked, Jasper refused to return certain objects Bruce claimed to have lent him when he had no furniture, most notably the half of Eileen Gray's map of Patagonia. Feeling bitterly rejected, Jasper kept away.

In July, Hugh Chatwin had wheeled Bruce into Jasper's showroom. Hugh was then unaware of his brother's relationship to the Princess of Wales's couturier. "Bruce wanted to give him a collection of 1920s Fortuny dresses to help with ideas for his own collection. I could see Jasper was backing off. He was cool, distant. There was a frisson." Jasper shuffled Bruce out and afterwards wrote a letter rejecting him once and for all. Elizabeth concealed this from Bruce, who was upset at Jasper's refusal to accept his gift. In his last months in hospital in Oxford he longed for a visit. "He minded frightfully that Jasper wouldn't come to see him," says Francis Wyndham.

AT SEILLANS, JASPER'S mother moved to fill the gap. "When I saw him entering the hall, his arms hanging around the two men who were carrying him, his neck no longer able to support his head, like the broken stem of a flower, Bruce released a flood of compassion in me." Shirley Conran had arranged for Bruce to occupy the games room, a former priest's room with a barrel-vaulted ceiling on the ground floor leading to the terrace. "It was like a little monk's cell. Just a low double bed which Bruce and Elizabeth slept in and one Van Gogh-style chair at the side. I would sit and read poetry and prayers. In the window embrasure opposite the bed he always had flowers."

By day, Bruce sat on the terrace on a sun bed, tucked into an eiderdown. "He had a hat like premature babies wear in incubators, and goggles. He looked like a Swiss gnome." For the first week he was able to hold a pen properly. He started making notes for his Russian novel, but he was becoming daily more resistant to le Fesvre's remedies. He had come to the south of France in a spirit of hope. The end was closer than anyone imagined.

On 19 December, Elizabeth wrote to Kath Strehlow on Bruce's behalf to say he was unable, after all, to write the foreword for *Songs of Central Australia*. "He is really too weak & ill to do anything. We've come here as it's warmer & brighter than England in the winter & he loves being away from there. He dictates to me occasionally the beginning of a new book, but hasn't the energy to do anything else. He is having some treatment from a doctor in Paris, which at first after an intensive 2 weeks of non-stop I.V.s had a very good effect. However, a lot of that has now worn off & he's very depressed . . . Keep up the prayers—all of them help."

He was a hopeless patient. At the Churchill, David Warrell had noticed how Bruce did not like to be reminded or to be given a realistic view of the inevitability of the process. "He systematically fell out with a number of my colleagues. One only had to make one pessimistic or realistic remark and he took against them. Ultimately, he took against me."

In France, Bruce continued to thwart his carers' attempts to ease his discomfort or make his treatment coherent. His behaviour stirred criticism. Without being aware of the background, outsiders jumped to conclusions. The fastidious Teddy Millington-Drake came to stay at Seillans, and found the conditions "most unsuitable": "There was no doctor, no nurse, and an Australian girl who walked around with no shoes on who

hadn't been told he had AIDS." He conveyed to Francis Wyndham and
Diana Melly his concern that Bruce might not be receiving proper medical treatment. "Seillans was not a bad place to be when you're ill, but it
was not a place in which to die of that illness," says Wyndham.

Public tolerance in the south of France was lower than in Paris.
(When, a month later, Wyndham stepped off the plane at Nice airport, he
walked into a crowd of Le Pen protesters, homophobic, right-wing and
holding up placards calling for AIDS to be purged, for everyone with the
disease to be isolated.) "We had great trouble with doctors in the south of
France paying attention," says Elizabeth. "They weren't interested." When
the local doctor found out about Bruce's illness, he refused to continue
treatment. "The doctor arrived in a rubber suit as if for a trip to the
moon," wrote Peter Adam of his experience with an AIDS sufferer in
France. On Boxing Day, in desperation, Elizabeth summoned André le
Fesvre for a swift visit from Paris. Latterly, she sought the help of a young
doctor near Grasse whom Bruce had chosen out of the telephone book for
his Alsatian name. Dr Bernard Prouvost-Keller had attended him in 1986.
"Bruce said he came from the North of France and would therefore be a
good doctor." Prouvost-Keller made his calls by motorbike, but he could
not come up as often as Elizabeth would have wished. Most of the time,
it was left to Elizabeth and a rota of friends to change Bruce's bedding,
turn him over, feed him his medicine.

Bruce twice left Seillans. He needed a blood transfusion before
Christmas and spent an awful weekend at a hospital in Draguignan. The
bed was too short and he was alarmed by the speaker above his head
through which the doctor spoke from his office. When Elizabeth's purse
was stolen while she went to the bathroom, they faced the prospect of being stranded in the ward with no money. "I'll commit suicide if I stay
here," he whispered. She sat up in a chair for two nights rather than leave
him.

In the New Year, in a van which a local boy fitted out for the purpose,
he was taken for another transfusion to the Sunny Bank Anglo-American
hospital in Cannes.

The remainder of the time he stayed in his priest's room.

"He should have gone into an AIDS hospice," says Kevin Volans.
"But since he didn't want to admit he had AIDS, Elizabeth was in the difficult position of trying to fulfil what he wanted." Had he submitted to
some formal palliative care as did Millington-Drake, who himself died of
AIDS five years later, his end would not have been so harrowing. The homosexual community was in many respects more sophisticated than the

first line of doctors in dealing with AIDS. Their losses had taught them quickly. But Bruce was not prepared to draw on their support.

The sicker Bruce became, the greater his denial. "I don't know why I'm not getting better," he said to Elizabeth. "It's probably the virus," she replied. "No, no!" Having faced up to his diagnosis in Switzerland, it was now a closed topic. "If you made the slightest reference, he was horrified. I couldn't discuss it."

"All the time he was ill," says Shirley Conran, "the word 'AIDS' was never mentioned."

On Elizabeth's shoulders fell the impossible task of wishing to honour Bruce's wishes while recognising that he was not in full possession of his faculties. Werner Herzog, whom Bruce invited to Seillans early in January, asked Elizabeth: "Why don't you help him die?" She replied: "Long ago we talked about it and we agreed we wouldn't."

But now he wanted to die. "It was the first thing he said: 'I want to die,' " says Herzog. "I said: 'How do I do that? Do I shoot you? Have you discussed it with Elizabeth?' 'No, I can't discuss it with Elizabeth because she's a Catholic'."

Bruce had summoned Herzog because he thought the director had healing powers. When they had first met in Melbourne in 1984, shortly after Bruce's visit to Swartkrans, their talks had begun with a discussion on the restorative powers of walking. "He had an almost immediate rapport with me," says Herzog, "when I explained to him that tourism was a mortal sin, but walking on foot was a virtue, and that whatever went wrong and makes our civilisation something doomed is the departure from the nomadic life." Herzog had written a short prose book, *On Walking in Ice*, which illustrated this theory and which Bruce loved.

Herzog had brought with him to Seillans a documentary he had made on the Wodaabe nomads of the Niger, *Herdsmen of the Sun*. These were Bruce's Bororo Peuls, "a people obsessed by the horizons and their own beauty". Bruce was eager to see the film. "I showed it to him only in bits of ten minutes," says Herzog, "and then he would just pass out, or become delirious, and then he would ask me to go on showing him the film. He was a skeleton, there was nothing left of him, and all of a sudden he would shout at me: 'I've got to be on the road again, I've got to be on the road again.' And I said to him, 'Yes, that's where you belong.' And he said: 'Can you come with me?' And I said: 'Yes, sure, we will walk together.' And then he said: 'My rucksack is so heavy.' And I said: 'Bruce, I carry it.' And we spoke about where we were walking and had a walk together and he all of a sudden had a lucid moment when his blanket was off him and every few minutes I turned him around because his bones were aching and he called his legs 'the boys'. He said: 'Can you put the left boy around to this side and the right boy?' And he looked down at himself and he saw the legs were only spindles and he looked at me in this very lucid moment and he said: 'I'm never going to walk again.'

"He said: 'Werner, I'm dying.' And I said, 'Yes, I am aware of that.' And then he said: 'You must carry my rucksack, you are the one who must carry it.' And I said: 'Yes, I will proudly do that.' And I have his rucksack and it's such a dear thing to me. Let's say if my house was on fire, I would throw my children out of the window, but of all my belongings it would be the rucksack that I would save."

IN PUBLIC, AND with Bruce, Elizabeth kept up a brave face, ruthlessly nursing him. They were on that expedition still, together on that Himalayan slope. She treated him like a lark with a broken wing. "Elizabeth's credo was what he wanted, he had," says Shirley Conran. "If it was poppy seed from the Crimea to scatter on his cornflakes or special teas sent by Paddy Singh from India, or honey from a special bee on Hymettus, Elizabeth got it."

"Instead of bursting into tears," says Francis Wyndham, "she'd go in a car miles and miles to get milk when no one else wanted to eat. She kept the front up, which was like her and what Bruce saw in her."

The others around the couple would never know the extent of Elizabeth's grief. Only once, at the very end, would she lose control.

Bruce deteriorated fast. When Shirley Conran left Seillans for her home in Monaco on 31 December, he was functioning "normally". She had showed him how her dictaphone worked so that he could continue with his novel. By the time Kevin Volans arrived a fortnight later, he was "dreadfully far gone". He was incontinent, thin, exhausted by the coughing. The white fungus in his mouth made speaking difficult. When Volans played him *The Songlines* quartet, which had premièred at the Lincoln Centre in November, all he could say was: "Lovely."

Shirley Conran arrived back the same afternoon in a black Jaguar. "She took one look at Bruce and climbed into bed with him and cradled him," says Volans. "That took guts because he didn't smell nice." Shirley says: "He could not move. His face looked liked melted wax. He could just say 'Granny' which meant the rubber ring for his bottom and 'Burnie' which meant he needed the bottle. He had christened the pee-bottle

'Birdie' because it was shaped like a Picasso bird-vase, but it came out as 'Burnie'."

That night she read him the Lord's Prayer. "Afterwards, he said: 'So simple'."

Later, he asked Volans to cradle him too. "I lay down with him and held him and he'd say, 'Hold me, hold me, not enough . . .' "

FRANCIS WYNDHAM AND the Mellys arrived before lunch the next day, Saturday 14 January. Worried that Bruce would not last long, Millington-Drake had urged them to hasten immediately to Seillans. Wyndham says: "We stood making nervous conversation on the terrace and Diana asked: 'Do they know he has AIDS?' " This, Shirley told Wyndham, was the first time the word had been used. He says: "We realised the extent to which it had been covered up. It was such an odd situation that everyone was inconsistent. We were all neurotic and not making sense. Shirley was very much the hostess, but with three women in the same kitchen all trying to help, there was a clash of personalities. We got on about as well as people on the *Titanic*."

Also at Seillans was a homeopathic doctor from London, David Curtin. Elizabeth had contacted Curtin to oversee Bruce's return to England. She was hoping to fly back with Bruce on Monday and put him in The Lighthouse, an AIDS hospice off Ladbroke Grove.

They took turns to sit at his bed. Diana Melly fed him a morsel of salmon. "It sat on his tongue and he wouldn't swallow." Volans likened the atmosphere to "a circus". At some point Prouvost-Keller arrived on his motorbike in his black leather bomber-jacket with "Do it to me, baby" patched to his sleeve. Shirley produced a crate of champagne and by Saturday evening everyone was slurring their words. Volans says: "Shirley, tanked up, would say: 'Bruce, I know you want to die, but I've got to disappoint you because you're *not* dying.' And every time she said 'dying', he shrieked: he was petrified of dying."

"It was the most awful thing I've ever experienced," says Wyndham. "It was like being in hell and he was in hell."

Bruce had been having recurrent nightmares. At night he had visions of a face, frightening him. Shirley wrote in her diary: "On Sunday a.m. I heard screams and went to B's room at 6 a.m. before it was light. He was terrified of 'the face' that he saw in his dreams. Eliz slept in his bed, which comforted him . . ." Elizabeth says, "He would lie awake and didn't want the light turned off. It was a human face, like a personification of his pain." She would shout at him: "He's not here, Bruce! He's not here!"

Volans says: "She was trying to force him to hold on. She was doing everything she could to keep him alive." To Volans, it was at this point that Bruce's life most closely mirrored Rimbaud's. "As Rimbaud was passing through his '*saison en enfer*'," Bruce had written during his first journey to the desert, "he realised that the Beast was winning."

In *The Viceroy of Ouidah*, Father de Lessa also suffered Rimbaud's dark dreams. "He kept seeing an animal called the Zoo. The Zoo had the head of a monkey, a dog's body, leopard's claws, and it would sprawl lecherously across his path and twitter like a bird . . . Dom Francisco decided to ship him back to Bahia. But the Zoo was also in the sea; for when they strapped him aboard the canoe, he was still screaming: The Zoo! The Zoo!' "

BRUCE SPENT MOST of Sunday 15 January, his last day conscious, lying in sunshine on the terrace. "He had been very disappointed not to have won the Booker Prize," says Shirley. "Teddy Millington-Drake telephoned from Italy and said Alberto Moravia had loved *Utz* and had written a full page rave review. I went straight and told Bruce and he gave a long slow smile and he just said: 'Better than the Booker'."

That afternoon Shirley was alone with him on the terrace when the sun went in. "It grew cold very quickly. Somehow I humped him over the steps." She carried Bruce inside, into the summer salon and lay him on a chaise longue, kneeling beside him. "I said: 'I love you, Bruce,' and to my joy he clearly said with an effort: 'I love you, too.' They were his last words to me."

At 3 a.m. on the morning of Monday 16 January, Elizabeth came into Kevin's room. She needed his help urgently. Bruce's fingernails had turned blue. "He was in a coma. He was not responding and he never regained consciousness," says Elizabeth.

An ambulance was called. Diana Melly and Shirley Conran ran out in their nightgowns and helped a coiffed stretcher-bearer to support Bruce's body over the steps. Elizabeth climbed in the ambulance beside him and it disappeared, jolting down the steep, cobbled hill.

He was taken to the state hospital in Nice. "I was allowed to sit with him until the staff came, then told to leave," says Elizabeth. She sat in the waiting room until mid-morning when the others arrived from Seillans.

They filed in to see him. He was lying on a steel bed, peacefully asleep, his face attached to an oxygen tube. His skin had gone back to peach colour. "He looked suddenly so young," says Volans.

Elizabeth did not go back to the hospital that day. "We felt she had been generous in sharing Bruce," says Shirley. "When she didn't want to stay with him, nor should we. She was very quiet, in her own space." Shirley booked Elizabeth into the Acropolis Hotel, close by, while Wyndham, Volans and Diana Melly returned to London. Meanwhile, Hugh was telephoned and asked to fly out.

Bruce was kept on oxygen throughout Monday and all through Tuesday night. Elizabeth had promised him he would not have his life prolonged artificially. On Tuesday morning, she cracked for the first time: "He's already dead," she told the hospital staff. "That isn't Bruce. It's a shell. They're *making* it breathe."

On Tuesday afternoon shortly before five, Hugh Chatwin turned up at the hotel and then he and Shirley Conran went in to pay their last respects. "His eyes are closed. He is grey. He is quiet," wrote Shirley in her diary. They returned with Elizabeth to Seillans.

At 10.45 on Wednesday morning, 18 January, Shirley wrote: "Bernard has telephoned E. B is being taken off everything. There is no point. It is a matter of hours. He's breathing on his own." At 1.35 p.m. she telephoned the hospital.

"Awful Swiss yodelling while on hold on hospital phone. Died 5 minutes before. That golden child of fortune, whose christening was attended by all the good fairies, has now felt the bad fairies come true. The darting dragonfly has been trampled. And the world is truly a sadder place because BC is no longer in it."

"As far as I was concerned," says Elizabeth, "he had died two days before."

XLI.

ⁿⁿ

The Chatwin Effect

> *Heroic saga—a young man, bursting with vigour and*
> *often credited with superhuman audacity in*
> *childhood leaves home on a long journey. After a*
> *sequence of Walter Mitty-ish adventures in remote*
> *and fabulous lands, he faces the jaws of Death.*
> —BC, NOTEBOOKS

ON 19 JANUARY, James Lees-Milne wrote his final entry on his old neighbour and walking companion: "Bruce Chatwin is dead. Not surprising from all accounts. A grievous loss to literature, the papers say. For one so comparatively young and only recently acknowledged the obituaries are amazingly long and eulogistic. You would suppose Lord Byron had died."

When Bruce died many people felt a sense of loss out of all proportion to their expectation. "His energy, his enthusiasm, his passion was fructifying," says Colin Thubron. "He was expansive; he opened horizons; you always felt with Bruce he was capable of coming back with the key to everything."

On a train to Zurich, Clem Wood picked up a copy of the *Guardian* and saw a photograph of Bruce. "I was delighted. I thought it was another review: When I realised that I was reading his obituary, I burst into tears." The art historian Hugh Honour was in Venice. "We came down to breakfast and the whole of the middle section of the *Corriere della Sera* was taken up under a single banner headline: *Chatwin è morto.*" Jack Lang sent a telegram from Paris: *"J'apprends avec tristesse la mort de Bruce Chatwin. Avec lui, c'est un esprit multiple qui nous quitte. Un homme dont les livres nous avaient appris mieux connaitre les hommes."*

The condolence letters registered a note of collective disbelief. "I've minded so much about his death," wrote Ivry Freyberg. "I just haven't been able to realise it's true."

Richard Bull was moved to describe his impact: "Despite the large number of people one meets as a doctor, it is only the very rare person who can be said to influence your life; and I feel Bruce was one of those people for me." A friend from New York wrote: "He was a wild man, and somehow left everyone with two eyes in their head, working feet and a pen feeling that they had misspent their attention . . ." Peter Levi was inarticulate: "I can't write this letter, I'm afraid."

On 27 January a class of students from a junior school in Leicester sent Elizabeth a package of letters and drawings. "My teacher Mrs Fawcett told us about Bruce Chatwin and told us he liked books," wrote one of the girls. "I like books too and I hope your [*sic*] feeling well." Sirish Patel told her: "We did a play in our school about the Aborigines and how the world began. It was very good. Your husband's book made it happen." Farren Sunley was one of the actors: "I held the map up and shouted 'I am a member of the Koala clan', I started at Shark Bay and ended at Sydney."

"He was one of the nicest men I ever met," wrote Anne-Marie Mykyta from Adelaide. "It is not too much to say that I loved him. On the day I heard of his death, I lay on my bed and read *Songlines* again and wept." Many of the letters were signed by unknown names. Elizabeth wrote back to one: "It comes as rather a shock to find that people think of him as a great man. I think he would have been surprised too."

On 20 January, Leo Lerman cabled her from New York: "The longest journey this one, and he always loved journeys."

"THE STARS KNOW the time when we die," Bruce had written in his notebook. Several saw an inevitability about his end. "Great people have an inbuilt instinct about how long they're going to live," said Pam Bell, "a sort of rhythm to the way they rule their life." This explained the disciplined economy of his writing, his manic behaviour, his impatient appetite for experience. "He was like a little firework all the time," says Barbara Bailey. "He never could stay long because he'd wear you away. That is why he died. You can't be a beautiful firework and live on and on." His dense, intense, short life had a preordained and mythic quality. It delighted him to lead everyone in his fantasies. By the end they had become a reality.

He died young; but not so young as most people think. At 48, he had outlived many of his influences: Humphrey Chatwin, Robert Louis

Stevenson, T. E. Lawrence, Anton Chekhov, Robert Byron, Arthur Rimbaud. Had he lived, it is tempting to imagine Bruce as the polymathic André Malraux. He might have grown to resemble his description of Klaus Kinski playing the Viceroy of Ouidah: "a sexuagenarian adolescent all in white with a mane of yellow hair". And behaved, perhaps, like Charles Milward the Sailor, home from the sea. "Charley the Pioneer with his restlessness gone, pottering round his garden, the Elms near Paignton." Yet few of his friends could picture an elderly Chatwin. "I have great difficulty imagining him as an old man," says Robert Hughes. "I think he would have been very crabby."

Dying early, his good looks for the most part intact in the public mind, Bruce stood for the promotable ideal of the literate adventurer. In Berlin, a travel bookshop, "Chatwins", opened up in Goltzstrasse. In Amsterdam, an art gallery in Houweg called itself "Songlines" while in Paris a publishing house took the name "Utz", publishing an edition of Walter Ralegh's *El Dorado* in 1993. Patagonia, once a joke, has become the brandname of an upmarket range of French wind and rainwear and a company in Italy now manufactures his moleskine notebooks, a Chatwin quotation in the back flap.

He was emblematic of a way of thinking and of being. He was inquisitive, spiritual and global and the grass was always greener where he had travelled. He incited others to follow him. The Land Council in Alice Springs received requests from the French Foreign Legion for permits and maps "to walk the songlines". He became an archetype for the urban traveller and a voice for Generation X. "You know Bruce said we should keep moving around," sang the English pop group Everything But the Girl in their 1991 song "One Place". He appealed to the world of youth, healthy-living, alternative life-styles; to both men and women. In Montreal, the Chatwin marriage was held up to an impatient girlfriend by a restless young traveller Patrick Blake, teaching now in Korea, as "the perfect marriage". To others, he represented the transforming potential of a chance encounter. A few weeks after his death, an advertisement appeared in the *Village Voice*, between a message to Doris to throw away her sandwich board and a thank you to St Jude: "*Bruce Chatwin aficionado* now studying law, we talked for a block on 7th Street. Meet again?"

ONE OF BRUCE'S inimitable legacies was "the campaign chair". In July 1983, Clinton Tweedie, the art dealer from Brisbane, was in a queue in the

Lix ice-cream parlour in the Piccadilly Arcade. Bruce, standing in front of him dressed in a lemon-coloured sweater, spun round. "You're French, obviously." "No, Australian." Waiting for Tweedie when he came outside, Bruce invited himself to tea. Extraordinarily, Tweedie was staying in the Covent Garden flat belonging to Bruce's old boy friend Donald Richards. Copies of Bruce's books lay scattered about, although Tweedie had never heard of their author. That afternoon Bruce took Tweedie to the Essential Cubism exhibition at the Tate and then showed him his attic flat in Eaton Place. There Tweedie sat in a comfortable deck-chair with a sweat-stained leather seat. Bruce, who had unfolded it from nothing, explained how it was designed in London in 1856. He had acquired the chair from Mussolini's daughter in Capri and the sweat was that of Il Duce himself, who had used the chair while directing his conquest of Ethiopia.

Visiting London again some years later, after Bruce's death, Tweedie recognised the chair when he walked into Lord Macalpine's gallery in Cork Street. Remembering Bruce's story, he bought it for £1,000 took it back to Australia and now manufactures copies from a factory in Djakarta with canvas seats designed by Mambo.

The chair story is quintessential Chatwin: several bizarre coincidences, an arresting provenance, a stylish object. In her memoir *With Chatwin*, one of Bruce's editors, Susannah Clapp, invoked an adjective to describe this phenomenon: ". . . at about the time the word 'Thatcherite' entered the English language, so did the term 'Chatwinesque'."

BRUCE'S POPULARITY WAS reflected in posthumous sales of his books. Published the spring after his death, his collected journalism *What Am I Doing Here* sold 31,688 in hardback in the British market, more than any of his other books.

The success encouraged Maschler in 1993 to publish an edition of Bruce's photographs, with extracts from his notebooks edited by Francis Wyndham. Three years later, Cape published a further selection of essays and stories: *Anatomy of Restlessness*. In Italy, Adelphi sold more than 50,000 copies of both of those books. But in London and New York there grew concerns that Bruce in death was threatening to be more prolific than he was in life. His American editor Elisabeth Sifton, who had worked with him line by line on *On the Black Hill*, articulated the difficulty of speaking about "the published Chatwin" in that, she felt, "some of it was not ready for publication". In the *New York Times*, Michiko Kakutani reckoned that *Anatomy of Restlessness* did nothing to enhance his reputation. "Sounding a lot like a flower child with a smattering of scholarly training, Chatwin is decidedly not at his best in this sort of theoretical writing." There was, she hinted, the whiff of a fully-scraped barrel.

In *What Am I Doing Here*, Bruce wrote of how "Malraux's breathless career has left lesser spirits far behind—and irritated." Bruce, who was himself an exceptionally generous author when it came to discussing the works of others—"I have no memory of Bruce ever saying anything nasty about anyone," says Rushdie—was perhaps inevitably the victim of jealousy. Wyndham, who had launched Bruce on his writing career, was among the first to worry about a backlash. He feared that Bruce's premature death and the quality of his early books had inflated his reputation, created a cult. "He is right to worry," wrote John Ryle in the *Independent on Sunday* on 24 October 1993. Ryle referred to a memoir by Paul Theroux in *Granta 44*.

Theroux insisted he had written his memoir as a friend. ("He was an inspiration to me," Theroux had written to Elizabeth.) The article was described by Graham Coster in the *London Review of Books* on 8 February 1996 as "an assassination"—a "fierce appreciation of a bore, an incessant chatterer, an embellisher of fact, a callow enthusiast for pretentious sentences and bogus science, and someone who whinged with unattractive self-absorption about the difficulty of writing anything, when no one was asking him to anyway".

Casually approaching a subject that neither Bruce nor Elizabeth took casually ("we had met his wife, but the fact of Bruce having a wife was so improbable that no one quite believed it"), Theroux recorded Bruce's "lively belief in homosexuality". He found "rather disturbing" Bruce's decision never to speak about his private life—although, as Ryle pointed out, it was questionable whether the fact that Theroux had chosen to write about his own sex life had any bearing on Chatwin's right not to talk about his.

A sense that he had lied about his illness hatched the suspicion that he might have lied in his art. Under the headline "Chatwin accused of hit and myth" the *Daily Telegraph's* Peterborough column reported the exaggerations which John Pilkington claimed to have uncovered in *In Patagonia:* "To be blunt, much of this book was invented." Bruce in death was starting to resemble, in some minds, *In Patagonia's* mythomaniac hero Louis de Rougemont, compère of the show "The Greatest Liar on Earth" for whom "dream and reality had fused into one". A critical perception in England, that Bruce was engaged in a similar hoax, was not one that would find fertile ground on the Continent where there is much less obsession with category. "If one had to object to people making things up, we'd kill literature," says his Italian publisher and author, Roberto Calasso. Nor was this attitude encountered in America. "Americans by force of their history and landscape do not think like that," says Elisabeth Sifton. In Sifton's view Bruce actually made up very little. He had the imagination to tell stories, to connect them, to enlarge, colour and improve them, but not to invent. "He was an artist, not a liar."

David Plante, who wrote a portrait of him for *Esquire* in 1990, attributed the backlash to an English desire to knock Bruce down a peg. "There might have been something devilish about Bruce—that he wanted people to envy him. But he was a magical person and he was enviable and if you envy someone you want to see them destroyed."

"Something about Bruce infuriates other writers," says Wyndham, "as if he's getting away with something and never did the things he said. But Bruce wasn't a *mythomane*. Why shouldn't he turn something that does happen into something with shape and story? It's not as if he had a tremendously successful and happy life. He wasn't a darling of the gods. His life wasn't particularly enviable. He had great depressions." Wyndham assigns at least part of the envy to the fact that Bruce thought internationally. "It's the parochial resentment for the brilliant villager who goes and makes it in the big city." As for the charge that Bruce might have hurt people: "Writers *do* hurt other people. Bruce's record is much better than a lot of others."

"He was so individual, so much himself. That's bound to polarise people," says Rushdie. "When the self is as multi-faceted as Bruce, I guess there's more to get up people's noses. That's the small change of being any good at what you do. And being an interesting person. Of my contemporaries he had the most erudite and possibly the most brilliant mind that I ever came across."

Inevitably, it was a foreigner who asked the question: "Why should the disappearance of Bruce Chatwin make such a difference?" Writing in the *Times Literary Supplement* in June 1989, Hans Magnus Enzensberger said that it was not enough to say that Bruce died young or was full of promise. "Chatwin never delivered the goods that critics or publishers or the reading public expected. Not fearing to disappoint, he surprised us at every turn of the page." What Enzensberger perceived was Bruce's Englishness, not his foreignness. He concluded: "it is surely as a story-teller that Chatwin will be remembered, and missed—a story-teller going far beyond the conventional limits of fiction, and assimilating in his tales elements of reportage, autobiography, ethnology, the Continental tradition of the essay, and gossip. Underneath the brilliance of the text, there is a haunting presence, something sparse and solitary and moving, as in Turgenev. When we return to Bruce Chatwin we find much in him that has been left unsaid."

A decade after his death, Bruce's reputation abroad continues to grow. "Of all the English writers in the last 30 years, the only one I take down and re-read is Bruce," says Susan Sontag. "It's a very valuable and enthralling voice." Although old-fashioned, he is seen as ahead of his time because of this cultural daring which is today not only accepted but demanded. "His nineteenth-century energy and zest are valued and cherished," says Elisabeth Sifton. "People are now rediscovering deep relationships between cultures over time and space. They are reconsidering the idea of a big unifying theme in a more modern way." His work has gained currency in anthropological departments, to correct the paternalism of previously undisputed western methodologies. Ruth Tringham, his Marxist colleague at Edinburgh and former adversary, now uses *The Songlines* in her teaching at Berkeley. "It amazed me that he managed to transcend the other Bruce I knew and get further into the landscape and people than I ever imagined he could. It's not the truth, it's Bruce's story, but as an idea of trying to grasp an entirely different way of thinking about space and time it's just as good as anthropology."

He has set free other writers and encouraged them not to be tamed by conventional boundaries. "People who study Chatwin feel liberated by him," says Sifton. "Reading him gives you the courage of your own convictions." The German anthropologist Michael Oppitz, now director of the Zurich Museum of Ethnography, knew him in Nepal. "The thing about Chatwin is that through his life he gave a new definition of the Writer as Hero." An icon of the back-packer, he inspired myriads of young people to set off and live in Calcutta or Patagonia—"and then come out with a diary that no one publishes". Oppitz believes this tailoring of the hero figure was a conscious desire. "On a sociological level it is at least as important as his books."

He made life difficult for booksellers, but vastly more interesting to readers. He is perceived to be the most glamorous example of a genre in which so-called "travel writing" began to embrace a wider range: autobiography, philosophy, history, *belles lettres*, romantic fiction. But unlike Colin Thubron, Jonathan Raban, Redmond O'Hanlon, Paul Theroux, Andrew Harvey, he does not put his travelling self at the centre. His stance is unflappable, detached, discreet—"a pose rather than a subject," writes Manfred Pfister, the result of a "brilliant self-stylization rather than the self-reflective depth and emotional richness of subjectivity". Bruce's lack of introspection is old-fashioned, but his style is contemporary. This unusual blend accounts for his distinctive voice. "He does not seem to owe anything to anybody," says Thubron. Yet other writers are open about their indebtedness to him. The Italian philosopher Claudio Magris turned to Patagonia for his first novel *Un altro mare*. In *Mundo del Fin del Mundo*, the Chilean writer Luis Sepùlveda has his hero set out from Hamburg airport to South America with Chatwin's *In Patagonia* in his hands. In Britain, he has inspired a younger generation of "travel writers" like Philip Marsden and William Dalrymple. "In many ways *In Xanadu* would never have happened without my having discovered and loved his writing" Dalrymple wrote to Elizabeth. "His inheritance was actually his adventurousness," says Thomas Keneally. "Modern fiction is sometimes too house-trained. Chatwin's fiction was not house-trained."

Keneally, whose own fiction is stimulated by history, is aware of the penalty for transgressing genres. "There is a link between all fine writers and Prometheus. Critics know that creative people have stolen fire, that's why they are so mean to them. Chatwin had stolen the fire—if you think of fire as the trigger for the tribal circle and stories. He had certainly plundered stories, but I mean, what do you want writers to do? That is almost the job description of writing. Economists think that economic indicators are the metaphor for humanity. Novelists think that stories are the true indicators of human existence. Chatwin correctly saw stories as paradigms of humanity."

Bruce died on the eve of the transformation of Central Europe, bringing down the barriers of the old and new worlds. Missing are his despatches from the Berlin Wall, the Iron Curtain, Poland, Prague in the Velvet Revolution. He died, too, before the revolution in information technology. He hated computers almost as much as he did the combustion engine, but he was in a sense a precursor of the Internet age: a connective super-highway without boundaries, with instant access to different cultures. The thirst for international experience and encounters may account in part for his appeal. He holds out the possibility of something wonderful and unifying. He inundates us with information and the promise that we will one day get to the root of it. "He posed questions that we all want answered," says Robyn Davidson, "and perhaps gave the illusion that they were answerable."

Bruce was not intimate, but he valued the personal encounter. This is one quality that makes his unwritten books such a loss. His compelling narrative voice was cut off just as he had found it. "I wish there was so much more in a way I don't wish with Robert Byron," says Sontag. Jean-François Fogel says, "At long last he had accepted the fact he was a novelist. He was now going to look into the human heart and tell us how it works."

In *Anecdotage*, Rezzori asks the question: "What would his life's work have looked like if he hadn't died in his 40s after *Utz* but had gone on living and writing until the blissful age of 80?"

Throughout his writing career Bruce flirted with the idea of chucking in his pencil. "I wish I could give up writing, don't you?" he wrote to Bail. "More and more this book business tempts me into silence." Driving through the outback near Broken Hill, he told Nin Dutton that nothing was permanent. "He said he mightn't be a writer forever. He might be a truck-driver—and he meant it half seriously."

Salman Rushdie does not believe his friend's protestations. "Bruce had just begun. We didn't have his developed books, the books that might have come out of falling in love with his wife. We only saw the first act. He was just creating himself into a person he'd be happy to be. Out of all the people he'd experimented being, he quite liked being the writer Bruce Chatwin."

AND WHAT OF ELIZABETH? "I think you know what you meant to him, which is everything," Peter Levi wrote.

Few understood Elizabeth's role in Bruce's life better than Gillian Walker. "This delight which we have all had from him in life and in his writing has had much to do with his relationship with you—your belief in him from the beginning—the support you gave him to find what he wanted to do and do it—at Sotheby's—those gloomy cold days in Edinburgh with your hands red and swollen from the raw Scottish winter—bicycling laden with food out to the end of no-where in Fisher's Island so that he could have the endless, unfettered time he needed for *In Patagonia*—you storing away his treasures so that he could have the illusion of nomadic existence while not having to give up his collector's passion." *Utz* had captured his mood of return. "He said on the phone that he didn't want to travel again but rather to be at home with you, this after, I think, that first serious bout of illness—illness which ironically teaches appreciation for what one has rather than what one journeys looking for—his Penelope, your love for him and his for you, home.

"I believe you made his life bearable, centred enough so that he could be as productive as he was—become what he had it in him to be—the

magical writer—you protected the joyful child-like person he always was
. . . I still believe he is 23 or younger—when we all first met—utterly
beguiling—in some mad white kaftan he had found. He kept that extraordinary quality of a child's humour, vision and mischief—curiosity—
qualities he very much shared with you."

Shirley Conran wrote: "Real love was what I observed between you
and Bruce, and whether or not or how it existed before between you, I observed the strength of it & the strength you gave him . . . It seems to me
that what unhappiness has gone before is minor compared to this final relationship you had . . . It would be wrong to attribute this to Bruce's physical dependence on you: but perhaps it was this dependence that enabled
him to stay still and see you for the extraordinary person that you are."

Elizabeth was and remains reluctant to assume an elevated mantle.
She was not indispensable to Bruce, she told Shirley. "He would have
found someone somewhere to look after him while he was writing, as he
certainly did while writing *On the Black Hill*. You probably don't know
that we hardly saw each other for years . . . When I got this house in September '81, he helped me move in and then fled after a week and I hardly
saw him until May '83, though he came up to London. That was the beginning of a reconciliation; we got together late on and it was only the beginning of a proper relationship."

BRUCE WAS CREMATED on 20 January in a non-denominational
chapel at the end of a rocky *cul-de-sac* with evergreen trees near Nice. His
body was taken from the hospital in an undertaker's maroon station-
waggon with a gold felt curtain at the window and appliqué stars. Elizabeth had found a young Greek Orthodox priest to officiate, who came
from refereeing a football match and rapidly changed into his vestments
which he carried in an attaché case. He chanted ancient chants and then
they all went out to lunch.

On 14 February, a memorial service was held at the Greek Cathedral
of Saint Sophia in Bayswater. Shortly before 3 p.m., to an astonished congregation, Bishop Kallistos Ware spoke of Bruce's plans to travel to Mount
Athos in September 1988, there to be baptised into the Orthodox Church.
"The rapid progress of the illness made this impossible, but God judges
our intentions, not only our deeds. In intention and desire Bruce was indeed an Orthodox Christian and that is why we are celebrating. In the funeral service we say, 'Blessed is the road on which you are travelling today.'

Bruce was always a traveller and he died before all his journeys could be completed and his journey into Orthodoxy was one of his unfinished voyages. What he did not complete in this life may he complete after death."

Apart from these words, the service was conducted in Greek. "I was surprised there were so many people," says Bishop Ware. "It was a weekday in the middle of the day and not possible to get a full choir."

The congregation reflected the range of Bruce's acquaintance. "One of the many things about that memorial service which was really striking to me," says Salman Rushdie, "was how many groups of people there were who all believed themselves to be close to Bruce—and most of them didn't know each other. It's as if all these different bits of Bruce came together in that room which he had quite deliberately kept very separate in his life." Few of them were aware of Bruce's conversion to the Greek Church.

Rushdie listened to the chanting beside Martin Amis, with Paul Theroux in the row behind. He was making his last appearance as a free man. At 10.30 that morning he had received a telephone call from a young woman reporter on BBC radio news. "How do you feel, Mr Rushdie, about the fact you've been sentenced to death by Ayatollah Khomeini?"

"Excuse me?"

"Oh, don't you know?"

She read out the *fatwa* and asked Rushdie to comment. "I've no idea what I said. I ran downstairs, shutting the windows and locking the front door." Rushdie spent the rest of the morning at the office of Gillon Aitken, the agent he shared with Bruce, avoiding camera crews. At 2.30, he was the last to arrive at Saint Sophia. "I was thinking very much about Bruce, especially as you couldn't understand a word being said. It was all in Greek, swinging censers and cantating and every now and then the words 'Bruce Chatweeeen'. Nobody said a word about Bruce in English. It was his last practical joke on all of us."

At some point in the service, Paul Theroux leaned over and said: "Well, Salman, I guess we'll be here for you next week."

"By the time we left, the world's press was outside."

A YOUNG WOMAN of the Altai region known as the "Ice Maiden" was buried 2,500 years ago in Pasyryk. Miranda Rothschild watched a television documentary about her excavation. She says: "The coffin, made of a single acacia trunk, was immensely long in order to accommodate her high, woollen and golden head-dress—deer inspired, as were her long tattooed hands. Her clothes were of wild silk and wool, and dyed red. She was encased in ice. She was a storyteller, they said.

"Of course, I thought of Bruce: how he would have been humbled, magnetised, adoring of her. Thinking of how some people seem to have considered him 'empty' and of why empty is used as a derogatory term rather than a complimentary one. He was receptive, permeable, objective: a true witness to the beautiful, the ancient, the elegant. He was permeable like a clay pot. You fill it and it becomes empty—the water drains away and leaves a residue. In retrospect, I shouldn't have been hurt when he neglected me—he had to keep filling himself up with new waters, and draining it all away by travelling along whatever track."

A fortnight after Bruce's death, Miranda wrote to Elizabeth encouraging her to stay with the Leigh Fermors in Kardamyli. "It is nearly springtime now and it is a peaceful place to go—also they are among those rare people who do not disturb one in spirit or in person, yet give a kind of comfort which is not burdensome."

ON 15 FEBRUARY, the day after the memorial service, Elizabeth flew to Greece. In accordance with his wishes, she brought Bruce's ashes to one of his favourite places: the ruined Byzantine chapel dedicated to St Nicholas in Chora. The tenth-century church, its masonry topped with battered blue and russet tiles, was reached two miles up a mountain on the Mani not far from where he had written *The Songlines*.

"You wouldn't know where the ashes are," says Paddy Leigh Fermor. Elizabeth had transported them to Kardamyli in an oak casket. He says, "The ground was too hard to bury that, so we dug a hole with the trowel under an olive tree very close to the church and put Bruce's ashes in and we poured a libation of Retsina and said a prayer in Greek: 'May the earth rest light upon him and may his memory rest eternal.' Then we had a picnic, which I think he would rather have liked.

"The place is surrounded by olive woods dropping away quite steeply and full of the most wonderful flowers in spring: anemones, wild geraniums, wild garlic, seasquills, asphodel, celandin, star of Bethlehem, graveswell. He was amazing on botany. I remember at Kardamyli somebody coming into the room and asking, 'What is that flower called?' and Bruce looking up and saying '*Magnolia grandiflora Angustifolia*'—and going on writing."

Epilogues

~~~

> *Ah, Chatwin . . . the English god.*
> —ELDERLY GREEK WAITER,
> KARDAMYLI, 1997

MARGHARITA CHATWIN told Hugh that she wanted to die before Bruce's biography was published. She went with Charles for a last journey in Italy. On 15 October 1995, the morning after returning to their mobile home in Gassin, she woke up and clasped her side: "Oh, I think I'm going to die." Her ashes were scattered outside the English church in Les Chênes-Lièges in the south of France, not an hour's drive from where Bruce died.

THE SEVENTEENTH-CENTURY CABINET, made for a Burgher of Antwerp. It had been bought by Bruce's great-grandfather, the architect-builder Julius Alfred Chatwin. Margharita stuffed it with wools, tapes, cottons, bobbins, buttons, elastics, needles and nappy pins. It had become known as The Spanish Cabinet and had always been earmarked for Bruce. "Once Margharita died, Charles regarded it as expensive junk," says Hugh. "Like Bruce, he had no interest in repossessing the past." It was sold by Phillips of Knowle, in September 1996, for £28,000, the proceeds being invested to fund a small, family gift-giving charity.

CHARLES CHATWIN had just taken delivery of his new, diminutive, single person camper van. Elizabeth was staying for Christmas in 1996. With Hugh, they drank a bottle of port together, Cockburn 1967, which Charles and Margharita had bought that year in the Douro. On Christmas Eve, while Elizabeth was at Midnight Mass, Charles was filling a hot water bottle for his lumbago when he suffered a heart attack. He was taken to Warwick Hospital. On Boxing Day, he said: "I just want to make one thing clear: where are we?" He died on 27 December. He had left his affairs in impeccable order. His last work as a lawyer had been to sort out Elizabeth's will and to arrange the Chatwin Family Charitable Trust.

LOT 165, an auction at Sotheby's in 1989: 700 pages of miscellaneous papers by Bruce Chatwin (estimate £3,000—£5,000). Bruce had given these in a rubbish sack to Justine Tomlinson, his neighbour, when leaving Holwell for the last time. On 17 July, Hugh Chatwin wrote to Bruce's agent Gillon Aitken: "Elizabeth's disbelief and mine is that Bruce would never have given away such personal and varied material as a gift to *anyone*. An over-riding consideration is that he was always so particular NOT to allow other people to lever any meaning out of his writings—other than by finished work. It was his abiding practice to destroy papers for which he had no further use." The sale went ahead. Lot 165 was sold (to Elizabeth) for £14,300, the money being used to buy Justine a violin.

THE MANUSCRIPT PAGES included notes on the Animal Style. After Bruce's death, Emma Bunker, his fellow curator of the Animal Style Exhibition in 1970, was making a trek through eastern Mongolia. "I came over a low rise and saw votive rags strung around the waist of an ancient, weather-worn statue. I had the strange sensation that Bruce might just materialise, and tell me some outrageous tit-bit of local lore."

THE PITT-RIVERS CATALOGUE, listing accessions to the Farnham Museum between 1880 and 1900, has since been found and is now in Cambridge University Library, but not yet gifted.

PETER WILSON died in Paris, 3 June 1984. Bruce had visited him a few months before. "I'm glad B. went to see him," wrote Elizabeth to Gertrude, "so they ended on a good note. They hadn't spoken for nearly 18 years & both were a bit nervous, but it was all right."

JOHN HEWETT died in 1994, STUART PIGGOTT in 1996.

FRANCIS BRADY, Elizabeth's first fiancé, died in 1987, Robert Mapplethorpe in March 1989, Donald Richards in 1990, Sebastian Walker in June 1991, Teddy Millington-Drake in 1994—all from AIDS.

AKBAR KHAN went back to Afghanistan, married an American girl and went to live with her in Shawnee, Kansas. Joyce Khan wrote to Elizabeth: "Kansas is a 9–5 prison of apt. complexes, suburban shopping centres, neighbourhood parks & decent schools. But it is so empty at our economic level . . . Akbar says we are too much affected by the six o'clock news—its media hype." Akbar's goal was "to get the hell out of here—as soon as possible" and go back to Afghanistan to help refugees. He would run a rickshaw to earn money. "We talked late into the night, arguing whether or not we, too, have journeys mapped out in our central nervous systems; it seemed the only way to account for our insane restlessness."

MA UTZ. In 1989, David Sulzberger was eating breakfast at a café in Washington. "What should I find but 'Ma Utz's home-made potato chips'. I felt it was a solution to what had happened to the old concierge."

REBECCA HOSSACK called her next show "Songlines".

THE STREHLOW COLLECTION. On 29 May 1992 government agents raided Kath Strehlow's house in Adelaide and seized books, papers and objects pertaining to Australian Aborigines. "One of the things bugging them," she says, "was my friendship with the English writer Bruce Chatwin." One of the last things Theodor Strehlow had said to his wife was that he regretted ever having had anything to do with the Aboriginals.

In Patagonia, Bruce's first book, has had a positive effect on the Welsh community in Argentina. In 1980, six years after Bruce was there, Gaiman was a dusty grid of pale red houses, two of them tea-rooms. The Welsh language was spoken by fewer than 2,000 in the region and in danger of disappearing altogether. In the burial ground at Chapel Moriah, the headstones of the founders were pitched at an angle and vandalised plastic roses lay melted under the sun. The place was sinking back into the desert.

Today, the village spreads in a new development beyond the Bethel chapel. There are seven tea-rooms, including the ranch-style "Caerdydd" which was favoured with a visit from Diana, Princess of Wales, in November 1995. Twice a week in January, a Welsh choir performs to bus loads of tourists, among them 500 Americans on a Cunard cruise down the coast. Gaiman is firmly on the map and the eight pages Bruce wrote about it are quoted on board by the lecturer on the evening the ship docks in Puerto Madryn.

In August 1998, one of the smaller Channel Islands was invaded, in the name of the King of Patagonia, by a small group led by the French novelist, and one-time Patagonian consul in France, Jean Raspail.

THE RUCKSACK, bequeathed to Werner Herzog. In the summer of 1998, Herzog went on an expedition into the Peruvian Amazon in search of an aeroplane that had crashed 27 years before. "I was booked on that flight, with eight actors, Klaus Kinski and some musicians. We were all taken off the list at the very last moment. We were totally disappointed."

The plane exploded mid-flight and 92 people died. There was one survivor, a girl. She was strapped into her seat, spinning through the sky towards the jungle, which she remembers as looking like cauliflowers. She was ten days on her own. Fortunately she was the daughter of a German biologist who had taught her the ways of the jungle. She knew that when the caymans splashed in the water there was no threat: they were running away from her. When she swam down the river to safety, she knew not to put her feet on the river bed because of sting-rays. Herzog found her in Bavaria and persuaded her to help him look for the site of the crash, which three previous expeditions had failed to locate. He put into Bruce's rucksack the fragments that they found: part of a grey plastic food tray, a woman's hair-roller, the high-heel of a shoe, a metal disc from the flight deck—and brought out of the jungle film of the girl describing her nights alone.

In 1998, paperback sales of BRUCE CHATWIN'S works in Britain exceeded one million copies. He is published in 27 languages, earning more for his estate than he was ever able to achieve in his lifetime.

BOB BRAIN'S discovery, in Bruce's presence, of the "earliest use of fire" was the cover story of *Nature* magazine in December 1988. Bruce did not live to read it.

Brain continues his search for the roots of predation. He is now digging in Namibia for microscopic fossils about 550 million years old. "Humans are a flash in the pan," he says. "We wouldn't even register on the fossil record."

Notes

∽

Abbreviations

AOR = *Anatomy of Restlessness*
CT = Colin Thubron
CW = Cary Welch
DM = Diana Melly
DR = Deborah Rogers
EC = Elizabeth Chatwin
FW = Francis Wyndham
GC = Gertrude Chanler
IF = Ivry Freyberg
IP = *In Patagonia*
JI = James Ivory
JK = John Kasmin

MB = Murray Bail
NA = *The Nomadic Alternative*
ND = no date
OTBH = *On the Black Hill*
PLF = Paddy Leigh Fermor
SH = Suzanne Hayes
SL = *The Songlines*
SP = Stuart Piggott
SS = Sunil Sethi
TM = Tom Maschler
VOO = *The Viceroy of Ouidah*
WAIDH = *What Am I Doing Here*

I: FIRE

Was he a . . . *AOR*, 161

This is a detective story . . . C. K. Brain, *The Hunters or the Hunted?: An Introduction to African Cave Taphonomy* (Chicago, 1981), 3

The most compelling . . . *SL*, 268

the most stimulating . . . BC to GC, 3.11.84

Good feeling at Swartkrans . . . BC notebooks, Box 35.2.2.84

This bone is . . . BC to GC, 3.11.84

When visiting the excavation . . . BC to CT, 9.7.87

Do I take it . . . BC to BB, July 87

the earliest use of fire . . . *Nature*, vol. 336, December 1988

Shamanism has always . . . *AOR*, 99

Aren't all true healers . . . Box 34, 1988

Man is a talking animal, a story-telling animal . . . Box 30

I hate T. E. Lawrence . . . BC to CT, taped interview June 1987.

Being an Englishman . . . *Granta 21*, 1987

To be unfindable . . . *Independent on Sunday*, 14.5.95

le tombeau vert . . . BC to Sunil Sethi, 18.6.78

a quick note . . . BC to Murray Bail, December 1984

but *mon cul* **is international** . . . Stella Wilkinson

The moment he got out . . . From "A Nomad Collector" in *Bruce Chatwin: Searching for the miraculous*, ed. Alessandro Grassi & Neri Torrigiani (Arti-Grif, Florence, 1995)

I'm at my happiest . . . BC to NS, June 1987

I fixed her . . . BC to EC, August 1970

slaves to a rare, authentic . . . James
Pope-Hennessy, *Robert Louis
Stevenson* (Jonathan Cape, 1974), 18

I've always loved . . . BC to CT, June
1987

I always feel . . . Anthony Powell,
Journals 1990–92 (Heinemann, 1997)

Nearly every writer . . . New York *Times*,
2.8.87

He wanted to *be* there . . . From "A
Nomad Collector"

II: "LET'S HAVE A CHILD," I SAID

He really is splendid . . . SP diary, 1.7.68

On the Yorkshire Moors . . . BC to CT,
June 1987

This book is written . . . Box 34

This is a strange country . . . H. E.
Chetwynd-Stapylton, *The Chetwynds
of Ingestre* (Longmans, 1892), 231

My trouble is . . . BC to DR, 25.9.87

Peter was scorning Birmingham . . .
1969, Box 34

The extraordinary thing . . . BC to
parents, 25.8.75

They are the eyes . . . *WAIDH*, 9

I adored him . . . Box 41

I like to think . . . Box 35

When people start talking . . . BBC2,
The Book Programme, 26.9.79

A swaying nipple . . . *SL*, 203

I watched the convoys . . . *AOR*, 4

the carriage door closing . . . BC to CT,
June 1987

fantastic homelessness . . . *SL*, 7

All my early recollections . . . BC to CT,
June 1987

I knew that once . . . *SL*, 7

Quite definitely a scar . . . Box 34

Long before I could read . . . Box 35

She was a tireless reader . . . *AOR*, 7

My old great-uncle . . . BC to Sarah
Bennett, 11.11.88

III: THE CABINET

The mother gives . . . *NA*, 250, Box 12

Two snippets of red and green plaid . . .
From Philip Chatwin's unpublished
essay, "Traditional Stories about the
'15 and the '45"

Richter's Anchor Blocks . . . Information
on Julius Alfred Chatwin from
Philip Chatwin's *J. A. Chatwin*
(Oxford University Press, 1952)

the *beau idéal* of the family lawyer . . .
Birmingham Daily Mail, 19
September, 1903

for grose incompitanse [sic] . . .
Information from John Crowder,
Milward's grandson

He was a friend of Richter . . . *IP*, first
edition only, 148

were of a most grave character . . .
Birmingham Daily Mail, 12
December, 1902

Dressed as a courtier . . . *AOR*, 4

All were very intrigued . . . Box 30

Bruce tells us . . . Kenneth Rose, diary

A real operator . . . BC to KR, April
1968

Every writer is a cut-purse . . . BC to
CT, June 1987

off it . . . a wild one! Mary Crowder to
BC, ND

You know how . . . BC to Uki Goni,
taped interview, 30.1.80

**Never in my life have I wanted
anything** . . . *IP*, 2

For those who . . . Box 35

things on holiday . . . Steven Mullaney,
"Strange Things, Gross Terms,
Curious Customs: The Rehearsal of
Cultures in the Late Renaissance" in
Representing the English Renaissance,
Stephen Greenblatt, ed., (University
of California Press, 1988)

If nature speaks . . . Anthony Alan
Shelton in "Cabinets of
Transgression: Renaissance
collections and the incorporation of

the New World" in *The Cultures of Collecting*, John Elsner and Roger Cardinal, ed., (Harvard University Press, 1994)

The Imperial mantle of *1125*! . . . BC to EC, July 1967

I want him . . . *Utz*, 18

a chronic restiveness . . . Werner Muensterberger, *Collecting: An Unruly Passion* (Princeton University Press, 1994)

Things are substitutes . . . Box 31

this world of little figures . . . *Utz*

IV: WAR BABY

To Freud we owe . . . Box 31

desperate attempts . . . Box 34

gazing squarely at the camera . . . *WAIDH*, 9

didn't quite belong . . . BC to CT, June 1987

He took us bicycling . . . *WAIDH*, 9

found a family . . . BC to CT, June 1987

The place I liked most . . . From "A Place to Hang Your Hat", *AOR*, 15

He said you could hear . . . BC to Valerian Freyberg, Easter 1978

Now moved to tears . . . Box 35

The house and garden . . . School prospectus, 1943

the arrival of . . . rejection *NA*, Box 12, 250–1

a small and hideous cottage . . . Box 42

This is the room . . . Box 31

a pivotal point . . . Box 41

Sam said there was . . . *OTBH*, 52

I became convinced . . . Box 41

My subsequent travels . . . Box 41

V: FROM BROTHEL TO PIGGERY

These restricted horizons . . . *OTBH*, 13

on the wrong side . . . Charles Chatwin

My bedroom window . . . *Sydney Morning Herald*, 15.1.83

The house absorbed . . . *OTBH*, 35

The absolute hideousness . . . Box 35

fairly derelict . . . CC

Old Sam had come to live . . . *OTBH*, 46

Once a year . . . BC Marlborough essay, family papers

absolute fairness . . . BC to MB, 9.2.86

Imagine the horror . . . Box 31

a buxom woman . . . *OTBH*, 58

I was a tremendous fabulist . . . Box 41

the boy who never smiled . . . From Margaret Chatwin's broadcast, "Life on the Gold Coast No 1.", *Daily Life*, ND

sad end in Africa . . . *AOR*, 4

He was his mother's darling . . . 4.10.71

One drizzly morning . . . *OTBH*, 64

golden headdress . . . *AOR*, 4

I am starting for a long journey . . . The figurine is in Box 40

VI: I KNOW WHERE I'M GOING

Old Hall, Wellington . . . BC to parents, 2.5.48, family collection

Dear Mummy, this is . . . BC to Margharita, 4.5.49

He is rather . . . Fee-Smith, summer report 1948

In a low liturgical voice . . . *OTBH*, 85

The Broad and Narrow . . . *OTBH*, 89

a hard, relentless hitter . . . *Old Hall School Record*, Lent 1951

do or die spirit . . . *Old Hall School Record*, 1951

Dear Mummy, Please . . . BC to Margharita, 23 January, ND

We had a film called . . . BC to parents, 10 October, ND

Please could you get me . . . BC to parents, 29 February [1949?]

I have just got a book . . . ND

I took a very . . . ND

Please don't send me . . . 4 February, ND

the odd ones, the Victorian ones . . . BC to CT, June 1987

one of the surrealist books . . . BC to CT

Some children obviously . . . BC to CT

sort of one's back door . . . *Washington Post*, 4.11.87

Conjuring has taken . . . BC to parents, 4 March [1951?]

I am sure he . . . Fee-Smith, report Lent 1951

On Monday I had the wacking . . . BC to parents, 3.10.50

I was awfully embarrassed . . . ND

The play is going . . . BC to parents, 10.12.50

Yesterday the fireworks . . . BC to parents, 6 November [1949?]

I enjoyed the fireworks . . . BC to parents, November, 1951

hold on to . . . Reprinted in *Old Hall School Record*, 1957–58

VII: THE ENGLISH SCHOOLBOY

he had to sell . . . Celestine Dars

Although the boys . . . Marlborough College archives

mostly ignored . . . Elaine Pyke, *The Marlburian*, 1989

They made the classics . . . Maureen Cleave, *Observer* magazine, 31.10.82

Jane Austen was . . . BC essay, family collection

the lineal descendant . . . *Portrait of a Public School*, BBC documentary, 1954

He is somewhat dreamy . . . Housemaster's report, Michaelmas 1953

I am thoroughly enjoying . . . BC parents, autumn 1953, ND

There were Roman Emperors . . . Redmond O'Hanlon, *Tatler*, May 1989

I was hopeless at school . . . ABC, 25.1.83

We are what . . . Box 41

Chatwin's Mrs Candour . . . *Wiltshire Herald and Advertiser*, 19.11.54

He has a smooth . . . Roman History report, Lent 1957

at least in the . . . Introduction to *The Road to Oxiana* (Picador, 1981)

Robert would have . . . *Fourteen Friends* (John Murray, 1996), 135

here in the first . . . Louis MacNeice, *Collected Poems*, (Faber & Faber, 1979)

forming a very vivid impression . . . *WAIDH*, 271

I always had an idea . . . BBC Radio 4, January 1989

How he longed . . . Robert Louis Stevenson, *An Inland Voyage*, At Mauberge (Falcon Press, 1949), 31

And another who . . . BC to Margharita, summer 1954, ND

chandeliers . . . Box 14

HC said I had the MAD MAD EYES . . . Box 35

snobismus . . . Peter Medawar, *Memoir of a Thinking Radish* (Oxford University Press, 1986), 4

It is fearfully select . . . *The Marlburian*, December 1957

Gentleman, I think . . . *The Marlburian*, 1989

Ripped off by taxi-driver . . . BC to parents, 2.4.57

Firstly that it is . . . BC to parents, ND

He was one . . . BC to Ivry Freyberg, 24.10.66

It was as though . . . BC to IF, 17.5.71

I had to assist Prince William . . . BC to CW, 17.5.71

Awfully nice to . . . Raulin Guild to IF, 21.7.58

Cars & character . . . Family papers

the stabilising influence . . . Housemaster's report, Michaelmas 1956

When it was decided . . . Family papers

I congratulate him . . . Housemaster's report, Lent 1958

of a train going . . . *Observer* magazine, 31.10.82

If there does happen . . . BC to Peter Wilson, 13.6.58

I was sent to Sotheby's . . . BC to Suzanne Hayes, March 1984

VIII: THE SMOOTHER BOY

You were panting . . . John Herbert, *Inside Christie's* (Hodder & Stoughton, 1990), 231

I suddenly had a horror . . . BC to Nigel Acheson, ND, 1978/9?

In a phenomenally . . . Guy Norton

Whenever there was a sale . . . *WAIDH*, 358

loitering near a Picasso . . . Susannah Clapp, *With Chatwin* (Jonathan Cape, 1996), 80

Wilson's text told stories . . . Robert Lacey, *Sotheby's Bidding for class* (Little, Brown, 1998), 97

A Syrian limestone . . . Antiquities catalogue, 12.12.60

A Bajokwe wooden . . . 12.12.60

The cataloguer's habits . . . *With Chatwin*, 88

When I was there . . . BC to CT, June 1987

like watching a young puppy . . . Judith Small

The eye is indefinable . . . Brian Sewell, *The Society of London Art Dealers 1995/6*, Yearbook, 30

with literally about ten . . . BC to Murray Bail, 1.3.85

when it is really English . . . *WAIDH*, 130

IX: THE IMPS

How long did it . . . BC to SH, Adelaide, March 1984

Why were you . . . Nigel Craig to Sarah Hunt, May 1960

There came a moment . . . BC to SH

a lot of Birmingham colonels . . . David Nash

Henry Moore is a fake . . . *Sunday Telegraph*, 22.1.89

terribly obvious . . . BC to SH

I had a marvellous morning . . . BC to CT

Had amusing time . . . BC to parents, 24.6.59

Went to Matisse chapel . . . BC to parents, 25.5.61

An average of 4 parties . . . BC to parents, 3.1.61

from a needle . . . BC to Nigel Acheson, ND, 1978/9

The talk that summer . . . From "A Nomad Collector"

a Germanic folk-tale hero . . . , From Emma Tennant's, *Girlitude: A Portrait of the 50s and 60s* (Jonathan Cape, 1999), 121

Lansberg was delighted . . . John McEwen, *Shapes on the Horizon: Teddy Millington-Drake* (London, 1996), 24

became the wretched jackdaws . . . *SL*, 124

The antique dealer was . . . *OTBH*, 220

I've always heard . . . *WAIDH*, 356

X: THE ART SMUGGLER

I suppose it's because . . . BC to John Pawson, 23.1.86

the chase, the recognition . . . *AOR*, 172

He was a split personality . . . From "A Nomad Collector"

the texture of . . . Box 34

entertaining sparely, deliciously . . .
  Christopher Gibbs, *Tatler*, October
  1982
It was terrifying to walk . . . BC to
  Murray Bail, 8.2.88
My nose bled . . . BC to parents, 29.7.59

XI: A GOÛT DE MONSTRES
The ugliest men . . . *Utz*, 91
1. When Bruce dictates . . . SG to Sarah
  Inglis-Jones, 1964
Rotting Fruit . . . Box 31
He didn't appear . . . James Crathorne
I have a *goût de monstres* . . . BC to
  James Ivory, 12.7.71
a blonde innocent . . . *WAIDH*, 168
bi-sexual since youth . . . Churchill
  medical records, 14.9.86

XII: ELIZABETH
The one truly . . . EC papers
like two warm rabbits . . . James Fox
the only truly cultured . . . *Harper's
  Bazaar*, February 1948
I am Admiral Chanler . . . BC to CW,
  ND, 1966
a volatile mixture . . . *A Pride of Lions:
  The Astor Orphans*, Lately Thomas
  (Morrow, 1971)
one of the most . . . *Evening Star*,
  25.10.37
Why didn't you . . . Hubert Chanler to
  EC, 20.8.49
Did you take . . . GC to EC, 25.9.56
She would steal . . . *OTBH*, 131
You might drop . . . Hubert Chanler to
  EC, ND, May 1957
having found that . . . EC to GC, 16.6.59
It's the most . . . EC to GC, 22.1.64
The house is heated . . . EC to GC,
  14.11.62
he is apt to . . . EC to GC, 6.9.63
I like having . . . EC to GC, 14.1.63
I wish I could . . . EC to GC, 6.9.63

so I spend . . . EC to GC, 23.10.62
Dearest Liz . . . Bufton Brady to EC,
  25.11.62
He walked ahead . . . *OTBH*, 24
They visited megalithic . . . *OTBH*, 191
I like getting mail . . . EC to GC, ND
Is it love . . . EC to Eleanor Macmillan,
  July 1964
He will live . . . SG, private collection

XIII: AFGHANISTAN
I come from . . . *Granta* 21, 1987
with its pale green . . . *WAIDH*, 135
Sotheby's sounded healthy . . . 17.8.63,
  Box 30
Yesterday afternoon confirmed . . . Box
  35
The mother is . . . 21.8.63, Box 30
To the bazaar . . . 22.8.63
Do you live . . . ND, [26.8.63?]
The most useless . . . 1.9.63
In half a minute . . . 3.9.63
On to Beirut . . . RE to mother, 8.9.63
I have refused . . . 3.9.63
Considering the very . . . RE to mother
He cannot find . . . 4.9.63
We drove with . . . BC to MC, 10.9.63
culled no doubt . . . RE to mother
an Afghan truck . . . 9.9.63
No sumptuary laws here . . . 10.9.63
From Maine to . . . BC to MC
Furiously impatient . . . 10.9.63
'Why,' we asked . . . 18.9.63
Robert is sick . . . 18.9.63
We pray that . . . 24.9.63
I wake up in . . . 17.8.64
clutching a . . . DN diary, 18.8.64
The driver was . . . 19.8.64
The whole of her . . . 22.8.64
The reservations of . . . 11.7.69, Box 34
Having been reduced . . . 25.8.64
I collected a . . . 25.8.64
We are leaving Afghanistan . . . 27.8.64

XIV: THE CHATTYS

Am given over . . . BC to CW 27.7.64

Poor thing . . . Katherine Maclean to EC, 12.8.65

He never got . . . EC to GC, 21.9.64

I felt sort . . . BC to CT

However enthusiastic . . . Box 41

Bruce Chatwin . . . *New York Times*, 21.11.64

a deafening barrister . . . BC to MB, 1.3.85

I manufactured a nervous . . . Box 41

Am rather depressed . . . BC to CW, ND

It was all . . . **at all** . . . BC to CT

Collectors, after all . . . CW to BC, 28.5.66

Things are tougher . . . *Utz*, 113

What I really . . . EC to GC, 16.1.65

I asked if I could . . . Box 31

great turning point . . . BC to CT, June 1987

women who sent . . . Box 31

He was the utter . . . BC to CT

the joy of going on and on . . . Box 31

The word homecoming . . . BC to CT

They are sensationally idle . . . *AOR*, 80

The hair would contract . . . ABC, 25.1.83

They started my . . . *Granta* 21, 1987

The Danakil journey . . . *AOR*, 110

As Rimbaud was . . . Box 10

Not entirely suitable . . . *WAIDH*, 361

Could you live . . . *OTBH*, 28

The deed is done . . . BC to IF, 8.6.65

Everything is perfectly . . . EC to GC, 22.6.65

partly because Bobby . . . GC to EC, 2.3.65

We are so pleased . . . GC to MC, 26.6.65

One thing you . . . GC to EC, 4.7.65

I do hope you . . . BC to GC, 22.6.65

We're getting married . . . BC to IG, ND

I thought I'd drown . . . EM to EC, 27.6.65

Letters are all . . . BC to EC, ND

Father Murray . . . BC to EC, 15.7.65

Am much cheered . . . 30.7.65

as one day . . . EC to GC, 29.6.65

My Dear Liz . . . 22.7.65

I hate to be trite . . . JL to EC, 9.11.65

I still think . . . MC to GC, 7.10.65

There was a . . . *WAIDH*, 26

XV: OUT OF HIS DEPTH

My career was . . . *Granta* 21, 1987

as she will be . . . MC to GC, 18.10.65

31 cents annually . . . John Chanler

Our situation is not . . . EC to GC, 17.10.65

No luck with . . . BC to GC, 23.10.65

Wilson told him . . . KR diary, 19.4.68

I've discovered there's . . . EC to GC, 28.10.65

Lady Rosse is . . . EC to GC, 24.11.65

John Hewett and . . . BC to GC, 23.10.65

We are sitting . . . BC to GC, 7.1.66

All the bluebells . . . EC to GC, ND

The main thing is . . . O'Donnell Iselin to EC, 19.4.66

He realised then . . . BC to Kasmin

I was never . . . BC to CT

I decided I didn't . . . SH, ABC, March 1984

Two days in . . . BC to JI, 8.12.69

Sotheby's name must . . . BC to EP, 30.6.60

You must tell . . . LL to EC, 29.8.66

fraudulently . . . BC to NS, 27.8.88

a nasty novel . . . CW to BC, 24.8.66

to guide Goering's *Luftwaffe* . . . Patrick Wright, *The Village that Died for England* (Jonathan Cape, 1995), 163

rather terrifying . . . Julian Pitt-Rivers

Bruce used to . . . EC to GC, April 21, ND.

an odd young . . . 7.7.68
a lady Marxist . . . *WAIDH*, 59
I now dread . . . 11.5.68
who is running . . . 3.7.68
Could you try . . . BC to EC, July 5
may well be . . . BC to EC, ND
Every plan was . . . BC to PI., 15.10.68
Reading Chatwin . . . *With Chatwin*, 42
reciting a Shakespeare . . . BC to PL
Liver pains and . . . BC to Joan Leigh
    Fermor, 30.11.71
Although Ruth . . . 16.7.68
I got very depressed . . . 9.7.68
Bruce & George went . . . 9.7.68
Nearly half way through . . . 10.7.68
When one speculated . . . *AOR*, 178
Moscow is an . . . 16.7.68
Most archaeologists interpret . . . Box 31
If an archaeologist has . . . Box 31
I began to feel . . . BC to NS
two supermale ladies . . . BC to JI,
    8.12.69
Emma is fine . . . BC to EC, ND
He is dreading . . . EC to GC, 14.7.68
His mounting contempt . . . *Tatler*,
    October 1982

XVIII: THAT WRETCHED BOOK
Wild horses . . . EC to GC, 21.3.69
Bruce went mad . . . 6.11.68
What you really . . . ABC, 25.1.83
Following their passion . . . *AOR*, 91
other forms of . . . BC to CW, 8.12.69
Mr Chatwin, an anthropologist . . .
    Foreword to *Art from East to West*,
    Bruce Chatwin, Emma Bunker, Ann
    Farkas (Asia Society, 1970)
pretty pretentious, but not bad . . . BC
    to NS, June 1987
He seemed to . . . my roots . . . Box 11
At present I . . . BC to CW, 1.2.69
the whole basis . . . *AOR*, 83
The idea is emerging . . . DR to TM,
    26.2.69
I do just want . . . TM to BC, 13.3.69

What exactly is . . . DM to TM, ND
    April 1969
The first will . . . BC to TM, 12.5.69
As I said . . . TM to DR, 2.5.69
The argument, roughly . . . *AOR*, 12
a nebulous no-man . . . Box 31
It was so much . . . BC to NS
His interest became . . . Ifan Kyrle
    Fletcher, "Ronald Firbank: A
    Memoir" (London, 1930), reprinted
    in Mervyn Horder (ed.), *Ronald
    Firbank: Memoirs and Critiques*
    (Duckworth, 1977), 3–5
In a moment of . . . BC to JI, 8.12.69
the kind of topographical . . . PL
    proposal, ND, Burns Library
Peter Levi is . . . EC to GC, 4.6.69
I've never felt . . . BC to GC, 4.10.67
Christie's are crazy . . . EC to GC,
    6.11.68
He found the pair . . . 25.9.67
for which he . . . 30.6.68
I hate having . . . 21.4.68
Where is the face . . . BC to CT
They are, if the . . . Box 35
The Times . . . 5.8.71
No spectacle . . . BC to JI, 12.8.71
odd little incident . . . *The Light Garden
    of the Angel King* (Collins, 1972), 36
A refreshing spot . . . 7.7.69, Box 35
We looked and . . . *LGAK*, 63
the moment of sitting . . . Box 35
A Crested lark . . . Box 35
It will be obvious . . . *LGAK*, 15
drove me wild . . . BC to EC, 14.9.72
Peter is being . . . Box 35
It was one . . . BC to NS
I declared loftily . . . *LGAK*, 133
Bruce had mild . . . *LGAK*, 72
small, elfin, mischievous . . . Box 35
I am always moved . . . Box 30
Officer in charge . . . Box 35
an ecstatic dance . . . Box 35
One cannot adequately . . . Box 30
Bruce has been . . . PL journal
The main question . . . Box 35

I hope he'll be . . . 2.4.71
Saw the Qashgais . . . BC to CW, 17.5.71
But with very truble . . . Akbar to EC, 4.5.71
Miranda is really . . . EC to GC, 28.5.71
Rang up Miranda . . . EC to GC, 5.7.71
Elizabeth's young Pakistani . . . BC to CW, 17.5.71
You must try . . . BC to IF, October, 1966
quite broken . . . BC to JI, ND, May 1971
The weather is so . . . BC to CW, 11.6.71
It's quite beautiful . . . BC to EC, 22.6.71
I do badly . . . BC to JI, 12.7.71
Also on the path . . . CW to BC, 28.5.66
to try and finish . . . EC to GC, 5.7.71
Never never never . . . BC to JI, 2.8.71
I have in the rough . . . 12.7.71
That Andrew story . . . ND, 1972
That really is worth a filum . . . 12.8.71
Once I'm through . . . 15.9.71
ACTION in film . . . ND, 1971
Perhaps I could go . . . 12.7.71
with a car *plus* another typewriter . . . BC to EC, ND, June 1971
a great expert on birdsong . . . BC to JI, 12.7.71
Very unusual for . . . 12.7.71

XX: DELIVERANCE
Bruce came in . . . James Lees-Milne, *A Mingled Measure: Diaries, 1953–72* (John Murray, 1994), 135
the husband who . . . Box 31
I spend the week . . . BC to JI, 21.5.70
Found myself lecturing . . . Unpublished diary, 1.8.80
I'm so broke . . . EC to GC, 29.1.72
Dear Max, well here . . . EC to BC, 4.7.75
I have just read . . . BC to JI, ND, autumn 1971

Bruce Chatwyn [*sic*] is . . . Jonathan Cape Archives, 23.3.70
Yesterday the phone . . . BC to JI, ND
At the moment . . . EC to GC, 4.11.71
rather disgruntled . . . BC to CW, December 1971
I am at my lowest ebb . . . December 1971
Feeling very Beau Geste . . . BC to EC, ND, January 1972
At the moment . . . BC to EC, 5.2.72
Bruce has been talking . . . EC to GC, 3.6.72
Most aesthetic market . . . BC to EC, ND
a language which . . . BC to JI, ND, 1972
Jeudi, Tahoua, Niger . . . Box 34
Have just returned . . . BC to EC, 2.2.72
I have started writing . . . 2.2.72
Don't know why . . . BC to EC, ND
I have a moustache . . . BC to JI, ND [March?] 1972
I always think . . . BC to parents, 30.8.72
I have been mouldering . . . BC to JI, 8.4.72
I'm sorry I left . . . 30.8.72
There is a canoe . . . 30.8.72
The Book is . . . BC to EC, 28.8.72
I hope he'll get . . . EC to GC, 1.9.72
one of the most unpleasant . . . BC to EC, 14.9.72
I am convinced . . . 13.3.69
The best travellers . . . *NA*, Box 12
The style alone . . . *SL*, 266

XXI: THE JOURNALIST
PHONE HOPELESS . . . 1973, Box 35
The idea of a job . . . BC to EC, 28.8.72
a colossal inspiration . . . ABC, 11.5.83
I felt that for writing . . . BC to CT
The *Sunday Times* things . . . EC to GC, 29.10.72
Journalism does help . . . ABC, 11.5.83

The feeling as one . . . Philip Norman, unpublished article

articulated pipe-cleaners . . . *Everyone's Gone to the Moon* (Hutchinson, 1995), 15

If a thing's worth doing . . . *EGTTM*, 59

We have frequently . . . *Sunday Times* magazine, 26.8.72

They've lost all . . . *EGTTM*, 205

le corset, c'est une . . . *WAIDH*, 89

The interior is as . . . *WAIDH*, 87

in a bedroom which . . . *Sunday Times* magazine, 4.3.73

There was never any . . . BC to CT

a man of about 40 . . . *EGTTM*, 68

barbed observation . . . PN, op. cit.

We soon forgot . . . *AOR*, 13

The *Sunday Times* still . . . EC to GC, 28.12.72

the mad Greek . . . *WAIDH*, 154

I fear I intended . . . Box 34

encouraged, criticised, edited . . . *AOR*, 13

I'm always seeing things . . . BC to CT

No whiches, thats and whos . . . Box 35

The rumours were true . . . *Utz*, 24

His eyes are a . . . *WAIDH*, 297

An observed detail . . . *New Yorker*, 23.6.87

In interview, he . . . *WAIDH*, 261

the interview was . . . *WAIDH*, 323

In answer to questions . . . *WAIDH*, 314

He was extremely nasty . . . BC to Sunil Sethi, 26.7.78

Personally, I would . . . PN, op. cit.

one of the most . . . *WAIDH*, 114

Malraux was there . . . February 1970, Box 34

In Lawrence's career . . . *WAIDH*, 122

adventurers of . . . *TLS*, 16.6.89

I do not want to . . . BC to EC, 6.9.78

I go through . . . *WAIDH*, 329

Bruce, you have . . . BC to CT

the 23-yr-old whizz-kid . . . BC to Nigel Acheson, 25.8.78

an exhilarating companion . . . *WAIDH*, 333

A bitch to write . . . BC to parents, ND, 1978

She's far worse . . . BC to CW, 21.5.78

The copy came back . . . BC to SS, 18.6.78

Resolution of the month . . . 18.6.78

Quotation of the Month . . . 18.6.78

XXII: "GONE TO PATAGONIA"

I have done . . . BC to FW, 11.12.74

the most enjoyable . . . BC to EG, 21.12.72

Allez-y pour moi . . . Peter Adam, *Not Drowning but Waving* (André Deutsch, 1995), 353

anyone would be . . . BC to CT

She said that Bruce . . . MC to EC, 4.2.75

Charles Milward's life . . . Box 35

I like my cousins . . . BC to EC, 12.12.74

It was like . . . ABC, 14.3.84

In all their minds . . . Box 35

Buenos Aires is . . . BC to EC, December 1974, ND

Here am I . . . Box 31

Last night dreamt . . . In museum, Trelew

Whether it is the . . . Tom Jones, *A Patagonian Panorama* (The Outspoken Press, 1961)

The further one . . . Box 31

I always try . . . *The South Bank Show*, September 1982

absolute constant . . . BC to UG, 1980

His lack of roots . . . Notice in Harberton

My business was . . . BC to Millicent Jane Saunders, 27.9.79

I'm not interested . . . ABC, 14.3.84

you could imagine . . . IP, 28

rolled off her tongue . . . IP.60

England in full . . . Box 35

spending nights in . . . Box 6

Dying of tiredness . . . BC to EC. 21.1.74
Difficulties of Patagonia . . . Box 35
Basically, God is . . . Box 35
Tourists always wave . . . Box 35
Day of disasters . . . Box 35
the tragedy of . . . Box 35
N.G. sounded . . . Box 35
live in a . . . Box 35
Mother remained on . . . MB to BC,
   28.11.77, Box 6
He was German . . . BC to CC. 15.3.75
a foppish man . . . Box 31
Said they were . . . Box 35
When the war . . . *Magellan Times*,
   12.12.28
We met this . . . Judith Jesser, ND 1975
On a wet and . . . 2.3.75
I tried to picture . . . IP, 181

XXIII: I DON'T KNOW WHAT
YOU'LL MAKE OF IT
stuffy as all hell . . . BC to EC, 7.6.75
It is slightly . . . 7.6.75
I'm sorry I'm . . . BC to parents, 25.8.75
I don't want . . . 11.12.74
I am going . . . 25.8.75
not quite sure . . . EC to GC, 25.10.75
The fatal thing . . . BC to UG 30.1.80
Like old lacquer . . . *Tatler*, October
   1982
Writing is the painting . . . Box 34
his splashed ink . . . Box 30
the essence of . . . Introduction to *John
   Pawson* (Gustavo Gili, 1992)
whittles his possessions . . . Box 12
One of his obvious . . . Gregor von
   Rezzori, *Anecdotage* (Farrar Straus,
   1996), 41
This *is* very extraordinary . . . 11.8.76
To my immense . . . BC to Gerald
   Brenan
I'm chicken about reviews . . . ABC,
   25.1.83
It is rare indeed . . . TM to BC, 25.10.77

It's an athlete's book . . . Harold Beaven,
   ND
without writing to . . . PLF to BC,
   18.1.78
in a state of emotion . . . JR to BC,
   5.6.79
My problem with . . . GS to TM, 13.9.77
Perhaps none of them . . . FW to BC,
   25.10.77
Don't flap too . . . BC to KM, ND,
   [1979?]
peculiarly dotty book . . . BC to DR,
   1.12.77
the FORM of . . . BC to CW, 5.11.77
in poetry, but more . . . BC to SS,
   26.7.78
For what it's worth . . . BC to CB,
   14.4.79
VERY VERY slowly . . . CW to BC,
   19.10.77
He spent many . . . Charles Milward,
   Journals, 182
I once made . . . *Granta 21*, 1987
on a cursory glance . . . Box 35
how he was . . . Oswaldo Beyer,
   Introduction to *Memorias del Uno
   Carrero Patagonico*, by Asencio
   Abeijon (Editorial Universitaria de
   La Patagonia, 1994)
I have always . . . BC to JZ, 16.6.83
set up on . . . Journals, 199
a worthy recognition . . . CC to BC,
   17.10.77
Surely it cannot . . . MB to BC, 28.11.77
If I am in . . . BC to MB, 10.6.78
With little exaggeration . . . Manfred
   Pfister, "Bruce Chatwin and the
   Postmodernization of the
   Travelogue", *LIT*, Vol 7, 1996,
   253–267

XXIV: "KICKED BY AMAZON"
He operated several . . . Box 35
How much did it . . . ABC, 8.5.84

They were mostly elderly . . . Fawn Brodie, *The Devil Drives: a life of Sir Richard Burton* (Eland, 1987), 213

Do descend if . . . BO to BC, ND

wandering among . . . Box 31

half open . . . SH, Adelaide, March 1984

le tabac est le produit . . . Pierre Verger, *Flux et Reflux de la traite des Nègres entre le Golfe de Bénin et Bahia de Todos os Santos, du XVII au XIX siécle* (Mouton, 1968), 30

a magic nose . . . Hugh Thomas, *The Slave Trade: the history of the Atlantic slave trade 1440–1870* (Picador, 1997), 354

After staging a . . . *WAIDA*, 136

This town, an old . . . BC to parents, February 1972

as thick as . . . *The Slave Trade*, 356

that most resembled . . . A. B. Ellis, *The Land of Fetish*, 1883

Whenever a woman . . . Joseph Skertchley, *Dahomey As It Is*, 1874, 458

A man came in . . . Box 23

He was a tall man . . . *VOO*, Preface

The story is wonderful . . . BC to EC, 29.12.76

quite exhausting . . . BC to EC, 14.1.77

One or two . . . 14.1.77

his self-discipline . . . Keith Nicolson Price, unpublished memoir

the allure of otherness . . . *TLS*, 31.7.98

I met the famous . . . BC to EC, 14.1.77

a French scholar . . . *Sunday Times*, 29.1.77

story . . . *WAIDH*, vii

Sunday morning began . . . Box 35

the badge of a mercenary . . . ABC, 14.3.84

Amazon . . . *Granta 10*, 1984

In one little country . . . James Lees-Milne, 3.2.78

XXV: BRAZIL

I want to forget . . . Box 34

Will walk off . . . Box 35

the cat-like figures . . . Box 35

infinitely alluring . . . 16.2.70, Box 34

solitary wanderings . . . *VOO*, 56

unburden his load . . . 57

cowed and lacking . . . BC to FW, 10.3.77

I want more . . . February 1972, Box 34

The architecture is wonderful . . . BC to JK, 7.3.77

a world where . . . *TLS*, 31.7.98

the 'daughters of the god' . . . BC to JK, 7.3.77

Her shoulders shuddered . . . *VOO*, 81

He came in off . . . Box 35

His green eyes . . . *VOO*, 63

The lineaments of . . . 64

yet he could . . . 57

I have to say . . . BC to JK, 7.3.77

I am heartily sick of it . . . BC to EC, 7.3.77

Everything's gone wrong! . . . BC to JK, 7.3.77

unstuck for me . . . BC to Belinda Foster, 9.3.77

the de Souza's are . . . BC to JK, 7.3.77

None of the black . . . BC to EC, 7.3.77

who was sold . . . BC to EC, 7.3.77

the terror of Brazilian life . . . Box 35

What to make . . . Journal, Box 35

know such expressions . . . Pierre Verger, *Les affaires Americains*, 1954

vaguely second-rate . . . Box 35

The Director wishes . . . Box 35

the Brazilian secret police . . . *SL*, 180

with a neat arrow-head . . . Box 35

I'm not entirely sure . . . BC to NA, 25.8.78

One with sub-machine . . . Box 35

XXVI: NEW YORK

The Greeks . . . *Granta 21*, 1987

Like the evolution . . . Walker Books, 1980

Cats have personalities . . . Walker Books, 1980

I can't think . . . BC to CW, 5.11.77

Talked to DR . . . 1.5.80, Box 35

I do love the borders . . . DR to BC, ND

Such a monumental . . . BC to SS, 18.6.78

is Australian . . . BC to SS, 26.7.78

England more depressing . . . 9.12.78, Box 35

Two friends of ours . . . EC to GC, 17.6.78

The dandy confronts . . . Introduction to *On the Marble Cliffs* (Penguin, 1969)

DR easing up . . . Box 35

committed every outrage . . . *AOR*, 85

They dressed up as women . . . Patricia Morrisroe, *Mapplethorpe* (Random House, 1995), 201

by far the best essay . . . *TLS*, 14.2.97

a black bedroom . . . "An Eye and Some Body" in *Lady Lisa Lyon* (St Martin Press, 1993), 9–14

I really don't . . . Box 35

Maybe it was . . . *TLS*, 14.2.97

By pushing back . . . *NDBW*, 499

the image of people . . . SW to Colin Thubron

As if to purge himself . . . Box 35

the pleasures of pain . . . Box 35

I live with that . . . *SL*, 147

On Monday, stuck . . . BC to SS, 18.6.78

Reviews from U.S. . . . BC to EC, 12.9.78

Who knows . . . BC to MC, 17.8.78

my mother's namesake . . . Chanler Chapman to GC, ND

Ushered into a . . . Box 35

The BIG NEWS . . . BC to EC. 16.2.79

Paul Theroux . . . BC to SS, 29.4.80

Called at 1040 . . . Box 35

Was it John . . . Box 35

Dear Maxine . . . BC to EC, 16.2.79

All our encounters . . . CW to BC, 19.10.77

Bruce loved to . . . JI to NS, 22.10.98

XXVII: OH, MAIS C'EST DU FLAUBERT!

He felt a slight . . . Draft of "November", EC collection

I wanted to . . . SH, Adelaide, March 1984

this mythical beast . . . BC to JK, 27.1.86

I think I'll sit . . . BC to JK, 7.3.77

As you know . . . BC to EC, 14.1.77

the state of hysteria . . . BC to JK, 1.10.77

wherever I go . . . BC to NA, ND [1979?]

I just pace up . . . BC to Peter Eyre

At the end . . . Box 34

Those of us . . . *AOR*, 22

It's not far . . . EC to GC, 29.5.77

The whole of . . . BC to EC, 24.10.77

Flat is exactly what I wanted . . . BC to JK, 1.10.77

cosy reading corners . . . JK diary

He was a cuckoo . . . *Shapes on the Horizon*, 122

This is better . . . BC to FW, 20.10.77

I know exactly . . . BC to EC, 11.3.77

I had thought . . . BC to CW, 5.11.77

Kas mentioned to me . . . TM to BC, 5.12.77

At its best . . . TM to BC, 16.1.78

The greatest master . . . SH, Adelaide, March 1984

I am *very* serious . . . ND

As an Englishman . . . BC to NS, June 1987

the Flaubertian *conte* . . . BC to KM, [1979?]

how to string . . . BC to Margharita, 17.8.78

At all costs . . . BC to BB, ND

A trick I learned . . . BC to NS, 27 August, 1988

One quite useful . . . BC to NS

an exquisite neo-Classical . . . BC to SS, 26.7.78

Ow! the strains . . . BC to FW, 2.9.78

Five hours of . . . BC to SS, June 1978

I have a huge . . . BC to EC, 6.9.78

Apparently when . . . BC to EC, 12.9.78

Xannikins has gone . . . BC to EC, 16.9.78

Bruce came in . . . 10.8.79

A house is . . . Box 35

Everyone, in . . . BC to JP, 23.1.86

I think we'd better . . . BC to GB, 26.8.76

As one gets older . . . BC to EC, July 1970

Patmos is the most . . . BC to EC, 30.8.70

She insisted on . . . FW to TLS, 21.5.99

The strain of living . . . VOO, 55

she carried her devotion . . . OTBH, 153

I simply can't begin . . . BC to EC, 6.9.78

I left England . . . BC to JK, 7.9.78

the ugliest little . . . EC to GC, 10.11.78

I have to say . . . BC to EC, 16.2.79

XXVIII: BORDER COUNTRY

NO LIVING WRITER'S . . . TM to BC, 23.10.80

bemusement of reviewers . . . WAIDH, 138

It's very good . . . GB to DR, 3.12.79

I had the distinct . . . TLS 14.2.97

on a pair of Welsh . . . BC to SS, 29.4.80

No man can . . . SH, Adelaide, March 1984

a penny a pound too much . . . Paths of Progress: A History of Marlborough College, Thomas Hinde (James & James, 1992), 189

We set off . . . 25.7.55, Marlborough College archive

I remember Penelope . . . Independent, 14.5.87

She was a . . . OTBH, 219

I think she was . . . EC to Michael Cottrill, 1989

The loss is hardly . . . BC to MC, July 1986

The story she told . . . BC to Graham C. Greene, 8.6.82

Two or three . . . David Plante, "The Restlessness of Bruce Chatwin" in Bruce Chatwin: Searching for the miraculous.

It was a squint at the nineteenth . . . ABC, 8.5.84

musty masculine smell . . . Box 35

exactly like the . . . Box 35

air of saintly detachment . . . Box 35

They went to . . . mad Box 35

We never went . . . SH, Adelaide, March 1984

The two brothers . . . Box 35

which of course . . . BC to Murray Bail, 23.10.83

I look forward . . . ND

were pretty gay . . . TLS, 14.2.97

Novel is of incest . . . Box 35

Some of the details . . . SH, Adelaide, March 1984

when I went . . . BC to FW, ND 1981

For example, you . . . SH, Adelaide, March 1984

Another coincidence . . . RZ to BC, 28.3.85

Before the War . . . BC to GCG, 8.6.82

The dogs howled . . . Box 35

I hope 'e comes . . . Box 35

I don't see . . . The South Bank Show

a lovely place . . . BC to EC, 25.10.83

believed, seriously, the road . . . OTBH, 90

When someone else . . . Esquire, October 1990

Bruce rings up . . . EC to GC, 24.4.81

a sort of 'monastery' . . . BC to MW, 27.4.81

When Bruce Chatwin . . . From "A
   Nomad Collector"
I could see . . . *Anecdotage*, 246
a place where . . . *AOR*, 26
One morning she . . . *Anecdotage*, 35
I think it an . . . TM to Fred Gibb,
   17.6.82
Bruce will be . . . Rupert Lancaster, ND
Reluctantly I began . . . 19.12.82
Some good . . . EC to GC, 3.10.82
general herbaceousness . . . Karl Miller,
   Doubles: Studies in Literary History
   (Oxford University Press, 1985),
   402–9
WITHOUT MY PERMISSION . . . BC
   to GCG
There's very . . . ABC, 8.5.84
You meet her . . . Box 35

XXIX: A JUDICIAL SEPARATION
Lunch with Elizabeth . . . Box 35
frantically looking . . . EC to GC,
   24.4.81
Bruce is v. busy . . . 15.5.80
there is a gap . . . EC to BC, ND
E seems to . . . BC to MW, 27.4.81
It's much better . . . EC to GC, 16.8.81
Spent a week . . . BC to parents, 22.9.81
Some of what . . . C-T to BC, 15.12.80
I realised, battling . . . BC to parents,
   7.11.81
The trouble with . . . BC to parents,
   7.2.82
Coughing of a leopard . . . Box 33
I do think . . . GC to EC, 6.4.82
I suggested that . . . BC to Jorge
   Zavaleta, 16.6.83
Bruce is in . . . EC to GC, 12.7.82
I have to man . . . 5.8.82
But don't say . . . 10.11.82
I'm so sorry . . . 6.9.82
Thank you for . . . SB to BC, 17.9.83

XXX: AUSTRALIA
Shanghai! Montevideo! . . . *The Moor's
   Last Sigh* (Jonathan Cape, 1994), 382
my tremendous difficulty . . . BC to EC,
   12.1.83
With so many . . . BC to parents, 12.1.83
I'm glad he's . . . EC to GC, 3.1.83
I am turning . . . BC to RR, 25.6.82
a mindless time . . . ABC, 23.1.83
The reviews such . . . BC to EC, 12.1.83
Good for Sir Victor! . . . BC to FW,
   11.1.83
Can I speak . . . Box 35
constantly being jolted . . . ABC, 25.1.83
concierge of Brigitte Bardot . . . ABC,
   12.8.87
beautiful, resilient and resourceful . . .
   ABC, 25.1.83
She, as you . . . BC to parents, 12.1.83
It was absolutely . . . BC to DM, 1.3.83
The sky is so . . . BC to DR, 23.1.83
sustained meditation . . . ABC, 12.8.87
indeed perhaps the reason . . . BC to
   Elisabeth Sifton, 7.2.83
ancient and traditional . . . TS,
   Australian Aboriginal Songs, 1955
It is a 20th century . . . BC to KS,
   24.8.83
was a real . . . BC to Anne-Marie
   Mykyta, 26.11.84
Sometimes, when . . . BC to KS, August
   1983
Things never seen . . . Box 35
I sat down . . . BC to CT
A man set out . . . Epilogue, *El Hacedor*,
   1960
vastly grander . . . comparison ABC,
   11.5.83
When you confronted . . . BC to CT
At last! I've . . . BC to EC, 28.9.83
So you're a . . . *SL*, 91
good-looking in . . . *SL*, 46
A good deal . . . Box 35
Whether it happened . . . ABC, 12.8.87
For myself, I . . . *SL*, 116
So what was . . . *SL*, 112

Never have I caught . . . BC to PVM, 8.1.84

Then she strolled . . . *SL*, 112

They were two . . . 316

XXXI: THE BAT CAVE

Tous les anglais . . . Box 34

hideous food poisoning . . . BC to DR, 18.4.83

I am terribly sorry . . . BC to PVM, 8.1.84

flat, dried-out, alienated . . . BC to DR, 18.4.83

XXXII: AN HOUR WITH BRUCE CHATWIN

Everyone—especially . . . Box 35

We walked off and . . . EC to GC, 3.6.83

He's having a bad . . . EC to GC, 12.11.84

I come from . . . Obituary, Radio 4, January 1989

I made the experiment . . . Box 35

To understand human . . . ABC, 8.5.84

A few years ago . . . BC to parents, February 1982

the point where . . . ABC, 8.5.84

should be given . . . BC to FW, 19.2.84

a man of infinite gentleness . . . Box 35

which appeared . . . Box 35

Black mood . . . Box 35

There is a point . . . ABC, 8.5.84

Australia, I find . . . BC to MB, 20.10.83

Aboriginal Australia . . . BC to MB, ND

What do you . . . BC to PVM, 8.1.84

Thinking of you . . . BC to Lydia Livingstone, [January?] 1984

They wrote to me . . . BC to MB, 20.10.83

I agree with you . . . BC to MB, 11.12.87

his sincere disgust . . . TLS, 16.6.89

There have been . . . BC to MB, 8.2.88

I'm fed up . . . BC to A-MM, ND

Llosa and I . . . BC to MB, 20.10.83

I said (realising . . . BC to MB, 20.10.83

Bruce, Salman Rushdie . . . GB to PVM, March 1984

He left his wife . . . BC to ND, 1.11.84

The spirit of generosity . . . Box 35

The craziest thing . . . BC to CT

SR kept audience . . . Box 35

I still cannot . . . Box 35

Mrs Houston worked . . . *SL*, 288

XXXIII: A SINCERE FUMBLING

It is ironic . . . BC to JP, February 1986

I'm longing . . . JC to BC, 24.3.84

The novel, if such . . . BC to MB, 20.10.83

I assume it *is* the . . . TM to BC, 4.2.85

Should we say . . . BC to TM, 1.3.85

The book is not . . . BC to ND, 6.3.86

soupy pre-Fascist . . . BC to MB, 4.6.83

Without wanting to . . . BC to MB, 1.3.85

I'm only capable . . . BC to MB, 11.3.86

this promenade-deck . . . BC to MB, ND

This a.m. there . . . EC to GC, 23.8.84

This peripatetic existence . . . BC to JK, 17.2.86

and needed clearance . . . EC to GC, December 1984

the most beautiful . . . BC to DM, 30.1.85

I've put a block . . . BC to MB, 1.3.85

I have a room . . . BC to MB, 1.3.85

a really good egg! . . . BC to ND, 1.11.84

It's ambitious, difficult . . . 24.8.84

I feel I must . . . BC to MB, December [1984?]

A disaster with . . . BC to PT, 2.7.84

Although Bruce's mind . . . From "A Nomad Collector"

It would be terrific . . . BC to MB, 1.3.85

The whole Taygetus . . . BC to EC, 30.8.70

weathered and faded . . . *A Time of Gifts* (John Murray, 1977), 23

Abstruse art-forms . . . *Spectator*, 18.2.89

Up behind Kardamyli . . . BC to DM, 30.1.85

crackpot theory . . . BBC2, *The Book Programme*, 26.9.79

is not simply . . . *WAIDH*, 139

To saunter . . . David Plante, "The Restlessness of Bruce Chatwin"

a hollow-chested figure . . . *OTBH*, 17

Nothing can be more . . . Box 12

Compression is what's . . . BC to PLF, August 1985

XXXIV: THERE IS A GOD

And I will be . . . Robert Byron, *The Station*, Duckworth, 1928, 143

"Golden Boy" . . . *Anecdotage*, 85

To anyone who . . . *The Station*, 148

his entrenched aesthetic . . . *Fourteen Friends*

No, Bruce, I said . . . 1.8.80

My whole life . . . BC to MB, April 1985

Athos is obviously . . . *WAIDH*, 282

Some form of religion . . . Box 34

The search for . . . Box 35

religion is a technique . . . Box 31

in the Greek . . . Box 35

Paddy says . . . Box 34

a sweet freckle-faced novice . . . Box 34

There must be a God . . . Box 34

XXXV: INDIA

Catarrh started in . . . BC to DR, 27.7.85

I went wind-surfing . . . BC to PLF, August 1985

The house we were . . . BC to parents, 1.2.86

My biggest worry . . . EC to GC, 8.12.85

The house, it turned out . . . BC to parents, 1.2.86

The palace in Jodhpur . . . BC to parents, 1.2.86

The first stab . . . BC to JK, 27.1.86

Murray was a . . . BC to JK, 27.1.86

the maharanee choked . . . BC to parents, 1.2.86

almost to the day . . . BC to MB, 9.2.86

He is the 'identical twin' . . . BC to DM, 15.2.86

I did my usual babble . . . BC to parents, 1.2.86

One is so well . . . BC to SS, 5.3.86

A cool blue study . . . BC to JK, 27.1.86

I've not seen her . . . BC to DM, 15.2.86

I adore it here . . . BC to JK, 17.2.86

Well, I have to . . . BC to the Bails, 9.2.86

I've had a terrible . . . BC to RC, 18.2.86

I've decided the . . . BC to PLF, ND

Old English tea . . . BC to JK, ND

On the mountain above . . . BC to EC, 27.3.86

What was this? . . . Box 31

Felt dazed . . . Box 31

XXXVI: AN AI MEDICAL CURIOSITY

On the way back . . . EC to GC, 4.8.86

allergy to dust . . . EC to GC, February 1986

He can only go . . . EC to GC, 4.8.86

I put this into . . . *The Times*, 20.1.89

which to all the publishers . . . BC to MB, 3.11.86

I'm going to . . . BC to CT

thinking that a . . . BC to MB, 3.11.86

He was in . . . Medical records

The fact is I . . . BC to MB, 30.11.86

definite glimpse of . . . Matthew Spender, *Within Tuscany* (Viking, 1992), 159

I saw green-capped . . . BC to NS

the occasional inappropriate . . . Medical records, 12.9.86

the self is all . . . BC to MB, 3.11.86

One point cannot . . . Letter to *LRB*, summer 1988

has previously only . . . 27.2.87

an extremely rare . . . BC to ND, 17.10.86

an A1 medical curiosity . . . BC to MB, 3.11.86

In the summer . . . BC to CW, 12.12.86

My illness was . . . 12.12.86

XXXVII: THE HARLEQUIN

Where in your . . . *Granta 21*, 1987

self-styled great lover . . . BC to EC, June 1967

I had thought . . . BC to CW, 22.2.88

You know that . . . Dr Rudolf Just to KF, 9.2.67

Under the heading . . . *Utz*, 32

Rudolf's treasures . . . *Utz*, 13

The shelves were . . . *Utz*, 49

the arch improvisor . . . *Utz*, 114

No idea of . . . BC to TM, March 1988

Ja! Ja! . . . *Utz*, 46

a man's relation . . . Box 35

on the bourgeoisie . . . Georges Borchardt to DR, 12.3.79

I'm riveted by . . . BC to A-MM, ND, 26.11.84

Hoffmann-like tale . . . BC to CW, 12.12.86

My legs . . . are BC to ND, 19.1.87

it was a city . . . *Utz*, 119

Smells of dustbins . . . Box 35

Cellini, Montezuma, Noah . . . C. Holdefer, "The Spoils of Utz" in *Bruce Chatwin*, Claudine Verley, ed., *Les Cahiers Forell 4*. (Poitiers, 1994), 68

names that meant . . . *Utz*, 92

Wry, evocative, sensitive . . . *Private Eye*, October 1988

By April . . . *Utz*, 88—9

there was never . . . *Utz*, 138

Plagues and wars do . . . Andrew Sullivan, *Love Undetectable* (Chatto, 1998)

And from that hour . . . *Utz*, 152

Elizabeth is being marvellous . . . BC, 17.10.86

Have been giving . . . EC to GC, 25.2.87

Elizabeth and I . . . BC to EC, 6.5.88

XXXVIII: A COSMIC BOOK

Are you a traveller . . . ABC, 14.3.84

the Cyclades Islands . . . ABC, 11.5.83

Look at the greatest . . . ABC, 11.5.83

The journey it describes . . . 8.2.88

Not many authors . . . TM to GA, 5.2.88

Reading your *Songlines* . . . SH to BC, 23.11.88

If there is one . . . Stewart Harris, *The Myth of Primitivism* (Routledge, Keegan & Paul, 1991)

One wonders where . . . PW to TM, ND

It's a low, rather . . . BC to NS, June 1987

Because to pass off . . . "Gentleman of the Road", *El Pais*, 26.9.93

the burden he's been carrying . . . *Observer*, 19.11.89

There are masses . . . BC to ND, 19.1.87

in semi-hallucination . . . BC to CW, 22.2.88

All in all *The Songlines* . . . BC to C & BT, 14.7.87

You called what . . . TM to BC, 13.10.86

XXXIX: MY INEXPLICABLE FEVER

I apologize that . . . Medical records, 7.7.87

He has no side . . . ND [July?] 1987

'remarkable' improvement . . . 7.7.87

Jasper thought it . . . BC to SC, ND

would appear to . . . Box 35

Je vais vous . . . BC to RC, 20.2.87

This poses problems . . . Medical records, 17.3.87

A wheelchair will . . . *WAIDH*, 141

He's really awfully . . . EC to GC,
18.5.87

Then to Prague . . . EC to GC, 30.5.87

I *am* sorry . . . BC to GO, 7.8.87

Then . . . ? Madrid? . . . BC to MB, ND

There's something about . . . BC to GG,
20.9.87

febrile illness . . . Medical records,
February 1988

I fear that all . . . 24.11.87

We went first . . . BC to MB, 8.2.88

highly suspicious . . . Medical records,
25.2.88

Suppose that I . . . Gillian Rose, *Love's
Work* (Vintage, 1997), 70

I've been on . . . BC to NS, June 1987

AIDS and the prowling . . . *Guardian*,
"When sex becomes sin", 1.12.89

With AIDS came also . . . *NDBW*, 497

his impenetrable aura . . . 417

There was a kind . . . 416

The first news is . . . BC to EP, 29.2.88

Still convinced that . . . Medical records,
13.6.88

Last night Sister Patterson . . . Box 34

That's it . . . Box 34

Perhaps this will be . . . TM to BC

The heart is there . . . *NDBW*, 414

I can honestly say . . . RH to GC,
23.1.89

Can I take a . . . BC to BB, ND

sapphire-blue visionary's . . . *Anecdotage*,
33

manic depression . . . GC to EC

Ma, I have very . . . JC to GC, ND

Profound loss of walking . . . Medical
records, 10.6.88

I am entirely paralysed . . . Charles
Nicholl, *Somebody Else: Arthur
Rimbaud in Africa, 1880–91*
(Jonathan Cape, 1997)

makes himself a seer . . . Kay Redfield
Jamison, *Touched with Fire*
(Macmillan, 1993), 110.

incoherent prophecies . . . *VOO*, 119

a kind of Middle . . . BC to MB, 11.12.87

He spread out . . . Box 30

What I've kept . . . SH, Adelaide, March
1984

But he knew that . . . Box 30

I have been buying . . . BC to GC,
26.6.88

I would like . . . 25.7.88

Any 'new' species . . . Box 34

Mr Chatwin is, of course . . . Medical
records, 10.8.88

Let me put it in . . . TM to BC, 17.7.87

I've said it before . . . TM to BC, 11.2.88

XL: FALLEN ANGEL

possession by the *Beast* . . . Box 34

thereby *completely* screwing . . . BC to
ND, 28.8.88

The promise of a . . . *NDBW*, 498

The only group . . . MEM to NS,
1.10.96

He seems better . . . EC to KS, 18.10.88

It will be just . . . EC to GC, 14.11.88

incorrigibly stylish . . . *Independent*,
19.1.89

XLI: THE CHATWIN EFFECT

Heroic saga . . . Box 34

I was delighted . . . CW to EC, 23.1.89

J'apprends avec tristesse . . . JL to EC,
20.1.89

Despite the large . . . RB to EC, 22.1.89

I can't write this letter, I'm afraid . . .
PL to EC, ND

The stars know . . . Box 35

a sexuagenarian adolescent . . . *WAIDH*,
143

Charley the Pioneer . . . *IP*, 162

at about the time . . . *With Chatwin*, ix

Malraux's breathless career . . . *WAIDH*,
119

He was an inspiration to me . . . PT to
EC, 26.1.89

Chatwin never delivered . . . *TLS*, 16.6.89

a pose rather than . . . Pfister, "Bruce Chatwin and the Postmodernization of the Travelogue"

In many ways *In Xanadu* . . . WD to EC, 11.10.89

What would his life's . . . *Anecdotage*, 88

I wish I could . . . BC to MB, 8.2.88

I think you know . . . PL to EC, ND

This delight which . . . GW to EC, ND

Real love was . . . SC to EC, 10.3.89

He would have found someone . . . EC to SC, ND

The coffin . . . MR to NS, 1.2.97

It is nearly springtime now . . . MR to EC, 1.2.89

Epilogues

Ah, Chatwin . . . told to Mary Henderson

Elizabeth's disbelief . . . HC to GA, Box 38, 17.8.89

Kansas is a . . . JK to EC, ND

The most complete Bruce Chatwin bibliography appears in *Anatomy of Restlessness: Selected Writings 1969–89* (Jonathan Cape, 1996).

A Chatwin Reading List

Sergei Aksakov, *A Russian Gentleman; A Russian Schoolboy; The Family Chronicle*
John Aubrey, *Brief Lives*
W. H. Auden, *A Certain World*
The Babur-Nama
Murray Bail, *Ian Fairweather*
Basho, *The Narrow Road to the Deep North*
Walter Benjamin, *Illuminations*
Thomas Bernhard, *Wittgenstein's Nephew, Gargoyles*
Jorge Luis Borges, *Ficciones*
Ivan Bunin, *Dark Avenues, The Gentleman from San Francisco*
Richard Burton, *A Mission to Gelele, King of Dahomey*
Robert Byron, *The Road to Oxiana*
Celtic nature poetry
Blaise Cendrars, *Moravagine, Prose du Transsibérien*
Anton Chekhov, stories
E. M. Cioran, *"De L'inconvenience d'Être Né"*
Cyril Connolly, *The Unquiet Grave*
Richard Henry Dana, *Two Years Before the Mast*
E. R. Dodds, *The Greeks and the Irrational*
John Donne, poems
Eleanor Doorly, *The Radium Woman, The Insect Man*
Gustave Flaubert, *Un Coeur Simple, Madame Bovary*
Carlo Emilio Gadda, *That Awful Mess on via Merulana*
Martin Heidegger, *Being and Time*
Ernest Hemingway, *In Our Time, To Have and Have Not*

Werner Herzog, *On Walking in Ice*
Alain Jerbauld, *In Quest of the Sun*
James Joyce, *Dubliners*
Ernst Jünger, *On the Marble Cliffs, Storm of Steel*, war diary from Paris occupation (not in English)
D. H. Lawrence, *Sea and Sardinia, Etruscan Places*
Mikhail Lermontov, *A Hero of Our Time*
Claude Lévi-Strauss, *Tristes Tropiques*
Mario Vargas Llosa, *The Perpetual Orgy*
E. V. Lucas, *The Open Road*
Curzio Malaparte, *Kaputt*
Osip Mandelstam, *Journey to Armenia, The Prose of Osip Mandelstam* (trans. Clarence Brown)
Carson McCullers, *The Ballad of the Sad Café*
Herman Melville, *Typee*
Henri de Monfried, *Hashish*
Paul Morand, *Close the Night*
Michele Neri, *Afrique Fantôme*
Flannery O'Connor, stories
George Orwell, *Homage to Catalonia*
Boris Pilnyak, *Chinese Story and Other Tales; Tales of the Wilderness; The Naked Year*
Dilys Powell, *An Affair of the Heart*
Raymond Radiguet, *Le Bal du Comte Orgel*
Tayeb Salih, *Season of Migration to the North*
Salvatore Satta, *The Day of Judgement*
Gaylord Simpson, *Attending Marvels*
I. B. Singer, stories
Andrei Sinyavsky, *A Voice from the Chorus*
Edith Sitwell, *Planet and Glow-worm, A Poet's Notebook, A Book of the Winter*
Joseph Skertchley, *Dahomey as It Is*

Joshua Slocum, *Sailing Alone Around the World*

Oswald Spengler, *The Decline of the West*

The Pillow Book of Lady Shonagon (trans. Ivan Morris)

Robert Louis Stevenson, *An Inland Voyage*

T. H. Strehlow, *Songs of Central Australia*

Jeremy Taylor, *Holy Living, Holy Dying*

Wilfred Thesiger, *Desert, Marsh and Mountain*

Leo Tolstoy, *The Death of Ivan Ilyich*

Michel Tournier, *Friday, The Other Island, The Erl King*

Ivan Turgenev, *A Sportsman's Sketches*

John C. Voss, *The Venturesome Voyages of Captain Voss*

Edmund Wilson, *Red, Black, Blond, and Olive*

Index

GORE VIDAL
A Biography
by Fred Kaplan

No writer since Ernest Hemingway has lived his life on as ambitious or as international a scale as Gore Vidal, a novelist whose work, like Hemingway's, has become a prominent landmark in twentieth-century American literature. This meticulously researched biography has all the glamour, sex, gossip, and family scandal one would expect. But more than that, Kaplan ties together the diversity and variety of his subject's work and life in a highly satisfying study that will be the starting point for any critical and cultural analysis of Gore Vidal for years to come.

Biography/0-385-47704-X

TRUMAN CAPOTE
*In Which Various Friends, Enemies, Acquaintances,
and Detractors Recall His Turbulent Career*
by George Plimpton

He was the most social of writers, and at the height of his career, he was the very nexus of the scintillating world of the arts, politics, and society. Truman truly knew everyone, and now the people who knew him best tell his remarkable story. Using the oral-biography style, George Plimpton has blended the voices of Capote's friends, lovers, and colleagues into a captivating narrative.

Biography/Autobiography/0-385-49173-5

GOOD-BYE TO ALL THAT
An Autobiography
by Robert Graves

Tracing his upbringing from his solidly middle-class Victorian childhood through his entry into World War I at age twenty-one as a patriotic captain in the Royal Welsh Fusiliers, poet Robert Graves goes on to depict the horrors and disillusionment of the Great War in this dramatic, poignant, often wry autobiography. An enormous success when it was first issued in 1929, it continues to find readers and has earned its designation as a true classic.

Biography/Autobiography/0-385-09330-6

THE LAST AVANT-GARDE
The Making of the New York School of Poets
by David Lehman

Greenwich Village, New York, circa 1951. Every night, at a run-down tavern, a group of painters, writers, poets, and hangers-on arrives to drink, argue, start affairs, and bang out a powerful new aesthetic, bringing about the works of art and poetry that will define New York City as the capital of world culture. *The Last Avant-Garde* covers the years 1948–1966 and focuses on four fast friends—the poets Frank O'Hara, James Schuyler, John Ashbery, and Kenneth Koch. Lehman brings to vivid life the extraordinary creative ferment of the time and place and gives both a definitive view of a quintessentially American aesthetic and an exploration of the dynamics of creativity.

Literary Criticism/Essays/0-385-49533-1

ANCHOR BOOKS
Available at your local bookstore, or call toll-free to order:
1-800-793-2665 (credit cards only).